Missouri

ROADSIDES

Missouri ROADSIDES

the traveler's companion

Bill Earngey

University of Missouri Press   Columbia and London

For my wife, Mary Sims, and blacktop roads—both true friends.

For my mother, whose wholeheartedly unpretentious name, Ada Sue, fits her.

For Lydel Sims (1916-1995), a damn good writer and a tough intellectual gentleman.

Copyright © 1995 by
The Curators of the University of Missouri
University of Missouri Press, Columbia, Missouri 65201
Printed and bound in the United States of America
All rights reserved
5 4 3 2 1   99 98 97 96 95

Library of Congress Cataloging-in-Publication Data

Earngey, Bill.
    Missouri roadsides : the traveler's companion / Bill Earngey.
        p. cm.
    Includes bibliographical references (p. 313) and index.
    ISBN 0–8262–1021–X (paper : alk. paper)
    1. Missouri—Guidebooks. 2. Automobile travel—Missouri—Guidebooks. I. Title.
F464.3.E27 1995
 917.7804′43—dc20

                                                    95-616
                                                    CIP

♾™ This paper meets the requirements of the
American National Standard for Permanence of Paper
for Printed Library Materials, Z39.48, 1984.

Designer: Stephanie Foley
Printer and binder: Edwards Brothers, Inc.
Typeface: Palatino

Unless otherwise indicated, all photographs are courtesy the State Historical Society of Missouri, Columbia.

Contents

Main Entries

About This Book

MISSOURI ROADSIDES IS ABOUT adventure: about roads and the towns along them—their names (like Monkey Run and Noel), histories, architecture, museums, parks, points of interest, and oddities—and their locations by prairies, mountains, rivers, valleys, lakes, and forests that provide wildlife habitats as well as outdoor recreation like picnicking, camping, hiking, canoeing, swimming, boating, fishing, hunting, and the chance to explore geological wonders and curiosities.

Missouri Roadsides is also about getting there being half the fun. It's a guide to the leisure part of travel and leisure, where a detour to see an old mill is the shortest distance between you and a good time. Relax, picnic, nap, and drive on down the road. This guide will always get you where you want to go, but more than occasionally it will tug at your sleeve, tempting you down a narrow stretch of country blacktop that promises the wicked freedom of the open road.

FROM "REPORT BOARD OF EDUCATION," ST. LOUIS, 1934-1935

In addition to city, state, and federal agencies, hundreds of Missourians contributed to this book, and it is to their credit that this guide has a greater variety of detailed information about the state than any other single source. My part in the project was to accumulate suggestions, cross-check facts, and then organize material. The result is actually a consensus of what local residents think is most interesting about their towns and counties.

The criteria for listing towns and sites in this guidebook are physical: *something* has to be there to write about. Towns were selected as guideposts to specific locations. Sites mentioned must be physically present (remnants are fine), and they must be on, or easily seen from, public property. There are a few exceptions when I desperately wanted to include a famous or infamous personality, like Calamity Jane. Sometimes a great town name like Monkey Run wouldn't take no for an answer and I found a hook to hang it on, but for the most part places like Shake Rag Hollow didn't make the cut. Pity.

Missouri Roadsides was a pleasure to write. I hope you find it entertaining and useful.

The Book is arranged alphabetically in two sections. Part I lists towns and also subjects associated with Missouri's history or physical environment—for example, the Civil War, Indians, Glacial Erratics. Part II is about recreation—lakes, trails, state and national parks. In the back are two indexes. The first is a standard index. The second is laid out by map coordinates. Towns, sites, natural areas, and recreation areas such as state parks are listed in this index in geographical groups to help with organizing touring plans.

FORMAT EXPLANATIONS

Main Entry • For each city listed as a main entry, the heading includes: general location in the state, name, 1990 census population, and coordinates on the state maps (pp. xvi–xix).

Subentries • Points of interest within or near to the main entry are listed in alphabetical order beneath the main entry.

Cross references • *Italicized Word(s)* refer to another main entry with more information about a topic (like "see also"). Note that references to Float Streams, Lakes, National Forests, National Parks, National Wildlife Refuges, State Forests, State Parks, Trails, and Wildlife Areas all refer to entries in Part II, Recreation. References to additional information within the same main entry are indicated by nonitalicized instructions to look above or below.

County profiles • Profiles of all of Missouri's counties are included in the section titled County Profiles. Because references to county names are so frequent in the entries for cities, a cross reference to this section is not indicated every time a county is mentioned.

Place-names • A caution is necessary about place-names. First, some places appear to have more than one namesake, which can be characterized as accidental, generous, fainthearted, or just plain politic. Second, pioneers were not aware they were making history. Often no official public records were left behind to explain the sentiments or hopes or heroes that named Missouri's towns. Family possessions such as Bibles, diaries, and letters are what helped preserve the towns' histories, as did memories that often added and dropped information while weaving a good story. When multiple accounts are equally disputed, all are mentioned here. When no reliable evidence was found, the place-name is annotated as "origin unknown."

Post offices • Recently established towns were often served by another town's post office, or the post office name was not the same as the town's. The names and dates of all post offices serving a town are listed. Most of the post office dates listed in this book are from "Missouri Post Offices, 1804–1981." Dates reflect the year the application was approved by the postmaster general and the year of official discontinuation. A date of "Now" indicates the post office was still active in 1981. Substations and other subordinate post offices are not listed. Post offices assimilated by a newly organized county are not traced through those changes, e.g. *Ozark,* formerly in Greene County, became county seat of Christian County. *(Post Offices)*

Directions • All directions are given from the main entry using the following abbreviations: CR, county roads; FR, forest roads; GR, unmarked gravel or low bituminous roads; I, Interstate highways; SR, state roads; US, federal highways. Cardinal compass directions are used (N, E, S, W), and distances are in miles (m.) as measured from county and state maps. Note that odometer mileage can vary among vehicles.

Footnotes • Place-names and dates of post offices are indicated in footnotes for sites mentioned in descriptions that do not have main entries or subentries of their own. If those sites still exist and their location is not indicated in the text, directions from the main entry are given as well.

About Missouri

DURING THE EARLIEST STAGES of geological history, igneous rocks were formed by magma, molten lava under the earth's crust. Missouri's only evidence of these rocks is found in the St. Francois Mountains of southeast Missouri (Sam A. Baker *State Park*, Johnson's Shut-Ins Natural Area). After the lava hardened, the St. Francois Mountains were gradually lifted about 2,000 feet. Southern Missouri's Ozarks rose with the mountains, and after a long series of erosions, the Ozark's characteristic tight valleys and steep canyons were formed.

About 500 million years ago, the St. Francois Mountains sank back to their former level and were then inundated by seas that covered nearly a third of the continent. Along with the water, rock strata were deposited on top of the igneous layer. During the Cambrian Period, about 20 million years later, the seas from the Gulf of Mexico and the Arctic regions began a cycle of advancing and retreating, bringing seashells as well as organisms from adjacent land masses. Additional sediment was produced by precipitation of mineral matter dissolved in the water. The pressure of successive layers of deposits slowly hardened these materials, which are seen today as layers of mostly limestone, dolomite (a magnesia-rich rock resembling limestone), chert, conglomerates, sandstone, and shale. These layers are dramatically revealed by road cuts *(Doniphan: SR 142 Road Cut)*.

After about 460 million years of cataclysmic changes—warm seas, arid deserts, massive erosion, violent fractures, and the slow dissolution of rocks by carbonic acid *(Collapsed Cave Systems)*—most of Missouri's present topography took shape, including the Ozarks, the Springfield Plain, the Bootheel's floodplains, faults, cave systems, limestone and dolomite outcroppings, and the 1,800-foot St. Francois Mountains uplift, which was then eroded by streams and winds wearing away millions of years of rock to reveal the igneous granite and porphyries that form Taum Sauk Mountain, the highest point in Missouri

(1,772 feet; Taum Sauk *State Park)*. The Osage Plains of west-central Missouri, similar in subsurface composition to the Dissected Till Plains (below), are partly a result of the St. Francois Mountains uplift and subsequent erosion. Their Pennsylvania-era sediment of 210–230 million years ago dips gently westward on rolling prairies that, in some areas (Jackson, Johnson, Vernon, and Barton Counties), begin from relatively steep escarpments.

After another 40 million years, or about 1 million years ago, two separate sheets of ice, ranging from several hundred feet thick to several thousand, spread from the northern part of what is now the United States to, and slightly below, the Missouri River, grinding and crushing the land into the Dissected Till Plains *(Glacial Erratics)*. Melted ice coursed in torrential rivers, contouring land later covered with *loess* that eventually formed strange earthen hills *(Crowley's Ridge; Forest City;* Van Meter *State Park)*.

The first human habitation of Missouri is currently dated at c. 9500 B.C. *(Indians)*. Explorers like Hernando de Soto in 1541 and Marquette and Jolliet in 1673 reported encounters with indigenous people living in extreme eastern Missouri, but it was Étienne Venyard de Bourgmont who first reported meeting Historic Period Indians when ascending the Missouri River in 1714 (Van Meter *State Park)*.

The first permanent European settlement in Missouri was established by French Canadian farmers from nearby Kaskaskia, Ill., at *Ste. Genevieve* during the late 1740s. It was followed in 1764 by a trading post established at *St. Louis* and in 1769 by a Spanish post built at the future site of *St. Charles*. From Ste. Genevieve a successful lead mining operation was developed c. 1773 at Mine au Breton *(Potosi)*. From St. Louis and St. Charles developed a fur trading route that encouraged more immigration, which in turn precipitated settlements like Daniel Boone's in 1799 near today's *Defiance*.

When America acquired the *Louisiana Purchase*

land in 1803, the floodgates of western immigration were opened by *Lewis and Clark.* By the time Missouri was granted statehood in 1821, its population was more than 66,000.

The state's name derives from French translations of the Algonquian term applied by Fox Indians to their enemies (known now as the Missouri Indians) who lived near the confluence of the Missouri and Mississippi Rivers. The exact Algonquian meaning of the name is probably irrelevant (possibly People with Big Canoes, Town of the Large Canoes, or People with the Wooden Canoes) since the Missouri Indians, who spoke Chiwere Sioux, called themselves Niutachi, reportedly meaning People Who Dwell at the Mouth of the River. Regardless of what either Indian name is supposed to mean, the French, and later the English, in order to identify a location and a group of people, spelled the Indian name in various euphonious ways: Massorites, Messorites, Emissourita, Missourita, etc. The first written English reference (by Robert Rogers in 1765) spelled the river's name as Misauri and the name of the people along it as Misauris. Unlike Arkansas, Missouri has no state legislation prescribing pronunciation of its name. Residents are nearly equally divided between those saying Missour-ee and those saying Missour-uh. Regardless of how loudly advocates assert their preference, there is no correct pronunciation.

State Symbols

Great Seal (January 11, 1822)

Flag (March 22, 1913)

Flower, the white hawthorn blossom (March 16, 1923)

Bird, the bluebird (March 30, 1927)

Song, the Missouri Waltz (June 30, 1939)

Tree, the flowering dogwood (June 20, 1955)

Mineral, galena (July 21, 1967)

Rock, mozarkite (July 21, 1967)

Insect, the honeybee (July 3, 1985)

Musical instrument, the fiddle (July 17, 1987)

Fossil, crinoid (June 16, 1989)

Nut tree, eastern black walnut (July 9, 1990)

Animal, mule (May 17, 1995)

State Facts

Nickname: Show-Me State

Population: 5,117,073

Capital: Jefferson City

Admitted to the Union: August 20, 1821, the 24th state

Area: 69,686 square miles, the 19th largest

Length and Width: c. 300 miles long, c. 240 miles wide

Geographic center: 20 miles SW of Jefferson City

Highest Point: Taum Sauk Mountain, 1,772 feet

Lowest Point: St. Francis River at Arkansas, 230 feet

Time Zone: Central, Daylight Saving Time

Map Legend

Airport

Archaeological site

Bridge)(

Cemetery †

Church

Civil War battle site ✕

   Confederate victory

   Federal victory

   Battle inconclusive

College, university

Courthouse

Creek, river, etc.

Former site ⊡

Garden

Historic commercial district

Historic district ▢

Historic Route 66   ⑥ Rt. 66

Historic structure

Information ⓘ

Interstate exit ◆

Mill

Modern building

Mountain / altitude ▲ 1772

Nature center

Observation Deck ■

Park

Railroad

Railroad depot

School

Site area

Site off map   To →

Stadium

Statue

Town location •

Water

Zoo

MAP 1 NORTHEAST QUARTER

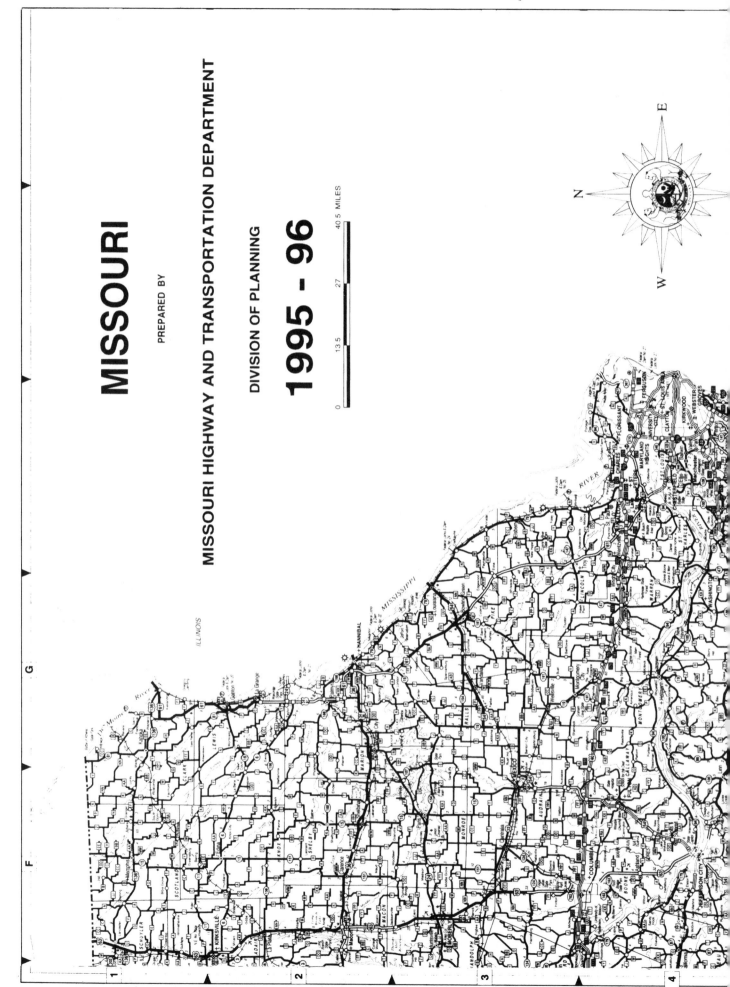

MISSOURI

PREPARED BY

MISSOURI HIGHWAY AND TRANSPORTATION DEPARTMENT

DIVISION OF PLANNING

1995 - 96

0   13.5   27   40 5 MILES

MAP 2   SOUTHEAST QUARTER

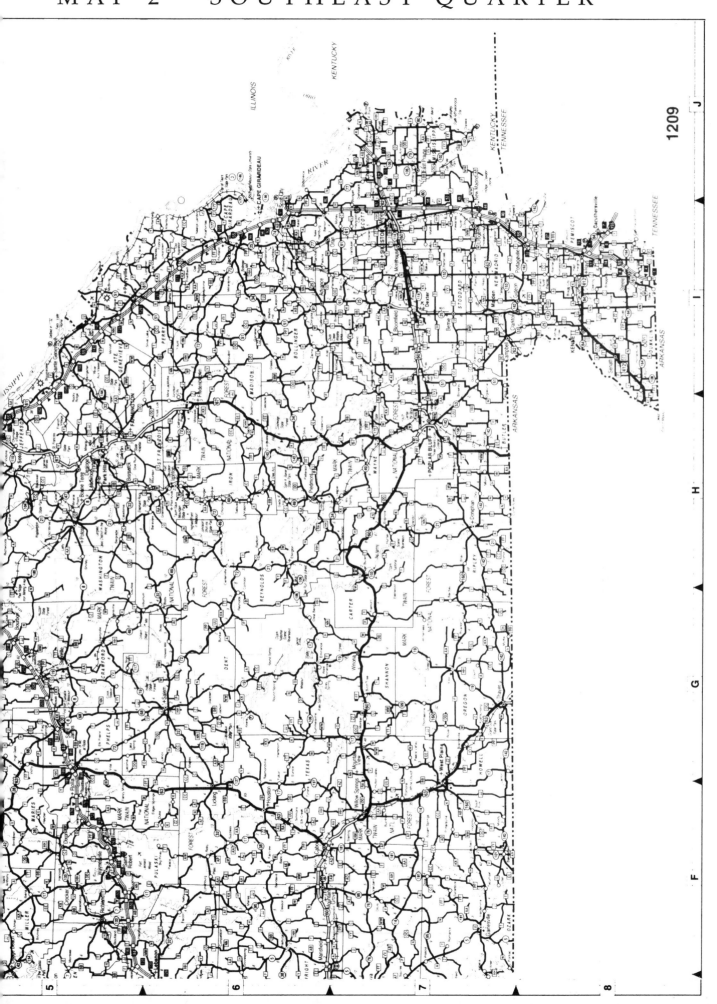

MAP 3 NORTHWEST QUARTER

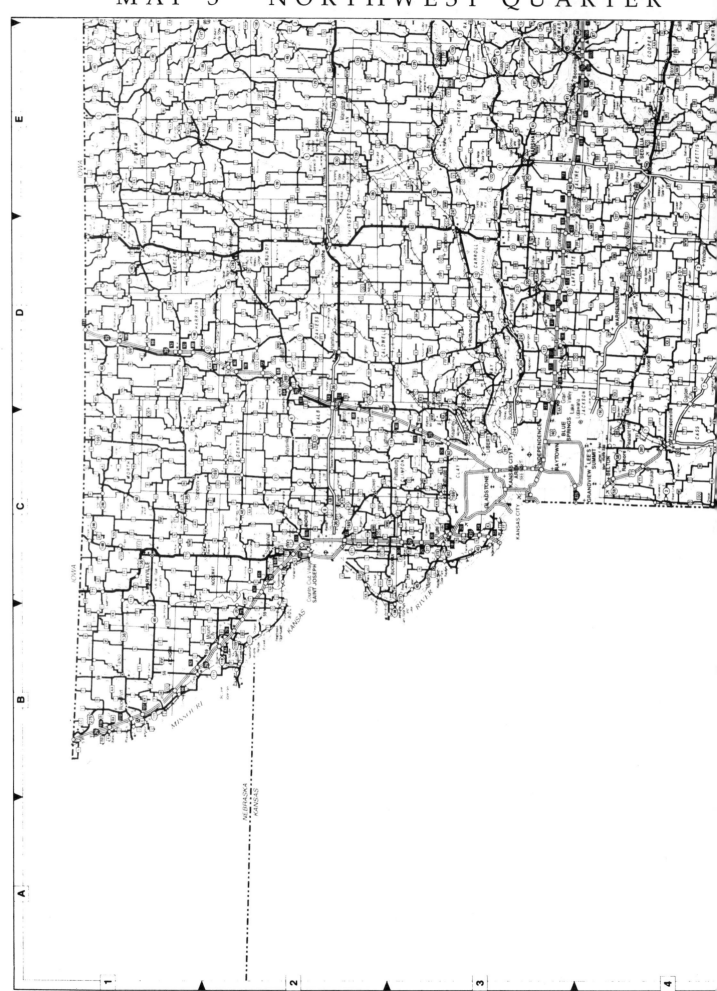

MAP 4 SOUTHWEST QUARTER

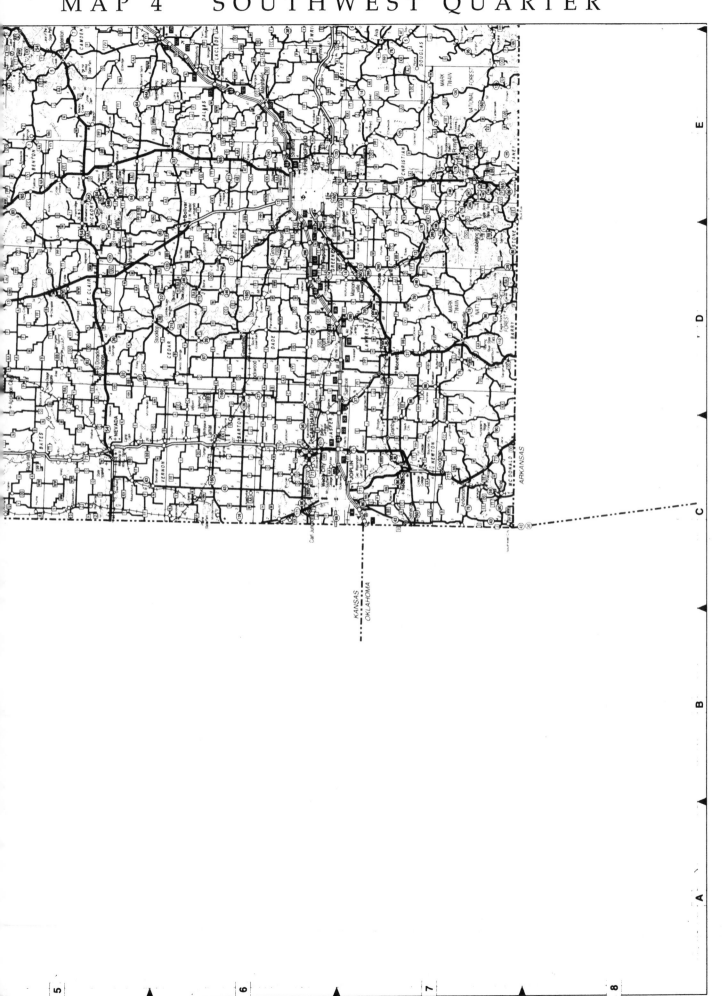

MAP 5 KANSAS CITY

MAP 6 SAINT LOUIS

Towns and
Other Subjects

Overleaf: Two men appear to fly over Joplin. Trick photography, early 1900s.

ADRIAN

Population: 1,582   Map C-4

When Crescent Hill[1] was bypassed in 1880 by the Missouri Pacific *Railroad,* Adrian was platted three miles south at the tracks, drawing away the population and businesses of Crescent Hill, whose townsite was converted into farms in 1883. Along the railroad's route in western Missouri, four towns—Adrian, Archie,[2] Arthur,[3] and Sheldon[4]—were named for sons of the railroad's general passenger agent, Talmage. Post office: 1880–now.

Gen. Joseph Shelby's House. Folk Victorian, c. 1878; one-story frame, U-shaped. Until the *Civil War,* Shelby lived in Waverly.[5] Reportedly the only ranking Confederate who never surrendered to the Union, Shelby established a farm near Adrian after the war, where he served as U.S. marshall for Missouri's western district from 1893 until surrendering to death in 1897. SR 18, W 6 m.; GR, S 1.25 m.

Western Missouri Antique Tractor and Machinery. 25 acres. Vintage farm machinery, household items, memorabilia, restored one-room schoolhouse, blacksmith's shop, general store. US 71, city park; signs.

Wildlife Areas. Amarugia Highlands; Settle's Ford. *(Wildlife Areas)*

1. Landmark; p.o. 1858–1861, 1866–1880.
2. US 71, N 6 m.; p.o. 1880–now.
3. US 71, S 25 m.; p.o. 1881–1936.
4. US 71, S 51 m.; p.o. 1881–now.
5. After Sir Walter Scott's "Waverley Novels," usually "e" omitted; p.o. Mount Hope, a commendatory, 1833–1854, 1860–1861, 1865–1879; Waverly 1854–now.

AGENCY

Population: 642   Map C-2

First known as Agency Ford for the Sauk and Fox *Indian* agency established here c. 1825 at a Platte River ford (below) that was used mostly by *St. Joseph*–bound travelers. When the city was platted in 1863, the name was shortened to Agency. Post offices: Walnut Hill[1] 1849–1872; Agency 1872–now.

The Ford. Until Robert Gilmore began operating a ferry in 1839, the Platte River was forded at this point, where it flowed over a bed of limestone. Inquire locally.

Frazier Store, Inc. General Store, turn-of-the-century. When the former owner recently went out of business, no buyer could be found. Rather than close its only store, the community bought it. In 1990 it had 41 stockholders, 351 shares outstanding, and a six-member board of directors. SR H, E 4 m.; SR E, S 0.5 m.

Pigeon Hill Wildlife Area. *Wildlife Areas.*

Ratcliffe Manufacturing Plant. During the late 19th and early 20th centuries, it manufactured wooden stirrups, which were sold internationally. In town.

1. Descriptive.

AKERS

Population: 25   Map G-6

This 1830s community at the Current River and Gladden Creek grew around a historic crossing. Its *post offices* changed names, lapsed, reorganized, and wandered a little. Carpentersville[1] and Current River[2] preceded this post office organized by George W. Cox, who named it Akers for a local 1850s pioneer family. Post office: 1884–1965.

Akers Ferry. Said to be the last of the downstream ferries that use river current for most of their power, it was reportedly established when automobiles became popular. Before then, wagons forded the river. *(Ferryboats)*

Devil's Backbone / The Narrows. Reportedly the narrowest narrows used by a Missouri state highway. The 250-foot elevation above flanking streams gives new meaning to the term "scenic." SR K, at town.

Devil's Well. Once a commercial attraction, now part of the Ozark National Scenic Riverways *(National Parks),* this narrow 100-foot vertical hole in limestone and sandstone (eroded by groundwater) gives a view of a 100-foot-deep lake below. The lake is connected to Cave Spring (at nearby Current River, S 1 m.), which flows at about 50 million gallons daily. SR KK, E approx. 3.9 m.; GR, S approx. 1.8 m.; signs.

Natural Areas. MONTAUK UPLAND FOREST: *Salem.* THE SUNKLANDS and BURR OAK BASIN: 160 and 230 acres, respectively. Close together, they offer excellent examples of *collapsed cave systems* and unique communities of plants like the yellow lotus. The Sunklands (about 0.75 miles long and 200 feet deep) is Missouri's longest conspicuous sinkhole and features forested sinkholes and a sinkhole pond. At first it appears to be a valley, but both ends are blocked (drainage is internal). Burr Oak has three very large sinkholes (one boggy, two dry). Requires a vehicle with good ground clearance; inquire about road conditions. Box G (SR 19N), Eminence 65466. SR K, S approx. 7 m.; GR, E approx. 4.3 m; signs.

Pulltight, Mo. This post office community, now defunct, was near a large spring and *gristmill.* The name reportedly derived from wagon drivers having to pull tight on the draft animal's reins while descending the steep hill to the mill. Post office: 1889–1907. SR KK,

E 6 m.; SR 19, S 7 m.; SR EE, W 2.6 m. *(National Parks: Ozark National Scenic Riverways)*

Recreation. *FLOAT STREAMS:* Current and Jacks Fork Rivers. MONTAUK *STATE PARK:* SR K, N to SR E, W to SR 119, then S; total 18.7 m. OZARK NATIONAL SCENIC RIVERWAYS *(National Parks):* Devils Well and Welch Landing river access. *STATE FORESTS:* Cedargrove (four tracts: 1. from Cedargrove:[3] SR B, E 1 m. to GR; sign; 2. from Cedargrove: NW of town on N side of county line, S of Current River; inquire locally; 3. from Akers: SR K, N 5.3 m.; 4. from Akers: SR KK, E 6 m.; SR 19, N 2 m.; SR WW, W 1 m.; sign) and Hartshorn. **The Sinks Natural Tunnel.** *Eminence.*

1. The family; p.o. 1870–1871.
2. The river's motion via French (Rivière Courante) and Spanish (Rio Corrente); p.o. 1871–1875.
3. Location in grove of cedars; p.o. Riverside, at Current River, 1883–1890; Cedar Grove 1890–1895, Cedargrove 1895–1957.

ALBANY

Population: 1,958   Map C-1

Selected in 1845 as a county seat for newly organized Gentry County, the town was platted in 1845 and first named Athens. Due to an existing Athens in Clark County, it used nearby Sandsville[1] post office until establishing Gentry Court House post office in 1847. The county court changed the town name to Albany when incorporating it in 1851, but it took an 1857 act of the Missouri legislature to finalize both procedures. Since 1857, the town and post office have remained Albany, a stock name honoring the capital of New York (some early settlers came from there), which derives its name from the Duke of York, whose Scottish title was Duke of Albany. Post offices: Sandsville 1845–1847; Gentry Court House 1847–1857; Albany 1857–now.

Architecture. Many late 19th- and early 20th-century structures, including Queen Anne and Eclectic, as well as an 1840s log cabin stagecoach depot. Downtown; south of SR 136 on SR 85.

Gentry, Mo. Platted in 1899 at the Chicago, Burlington & Quincy *Railroad* and named for Gentry County, this community (pop. 123) sponsors an annual pig roast and flea market (second Saturday in August). Post office: 1899–now. US 136, W 5 m.; US 169, N 6 m.

Gentry County Courthouse. Second Empire, 1884–1885; National Historic Register. The county's third, a good example of its type, this massive three-story brick courthouse has a mansard roof with dormers, an imposing clock tower with bracketed eaves, and decorative arched drip molding. Cost: $29,100. Grounds: two war

memorials, a large elaborately landscaped fountain, and a WWI doughboy statue with fixed bayonet. Downtown; 1 block W of SR 85. *(County Profiles)*

Grand River Shut-Ins. The river valley narrows to about 660 feet, creating these *shut-ins.* Downstream, S 5 m.; inquire locally.

Stanberry, Mo. Platted in 1879 by the Western Improvement Company at the Council Bluffs & Omaha division of the Wabash, St. Louis & Pacific *Railroad,* the town was named for John J. Stansberry, a prominent farmer who donated 40 acres for the railroad right-of-way. No records explain the spellings change from Stansberry to Stanberry. Post offices: Mount Pleasant[2] 1862–1879; Stanberry 1879–now. US 136, E 13 m. CITY PARK: Restrooms, picnic facilities, Civil War–era cannon, bandstand, croquet court. DOWNTOWN: Brick streets; buildings reflect the town's 1890s prosperity (1890 pop. c. 3,000). KING LAKE *WILDLIFE AREA.*

1. First postmaster D. Saunders.
2. Commendatory; E 2 m.; inquire locally.

ALTENBURG

Population: 256   Map I-6

Founded and platted in 1839 by the congregation of Trinity Lutheran Church, the town was named by Rev. G. H. Loeber for Altenburg, Germany, where he was baptized. Said to be one of the first settlements in Missouri established solely for religious reasons (Saxon Lutheran Settlements, below), it is the home of the Lutheran Church–Missouri Synod. Post office: 1854–now.

Darnstaedt House. Log, c. 1839. Representative of the first homes here, this one-room cabin (hand-hewn oak, limestone foundation) has a cellar and sleeping loft. Slick clay was used as plaster inside. In 1840 it accommodated Johann Darnstaedt, his wife, and their four children. Private; inquire locally.

Log Cabin College. Log, 1839; National Historic Register. The first Lutheran seminary west of the Mississippi was moved here in 1912 from nearby Dresden (Saxon Lutheran Settlements, below). From this one-story cabin evolved Concordia Seminary (transferred 1849 to St. Louis), the oldest Lutheran institution of higher learning in Missouri. The 1839 classes included six languages, math, physics, history, geography, philosophy, religion, music, and drawing. Displays. Across from Trinity Lutheran Church (below).

Mini-Central Park. Log house, c. 1839. Small with squared logs, it was possibly the home of Miss J. C. M. Loeber, whose brother founded Trinity Lutheran Church. Neatly cut grass, picnic tables, and large shade trees. Across the street is Schmidt's Haus (1840 with 1890s additions). In town.

Old Trinity Lutheran Church. Vernacular, 1845; remodeled 1929. Built with random-size limestone, this one-story structure was converted in 1867 to a school; closed 1969. Now a museum, it displays local church items, including an 1838 baptismal tray and its original bell, cast in Spain in 1761. In town.

Saxon Lutheran Settlements of 1839. Of seven closely grouped Saxon Lutheran settlements, only Altenburg, *Frohna,* and Uniontown *(Old Appleton)* remain; Dresden, Seelitz, Johannisberg, and Wittenberg (below) declined. Led by Rev. Martin Stephens and financed from a communal treasury of $88,000, Lutherans from Saxony, Germany, hoping to establish the Church of Martin Luther in America, arrived in 1839 at nearby Wittenberg to farm about 4,500 acres. Consisting mostly of students and professional men unaccustomed to farming, the settlements floundered. The Reverend Stephens, accused of "voluptuous living and dictatorial conduct," was exiled to Illinois. From these troubled beginnings the Lutheran Church–Missouri Synod, one of America's largest, was established in 1847.

Trinity Lutheran Church. Romanesque, 1866–1867. Built from locally quarried sandstone, its footings are 8 feet deep and 8 feet wide, its walls 24 inches thick. The 16-by-5-foot Roman-arch windows and 120-foot steeple capped by a 6-foot gilded cross complete the impression of a building built to last an eternity. Inside, framed by a barrel-vaulted ceiling, the pulpit appears to be suspended over the altar, which is typical of 18th-century German Lutheran designs intended to give everyone a view of the speaker. In town.

Wittenberg, Mo. Saxon Lutherans, who settled this region, landed here first (Saxon Lutheran Settlements, above). Established in 1839 at the Mississippi River, the town was named for Wittenberg, Germany, the center of the Reformation led by Martin Luther. A successful river landing (1874 pop. c. 500) that changed in 1904 to a St. Louis & San Francisco *Railroad* shipping point, its decline was precipitated by the 1930s Depression. Its demise followed a 1986 flood that destroyed the town. Post office: Wittenberg(h) 1862–now. SR A, E 4.2 m. GRAND TOWER ISLAND AVULSION: Just south of Grand Tower, Illinois, a roughly three-by-two-mile island, separated by channels of the river, belongs to Missouri despite its location on the Illinois side of the Mississippi. MIDCON CORP. PIPELINE SUSPENSION BRIDGE: The world's longest pipeline *suspension bridge* (2,150 feet), it was built in 1953–1955 to supplement existing underwater lines. These two 30-inch pipes are part of a system delivering natural gas from the Texas Gulf Coast to the Chicago market. CR 460, S 0.2 m. TOWER ROCK:

National Historic Register; dedicated in 1871 for public use by president U. S. Grant. First noted in 1673 by French Jesuit explorers Jacques (Père) Marquette (1637–1675) and Louis Jolliet (1645–1700), this impressive erosional remnant, a quarter-acre limestone island, thrusts 60–80 feet above the water. The rough horizontally grooved rock is sparsely covered on top by oaks, grass, and cedars. During low water, access is by foot; during high water, by boat. Warning! A treacherous eddy and whirlpool are on the downstream side. CR 460, S along shore 1.5 m.

ALTON
Population: 692   Map G-7

Alton was platted in 1859 to replace Thomasville (below) as the county seat of Oregon County after the county was reduced in size. Although local tradition insists the town was named to accommodate county clerk William "Uncle Billy" Boyd's notoriously poor spelling, it was named for Boyd's previous residence, Alton, Ill. *(St. Charles: Portage Des Sioux),* which was named for Alton Easton, son of that town's founder, Rufus Easton. (Boyd was the first postmaster of Alton, Mo.) Post offices: Huddleston[1] 1855–1860, defunct; Alton 1860–now.

Bardley, Mo. Established in 1895 during the timber boom *(Doniphan: Grandin),* Bardley was supposed to be named for merchant J. P. Wooding's Kentucky hometown, Bordley, whose 1828 postmaster named it for a friend in England, but the postal department returned it as Bardley, which was not an uncommon error—e.g. nearby Handy's[2] post office name was to honor store owner Noah Haney, but the postal department could not read the writing and returned it as Handy, a name locals agreed was appropriate because receiving the mail there was more handy than traveling elsewhere. Bardley post office: 1895–1966. US 160, E 19 m.; SR J, N 1.8 m. IRISH WILDERNESS: Land located a few miles north was bought by the Catholic church in *Old Mines* for destitute Irish railroad workers and immigrants affected by the Panic of 1857. About 40 families had settled the area by 1859 but were forced out (never to return) by marauders during the Civil War *(West Plains).* The communities in the area today were established because of the timber industry. NATURAL AREAS: Cupola Pond and Red Maple Pond (Natural Areas, below). GR, E approx. 3.5 m.; SR C, S approx. 5.4 m. WHITES CREEK *TRAIL* / CAMP FIVE POND PICNIC AREA *(National Forests):* Vault toilets, pond fishing. SR J, N 5.5 m. WILDERNESS, MO.: Descriptive of the area even today, the name is derived from the former

Delivering the mail, c. 1910.

Irish Wilderness Settlement (above) that is now part of Mark Twain *National Forest*. A former school (WPA Folk, 1935; now a Baptist church), one grocery, and one former gas station compose the community buildings. Post office: 1882–1954. SR J, N 10.8 m.; SR K, S 2.9 m.

Greer Spring / Mill. GREER MILL: Vernacular, 1885. When built at Greer Spring c. 1852, today's three-story clapboard structure housed machinery powered by the spring, with one-inch drive cables strung through towers. Closed c. 1920. Private; visitors welcome. Approx. 200 ft. uphill from spring. GREER SPRING: National Natural Landmark. This scenic two-part spring (from a cave and from underground 50 feet away) is reportedly the second largest in Missouri (*Van Buren: Big Spring*). At 214 million gallons per day, it provides a third of the Eleven Point River's volume (*Float Streams*). SR 19, N 6 m. to Greer;[3] signs.

Natural Areas. BRUSHY POND: 28 acres. An excellent example of a sinkhole (*Collapsed Cave Systems*) pond marsh, featuring three types of sedges and manna grass found only at Missouri sinkhole pond marshes. Rt. 1, Box 182, Winona 65588. SR 19, N 6 m. to Greer (above); continue SR 19, N approx. 7.7 m. (approx. 1.8 m. N of W junction with a blacktop road). TUPELO GUM POND: 32 acres. Features a five-acre sinkhole (*Collapsed Cave Systems*) ringed by swamp tupelo (uncommon in the Ozarks), swamp vegetation, rare plants, and Missouri's largest tupelo gum (67' tall; 7'7" in diameter). Hard to locate; inquire: U.S. Forest Service, Rt. 1, Box 189, Winona 65588.

Oregon County Courthouse. Moderne, 1939–1942. The county's fourth, this is Missouri's only red granite courthouse. Local stone was preferred, but Iron County's red granite was cheaper. Today, red granite is too expensive to use except for trim. Cost: $100,000 ($10,000 from bonds, $75,000 from *WPA*). Downtown. (*County Profiles*)

Oregon County Springs. Reportedly the area around Alton has Missouri's largest daily volume of flowing spring-water. Inquire locally. BLUE SPRING: 47 million gallons; SE 14 m. BOZE SPRING: 12 million gallons; E 10 m. FALLING SPRING: Recreation, below. THOMASON MILL SPRING: 21 million gallons; 5 m. NW of Blue Spring. TURNER SPRING: Recreation, below.

Recreation. All are in the Mark Twain *National Forest*; all except McCormack and Falling Spring are also part of the Eleven Point National Scenic River (*Float Streams*). CANE BLUFF PICNIC AREA: Vault toilets; Eleven Point fishing, swimming, and access. SR 19, N 5 m.; GR, W 0.5 m; GR, N 3 m. FALLING SPRING PICNIC AREA: Year-round spring (0.9 million gal./day), historic mill. *FLOAT STREAM*: Eleven Point River. GREER CROSSING CAMPGROUND / PICNIC AREA: Water, vault toilets, Eleven Point River access. SR 19, N 9.2 m. MCCORMACK LAKE / CAMPGROUND / PICNIC AREA: Hiking *trail*, 11-acre lake, fishing (bass, sunfish, catfish), water, vault toilets. RIVERTON WEST PICNIC AREA: Vault toilets; Eleven Point fishing, swimming, and access. US 160, E 13 m. to Riverton;[4] continue US 160, E 2 m. TURNER MILL NORTH PICNIC SITE: Vault toilets, Eleven Point fishing and access. SR 19, N 2 m.; SR AA, E 4.5 m.; FR 3153, N 4.5 m. TURNER MILL SOUTH PICNIC SITE: Vault toilets, Eleven Point fishing and access; Turner Spring: 1.5 million gal./day. SR 19, N 11.2 m.; FR 3152, E 7 m.; FR 3190, S 3 m.

Thomasville, Mo. Located at the Eleven Point River (*Float Streams*), this former county seat, first called Rich Woods,[5] was platted in 1846 and named for 1817 settler George Thomas. The Howell family (*County Profiles: Howell*) settled here in 1818; reportedly, Charles Hatcher made the first settlement in 1803. Post office: 1846–1979. SR 160, N 11 m.; SR 90, N 1.3 m.

1. Family name.
2. SR J, N 8.6 m.; GR at sign to Handy Baptist church, E approx. 2 m.; p.o. 1913–1954.
3. Via p.o. for early settler Samuel Greer; p.o. 1890–1941.
4. C. R. Jones established the first store here in 1923, naming the site Riverton (town at river; no p.o.) for his former Wyoming business location.
5. Commendatory; no p.o.

ARCADIA
Population: 609   Map H-6

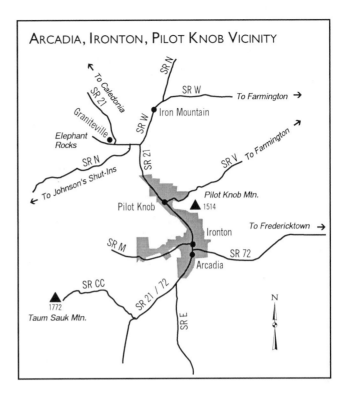

ARCADIA, IRONTON, PILOT KNOB VICINITY

One of three mining towns (*Pilot Knob; Ironton*), joined today by their city limits along SR 21, Arcadia grew around Arcadia High School (Ursuline Academy, below), was platted in 1849, and was named for its 1841 post office, which honors the classical Greek Peloponnisos region, an elevated plateau surrounded by mountains. Reportedly, a New England woman who came with the first mining company suggested the name in remembrance of the "Greek grazing country, which has furnished the word Arcadian for poets," referring to Sir Philip Sidney's "Arcadia," the 1590 prose romance that made the term synonymous with rustic simplicity and innocence and often with Eden. The town declined c. 1858 after the Iron Mountain *Railroad* reached *Pilot Knob* but revived when the line was extended south c. 1871. Incidentally, America's first excursion train to organize a "mystery theme" was between here and St. Louis on May 21, 1932. Post offices: 1841–1858, 1871–now.

Architecture. Gardner Bros. Store (1888), 123 Main; Walton House (1860), 315 College; Pollock House (1843), SR 72, E 0.6 m.; Missouri-Pacific Depot (1941, red granite), SR 21.

The Baptist Home. Neoclassical, 1920–1923. The Riggs-Scott building is the third location in Ironton of what was formerly called The Missouri Home for Aged Baptists. Moved to this site in 1923, the institution is the oldest Southern Baptist home for the aged west of the Mississippi and is supported by donations and the residents' assets. Residents receive lifetime care. The red granite building with full-height entry porch and triangular pediment is set on 175 landscaped acres; visitors welcome. SR 72, E 1.5 m.

The Maples. This granite house has its own conical watertower (part wood and shingle, part stone). Private. SR 72, E 0.7 m.

Recreation. CRANE LAKE PICNIC AREA / TRAIL (*National Forests*): 100-acre lake (electric motors only), pit toilets, fishing (bass, bluegill, redear, catfish), Crane Lake *Trail*, *shut-ins*. KETCHERSIDE MOUNTAIN *STATE FOREST*: includes Taum Sauk and Ketcherside Mountains. MARBLE CREEK CAMPGROUND / TRAIL (*National Forest*): Water, pit toilets, creek fishing; part of Ozark *Trail*.

Royal Gorge Natural Area. 80 acres. Part of Ketcherside Mountain *State Forest*. Features a canyon-like *shut-in* that rises 100 feet above the roadbed, scenic igneous rock glades and cliffs, a headwater stream, and forests. Rt. 1, Box 1 (Hwy. 34), Piedmont 63957. SR 21, S 4.8 m.

SR 49 Towns. Paralleling the St. Louis & Iron Mountain *Railroad's* 1871 route, the highway has attracted towns with colorful names: Chloride,[1] Sabula,[2] Annapolis,[3] Vulcan,[4] Des Arc,[5] and Gad's Hill (*Piedmont*), site of Missouri's first train robbery.

SR 72 Guardrails. Between Arcadia and *Fredericktown* is one of the state's oldest highway guardrails, a low native stone wall built using *WPA* funds by Reichert Brothers during the late 1930s.

Stouts Creek Shut-Ins (Lower). Road cuts near these *shut-ins* show purple and red volcanic rock. Here, just north of SR 21, was the first (1816–1819) iron furnace west of Ohio. SR 72 at SR 21; SR 72, E 2.3 m.

Taum Sauk Generator / Reservoir. This unique 50-million-dollar hydroelectric plant, built in 1960–1963 for use during peak demand (usually warm months), can generate 350,000 kilowatts. A 55-acre reservoir on top of 1,590-foot Proffit Mountain holds 1.5 billion gallons of water that flows down a 7,000-foot shaft through a powerhouse, spinning turbines to generate electricity, then into a lower reservoir where the water is pumped back to the top during low-demand periods (usually nights and weekends). Geological and natural science museum, picnic area, tours. SR 21, S 7 m.; SR AA, W 2.8 m.; signs.

Taum Sauk Mountain State Park. The park is located in the St. Francois Mountains among thick woods with igneous rock outcroppings and isolated glades supporting *prairie* grasses. Various legends try to explain the names of the park and its geological wonders. The consensus is that Taum Sauk, chief of the Piankashaw

Indians, had the suitor of his daughter Mina Sauk thrown from the top of the mountain; Mina jumped after him. A bolt of lighting then cleaved the mountain, causing water to pour over them, washing away their blood except that which remains today as crystals (pink porphyry) and as flowers (Indian pinks). Factual discrepancies detract from this romantic story: Sauk *Indians* lived in northeast Missouri, Taum and Mina are not recorded names, and the Piankashaw briefly lived in southwest Missouri. Regardless, the area is as picturesque as the legend. SR 21, S 3 m.; SR CC, W 3 m. DEVIL'S TOLL GATE: About 0.75 m. down the trail from Mina Sauk Falls (below). Most likely formed by weathering, this eight-foot-wide gap in a ridge of orange and red porphyry is about 50 feet long and 30 feet high. MINA SAUK FALLS: The highest waterfall in Missouri has a nearly vertical fall of 132 feet. Its jagged rocks are highlighted by pink crystals. OZARK TRAIL: *Trails: Ozark Trail (Taum Sauk section).* TAUM SAUK MOUNTAIN: At 1,772 feet it is the highest point in Missouri *(Mansfield: Lead Hill; Caledonia: Buford Mountain);* lookout tower. The mountain is composed mostly of Precambrian rocks; from the oldest geological era, they are over 1 billion years old. A trail from the parking lot leads to Mina Sauk Falls (above). *(State Parks)*

Ursuline Academy. Vernacular, 1913. Originally built in 1847 as a Methodist Episcopal high school, briefly Arcadia Seminary (1870), it was bought in 1876 by the Ursuline Order and operated as a Catholic girls school until closing in 1970. Vacant. E. Maple and College.

1. Possibly for the ore, silver chloride; p.o. 1904–1953.
2. Possibly a woman's name, but probably from Latin for sand or gravel; p.o. Ozark Mills *(Ozark)* 1871–1887; Sabula 1884–1952.
3. Formerly Allen; RR president T. Allen's wife, Anna, + apolis, Greek for city; p.o. 1871–now.
4. Roman god of fire; p.o. 1895, 1913–now.
5. French-Indian, to the arcs or bows as in a river, but in this case where the railroad curves abruptly; p.o. 1871–now.

ARROW ROCK

Population: 70   Map E-3

National Historic Site, State Historic Site, National Historic Register. Adjacent to a prehistoric ford of the Missouri River described by the *Lewis and Clark Expedition* as "confined within a [river] bed of 200 yards" and offering "a fine landing on a Rocky Shore under the Clift [*sic*]," the townsite began as a ferry crossing established in 1811 by Henry Becknell; licensed in 1818, the ferry was used 1821–c. 1826 during the first regular trading expeditions along the *Santa Fe Trail,* which crossed the Missouri here from Franklin

(New Franklin). Platted in 1829 as Philadelphia[1] by M. M. Marmaduke (Sappington Cemetery, below), the town was renamed in 1833 for its post office. The name Arrow Rock supposedly derives from reports of flint found near the rock bluff by early explorers, who assumed its use was for making arrow points. A colorful version claims the bluff was originally called Airy Rock because of the cool high wind at its top *(Huntsville: Mount Airy)* and that local pronunciation of "arrow" as "arry" later led to the interpretation of "arrow" in place of "airy." The town grew as a trade center (mid–1800s pop. 1,000), then declined after being bypassed by railroads to the north and south. Post office: 1821–now. Facilities: Picnicking, trails, basic and improved camping, RV services (dump station, electricity, showers, water). Summer: walking tours, demonstrations (art, gardening, craft, music).

Architecture. Over a dozen historic buildings can be toured. CHRISTIAN CHURCH: 1872. Has its original furnishings. FEDERATED CHURCH: 1849. Still active. HALL HOUSE: 1846. Furnished. SITES GUN SHOP: 1840s. Contains tools and parts arranged to show procedures for repairing 19th-century weapons. SITES HOUSE: Probably Adamesque when built in the 1830s. Bought by John Sites in 1866; enlarged and remodeled 1874–1876. Furnished. ZION UNITED CHURCH: 1857. Still active.

Arrow Rock Jail. Vernacular, 1871. This one-room jail with limestone walls and iron door reportedly confined only one prisoner, who lamented his plight so loudly he was released. In town.

Arrow Rock Tavern. Adam, 1834; National Historic Register. Built by Judge Joseph Huston as a four-room two-story brick tavern, it was expanded several years later by two additions and served as a general store, meeting hall, ballroom, and hotel until bought and restored in 1923 by the state. Two portraits by George Caleb Bingham (below) are on display. In town.

Country Doctor's Museum. Log, 1830s. Medical instruments from the 19th to early 20th century depict the fast growth in medical knowledge. In town.

George Caleb Bingham House. Adamesque, c. 1837; additions, restored twice by the state (1936, 1964–1965); National Historic Register, National Historic Landmark. The original layout is still uncertain; furnished. Bingham (1811–1879), recognized for depicting everyday Missouri life, was the first painter to seriously interpret this region. Self-taught at first, he began painting portraits before he ever saw one. Although he built this house for his wife, neither lived here long. She lived in *Boonville,* while he worked back east from 1837 to 1844. He sold the house in 1845. In town.

Lyceum Theater. Built in 1872 as a Baptist church, this is now Missouri's oldest (since 1961) summer repertory theater; evening and matinee performances. In town.

Old Saline County Courthouse. Vernacular Greek Revival, 1839; restored. Arrow Rock was Saline County's third seat of justice in 1839–1840 (*Marshall*). This one-story clapboard structure was reportedly used as a setting for George Caleb Bingham's (above) 1852 painting "County Election." In town. (*County Profiles*)

Sappington Cemetery. State Historic Site. Shaded by large cedars at a scenic site near Flat Creek, this two-acre cemetery has more than 100 headstones, some of them elaborate. Buried here are CLAIBORNE F. JACKSON (1806–1862), pro-Southern governor (1861) who, while in office, took up arms against the Union at the onset of the *Civil War*; MEREDITH M. MARMADUKE (1791–1864), governor (1844), whose son, John S., was a Confederate general (*Civil War: Battle of Boonville; Price's Raid*) and governor (1885–1887); DR. JOHN SAPPINGTON (1776–1856), who pioneered the use of quinine to replace bloodletting for treatment of malaria. Sappington is the grandfather of John Sappington Marmaduke, the father of Thomas Sappington (*Crestwood*), and the father-in-law of both M. M. Marmaduke and C. F. Jackson, who married three of Sappington's daughters. When Jackson asked for the third, Sappington's legendary response was, "You can take her, but don't come back after the old woman." SR TT, S 4.7 m.; SR AA, S 0.2 m.; first road E after Flat Creek, 0.4 m. (*Cemeteries*)

Sappington House. Early Classical Revival, 1844; National Historic Register. Built by William B. Sappington, son of Dr. John Sappington (above), this brick mansion with a two-story portico is a fine example of its style. SR TT, S 3 m.

---

1. *Palmyra: Marion City;* p.o. Arrow Rock.

ASH GROVE

Population: 1,128   **Map D-6**

The first settler in the area was Daniel Boone's youngest son, Nathan (below), who became interested in the area while surveying for the government c. 1834. Founded in 1853 by Joseph Kimbrough as Kimbrough and platted in 1870, the town was reincorporated in 1871 (due to a defective 1870 charter) as Ash Grove in honor of its 1849 post office, which was named for a nearby grove of ash trees. An agricultural town, it prospered with the arrival c. 1881 of the Springfield & Western *Railroad*. Post offices: 1849–1864, 1866–now.

Bois D'Arc, Mo. The Osage orange, hedge apple, or bois d'arc (French, literally wood-of-bow) tree was used by *Indians* for making bows because of the wood's flexibility and strength. The place-name Bois D'Arc is usually used for a forest or grove. Various spellings (Bowdark, p.o. below) are usually attributed to phonetic renderings. Later, settlers planted these trees as living fences, making their stout thorns a virtue. Found throughout Missouri, they flower May–June; the rough-textured softball-size inedible fruit falls in October, turning from green to yellow. Post offices: Grand Prairie[1] 1846–1847; Bowdark 1847–1863, 1867–1868; Bois D'Arc 1868–now. US 160, E 4.9 m.; SR UU, S 4.9 m. BOIS D'ARC *WILDLIFE AREA.*

Frisco Railroad Museum. Over 1,000 items related to the St. Louis & San Francisco *Railroad*, including a wooden passenger coach and a Pullman compartment and dining car. In town.

Nathan Boone Homestead. Log, 1837; National Historic Register, State Historic Site. This four-room cabin with stone chimneys at either end is divided by a hallway. After retiring in 1853 from the 1st Regiment of the Dragoons (America's first cavalry unit, organized in August 1833 at Jefferson Barracks in *St. Louis*), Boone lived here until his death in 1856. He and his wife, Olive Van Bibbler (*Mineola*), are buried close to the cabin (*Boonslick Trails; Defiance: Boone Home*). Protected site. Contact: Missouri Department of Natural Resources, Box 176, Jefferson City 65102.

Walnut Grove, Mo. Formerly known as Possum Trot,[2] the town was platted in 1859 as Walnut Grove, whose name, like the post office's, is for the locally abundant black walnut trees. Post office: 1853–now. SR V, N 8 m. PHENIX MARBLE QUARRY: Once one of America's largest marble-producing quarries, its adjacent community (1910 pop. 250) was named Phenix.[3] Marble from here was used in the Missouri State Capitol, the Russ building in San Francisco, and the Petroleum Securities building in Los Angeles. Abandoned. FR 43, S approx. 3 m.; inquire locally.

---

1. Location (*Prairies*).
2. A common derogatory name indicating an area so remote that opossum trails (trots) run through it.
3. A shortened version of Phoenix, the mythological bird that rose from its own ashes; connotes hope for the future; p.o. 1886–1942; defunct.

ATHENS

Population: 15   **Map G-1**

Platted in 1844 at the Des Moines River by pioneer settler Isaac Gray, this port town had eight dry-goods stores before a Civil War battle here (below). The town declined after the war when bypassed by railroads. Its classical name, derived from Athens, Greece, was first popularized in America by Athens, Ga. (founded

1801). Post offices: Sweet Home (below) 1835–1841; Athens 1841–1922.

Architecture. Restoration is being conducted on 19th-century homes. One example is the Benning House; during the Battle of Athens (below) a cannonball was shot through it, brushing past John Benning (the hole remains).

Battle of Athens / Park. Battle of Athens State Historic Site. This August 5, 1861, skirmish was part of Federal strategy to stymie Confederate control of port towns in the state *(Lexington)*. Federal Col. David Moore defeated pro-Southern Missouri State Guard Col. Martin E. Green here in what is reported to be the northernmost *Civil War* battle west of the Mississippi. Federal, 3 killed, 8 wounded; Confederate, 14 killed, 14 wounded. Interpretive trails, picnic area, basic camping (water and electricity), boating, sailing, fishing. (Architecture, above; Des Moines River, below)

Des Moines River Ravines Natural Area. 40 acres. Part of the Battle of Athens State Historic Site. Features ravines along steep north-facing slopes overlooking the Des Moines River. The slopes support unusually rich flora, including ferns, snow trillium, and blue cohosh. Revere 63465.

Iliniwek Village State Park. State Historic Site. To date, this former village is the only evidence in Missouri of habitation by the Iliniwek or Illinois *Indians*. Reportedly it was visited in 1673 by Marquette and Jolliet during their historic exploration of the Mississippi River *(Altenburg: Wittenberg)*. Acquired 1992; no facilities; protected site.

Sweet Home, Mo. A trading post established near here in 1832 grew into a steamboat port community by 1836 that prospered until overshadowed by Athens. Its name is commendatory; it is not known which came first, the popular song title or the place-name. Defunct. Post office: 1835–1841. GR, S 2 m. along the Des Moines River to Cedar Creek.

AUGUSTA

Population: 263   Map H-4

Patent deed #63 for the original townsite was issued to Leonard Harold, who platted a town in 1836, naming it Mount Pleasant. Due to an existing Mount Pleasant, this Mount Pleasant, when applying for a post office, used the name Augusta. When incorporated in 1855, the town adopted the post office name. Although local tradition claims the name honors Harold's wife, records indicate that neither of his two wives was named Augusta, which obscures the origin. The town was primarily a Missouri River port until the current

changed in 1872, shifting the channel one mile south and ending its prosperity. Arrival of the Missouri, Kansas & Eastern *Railroad* c. 1892 helped replace the loss of river traffic. Post offices: Dardenne[1] 1820–1842; Augusta 1842–now.

Architecture. This small town has about 50 good examples of 19th-century structures, including commercial, residential, and church architecture of the 1840s–1860s.

Femme Osage, Mo. The site was settled in 1832 primarily by German immigrants along an alternate *Boonslick Trail* route and named for nearby Femme Osage Creek (French, meaning Osage wife or woman), which previously was the namesake for a territorial post office *(Defiance: Missouri / Missouriton)*. The local pronunciation is Fem'me (rhymes with Jimmy). This well-preserved community in a pastoral setting has fine examples of 19th-century rural architecture. Post office: 1839–1908. SR 94, W 1 m.; SR T, N 5.2 m. EVANGELICAL CHURCH *CEMETERY:* Established in 1837 at the site of the first (1833) Evangelical church west of the Mississippi. GENERAL STORE: Vernacular, c. 1842. Part of the original store can be seen inside a later general-store-style architectural addition. GERMAN SCHOOL: Vernacular, 1887. The stones for this one-story school were taken from an 1841 church.

Katy Trail State Park. S end of Public St. *(State Parks)*

Original Townsite. Harold's original plat included the blocks at the southeast corner of town, bounded on the north and west by High and Water Streets. Steamboats once docked across from the Sander Hotel (built 1849; S end of Public Street).

Wineries. MONTELLE WINERY: Its 1970 vineyards offer award-winning dry and semidry table wines, as well as dessert wines and a multifruit spiced wine. Overlooks the Missouri valley. SR 94, E 1.5 m. MOUNT PLEASANT WINE CO.: Its 1860 vineyards produce wines that have won national and international awards. Vaulted brick and stone cellars built in 1881–1887 are used for storage. Specialties: French- and German-style dry wines, America's first ice wine, and sparkling mead. Overlooks the Missouri valley. In town. OSAGE RIDGE WINERY: Overlooking the Missouri valley, it features dry and semidry wines. SR 94, E 1.5 m.

---

1. For a creek, via family name.

AUXVASSE

Population: 821   Map F-3

Platted in 1873 by T. B. Harris along the tracks of the Chicago & Alton *Railroad* at the site of the Clinton City[1] post office, the town was named for the nearby Aux

Vase River (American French, meaning at the swamps or muddy places). The name is also carried by the county's first (1826) township, as well as a river and town near *Ste. Genevieve*. Post offices: Clinton City 1872–1874; Auxvasse, 1874–now.

Mules. The legendary Missouri mule was first (c. 1823) introduced to the state by pack trains returning from Santa Fe *(Santa Fe Trail),* and soon Missouri had more mules than it needed. One of the first recorded advertisements (in the "Columbia Statesman," 1830) announced 42 mules for sale in the neighborhood of Aux Vasse Church. Quickly proven to be stronger and more reliable draft animals than oxen or horses, mules were shipped south for plantation work and west to *Independence* and *St. Joseph* for use in pulling wagon trains. Gaining international reputations even before their wide-scale publicity during the 1904 St. Louis World's Fair, Missouri mules were bought in large numbers by countries such as England, who used them in the 1899–1902 Boer War and in WWI *(Plattsburg: Lathrop).*

Whetstone Creek Natural Area. Part of Whetstone Creek *Wildlife Area.* Features 1.75 miles of the creek that is bordered on one side by steep wooded bluffs. The creek has short well-defined riffles and long deep pools and supports at least 34 different species of fish. Water willow and spike rush are common plants. Box 2, Williamsburg 63388. SR B, E 7.4 m.; SR A, S 1.8 m. to Bachelor;[2] GR E 1.2 m.; GR, S approx. 2 m. to parking lot; walk N 0.5 m.

1. Origin unknown.
2. For the creek, via unmarried men who settled beside it; p.o. 1875–1959.

AVA

Population: 2,938   Map F-7

Settled in the early 1830s, the area was known as California Barrens/Springs[1] and Militia Springs.[2] After Douglas County was organized in 1857, boundary changes led to bitter rivalries for county seat (Arno, Vera Cruz, below) that continued into the 20th century and included numerous elections, the burning of courthouses, and the theft of court records. Early historical records have been destroyed. Ava, selected in 1870 as a compromise central location for a new county seat, was platted and named in 1871 by James Hailey. Tradition claims the site was known as Militia Springs, but the name was too hard to spell (actually, Ava is 1.5 m. N of the springs). Reportedly, Hailey found "Ava" in the Bible (II Kings 17:24) and chose it because the name was short and, some say, because the

interpretation of the biblical reference could mean "overthrowing," which is what Ava did to its rivals for county seat. Another version says a doctor, Sellers, named it for his birthplace in England. Ava is also a woman's name. The town grew as a trading and political center. Post offices: Cow Skin[3] 1849–1865, 1867–1872, defunct; Ava 1872–now.

Arno, Mo. The origin of Arno's place-name is uncertain. According to "American Place-Names," Arno, Calif., was named for a person or the Italian River that originates northeast of Florence and empties into the Ligurian Sea near Pisa. Established c. 1857 near the confluence of Beaver and Cow Skin Creeks in Taney County, Missouri's Arno was shifted by boundary changes into Douglas County, where it was selected in 1869 by western county residents as a central location for a county seat, replacing Vera Cruz (below). Immediate objections from eastern county residents resulted in the 1870 compromise selection of Ava. Defunct. Post offices: 1857–1863 (in Taney County); 1867–1933 (in Douglas County). SR Y, W 5.8 m.; GR, S approx. 2 m. near cemetery and between creeks.

Assumption Abbey. This Cistercian (Trappist) monastery was founded in 1950 by monks from the Melleray Abbey of Dubuque, Iowa. Their intention is "to make their very lives a prayer" through common and private worship, Scripture study, and manual labor. Guest facilities available for prayer and reflection. SR 5, S 10 m.; SR P (becomes SR N), E 10 m.; SR OO, N 1.5 m.

Douglas County Courthouse. Moderne, 1937. The county's fifth (Ava's fourth), this two-story red-brick courthouse is trimmed with a mixture of crushed stone and cement polished to look like quarried stone. Of Ava's three courthouses in 65 years: the first (1872) was burned by vandals, the second (1873–1886) was burned by the assessor-treasurer to hide evidence of embezzlement, and the third (1888–1937) was condemned due to structural weakness. Today's is not on the town square (now a public parking lot) because the site was too small and traffic noise from the highway built in 1923 interfered with court business. Cost: $53,545. Downtown. *(County Profiles)*

Glade Top Trail / Fractures. This 60-mile round-trip trail in the Mark Twain *National Forest* can be hiked or driven in small portions that offer dense wildlife populations, smoke trees and junipers, picnic areas, *balds,* and spectacular views. The glade is a fracture system in which the vegetation, particularly junipers in this case, marks the angles in the dolomite. Appearing to be planted along a fence line, cedars cut straight edges trending northwest, growing from crevices that offer a better environment than the mostly barren rock. Trail marker #2 features Haden Bald (Natural Areas, below). SR 5, S 5 m.; SR A, W 3.7 m. to Smallett;[4] GR (follow

Glade Top Trail signs), S 3.7 m. to turnout with large map of tour area. Maps: Ava chamber of commerce, Box 88, 65608. Note: the trail essentially runs along FR 162 and FR 147 to Longrun *(Gainesville: Recreation, Glade)* from SR A to SR 95. GLADE TOP FESTIVAL: Established 1960, mid-October. Arts and crafts, food, guided hikes along Glade Top. Mid-October at Caney Picnic Area *(National Forests)*, which has an amphitheater and three picnic sites with grills and toilets but no drinking water. Box 23, Ava 65608.

Honey Branch Cave. *Sparta.*

Natural Areas. BRYANT CREEK: About 18 acres. Part of Rippee *Wildlife Area*, this high-quality headwater stream supports fauna and flora typical of this area. Box 138, West Plains 65775. SR 14, E approx. 11.1 m.; GR, S 0.8 m.; sign: Rippee Public Access. HADEN BALD: 40 acres. Part of Mark Twain *National Forest*, the bald features dolomite glades on slopes facing west, north, and east. Plants and animals are characteristic of the area, e.g. smoke trees and Bachman's sparrow. Box 188, Ava 65608. (Glade Top Trail, above; *Balds and Knobs*)

Pilot Knob. This area landmark, an erosional remnant capped by sandstone, is about 450 million years old. SR 14, W 5 m. *(Balds and Knobs)*

Rockbridge Mill. *Gainesville.* SR 5, S 17 m.; SR 95 E 9 m.; SR N, N 2.6 m.

Vera Cruz, Mo. Established at Bryant Creek c. 1850 and named for the Mexican town brought to national attention during the 1846–1848 *Mexican War*, this town served during 1857–1869 as county seat of newly organized Douglas County (Arno, above). Post offices: 1859–unknown, unknown–1870, 1873–1879, 1881, 1883–1936. SR 14, E 9 m.; SR AB, N 3.6 m.; GR, E 0.3 m. *FLOAT STREAM:* Bryant Creek. OLD VERA CRUZ: Original town remnants include a rock building and the dam of a former mill. GR at SR AB; GR, S 0.5 m. at creek and *cemetery*. VERA CRUZ ACCESS: Steep bluffs, clear water at end of SR AB at junction of Hunter and Bryant Creeks.

1. An 1850s camp for California-bound immigrants.
2. Civil War camp.
3. Via the creek, origin unknown, but cow prefixes are common, usually referring to an incident—e.g. Cowskin Island, Calif., where people built cowhide shelters.
4. First postmaster James Small; p.o. 1888–1967.

BALDS AND KNOBS

Depending on the region, the terms "mountain," "hill," "mound," "bald," and "knob" are used indiscriminately to define a noticeable difference in elevation. BALDS: Mountains (actually prominences)

characterized by a glade, an open area of rock or vegetation surrounded by timber. Generally of Lower Ordovician dolomite, some are capped by Mississippian limestone. Trees are commonly cedar due to their adaptability to thin soil and carbonate rocks. KNOBS: Erosional remnants of various ages (generally Ordovician). They are occasionally capped by Pennsylvanian limestone and/or conglomerate (a gravel naturally cemented to form a rock). Usually distinctive because of rising to a point, they were often used as navigational references—e.g. *Pilot Knob*. (Baldknobbers, reportedly named for their meeting place on Bald Knob near *Branson* and *Forsyth*, were organized c. 1884 as vigilantes to combat post–Civil War violence. After they became a problem rather than a solution, three Baldknobbers were hanged for murder in 1889 at *Ozark*, which effectively disbanded the group.)

BARING
Population: 182   Map F-1

Platted in 1888 along the tracks of the newly arrived (1887) Atchison, Topeka & Santa Fe *Railroad*, the town was named by the Santa Fe Town & Land Company for the Baring Brothers of London, England, who loaned $70 million for the railroad's construction. Post office: 1888–now.

Baring Depot. Vernacular, c. 1889. Built by railway workers, this small rectangular structure, originally twice the present size, stayed open 24 hours a day and employed three telegraph operators.

St. Aloysius Catholic Church. Vernacular (some Romanesque and Eastlake affinities), 1893; remodeled 1927. This church reflects the town's Irish Catholic roots. In town.

St. Mary's. Vernacular, 1904; National Historic Register. This noteworthy frame church has a commanding elevation, ornate tin ceilings, and mismatched towers: one square with a pyramidal roof, the other octagonal with a dome. SR 11, W 9 m. to Adair.[1]

1. Adair County namesake *(County Profiles)*; p.o. 1878–1900.

BARNARD
Population: 234   Map C-1

Platted in 1870 at the grade of the Kansas City, St. Joseph & Council Bluff *Railroad*, the town was named for B. F. Barnard, superintendent of the line. Post offices: Prairie Park[1] 1862–1872; Barnard 1871–now.

Depot Museum. Railroad, 1870. With wood pilings and overhanging roof, this frame structure is typical of Mid-American depot architecture. Local historical items. In town.

Groves Cemetery. One of Nodaway County's oldest cemeteries, its first interment was Elion Smith in 1846. SR M, E 4.6 m. to Guilford;[2] continue SR M, E 0.8 m. to 1st S GR, S 0.2 m. *(Cemeteries)*

One Hundred and Two River Shut-Ins. Upstream from town the valley is a quarter-mile wide; downstream it is two miles wide. Inquire locally. *(Shut-Ins)*

1. Location *(Prairies)*.
2. Via Guilford Court House, N.C., which takes its name directly from England's Lord North, Earl of Guilford; p.o. Carterville, family name, 1853–1856; Guilford, 1856–now.

BELL AIR
Population: 25   Map E-4

The original stage stop on the 1820s Boonville-Warsaw Trail *(Roads and Traces)* was settled c. 1825 by Nathaniel Leonard (Ravenswood Farm / House, below) and named Bellair for unknown reasons. The last post office (1906) spelled the name Bell Air, today's maps list the town as Bellair, and 19th-century maps used various spellings, including Belle Air. Any of these combinations could be a transferred place-name or locally inspired. Traditionally, the derivation is from the personal name Bell or the French for beautiful air. Post offices: Palestine[1] 1835–1836, 1838–1849 (Speed, below); Bellair 1849–1864; Bell Air 1864–1906.

Briscoe Cemetery. Grave of Hannah Cole, 1810 founder of *Boonville*, who was reportedly one of the first white settlers on the south side of the Missouri River west of St. Louis. DAR marker; roadside park adjacent. SR 5, S 3 m. *(Cemeteries)*

Mt. Nebo Church. Vernacular, 1856; National Historic Register. Small brick church with separate entrances for men and women that corresponded to sanctuary seating. The *cemetery* dates from 1868. SR 5, S 2 m.; SR E, W 2 m.

Ravenswood Farm / House. Established in 1825 by Nathaniel Leonard, this farm in 1839 became the first west of the Mississippi to breed purebred Shorthorn cattle; by 1919 the third generation of Leonards reportedly owned the world's oldest Shorthorn stock farm. HOUSE: Eclectic Victorian, 1880; National Historic Register. This two-story house has ornate columns, mansard roof, central tower, and 30 rooms; tours. SR 5, S approx. 0.6 m.

Speed, Mo. In 1869 the 1833 town of Palestine (Bell Air, above) was moved a mile east to the Boonville branch of the Pacific & Missouri River *Railroad*, where it was renamed New Palestine. In 1898 a *post office*, Speed, was established, and the town's name was changed to match that of the post office. Usually Speed is a person's name. Post offices: New Palestine[2] 1869–1898; Speed 1898–1955. SR 5, N 0.8 m.; SR F, E 2.7 m. ADELINE RAY: Born a slave on June 10, 1810, in Virginia, she was brought to Missouri in 1850, freed after the Civil War, died at her son's house in *Sedalia* on April 8, 1920, and was buried near her former home at Speed. *Cemetery:* GR, W 1 m. near Stephens Branch of Petite Saline Creek.

1. Biblical Canaan.
2. New town location via biblical Canaan.

BELLE
Population: 1,218   Map G-5

Today's 1st Street is the Maries–Osage County line, which leaves about 12 percent of the population in Osage County. Before J. W. Terrill platted the town in 1901 for the St. Louis, Kansas City & Colorado *Railroad*, the post office changed locations four times (below), keeping the same name, Belle. In an area known as Gallaway's *Prairie*, the town was established in 1901 by J. S. Ridenhour, a local merchant since 1873, who gave the railroad every other town lot and reportedly named the town Belle, because establishing it reminded him of a Southern lady making her debut. Another version claims it was named for the only single girl (or a pretty girl) in town, Belle Wallace. Both versions ignore the fact that the post office name predates the founding of the town, which leaves the origin uncertain. Post offices: 1878–1895, 1900–1901 (in Osage County); 1895–1900, 1901–now (in Maries County).

Canaan State Forest. *State Forests.*

Paydown, Mo. The community that grew around this *gristmill* site, first used c. 1830 alongside a large spring (about 11.5 million gallons daily), was named in 1850 for the post office established by mill owner Thomas Kinsey, whose policy was pay-down-or-no-deal. Today, the former post office, a store, the mill (c. 1892), and a 19th-century house built by the Bray family *(Iberia: Bray's Mill)* still stand; private. Post office: 1850, 1855–1862, 1866–1932. SR 42, W 5.9 m.

Tunnel Cave. In a classic example of *stream piracy*, this 110-foot-long natural tunnel captured two streams on the east side of a ridge and funneled them underneath the ridge to join a third stream on the west side. Previously, the east-side streams joined the west-side stream at the north end of the ridge. Today, the northeast side of the ridge has no water. From the road on top of the *cave*, the piracy process is apparent. SR 89, N 3.6 m.; at Pilot Knob sign, W 1.7 m.; 1st junction, S 1.3 m.; 2d junction, W 0.6 m. to a hump in the road near a house.

BELTON
Population: 18,150   Map C-4

Platted in 1871 along the grade of the Kansas City, Clinton & Springfield *Railroad* by former Confederate soldiers G. W. Scott and W. H. Colbern, the town was most likely named for Confederate Capt. Marcus Lindsey Belt, who helped survey it. Proximity to *Kansas City* helped establish today's economy. Post office: 1872–now.

Belton Cemetery. Two notable personalities are buried here. DALE CARNEGIE (1888–1955): Born in *Maryville*, he was most famous for "How to Win Friends and Influence People" (1936). His grave is marked by eight stone pillars with chains between them; east cemetery entrance, center section. CARRY AMELIA MOORE NATION (1846–1911): Characterized as an ax-wielding temperance leader, she began her crusade in 1889 at Medicine Lodge, Kans., progressing from stones to bricks to her famous ax—first used in 1900 to destroy Wichita's Hotel Carey bar. Her last public words, "I have done what I could," are paraphrased on her marker. East cemetery entrance, midway, first section. 2.5 m. from SR 58 at SR Y: S on SR Y, W on Cambridge. *(Cemeteries)*

City Hall / Belton Museum. Vernacular, 1906. Built as a city hall, the building had no city offices until 1940. Until then, it housed community activities, including basketball, and even served as a factory for The Grace Company (moved here in 1936 and now known for youth fashion designs). Local historical items and exhibits about Truman, Carnegie, and Nation (Belton Cemetery, above). 512 Main St.

Harry S. Truman House. In 1886, Truman *(Grandview; Independence; Lamar)* briefly lived four and a half miles south of Belton (private; inquire locally). In 1908 he was accepted for membership in Belton Lodge #450.

Peculiar, Mo. Platted in 1868, the town reportedly gained its peculiar name, as did Peculiar, Wis., as a result of frustration and wry wit. Local tradition claims that after submitting several names to the postal department that were rejected as already in use, postmaster E. T. Thompson sent a final suggestion with an addendum, asking that if this suggestion was also unacceptable, the department suggest a "peculiar" name (in the sense of one out of the ordinary). By return mail, without explanation, Thompson received

his commission as "postmaster of Peculiar, Cass Co., Mo." *Post office:* 1868–now. US 71, S 7 m.

BENTON
Population: 575   Map J-6

Platted in 1822 as county seat of newly organized Scott County, the town was named for one of Missouri's first U.S. senators, Thomas Hart Benton *(County Profiles: Benton)*, whose daughter Jessie married explorer John C. Frémont *(Stockton)* in 1841. In 1856, Benton unsuccessfully tried to block Frémont's Republican nomination for president. Repeated raids during the *Civil War* destroyed most of the county records and caused the county seat to be moved in 1863 to Commerce,[1] where it remained until returned here by popular vote in 1878. Because Benton was bypassed by railroads until the 20th century, its economy was based on county politics. Post office: 1823–1864, 1867–now.

Chaffee, Mo. Platted in 1905 by the St. Louis & San Francisco *Railroad* as a division point, the town was named for Gen. A. R. Chaffee (1842–1914), who was commissioned an army lieutenant during the Civil War, served with distinction during the 1898 Spanish-American War, and was U.S. Army chief of staff in 1904. Post office: 1905–now. US 61, N 2 m.; SR A, W 8 m. TWYAPPITY COMMUNITY LAKE: 37 acres. Bass, sunfish, crappie, catfish. This curious name also appears nationally as Tywhapita and Tyewhoppety. Reportedly first used in Missouri c. 1789 for this area's Twyappity Bottoms (also known as Zewapeta), it was probably transplanted from Kentucky and is probably Algonquian in all its spellings, loosely meaning a point of no return in the sense of a halfway mark. A Tywappidy post office (1805–c. 1811) in Cape Girardeau District *(County Profiles)* may be yet another spelling or a typographical error. SR A, E 0.7 m.; SR RA, N 0.9 m.

General Watkins State Forest. As on much of *Crowley's Ridge*, trees here are similar to those of the Appalachians, e.g. beech, sweet gum, tulip poplar. Erosion has cut the *loess* into ravines up to 50 feet deep in places. *(State Forests)*

St. Lawrence Catholic Church. Vernacular, 1857–1861; Romanesque-style tower and facade added 1909. Built by Belgian immigrants who used locally quarried stone, the church was burned during the Civil War, leaving only the walls intact. US 61, N 2 m.; SR A, W 2 m. to New Hamburg.[2]

Scott County Courthouse. Italian Renaissance, 1912–1913. The county's sixth and longest serving courthouse was designed by H. H. Hohenschild, whose work is also found in Barry, Pemiscot, and Christian Counties. The three-story brick building, with quoins and balustrades, has a two-story colonnaded porch, two 52-by-55-foot wings, and a central projecting 56-by-122-foot entry. Estimated cost: $100,000–140,000. Downtown. *(County Profiles)*

Sikeston, Mo. Platted in 1860 by John Sikes along the Cairo & Fulton *Railroad* and the former King's Highway *(Roads and Traces)*, the town was about a half-mile north of the then-defunct town of Winchester, a former county seat of *New Madrid* County. Two years later Federal general John Pope used the town as a garrison while waiting for heavy guns from Cairo, Ill., to use at the siege of *New Madrid*. The town's location by a major road and railroads (the St. Louis & San Francisco arrived c. 1906) helped it to grow as a shipping point for agricultural products and, briefly, timber *(Bunker)*. Post offices: Pleasant Plains[3] 1834–1860; Sikeston 1860–1864, 1867–now. SR 77, E 1.5 m.; I-55, S 16.7 m. Home of Sikeston Area Vocational School. DOWNTOWN: Reminders of the former commercial district, once oriented to the depot, remain near the public square platted one block west. US 61B.

1. Commendatory; p.o. 1834–now.
2. The German city-state; p.o. 1874–1972.
3. Commendatory, descriptive.

BETHANY

Population: 3,005   Map D-1

Founded by John Allen in 1841 (First Christian Church, below), the town was platted in June 1845 at Big Creek as Dallas,[1] county seat of newly organized Harrison County. Reportedly the name was unpopular, and six months later the county court changed it to Bethany, after the town (today, El Azareyeh, 2 m. E of Jerusalem) revered by Christians as the home of Lazarus and Mary Magdalene and the place where, according to Luke 24:50–51, Christ's disciples witnessed the Ascension. The arrival in 1880 of the Chicago, Burlington and Quincy *Railroad* helped establish the town as a trading center. Initially, both Dallas (Greene County 1844–1857) and Bethany (Clay County 1844–1848) were already in use as post office names. Post offices: Bethpage[2] 1846–1850; Bethany 1850–now. Maps: chamber of commerce, E side of square.

Brooklyn, Mo. Settled in 1830 as Snells Mill,[3] the town was platted as Brooklyn in 1854 and named for one of New York City's five boroughs, which in turn was named for Breuckelen, the Netherlands. Post office: Snells Mill 1856–1868; Brooklyn 1868–1908. US 69, N 7 m.; SR Z, W 2.6 m. BROOKLYN BRIDGE: This 14-foot-wide WPA-era iron bridge spanning Big Creek is set on cut-limestone piers; high railings, 8-ton limit. SR Z, W edge of Brooklyn. BROOKLYN FALLS: This site near Snells mill has been popular for picnics since the 1830s. Water cascades over a broad rock shelf that is also a natural ford; good swimming hole. Just W of bridge. PROPOSED BROOKLYN LAKE: About 279 acres for flood control and drinking water. W 2 m., N on SR W; inquire locally.

Eagleville, Mo. The town was called Eagle from its first settlement c. 1844 until 1881. Local tradition claims it was named for eagles nesting in the area. Post offices: Eagle 1853–1881; Eagleville 1881–now. US 69, N 14 m. LOG CABIN: Log, early 1830s. Features keystone cuts on the corner joints and walnut window trim. Inquire locally.

Edna Chuddy House. Italianate, 1882; National Historic Register. This two-story 12-room house features pink brick, tall narrow windows, and bracketed eaves. US 69, W on Main to 14th.

First Christian Church (Disciples of Christ). Gothic, 1900. Established in 1841 by town founder and 1845 county seat commissioner John Allen, today's brick church with elaborate stained-glass windows and a square corner tower is the fourth structure, the third at this site since 1855. US 69, W on Main, N on 17th.

Geodesic House. Built in 1984, this 3,000-square-foot three-story structure is set on a concrete slab with a wooden foundation. Triangular windows are positioned to catch the winter sun; an overhang blocks summer sunlight. US 69, E on Parkview to 28th.

Grant House. Greek Revival affinities, 1861–1866 (construction interrupted by Civil War). Built by Thomas Grant, who immigrated from England in 1857, this three-ranked, two-door, rectangular limestone house features two-foot-thick walls, three-foot-thick doorsills, interior fireplaces at either end, a ranking cornice with returns at the gable ends, and stone lintels; no porch. I-35, N 7.6 m.; SR A, E 3.5 m. to Ridgeway;[4] continue SR A, E 2 m.; GR, N 0.75 m.

Harrison County Courthouse. Moderne, 1938–1940. The fourth courthouse, this 87-by-83-foot limestone building, set on a slight elevation, has broad temple-style steps and marble corridors. After Bethany lost its central location when the Missouri–Iowa *boundary line* was moved about 10 miles south in 1851, it successfully defeated five attempts (1870–1912) to relocate the county seat. Cost: $124,000. US 69, W on Main. *(County Profiles)*

Harrison County Historical Museum. Displays of pioneer life and local items like corn-shuck dolls, farm tools, and a portable anesthetic device patented in 1919 by a local dentist. US 69, W on Main, S on Fuller to 17th.

Helton Prairie Natural Area. 30 acres. Part of Helton

Wildlife Area, this is this region's largest high-quality mesic *prairie*. 722 E. Hwy. 54, El Dorado Springs 64744. US 136, E 9 m.; SR CC, S 2.8 m.; GR, W 2 m.; sign.

Mitchelville Church. Vernacular, 1870. This simple clapboard church with double doors was turned around to face US 69 when the road was built in 1920. SR 136, W 2 m.; US 69, S 2.3 m.

Northwest Missouri State Fair. Since 1916; Labor Day.

Parks. ALLEN PARK: Rose garden; fountain with a 1904 statue, "Two Children Under an Umbrella." US 69, W on Main, N on 22d. BETHANY MEMORIAL PARK: Gardens, picnic area, grills, tennis, croquet, ball fields, pool, nature trail, and covered bridge over a stream. US 69, E on Parkview, N on 28th. TENTH STREET PARK: picnic tables, playground along Big Creek. US 69, W on Main to 10th.

Recreation. GRAND TRACE *STATE FOREST*. HELTON *WILDLIFE AREA*. LAKES: Fishing, picnicking. Old City Lake (US 69, N 0.5 m.); New City Lake (US 69, N 4 m.).

WPA Mural. Depictions of rural life painted in the heroic style of the era. Post office; W on Main, N on 15th to Central.

1. Powerful Pa. Democrat George Mifflin Dallas, U.S. vice president under James Madison.
2. A town near Jerusalem mentioned in the New Testament (Matt. 21:1).
3. Mill owner Noah Snell; p.o. 1856–1868.
4. Location on north–south ridge through county; p.o. 1880–now.

BETHEL

Population: 117   Map F-2

During the religious fervor of the late 1830s and early 1840s, the townsite was selected in 1844 by Prussian immigrant William Keil, who had recently recruited dissidents from The Harmony Society of Economy Village, Pa. (a communistic theocracy predating Karl Marx's 1848 Communist Manifesto). Keil's vision of a *utopian society* was Christian without church requirements, based on "from every man according to his capacity, to every man according to his needs." Biblical Bethel, "the house of God" 11 miles north of biblical Jerusalem, was named by Jacob after he dreamed of God. This Bethel's population of 650 owned over 4,000 acres, a steam-powered mill, a distillery, and industries like glove manufacturing that won first prize at the 1853 New York World's Fair. The town's decline began in 1855, when Keil led a resettlement group to Oregon to reportedly lessen contact with the world *(Oregon Trail)*. Keil never returned. Three other groups followed (1862–1867), but 340 people elected to stay. The colony disbanded in 1879, two years after Keil's death,

dividing the common property proportionally, according to the years spent there. Bethel remained vital (incorporating in 1883) until the Depression, when it declined severely. Since 1972, the town has been restored by another communal effort, Bethel Communal Colony, Inc., directed at tourism. Post office: Bethel 1848–now. Walking tours, maps, camping.

Architecture. The downtown is listed on the National Historic Register. Concentrated in a small area are over 30 structures dating from 1844. The first houses, some of which still stand, were prefabricated: doors, flooring, windows, etc., arrived as numbered, prefitted parts to be assembled on a limestone foundation. Originally stucco was used on exterior walls, but severe weather caused such quick damage that clapboard replaced the stucco. The brick houses usually have two stories and four rooms and are set snugly at the sidewalk. Tours.

Bethel Colony Band. The music played from a Victorian-style bandstand behind a picket fence is characteristic of German "oompah" bands. The town has maintained a band since 1844, but today's plays mostly c. 1900 music. Main St.

Bethel-Style Communities. These towns, now defunct, were founded soon after 1845: Mamri[1] [*sic*] (S side of North River), Elam[2] (1 m. E), and Hebron[3] (Cemetery, below). The largest, near *Novinger*, was Nineveh[4] (1876 pop. 30).

Cemetery. At Hebron (Bethel-Style Communities, above); colony members were buried by date of death, in rows, with no family plots. SR 15, N 0.5 m.; then W 0.5 m. and N 0.25 m. *(Cemeteries)*

Cherry Box, Mo. This late 1850s German community of *Mennonites* echoes the era's religious fervor. Their beliefs included rejection of war and violence, a literal following of Christ's teachings, and the practice of nonresistance and love, the latter being celebrated twice each year (as late as 1940) at a "love feast." They were known locally as Dunkards (corrupted from German, "dunker," to immerse) because of adult baptisms. The town name reportedly stems from the mail service box being either made of cherry or nailed to a cherry tree; however, a contemporary oral history claims the postmaster liked the word "cherry" and used "box" (for no given reason) as a combination not already in use as a post office name. Post office: 1858–1943. SR M, W 12 m.; SR B, N 2 m.

1. The Oak of Mamre at Hebron where Abraham went after separating from Lot (Gen. 13:18); no p.o.
2. Son of Shem and grandson of Noah (Gen. 10:1, 10:22); later a kingdom warring with Sodom (Gen. 14:1–16); no p.o.
3. Important biblical town; Abraham's wife Sarah died here (Gen. 23:1–2); no p.o.
4. *Novinger.*

BEVIER

Population: 643   Map F-2

Platted in 1858 by John Duff along the Hannibal & St. Joseph *Railroad*, the town was named for the township, which was settled in the 1830s by William Green of Kentucky, who honored fellow Kentuckian Robert Bevier, a pro-Southerner and later a Confederate colonel. Coal was discovered here in 1860, but the Civil War delayed mining. As the center of Macon County coal mining, the town attracted Welsh and Italian immigrants c. 1880, and its population boomed to 2,200 by 1889. Large-scale mining became unprofitable c. 1930, and the town declined. Post office: 1858–1860, 1863–now.

Bevier & Southern Locomotive. Used for hauling coal; displayed downtown.

Our Lady of the Highway Shrine. Built c. 1957 by Charles Bianchi for his wife, Tracey, and set beside a roadside park he donated to the state, the shrine was moved to St. Charles Cemetery after the highway was rerouted. Just S of Shoemaker's Museum (below).

Recreation. LAKES: Long Branch *(Lakes: Corps of Engineers)*; Thomas Hill: SR C, S 9.1 m.; SR T, W 2.7 m. *(Macon)*. STATE PARK: Long Branch. US 36, E 3.5 m.

Shoemaker's Museum. Large collection of miniature Navy vessels, photographs, and items related to the history of Bevier and its mines. US 36 at SR C.

BIRDS POINT

Population: 50   Map J-7

Never a large town, but strategically located near the confluence of the Mississippi and Ohio Rivers, Birds Point has served as a transfer point for both river and rail traffic. Abraham Bird acquired a Spanish land grant in 1798 and temporarily established a home here c. 1805. An 1811 record mentions him as "agent at Bird's Point near the mouth of the Ohio," but it could be referring to property of that name on the Illinois side. "Bird," in various combinations, has been used as a place-name for sites on both sides of the river. Abraham Bird's son, John, founded the town in 1824, but it was not platted until 1889 after construction began in 1881 on the Texas & St. Louis *Railroad*. The terminal here served as a transfer point for shipping railroad cars to Cairo, Ill., by ferryboat. Extreme fluctuations of the river in 1882–1907 contributed to the town's decline. Unprotected by levees, a reported 1,000 feet of land fell into the river during 60 days in 1908. Derelict. Post offices: Birdsville 1854–1859, 1863–1868,

1873; Bird's Point 1859–1863, 1878–1893; Bird Point 1893–1913.

Battle of Belmont. *East Prairie.* US 60, S 4 m.; SR 77, S 10 m.; SR 80, E 8 m.

Birds Point–New Madrid Floodway. *East Prairie.*

Mississippi River Bridge. The approach is a levee road at nearly telephone-pole height. This bright blue-green truss bridge can be seen for miles, as can the silver-colored truss bridge over the Ohio River beyond it.

Old Highway 7-A. Completed in 1921, this 16-foot-wide road between *Charleston* and Birds Point was one of Missouri's first concrete highways. Portions of the original road can still be driven: CR 205 between SR K and the river; CR 307 between US 60 and SR HH (SR 60, S approx. 1.5 m.); other remnants: N, S, and E of Wyatt[1] on US 60, SR EE, and SR HH.

1. Family name; p.o. 1895–now.

BLACK HAWK WAR, 1832

Black Hawk (1767–1838) was a subchief of the Sauk and Fox *Indians* who, along with Tecumseh *(Gainesville: Tecumseh)*, fought for the British in the *War of 1812.* Sauk and Fox land once included Illinois and northeast Missouri. Black Hawk, claiming that an 1804 treaty had deceived the Indians into ceding all land east of the Mississippi, organized 500 men to attack Illinois settlers. Expected attacks in Missouri did not occur. Black Hawk was captured and released in 1833 after meeting with President Andrew Jackson. The war resulted in the final removal in 1832–1833 of the Sauk and Fox from Illinois. Black Hawk's autobiography defending his people and himself is called an American classic.

BLACKWATER

Population: 221   Map E-3

Reportedly this was one of the oldest trading points in Cooper County (salt was manufactured here in 1808), but there was no post office until 1873 when a lead mine was established to the northeast. One owner of the future townsite, John Trigg, attempted to disinherit his son by leaving him only a dime as punishment for following the advice of "evil, wicked and traitorously affected persons" during the Civil War. Trigg's 1865 will also directed that his own tombstone (d. 1872) read: "He loved his whole Country." The son contested the will, won, and sold the land; it was later bought by W. C. Morris, who platted the town in 1887 along the recently completed tracks of the Missouri-Pacific *Railroad*. The town was named for the post office, which took its name from nearby Blackwater River (descriptive). Post office: 1873–1874, 1877–now.

Architecture. DOWNTOWN: Late 19th- and early 20th-century brick and frame. OTHERS: Cotton Patch School (frame, 1903, private), SR Z at SR AE. Peninsula Baptist Church (frame, 1873). SR K at SR Z.

Mozarkite. Philip Widel, a lifelong Blackwater resident, successfully lobbied in 1967 to have this colorful rock unique to Missouri and northern Arkansas adopted as the official state rock.

BLOOMFIELD
Population: 1,800   Map I-7

Reportedly a former Shawnee *Indian* village, this town on *Crowley's Ridge* was platted in 1835 as county seat of newly organized Stoddard County. Although this popular place-name is often derived from a personal name, in this case local tradition claims it was for the area, which reportedly was in full bloom at the time. A Federal military post during the *Civil War*, the town was mostly destroyed. Landlocked and without a railroad until the early 1890s, it successfully kept the county seat from *Dexter*, maintaining itself as the center of county business. Post offices: Castor[1] 1834–1836, defunct; Bloomfield 1836–now.

Architecture. Miller House: Greek Revival, 1843; State Historic Register. Private. Cape Rd. (W, 1st street S of SR AA).

Natural Areas. BEECH SPRINGS: 35 acres. Features trees common to *Crowley's Ridge*, a small stream, springs, and a natural ephemeral pond. HOLLY RIDGE: 84 acres. Features a natural stand of American holly, rare and interesting plants, and several small springs. Both areas: Holly Ridge *State Forest*, Box 631, Poplar Bluff 63901. 3 m. SE of town; inquire locally.

Park. Tennis, ball field, playground, picnic area, two restored log cabins (one story, c. 1862; two-story dogtrot, 1888), S side; W of SR AA.

Recreation. CROWLEY'S RIDGE *WILDLIFE AREA*; MINGO *NATIONAL WILDLIFE REFUGE*.

Stars & Stripes. Today's official newspaper of the Overseas Department of Defense was first printed here November 9, 1861, as "The Stars & Stripes" (*Hillsboro: De Soto; Macon*) by four Federal soldiers whose editorial page began, "The Stars And Stripes.—Once more wave over a town lost to patriotism and Honor." Plaque at courthouse; museum (below).

Stoddard County Courthouse. Italianate affinities,

1867–1870; extensively remodeled and enlarged to Italian Renaissance, 1909; National Historic Register. In 1910 cattle drives passed along unpaved streets beside this two-story brick building with its domed cupola, the county's third courthouse. Remodeling and enlargement added bracketed eaves, a pedimented and colonnaded projecting central entry, and arched windows. Original cost: $18,000; remodeling: $28,325. Architect P. H. Weathers also designed early-20th-century courthouses in Cape Girardeau and Daviess Counties. Downtown. (*County Profiles*)

Stoddard County Museum. Housed in a red-brick church building are local historical items: tools (for pottery, farming, etc.), furniture, one of three existing original issues of "The Stars & Stripes." Center and Delaware. SR AA to Center; W to Delaware.

1. For the river via French for beaver.

BLUE SPRINGS
Population: 40,103   Map C-3

Settled in the 1840s as an agricultural community along a major *road* that intersected the old *Santa Fe Trail* at *Independence*, the town was destroyed as a result of Civil War *Order No. 11*, rebuilt, and then moved east about a mile and platted in 1878 along the grade of the Chicago & Alton *Railroad*. An agricultural town until the 1920s, it developed into a suburb of the *Kansas City* metroplex. Named for its post office, which took its name from a popular spring-fed watering hole of the mid-1820s that formed a tributary of the Little Blue River. Post office: 1848–1864, 1867–now.

Burr Oak Woods Natural Area. 33 acres. Part of Burr Oak Woods *State Forest*. Features a mature and old-growth upland forest and limestone exposures with six-foot-deep mazes. Trails and wildlife refuge; 3,000-gallon native fish aquarium at the state forest nature center. Box 54, Blue Springs 64015. I-70; exit SR 7, N 1 m.

Lakes. BLUE SPRINGS: *Lakes: Corps of Engineers*. JACOMO: 970 acres. Fishing (bass, crappie, catfish), boating, swimming, picnicking, camping, sports. I-70 and SR 7; SR 7, S 4.75 m.; Cowherd Rd., W 2 m.; Cyclone School Rd., N 0.8 m. LONGVIEW: *Lakes: Corps of Engineers*.

Missouri Town 1855. Over 30 original 1820s–1850s structures from eight western Missouri counties were dismantled and reassembled here to create a typical 1850s farming community. Houses, barns, a school, a church, a tavern, a blacksmith shop, gardens—all facets of community life are represented in a natural setting. The staff dresses in period attire. E side of Lake Jacomo (above).

BOLIVAR
Population: 6,845   Map E-6

Although selected and named in 1835 as county seat of newly created Polk County, the town was not platted until 1841 (a city plan was drawn in 1835). The names of the county and town have similar origins. Col. Ezekiel Polk, the grandfather of settlers William and Ezekiel Campbell (also the grandfather of their cousin, President James K. Polk), was a pioneer settler of Hardeman County, Tennessee, whose county seat, Bolivar, was named for Venezuelan Simon Bolívar (1783–1830), leader of the 1817–1825 South American revolution that freed his country and four neighboring ones from Spain. The town had no frame houses until c. 1860. Arrival of the St. Louis & San Francisco *Railroad* in 1884 helped establish it as a trading center. Post office: 1836–now. Home of Southwest Baptist University. The town's alignment with a major 1830s north–south *road* (today's Main Ave.) reportedly caused the original plat to be drawn 22°W of north. (*Overland Mail Company*)

Brighton, Mo. Brighton had a Butterfield stagecoach (*Overland Mail Company*) way station (SR 13, N 1 m.; marker) and the first (1860) telegraph office in southwest Missouri. Named for Brighton, Tenn., which probably honors Brighton Beach, England (11th-century Brighthelmstone). Post office: 1852–now. SR 13, 11 m. S. PLEASANT HOPE *WILDLIFE AREA.*

Dunnegan, Mo. Bolivar resident and judge T. H. B. Dunnegan asked the manager of the Kansas City, Clinton & Springfield *Railroad* to name the 1885 railroad station Dunnegan Springs after his family, the first settlers there. The name was shortened after the *post office* was established. Post office: 1886–now. SR 32, W 9 m.; SR 123, N 6 m. SPRINGS: Picnic facilities. SR 123 at SR A.

Dunnegan Memorial Park. Five-acre lake, 60 wooded acres, picnic area, shelters, trails, playground. SR 83, NW city limits (Dunnegan, above).

Fair Play, Mo. A store owner named Owens, intending to establish a community just south of today's site, applied for a post office with the name Oakland but was refused because the name was taken, after which John Wakefield and Millard Easly donated land for today's townsite. Wakefield, probably because of the competition for a townsite, reportedly said, "We'll just call it Fair Play." This popular place-name is often associated with apocryphal stories, usually entangled with fighting fairly. Another Fair Play was briefly established c. 1860 near *St. Elizabeth* (no p.o.). Post office: 1852–now. SR 32, W 8 m. STOCKTON LAKE / *STATE PARK: Lakes: Corps of Engineers.*

Flemington, Mo. Named for Robert Fleming, who donated land for the town in 1898 along the St. Louis & San Francisco *Railroad.* The town's resemblance to a Western town inspired its use as a Hollywood set in 1910 for "The Range Rider," Tom Mix's first feature role. Post office: 1898–now. SR 83, N 14 m.; SR V, W 3.1 m.

Greenwood Cemetery. Established in 1887, the cemetery is extensively landscaped with flowers (e.g. peonies, irises, lilies) and over 50 varieties of trees. Among those interred here is Dr. A. H. Lewis, whose company manufactures Tums. SR 32 to Dunnegan Ave., S 4 blocks; W city limits. (*Cemeteries*)

Halfway, Mo. Named for its location approximately halfway between two county seats, Bolivar and *Buffalo,* the town is also about halfway between two other county seats, *Springfield* and *Heritage,* but this observation was not considered at the time. Post office: 1850–now. SR 32, E 10 m.

Humansville, Mo. Also known as Big Spring. Settled in 1834 by James Human at a large spring near one of southwest Missouri's two major north–south *roads.* Post office: 1839–now. SR 32, W 2 m.; SR 13, N 12 m.; SR 123, N 3 m. POMME DE TERRE LAKE: *Lakes: Corps of Engineers.*

La Petite Gemme Prairie Natural Area. 37 acres. The name, which translates as The Little Gem, reportedly describes the quality of wildflowers in this scenic upland *prairie.* SR 13, S 2 m.; GR, W 1 m.

North Ward School Museum. Vernacular, c. 1904. Displays include a restored schoolroom and exhibits relating to the school, the military, pioneer families, and a two-story log cabin. Main and Locust, N of courthouse.

Old Jail Museum. Vernacular, 1879. Replacing one razed in 1879, this building served as a jail until 1978. Today it houses local historical items: Indian artifacts, antique furniture, unusual household articles, tools, a Civil War–era newspaper printed on wallpaper. Downtown; 1 block S of courthouse.

Polk County Courthouse. Richardsonian Romanesque, 1906. One of the last two of its style built in Missouri (*Nevada*), this stone structure is nearly identical in its design and central clock tower to courthouses in Vernon, Carroll, and Adair Counties. Cost: $41,950. SR 83; W on Broadway to Main; court square. (*County Profiles*)

Polk County Ghost Towns. Many ghost towns have just histories; the following have a few structures. BURNS:[1] SR 32, E 6 m.; Pomme de Terre River. CLIQUOT:[2] SR 83, N 4 m.; SR B/BB, W 2.8 m.; SR O, N 1.8 m. RONDO:[3] Formerly *Rolla.* SR 83, N 12 m. TIN TOWN:[4] Once called Klondike (no p.o.) and then Gold. SR 13, S 11 m.; SR 215, E 8.5 m.

Statue of Simon Bolívar. Built in heroic proportions,

the statue was given to the city by Venezuelan president Romulo Gallegos and dedicated in 1948 by U.S. president Harry S. Truman. Neuhart Park: SR 83 at College St.

1. Named for Capt. Joseph Burns; p.o. 1884–1920.
2. The town founder's racehorse; p.o. 1893–1957.
3. Postmaster's name; p.o. *Rolla* 1858; Rondo 1858–1864, 1866–1919.
4. Klondike and Gold because of the gold prospecting in the area; changed due to the tin covering on the buildings; p.o. Gold 1900–1915.

BONNE TERRE
Population: 3,871   Map H-5

This area was referred to as Bonne Terre (French for good earth, especially for mining) c. 1825 by surface miners, but the town's beginnings can be traced to the 1864 incorporation of the St. Joseph Lead Co. in New York City. Surface mining began the next year on a 964-acre tract; subterranean mining began with the introduction of the diamond drill in 1869. First called St. Joe Lead Mines (or St. Joe Mines), the community's name was changed after the post office was established in 1868. It was first platted in 1880 as Bonne Terre. The purchase of other mines and the completion c. 1890 of the Mississippi River & Bonne Terre *Railroad* to haul ore to *Herculaneum's* smelters helped establish the company as the largest in southeast Missouri by 1900. Post offices: Bontear 1868–1876; Bonne Terre 1876–1895, 1906–now; Bonneterre 1895–1906. (*Desloge; Flat River*)

Architecture. All located in the old section of town; maps: Bonne Terre Mine. BONNE TERRE DEPOT: Railroad, 1909; National Historic Register; built by the Mississippi River & Bonne Terre *Railroad;* restored. CONGREGATIONAL CHURCH: 1910; reportedly patterned after an English cathedral. FORMER POST OFFICE / SAMARITAN LODGE: c. 1878, frame; also served as a meat market stocked by company herds. NATATORIUM: 1889, frame; used principally as a bathhouse. ST. JOSEPH CATHOLIC CHURCH: 1908–1917, stone; imposing central clock tower with dome. SHEPARD HOUSE: 1869, frame; reportedly the oldest structure in town.

Bonne Terre Memorial Library. Italian Renaissance, 1905. Small but remarkably detailed, the library was built from dressed limestone by St. Joseph Lead Co. president Dwight Jones. Features include a marble fireplace, an oak interior, and an 18th-century grandfather clock. Downtown; SR 47, S on School to Main.

Bonne Terre Mine. National Historic Site, National Historic Register. Legend claims that when the mine closed in 1961, the miners walked off, leaving tools, equipment, and personal items that ranged from eyeglasses to ore carts to a pneumatic jack stuck in a wall. Rain and underground springs have nearly filled what is called the largest man-made cavern in the world. Three tours: BELOWGROUND: Entering the cavern via a mule trail, this tour features mining equipment, a trout pond, a flower garden nurtured by the cavern's constant 62°F, and the smooth ceilings and huge stone pillars created by the flooding within the mine. SURFACE: Features a mining museum, barbershop, post office, and mining-related items. UNDERWATER: Billed as one of America's largest scuba diving resorts, the mine was explored in 1983 by Jacques Cousteau's "Calypso" crew for a Mississippi River valley documentary. More than 17 miles of navigable waterways are well lit, with deep chambers and tunnels, 200-foot pillars (some 50 feet in diameter), and abandoned tools and equipment. The experience has been compared to swimming over a shipwreck in Carlsbad Cavern. Visibility 80 feet, water temperature 58°F, diving depth 40–80 feet. US 67 and SR 47; 33 N. Allen.

City Hall. Tudor style, 1909. Reportedly a replica of William Shakespeare's home, today's city hall was built as the Cash and Carry Store, a typical company store, where miners bought on credit against their earnings. Downtown; SR 47, S on School (118).

Coonville Creek Natural Area. Eighteen species of fish, including the southern redbelly dace and the fantail darter, swim in this headwater stream. Numerous seeps feed the creek and also create boglike meadows that support rare plants like queen-of-the-prairie. Bonne Terre 63628. U.S. 67, N approx. 3.5 m. to St. Francois *State Park.*

French Village, Mo. Used as a campsite by late 18th-century French Canadian explorers, missionaries, and lead miners on a trail branching off El Camino Real (*Roads and Traces*), the site was first called Petit Canada;[1] the name was changed to French Village for its residents' nationality when the post office was established. The community was founded in 1825, after which the first Catholic chapel in St. Francois County was built here in 1828 (St. Anne, below). Post office: 1857–now. US 67, N 8 m.; SR Y, E 6.9 m. ST. ANNE CATHOLIC CHURCH / *CEMETERY:* Vernacular, 1870–1874. The front-gabled one-story limestone structure has an aboveground basement and stained-glass windows. The cemetery has several elaborate wrought-iron crosses and the grave of G. W. Brooks (1854–1937), a former slave who served six generations of the same family and whose epitaph reads, "Faithful In All Things." SR Y at Brickey Rd.

Missouri Mines State Historic Site. *Flat River.*

St. Joe Lead Co. Administration Building. Tudor, 1909; National Historic Register. From this two-story red-brick building trimmed in limestone, the company directed operations in the closely spaced mining towns of *Desloge,* Elvin, *Flat River,* and River Mines. W on SR 47, S on School.

St. Joseph Lead Co. Cottage. Now Mansion Hill House. Italian Renaissance, 1902. Built to accommodate company executives, this 32-room two-story "cottage" with Victorian furnishings sits on 130 acres and has a 45-mile view. Tours. SR 47 to Summit.

1. French for little Canada; no p.o.

BONNOT'S MILL
Estimated population: 175   Map F-4

Threatened by flooding at Côte sans Dessein *(Jefferson City)* in the early 1800s, French Canadians began crossing the Missouri River to settle at the Osage River just downstream from today's townsite, establishing a new community known as French Village.[1] Ironically, the great Missouri flood of 1844 destroyed this community, forcing residents uphill to today's site, which they named Dauphine.[2] French immigrant Felix Bonnot platted the town in 1852; c. 1855 he established a saw/ *gristmill* c. 1855, and people began to speak of going to Bonnot's mill. The town officially became Bonnot's Mill when the Pacific *Railroad* built a station here in 1868, but the post office name flip-flopped until 1892. *Post offices:* Bonnot's 1857–1869; Dauphine 1869–1892; Bonnot's Mill 1892–now.

Architecture. The entire town is listed on the National Historic Register. Set close together along narrow hilly streets at the river's edge are turn-of-the-century frame and brick buildings.

The Dauphine Hotel. Vernacular, c. 1890; National Historic Register. This two-story frame hotel has deep front porches on each level and a tin roof.

Frankenstein, Mo. This nearby hilltop community, centered around Our Lady of Help, a massive limestone Catholic church (Romanesque, 1922–1923), has provided an elementary school for Bonnot's Mill since the early 1970s; the secondary school is at Westphalia *(Freeburg).* Named for either Gottfried Franken, who donated land for the previous (1892) frame church here, or a church benefactor in Germany named Frankenstein. Post office: 1893–1921. SR C, E 7.2 m.

St. Louis Parish. Vernacular, 1906; remodeled/ enlarged. During the 1800s, the town had no church. Services were held six miles south at Loose Creek *(Linn).* After 1900, Germans began settling the area and, like Father Even, who established this parish, they were initially resented because they did not speak French. Top of Church Hill St.

1. The inhabitants; no p.o.
2. Former province in SE France, Dauphiné, one of the first to embrace the principles of the 1789 French Revolution; p.o. 1869–1892.

BOONESBORO
Population: 50   Map E-3

Platted in 1840 along the *Boonslick Trail* a few miles east of Boon's Lick (below), the town was reportedly named for Daniel Boone *(Defiance: Daniel Boone Historic Area)* but could have been named for one of his sons, Daniel Morgan or Nathan. Like the family name *(Boonville: Daniel Boon[e]),* the town name has been spelled both with and without the "e." The first store (which sold mostly tobacco and whiskey) was built by one of the town founders, Achilles Callaway *(County Profiles: Callaway).* With the shift in roads and the arrival of railroads, the town declined (1880s peak pop. 250). Post office: Boonesboro(ugh) 1871–1953.

Boon's Lick State Historic Site. This site, part of James Mackey's 1797 Spanish land grant, was the location for one of central Missouri's earliest industries, a salt-manufacturing business that was run from 1806 to 1811 by Daniel Boone's sons Daniel Morgan and Nathan in partnership with the Morrison brothers, who continued the operation until 1833, when plentiful salt eroded their business. The site produced about 100 bushels a day (a bushel, about 50 pounds, sold for $2–2.50; *County Profiles: Saline).* Facilities: wooded trail leading to the salt springs, interpretive material, picnic shelter. SR 87, N 1 m.; SR 187, S 2.2 m. *(Boonslick Trails)*

Loess Badlands. These badlands were formed by erosion and gullying of windblown deposits of claylike silt *(loess).* The stark and nearly vertical pinnacles and ridges reach heights of 30 feet. SW side of SR 87, 0.8 m N of junction with SR 187.

BOONSLICK TRAILS

BOONSLICK TRAIL: Cut in 1807 by Daniel Morgan and Nathan Boone, who probably used a combination of existing animal and Indian trails *(Roads and Traces),* this trail extended from west of *St. Charles*[1] through the northern part of the 1795–1820 Boone Settlement[2] *(Defiance: Daniel Boone Historic Area)* to Boon's Lick *(Boonesboro).* In 1808 Nathan Boone acted as a guide for Gen. William Clark *(Lewis and Clark Expedition),* escorting him along this route to Boon's Lick and then cross-county to the site of Fort Osage *(Sibley).* This Boon's Lick route was used more freely after the *War of 1812*

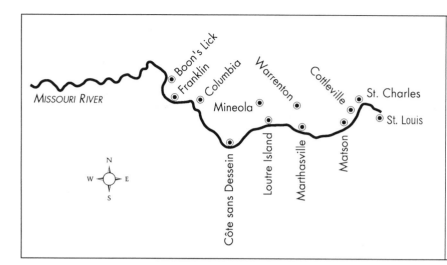

BOONSLICK TRAILS

Northern Trail: As cut by the Boones in 1807, it passed through or near the following towns, some of which were later established:

Cottleville, Warrenton, Mineola (formerly Loutre Lick), Columbia, and Franklin.

Southern Trail: Used nearly exclusively until after the *War of 1812*, it passed through or near the following towns, some of which were later established:

Matson, Marthasville, Loutre Island, Côte sans Dessein, and Franklin.

(Old Boone Trace, below) when it was less vulnerable to Indian attacks. The 1807 route, along with an older trail from St. Charles to west of Cottleville *(Defiance)*, generally approximated today's SR N (at SR 94) west through Cottleville to SR OO and SR M to *Warrenton*. From Warrenton it approximated I-70, passing through Loutre Lick *(Mineola)* to near the Callaway–Boone County line, where the trail arced above *Columbia's* corporate limits to Brown's Station and then slowly dropped down to Franklin, at which point it angled northwest to Boon's Lick. In about 1822, the trail shifted, running southwest from the Callaway–Boone County line through Columbia to a point several miles north of *Rocheport*, thereby approximating today's I-70 and US 40 to Franklin, which by 1822 commanded more interest than did Boon's Lick *(Santa Fe Trail: map)*. OLD BOONE TRACE OR BOONE TRAIL: An older southern route has recently been proposed that convincingly plots an alternate trail to Boon's Lick. It began at Daniel Morgan Boone's grant land at Matson *(Defiance: Boone Fort)* and traveled west through Femme Osage *(Augusta)* to SR D and then to *Marthasville*, where it paralleled today's SR 94 to east of SR U/SR 94 at Pinckney *(High Hill: Lewiston)*; from there it followed the Missouri River past the 1807 settlement of Loutre Island *(McKittrick)* and the 1808 settlement at Côte sans Dessein *(Jefferson City)*, continuing along the north side of the river to Boon's Lick. This route was possibly relied on extensively before and during the War of 1812, after which the northern route was used most. A connecting route to the northern Boonslick Trail turned north at Loutre Island (at SR EE) to follow a series of today's back roads past the Callaway Grave Site *(Mineola)* to Loutre Lick.

1. Although joined with the Boonslick Trail, the section from St. Charles to near *War of 1812*–era Fort Pond (several miles west of Cottleville *[Defiance]*) was established during the late 1700s.

2. A broad area of the region's earliest settlers who lived on both sides of the Missouri River, from *St. Charles* to Boon's Lick *(Boonesboro)*.

BOONVILLE
Population: 7,095   Map E-3

Set on bluffs overlooking the Missouri River where Ozark uplands meet the *prairie*, the townsite was settled in 1810 by Hannah Cole *(County Profiles: Cole)* and her nine children. She was reportedly the first to settle on the south side of the Missouri River west of St. Louis, and the site was known as Fort Cole during the Sauk and Fox Indian hostilities of c. 1814–1816 *(War of 1812)*. Platted and named Boonville *(Daniel Boone, below)* in 1817 by Asa Morgan and Charles Lucus, who was killed that year in a duel with Thomas Hart *Benton*, the town was incorporated in 1818 by the Territory of Missouri and selected in 1818 as county seat of newly created Cooper County *(County Profiles)*. A trading center, it made a successful transition from *roads* to steamboats but declined after hesitating to encourage rail transportation *(Kurtz Memorial Dogs, below)*. Post offices: Cooper Court House 1819–c. 1825; Boonville c. 1825–now. Home of Kemper Military School and College *(below)* and Boonslick Area Vo-Tech.

Architecture. DOWNTOWN: 1840s–1900 buildings (second stories original). Note: early and mid-1800s structures can be recognized by their large chimneys; small windows (compared to wall size); long, low design; symmetrical facades; nearness to the street; and irregularly shaped foundation stones. HISTORIC DISTRICTS: Seven districts contain 375 National Historic Register structures. The densest concentration is east of Main (SR 87) and bounded by High, 8th,

Morgan, and Main, with a larger area being bounded by High, 8th/7th, Spruce, and 3d. Tour maps: chamber of commerce, 1st floor, courthouse (Main at High).

Art Glass Canopy. At the entrance to Gmelich & Schmidt Jewelry Store (founded 1860) is a 1923 opaque glass canopy (8 feet wide, 4 feet long) patterned after a Tiffany lamp shade. 309 Main (SR 87).

Bell's View Park / House. Romanesque Revival, 1886. John Bell gave the city this park after he tore down a house at the site to improve his view of the river valley. On the park's steps is his motto: "Get busy, stay busy, avoid vice, waste, tobacco & booze and you will have Health, Honor & Plenty." E of Main (SR 87), High (713) at 8th.

Christ Episcopal Church. Gothic-Revival, 1844; extensively remodeled. Reportedly the oldest standing Episcopal church west of the Mississippi. W of Main (SR 87), 4th at Vine.

Cobblestone Road. Built in 1832 on the c. 1825 Wharf Hill Road, using no binding materials, this is reportedly Missouri's oldest paved road west of St. Louis. Between Water and High Streets, beneath the approach to Boonville's first highway bridge (1924).

Cooper County Courthouse. Beaux Arts, 1912. The county's third, this three-story courthouse of light-colored smooth stone, unassuming for its style, has few decorative details. It replaced one built 1838–1840. Cost: $95,000. Main (SR 87) at High. (*County Profiles*)

Daniel Boon(e) / Boonville. Maps from the 1820s–1850s carry the town name with and without the "e." In the recent past, spelling was a personal choice, often a phonetic transcription.[1] Reportedly, Daniel spelled his name both ways, in general using "Boon" when carving his name on trees while blazing trails and "Boone" when signing documents (his grandfather and his descendants spelled it Boone). Distant relatives of Boone's spelled the name "Boon," which could account for this town's spelling. Curiously, his tombstone reads "Boon" (*Fayette: Stephens Museum*), most likely a common error but appropriate as blazing his last trail. (*Defiance: Daniel Boone Historic Area*)

First Land Battle of Civil War. June 17, 1861 (Historic Bluff, below). Following Fort Sumter (April 12) and preceding First Manassas (Bull Run, July 21), this skirmish, in which Federal Brig. Gen. Nathaniel Lyon routed the Missouri Home Guard commanded by Col. John S. Marmaduke, was reportedly the *Civil War's* first land battle (*Carthage*). More important, it secured the Missouri River and all land north of it for

the Federals and eventually helped secure Missouri for the North (*Springfield: Wilson's Creek*). Federal, 2 killed, 14 wounded; Confederate, 14 killed, 20 wounded. GR, E 4 m., near Merna,[2] which was known then as Elliot's Landing;[3] inquire locally. No remnants.

Hain House. Built in 1836 by Swiss immigrant George Hain, the house remained in the Hain family until 1981. The original two-room structure of walnut logs grew with the family (additions 1843–1908). Grounds: herb gardens and flower beds. W of Main (SR 87), 4th and Chestnut.

Harley Park. Given to the city in 1887, the park overlooks the Missouri River and the *Santa Fe Trail*. Preserved here are four Woodland Period *Indian* mounds. W of Main (SR 87), Water St. to dead end.

Historic Bluff. On this bluff are three historic sites at the old Cooper County Hospital. Main (SR 87) at Water; Water and Rura E, at river. FAIRGROUNDS: antebellum forerunner of the Missouri State Fair (*Sedalia*). HANNAH COLE FORT: 1814 (Boonville history, above); site of first (1816) court of Howard County. SECOND BATTLE OF BOONVILLE: September 13, 1861. Federal, 1 killed, 4 wounded; Confederate, 12 killed, 30 wounded. Morgan St.

Katy Railroad Bridge. Built in 1930 to replace the 1874 bridge, this bridge's 480-foot lift-span was then America's longest. W of Main (SR 87), Water St.

Katy Trail State Park. Parking: Main (SR 87) at Spring; W on Spring to the depot near 2d. (*State Parks*)

Kemper Military School. Founded in 1844 by Fredrick T. Kemper, this is the oldest boys' school (now coed) and military school west of the Mississippi River. Alumni include Will Rogers. W of Main (SR 87), Center at 3d.

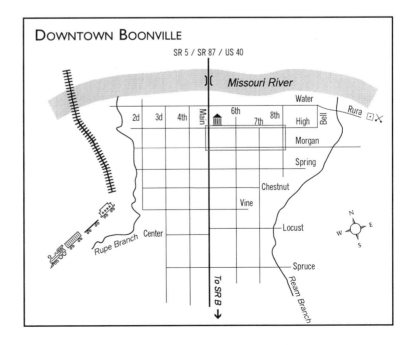

DOWNTOWN BOONVILLE

Kurtz Memorial Dogs. These cast-metal dogs were given to Boonville banker Joseph Stephens in the 1860s by Missouri-Pacific *Railroad* builder Jay Gould, after Stephens, a steamboat advocate, lobbied for a railroad to Boonville despite opposition from most local businessmen, who saw railroads as a threat to river trade. The Boonville branch of the Pacific & Missouri River Railroad arrived in 1869, and the Missouri, Kansas & Texas arrived in 1874. In 1937 the dogs were set at the entrance to the high school as a memorial to Fredrick Kurtz and his wife, recognizing 50 years of janitorial service there. Main (SR 87) at Locust.

Old Jail. Until closed in 1978 by a federal court, citing cruel and unusual punishment, this 1848 two-story limestone building was Missouri's oldest continuously used county jail. Altered once in 1871 when iron box cells replaced a shackles-and-iron-rings form of confinement, the jail remains intact, including the graffiti. Other structures include the sheriff's residence (1871) and a barn (1878), wherein one of Missouri's last public hangings took place in 1930. E of Main (SR 87) on Morgan (614).

Prairie Home, Mo. Established in 1874 around the Prairie Home Institute (a college preparatory school chartered in 1864) on the main road between *Jefferson City* and Boonville, the town assumed the school's sentimentally descriptive name, which promoted the school's intent of being "separated from the expense and vice of city schools." Post office: 1874 – now. SR 87, S 15 m. PRAIRIE HOME *WILDLIFE AREA. (Prairies)*

Santa Fe Trail. A portion of this historic route can be seen from Harley Park (above). Boonville, because of its strategic location, was an important early 1800s outpost, a jumping-off place for explorers, trappers, and traders. *(New Franklin; Santa Fe Trail)*

Sunset Cemetery. Two gravestones in this 1841 cemetery encapsulate the hardships and sentimentality of 19th-century frontier life. The William Colt family, returning to New York in 1856 from a failed Kansas homestead, stopped in Boonville, ill, worn-out, and without money. On September 21, a son died. Mrs. Colt sowed the grave herself. A donated marker was inscribed by townspeople, "Willie, the little Stranger." On October 3, William Colt died. His marker, beside his son's, reads: "Where Sleeps My Husband beside My Little Willie." The remaining family continued to New York. SR 87 at SR B, S on SR B, W on South to 3d. *(Cemeteries)*

Thespian Hall. Greek Revival, 1855–1857; renovated 1901. This four-story brick structure was built by the 1838 Thespian Society (initially a 66-member, all-male dramatic group). Called the oldest theater still in use west of the Alleghenies, it has remained flexible through many transitions: from theater, opera house, nickelodeon, and movie house to today's visual and performing arts center. Main (SR 87) at Vine.

1. "I do Cartify that I gave Benjamon Gardner purmistion to Satel on a pees of vacant Land" (signed Daniel Boone).
2. Origin unknown, but there are Mernas in Neb., Wyo., and Ky.; no p.o.
3. Plantation owner; no p.o.

BOUNDARY LINES

Many states were required to adjust their original statehood boundaries, but Missouri ran the gamut of border disputes and adjustments, including the creation of an awkwardly shaped addition to its southeast corner in deference to a wealthy landowner who did not want to be part of Arkansas *(Caruthersville: Missouri's Bootheel)*. With the 1837 *Platte Purchase* of the northwest corner, it also added about 2 million acres in defiance of federal legislation *(Missouri Compromise)* and claimed nearly 10 miles of southern Iowa, which was later returned to Iowa by an 1851 U.S. Supreme Court decision *(Sheridan: Iowa–Missouri Marker)*. Although the Mississippi River should have been a stable boundary line for the eastern border, Missouri lost two disputes over territory with Kentucky and Illinois: Wolf Island *(East Prairie)* and Arsenal Island, respectively. The maps indicate the boundaries of Missouri as proposed by the state legislature before statehood, as accepted at statehood in 1821, and as adjusted afterward: (1) the first proposal excluded today's northwest and southwest corners; (2) the second proposal included all but a small tip of the northwest corner and added lands now part of Oklahoma, Kansas, Iowa, and Arkansas; (3) the borders accepted at statehood excluded the northwest corner; (4) the *Platte Purchase* added the northwest corner; (5) an 1851 U.S. Supreme Court decision deleted nearly 10 miles of northern Missouri. Incidentally, the original southwest corner survey marker as set by the 1820 Missouri Compromise is still in place at South West City *(Noel)*.

BOWLING GREEN
Population: 2,976   Map G-3

Settled by Kentucky and Virginia immigrants in the early 1800s, the town was named for Bowling Green, Ky., which was established as Bolin Green[1] and probably named for the county seat of Caroline County, Va., which in turn was named by townsite donor Col. John Hoomes for his estate where a large lawn was used for

MISSOURI'S BOUNDARY LINES

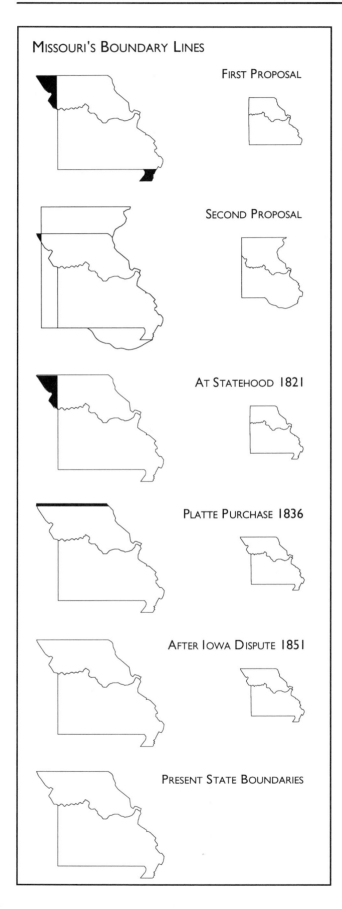

FIRST PROPOSAL

SECOND PROPOSAL

AT STATEHOOD 1821

PLATTE PURCHASE 1836

AFTER IOWA DISPUTE 1851

PRESENT STATE BOUNDARIES

bowls or lawn bowling, an ancient game featuring an irregularly shaped wooden ball rolled down a lawn alley at a smaller ball.[2] Bowling Green, Mo., was selected as a central location for Pike County seat in 1822, replacing *Louisiana*, and was reportedly platted in 1823, although the plat itself is dated 1826. The junction here of the Chicago & Alton and the St. Louis, Hannibal & Keokuk *Railroads* in the late 1870s helped establish the town as a trading center. Post office: 1824 – now.

Champ Clark's Honey Shuck. Folk Victorian, 1880s; National Historic Register, National Historic Landmark. This two-story front-gable-and-wing frame house with decorative spindles was the home of James Beauchamp "Champ" Clark (1850–1921), U.S. congressman (1893–1895, 1897–1921), speaker of the House (1911–1919), and 1912 Democratic presidential hopeful (defeated by Woodrow Wilson on the 46th ballot). Set on a tree-shaded lawn, the house displays furnishings and memorabilia. The name "Honey Shuck" reportedly comes from the yard's honey locusts, whose shucks fall to the ground. Champ Clark Dr.; 3 blocks E, 1 block S of square.

Eolia, Mo. The town was platted in 1881 along the St. Louis, Hannibal & Keokuk *Railroad* a mile south of the 1837 town of Prairieville[3] on what county surveyor F. T. Meriwether claimed was one of the windiest days he ever experienced, so he named the town for the Greek god of winds, Aeolus. As with other similarly named towns (Eoia, Eolian), the "A" was deleted. Post office: 1881– now. US 61, S 14 m. ST. JOHN'S EPISCOPAL: Early Classical Revival style, 1856; restored 1940; National Historic Register. This front-gabled one-story brick church, reportedly the oldest building in Missouri's Episcopal Diocese, has small Georgian-style panes topped by Gothic-arch windows. SR D at SR H; SR H, E 0.25 m.

Pike County Courthouse. Italian Renaissance, 1917–1919. The county's sixth, this Bedford stone and Georgia granite courthouse forms an 85-foot square; it has a parapet and a second-story pedimented entry with Ionic columns and balustrade. Cost: $100,000. Grounds: life-size bronze statue of Champ Clark (above); memorial for county veterans who died during any war. Downtown. *(County Profiles)*

Recreation. BOWLING GREEN LAKE: 20 acres. Fishing (bass, crappie, perch, catfish), camping, picnicking. NE of town; inquire locally. RANACKER *WILDLIFE AREA.*

US 61. *New London: US 61 / Red Ball Road.*

1. P.o. Bowling Green 1802; incorporated Bowling Green 1810.
2. The closest scored 1 point; 21 points won the game.
3. *Prairie* location; p.o. 1843–1861, 1865–1887, 1890–1892.

BRANSON
Population: 3,706   Map E-7

In 1880, newly married Reuben S. Branson moved from just southwest of Springfield, Mo., to this location along the White River, about four miles east of a historic wagon road and seven miles southwest of the Taney County seat, *Forsyth*. He established a general store, adding a community post office in 1882. There was little growth until about 1902, when news of the approaching White River *Railroad* encouraged new businesses. Two towns were platted in October 1903, Lucia[1] and Branson (the plat for Branson was filed in December), which were divided by Commercial Street, with Branson being north and east of Lucia. In 1912 they were incorporated as Branson. After completion of Powersite Dam, creating Lake Taneycomo in 1911–1913 (Recreation, below), the town began catering to tourists, which remains its only enterprise. Post offices: Branson 1882–1901, 1904–now; Lucia 1901–1904. Maps and information: chamber of commerce, SR 248, just W of US 65.

Bear Mountain Cut. At more than 150 feet deep, this 0.3-mile-long road cut for US 65 is Missouri's deepest of its kind. US 65, N 7.8 m. (0.8 m. N of junction with US 160).

Branson Scenic Railway / Depot. Established in 1993, the *Ozark Zephyr* is the only privately owned passenger train in America that is Amtrak certified. In fact, the 1940s–1950s engine and rolling stock can be chartered to go anywhere Amtrak does. Hour-and-a-half scheduled excursions, either northwest to *Galena* or southeast to nearby Bergman, Arkansas, travel through rural Ozark countryside on Missouri and Northern Arkansas Railroad trackage, crossing two 100-foot trestles and through two solid-rock tunnels. WHITE RIVER RAILROAD DEPOT: Railroad, 1906. Now home of the *Ozark Zephyr*, this one-story white frame structure, except for its c. 1922 addition, is original. Downtown; SR 76B at Main.

The College of the Ozarks. Established in 1906 at *Forsyth* to provide secondary and elementary education for "the financially underprivileged," the school was moved here to Point Lookout, overlooking Lake Taneycomo (p.o. 1931–now) after a 1916 fire. Today, as a four-year liberal arts college, it is called the college that works: 65 different kinds of jobs are available to full-time students who work 20 hours each week to contribute toward room, board, and tuition; remaining expenses are provided by scholarships. The school runs a dairy and beef herd, operates a corn and flour mill (Edwards Mill, below), and maintains its own airport, fire department, processing plant, post office,

print shop, radio station, and greenhouses (with a large orchid collection); it is also one of Missouri's largest producers of fruitcakes. Also produced on campus are handmade baskets and woven goods (from dirndl skirts to place mats) made on looms donated by the *WPA*. EDWARDS MILL: Built in 1973 as a replica of a late 19th-century *gristmill*, partially using salvaged materials from three derelict mills, this three-story stone and timber structure has a 14-foot waterwheel that powers two 30-inch 125-year-old buhrstones. RALPH FOSTER MUSEUM: Displays include North and South American Indian artifacts, a gun collection, Ozark memorabilia, the original truck from the TV series "The Beverly Hillbillies," and Kewpie dolls, which were originally inspired by the turn-of-the-century illustrations of Rose O'Neill, whose parents moved near Branson in 1896 (O'Neill Homestead, National Historic Register; inquire in Branson). Visitors welcome; tours. SR 65, S 3 m.; SR V, W 0.7 m.

Parks. Ten city-owned parks include two lakeside campgrounds with full hookups, fishing docks, boat ramps, restrooms, and showers. US 65 at SR 76B; SR 76B, E to Main, then E past railroad depot (above) to the river.

Recreation. BULL SHOALS LAKE: *Lakes: Corps of Engineers;* LAKE TANEYCOMO: 2,080 acres. Missouri first major artificial lake (1912–1913), impounds 22 miles of the White River between Table Rock and Bull Shoals Lakes. Branson and nearby towns—*Forsyth, Hollister,* and Rockaway Beach (below)—provide food, lodging, boat rentals, and supplies for recreation, including the lake's best-known sport, trout fishing. Adjacent. TABLE ROCK LAKE / *STATE PARK: Lakes: Corps of Engineers; WILDLIFE AREAS:* Drury-Mincey; Shepherd of the Hills.

Rockaway Beach, Mo. Proposed construction of Lake Taneycomo prompted Kansas City realtor William Merriam to buy over 600 acres for a summer resort he called Rockaway Beach. Tourists arriving by railroad were bought here by boat from Branson and *Hollister*. Reaching its height of popularity in the 1930s–1940s, Rockaway Beach site today nostalgically reflects that era. The name reportedly comes from the relaxation of rocking away the time (Merriam named his own house Whileaway), but other possibilities are Rockaway, N.J. and N.Y., derived from Algonquian for sandy place. Post offices: Taneycomo[2] 1919–1933; Rockaway Beach 1933–now. US 65, N 3.4 m.; SR F, E 3.7 m.; US 160, E 0.3 m.; SR 176, S 1.6 m. LAKE TANEYCOMO: Adjacent (Recreation, above).

Shepherd of the Hills Homestead. Features a museum, Old Matt's Cabin (frame and log; National Historic Register), and an outdoor drama based on Harold Bell Wright's enormously successful 1907 book about

Ozark life, "Shepherd of the Hills," which was based on this area and its residents. US 65 at SR 76; SR 76, W 7 m.

Shepherd of the Hills Trout Hatchery. Nearly 1 million rainbow and 10,000 brown trout are reared annually at Lake Taneycomo (Recreation, above), using water drawn from the lower level of Table Rock Lake (14 million gallons daily). Exhibits describe spawning, egg development, and rearing techniques. A 3,500-gallon aquarium holds trout, and two smaller aquariums stock native Ozark fish. Guided tours, boat ramp, fishing area, nature trails. US 65, S 4.1 m.; SR 165, W 6.5 m. (just below dam).

Silver Dollar City / Marvel Cave. This is Missouri's largest entertainment complex of its kind, and one of the largest in America. The attractions include a working Ozark craft village, sophisticated amusement rides, and Marvel Cave, a National Natural Landmark and America's third largest cavern, featuring a waterfall 505 feet belowground and the 20-story Cathedral Room, America's largest cave entrance room. Silver Dollar City evolved from a mining town, Marble City (the name was changed in 1886 to Marmaros), established in 1884 by the Marble Cave Mining and Manufacturing Company, which mistakenly identified the cave's limestone as *Carthage* marble. Undaunted, the company began mining another cave asset, bat guano (at $700 per ton), which was used as nitrate for gunpowder and fertilizer. After exhausting the supply, it sold the site in 1889 to Canadian William H. Lynch, who, along with his two daughters, Miriam and Genevieve, developed the cave as a tourist attraction. When Lynch died in 1927, his daughters continued showing the cave, changing its name to Marvel Cave. In 1950 they leased it to Hugo and Mary Herschend of Wilmette, Ill., who were frequent visitors. Hugo died in 1955. Mary and her sons continued improving the tourist attraction, initiating an advertising strategy of giving silver dollars as change. Customers using the rarely seen silver dollars in other areas were invariably asked where they got them. Silver Dollar City opened on May 1, 1960, with an attendance of 60,000. Miriam Lynch died in 1962. Genevieve died in 1972, leaving the property to The College of the Ozarks (above) and the Branson Presbyterian Church, which still holds the lease. Post offices: Marmaros[3] 1886–1929 (p.o. moved to another location after 1889); Silver Dollar City (substation of Branson) 1967–1980; Marvel Cave Park[4] 1980–now. US 65 at SR 76; SR 76, W 9 m.

Tourism. Millions visit Branson annually. Entertainment—large and small, serious and silly—makes this town one of Missouri's largest tourist attractions. Attractions include high-caliber country and western music shows, museums of all kinds, waterside resorts, carnival-style rides, lake cruises, arts and crafts exhibits, Ozark-life plays, a scenic railroad, fishing, camping, and even a wilderness safari. *(Forsyth; Hollister)*

White River Balds Natural Area. 362 acres. This part of Henning *State Forest* features smoke trees, Ashe's juniper, collared lizards, six-lined racers, an intermittent stream, and wildflowers among large glades. 1675 E. Seminole, Suite 100, Springfield 65804. SR 76, W 4 m. *(Balds and Knobs)*

Wineries. OZARK VINEYARD: Native labrusca grapes crossed with European varieties produce ten wines ranging from semidry and sweet to fruity. Tasting. US 65, N 10 m. to Chestnutridge.[5] STONE HILL: Produces fruit and sparkling wines locally, and stocks those from the parent winery in *Hermann*. Tasting and tours. SR 76, W 4 m.; SR 165, S 2 blocks.

1. Reportedly, wife of postmaster E. P. Brice.
2. The lake via Taney County, Missouri.
3. Greek for marble; town name changed to suit *post office* regulations.
4. Named changed to keep trademark rights of Silver Dollar City; substation of Branson.
5. Local tradition claims a man named Chestnut hauled freight from this ridge to Springfield in late 1800s; p.o. 1902–now.

BRUMLEY
Population: 81   Map F-5

The future townsite was recorded in 1858 by Charles Sheppard via Cpl. Z. E. Cheatham's *War of 1812* bounty certificate *(New Madrid: New Madrid Earthquake)*. During the Civil War, Federals maintained a base of operations (Camp Union) close to the recently established Brumley post office, which was named for John Brumley, an early settler. Later a community began to grow around Mark Lessem's 1868 store along a north–south *road*. A plat was filed in 1877 for the town of Brumley. Post office: 1863 – now.

Kliethemes Bridges. AUGLAIZE CREEK: Suspension Bridge, 1931; this 400-foot-long bridge rises to a hump in the middle; one lane, four-ton limit. Approx. 0.2 m. W of Mill Creek bridge. MILL CREEK: Suspension Bridge, 1931; remodeled; one lane, 100 feet long, no side rails, 15-ton limit. Junction SR C at SR 42; SR 42, W approx. 1 m.; CR 42-10, W approx. 2.5 m. *(Suspension Bridges)*

Toronto Springs Wildlife Area. *Wildlife Areas.*

Ulman, Mo. The town is named for founder Joseph Ulman, but a storefront still carries its nickname of Needmore, a popular frontier name (sometimes humorous, usually derogatory), referring to a continuous shortage of nearly everything *(Springfield: Needmore)*. Post offices: Ulman's Ridge[1] 1857–1861, 1866–1895;

Ulman 1895–now. SR C, N 4.7 m. ULMAN HOTEL: Folk Victorian, 1871. Eleven rooms, two-story frame. Private; in town.

1. Location.

BUCKNER
Population: 2,885   Map D-3

Platted in 1875, this depot town for the Missouri-Pacific *Railroad* was named either for A. M. Buckner, a member of the 1820 state constitutional convention and a U.S. senator (1830–1833), or for real estate operator Simon Buckner. Post office: 1876–now.

Fort Osage Historic Site. SR 24 and SR BB; Sibley St., N 3.25 m. *(Sibley)*

Lake City Stream Piracy. Railroad and highway builders took advantage of this valley left behind when the Little Blue River was captured by a tributary of the Missouri River and diverted north. Formerly the Little Blue flowed east through the area now occupied by Fire Prairie Creek. SR 24, E and W of Buckner. *(Stream Piracy)*

BUFFALO
Population: 2,414   Map E-6

Platted in 1838 as a crossroads town and selected in 1841 as county seat of newly formed Niangua County (renamed Dallas County), the town was reportedly first named Buffalo Head for Buffalo Head *Prairie*, which was named for a buffalo skull impaled on a stake marking a trail just southwest of the future town. An 1844 map identifies the town as Buffalo Head, but late 1840s and early 1850s maps list Buffalo. Incorporated as Buffalo in 1854, the town grew as a trading and political center; its county was bypassed by railroads. Post office: 1840–now.

Architecture. BUFFALO METHODIST CHURCH: 1889; Madison and Pike Streets. DALLAS COUNTY BANK: 1848; two-story, brick, built by Levi Beckner, who built the first (1846) Dallas County courthouse. SW corner of square.

Dallas County Courthouse. Fifties Modern, 1956–1958. The county's third, this one replaced the 1868 courthouse (destroyed by fire) featured in Thomas Hart Benton's painting "County Politics" *(Neosho: Thomas Hart Benton).* Cost: $241,114. Downtown. *(County Profiles)*

Hanging Fern Natural Area. 5 acres. On a steep slope along a bluff, ferns are perpetually saturated by cool mineralized groundwater, which nurtures unusual flora like swamp dogwood, boneset, umbrella grass, and cowbane. Bennett Spring *State Park*, Brice Rt., Lebanon 65536. SR 73, N 8 m.; SR 64, E 14 m.

Lead Mine State Forest. *State Forests.*

Long Lane, Mo. Established in 1845 along a stretch of road between hills and hollows. In 1873, W. H. Bennett founded the Bennett Cooperative Company here, a *utopian* venture that failed in 1877. Post office: 1850–1861, 1864, 1866–now. SR 32, E 12 m. NIANGUA RIVER PARK: From Windyville, below: GR, E 2.7 m. to low-water bridge (to join SR OO, continue E 1.5 m.). WINDYVILLE, MO.: Established in 1858 and probably named for prevalent winds, although local wits, as is the case with most uses of this place-name, attribute it to tall tales told by resident benchwarmers. Post office: 1921–now. SR P and K, N 7.4 m. to junction SR MM.

Louisburg, Mo. After the town was settled c. 1847 as Round Prairie,[1] the name was changed for unknown reasons to Louisburgh[2] c. 1858. Its namesake is not known. Post offices: Round Prairie 1847–1858; Louisburg 1858–now. US 65, N 9 m. OLD SETTLERS REUNION: Held on July 24–25 since 1891, this is reportedly Missouri's oldest continuously held community reunion. Music, games, carnival rides, food; public welcome.

Red Top All Day Sing. Held since 1892 at Red Top Missionary Baptist Church on the last Sunday in June. Originally the gospel music was sung using shape[3] notes and no musical instruments, but today there is some piano accompaniment. US 65, S 9 m.; SR TT, W approx. 2.1 m.

1. Location.
2. The older style "burgh," distinctively British, was probably shortened, like others, through being spelled as it was pronounced.
3. A system of written notes (do, re, mi, fa, sol, la, ti, do) showing the musical scale by the shape of the note head.

BUNCETON
Population: 341   Map E-4

Platted by Harvey Bunce in 1868 close to the geographical center of Cooper County, the town grew, aided by the Missouri-Pacific *Railroad*, as a trading center (1919 pop. 1,000). Post offices: Coal Bank[1] 1854–1868; Bunceton 1868–now.

Architecture. AREA: Ravenswood *(Bell Air).* TOWN: Bunceton Jail (log, c. 1869), about 15 feet square. Vick House (1868), the town's first house; one-story frame.

"Battle" of Bunceton. The name refers to a legendary 1924 political picnic/rally (estimated attendance 75,000) held at the 27-room mansion of gubernatorial candidate Dr. A. W. Nelson, who was joined by

Democratic presidential candidate John W. Davis (Nelson lost to Sam A. Baker; Davis to Calvin Coolidge). An uncounted number of people were stranded in central Missouri by heavy rains and mud. The 1913 mansion is still in use (private). SR J, W 3.3 m.; SR 5, S 3.1 m.; GR, W 1.3 m.

Bunceton Historical Library. Monthly displays of local historical items. In town.

Concord Church / Cemetery. Organized in 1817; no structure now. *CEMETERY:* Reportedly the county's oldest church cemetery. SR J, E 1 m.; GR extending from SR B, N approx. 2 m.; W side.

Dick's Mill / Cotton, Mo. Presumably named for the plant, Cotton was first called Dick's Mill when Adolph Dick built a *gristmill* here in 1868; his wife ran a store. The mill (restored) and store still stand. Post offices: Dicks 1887–1899; Cotton 1899–1906. SR J, E 3.1 m.; SR T, S 5 m.

Pisgah, Mo. Platted in 1830 by Rev. James A. Reavis and named for Pisgah Baptist Church (below), whose name comes from a mountain peak in biblical Moab from which Yahweh allowed Moses to see, but not enter, the Promised Land (Num. 3:27). Post office: 1828–1910. SR J, E 7.9 m.; SR O, S 0.5 m. PISGAH BAPTIST CHURCH: Vernacular, 1926. Organized in 1819, reportedly it is the second oldest Baptist church west of the Mississippi. This is the fourth structure; *cemetery* adjacent. In town.

1. Descriptive, like Coalgood, Ky.

BUNKER

Population: 390   Map G-6

Platted in 1907 in the center of a 30,000-acre forest, whose timber options were held by the recently (1907) incorporated Bunker-Culler Lumber Company, the town was named for lumberman S. J. Bunker, who began cruising timber here in 1906 in one of the few virgin forests untouched by the lumber boom of c. 1885–1915. The forests were remote and had no year-round waterways for shipping, so Bunker helped the Missouri Southern *Railroad* build about 10 miles of track to the new town. Like most sawmill boomtowns, its future dwindled with every milled board foot of lumber (about 60,000 feet a day); unlike most, it survived the mill's 1921 closing by switching to trade and production of light wooden products such as handles and chairs. Post office: 1907–now.

Blair Creek Raised Fen Natural Area. 3 acres. Missouri's only known raised fen, or marsh, features rare plants like blue violet and glossy-leaf aster, as well as sedges and shrubs. Salem Ranger District, Salem

65560. Located in Blair Creek valley on a wooded slope. Access: Ozark *Trail.*

Rat, Mo. The postal department advised local postmaster James Swiney to keep the suggested names short and simple (*Post Offices*). After several suggestions were turned down (some names were already in use), Swiney reportedly chose Rat as a name no one would want (*Eminence: Ink*). Post office: 1898–1954. SR 72, S 4 m.; SR P, W 6.1 m.

Recreation. LITTLE SCOTIA POND CAMPGROUND / PICNIC AREA: Water, vault toilets, pond fishing. LOGGERS LAKE CAMPGROUND / PICNIC AREA / TRAIL: 25-acre lake, swimming, fishing (electric motors only; bass, sunfish, crappie, catfish), hiking, water, vault toilets. (*National Forests*)

Turner Natural Arch. Part of a *collapsed cave system*, the arch has a 50-foot span and a 10-foot-high ceiling. Above it is a small *cave*. Visible from the road except during summer; beaver dams. SR 72, S 4 m.; SR P, W 4.7 m. On N bluff of Big Creek.

BUTLER

Population: 4,099   Map C-5

Most of the early town and county records were destroyed in 1863 during the *Civil War*. First platted in 1853 as a proposed central location for the county seat of Bates County in anticipation of the creation of Vernon County from Bates (which occurred in 1855), Butler was designated county seat in 1856, replacing Papinsville (below). It was named for William Orlando Butler (*County Profiles: Butler*). Destroyed in 1863 in accordance with Civil War *Order No. 11*, it was platted again in 1866 about half a block from its original site and prospered as a trading center aided in 1880 by the arrival of the Missouri-Pacific *Railroad.* Butler's 19th-century nickname, Electric City, comes from four arc lights placed on top of the courthouse in 1881, which could be seen from 20 miles away. According to "Power Magazine" (1986), Butler has America's oldest continuously operated municipal power system (since 1881) and was the second city, after St. Louis, west of the Mississippi to have electricity. Post office: 1853–1863, 1866–now.

Architecture. The town square with its brick streets and commercial buildings is a 19th-century set piece. Representative of late 19th-century Folk Victorian residences is the 1907 birthplace of science fiction writer Robert L. Heinlein (1 block W of downtown, N on Fulton).

Bates County Courthouse. Richardsonian Romanesque, 1901. The county's fourth (the third at Butler), this 80-by-105-foot three-story *Carthage* stone courthouse has rusticated stonework, ornate square corner towers, spring arches, and a domed central tower. Architect G. E. McDonald designed similar courthouses for Andrew, Johnson, and Lawrence Counties. Cost: $50,000. Downtown. *(County Profiles)*

Bates County Fair. Late July.

Museum of Pioneer History. Folk Victorian, 1893. This three-story red-brick former county jail and sheriff's quarters contains thousands of items, including 18th–20th-century military weapons and uniforms, gowns and accessories, jewelry, dolls and toys, and rooms furnished to resemble 19th-century daily life, like a schoolroom, chapel, and kitchen. Grounds: other exhibits include a furnished log cabin, a restored stagecoach depot, a blacksmith's shop, and a print shop. Downtown; 106 E. Fort Scott St.

Oak Hill Cemetery. At the northeast corner of this peaceful and well-landscaped cemetery is possibly the world's smallest tombstone: about five by six inches and mounted on a rotating board at ground level, it reads "Linnie Crouch" on one side and "April, 26, 1898" on the other. SR 71B at Mill (SR H), E approx. 1 m. on Mill. *(Cemeteries)*

Papinsville, Mo. Established c. 1841 as Batesville,[1] about three miles above the Osage River at the Marais Des Cygnes River, the town was platted in 1847 as the Bates County seat, replacing Harmony Mission (below), and was named for French trader Melicourt Papin. Post offices: Batesville 1841–1848; Papinsville 1848–1862, 1866–1906. SR 71, S 11 m. to Rich Hill (below); SR B, E 7.2 m.; SR N, S 2 m. CEMETERY: Platted on a grassy knoll in 1847, this peaceful cemetery has ornate and interesting markers among towering old cedars, some of which touch and occasionally envelop the stones. Many of the carved sentimental inscriptions and symbols are familiar and endearing. SR N at Green St.; Green, W 100 yards *(Cemeteries)*. HARMONY MISSION, MO.: Established in 1821 a few miles upstream from today's Papinsville by the American Board of Home Missions for the Osage *Indians*. The commendatory name was carried forward after the removal of the Osage and the subsequent establishment in 1838 of a secular community, which was selected in 1841 as the county seat of newly organized Bates County. No courthouse was built; no remnants or public access. Post office: 1838–1839. PECAN GROVE: Just across the Marais Des Cygnes River are hundreds of acres of pecans. SR N at Main; Main, W 0.3 m.; cross over steel truss bridge (note 1951 high-water mark on bridge). SITES: Many of the town's former sites are marked with homemade signs, including the court square that was never developed.

Rich Hill, Mo. Platted in 1880 by a corporation composed mostly of Bates County businessmen, this former boomtown was named by first postmaster E. W. Ratekin for the rich coal that helped build it (1883 pop. 8,000); the town declined after mining played out c. 1900. Post office: 1871–now. SR 71, S 11 m. PARKS: Two large and well-kept parks testify to the town's former prosperity. In town, SR A. *WILDLIFE AREAS:* Four Rivers; Harmony Mission; Peabody.

Ripgut Prairie Natural Area. 136 acres. This high-quality example of a wet-mesic *prairie* includes big bluestem grass, cordgrass, and cottonwood. 722 E. Hwy. 54, El Dorado Springs 64744. SR 71, S 11 m. to Rich Hill (above); SR B, E 0.4 m.; GR, N 0.6 m. to E turn; continue N on dirt lane, approx. 0.3 m.

1. Bates County namesake *(County Profiles)*.

CALEDONIA
Population: 142   Map H-5

Tennessean Alexander Craighead came to Bellevue valley in 1816 and built a two-story cabin in a small settlement near Goose Creek (today's townsite), platting a town in 1818 on 34 acres and selling lots in 1819, mainly to residents of nearby Bellevue (Methodist Cemetery, below), which was founded in 1798 on Spanish land grants. Caledonia, a popular place-name, the Roman name for the northern part of Britain and a poetic synonym for Scotland, was reportedly used by Craighead out of pride for his Scottish heritage. The town is home to Missouri's oldest Masonic Lodge with a continuous charter (1825), Tyro Chapter #12. Post offices: Caledonia, 1819–1822, 1826–now; New *Bowling Green* 1822–1825; New Caledonia 1825–1826.

Architecture. Easily walked, the historic district (33 structures, National Historic Register) is roughly bounded by Patrick, College, Alexander, and SR 21. Structures range from c. 1816 to mid-1800s.

Bellevue Collegiate Institute. About 1868–1895. A strip of concrete walk that once led to the front door is all that remains of the first college owned by the St. Louis Methodist Conference (deed recorded in 1871). SHOW-ME STATE: W. D. Vandiver, the former president of the institute and a U.S. congressman from 1897 to 1905, is credited with popularizing Missouri's nickname, the Show-Me State, after using the phrase during an 1899 speech in Philadelphia. Vandiver does not claim credit for coining the nickname, and there is no factual basis for its origin. While the consensus is that the slogan first gained attention during the late 1890s, the initial meaning of "Show Me" ranged from an epithet (Missourians are slow, you have to show them) to a no-nonsense posture of "I'm from

Missouri, you'll have to show me." Undoubtedly, the latter is today's usage.

Bellevue Presbyterian Church. Gothic Revival, 1864–1872. Organized in 1816, this is reportedly the oldest Presbyterian church west of the Mississippi. The red-brick structure, the church's third, features a cupola-style bell tower and a steeply pitched roof. College St., across from the Craighead House (below).

Buford Mountain. At 1,740 feet, Buford rivals Missouri's tallest mountain, Taum Sauk (*Arcadia*). Paralleling SR 21 south of town.

Cedar Creek Shut-In. One of seven in the area, this *shut-in* is the most accessible. The most scenic part is 200–300 yards east of the highway. SR 21, S approx. 1.7 m. to Cedar Creek.

CONOCO Service Station. Corporate Colonial Revival, 1930. Originally painted green and white, this small brick building is typical of its 1920s–1930s style. Main and Webster.

Craighead House. Log, c. 1816. This two-story dogtrot structure built by town founder Alexander Craighead served as a home, store, and Caledonia's first post office. 304 College.

Hughes Mountain Natural Area. 240 acres. Features Devil's Honeycomb, which consists of igneous glades formed by the polygonal joining of once-molten rhyolite, giving the appearance of huge slabs of cut stone staggered together vertically. Small in comparison to Devil's Tower in Wyoming, it is a unique example of this phenomenon in Missouri. Surrounded by a stunted forest, the glades support little bluestem grass, prickly pear cactus, rushfoil, pinweed, and rough buttonweed. Meramec Forest District, Box 248, Sullivan 63080. SR 21, N 3 m.; SR M, E approx. 4 m.; signs.

Methodist Cemetery. A red granite marker approximates the site of Bellevue[1] (Caledonia history, above) and of Shiloh Meeting House, built before 1814 and reportedly the first Methodist church building in Missouri. A folk-art marker, made of mineral blossom quartz and granite, cites the area's history. SR 21 now divides the cemetery. SR 21, N 1 m. to SR C. (*Cemeteries*)

Palmer Fault Zone. Faults are cracks in the earth's crust that involve some noticeable movement. Although movement at the New Madrid fault has not been noticed recently, it did make itself apparent in 1811–1812 (*New Madrid: New Madrid Earthquake*). Palmer Fault, crossed by SR 21 at Big River, is actually four faults that comprise a zone about 2 miles wide and 45 miles long tending easterly, with a 1,000-foot vertical displacement. To the south is rolling farmland; to the north, rugged country with lean soil. Notice the shattered rock (E side of hwy., N of bridge). SR 21, N 4.2 m. to Big River.

Presbyterian Cemetery. An ornate iron arch marks the entrance and records the first burial as 1798. The site of the first (1807) recorded Sunrise Prayer Meeting west of the Mississippi, this cemetery contains the grave of Comfort Ruggles (participant in the 1773 Boston Tea Party; d. 1833), ornate red granite markers, and a maple tree estimated to be over 200 years old. SR 32, E 0.5 m.; inquire locally. (*Cemeteries*)

Recreation. COUNCIL BLUFF RECREATION AREA (*National Forests*): 440-acre lake, fishing (bass, sunfish, catfish), improved camping, picnic, toilets, boat launch, change house, playground, tables, grills. HAZEL CREEK TRAIL CAMP (*National Forests*): fireplaces, tables, vault toilets, small creek; trailhead for Trace Creek. *TRAILS:* Bell Mountain Wilderness; Ozark Trail (Trace Creek section).

1. Commendatory; no p.o.

CALIFORNIA
Population: 3,465   Map F-4

Boonesborough,[1] platted in 1845 as the county seat of recently organized Moniteau County, was denied that post office name due to an existing Boonsboro.[2] An 1840 California post office in a small town also called California, about a mile west of Boonesborough, was moved to Boonesborough in 1847, and the county seat was renamed California. Reportedly the former California was named in 1835 for California Wilson, who tradition claims donated two gallons of whiskey for the honor. Another version claims it was named for Mexican California, which would become a U.S. state in 1850 and was receiving national attention because of U.S. expansion (*Mexican War*). According to "American Place-Names," the name "California" was probably coined by 16th-century Spanish poet Garcí Ordóñez de Montalvo in a poem about an island of giant women and fabulous wealth. It was first applied to today's state when 16th-century explorers mistakenly thought Baja California was an island. Arrival of the Pacific *Railroad* in 1858 helped establish this town as a trading center. Post office: 1840–1847 (former California), 1847–now (relocated).

Architecture. Good examples of 19th-century styles include AMERICAN LEGION HALL: Greek Revival (bracketed), c. 1860s; two-story brick. EITZEN HOUSE: Queen Anne, c. 1898; occupies a city block; widow's walk, stained-glass windows. NATIONAL HISTORIC REGISTER (all on High Street): old City Hall and Fire Station (101 N.), Barnhill Building (301 N.), Gray-Wood Buildings (401–407 N.), and the courthouse (below).

Burgers' Smokehouse. Established in 1956 on the family's 1886 farm, today the firm ships smoked meat products nationwide. Visitor center: meat processing items and dioramas of the seasons, of which "Summer" is reportedly the world's second largest of its kind (2.5 stories tall, 40 feet wide). Tours. SR 87, S 3 m.

Enon, Mo. The familiar story of railroad surveyors possibly stumped for a name or in a fit of good humor using "none" spelled backward does not apply here or probably anywhere else. The name is a simplified form of Aenon, a place mentioned in the Bible, John 3:23, "because there was so much water there" (Burkes and S. Moreau Creeks in this case). Post office: 1882–1968. SR 87, S 13 m.; SR A, E 3.8 m. ENON SINK (*Collapsed Cave Systems*): This sinkhole acted as an Ice Age tar pit, preserving remains of large turtles, extinct horses, tapirs, and sloths. SW 1 m.; inquire locally. ROCK ENON FARM: Vernacular, farm complex, 1871–1876. The two-story house, barn, granary, and springhouse are built from dressed limestone. The privy is brick. Small pastoral pond in front. SR A, W 0.75 m.; SR V, N 0.5 m.

High Point, Mo. Named for its location on Moniteau County's highest point (904 feet). Post office: 1852–1973. SR 87, S 10 m.; SR C, W 1 m. KELLY-TISING STORE: Vernacular, 1843; two additions. High Point's first store and still in business (the third room is the original). In town. MINES: The town prospered from nearby Sterling Lead Mine (1843–1880; 90 feet deep) and Simpson Coal Mine (1875–1945), which was reported in 1867 as the world's deepest, when no bottom was found at 80 feet (in 1945, no bottom was found at 150 feet). Remnants; inquire locally.

Moniteau County Courthouse. Early Classical Revival, 1867–1868; remodeled 1905; National Historic Register. This impressive two-story brick structure has a bracketed cupola and domed semicircular portico with brick columns. Designed like the 1840–1911 Missouri State Capitol, it features an early application of structural cast iron, as do the nearby contemporary buildings. Cost: $40,433. SR 87 at Main. (*County Profiles*)

Moniteau County Fair. Organized in 1859, this is reportedly the oldest continuous county fair west of the Mississippi; it had a lapse of only six years due to the Civil War (*Platte City: Tracy*). First full week of August.

Moniteau County Historical Museum. Local historical items, genealogical material. 308 Oak.

Parks. CITY PARK: Tennis, bird sanctuary, rest area. SR 87 at US 50; US 50, E 1 block. PROCTOR LAKE: Built by the Pacific Railroad as a water supply for its steam engines: *thong tree*, fishing, shelter houses, dutch ovens; no swimming or boating. SR 87 at US 50; SR 87, S to Parkway.

Salem United Church of Christ. Vernacular (two structures), 1851 and 1858. The church was organized in 1843 as the North Moreau Evangelical Church; its

original structures, now covered with siding, stand side by side. The smaller one, built in 1851 of log, was used as a school after the larger one was built in 1858. Christmas programs have been omitted only twice: due to the Civil War and the 1918 flu epidemic. *Cemetery* established 1850. US 50, E 4 m.; SR K, S 2 m.

Tipton, Mo. Platted in 1858 at a major crossroads and along the Pacific *Railroad* by William Tipton Seely, a merchant and banker of nearby Round Hill,[3] the town experienced an immediate boom as the eastern terminus of the Butterfield (*Overland Mail Company*) Stage in 1858–1859; its station was also the line's first. Post offices: Fairfield Station[4] 1858; Tipton 1858–now. US 50, W 12 m. MACLAY HOUSE: Greek Revival, bracketed, 1858; National Historic Register. This three-story brick structure with Doric columns, wide trim beneath the cornice, a narrow transom, and sidelights was built as a girls' school, Rose Hill Seminary, and used in 1863 by Civil War general John C. Frémont as his headquarters. Furnished; infrequent tours. Howard at Moreau. MANITO LAKE *WILDLIFE AREA*.

1. Daniel Boone.
2. Daniel Boone; p.o. 1839-1850.
3. Descriptive; 3 m. N; p.o. 1837-1864; defunct.
4. RR depot (*Post Offices*); popular commendatory place-name.

CALLAO
Population: 332   Map F-2

The town was platted in 1858 by Samuel and Enoch Humphreys and James Kem along the right-of-way of the Hannibal & St. Joseph *Railroad* (which arrived in 1859). Legend claims they were undecided about a town name, so they blindfolded a railroad man, Samuel Kinney, and spun a globe. Kinney's finger landed at Callao, Peru (locally, Cal'-e-o). Other sources point to Missourians' favoring exotic names during this era, e.g. *La Plata* (18 m. N). The town prospered as a tobacco shipping center (record year: 700,000 lbs.) until early in the 20th century when tobacco prices declined. Four fires between 1885 and 1934 destroyed most of the historic structures. Post office: 1859–now.

Christy's Camp. Camps and courts were the forerunners of motels as highway accommodations. In 1928, George Christy, anticipating the paving of US 36 (completed here in 1929), built a gas station and 14 frame structures, some with bathrooms and attached garages. This was reportedly the first camp on US 36 in Missouri. Several structures remain; derelict. In town; SR 3, E 1 block on old US 36; near hog market.

Grand Divide. *Grand Divide.*

New Cambria, Mo. Beginning in 1858 as a post office

(NW of Mechanicsburg[1]) along the Hannibal & St. Joseph *Railroad*, the town was platted in 1861 as Stockton[2] by railroad official C. O. Godfrey. Welshmen J. M. Jones and W. B. Jones began promoting the town. Either to attract Welsh settlers or because of mass immigration of Welsh families to this area, the town was renamed New Cambria in 1864 (Cambria: from the Latin for Wales, land of the Wealas, i.e. Celts and Britons but not Saxons). Post offices: Mechanicsburg 1847–1858; Stockton 1858–1859; Summit[3] 1859–1864; New Cambria 1864–now. US 36, W 5.6 m.; SR 149, N 1 m. CITY PARK: Town founder Godfrey donated this land for resort use only, stipulating other purposes would result in its reversion to his heirs. Bandstand, picnic area. In town. GRIFFITH *WILDLIFE AREA*.
Recreation. LONG BRANCH LAKE / *STATE PARK*: US 36, E 6 m. *(Lakes: Corps of Engineers)*. THOMAS HILL RESERVOIR: *Macon*. WILDLIFE AREA: Griffith.

1. Origin unknown, but usually commendatory due to factory workers.
2. James Stocks, RR contractor; 1858–1859.
3. Origin unknown; usually the location but not necessarily a great height; located 4 m. W of today's New Cambria.

CAMDEN
Population: 238   Map D-3

Nearby Bluffton,[1] an 1817 fort, river port, and temporary Ray County seat (1821–1827), attracted the initial population, but frequent floods and unclear land titles began to stunt its growth. Aided by abundant coal, fur trading, fertile land, and the arrival of the steamboat in 1830, a new townsite with clear land titles and better elevation was selected just east of Bluffton and platted in 1838 by E. M. Samuels and Amos Reeson on land from a *New Madrid Earthquake* certificate. Camden's namesake is not known, although Camden County and *Camdenton* were both named for British statesman Lord Camden (Charles Pratt, 1714–1794), the chancellor of England (1766–1770) who supported the colonies' stand against taxation without representation. This transportation center grew steadily (c. 1900 est. pop. 1,000), aided by the west branch of the North Missouri (1868) and the Wabash, Chicago, Santa Fe & California (1888) *Railroads*. And then the river abandoned the town. No one heard or saw anything unusual, but during the night of July 3, 1915, the Missouri River broke through the bottom of its horseshoe bend—ironically along a line from Napoleon to Waterloo to Wellington *(Lexington)*—cutting a new channel that eliminated a 10-mile bend by straightening out the river and leaving Camden three miles to the north, high and dry. It was

the Missouri River's most dramatic change *(Augusta; Weston)*. Six months later, wagons rolled along the former riverbed. The county line dividing Lafayette and Ray (Camden's county) had been defined by the river. Ray County argued that it owned the land now included by the river's shift southward, but Lafayette won the dispute, creating a Lafayette County island inside Ray County. Post office: 1838–now.
Architecture. Four blocks of 19th-century commercial buildings, now in disrepair, once fronted the river. Front St.
Elliot/Vandiver House. Greek Revival, 1856; remodeled 1911. The two-story brick (now stucco) house, with a full-facade porch and gallery, retains its original classical lines. N of town; inquire locally.
King House. Vernacular, 1828; extensively remodeled. Built as a two-story dogtrot log cabin before Camden was established. In town; SR 210 at the stop sign.
Sunshine Lake. This c. 300-acre oxbow lake bordered by marshes was created when the river shifted channels (Camden history, above). Fishing (catfish, bluegill, bass) and hunting (duck, quail, dove). SR 210, E 0.7 m.; SR H, E approx. 2.2 m.; GR, S.

1. Location; p.o. 1820–c. 1830.

CAMDENTON
Population: 2,561   Map E-5

The establishment of one of Missouri's newest county seats was precipitated by construction of Bagnell Dam (below), which required the relocation of the former county seat, *Linn Creek*. When residents were forced to move before Linn Creek was covered by the lake, some chose to settle in a valley at the site of today's Linn Creek; others chose a flat summit near the recently surveyed highways 54 and 5 where Clint Webb and Jim Banner had bought a 160-acre farm in 1930 and begun platting a town that was selected that year as the new county seat (effective 1931) of its namesake, Camden County *(County Profiles)*. Today the lake area provides recreation for millions of vacationers. Post office: 1931–now. Chamber of commerce: SR 5, N 1 m. from junction with US 54.
Bagnell Dam / Lake of the Ozarks. In 1931 Union Electric Light and Power Company was the world's largest privately owned power plant; by damming the Osage, Niangua, and Galiza Rivers in 1931, it formed what was at that time the world's largest artificial lake, with 1,375 miles of shoreline (longer than the California coast). Approximately 20,000 men working round-the-clock, often seven days a week, completed the project in just over two years (1929–1931). Towns

and homesteads disappeared, thousands of graves were relocated, postal systems were rezoned, and roads were rerouted. Today, except for two new generators, the power plant and dam remain the same. The dam, Missouri's largest (2,543 feet long, 148 feet above Osage River bedrock), supplies electricity as far away as St. Louis and Kansas City. Tours. US 54, N 15.4 m.; US 54B, N 3.9 m. LAKE FACILITIES: Lake of the Ozarks *State Park*; Camdenton and nearby towns such as Osage Beach *(Linn Creek)* and *Gravois Mills* provide food, lodging, and boat rentals for water recreation, including fishing (bass, striper, catfish, crappie).

Camden County Courthouse. Moderne, 1931. One of Missouri's first modernistic courthouses, the county's fourth, this two-story yellow brick and tile building is trimmed with white stone. Its location on a triangle rather than a square (because of two intersecting highways) adds emphasis to its break with tradition. Cost: about $50,000 (Union Electric compensated the county $60,000 for the former courthouse). SR 5 at US 54. *(County Profiles)*

Caves. BEAR: Associated with Bridal Cave (below), it features lantern tours and a lakeside nature trail; boat dock available. BRIDAL: Opened in 1948, it claims to hold the world's record for the most underground weddings: 1,110 in the first 40 years; massive and colorful onyx formations. Both caves: SR 5, N 2.2 m.; Lake Road 5-88, W approx. 2 m. FANTASY *(Eldon: Fantasy World Caverns)*.

Climax Springs, Mo. This former spa town (1882–1911), platted in 1882, advertised its "fizz water" as America's only cure for epilepsy. The springs, charged with large amounts of magnesium and sodium chloride, still flow, and most of the original spa's two-story frame hotel (now private) still stands. The town's name reportedly indicates the superlative pride of its founder, W. H. Hockman, who said when seeing the spring: "This caps the climax!" In town. Post offices: Climax 1883–1886; Climax Springs 1886–now. SR 5, N 9 m.; SR 7, W 14 m. FIERY FORK *STATE FOREST*.

Decaturville, Mo. Established in 1854 by store owner James Farmer, the town was named for Capt. Steven Decatur (1779–1820), the American naval hero best remembered for his highly romantic and successful expedition into Tripoli's harbor during the 1804–1805 Tripolitan War and for coining the slogan "our country, right or wrong." Post office: 1860–1957. SR 5, S 9 m. DECATURVILLE CHURCH: Vernacular, Italianate affinities, 1895. Frame with a plain but Italianate-style bell tower and windows; picnic area adjacent. Inquire locally. DECATURVILLE STRUCTURE: Within a radius of several miles are rocks described by geologist Thomas Beveridge as "intensely fractured, crushed and folded in an annular and polygonal pattern." Whether

the structure was caused by meteorite impacts or explosive (possibly igneous) activity is still debated by geologists *(Steelville: Crooked Creek Structure)*. W edge of town; W edge of SR 5.

Ha Ha Tonka State Park. US 54, W 2.3 m.; SR D, S 3 m.; sign. (Natural Areas, below; *State Parks*)

Hurricane Deck Bridge. Truss, 1936. A toll bridge until 1953 (a remnant of the booth remains at the north end), the structure, with its delicately arched truss support underneath, won first prize in 1936 from the American Institute of Steel Construction as the most beautiful of its size. SR 5, N 12 m.

Natural Areas. COAKLEY HOLLOW FEN NATURAL AREA: *Linn Creek.* The following are located in Ha Ha Tonka *State Park.* Trail and natural area maps: Rt. 1, Box 658, Camdenton 65020. HA HA TONKA KARST: 70 acres. Always described in superlatives, this is one of America's most outstanding geological areas. A classic example of a complex karst site formed by the collapse of a major cave system *(Collapsed Cave Systems)*, it includes a large spring (48,000,000 gallons daily), several sinkholes, caves, and a natural bridge (60-foot span). HA HA TONKA SAVANNA: 953 acres. This high-quality chert, dolomite, and sandstone savanna, interspersed with dolomite glades, is reportedly Missouri's largest publicly owned savanna landscape, with highly diverse native *prairie* and woodland species, e.g. royal catchfly and ladies' tresses. LODGE GLADE: 20 acres. This dolomite glade, interspersed with seeps and savanna forest, supports Missouri evening primrose, compass plant, and silky aster, as well as plains scorpion, fence swift, and six-lined racerunner. RED SINK: 8 acres. The south wall of this oval-shaped sink rises nearly 200 feet above a mature sinkhole-floor forest. Its rimrock is Gunter sandstone that weathers to a deep red. *(Collapsed Cave Systems)*

Standing Rock. More than one standing rock is in an area about 40 yards long and 15 yards wide. Fractured sandstone pinnacles (10–20 feet high) have patterned surfaces that seem to contain cast impressions of what might have been a former cave. SR 5, N 10 m.; GR (Lake Road 5-61), E 0.75 m. (bear right; signs).

Tunnel Dam Natural Tunnel. A natural tunnel through a high and scenic narrow ridge allows the Niangua River to fall 22 feet from its upper to its lower end. In 1909 engineers thought to use this phenomenon to power a hydroelectric plant, but after initial enlargement of the tunnel, the idea was dropped when branching passageways (similar to leaks) were discovered. Today's power plant is driven by water from an excavated tunnel just upstream from the natural one. US 54, W 10 m.; SR U, S 2.9 m. to Edith;[1] GR, S and E approx. 2.5 m.

---

1. Origin unknown; p.o. 1884–1918.

The intersection of Old Highway 36 (Grand Avenue) and Walnut Street (US 69), in Cameron. ("CAMERON CITIZEN OBSERVER")

CAMERON
Population: 4,831   Map D-2

When Samuel McCorkle learned that his newly (1854) platted town, Somerville,[1] was on a grade too steep to serve as a stop for the planned Hannibal & St. Joseph *Railroad* (which arrived in 1858), he moved the town's three buildings one and a half miles west to today's site straddling the De Kalb–Clinton County line. He formed a five-member company, platted a town in 1855, and sold lots in 1856. The name honors the Cameron family; most sources divide the honor between McCorkle's wife, Malinda, and her father, Judge Elisha Cameron. Post office: 1855–now.

Coberly House. Queen Anne, 1890. This house uses all the architectural devices of its style, including Eastlake detailing, roof cresting, shingle siding, delicately turned porch supports, complicated cross-gabling, and a variety of first- and second-story porches. Chestnut at Seminary, 1 block W of US 69.

McCorkle Park / Band Concerts. Donated by Samuel McCorkle in 1855, this city-tax-supported park is the site of a brass band concert every Thursday evening during the summer. US 69B to 4th, W 3 blocks; sign.

Recreation. CAMERON RESERVOIRS: 156 acres. Bass, bluegill, catfish. PONY EXPRESS LAKE: US 36, W 6 m.; SR 33, N 2 m.; SR RA, W 1 m. *(Maysville: Recreation).* WALLACE *STATE PARK:* US 69, S 4.5 m.; SR 121, E 0.6 m.

Stewartsville, Mo. The town was established in 1853 as Tetherowtown by George Tetherow *(Trenton)* along the proposed grade of the Hannibal & St. Joseph *Railroad.* Today's name, like that of the post office, honors Robert M. Stewart (governor 1857–1861 and first president of the railroad), who as a state senator in 1846–1857 lobbied for the railroad's route through this area. Post offices: Porasia Point[2] 1853; Stewartsville 1855–now. US 36, W 12.5 m. TETHEROW HOUSE: Log (covered by clapboard), 1853. This one-and-a-half-story structure, lived in continuously since 1853, first served as a home, inn, and store. S of railroad, 2d at Castile.

1. This town failed twice: once as a paper town c. 1849 (p.o. 1849–1850 in De Kalb County) and again in 1854–1855 (no p.o.) after the plat was filed in 1854 and three buildings were erected. Named for the firm of Ray & Somerville, which built a store in the second Somerville.
2. Origin unknown.

CANTON
Population: 2,623   Map G-2

Formerly a trading post known as Cottonwood Prairie c. 1821, Canton was platted in 1830 at the Mississippi

River's widest westward sweep. The town literally held the high ground in a rivalry with Tully,[1] which was platted in 1834 about a mile north and whose former riverside site is now in Canton (between the dam and Henderson Ave.). The rivalry peaked c. 1847 after the towns balked at combining with a proposed name of De Soto. After Tully was inundated by an 1851 flood, it began losing population to Canton, which was incorporated that year. Canton's growth, slowed during the Civil War, continued in 1871 as it made a successful transition from river to rail transportation. The stock place-name has two main derivations; sources claim both in this case: (1) Canton, China, established in 1053 at the Pearl (or Canton) River, and (2) other Cantons (in this case Canton, Ohio). A third possibility is the French term for district or subdivision, as applied in Canton, Tex. Post offices: Canton 1831–1835, 1847–now; Tully 1835–1847, 1849–1859. Home of Culver-Stockton College (below).

Architecture. DOWNTOWN: Good examples of 19th-century brick commercial buildings include a button factory and a broom factory. Near the river, 400 block of Clark St. (part of the original plat). NATIONAL HISTORIC REGISTER: Henderson Hall (1903), on the Culver-Stockton College campus (below). Lincoln School (1880; restored), a black school built near Martin Park, S end of 4th.

Canton Ferry. Established in 1853, this is reportedly the oldest continuously used ferry on the Mississippi. (*Ferryboats*)

Culver-Stockton College. Established on a bluff facing the river in 1853 as Christian College by the Disciples of Christ, this is the oldest college west of the Mississippi expressly chartered as coeducational. Some Greek Revival architecture remains. US 61, S on 11th.

Fenway Public Landing. Boat ramp, camping, picnic area, restrooms. US 61, N 7 m.

Library. Reportedly Missouri's oldest (1868) lending library; local historical items and documents. 112 N. 4th (SR B).

Lock and Dam #20. Built in 1933–1936. Dam: 2,144 feet long; locks: 600 feet long, 110 feet wide. Launch ramp. SR B, N 1.3 m.; sign. (*Locks and Dams*)

Mounds Roadside Park. Prehistoric mounds, camping, picnic area. US 61, N 10 m.

Pickle-Separating Machine. Standard Machine Co., the world's only manufacturer of flatbed wooden pickle-separating machines, hand-makes about 35 of these 2,500-pound machines annually. Invented in 1906 by T. C. Yager, they grade pickles by diameter and are sold as far away as Japan and Israel. Visitors welcome. In town; SR B, W on Lewis (415).

Remember When Toy Museum. The self-proclaimed "home of the world's largest Marx Toy collection" features over 10,000 toys made during the past 60 years; guided tour of the museum, research lab, and plant. US 61B/SR B, S 1 m.

US 61. *New London: US 61 / Red Ball Road.*

Wyaconda Crossing State Forest. *State Forests.*

---

1. Origin unknown; popular as a classical name in N.Y., Americanized form of Tullius, Roman orator; p.o. 1835–1847, 1849–1859.

CAPE GIRARDEAU
Population: 34,475   Map J-6

Tradition claims that French Ensign Sieur Jean B. Girardot established a trading post here c. 1725 (± 5 years). Maps as early as 1765 identify the site as Cape Girardot or Girardeau and by its nickname L'anse à la Graisse (greasy cove).[1] About 1786, French Canadian Louis Lorimier, along with Shawnee *Indians* (his wife was Shawnee-French), settled near today's St. Mary *(Ste. Genevieve)*. Lorimier moved to Cape Girardeau c. 1793 as a Spanish agent to oversee trading with the Indians, as well as the immigration of Americans, who were being offered virtually free tax-exempt homestead land by Spain *(Defiance: Daniel Boone Historic Area)*. At about the same time (c. 1795), Andrew Ramsey built a plantation here (closely followed by families from Ky., Tenn., and N.C.). After the 1803 *Louisiana Purchase*, this trading post was platted in 1806 as an American town, Cape Girardeau, serving as the seat of government for the territorial district, later (1812) Cape Girardeau County. The seat of government was moved in 1815 to recently established *Jackson* after the federal government rejected Lorimier's Spanish land grants, invalidating titles to all city lots. Unable to function as a legal entity, Cape Girardeau declined until 1826, when the land grants were recognized. A river town, it had no railroad until Louis Houck organized the Cape Girardeau Railroad Company in 1880 *(Marble Hill: Zalma)*. Post office: 1806–now. Home of Southeast Missouri State University (SEMO, below) and Cape Girardeau Area Vo-Tech. Maps, downtown walking tour: chamber of commerce, N of Broadway at US 61 (601 N. Kingshighway). Incidentally, in 1908 local resident Marie (Watkins) Oliver helped design and sew the official Missouri State Flag, adopted in 1913 *(Richmond: Henrietta)*.

American Heritage Museum. Over 400 pieces of late 19th- and early 20th-century equipment are on display in 15 buildings, including about 35 tractors, a 1916 steam engine, a 1903 popcorn machine, a sawmill, a broom machine, and a wide assortment of farm equipment. A film shows operation of some equipment. S side, near airport; I-55.

Architecture. DOWNTOWN: good examples of 19th- and 20th-century styles are in an area bounded by Sprigg, North, the river, and Morgan Oak. NATIONAL HISTORIC REGISTER: Old St. Vincent Church (Gothic Revival, 1851–1853), SR 177 and Main. Thilenius House (1873), 9.5 acres; occasional tours; Themis at Keller. Oliver House (1898), 740 North St. (Deane Architecture, below)

Cape River Heritage Museum. Vernacular, 1908. This two-story, brick, slate-roofed building served the police and fire department until 1981. Exhibits focus on river traffic, vintage clothing and uniforms, fire and police history, and early town history. Downtown; Independence at Frederick.

Capetown Safari. This 150-acre drive-through wildlife park features over 700 exotic animals in natural settings, including llamas, antelopes, zebras, and camels. Petting zoo, feeding area, picnic area. US 61B at SR W; SR W, N approx. 7 m.

Court of Common Pleas. Greek Revival, 1854 (wings added 1889). Established in 1851 by Missouri's general assembly to hear local civil disputes, the court that meets here is one of the last of its kind still presiding. The steps (built 1900) leading uphill to the building's entrance are reportedly Missouri's first (S of St. Louis) use of concrete. Grounds: large cast-iron fountain with a Confederate soldier on top. Downtown; Spanish at Bellevue. *(Hannibal)*

Deane Architecture. Local architect-builder E. B. Deane (1813–1901) built many noteworthy houses here, beginning in 1839. Examples still standing include: CARUTHERS-BURROUGH HOUSE (1859), 2121 Bloomfield. GLENN HOUSE (below). REYNOLDS HOUSE (1857), National Historic Register; 623 N. Main. SHERWOOD-MINTON HOUSE (1846), 444 Washington.

El Camino Real. Marker, Spanish at Williams. *(Roads and Traces)*

Fort D. The largest of four Civil War forts built here during the 1861–1865 Federal occupation; commanding view of the Mississippi. Remnants: rifle pits, earthworks. SE side of town. SR 74, E on Elm.

Glenn House. Folk Victorian, 1883; remodeled as Queen Anne Free Classic, early 1890s; National Historic Register. Built by E. B. Deane (above) in gable-front-and-wing style, the house has been extensively remodeled to include paired columns and a tower. Interior: ceiling rosettes, stenciling, grained woodwork to resemble burled walnut, slate fireplaces; furnished in authentic and stylish detail. Tours. Downtown; SR 74, S on Morgan, N on Spanish (325).

Little River Drainage District. Big, Great, or Little River Swamp is what 19th-century cartographers

A dredge boat in the Little River Drainage District, c. 1908.

labeled an area along the Little River from south of Cape Girardeau, between Sikeston *(Benton)* and *Kennett*, to the Arkansas line. Reportedly one of the largest private projects of its kind (80 m. long, 12–25 m. wide, 500,000 acres), the drainage district was formed as a company in 1905, after the timber industry *(Bunker)* left the area a wasteland of swamps and marshes. Using state-sanctioned assessments that ranged from $4 to $40 an acre, the district was organized into a headwater diversion channel, three detention basins, and 900 miles of ditches spaced one mile apart. The nucleus of the project, the 30-mile headwater diversion channel, diverts runoff from the foothills of southeast Bollinger and Cape Girardeau Counties to the Mississippi at a point east of I-55 and N of SR AB (NE of *Charleston*). I-55, S 1 m. BIRDS POINT–NEW MADRID FLOODWAY: *East Prairie.*

Mississippi River Bridge. Truss, 1928. This 4,744-foot-span bridge was the first for vehicular traffic built between St. Louis and Memphis, Tenn.

Natural Areas. KELSO SANCTUARY NATURAL AREA: 23 acres. Used by SEMO for research and classroom projects, the area includes interesting fauna and flora; observation list available. Biology Dept., SEMO, Cape Girardeau 63701. SR 177, N at city limit. VANCILL HOLLOW NATURAL AREA: 300 acres. Features rugged river-brake terrain and a forest that includes American beech, tulip poplar, cucumber magnolia, and a luxuriant ground cover. Trail of Tears *State Park*, Rt. 4, Jackson 63755. SR 177, N 8 m.

Old Lorimier Cemetery. Established in 1808 by town founder Louis Lorimier, the cemetery contains ornate and interesting markers, including one for Lorimier (d. 1812) and his wife (d. 1808), an elaborate shelter supported by columns. His wife's inscription, in Latin, refers to her as "the noblest matron of the Shawnee race." Overlooking the Mississippi, downtown; Fountain at Washington. *(Cemeteries)*

Parks. CAPAHA: Features one of America's 100 display test gardens for roses (begun in 1956), a replica of the Statue of Liberty, and municipal band concerts (summer, Wednesday evenings). Pool, tennis, ducks. Midtown. Broadway at West End Blvd. CAPE ROCK: The site of the original trading post and the landmark namesake of Cape Girardeau, this rock is two tiers of limestone capped by *loess*. Once extending further into the river, it was excavated in the late 1880s by the St. Louis & San Francisco *Railroad* when track was laid along the river. Overlooking the river; picnic area. NE side of town; SR 177, E on Cape Rock Drive. RIVERFRONT: Benches, protected walkway to the river's edge, 320-by-14-foot mural depicting the town's history. Broadway at the river.

SEMO CAMPUS. Founded in 1873. KENT LIBRARY: an outstanding William Faulkner collection. SHOW ME CENTER: a 7,800-seat arena used for conventions, concerts, sports events, exhibitions. UNIVERSITY MUSEUM: major collections include kachina dolls, navaho rugs (some from the classic period), Maria pottery (San Ildefonso, N.M.), life-size statuary produced by August Gerber for the 1904 St. Louis World's Fair. NE side of town; SR 34 at West End Blvd, N on West End.

"Southeast Missourian" Newspaper Building. Vernacular, 1923. Features a pair of tile murals illustrating printing and newspaper publishing. Reportedly, the tiles, oil painting on clay, took ten years to design and the mural two years to produce. Downtown; Broadway at Lorimier.

Southeast Missouri State Fair. Since 1855. Agricultural exhibits, entertainment, midway, carnival. Late June.

Stream Piracy. Just northwest (0.75 m.) of the junction of US 61 and SR 34, a tributary of the Mississippi captured the Cape La Croix Creek, diverting it to today's course to the Mississippi. The two highways were laid in the creek's abandoned valley. Junction, S to I-55. *(Stream Piracy)*

Trail of Tears State Park. *State Parks.* SR 177 at Mississippi River bridge; SR 177, N 13.3 m.

1. A humorously derogatory nickname *(Ste. Genevieve)*.

CARROLLTON
Population: 4,406   Map D-3

Selected in 1833 as county seat of newly organized Carroll County, Carrollton was platted and named for county namesake Charles Carroll *(County Profiles)*. John Standley, an 1819 settler, donated the land, which was sold at auction in 1834. Narrowly bypassed in 1868 by the Western Branch of the North Missouri *Railroad*, the town was bisected by the Chicago, Santa Fe & California and the Chicago, Burlington & Kansas City during the 1880s. Post office: 1834–now.

Architecture. The town square has good examples of 19th-century structures, including these on the National Historic Register: Carroll County Jail and Sheriff's Quarters (1878, remodeled 1958), post office (1911), Wilcoxson Bank (late 1800s).

Carroll County Courthouse. Richardsonian Romanesque, 1902–1904. The county's fourth courthouse is typical of the style—rusticated stone, arched windows, corner towers, central clock tower—and nearly identical to courthouses in Vernon, Polk, and Adair Counties, which were also designed by R. B. Kirsch. Cost: $45,900. Grounds: 14-foot bronze statue of Gen. James Shields (St. Mary's Cemetery, below). Downtown. *(County Profiles)*

Carroll County Museum. About 30 rooms have specific themes—e.g. 19th-century parlor, doctor's office, log cabin, kitchen. NE side of town, US 65B, 0.25 m. N of junction with SR 24.

Coloma, Mo. Platted in 1858, Coloma was a successful trading point until bypassed by the Chicago, Burlington & Kansas City *Railroad* in the 1880s. The place-name, originally from California after a Maidu Indian village (meaning unknown), was probably transferred here by former California gold miners. Post offices: Mound[1] 1842–1848, 1857–1858; San Francisco[2] 1858–1861; Coloma 1861–1907. US 65, N 14 m.; SR Z, W 2.4 m. BUNCH HOLLOW *WILDLIFE AREA*.

Fort D'Orleans. Two markers. (1) US 24, E 14 m. to DeWitt,[3] then US 24, E 1.7 m. (2) US 24, E 4 m. *(Keytesville: Brunswick)*

Glacial Erratic. Buried about two and a half feet, the visible portion of this quartzite boulder measures 12 x 9 x 3.5 feet. US 65, N 7 m.; SR W, W 13 m.; SR D, N 2 m. to church; GR, W 1 m.; GR, turn N, look W. *(Glacial Erratics)*

Round Barn. This 1915 structure is one of only a few round barns remaining in Missouri. With a capacity of about 100 tons of hay, it is 70 feet tall and 190 feet in circumference. US 65, N 9 m.; SR M, E approx. 1.5 m.; inquire locally.

St. Mary's Cemetery. A 1910 bronze bust marks the grave of Gen. James Shields (1806–1879), who fought in three wars *(Black Hawk; Mexican; Civil)* and who is America's only senator elected from three different states (Ill., Minn., and Mo.). One of two memorials honoring him (Carroll County Courthouse, above), reportedly this is America's only Federal monument in a private cemetery. US 65, N approx. 1 m. *(Cemeteries)*

Wildlife Areas. Bunch Hollow, Little Compton, Schifferdecker. *(Wildlife Areas)*

1. Prominent landmark.
2. 1847 Calif. town after its bay named in 1769 for St. Francis of Assisi *(County Profiles: St. Francois)*.
3. DeWitt *Clinton*; p.o. Pleasant Park, commendatory, 1835–1882; DeWitt 1842–now.

CARTHAGE
Population: 10,747   Map C-6

Selected in 1841 as a central location for county seat of newly organized Jasper County, the town was platted in 1842 on a *prairie* plateau above the Spring River. Reportedly the river bluffs' light-colored building stone was reminiscent of the quarries near the classical city-state Carthage (the gray marble quarries here are the world's largest). Reduced to weeds and ashes by both sides during the *Civil War* (Battle of Carthage, below), Carthage began rebuilding in 1866 and was incorporated in 1868. Incidentally, county resident Annie Baxter was elected to a public office (Jasper county clerk) in 1890, 30 years before the 19th Amendment granted women the right to vote. Post offices: Jasper[1] 1840–1843, 1857–1863, 1867–1870, 1872–now; Carthage 1843–1863, 1866–now. Home of Carthage Area Vo-Tech. Walking/driving maps: chamber of commerce, across from courthouse. *(Route 66)*

Architecture. National Historic Register districts: CASSILL PLACE: 500 block of W. Central. COURT-HOUSE SQUARE: roughly bounded by E. Central, Lincoln, 5th., S. Maple. SOUTH DISTRICT: roughly bounded by Garrison (SR 571), 5th, Clinton, and Macon.

Battle of Carthage / Park. State Historic Site. This one-day *Civil War* battle (July 5, 1861) preceded First Manassas (Bull Run) by sixteen days and was reported by the "New York Times" as "The first serious conflict between the United States Troops and the Rebels." Federal Col. Franz Sigel was ordered to find and destroy deposed Gov. Claiborne Jackson's Missouri State Militia, which was retreating from *Boonville* and

trying to reach Gen. Ben McCulloch in Arkansas. About 1,100 Federals confronted over 6,000 Confederates (2,000 without weapons), optimistically hoping to defeat them, or hold them until reinforcements arrived. After a brief battle that morning at Dry Fork Creek, the outnumbered and nearly outflanked Sigel began a leapfrog skirmishing retreat that ended in the streets of Carthage, where, in the darkness, he retreated unchallenged 18 miles south to Sarcoxie (below). The next day, Jackson continued unopposed toward Arkansas to meet McCulloch *(Springfield: Wilson's Creek)*. Federal, 13 killed, 31 wounded; Home Guard, 35 killed, 125 wounded. Stone markers indicate sites along the eight-mile skirmish route. N side; SR 96 at US 571; SR 96, W to Francis; N on Francis to N on CR 15. CARTER PARK: This four-acre park is the site of the final confrontation in the 12-hour running battle. Confederates camped here that evening. Preserved intact. SR 571, E on Chestnut.

Belle Starr. A plaque identifies Carthage as the childhood home (1848–1863) of Myra Belle Shirley (1848–1889), the legendary postwar bandit queen, cattle rustler, and horse thief who was murdered by her son and sometime lover. Her parents, local merchants, moved to Texas just before the town was destroyed during the Civil War. Lawn of courthouse (below).

Jasper County Courthouse. Richardsonian Romanesque, 1894–1895; National Historic Register. This is the county's third courthouse. The previous one was destroyed by fire in October 1863 as a result of a Civil War incident and afterward the court met in temporary quarters (e.g. a remodeled jail and the Baptist

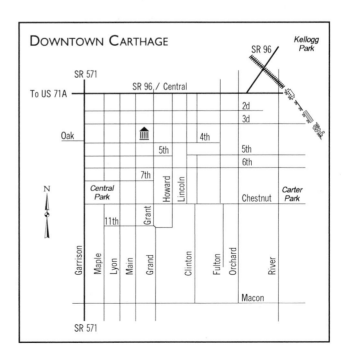

DOWNTOWN CARTHAGE

church) for 32 years. Today's structure is built of Carthage marble and features square towers, turrets, and a domed central clock tower with a cupola. Cost: $91,600. Grounds: Civil War marker (Battle of Carthage, above), Belle Starr plaque (above). SR 571, E on 3d. *(County Profiles)*

Museums. JASPER COUNTY: Local historical items. In courthouse. POWERS: Focuses on the careers of physician Everett Powers and his wife, Marian, a coloratura soprano, who performed regionally. Also: extensive female fashion collection, Civil War artifacts, quilts, nature walk. NW side; W on Oak (1617).

Parks. CARTER: Battle of Carthage, above. CENTRAL: Wading pool, Civil War battle site marker (Battle of Carthage, above), bronze statue of Marlin Perkins of "Wild Kingdom," who grew up here. SR 571 at Chestnut. KELLOGG LAKE: Small fishing lake (crappie, catfish), picnicking, RV camping, small portion of *Route 66*. SR 96, NE of town. MUNICIPAL: golf, pool, tennis, roller rink, baseball, picnicking, playground. SR 571, W on Oak to Robert Ellis Young Blvd.; sign.

Public Library. Neoclassical, 1905. Displays include vintage coins, pottery, African artifacts, dolls, miniature toys. Downtown; SR 571 at 4th.

Route 66 / Towns. *Halltown; Route 66.*

Sarcoxie, Mo. After the town was settled in 1831 as Centerville,[2] its name was changed due to an existing *Centerville*. Named for the Shawnee *Indian* chief[3] who once lived at the town's spring. ARCHITECTURE: Intact 19th-century commercial buildings. Post office: 1838 – now. US 71, S 8 m.; I-44, E 12 m.

Tour Homes. Postwar prosperity resulted in a large number of Victorian homes. The following are representative. HILL HOUSE: Queen Anne, 1886–1887. Features 10 fireplaces, 5 porches, stained glass, a slate roof, and copper gutters. Downtown; SR 571, E on Macon, N on Main (1157). MAPLE LANE FARM: Queen Anne, 1900–1904; National Historic Register. Conspicuously elaborate 22-room 10,000-square-foot house built by W. H. Phelps (below). Features Carthage marble, a tile roof, a ballroom, 64 doors, 76 windows, 5 fireplaces, and 3 types of original heating systems (electric, gas, and steam). SR 571/SR 96; SR 96, E 3.5 m.; 10th Road, N 3.75 m. PHELPS HOUSE: Queen Anne, c. 1890. Built by nationally influential lawyer-politician W. H. Phelps, who later built Maple Lane Farm (above), a similar high-style architect-designed structure. Downtown; SR 571, E on Macon, N on Grand (1146). (Architecture, above)

---

1. Jasper County namesake *(County Profiles)*.

2. Location; no p.o.

3. "American Place-Names" cites Sarcoxie, Kans., as named for a Delaware chief "who lived in this region."

CARUTHERSVILLE
Population: 7,389   Map I-8

This town has prospered because of the Mississippi River. To its south, nearby Little Prairie,[1] a French trading post established c. 1794 by François LeSieur *(New Madrid)*, was washed away in the late 1850s. G. W. Bushey and 1810 settler John Hardeman Walker (Missouri's Bootheel, below) platted a town in 1857 on Walker's plantation, naming it for Samuel Caruthers, a prominent southeastern Missouri politician who helped "in the legal establishment" of the town. In 1899 it was made county seat of Pemiscot County after nearby (to the north) Gayoso[2] could not control repeated flooding (it washed away in the early 1900s). Bypassed by railroads until the 1890s, Caruthersville prospered as a river port. Post offices: Lost Village[3] c. 1846–1856; Gayoso 1854–1900; Caruthersville 1856–1864, 1866–now.

Braggadocio, Mo. Reportedly settled c. 1847, the community shares with its township this officially unexplained name that entered the English language via Braggadocchio, Edmund Spenser's vainglorious knight from "The Faerie Queene." Because Braggadocio is the dictionary definition of empty bragging or pretentious cockiness, authorities disagree as to its inspiration for a town name: (1) an event or (2) a blanket judgment of its residents *(Gasconade)*. Post office: 1881–now. SR U, W 8.8. m. Home of Pemiscot County Vocational School.

Depot / Museum. Railroad, 1915. Pemiscot County historical items. W 3d at tracks.

Missouri's Bootheel. John H. Walker (Caruthersville history, above) is responsible for this irregularity in Missouri's *boundary line*. Learning that the proposed 1818 northern Arkansas Territory line would include his property, he successfully lobbied to set Missouri Territory's southeastern line at the 36th parallel between the St. Francis and Mississippi Rivers.

Pemiscot County Courthouse. Italian Renaissance, 1924–1925. The county's fourth, this three-story 136-by-96-foot brick courthouse with stone trim has a decorative facade, roofline balustrade, eight second-story ionic columns, first-story arched windows, and pedimented entries. Architect H. H. Hohenschild also designed courthouses for Barry, Christian, and Scott Counties. Cost: $114,000. Downtown. *(County Profiles)*

Stateline, Mo. This turn-of-the-century community was named for its location. THE OTHER ARCH: Older but considerably smaller and less elaborate than the one at *St. Louis*, this 1924 concrete arch across the narrow two lanes of US 61 might not clear the top of a tractor-trailer. The north side proclaims "Entering Arkansas"; the south side, "Entering Missouri." Post office: none. SR U, W 4.6 m.; I-55, S 13.5 m.; US 61, S.2.7 m.

Watertower. National Historic Register. Originally brick but now covered with concrete and white paint, this is reportedly one of the first (1902) of 15,000 watertowers like it built in America and is now one of two still known to be standing. Downtown.

Wolf Bayou Natural Area. 200 acres. Features an oxbow lake and cypress forest. 833 N. Kingshighway, Cape Girardeau 63701. SR 84, W 5 m.; I-55, N 10 m.; SR BB, E 3.2 m.; GR, S 0.7 m.

1. *Prairie* location; no p.o.
2. Spanish governor of Louisiana; p.o. 1854–1900.
3. After the *New Madrid Earthquake* of 1811–1812, now-deserted Little Prairie, which had a population of 200 c. 1803, became known as Lost Village.

CASSVILLE
Population: 2,371   Map D-7

Reductions in the size of Barry County required moving the county seat twice: first from Mount Pleasant[1] and then from McDonald.[2] Cassville, platted in 1845 along Flat Creek as the third county seat, was named for Lewis Cass (1782–1866), Michigan U.S. senator and American statesman who was known for his support of U.S. expansionist policies, the *Mexican War,* and squatter sovereignty that allowed residents of territories to decide the issue of slavery *(County Profiles: Cass; Kansas Border War).* The town grew as a trading and political center. Post offices: Flat Creek[3] 1840–1845; Barry Court House[4] 1845; Cassville 1845–now.

Barry County Courthouse. Italian Renaissance, 1913. This building's predecessor (1856–1907) was used by Civil War Federals as a hospital and fort. Today's stone-veneer courthouse, the county's fourth, has a full-height projecting central wing with Ionic columns, second-story arched windows, and a parapet. Cost: $45,720. Architect H. H. Hohenschild also designed courthouses for Pemiscot, Christian, and Scott Counties. Downtown. *(County Profiles)*

Capital of Confederate Missouri. During the first year of the *Civil War,* Cassville was occupied by both sides (more often by Federals) and was used as a staging area for battles, including the one at Wilson's Creek *(Springfield).* After the battle of Pea Ridge, Ark., in March 1862, the town was gutted by Federals. For one week (October 31–November 7, 1861) it served as the Confederate's state capital when the state assembly was forced out of *Neosho.* Markers at courthouse.

Cassville & Exeter Railroad. Located at an important north–south road during the 1850s–1870s, Cassville was narrowly bypassed in 1880 by the St. Louis & San Francisco *Railroad,* which helped establish nearby Exeter.[5] To compensate for the loss, this railroad was built in 1896; at 4.8 miles in length, it was, at that time, reportedly America's shortest broad-gauge railroad. Marker at courthouse.

Cassville Natural Bridge. Set 25 feet above Natural Bridge Hollow Creek, the bridge is 160 feet long with a 50-foot span and a 30-foot ceiling. SR 76, E 4 m.; SR 86, S 3.65 m.; forest trail, 0.1 m.; left fork, 0.5 m. *(Collapsed Cave Systems)*

Crystal Caverns. Open since 1924 and promoted as "one of ten largest show *caves* in Missouri," this living cave has a large variety of formations. Constant 54°F; 40-minute guided tour. SR 37B, N approx. 0.6 m.

O'Vallon Winery. Established in 1986, it specializes in dry and semidry wines, featuring a vineyard of Missouri wild grapes and hybrids. Tours and tasting. SR 37, S 6 m.

Recreation. FLAG SPRING *STATE FOREST. FLOAT STREAM:* Flat Creek. MARK TWAIN *NATIONAL FOREST:* multiple access, S and E. PINEY CREEK WILDERNESS HIKING *TRAILS.* ROARING RIVER *STATE PARK:* SR 112, S 6 m. ROARING RIVER *WILDLIFE AREA.* TABLE ROCK LAKE: *Lakes: Corps of Engineers.*

Roaring River Cove Hardwood Natural Area. 120 acres. Part of Roaring River *State Park.* Features old-growth stands of various types of oak, as well as shagbark hickory on rocky chert slopes; 66 species of birds have been spotted here. Box D, Cassville 65625. SR 112, S 6 m.

Roaring River Trout Hatchery. About 28 million gallons of water flow daily through this hatchery that produces 250,000 trout annually. Fishing, restrooms, nature center, camping (Roaring River *State Park).* SR 112, S 12 m.

Shell Knob, Mo. The site was first settled in 1835 by Henry and Elizabeth Schell as a White River trading post (SR Y Sites, below) near a prominent knob *(Balds and Knobs)* that served as a guide to the store and as the basis for the area's name. The name was changed (possibly misspelled) when the post office was established. Post office: 1872–now. SR 76, E 12 m.; SR 39, S 3 m. BIG BAY CAMPGROUND / PICNIC AREA *(National Forests):* Improved camping, fees, flush toilets, water, tables, fire ring, boat ramp; seasonal. Adjacent to Table Rock Lake; inquire locally. PINEY CREEK WILDERNESS HIKING *TRAILS.* SR Y SITES: Along this road, measured from the junction with SR 39, are: (1) Remnants of a WWII CCC Camp; E 1 m. (2) A large rock with a plaque commemorating the site of Schell's trading post; E 1.5 m. (3) A panoramic view of Table Rock Lake *(Lakes: Corps of Engineers);* E approx. 3 m., then GR (at mobile home park), N approx. 0.3 m.

(4) A late 19th-century school-house moved here in 1916 from Viola;[6] E approx. 3 m.

1. Stock name, commendatory; p.o. 1836–1846; co. seat 1835–1840.
2. Origin unknown; p.o. 1840–1851, 1854; co. seat 1840–1845; McDonald is today's McDowell, origin unknown; p.o. 1858–1868, 1872–1925.
3. Descriptive, via the creek (*Flat River*).
4. Barry County namesake (*County Profiles*).
5. Stock name, town in England; p.o. 1880–now.
6. Unidentified person; p.o. 1893–1918, 1921–1974.

Gourd Creek Cave, Phelps County.

CAVES

Missouri, known as the Cave State as well as the Show-Me State, reportedly has more caves than any state in America (over 5,000). All show caves (over 31) are lighted, most have guides, and each is unique. Not all caves listed in this book are developed. Exploring undeveloped ones is extremely dangerous. Do not go beyond the point of natural light. Check the ceiling and floor before entering. Signs of recent water (flooding) or imminent rain are serious warnings to keep out. Undeveloped caves also provide shelter for animals, reptiles, and insects, some of which can be harmful. (*Collapsed Cave Systems*)

CEMETERIES

"Remember friends, as you pass by / As you are now so once was I / As I am now so you must be / Prepare for death and follow me." Named from the Greek "koimeterion," meaning resting or sleeping place, cemeteries are a reliable source for town history. Beginning in the 19th century, death and cemeteries were romanticized, especially by the new concept of interment in secular garden cemeteries rather than churchyards. Gravestones for all members of society were often carved, using symbols and sentimental passages. Mozelle Hutchison of Vienna, Mo., contributed the following explanations for some of the more common symbols. ANGELS: to protect the soul in flight. BIRD: the soul flying to heaven. CLASPED HANDS (also index finger pointing upward): a sentiment usually reinforced by words, i.e. Farewell, Meet Me In Heaven, Gone Home. CROWN: the crown of righ-

teousness. DOVE: constancy and devotion. FLOWER BUD: being cut from life before blooming (a bud on a broken stem); unfulfilled potential (a broken bud). HEAVENLY GATES: welcome to heaven. LAMB: innocence. RECLINING CHILD: innocence, the sweetness of a short life. SCROLL: victory, the spiritual life of the mind. SHELL: rebirth. WILLOW TREE: mourning. (To determine the precise birth date from markers with only death dates, use the 8870 formula as published in the "Skagit Valley GS Newsletter." Example: Died 1889, May 6 at 71 years, 7 months, 9 days: death date [18890506] minus the life span [710709] minus the formula 8870 equals 18170927, or born September 27, 1817.)

CENTER

Population: 552   Map G-3

In 1871 James Mason platted the town in the center of a 12-mile *prairie* near the center of Ralls County, hoping in vain to attract the county seat from *New London*. About 20 years later the town did attract a spur of the St. Louis & Hannibal *Railroad*, which in turn attracted most of the businesses from nearby Madisonville[1] (SR P, S 3.3 m.; SR C, E 2 m.). Post offices: Center, 1844–1845, 1892– now; Centre, 1872–1892.

Mason Park. The land was originally set aside for a court square (Center history, above): playground, picnic facilities, tennis. Downtown; SR 19.

Perry, Mo. This 1837 community was known by its post office names (below) until platted in 1868 at Lick Creek by namesake Perry Crossthwait and A. Mayhall.

Post offices: Cove Springs[2] 1837–1846; Lick Creek[3] 1846–1866; Perry 1866–now. SR 19, S 7.5 m.; SR 154, W 2.1 m.; just S of Mark Twain Lake (*Lakes: Corps of Engineers*). ARCHITECTURE: Good examples of 19th-century commercial styles.

St. Paul Catholic Church / Cemetery. Vernacular, 1859–1860; National Historic Register. Deconsecrated 1966. Although the first resident priest, Father Peter Paul Lefever (later Bishop of Detroit), arrived in 1833 (St. Peter Catholic Church, below), the parish and cemetery date from 1828; this is reportedly the mother church of those in northwest Missouri, southeast Iowa, and western Illinois. The locally quarried stone walls of this church are two feet thick, and the foundation is set six feet deep. Features include Gothic-style windows and a 22-foot barrel-vaulted ceiling. SR 19, W 6 m.; SR EE, N 2.5 m. to curve; GR, N 0.25 m. (*Cemeteries*)

St. Peter Catholic Church / Cemetery. Vernacular, 1862, National Historic Register. Deconsecrated 1945. Father Lefever built this church (same materials and construction as St. Paul, above) for parishioners on the north side of the Salt River. Features include Gothic-style windows. Cemetery established c. 1833. SR H, N 4.8 m.; SR A, W 4 m. to curve N of Ely Creek; GR, N approx. 2 m. to fork; W 0.1 m. (*Cemeteries*)

1. Settler James Madison Crossthwaite; p.o. 1838–1906.
2. Descriptive.
3. The creek, which provided a source of salt for animals, who licked the saline solution there.

CENTERVILLE
Population: 200   Map H-6

The town was platted in 1845 as Centreville at a spring near the west fork of the Black River by property owner John Buford, who offered the site as a central location for the county seat of newly organized Reynolds County. The offer was rejected in favor of nearby Lesterville (below), which served as seat of justice until a reduction in the county's size and the town's 1862 destruction during the Civil War resulted in Centerville's 1865 selection as county seat. It prospered as a trading center during the county's c. 1885–1915 lumber boom (*Bunker*) and then declined. Post offices: Centreville 1846–1847, 1852–1863, 1865–1892; Centerville 1892–now.

Architecture. Examples of 19th-century styles include Bowles House (Gothic Revival), across from the courthouse.

Johnson's Shut-Ins Natural Areas. These following areas are all part of Johnson's Shut-Ins *State Park*. SR 21, N 5 m.; SR 49, E 0.5 m.; SR N, N 6 m. Middlebrook

63656. DOLOMITE GLADE: 18 acres. Glades are rare in the St. Francois Mountains. Plant species include the Missouri evening primrose, adder's tongue fern, and sandwort. FEN: 8 acres. Reportedly the least disturbed example in the state, these wetlands nurture notable flora, including an uncommon variety of blue flag iris. SHUT-INS: 180 acres. Valley walls converge dramatically to form one of the state's most spectacular *shut-ins* highlighted by billion-year-old igneous rock, gravel bars, igneous forests, glades, and talus slope communities.

Lesterville, Mo. Settled c. 1816 by Jesse Lester, this former county seat (Centerville history, above) and historic crossroads town is known today for its resorts and campgrounds along the Black River. Post office: 1838–1839, 1842–unknown, unknown–1863, 1865–now. SR 21, N 6 m.; SR 49/72, E 4 m. *FLOAT STREAM:* Black River. LOWER TAUM SAUK *WILDLIFE AREA. STATE PARKS:* Taum Sauk Mountain (SR 49/72, E 8 m.; SR 21, N 5 m.; SR CC, W 3 m.; signs); Johnson's Shut-Ins (above; SR 49, W 3 m.; SR N, N 6 m.).

Recreation. OZARK *TRAIL:* Blair Creek section. SUTTON BLUFF CAMPGROUND / PICNIC AREA / *TRAIL (National Forests):* Water, toilets, fishing and swimming in the West Fork of the Black River.

Reeds Spring / Gristmill. Built c. 1873, the *gristmill's* waterwheel was taken to the New York World's Fair in 1939. Today's log mill house and 11-foot wooden waterwheel are working replicas built c. 1973. The spring still flows (c. 9,700,000 gallons daily). Private. SR 21; Pine St., E 0.5 m. at S side of West Fork of Black River.

Reynolds County Courthouse. Vernacular Classical Revival, 1871. The county's third and one of Missouri's oldest functioning courthouses was built of handmade bricks. (Fire destroyed the previous two courthouses of 1846–1862 and 1865–1871; most records were lost.) Simply designed and set in a parklike enclosure fenced by a low stone wall, this front-gabled structure has brick quoins, dentils, and second-story arched windows with brick hood molds. A proposed dome and lantern were deleted from the original plan. Cost: $8,000. Grounds: JAIL: c. 1872. The walls have been covered with stucco; now used to store records. MEMORIALS: Several polished red granite markers commemorate "the Boys of Reynolds County" who served in wars since WWI. SR 21, in town. (*County Profiles*)

Town Spring. Springwater flows through town, emptying into the West Fork of the Black River. Until pipes were laid in 1965, the spring served the town's needs. City park; in town.

Victor Safe. Bought by the Bank of Reynolds County at the 1904 St. Louis World's Fair, where it had won first premium, this seven-ton Victor Spherical Manganese

Burglar-Proof Safe reportedly had foiled 10 burglary attempts in the previous 18 months *(Galena: Dewey J. Short Memorial Building)*, an accomplishment far less dramatic than the delivering of this 14,000-pound safe to Centerville: from the railroad station at Hogan[1] (15 air miles NE) at the base of Missouri's tallest mountain, Taum Sauk (1,772 feet), it was skidded over ice- and snow-covered mountain trails, using a wagon pulled by 14 mules. Daniel Building, NW corner of square.

1. Origin unknown; p.o. 1880–1887, 1897–1943.

CENTRALIA
Population: 3,414   Map F-3

The single-minded purpose of this town, platted in 1857 on a *prairie* along the North Missouri *Railroad's* proposed route from St. Louis to Ottumwa, Iowa, is indicated by its name, coined for its central location between the two cities (the suffix -alia was added for euphony). In a race with Sturgeon (below) to be the area's primary market town, it reportedly had 25 dwellings, 2 stores, a hotel, and a saloon waiting when the first train arrived in 1859. Post office: 1858 – now.

Centralia Historical Museum. Queen Anne, 1904; National Historic Register. This residence of A. B. Chance from 1920 until his death in 1949 highlights period furnishings, Civil War artifacts, a pioneer kitchen, and a garden (below). The Centralia-based A. B. Chance Company is the world's largest producer of earth anchors for telephone poles, etc. 319 Sneed, 3 blocks E of square.

Centralia Massacre. Although one of the worst of its kind, this atrocity typifies the violence of paramilitary marauders during the *Kansas Border War* and the *Civil War*. On September 27, 1864, Bushwhacker Bill Anderson *(Richmond: Orrick)* led 80 of an estimated 350 heavily armed men into undefended Centralia and began randomly looting the town. When the North Missouri *Railroad* arrived, he robbed it ($3,000 from the train's safe, $10,000 from the passengers' baggage), then ordered the removal of about 23 (accounts vary) unarmed Federal soldiers. Arch Clements stripped them naked, formed a firing squad, and, using pistols, killed them all. Half fell on the first volley. The rest, staggering around, were shot individually. Passengers were ordered off the train, which was set on fire, put at full throttle, and sent blazing down the tracks. Anderson and his men returned to a nearby base camp. Late that afternoon, Federal Maj. A. V. E. Johnson, who had been tracking Anderson, arrived in town with about 185 men (accounts vary widely). Johnson, underestimating Anderson's strength, left a rearguard and with mostly new recruits set out across the prairie for the guerrillas' base camp. Anderson's veterans caught them in the open. Reportedly, Jesse James killed Major Johnson. An estimated 12 Federals escaped (78 are buried at National Cemetery, *Jefferson City*). Marker at tracks 1 block N of square. *(Glasgow: Battle of Glasgow)*

Chance Gardens. National Historic Register. Established in 1935 by A. B. Chance (Centralia Historical Museum, above) as a retirement hobby, this half-acre garden is filled with flowers bordered by paths, rock walls, trees, and a stream. Beside museum.

Chance Guest House. Art Moderne, 1940; National Historic Register. An excellent example of its type, the house was built by A. B. Chance's son F. Gano. The curving and undecorated smooth concrete facade distinguishes it from the earlier Art Deco style. Private; 543 Jefferson, beside Centralia Historical Museum (above).

Parks. CENTRALIA PARK: 30 acres. Pool, tennis, picnic facilities, playground, fishing ponds, fitness trail. N side, SR 22, S on Jefferson, E on Head. TOALSON PARK: 10 acres. Picnic facilities, tennis, playground, outdoor ice rink. W side, SR 124, E on Lakeview.

Sturgeon, Mo. Platted along the railroad's grade in 1856 (one year before Centralia) and named for North Missouri *Railroad* superintendent Isaac H. Sturgeon, the town was established by draining the population, post office (Bourbonton, below), and structures from nearby Prairie City[1] and Buena Vista.[2] Due to slow growth and damage by an 1859 tornado, it lagged behind its rival, Centralia. Post offices: Bourbonton[3] 1849–1857; Sturgeon 1857–now. SR 22, W 7.5 m.

Tri-City Community Lake. 30 acres. Bass, sunfish, crappie, catfish. SR CC, W 3 m.; GR, S 1.5 m.

1. *Prairie* location; no p.o.
2. Spanish for good view.
3. For the French royal family, the Bourbons *(Cuba: Bourbon)*.

CHAMOIS
Population: 449   Map G-4

First settled in 1818 by French, Dutch, and German immigrants, the town was platted in 1856 along the tracks of the Pacific *Railroad* and named by Morgan Harbor, who reportedly thought the countryside resembled the Alpine regions of Europe and the local deer looked like Alpine chamois, highly prized hunting trophies that combine features of goats and antelopes. Post office: 1856–now.

Architecture. CHAMOIS SCHOOL: Vernacular, 1876.

Set on a hill, this three-story brick structure with a cupola appears to be a courthouse. Closed 1942; today used by the American Legion. In town. DR. J. M. TOWNLEY HOUSE / OFFICE: Weatherboard Log, c. 1834; additions prior to 1900. The one-room office had a second room added for use as the first Osage County school; three fireplaces. SR 89, S 3 m.; Shawnee Creek Rd., E 2 m. MCKNIGHT HOUSE (OLD BIRCH): Adamesque, 1840; restored 1952. Two-story brick with 15-pane double-hung sashes. McKnight Rd., S 4 m.; inquire locally.

Chamois Access. 1 acre. Picnic facilities, restrooms, camping, fishing, ramp. Missouri River.

CHARLESTON
Population: 5,085   Map J-7

Platted in 1837 on property owned by J. L. Moore, W. P. Barnard, and Mrs. Thankful Randol, the town was overshadowed by nearby Matthews Prairie[1] until selected in 1845 as county seat of newly organized Mississippi County. Charleston was slow to grow (there was no courthouse until 1852), but the arrival of the Iron Mountain & Southern *Railroad* in the late 1870s and the 1882 completion of the Texas & St. Louis from *Birds Point* via Charleston to the Texas border helped establish Charleston as a trading center. Proposed namesakes for the town include King Charles II via 1670 Charleston, S.C., and J. L. Moore's brother Charles, who was offered the honor if he would move here to help build the town; at various times the area was known as both Carlos Prairie and St. Charles Prairie. Post offices: Matthews Prairie 1828–1847; Charleston 1847–now.

Architecture. National Historic Register: Missouri-Pacific depot, downtown. Jacob Swank house (1839), US 62, W 0.2 m.

Little River Drainage District. *Cape Girardeau.*

Mississippi County Courthouse. Italian Renaissance, 1900–1901; remodeled 1938, after a fire. The county's second, designed by self-taught architect J. B. Legg, who designed similar courthouses in Gasconade and St. Charles Counties, this 114-by-70-foot brick structure has its style's hallmarks: quoins, balustrades, a rusticated first level, a different window treatment on each floor, pedimented and colonnaded projecting central entries, and corner towers projecting like wings. Cost: $25,000. Downtown. *(County Profiles)*

Moore House / Museum. Queen Anne, 1899–1900; National Historic Register. Highlights of this county museum include period furnishings, never-painted interior woodwork, local historical items, vintage clothing, and a piece of mile-long chain with 20-pound links used by Confederates in an attempt to contain Mississippi River traffic above the crossing from Columbus, Ky., to Belmont, Mo. *(East Prairie: Battlefield / Belmont)*. Downtown; 403 N. Main.

1. Family name, *prairie* location.

CHILLICOTHE
Population: 8,804   Map D-2

The townsite, near the confluence of the Thompson and Grand Rivers on land acquired by an 1830 treaty with the Sauk and Fox *Indians,* was platted in 1837 as county seat of recently organized Livingston County and named Chillicothe by the court (reportedly the clerk spelled it Chilicothe). This stock place-name (used also in Ohio, Ill., and Tex.), was first applied to the 1800–1803 capital of the Northwest Territory and the first (1803) capital of Ohio (originally spelled Chillicoathee c. 1774); it was an Indian tribal name, later used to describe the place where the tribe lived, and reportedly means "big town where we live" or "our big house." Although Missouri's Chillicothe was platted as the county seat, the federal government owned the townsite until 1839. As a result, the town was of little consequence and was overshadowed by Jessie Nave's nearby small store and post office (Spring Hill, below). Completion of the Hannibal & St. Joseph *Railroad* in 1859 (below) helped secure its prosperity. Post office: 1839–now. Home of Chillicothe Area Vo-Tech.

Bedford Limited Excursion Train. During the week, a diesel-electric locomotive hauls commercial products 37 miles to the Missouri River along one of the few railroad branch lines left in Missouri. On weekends it pulls a 1920s Pullman Standard coach for a 20-mile round-trip (2.5 hrs.) passenger excursion tour. S side; US 65, E on 1st, S on Elm to tracks.

Chillicothe Correctional Center. Vernacular, 1888. Built to house and educate, rather than punish, delinquent girls, these brick building are now Missouri's only prison for women. SW side; US 65, W on 3d to Dickinson.

Grace Episcopal Church. Gothic style, 1867–1869; National Historic Register. Still housing regular services, this frame church on a stone foundation is reportedly one of Missouri's earliest examples of prefabrication (the beams and wall sections were cut and constructed in St. Louis). Leaded, stained-glass, and painted-glass windows; black walnut furnishings. Downtown; 421 Elm.

 **CIVIL WAR**

Grand River Historical Museum. Displays include 100 years of wedding gowns, furniture, military uniforms, tools, and local items. N side; US 65, W on Polk, N on Fair, E on Irving to Forest.

Hannibal & St. Joseph Railroad Marker. A five-foot stone column enclosed by an iron fence marks where tracks from the east and west met in 1859, completing the first railroad to cross Missouri. Junction US 65 and 36; US 36, E 2.5 m.; GR, N 0.8 m.; railroad tracks, W 0.25 m.

Livingston County Courthouse. Italian Renaissance, 1913–1914. When the county's second courthouse was razed in 1864 as unsafe, proposed bond issues for a new one were rejected by voters. For over 50 years county offices were located in various buildings. The vacant lot on the square was named Elm Park by residents and used as such until a direct tax was approved for today's three-story 80-by-100-foot structure of Bedford stone with quoins, roof-line balustrades, a rusticated first level, second-story Ionic columns, and an entry with balustrades and paired Ionic columns. The structure and interior are in original condition. Cost: $97,890. Downtown. *(County Profiles)*

Poosey State Forest. *State Forests.*

Rocky Ford. Rapids running next to limestone bluffs mark this crossing. US 65, N to cemetery; GR, W to church; GR, N approx. 2 m.; at the Thompson River.

Simpson Park. 35 acres. Set aside in 1928. Pool, picnic tables, tennis, walking trail, playground, restrooms. US 65, near N city limits.

Spring Hill, Mo. First called Navestown or Naves Town (Chillicothe history, above), this ghost town was also called Knaves Town by accident or irony. Frustrated, Jessie Nave changed the name to Spring Hill, for the springs on the townsite's hill, when platting it in 1848. Post offices: Medicine Creek Post Office[1] 1837–1845; Naves Store 1838–1849; Springhill 1849–1901. SR 190, W 6 m.; SR A, N 2.6 m.; SR T, E 0.2 m.

1. The creek, origin unknown; usually the name is based on Indian lore, but it can be for an incident or for some reported medicinal property of the water.

After the fall of Fort Sumter on April 13, 1861, and after the sword-rattling and grandstand gestures of battles like the first one at Bull Run, a few sober-thinking Northerners began to confront the overwhelming evidence that no one single contest would bring the South back into the Union. It would be necessary to begin a protracted siege against a determined enemy on his home ground. The general strategy proposed by the Federals was to encircle and squeeze. In order to succeed, the Federals needed control of the coastlines and, to Missouri's misfortune, the Mississippi River.

During the first years of the Civil War communication and general planning were ragtag affairs left to the passions and pressures of the moment, creating the impression at times that anyone with money for a costume could be a general. It was not until 1863–1865 that practical battle-experienced men came forward, and then the Federals began to methodically pull the constricting circle tighter and tighter until a hopelessly surrounded and outnumbered Gen. Robert E. Lee symbolically surrendered the South, offering his sword to Gen. Ulysses S. Grant at Appomattox Court House on April 9, 1865.

Despite Missouri's vote in February 1861 not to secede, the state was the site of the Civil War's first land battle (June 17, 1861, at Boonville) and the first serious engagement (July 5, 1861, at Carthage). As testimony to the state's deep division of loyalties, by 1865 Missouri ranked third among states in total number of skirmishes.

The Federal strategy in Missouri of neutralizing the Confederates' ability to mass large armies and the subsequent policy of using a minimum number of troops to keep Missouri for the Union resulted in an undefended civilian population of fiercely divided loyalties stranded in an anarchy that spawned vicious personal vendettas and violent raids by irregulars from both sides. These irregulars, Northern jayhawkers and Southern bushwhackers, caused more suffering and destruction than the regular troops. While romanticized by legends like those surrounding Jesse James, many were hardcore criminals who continued preying on the countryside after the war *(Gallatin: Lyle Cemetery; Kearney: Jesse James Farm)*.

The war in Missouri can be generalized into three stages: (1) a series of Federal and Confederate attempts between 1861 and 1862 to keep or capture Missouri;

(2) an intensified guerrilla war from 1862 to 1864, in effect Missouri's own civil war, waged in a vacuum created by the withdrawal of Confederate regular troops and fostered by harsh Federal military authority, personal grudges, and resentment nurtured since the *Kansas Border War;* and (3) Sterling Price's Raid of September–October 1864, an attempt to recapture Missouri for the Confederacy.

April 20, 1861–Fall 1862. LIBERTY LANDING ARSENAL, APRIL 20, 1861: Military action began here when about 200 pro-Southerners captured the arsenal at *Liberty* Landing. As a result, nearby *Independence* was occupied by Federals until they were driven out in August 1862 (Battle of Independence, below). CAMP JACKSON, MAY 10, 1861: Capt. Nathaniel Lyon initially won a bloodless battle by capturing this proSouthern training camp that was ostensibly set up on May 3 to drill state militia but was seen by some as a preparation by Gov. Claiborne Jackson to resist Federal authority. A pro-Southern mob crowded Federal troops escorting the captured militia and was fired on by Federals, resulting in the deaths of approximately 28 civilians (*St. Louis: South Broadway Area Sights*). Lyon's capture of Camp Jackson earned him a promotion on May 17 to Brigadier General of Volunteers. JEFFERSON CITY PROCLAMATION, JUNE 12, 1861: On June 12, Gov. Jackson issued a proclamation stating in effect that the federal government's refusal to leave Missouri soil violated its states' rights. He called for 50,000 state militia to repel the "invaders." Gen. Lyon steamed up the Missouri River on June 13, arriving on June 15 and causing Jackson to retreat to Boonville. BATTLE OF BOONVILLE, JUNE 17, 1861: Lyon left Jefferson City to pursue Jackson, meeting him and Col. John Sappington Marmaduke on June 17 just east of Boonville; after a brief battle, the outnumbered and outgunned Confederate state militia retreated south, attempting to meet Gen. Ben McCulloch in Arkansas (*Boonville; Cole Camp*). BATTLE OF CARTHAGE, JULY 5, 1861: Lyon, in pursuit of Jackson, was delayed north of the swollen Osage River. Federal Col. Franz Sigel broke camp at Springfield and marched to Neosho, expecting to confront Confederate forces but entered the town unopposed on July 1. Learning that the Confederates had massed north of Carthage, Sigel marched north. When he met them on July 5, his outnumbered troops were forced to retreat after a sharp battle (*Carthage*). The next day Jackson continued unopposed toward Arkansas to join McCulloch; on July 22 he was replaced as governor of Missouri by a state convention that named Hamilton R. Gamble provisional governor. BATTLE OF WILSON'S CREEK, AUGUST 10, 1861: McCulloch and N. B. Pearce marched from northwest Arkansas and joined Price to form a combined Arkansas–Missouri army of

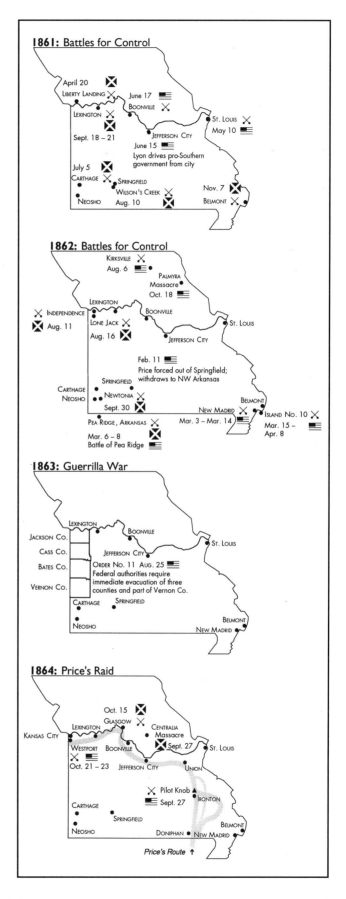

about 12,000 with the purpose of destroying Lyon's army camped at Springfield and recapturing the state. This was Missouri's largest battle and proportionately one of the Civil War's bloodiest. After the Confederate victory, Price occupied Springfield, recruiting troops for the siege of Lexington *(Springfield: Wilson's Creek)*. SIEGE OF LEXINGTON, SEPTEMBER 18–21, 1861: Price's victory here on August 21 gave the Confederates dominance in western Missouri, broke Federal control of the Missouri River, and appeared to give pro-Southern forces an opportunity to recruit and expand their holdings *(Lexington)*. That appearance diminished on September 30 when Price was forced to withdraw to Springfield to avoid being cut off from support in Arkansas. BATTLE OF BELMONT, NOVEMBER 7, 1861: In what was reportedly U. S. Grant's first battle, he was turned back from this Confederate position on the Mississippi River. Not until after the 1862 battles of New Madrid and Island No. 10 did the Federals gain control of this portion of the river *(East Prairie: Battlefield)*. WITHDRAWAL FROM SPRINGFIELD, FEBRUARY 11, 1862: All appearance of Confederate control vanished when Federal general Samuel R. Curtis advanced on Springfield, driving Price south, where he joined forces with McCulloch in Arkansas. Curtis continued to press south to Pea Ridge, Ark., where he met a 16,000-man army mustered by Price, McCulloch, and Gen. Earl Van Dorn

(commanding), who intended to advance on St. Louis. This March 6–8 battle, technically a draw (equal losses of about 1,300 each), was from historical hindsight the one that kept Missouri for the Union by denying the Confederates their best opportunity of capturing the state. Van Dorn withdrew unmolested and later was ordered east of the Mississippi; Price lost a large part of his army to urgent orders from the East; and Curtis continued into Arkansas, knowing Missouri was secure. SIEGE OF NEW MADRID / ISLAND NO. 10, MARCH 3–APRIL 8, 1862: Acting on Federal policy to gain control of the Mississippi River, Gen. John Pope and Flag Officer A. H. Foote were ordered to take this island fortress that successfully blocked all traffic sailing south from the confluence of the Ohio and Mississippi Rivers. Pope and Foote won control of both New Madrid and the Island *(New Madrid: Island No. 10 / Siege of New Madrid)*, thereby freeing the river between its confluence with the Ohio at Cairo, Ill., and the Confederate stronghold at Vicksburg, Miss., which was captured in July 1863. BATTLE OF INDEPENDENCE, AUGUST 11, 1862 / BATTLE OF LONE JACK, AUGUST 16, 1862: Confederate Col. Upton Hayes captured the Federal garrison at Independence, breaking Federal dominance of the river, and then turned southeast for Lone Jack, where his effort to recruit was challenged by Maj. Emory Forest. Casualties at Lone Jack were about even, but Confederates

Gen. Nathaniel Lyons's charge at Wilson's Creek, August 10, 1861.

remained in control of the area *(Lone Jack)*. BATTLE OF NEWTONIA, SEPTEMBER 30, 1862: Although the majority of the Confederate troops were ordered east of the Mississippi after the Battle of Pea Ridge, they still controlled the important roads in northwest Arkansas and parts of southwest Missouri, causing Federal general Curtis concern that the Confederates could quickly gather an army to attack his headquarters and supply depot at Springfield. This battle, technically a Confederate victory, precipitated Federal pursuit of Confederate forces into northwest Arkansas, where, at the Battle of Prairie Grove on December 7, 1862, Federal general James G. Blunt ended serious Confederate challenges to Federal dominance in Missouri until Price's Raid of 1864 *(Newtonia: Ritchey House / Battle of Newtonia)*.

Fall 1862–Fall 1864. After Confederate forces were driven out of the state, the vacuum was filled by bedlam. Today "bushwhacker" and "jayhawker" are used to describe pro-Southern and pro-Union irregulars, respectively *(Centralia: Centralia Massacre; Osceola)*, but "bushwhacker" at first applied to marauders loyal to no side, who rode under no flag and wore no set uniform: civilian clothes, Confederate gray, Federal blue, or a mix of all. They robbed and burned towns and sought out individuals, settling old grudges by murder and arson. So widespread was this kind of violence that whole counties were depopulated *(Houston; West Plains)*. Federal authority was weak, often overbearing, and sometimes brutal, as documented by the *Palmyra* Massacre and *Order No. 11*. During this period men like William Quantrill and Bill Anderson *(Centralia: Centralia Massacre)*, who claimed allegiance to the South, popularized the association of the term "bushwhacker" with pro-Southern marauders, who in fact were responsible for only a small part of the misery spread wholesale across Missouri. Sadly, the real horrors were committed by neighbors and were usually based on petty revenge masked as patriotism by both sides *(Harrisonville: Tarkington-Mockbee Home; Hollister: Murder Rocks)*. Ineffective Federal reprisals included burning the house nearest to the site of an incident and imprisonment based on gossip. Often those arrested lost their homes, farms, or businesses. Any civil war is a result of drastic and irreconcilable differences. When neighbors, saturated by emotional and physical violence, are left to settle their differences in a state of anarchy, the result is meanness fueled by unforgiving bitterness. The effects of this period of the Civil War in Missouri lasted well into the next century *(Lamar)*. Its traces still endure in monuments, songs, stories, and regional politics *(Springfield: Cemeteries)*.

Price's Raid, September–October 1864. Politician-soldier Sterling Price *(Keytesville: Sterling Price Monument)*, a pro-Southerner but a staunch Unionist, joined secessionists only after the Federals began hostilities in Missouri. Price led or took part in the region's most important battles, including Wilson's Creek, Lexington, and Pea Ridge. In the summer of 1864, Confederate general Robert E. Lee was under siege in Virginia and Federal general William T. Sherman was marching through Georgia toward Atlanta. Confederate Pres. Jefferson Davis ordered Trans-Mississippi commander Kirby Smith to help reinforce Alabama and Georgia, but Smith argued convincingly, some say deceitfully, that he had organized a major western campaign that would serve the same end by pressuring the Federals to send reinforcements to the West. Kirby's unspoken agenda was to recapture Arkansas and Missouri. On September 19, 1864, Price, in command of three mounted divisions led by generals James Fagan, John Marmaduke, and Joseph Shelby, entered southeast Missouri from Arkansas, advancing rapidly in three columns. Camped at Fredericktown on September 26 while finalizing plans for an attack on St. Louis, Price, not wanting to leave Federal troops at his rear, sent Shelby to destroy the railroad at Irondale and ordered Fagan to attack Fort Davidson at *Pilot Knob*. In spite of Federal losses of about 1,200 in the battle of Pilot Knob, the time spent there stymied Price, giving St. Louis defenders an opportunity to secure reinforcements. After a brief skirmish on the outskirts of St. Louis, Price turned toward Missouri's capital, Jefferson City, bypassing it at the last minute when it proved also to have reinforced. Price then turned toward *Glasgow* for supplies, most of which were destroyed by Federals before Price could capture the town. From Glasgow, Price marched to Lexington, where he was confronted on October 20 by Gen. James G. Blunt, who continued fighting and falling back toward Westport *(Kansas City)* in an attempt to hold Price for Generals Alfred Pleasanton, A. J. Smith, and S. R. Curtis. Price, forced to engage both Pleasanton and Curtis, was severely beaten and pursued south into Arkansas. While marching 1,434 miles and fighting 43 skirmishes in two months, Price lost about 10,000 men (killed, captured, or deserted), and both Missouri and Arkansas remained firmly under Federal control.

The End. The Battle of Westport (October 23, 1864) marked the end of any significant military engagements in Missouri or Arkansas. After Lee surrendered on April 9, 1865, Kirby Smith tried to form a military alliance with Maximilian, the French-backed emperor of Mexico, but his officers revolted, surrendering the Trans-Mississippi on May 24, 1865. Price was granted land in Mexico for an ex-Confederate colony, but it failed after Maximilian was overthrown, and Price returned to Missouri in 1866. Legend claims that

Shelby's Iron Brigade crossed the Rio Grande and buried its battle flag, never giving up *(Adrian: Gen. Joseph Shelby's House).*

CLARKSVILLE
Population: 480   Map H-3

Sparsely settled from 1800 to 1816, a community was permanently established in 1816 as a Mississippi River port by Tennessee, Kentucky, and Virginia immigrants and was known as Clarksville as early as 1817. Lots were reportedly surveyed and sold in 1818, but none were recorded until 1826. The town's namesake is either George Rogers Clark (1752–1818), a Revolutionary War hero *(Ste. Genevieve: Kaskaskia),* or his brother William Clark (1770–1838), a partner in the 1804–1806 *Lewis and Clark Expedition,* governor of Missouri Territory (1813–1820), and later an agent for all Indians west of the Mississippi River *(Platte Purchase; St. Charles: Portage Des Sioux).* Both brothers were reared in Virginia, lived in Kentucky, and became celebrated as American heroes. Post office: 1819–now. Tour maps: visitor center; SR 79, E side. Home of Pike/Lincoln Technical Center.

Annada, Mo. Named for early settler Carson Jamison's daughters Anna and Ada. Post office: 1880–now. SR 79, S 8 m. NATURAL AREAS: *Troy.* RECREATION: Clarence Cannon *National Wildlife Refuge.* GR, E 0.6 m.

Architecture. NATIONAL HISTORIC REGISTER: Clifford-Wirick House (c. 1876), 105 S. 2d. TOWN: Well-kept 19th-century structures, good examples of Greek Revival and Italianate.

Clarksville Museum. Exhibits on history, the river, and town firsts, such as the first bicycle built in America (by George Knightley, 1856) and America's first international bike race (1886). SR 79, S side.

Lock and Dam #24. Built in 1936–1940, this lock and dam completed the channelization of the Mississippi. Dam: 1,200 feet long; locks: 600 feet long, 110 feet wide. Launch ramp, overlook, wintering bald eagles. US 79, E on Howard, N on 1st. *(Locks and Dams)*

Museum / Skylift. ARCHAEOLOGICAL / GEOLOGICAL MUSEUM: Artifacts and displays illustrate local human and environmental conditions. SKYLIFT: This early 1960s cable-operated chairlift offers a bird's-eye view of the river valley while rising to Lookout Point (The Pinnacle), reportedly the highest (840 ft.) bluff along the Mississippi between New Orleans and St. Paul. US 79, in town.

Paynesville, Mo. In 1823 Andrew Forgey bought out 1819 settler Thomas Buchanan and established a general-store community that he named for St. Louis merchandiser William Payne, who reportedly sold Forgey his first stock of goods. Post office: 1833–now. SR W, S 7.9 m. ARCHITECTURE: 19th-century styles include a brick store and post office, two schools, three churches, and several houses. In town.

Riverfront Park. Restrooms, picnic facilities, birdhouses. US 79, E on Howard; at the river in front of downtown.

CLAYTON
Population: 13,847
Maps H-4 and St. Louis Area

Ralph Clayton and his neighbor Martin Hanley (Hanley House, below) donated 204 acres in 1877 for a new county seat to replace St. Louis, which opted in 1876 for home rule, an act that separated it from the county *(St. Louis).* The town was platted two miles west of St. Louis and an auction was announced in 1878, but the first residence was not built until 1880 (the second in 1882). The town floundered (dirt streets, no city government) until incorporated in 1913, after which development of subdivisions began (1920 pop., 3,000; 1925 pop., 7,000). Today, 52 of the "Fortune 500" and "Forbes 500" companies are based here, including the May Company's Famous-Barr, which was America's first (1949) suburban full-service department store. Post offices (another Clayton p.o. existed until 1885): Mount Olive[1] 1877–1885; Clayton 1885–1901, 1904–1913 (consolidated with St. Louis p.o.). Home of Washington University (below), Fontbonne College, and Concordia Seminary, the world's largest Lutheran Seminary *(Altenburg).* Maps and information: City Hall, 10 Bemiston; I-170, E on Forest Park, N on Bemiston.

Architecture. Good 19th-century examples, including several on the National Historic Register. CARRS-WOLD HISTORIC DISTRICT: 1–26 Carrswold. I-170,

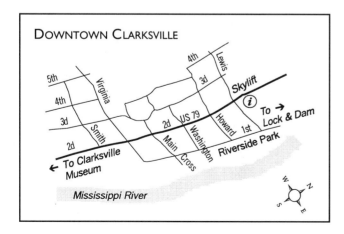

DOWNTOWN CLARKSVILLE

5th
4th
3d
2d
Virginia
Smith
4th
3d
2d
Lewis
Skylift
US 79
Main
Cross
Washington
Howard
1st
To Lock & Dam
Riverside Park
← To Clarksville Museum
Mississippi River

Bicycle racers, late 1800s or early 1900s.

E on Forest Park, S on Hanley, E on Wydown to Carrswold Dr. WASHINGTON UNIVERSITY: Hilltop Campus Historic District. I-170, E on Forest Park, E on Forsyth. Information: city hall (above).

Hanley House / Museum. Greek Revival, 1855; National Historic Register. The farmhouse of town cofounder Martin Hanley (Clayton history, above) remained in his family until acquired in 1968 by the city. Today its style remains authentic, including the exterior and interior paint, wallpaper, and furnishings. Grounds: Missouri's largest black oak (over 300 years old). Tours. Downtown; I-170, E on Forest Park, N on Hanley, E on Westmoreland (7600).

St. Louis County Government Buildings. Sixties Modern, 1968–1971. Organized in 1813, St. Louis County had no permanent courthouse until 1830. It was razed in 1852 and replaced by St. Louis's Old Courthouse (*St. Louis: Market Street Area Sights*). Built in 1852–1862, the Old Courthouse served the county until 1876, when the county seat was moved to Clayton in accordance with the reorganization of St. Louis County (Clayton history, above). Today's complex of buildings is the county's third courthouse at Clayton; the first, built in 1878, was replaced in 1949. Cost: $18,602,266. I-170, E on Forest Park, N on Central to Bonhomme at Carondelet. (*County Profiles*)

Washington University Art Gallery. Founded in 1881, this was reportedly the first fine-art museum west of the Mississippi. It features artists like Rembrandt,

Picasso, and Bingham. I-170, E on Forest Park to Forsyth at Skinker.

1. Biblical Mount of Olives, 2 Sam. 15:30.

CLEVER

Population: 580   Map D-7

Platted in 1905, the town was moved slightly to the surveyed grade of the St. Louis, Iron Mountain & Southern *Railroad* before being incorporated in 1909. Tradition claims that when store owner Frank Netzer applied for a post office for this crossroads trading post community, the postmaster general rejected his application (name and reason unknown). Tom Lentz's suggestion, Clever, was accepted. Today "clever" has an unflattering connotation, but in the 19th century it meant intelligence and resourcefulness, and local slang defined it to mean good-natured and hospitable. "American Place-Names" lists it (and other towns of the same name) as probably derived from a personal name. Post office: 1892–1905, 1908–now.

Butterfield Overland Stage Station. John Ashmore's station was located three miles northeast. Marker: SR 14, E 1.5 m.; SR ZZ, N approx. 0.5 m. (*Overland Mail Company*)

Wilson's Creek Battlefield. SR 14, E 1.5 m.; SR ZZ, N 6 m. (*Springfield: Wilson's Creek*)

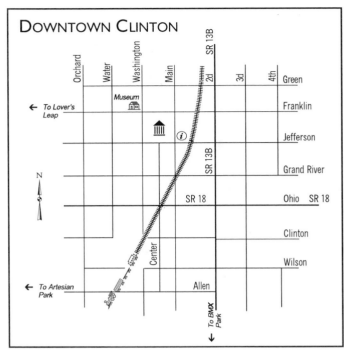

DOWNTOWN CLINTON

← To Lover's Leap

Museum

N

← To Artesian Park

Orchard | Water | Washington | Main | SR 13B | 2d | 3d | 4th | Green

Franklin

Jefferson

SR 13B

Grand River

SR 18 | Ohio SR 18

Clinton

Center

Wilson

Allen

To BMX Park ↓

CLINTON

Population: 8,703   Map D-4

Selected as county seat in 1836 of recently organized Rives (now Henry) County, Clinton was platted in 1837 and named for DeWitt Clinton (1769–1828), American statesman, vigorous sponsor of the Erie Canal (completed 1825), and 1812 U.S. presidential candidate defeated by James Madison. Slow to grow, the town boomed when the Missouri, Kansas & Texas *Railroad* arrived in 1870 (the population went from 640 to 2,868 by 1880). Post offices: Rives Court House[1] 1836–1850; Clinton 1850–now. (Although the county indignantly changed its name in 1841 when namesake William C. Rives changed parties from Democrat to Whig, this town, the county seat, kept its Rives Court House post office name, despite the indignation, the misnomer, and the availability of Clinton as a post office name.) Home of Clinton Area Vo-Tech. Walking/driving tours: chamber of commerce (Kansas, Missouri & Texas Depot, below).

Architecture. Walking/driving tour: 21 examples of 19th- and early 20th-century structures; 5 are located on 2d (between Wilson and Grand River), 4 on Franklin (between Washington and Orchard).

Artesian Park. Workmen drilling for natural gas in 1887 struck sulfur water at 800 feet. A short-lived resort (hotel, racetrack, dance hall, bathhouse, etc.) promoted the supposedly curative water until other wells diminished the water pressure c. 1902. Small

fishing lake, pool, ball field, picnic facilities. SW side; S on SR 13B, W on Allen.

Chinkerchek. The game now called Chinese checkers, developed from Chinese chess, became so popular by 1939 that local inventor Lawrence Brown hired three eight-hour shifts and bought 100,000 marbles every 10 days to keep up with the orders. Inquire locally for site.

Henry County Courthouse. Richardsonian Romanesque (truncated), 1892–1893. The county's second, reportedly set on one of America's largest town squares, this three-story sandstone courthouse originally had an elaborate 127-foot central tower framed by steel and covered with copper and stucco. The tower began leaking in 1893 and continued until 1969 when a county vote of 4 to 1 (the turnout was small) approved removing it. Spring arches, rusticated sandstone, gabled wall dormers, and recessed windows help preserve the building's architectural style. Cost: $47,221. NW side; SR 13B, W on Franklin. *(County Profiles)*

Henry County Museum. Vernacular, 1886. Displays housed in this former Anheuser-Busch distribution station include Indian and Civil War artifacts, dolls, Christmas ornaments, a child's room, parlor, kitchen, country church, and 1930s and 1940s industry-related items from when Clinton was "The Baby Chick Capital of the World." The red-brick limestone-trimmed building, used until prohibition, has many of its original fixtures. NW side; SR 13B, W on Franklin (203).

Kansas, Missouri & Texas Depot. Railroad, 1870; slightly remodeled. Moved to this site for use by the chamber of commerce. Restrooms, maps. NW side; SR 13B, W on Jefferson to Main.

Lover's Leap. Late 19th-century writers tell a familiar legend of an Indian couple jumping to their deaths from this 50-foot bluff at Town Creek after being refused permission to marry (by family or opposing tribes). Once a popular picnic site, this was also the location of early mills. NW side; SR 13B, W on Franklin, N on Urich to creek.

Urich, Mo. The town was settled in 1871 during the Franco-Prussian War and named for French general Uhrich (1802–1886), who had heroically but vainly defended Strasbourg in 1870. The resulting 1871 capture of Paris marked the rise of a unified Germany *(Flat River: Bismarck)* and sowed the seeds for WWI and WWII. Post office: 1872–now. SR 7, W 15 m. URICH *WILDLIFE AREA.*

Wildlife Areas. Fewel, Montrose Lake, Poague, Urich. *(Wildlife Areas)*

---

1. Former name of county; another Clinton post office existed.

COLE CAMP
Population: 1,054   Map E-4

The town was first platted in 1854 along a state road at William Blakey's farm (near today's watertower). Downtown businesses moved about five blocks northeast in 1880 to the tracks of the arriving Missouri-Pacific *Railroad*. The town was named for its post office, which was established in 1839 at Cole Creek near today's Union Church (below) by fur trapper and explorer Ezekiel (or Exachel) Williams, who was issued the county's first business license (1835). Williams moved the post office during 1839 to nearby Blakey Town,[1] and the community took the post office's name, which according to local tradition honors Capt. Stephen Cole (Cole County's namesake), who reportedly camped regularly at this creek. Cole Camp is also the name of the Cumberland County, Ky., magisterial district where Williams lived c. 1799. Plattdeutsch (low German dialect) is still spoken in this area by descendants of immigrants who arrived during the 1830s to 1850s and 1870s to 1890s, as well as after WWI and WWII. Post office: 1839–now. (*Overland Mail Company*)

Architecture. Downtown is remarkably intact and has good examples of late 19th- and early 20th-century commercial architecture.

Battle of Cole Camp. June 19, 1861; date disputed. Benton County was divided geographically by settlers from the Southern states (*Warsaw* area) and German immigrants (Cole Camp area). Local regular officer Federal Capt. A. H. W. Cook began recruiting on June 11, accumulating nearly a regiment, mostly Germans. After the June 17 battle of *Boonville*, Federals attempted to cut off retreating Confederates (*Carthage*). The Confederate objective here was to prevent these new recruits from joining the pursuing Federal forces. At dawn, Confederates from Warsaw attacked, catching the Federals by surprise. Most locals were away on furloughs while waiting for munitions and supplies. Those remaining were asleep in two barns outfitted as barracks. The Confederates fired point-blank into the barns, and the battle was a rout. Casualty estimates vary: Federals, 80–205 killed; Confederates, 4–9 killed. A mass grave at Union Cemetery (below) indicates that Federal losses were extremely heavy.

Unmarked site: SR 52, E 2 m. to railroad underpass; approx. 0.5 m. S in a field.

Mora Wildlife Area. *Wildlife Areas.*

Natural Areas. BIG BUFFALO CREEK HARDWOODS: 5 acres. Features a bottomland forest (sycamore, elm, walnut, and butternut) with wildflowers. BIG BUFFALO CREEK MARSH: 40 acres. This spring-fed marshy meadow provides a habitat for sedge, blue flag iris, orange coneflower, willow, and the rare bushy aster. Both part of Big Buffalo Creek *Wildlife Area*. SR 52, E 9.1 m.; SR FF, S 8 m. Box 180, Jefferson City 65102.

Union Church / Cemeteries. Sold in 1842 by Ezekiel Williams to the Methodist Church (he is buried here; d. 1844), the cemetery next to today's clapboard church (Vernacular, 1904) has a mass grave where an estimated 90–150 Federals are buried. SR F, S 3 m. Another church cemetery, Monsees, has a single mass grave of 18–19 Federals. SR 52, E 5.7 m. to Crockerville;[2] GR, S 1.9 m. (*Cemeteries*)

1. William Blakey; also known as Lick Skillet, usually derogatory, meaning a place so poor inhabitants had to lick their skillets; no p.o.
2. Origin unknown; no p.o.

COLLAPSED CAVE SYSTEMS

Usually caused by a stream going underground and following a cave passage to its mouth, these systems are best described in stages, which are interrelated. KARST TOPOGRAPHY: Missouri contains some of the

A natural bridge in Camden County. (FROM WILLIAMS, "THE STATE OF MISSOURI")

largest karst areas in the world. Rainwater absorbs carbon dioxide from the atmosphere to form a weak carbonic acid. When percolating through limestone, it dissolves the rock, especially along bedding planes and joints, forming sinks (or sinkholes), underground streams, springs, tunnels, and caves. SPRINGS: Formed when a cave system fills with water and is breached by surface erosion. NATURAL BRIDGES: Formed when a cave system has partially collapsed, leaving a portion of the roof connected by just the side walls. SINKS: Formed when a cave system totally collapses; steep bluffs indicate the remaining walls of the system. FILLED SINKS: The mechanics or chemistry of this phenomenon, occurring relatively late in sinkhole development, is not thoroughly understood. The filling can be beneficial both economically (surface deposits of lead, iron, fireclay) and aesthetically (colorful road cuts), as well as a nuisance (unstable road cuts, polluted and unstable water wells). TUNNELS: Often created by subterranean piracy (like *stream piracy),* wherein a stream goes underground, possibly via a sinkhole, and exits through a cave, thereby contributing to the cave's collapse. *(Caves)*

COLUMBIA

Population: 69,101   Map F-4

Platted in 1821 as county seat of newly organized Boone County, Columbia replaced nearby 1820 county seat Smithton,[1] which, anticipating formation of the new county, was platted about a half-mile from today's courthouse on land bought in 1818 by the Smithton Company. A stock place-name, Columbia was coined during the Revolutionary period as a latinized version of Christopher Columbus and used first in Philip Freneau's 1775 poem "American Liberty" as a euphonious substitute for the United States of America; it was first used as a town name for the 1786 capital of South Carolina and possibly transplanted here by early Kentucky settlers. Although the town grew as a political and trading center (the *Boonslick Trail;* the North Missouri *Railroad* in 1867), education has been its economic base since the 1830s, with today's student population at about 25,000. Post offices: Smithton 1820–1821; Columbia 1821–now. Home of Columbia College (below), Stephens College (below), and the University of Missouri–Columbia (below).

Architecture. Many of the town's best examples of 19th-century structures are located at the colleges and university (Stephens College, University of Missouri, below). National Historic Register sites include: MAPLEWOOD FARMSTEAD: below. MISSOURI

STATE TEACHERS ASSOCIATION: America's first building erected by a state teachers association; 407 S. 6th. MISSOURI THEATER: 201–215 S. 9th. MISSOURI UNITED METHODIST CHURCH: 204 S. 9th. MKT DEPOT (Katy Station): 402 E. Broadway. PIERCE PENNANT MOTOR HOTEL (Candlelight Lodge): 1406 old US 40 West. TIGER HOTEL: 23 S. 8th. WABASH RAILROAD STATION: 126 N. 10th.

Boone County Courthouse. Neoclassical, 1906–1909. Organized in 1820, the county had no finished courthouse until 1828; that building was replaced by an 1846 structure whose four massive entrance columns (standing today) were set facing the six columns of Academic Hall (University of Missouri, below), which accounts for their placement at the corner of the court square. Townspeople lobbied to preserve the building when today's courthouse (the county's third) was near completion, but only the columns remain. The two sets of freestanding columns (government and education) are still aligned in their 19th-century positions and are figuratively joined to the present courthouse's four columns by the front entrance sidewalk. Cost: $100,000. I-70 at Providence, S to Walnut, E to 8th. *(County Profiles)*

Boonslick Trail. Just behind buildings fronting old US 40 at Perche Creek just east of the I-70 bridge is a remnant of this historic trail that was deeply etched by the heavy traffic. The I-70 bridge is the third at this site: one built in 1852 by William Jewell (Jewell Cemetery, below) and the old US 40 one built in 1925. From here, the route west parallels US 40 to the later *Santa Fe Trail.* Junction I-70 and SR 740; old US 40, W 2.1 m. *(Boonslick Trails)*

Chimney Rock. Barely visible from the highway, about 75 feet tall and 20 feet in average diameter, it was formed from Burlington limestone sliced by vertical fractures at right angles to each other. US 63, S 10 m. to Ashland;[2] SR Y, E 4 m. to bridge; W bank of Cedar Creek, N 0.5 m. to elbow.

Columbia College. Founded in 1851 as Christian Female College by the Disciples of Christ, this was the first state-chartered four-year college for women west of the Mississippi. It was renamed Christian College in 1929, then Columbia College in 1970, when male students were admitted. I-70 at US 763; signs. ARCHITECTURE: Red-brick 19th- to early 20th-century buildings are mostly Romanesque and Tudor (Eclectic). MISSOURI BASKETBALL HALL OF FAME: Dedicated in 1988 and housed in the college's former gymnasium, Dorsey Hall (built 1911), it displays memorabilia of Missouri's exceptional athletes, coaches, and teams, including Forrest "Phog" Allen, Henry Iba, Bill Bradley, Edward C. Macauley, Cotton Fitzsimmons, and Bertha Teague, America's most successful high

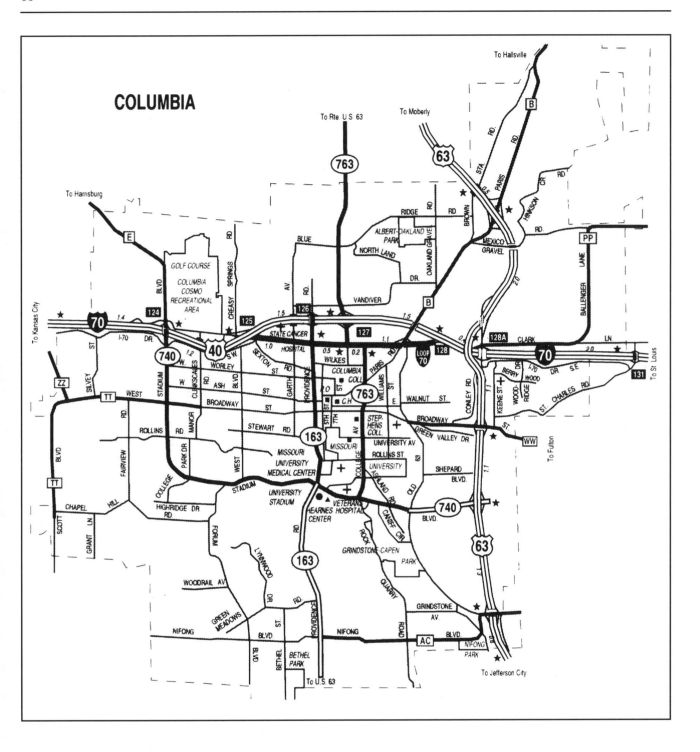

school girls' basketball coach (won 1,152; lost 115). WILLIAMS HALL: The college's first building was bought in 1851 as an unfinished brick house and is the oldest women's college building in continuous use west of the Mississippi.

Devil's Backbone. Formed as a limestone neck in a meander loop of Cedar creek, this half-mile narrow crest is about 175 feet above the streambed; crinoid fossils. US 63, S 6 m.; SR H, E 4.1 m. to Englewood;[3] GR, E 1.8 m.; GR, S 1.1 m. to parking area (slippery in wet weather).

Jewell Cemetery. State Historic Site. The text on the plaque at the entrance—"No one, not the husband, wife or child of a descendant of George Jewell can be buried here"—is a double negative, meaning only those mentioned can be buried here. Among them are noted Missouri educator and mayor of Columbia Dr. William Jewell (1789–1852), his son (called the

Thomas Jefferson of Boone County), and his grandson C. H. Hardin, governor from 1875 to 1877. SR 163, about 2 m. S of SR 740. *(Cemeteries)*

Maplewood Farmstead / Park. MAPLEWOOD FARM-STEAD: Italianate, 1877; National Historic Register. This center-gabled, two-story brick house has a bracketed cornice and paired central windows. Original furnishings. Tours include barn and carriage house. Open-air theatrical performances in the summer. SR 163, E on Nifong (SR AC) to NIFONG PARK: picnic facilities, fishing, restrooms, hiking, playground, recreation.

Natural Areas. THE PINNACLES: 77 acres. In this geologically and aquatically significant area, Rock Ford and Silver Creeks have formed narrows (a very sharp ridge between two streams), Western-looking pinnacles, cliffs, and arches in Burlington limestone. The Pinnacles, set at the water, are 75 feet high and 1,000 feet long, with a crest barely several feet wide. Extension Service, 1708 I-70 Dr. SW, Columbia 65201. US 63, N 10.5 m. (0.5 m. N of W junction of SR 124); paved road, E 0.5 m. to bridge and small park. Trail, NW bank. SCHNABEL WOODS: 80 acres. This old-growth forest's overstory is mostly maple, oak, and hickory. Two streams cross the area before joining Perche Creek. Fisheries and Wildlife, UMC, Columbia 65201. SR 163 at SR 740, SR 163 S 3.2 m.; SR K, W 7.3 m. to railroad track at McBaine;[4] walk 1.7 m. SE (to where Perche Creek parallels railroad).

Parks. Over 1,400 acres (40 parks) offer recreation. MKT TRAIL: 100 acres. Walking, jogging, biking. I-70, S on Providence. TWIN LAKES: 6 acres. Swimming, sand beach; 20-acre fishing lake. In town; SR TT (West Broadway), S on Fairview to Chapel Hill.

Performing Arts / Galleries. Nine museums and galleries; ten performing arts centers. Chamber of commerce: Box N, Columbia 65205.

Recreation. ROCKY FORKS LAKE *WILDLIFE AREA.* STATE PARKS: Rock Bridge Memorial (I-70 at SR 163; SR 163, S 6.1 m.); Katy Trail (parking at McBaine [Natural Areas: Schnabel Woods, above]); Finger Lakes (US 63, N 7.5 m.). THREE CREEKS *STATE FOREST.*

Shelter Insurance Gardens. Five landscaped acres at the company's home office are billed as a miniature mid-American environment. Features include over 300 varieties of trees and shrubs, 15,000 annuals and perennials, a one-room 19th-century schoolhouse, fern garden, lily pond, rock garden, and rose garden; free concerts on Sunday evenings (June–July); lawn picnics. I-70, S on SR 163 to W. Broadway (1817).

Stephens College. The oldest women's college west of the Mississippi was founded in 1833 as the Columbia Female Academy by local businessmen. It closed in 1855 because of poor financing, reopened as the Baptist Female Academy in 1856 (Senior Hall, below), and

then changed its name in 1870 to honor James L. Stephens, who endowed the college with $20,000. Four-year private college. I-70, S on US 63, W on Broadway. FIRESTONE BAARS CHAPEL: Modern, 1956. Designed by Eero Saarinen, who also designed the St. Louis Arch, this nondenominational chapel is a square brick building with a modified lamella roof of aluminum that features an aluminum center spire capped with gold. Walnut, just E of College. GORDON MANOR: Adamesque, 1823; remodeled with Italianate cornice and brackets; National Historic Register. The two-story 14-room brick house features an elliptical fanlight, Palladian window, and keystone lintels. Sold to the college in 1926, it is part of a recreation area (golf, 11-acre lake) shared by club members and students. E. Broadway at Old 63 N; sign. SENIOR HALL: Built c. 1841 as a two-story brick house on eight acres, it was bought in 1857 by the Baptist Female College; major additions 1870, 1890; renovated 1987–1989. Waugh St. VISITOR CENTER: Modern, 1979. This four-story 13,900-square-foot building derives 75 percent of its heat from solar energy, utilizing 180 chrome-plated tempered-glass solar collectors along with sheet metal, copper tubing, water, and antifreeze. Broadway at College.

University of Missouri–Columbia. Founded in 1839 as the first state university west of the Mississippi. Chartering the university in 1835, Maj. J. S. Rollins directed a competition, which was compared to a heated political campaign, to gain federal government funds promised to the town that offered the "highest material inducements." The university won in 1839 by raising $117,900 and then in rapid succession laid the first cornerstone in 1840, opened classes in 1841, and graduated two students in 1843. (Its teams' nickname, Tigers, honors the local *Civil War* home guard Missouri Tiger Squadron.) I-70; signs. ARCHITECTURE: Francis Quadrangle District (National Historic Register). GREENHOUSES: Tropical, desert, and jungle flora. Tucker Hall, Hitt St. IONIC COLUMNS: Six freestanding columns are remnants of the first building, Academic Hall, destroyed by fire in 1892 (Boone County Courthouse, above). Francis Quadrangle. MUSEUM OF ART AND ARCHAEOLOGY: Egyptian, Greek, Roman, Asian, African, pre-Columbian, American, European. Pickard Hall, 9th and University. RESEARCH REACTOR: America's largest university-owned nuclear research reactor; tours (two-day notice required). Research Park *(Rolla: University of Missouri).* SANBORN AGRICULTURAL EXPERIMENTAL FIELD: National Historic Landmark. Established in 1888, this is the oldest plot of its kind west of the Mississippi. The organism needed to make the antibiotic aureomycin was first found here in soil samples. 700 College.

SCHOOL OF JOURNALISM: The world's first school of journalism was established here in 1908. Today it is the world's only school that publishes a daily commercial community newspaper. Neff and Williams Halls, Francis Quadrangle. STATE HISTORICAL SOCIETY OF MISSOURI: Founded in 1898, the state's second largest research library has changing exhibits; America's largest collection of state newspapers, rare manuscripts, and books; and artwork by George Caleb Bingham, Thomas Hart Benton, and John J. Audubon. In Ellis Library at Hitt and Lowry. THOMAS EDISON'S ELECTRIC DYNAMO: Donated in 1892 by Edison, it was used on campus in 1893 for the first demonstration of incandescent lighting west of the Mississippi. Electrical Engineering Building, 6th St. THOMAS JEFFERSON'S TOMBSTONE: Designed by Jefferson in sketches and descriptions before his 1826 death, this coarse stone monument (a three-foot base with a six-foot obelisk) stood at his grave until 1883, when Congress voted to replace the neglected and vandalized marker. The university persuaded his family to donate the tombstone, citing Missouri as the first state of Jefferson's *Louisiana Purchase* and this, its first public university, as an appropriate site because of Jefferson's passion to "Educate and inform the whole mass of people." Francis Quadrangle.

1. Gen. T. A. Smith, register of public lands in old *Franklin*; p.o. 1820–1821.
2. Henry Clay's Ky. estate; p.o. Wisemans, personal name, 1837–1856; Ashland 1856–now.
3. From Ill. town, stock name via Ingle, Scottish for nook or corner, first used in 1859 in N.J. suburban development; p.o. 1892–1906.
4. Personal name; p.o. 1894–1958.

CONCEPTION
Population: 355   Map C-1

The town was platted in 1860 by Irish-Catholic railroad workers from near Reading, Pa., who lost their jobs during a late 1850s depression (*Alton: Bardley*). With aid from their local priest and from contractors for the railroad, 58 men formed the Reading Colony to buy a large tract of land near the Platte River. Named for Mary's miraculous conception of Jesus. Post office: 1864–1865, 1868–now.

Benedictine Convent of Perpetual Adoration. Romanesque, 1901–1911. Founded by three Swiss Benedictine nuns in 1874, the convent occupied its first brick buildings in 1882. The present three-story Bedford stone structure with turrets, tower, spire, stained glass, and mosaics of Christian life was once the nucleus of an orphanage and girls' school. Today the nuns dedicate their lives to prayer for all people.

SR 136, N 2 m.; SR AF, E 0.5 m.; SR P, S 0.3 m. to Clyde.[1]

Conception Abbey. Romanesque Basilica, 1882–1891; towers added c. 1895 (one hides a watertower). The abbey and seminary were established in 1873 by Benedictine monks from near Lucerne, Switzerland. Today's three-story brick structure with a 56-foot interior height, built by 40 monks and local parishioners, was given the status of Minor Basilica in 1941 by Pope Pius XII, designating it as an official place of worship for the Pope. Noteworthy features of this 206-by-66-foot building include handmade bricks, walls from three to six feet thick, painted glass, and murals painted by the monks in the style of Paolo Veronese. The abbey library has 10th-century manuscripts and a large collection of Plains Indian art and artifacts. Daily midday mass.

Conception Junction, Mo. Notable for the pun of its name, the town was platted in 1895 at the junction of the Chicago Great Western and Omaha & St. Louis *Railroads*. Post office: 1907–now. US 63, N 1.5 m.; SR T, W 0.7 m.

1. For the Clydesdale horse, some of which had recently been imported here from Canada; p.o. 1880.

CONCORDIA
Population: 2,160   Map D-3

What began in the 1840s–1850s as a settlement of German immigrants about two and a half miles east of the crossroads town Cook's Store[1] gradually grew into the 1865 post office community of Concordia. The town of that name was platted in 1868 at the site of about a dozen houses and a few vacant stores formerly known as Humbolt.[2] Local tradition claims that the name was chosen by the town's first postmaster, Rev. F. J. Blitz (a German Lutheran), "in gratitude for the peace" following the misery of the *Civil War,* but Lutherans in Dresden, Germany, as early as 1580 held Concordia-hours to discuss the Lutheran Formula of Concord. More recent and geographically closer was Concordia Seminary, established in 1839 at *Altenburg.* Another source claims the namesake is Rev. Blitz's alma mater, Concordia College of Fort Wayne, Ind. The arrival in 1871 of the Lexington and St. Louis *Railroad* helped establish the town as a trading center. Post offices: Cook's Store 1851–1865; Concordia 1865–now.

Architecture. Good 19th-century examples are found in an area roughly bounded by 1st (old US 40), West, 14th, and St. Louis. (St. Louis, just east of Main, was originally the main street.)

Central Park. Features 1920s streetlights, c. 1906 bandstand, 1923 doughboy statue, picnic shelters, and historical markers commemorating (1) Civil War skirmishes and the murder of three men by bushwhackers, and (2) former resident Kathryn Kuhlman (c. 1910–1972), an evangelist and faith healer whose Pittsburgh-based foundation grossed $2 million in 1972. Main, across from city hall's freestanding clock tower (1976), which features a 19th-century clock and the town's original fire bell.

Concordia Fall Fest. Since 1899. Carnival, street dance, German beer garden, livestock show, parades with floats, and the Konkordia Komical Krew, a band founded in the late 1800s. Thursday, Friday, and Saturday following Labor Day.

Edwin A. Pape Lake. 245 acres. Completed in 1967 for recreation and city water; picnic areas, restrooms, playground, shelters, boat ramp, jetty, fishing (crappie, bluegill, bass, catfish), duck hunting. SR 23 (Main), S 2 m.; SR CC, W 0.5 m.

Lohoefener House Museum. Gothic Revival, 1872–1873. This two-story brick house with walls eight inches thick contains historical items, toys, handicrafts, rooms with period furniture, original fixtures, a pine floor painted to resemble linoleum, and unusual exhibits like a stuffed-frog band and a wooden leg with its own shoe. I-70, S on Main, E on 7th, S on Orange (710).

Perry Wildlife Area. *Wildlife Areas.*

St. Paul's Lutheran Cemetery. This cemetery reflects the ongoing strong German influence on this town. Among the ornate markers is a six-foot gray metal monument, square and hollow, trimmed as if draperies were falling in folds; angels in relief strike various poses; a German inscription commemorates the husband and wife buried here. Reportedly a compartment holds the couple's wedding picture. I-70 at SR 23; SR 23, S 0.1 m., then E 0.2 m. on Old Hwy. 40. The church (Gothic Revival style, 1905), at 5th and Main, has an impressive spire. *(Cemeteries)*

1. Store owner M. M. Cook; p.o. 1851–1865.
2. Probably a simplified version of Alexander von Humboldt, mid-19th-century German writer and traveler; stock name; no p.o.

COUNTY PROFILES

The American county was patterned after the territorial division used in Great Britain and Ireland (formerly Anglo-Saxon shires) for administrative, judicial, and political purposes. Part of the 1803 *Louisiana Purchase* was included in the 1804 District of Louisiana, under the jurisdiction of the Territory of Indiana *(Lancaster: Tippecanoe)*. In 1805 an area described as all land west of the Mississippi and above 33°N latitude was organized as the Territory of Upper Louisiana (Stoddard, below). Its 1810–1812 governor, Benjamin A. Howard (Howard, Lewis, below), divided what was to become part of Missouri into districts according to the original Spanish administrative units: St. Louis, St. Charles, Ste. Genevieve, Cape Girardeau, and New Madrid. In 1812 the U.S. Congress designated the area encompassed by these districts as the Territory of Missouri, and the five districts were organized as territorial counties; these, along with 20 later subdivisions, became state counties in 1821. Today, Missouri has 114 counties, as well as the city of *St. Louis*, which in 1876 opted (in line with the 1875 constitutional amendment permitting cities with populations exceeding 100,000 to adopt home rule) to function independently of its former county, St. Louis. Of the 50 states, Missouri ranks fourth in the number of counties. While petitioners could suggest names for new counties being proposed, state legislators had the ultimate authority in selecting names.

Adair. Organized on January 29, 1841, from Macon County. Named for John Adair (1757–1840), Kentucky's eighth governor (1820–1824). As a general during the *War of 1812* he fought at the Battle of New Orleans with Andrew Jackson (Jackson, below). COUNTY SEAT: *Kirksville* (elev. 981). POPULATION: 24,577. TOPOGRAPHY (567 sq. mi.): Rolling prairie in the east; remainder rougher terrain with steep-sided closely spaced hills, particularly west and south of the Chariton River.

Andrew. Organized on January 29, 1841, from the *Platte Purchase*. Its namesake is disputed: either president (1829–1837) Andrew Jackson or Andrew Jackson Davis, a former area resident and prominent St. Louis attorney. President Jackson is the more likely since two other counties are named for him:

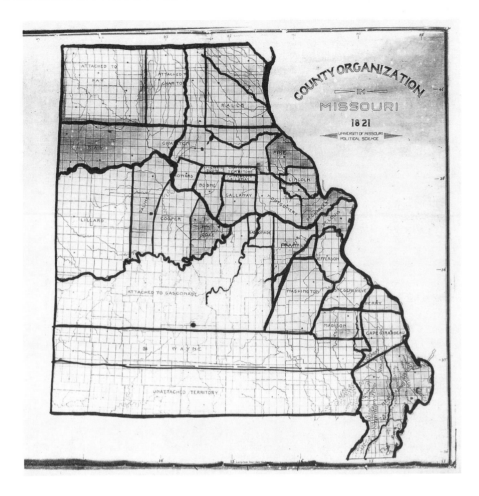

Hickory and *Jackson*. COUNTY SEAT: *Savannah* (elev. 1,115). POPULATION: 14,632. TOPOGRAPHY (435 sq. mi.): Bottomland along the rivers; remainder rolling prairie.

Atchison. Organized on February 14, 1845, from Holt County. Named for David Rice Atchison (1807–1886), U.S. senator from 1843 to 1854 (*Plattsburg*). COUNTY SEAT: *Rock Port* (elev. 935). POPULATION: 7,457. TOPOGRAPHY (542 sq. mi.): 30 percent bottomland along the rivers; remainder rolling prairie.

Audrain. Organized on December 17, 1836, from Callaway, Monroe, and Ralls Counties. Named for state legislator James H. Audrain (1782–1831) of St. Charles, who died in office. COUNTY SEAT: *Mexico* (elev. 801). POPULATION: 23,599. TOPOGRAPHY (697 sq. mi.): Mostly high prairie.

Barry. Organized on January 5, 1835, from Greene County. Named for Kentuckian William Taylor Barry (1785–1835), postmaster general from 1829 to 1835 under president Andrew Jackson (Jackson, below) and the first as such to be appointed to that office. COUNTY SEAT: *Cassville* (elev. 1,324). POPULATION: 27,547. TOPOGRAPHY (773 sq. mi.): Ozark mountain plateau with rugged hills; *balds and knobs* in the extreme south.

Barton. Organized on December 12, 1855, from Jasper County. Named for David Barton (1783–1837), president of Missouri's 1820 constitutional convention and one of Missouri's first U.S. senators (1821–1831). COUNTY SEAT: *Lamar* (elev. 985). POPULATION: 11,312. TOPOGRAPHY (596 sq. mi.): High rolling prairie.

Bates. Organized on January 29, 1841, from Van Buren County (name changed to Cass; below). Named for Frederick Bates (1777–1825), the 1814 Territorial secretary and Missouri's second governor (1824–1825). COUNTY SEAT: *Butler* (elev. 865). POPULATION: 15,025. TOPOGRAPHY (849 sq. mi.): Rolling prairie.

Benton. Organized on January 3, 1835, from Pettis and Greene Counties. Named for nationally prominent Thomas Hart Benton (1782–1858), one of Missouri's first U.S. senators (1820–1850), an ardent expansionist, patron of the western farmer, and advocate of free land for settlers (eight U.S. counties and many towns are named for him, including *Benton*). COUNTY SEAT: *Warsaw* (elev. 709). POPULATION: 13,859. TOPOGRAPHY (729 sq. mi.): About 30 percent steep hills with gentle slopes (mainly northwest); remainder Ozark mountain hills and valleys.

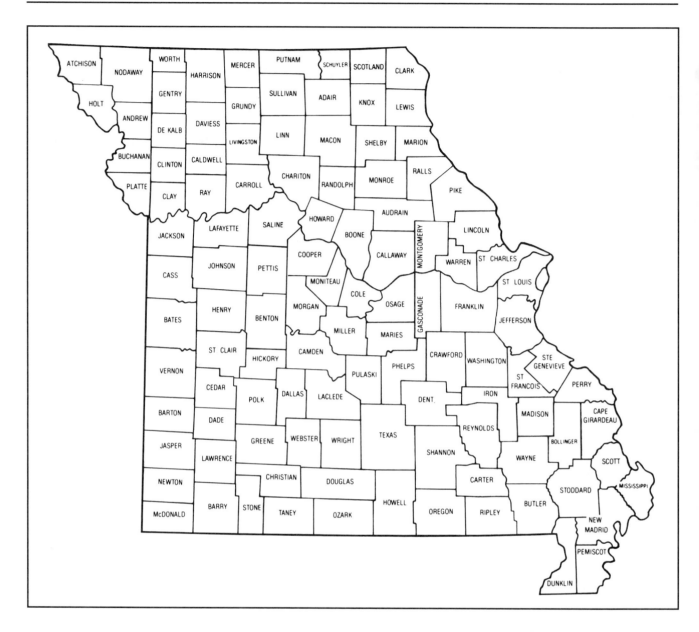

Bollinger. Organized on March 1, 1851, from Cape Girardeau, Madison, Stoddard, and Wayne Counties. Named for George Frederick Bollinger (1770–1842; *Fredericktown*), who c. 1796 was promised land concessions by Louis Lorimier (*Cape Girardeau*) in return for establishing a settlement, which Bollinger did in 1800 by recruiting about 20 fellow North Carolina German families. COUNTY SEAT: *Marble Hill* (elev. 422). POPULATION: 10,619. TOPOGRAPHY (621 sq. mi.): 80 percent wooded St. Francis mountains, tapering eastward to foothills and bluffs; lowlands in the southeast corner.

Boone. Organized on November 16, 1820 (effective January 1, 1821), from Howard County. Named for legendary explorer Daniel Boone (1735–1820; *Defiance: Daniel Boone Historic Area*). COUNTY SEAT: *Columbia* (elev. 730). POPULATION: 112,379. TOPOGRAPHY

(687 sq. mi.): Mostly low hills and rolling prairie; remainder Missouri River bottomland and bluffs.

Buchanan. Initially known as Roberts County for the first settler, Hiram Roberts; organized on December 31, 1838, as Buchanan from the *Platte Purchase*. Named for James Buchanan (1791–1868), statesman-politician, Pennsylvania Democrat, congressman (1821–1834), U.S. senator (1835–1845), and later U.S. president (1857–1861). (Buchanan was America's only bachelor president; he never married.) COUNTY SEAT: *St. Joseph* (elev. 841). POPULATION: 83,083. TOPOGRAPHY (409 sq. mi.): Western half hills and bluffs; remainder prairie.

Butler. Organized on February 27, 1849, from Wayne County. Named for Kentucky Democrat William Orlando Butler (1791–1880), a veteran of the *War of 1812*

(as a captain under Andrew Jackson) and the *Mexican War* (as a general under Zachary Taylor); as a vice presidential candidate with Lewis Cass (below), he was defeated in 1848 by Republicans Zachary Taylor and Millard Fillmore. COUNTY SEAT: *Poplar Bluff* (elev. 344). POPULATION: 38,765. TOPOGRAPHY (698 sq. mi.): Nearly equally divided diagonally into bluffs and rocky hills in the northeast and wet lowlands in the southwest.

Caldwell. Organized on December 29, 1836, from Ray County. Named for Matthew Caldwell, commander of Indian Scouts in Kentucky. COUNTY SEAT: *Kingston* (elev. 1,005). POPULATION: 8,380. TOPOGRAPHY (430 sq. mi.): Mostly high rolling plains; rougher land in the southwest corner.

Callaway. Organized on November 25, 1820 (effective January 1, 1821), from Howard, Boone, and Montgomery Counties. Named for Daniel Boone's grandson *(Defiance: Missouri Territory Village)*, Capt. James Callaway (1783–1815), who was killed near *Mineola* by Indians during the *War of 1812*. The county's nickname, Kingdom of Callaway, stems from a *Civil War* confrontation wherein Union forces, outnumbered by local Confederate partisans, agreed not to invade the county if the Confederates would disband. The legend of this independent truce is nurtured by the town name of Kingdom City.[1] COUNTY SEAT: *Fulton* (elev. 825). POPULATION: 32,809. TOPOGRAPHY (842 sq. mi.): Mostly wide prairies; Missouri River bluffs in the south.

Camden. Organized on January 29, 1841, from Pulaski, Morgan, and Benton Counties as Kinderhook, a name inspired by the slogan "Old Kinderhook" used by Democrat Martin Van Buren in his successful 1836 campaign for the presidency *(Van Buren)*. The slogan's abbreviation, O.K., is believed to be the origin of America's most familiar approbation. Van Buren's birthplace, Kinderhook, N.Y., was named from a 17th-century Dutch term meaning children's point. His overwhelming defeat for a second term, his political decisions affecting the South, and a continuing economic depression persuaded residents to change the county name in 1843 to Camden for British statesman Lord Camden, Charles Pratt *(Camden)*. COUNTY SEAT: *Camdenton* (elev. 1,043). POPULATION: 27,495. TOPOGRAPHY (641 sq. mi.): Mountainous with the northeastern portion nearly covered by the Lake of the Ozarks (the lake's fingers extend to the center of the county).

Cape Girardeau. Organized on October 1, 1812, as one of five districts that later became the original Missouri Territory counties (County history, above). Named for French Ensign Sieur Jean B. Girardot *(Cape Girardeau)*. COUNTY SEAT: *Jackson* (elev. 402). POPULATION: 61,633. TOPOGRAPHY (577 sq. mi.): Mostly hilly with bluffs 300–400 feet high at the Mississippi River; lowlands in the extreme south-southeast.

Carroll. Organized on January 2, 1833, from Ray County. Originally intended to be named Wakenda for the county's large east–west creek, which in turn took its name from a Siouan term for preternatural; the name was changed when news was received of the November 1832 death of Marylander Charles Carroll (1737–1832), the last surviving signer of the Declaration of Independence. COUNTY SEAT: *Carrollton* (elev. 754). POPULATION: 10,748. TOPOGRAPHY (695 sq. mi.): Rolling hills with broad floodplains along the rivers.

Carter. Organized on March 10, 1859, from Reynolds, Shannon, and Oregon Counties. Named for South Carolinian Zimri Carter, who in 1812 was the county's first settler and in 1859 was the county's richest resident. COUNTY SEAT: *Van Buren* (elev. 475). POPULATION: 5,515. TOPOGRAPHY (509 sq. mi.): Mostly rugged hills that are steeper in the northwest than in the east; flat woods in the southeast corner.

Cass. Organized on March 3, 1835, from Jackson County. Originally named Van Buren for then U.S. secretary of state Martin Van Buren; the name was changed in 1849 after Van Buren's political career failed (Camden, above). The name Cass was chosen to honor Lewis Cass *(Cassville)*, Michigan U.S. senator and in 1848 the Democratic presidential candidate (Butler, above). COUNTY SEAT: *Harrisonville* (elev. 904). POPULATION: 63,808. TOPOGRAPHY (701 sq. mi.): Gently rolling prairie.

Cedar. Organized on February 14, 1845, from Dade and St. Clair Counties. Named for Cedar Creek (with its cedar trees), a large stream stretching north–south through the center of the county. COUNTY SEAT: *Stockton* (elev. 965). POPULATION: 12,093. TOPOGRAPHY (470 sq. mi.): Steep hills in the north and northwest; rolling prairie in the west; Stockton Lake *(Lakes: Corps of Engineers)* covers the south-central and south-southeast section.

Chariton. Organized on November 16, 1820 (effective January 1, 1821), from Howard County. Its namesake, the county's first town, Chariton *(Glasgow; Keytesville)*, was named for the river via a French fur trader, whose identity is vague; possibilities include (1) Joseph Chorette (Charette, Charrette, Chariton), who drowned in the Missouri River in 1795, or (2) John Chariton, whose base camp reportedly was at the confluence of the Chariton and Missouri Rivers. COUNTY SEAT: *Keytesville* (elev. 709). POPULATION: 9,202. TOPOGRAPHY (758 sq. mi.): The central and east sections taper north–south through steep-sided closely spaced hills, rolling prairie, and bottomland; the western section has gently rolling uplands.

Christian. Organized on March 8, 1859, from Taney, Greene, and Webster Counties. Named for Christian County, Ky., which was named for Kentucky pioneer and Revolutionary War veteran Col. William Christian (1743–1786), who was killed during a battle with Indians. COUNTY SEAT: *Ozark* (elev. 1,178). POPULATION: 32,644. TOPOGRAPHY (564 sq. mi.): Rolling tableland in the panhandle and central-western sections; remainder rugged hills, some with heavy forests, ridges, *balds, and knobs.*

Clark. Organized on December 16, 1836, from Lewis County. Named for William Clark of the *Lewis and Clark Expedition (Clarksville)*. COUNTY SEAT: *Kahoka* (elev. 703). POPULATION: 7,547. TOPOGRAPHY (507 sq. mi.): Lowlands in the extreme southeast; hills in the extreme northeast; prairie running diagonally through the center but hilly near large streams.

Clay. Organized on January 2, 1822, from Ray County. Named for American statesman-politician Henry Clay (1777–1852) of Kentucky, who drafted the 1820 *Missouri Compromise*. COUNTY SEAT: *Liberty* (elev. 879). POPULATION: 153,411. TOPOGRAPHY (403 sq. mi.): Mostly rolling hills, rugged near streams, with Smith Reservoir covering part of the northwest corner; tighter hills in the southwest.

Clinton. Organized on January 2, 1833, from Clay County. Named for American statesman DeWitt Clinton *(Clinton)*. COUNTY SEAT: *Plattsburg* (elev. 953). POPULATION: 16,595. TOPOGRAPHY (423 sq. mi.): Rolling prairie, rugged near streams; Smith Reservoir covers part of the southwest corner.

Cole. Organized on November 16, 1820 (effective January 1, 1821), from Cooper County. Named for 1807 Virginia emigrant Capt. Stephen Cole, whose 1810–1814 fort was one mile east of his sister-in-law Hannah Cole's fort *(Boonville)*. Stephen Cole died in 1820 while on the *Santa Fe Trail*. COUNTY SEAT: *Jefferson City* (elev. 627). POPULATION: 63,579. TOPOGRAPHY (392 sq. mi.): Rolling hills with steep slopes; bottomland along streams.

Cooper. Organized on December 17, 1818, from Howard County. Named for Sarshall Cooper, who was killed by an Indian in 1814 during the *War of 1812*. According to the legend, the Indian removed some of the chinking from Cooper's log cabin at Fort Cooper[2] and shot him while he sat by the fire with a child in his lap. COUNTY SEAT: *Boonville* (elev. 660). POPULATION: 14,835. TOPOGRAPHY (567 sq. mi.): Steeply rolling hills, some with steep slopes; bottomland and bluffs along the Missouri River.

Crawford. Organized on January 23, 1829, from Gasconade County; reorganized on February 23, 1834. Named for Georgia U.S. senator and American statesman William H. Crawford, who was U.S. treasury sec-

retary in 1818, served as a member of president (1817–1825) James Monroe's (Monroe, below) cabinet, and in 1824 was a U.S. presidential candidate supported by Martin Van Buren (Camden, above) and defeated by John Q. Adams. Crawford died in 1834. COUNTY SEAT: *Steelville* (elev. 755). POPULATION: 19,173. TOPOGRAPHY (744 sq. mi.): 75 percent rugged wooded hills, nearly mountainous; remainder, between I-44 and the Meramec River, broader and more gently rolling.

Dade. Organized on January 29, 1841, from Polk and Barry Counties. Named for Maj. Francis L. Dade, who, along with his detachment, was ambushed and killed in 1835 by Osceola's Seminole guerrillas near today's Tampa, Fla., precipitating the 1835–1842 Second *Seminole War*. COUNTY SEAT: *Greenfield* (elev. 1,087). POPULATION: 7,449. TOPOGRAPHY (491 sq. mi.): High rolling prairie in half the western area; remainder tight hills, except for some prairie in the southeast corner; Stockton Lake *(Lakes: Corps of Engineer)* covers part of the central northeast and center.

Dallas. Organized on January 29, 1841, from Polk County. First designated Niangua, which is probably a Siouan word for the county's river (meaning not known). The name was changed on December 16, 1844, reportedly because it was difficult to spell and pronounce. Dallas honors George M. Dallas (1792–1864), a Pennsylvania Democrat who at that time was vice president elect as the running mate of James K. Polk. Incidentally, Dallas, Tex., had just been platted in 1844; its county, Dallas, was not named until 1846 (Texas, below). COUNTY SEAT: *Buffalo* (elev. 1,200). POPULATION: 12,646. TOPOGRAPHY (543 sq. mi.): rugged tight hills in most of the eastern half; prairies in extreme southwest and near Buffalo; remainder long rolling hills.

Daviess. Organized on December 29, 1836, from Ray County. Named for Col. Joseph H. Daviess (1774–1811), who was killed at Tippecanoe *(Lancaster: Tippecanoe)*, an Indian battle that helped precipitate the *War of 1812*. COUNTY SEAT: *Gallatin* (elev. 931). POPULATION: 7,865. TOPOGRAPHY (563 sq. mi.): Nearly all prairie, changing from undulating in the northeast to rolling in the northwest; rugged near large streams with some bottomland.

De Kalb. Organized on February 25, 1845, from Clinton County. Named for Johann Kalb (1721–1780), a German-Bavarian peasant who, after marrying into a wealthy political French family and retiring from the army as "Baron de Kalb," came to America with La Fayette (below), joined George Washington's army in 1777 as a major general, and was killed in 1780 in a battle charge near Camden, S.C. COUNTY SEAT: *Maysville* (elev. 974). POPULATION:

9,967. TOPOGRAPHY (425 sq. mi.): Mostly high prairie, some rolling; rocky broken land along Grindstone Creek in the southeast and extreme east.

Dent. Organized on February 10, 1851, from Shannon and Crawford Counties. Named for the area's first state legislator, Lewis Dent, who came to Missouri in 1835 to join his father, 1811 pioneer Mark Dent. Lewis Dent successfully promoted area mining and immigration to the region. COUNTY SEAT: *Salem* (elev. 1,182). POPULATION: 13,702. TOPOGRAPHY (755 sq. mi.): Mountainous; about 8 percent valleys and bottomland.

Douglas. Organized on October 29, 1857, from Ozark County. Named for American statesman and Illinois U.S. senator Stephen A. Douglas (1813–1861), who at that time had not begun his legendary series of debates with Abraham Lincoln and was best known for his ardent support of the annexation of Texas and Oregon *(Oregon Trail)*, the *Mexican War,* and the transcontinental railroad, and as sponsor of the 1854 Kansas-Nebraska Act that removed the *Missouri Compromise*'s restrictions on slavery above the Mason-Dixon line. COUNTY SEAT: *Ava* (elev. 1,283). POPULATION: 11,876. TOPOGRAPHY (841 sq. mi.): Mountains, which are highest along the north edge and center.

Dunklin. Organized on February 14, 1845, from Stoddard County. Named for Daniel Dunklin (1790–1844; *Herculaneum: Gov. Daniel Dunklin Grave),* Missouri's fifth governor (1832–1836). COUNTY SEAT: *Kennett* (elev. 258). POPULATION: 33,112. TOPOGRAPHY (547 sq. mi.): Level except for 400-foot *Crowley's Ridge* in the extreme north.

Franklin. Organized on December 11, 1818, from St. Louis County. Named for Benjamin Franklin. COUNTY SEAT: *Union* (elev. 545). POPULATION: 80,603. TOPOGRAPHY (922 sq. mi.): Mostly long, high rolling hills with broad valleys.

Gasconade. Organized on November 20, 1820 (effective January 1, 1821), from Franklin County. Named for the Gasconade River *(Gasconade).* COUNTY SEAT: *Hermann* (elev. 533). POPULATION: 14,006. TOPOGRAPHY (521 sq. mi.): Mostly steep hills and deep valleys; bluffs and bottomland along the Missouri and Bourbeuse Rivers.

Gentry. Organized on February 14, 1845, from Clinton County. Named for Col. Richard Gentry, a soldier-politician and the first mayor of Columbia, Mo. He was killed on Christmas Day 1837 in battle at Okeechobee, Fla., during the 1835–1837 Second *Seminole War.* COUNTY SEAT: *Albany* (elev. 915). POPULATION: 6,848. TOPOGRAPHY (493 sq. mi.): Mostly long rolling hills with bluffs and wide bottomland along larger streams, especially in the northeast and northwest; some prairie.

Greene. Organized on January 2, 1833, from Wayne and Crawford Counties. Named for Gen. Nathanael Greene (1742–1786) of Rhode Island, who fought in most of the important Revolutionary War campaigns, including, as commander of the southern department, the 1781 British surrender at Yorktown. As acting commander of the Continental Army, he efficiently quashed Benedict Arnold's 1780 plot to surrender West Point to the British (Wayne, below). COUNTY SEAT: *Springfield* (elev. 1,316). POPULATION: 207,949. TOPOGRAPHY (677 sq. mi.): Rolling tableland cut deeply by streams; some heavily forested steep slopes.

Grundy. Organized on January 29, 1841, from Livingston County. Named for Tennessee U.S. senator Felix Grundy (1777–1840), who served as U.S. attorney general (1838–1840) under President Martin Van Buren (Camden, above). COUNTY SEAT: *Trenton* (elev. 841). POPULATION: 10,536. TOPOGRAPHY (437 sq. mi.): Gently rolling uplands; rugged near larger streams.

Harrison. Organized on February 14, 1845, from Daviess County. Named for U.S. Congressman Albert G. Harrison (1800–1839) of Fulton, Mo., who died in office. COUNTY SEAT: *Bethany* (elev. 904). POPULATION: 8,469. TOPOGRAPHY (725 sq. mi.): Gently rolling uplands; rugged near larger streams.

Henry. Organized on December 13, 1834, from Lafayette County as Rives County. Originally named for William Cabell Rives (1793–1868), a Virginia U.S. senator (1833–1845). When residents learned c. 1834 that Rives had joined the new Whig Party, petitions were circulated to change the county name. The name officially became Henry on February 15, 1841, in honor of American statesman Patrick Henry (1736–1799) of Virginia, who is best remembered for his Revolutionary War oratory: "Give me liberty or give me death!" COUNTY SEAT: *Clinton* (elev. 800). POPULATION: 20,044. TOPOGRAPHY (729 sq. mi.): Mostly rolling prairie; rugged near streams; Harry S. Truman Reservoir *(Lakes: Corps of Engineers)* covers part of the east-southeast and south-central area.

Hickory. Organized on February 14, 1845, from Benton and Polk Counties. Named for Andrew Jackson (below), whose nickname "Old Hickory" was earned for his resolution, discipline, and success despite formidable obstacles during the Creek Indian Campaign of the *War of 1812.* COUNTY SEAT: *Hermitage* (elev. 822). POPULATION: 7,335. TOPOGRAPHY (379 sq. mi.): Prairies on both sides of the Pomme de Terre River; remainder heavily forested with some hills in the west and southwest; Pomme de Terre Lake *(Lakes: Corps of Engineers)* covers most of the south-central and part of the southeast area.

Holt. Organized on January 29, 1841, as Nodaway (below) from the *Platte Purchase.* The name was changed on February 15, 1841, to Holt, in honor of

Missouri state legislator David Rice Holt of Platte County (below), who died in office on December 7, 1840. COUNTY SEAT: *Oregon* (elev. 1,094). POPULATION: 6,034. TOPOGRAPHY (457 sq. mi.): Bottomland along the rivers, *loess* bluffs for ten miles up the Nodaway River from the Missouri; remainder mostly rolling prairie.

Howard. Organized on January 23, 1816, from St. Louis and St. Charles Counties. Named for Gen. Benjamin A. Howard (1760–1814) of Lexington, Ky., the 1810–1812 governor (County history, above) of the Upper Louisiana Territory. COUNTY SEAT: *Fayette* (elev. 700). POPULATION: 9,631. TOPOGRAPHY (465 sq. mi.): Mostly wide prairie; bottomland along the Missouri.

Howell. Organized on March 2, 1857, from Oregon County. Its specific namesake is uncertain, although two specific names are mentioned: Tennessean Josiah (some sources list James) Howell, the valley's first permanent settler *(West Plains)*, and his son Thomas Jefferson Howell, an 1840 settler who served as a state legislator from Oregon County and as Howell County's first sheriff. Thomas's brother Josephus was the first postmaster of West Plains. COUNTY SEAT: *West Plains* (elev. 991). POPULATION: 31,447. TOPOGRAPHY (928 sq. mi.): Streamless valleys of the Ozarks' southern slopes vary from rugged heavily forested hills to rolling upland prairies and plains.

Iron. Organized on February 17, 1857, from Madison, St. Francois, Washington, Reynolds, and Wayne Counties. Named for the vast amounts of iron ore found in the area. COUNTY SEAT: *Ironton* (elev. 914). POPULATION: 10,726. TOPOGRAPHY (552 sq. mi.): Mainly mountainous with *balds, knobs,* and dense forests.

Jackson. Organized on December 15, 1826, from Lafayette County. Named for folk military hero Andrew Jackson (1767–1845; *Jackson)*, who served as U.S. president from 1829 to 1837 *(Seminole Wars; War of 1812;* Taney, below). His popularity in Missouri is evident from the many place-names derived from his name and the places and people associated with him. COUNTY SEAT: *Independence* (elev. 988). POPULATION: 633,232. TOPOGRAPHY (611 sq. mi.): Rolling hills; heavily urbanized.

Jasper. Organized on January 29, 1841, from Barry County. Named for Revolutionary War soldier Sgt. William Jasper (1750–1779), who in 1776 replaced the fallen American flag at Fort Moultrie and was killed in 1779 while trying to replace the flag on Spring Hill redoubt near Savannah, Ga. Reportedly the namesakes of Jasper, Newton, and McDonald Counties all served under Francis Marion (Marion, below). COUNTY SEAT: *Carthage* (elev. 1002). POPULATION: 90,465.

TOPOGRAPHY (641 sq. mi.): Rolling tableland deeply cut by streams.

Jefferson. Organized on December 8, 1818 (effective January 1, 1819), from St. Louis and Ste. Genevieve Counties. Named for Thomas Jefferson. COUNTY SEAT: *Hillsboro* (elev. 802). POPULATION: 171,380. TOPOGRAPHY (661 sq. mi.): Mostly steep and rolling hills; bottomland along the rivers; bluffs along the Missouri River.

Johnson. Organized on December 13, 1834, from Lafayette County. Named for Richard M. Johnson, U.S. congressman and U.S. senator from Kentucky (1807–1829) and a *War of 1812* veteran who reportedly killed Tecumseh *(Gainesville: Tecumseh)* and was an advocate of pensions for service during that war; he later (1837–1841) was vice president under Martin Van Buren (Camden, above). COUNTY SEAT: *Warrensburg* (elev. 825). POPULATION: 42,514. TOPOGRAPHY (834 sq. mi.): Mostly rolling prairie; some steeply sloping ridges.

Knox. Organized on February 14, 1845, from Scotland County. Named for Gen. Henry Knox (1750–1806), a collateral descendant of Scottish Protestant reformer John Knox (c. 1505–1572). Henry Knox, highly respected by George Washington, served as commander of the army's artillery during the Revolution and as the first U.S. secretary of war (1785–1794). COUNTY SEAT: *Edina* (elev. 815). POPULATION: 4,482. TOPOGRAPHY (507 sq. mi.): Level uplands with bottomland along streams.

Laclede. Organized on February 24, 1849, from Pulaski, Wright, and Camden Counties. Named for French fur trader and *St. Louis* town founder Pierre Laclède. COUNTY SEAT: *Lebanon* (elev. 1,266). POPULATION: 27,158. TOPOGRAPHY (768 sq. mi.): Ozark plateau; mostly rolling uplands with some sharp hills, especially along the rivers.

Lafayette. Organized on November 16, 1820 (effective January 1, 1821), from Cooper County. Originally named Lillard for either one or both of the brothers James and William Lillard *(Lexington)*, Tennessee immigrants who as Missouri state legislators were instrumental in the formation of the county. After both the Lillards returned to Tennessee, the name was changed to Lafayette in 1825 to honor Marquis de La Fayette *(Fayette)*, whose 1824–1825 American tour renewed patriotic enthusiasm for his participation in the Revolutionary War. COUNTY SEAT: *Lexington* (elev. 849). POPULATION: 31,107. TOPOGRAPHY (632 sq. mi.): Mostly prairie, some rolling; bottomland and bluffs along the Missouri River.

Lawrence. Organized on February 14, 1845, from Dade and Barry Counties. Named for naval hero Capt. James Lawrence (1781–1813), who during a *War of 1812* sea battle with the British reportedly issued his last command, "Don't give up the ship," which today is the U.S. Navy's slogan. COUNTY SEAT: *Mount Vernon* (elev. 1,240). POPULATION: 30,236. TOPOGRAPHY (613 sq. mi.): Rolling prairie in the north and south; east and west somewhat hilly.

Lewis. Organized on January 2, 1833, from Marion County. Named for Meriwether Lewis (1774–1809), explorer *(Lewis and Clark Expedition)* and governor (1807–1809) of Upper Louisiana Territory (County history, above). His 1809 suicide in a central Tennessee tavern remains a mystery. COUNTY SEAT: *Monticello* (elev. 604). POPULATION: 10,233. TOPOGRAPHY (509 sq. mi.): Prairie with ridges near streams in the west; remainder hilly with bluffs and bottomland in the east, especially along the Mississippi River.

Lincoln. Organized on December 14, 1818, from St. Charles County. Named for Benjamin Lincoln (1733–1810) of Massachusetts, a Revolutionary War general, the secretary of war (1781–1783) of the Continental Congress, and a respected friend of George Washington, who deputized him to receive the British sword of surrender at Yorktown. The Missouri state legislator and first county settler Capt. Christopher Clark *(Troy: Moscow Mills),* who proposed the name, had previously lived in Lincoln County in Kentucky and North Carolina. COUNTY SEAT: *Troy* (elev. 572). POPULATION: 28,892. TOPOGRAPHY (627 sq. mi.): Gently rolling to steep with reliefs of 200–300 feet and karst landforms *(Collapsed Cave Systems);* bottomland along the Mississippi *(Lincoln Hills Area).*

Linn. Organized on January 6, 1837, from Chariton County. Named for Dr. Lewis F. Linn (1796–1843), who moved to Ste. Genevieve from Lexington, Ky., in 1815 and litigated titles involving Spanish land grants until appointed in 1833 to fill a vacancy in the U.S. senate. He served there until 1843 and was an influential lobbyist for the *Platte Purchase* and the development of Oregon Country *(Oregon Trail).* COUNTY SEAT: *Linneus* (elev. 837). POPULATION: 13,885. TOPOGRAPHY (620 sq. mi.): Rolling uplands in the east; hilly in the west with some bluffs and ravines.

Livingston. Organized on January 6, 1837, from Carroll County. Named for Edward Livingston (1764–1836), U.S. congressman from New York (1794–1801) and mayor of New York City (1801–1803); U.S. congressman (1822–1829) and U.S. senator (1829–1831) from Louisiana; and U.S. secretary of state (1831–1833) and minister to France (1833–1835) under President Andrew Jackson (Jackson, above). COUNTY SEAT: *Chillicothe* (elev. 798). POPULATION: 14,592. TOPOGRAPHY (537 sq. mi.): Gently rolling uplands in the north; hilly in the south; broad bottomlands along the Grand River and Medicine Creek.

McDonald. Organized on March 3, 1849, from Newton County. Said to be named for a Revolutionary War soldier named McDonald, possibly Alexander McDonald, reportedly a sergeant major in the South Carolina 7th Company who served under Francis Marion (below) and was personally decorated for bravery by Gen. Nathanael Greene (above). Four Arkansas McDonalds are listed in the "South Carolina Roster of Patriots" (one was convicted by court-martial for stealing soap). Reportedly, the namesakes of Jasper and Newton Counties also served under Marion. COUNTY SEAT: *Pineville* (elev. 899). POPULATION: 16,938. TOPOGRAPHY (540 sq. mi.): Steeply rolling tableland cut deeply by streams in the north; rugged forested hills in the south.

Macon. Organized on January 6, 1837, from Randolph and Chariton Counties. Named for Revolutionary War soldier and North Carolina politician Nathaniel Macon (1757–1837), a U.S. congressman during the ratification of the Constitution and adoption of the Bill of Rights. COUNTY SEAT: *Macon* (elev. 875). POPULATION: 15,345. TOPOGRAPHY (797 sq. mi.): Relatively level prairie in the east; remainder steep-sided closely spaced hills; Long Branch Lake *(Lakes: Corps of Engineers)* covers part of the center.

Madison. Organized on December 14, 1818 (effective January 1, 1819), from Ste. Genevieve and Cape Girardeau Counties. Named for James Madison (1751–1836), one of the chief architects of the U.S. Constitution and U.S. president from 1809 to 1817. COUNTY SEAT: *Fredericktown* (elev. 743). POPULATION: 11,127. TOPOGRAPHY (497 sq. mi.): Heavily forested with few secondary roads; eastern third hilly with reliefs of 200–300 feet; remainder rugged, nearly mountainous, with granite and felsite knobs *(Balds and Knobs).*

Maries. Organized on March 2, 1855, from Osage and Pulaski Counties. While the county's namesake is definitely the river that runs through it, the derivation of the river's name is uncertain. There are good arguments for "Marais," which in American French refers to a body of water (possibly pool, slough, bayou), and there was a Marais post office (1839–1855) at the river. However, early 19th-century maps usually spell the river's name "Maria," sometimes "Marie," and rarely "Marais," which points to a personal name, as in the case of the Marias (Maria's) River in Montana, which was named in 1804 by Meriwether Lewis (Lewis, above) for his cousin Maria Wood. COUNTY SEAT: *Vienna* (elev. 873). POPULATION: 7,967. TOPOGRAPHY (528 sq. mi.): Varies from steeply rolling hills to sharply hilly with deeply entrenched streams; bottomland along streams; some prairie in the east.

Marion. Organized on December 23, 1826, from Ralls

County. Named for Revolutionary War folk hero Francis Marion (1732–1795), who rose from private to general and was nicknamed the Swamp Fox for his guerrilla tactics of striking at night, then retreating to swamps and morasses. Reportedly the namesakes of Jasper, Newton, and McDonald Counties all served under Marion. COUNTY SEAT: *Palmyra* (elev. 603). POPULATION: 27,682. TOPOGRAPHY (438 sq. mi.): Mostly gently rolling to steep; reliefs of 200–300 feet.

Mercer. Organized on February 14, 1845, from Grundy County. Named for Dr. Hugh Mercer (1721–1777) of Maryland, who was graduated in 1744 from Marshall College in Scotland, which was unusual schooling for the era; as a general during the Revolutionary War, he was mortally wounded at the battle of Princeton. COUNTY SEAT: *Princeton* (elev. 932). POPULATION: 3,723. TOPOGRAPHY (454 sq. mi.): Gently rolling upland; rugged near streams.

Miller. Organized on February 6, 1837, from Cole and Pulaski Counties. Named for John Miller (1781–1846), Missouri's fourth governor (1825–1832) and a member of an influential political community in *Fayette;* he helped establish the first penitentiary west of the Mississippi, completed in 1834 *(Jefferson City).* COUNTY SEAT: *Tuscumbia* (elev. 742). POPULATION: 20,700. TOPOGRAPHY (593 sq. mi.): Tableland in the extreme northwest; remainder steeply rolling hills.

Mississippi. Organized on February 14, 1845, from Scott County. Named for the river that borders it, whose name was extrapolated from the Great Lake Algonquian Indians' name for their portion of the river (Messipi, big river). The name was uniformly applied to the whole river by later French explorers descending it, thereby eliminating other local Indian and Spanish names. COUNTY SEAT: *Charleston* (elev. 327). POPULATION: 14,442. TOPOGRAPHY (410 sq. mi.): Broad alluvial lowlands.

Moniteau. Organized on February 14, 1845, from Cole and Morgan Counties. Its name is the French spelling of an Algonquian term more widely spelled as Manitou (also Manito, Manido), which roughly translates as spirit (implying preternatural) and was first applied to a local creek. COUNTY SEAT: *California* (elev. 874). POPULATION: 12,298. TOPOGRAPHY (417 sq. mi.): Hilly in the north; rolling prairie in the south.

Monroe. Organized on January 6, 1831, from Ralls County. Named for James Monroe (1758–1831), principal negotiator of the *Louisiana Purchase,* secretary of state and secretary of war during the *War of 1812,* and U.S. president (1817–1825). His Monroe Doctrine, declaring the Western Hemisphere an American (and not European) sphere of influence, is still part of American foreign policy. COUNTY SEAT: *Paris* (elev. 696). POPULATION: 9,104. TOPOGRAPHY (670 sq.

mi.): Some hills; remainder mostly high prairie.

Montgomery. Organized on December 14, 1818 (effective January 1, 1819), from St. Charles County. Named for Richard Montgomery (1736–1775), a British officer who sold his commission in 1772 and settled as a farmer in New York. Appointed as an army general by the Continental Congress, he was killed in 1775 while assaulting Quebec with fellow commander Benedict Arnold (Greene, above; Morgan, below). COUNTY SEAT: *Montgomery City* (elev. 832). POPULATION: 11,355. TOPOGRAPHY (540 sq. mi.): Steeply hilly in the southern panhandle and extreme west; remainder wide upland and tableland.

Morgan. Organized on January 5, 1833, from Cooper County. Named for Daniel Morgan (1736–1802), a veteran of the 1754–1763 French and Indian War. In 1775 he assembled a company of frontier riflemen and fought at Quebec, where he was temporary commander when Benedict Arnold was wounded (Montgomery, above). Morgan was instrumental in the 1777 victory at Saratoga and, as a general and commander, won the 1781 Battle of Cowpens in South Carolina. COUNTY SEAT: *Versailles* (elev. 1,036). POPULATION: 15,574. TOPOGRAPHY (594 sq. mi.): Southern portion sharply hilly; remainder rolling prairie and hills with some steep slopes.

New Madrid. Organized on October 1, 1812, as one of five districts that later became the original Missouri Territory counties (County, above). Originally named Nuevo (New) Madrid for the capital of Spain, Madrid. COUNTY SEAT: *New Madrid* (elev. 298). POPULATION: 20,928. TOPOGRAPHY (658 sq. mi.): Broad alluvial lowlands.

Newton. Organized on December 31, 1838, from Barry County. Named for Revolutionary War soldier Sgt. John Newton (c. 1750–1799) of the South Carolina First Regiment, who rescued American prisoners from the British. Reportedly the namesakes for Jasper, Newton, and McDonald Counties all served under Francis Marion (above). COUNTY SEAT: *Neosho* (elev. 1,039). POPULATION: 44,445. TOPOGRAPHY (627 sq. mi.): Rolling tableland with deeply entrenched streams and steeply forested slopes.

Nodaway. Organized on February 14, 1845, from Andrew County. Named for the river, whose derivation is not known but is most likely Indian. Three opinions are: (1) Pattawattamie for placid water; (2) Indian (unspecified tribe) for tranquil; and (3) Souian with no known meaning. A similar place-name, Nottaway, Va., is from an Indian tribal name. Most early county settlers were from Kentucky, Tennessee, and Virginia. COUNTY SEAT: *Maryville* (elev. 1,136). POPULATION: 21,709. TOPOGRAPHY (875 sq. mi.): Rolling upland; rugged near streams.

Oregon. Organized on February 14, 1845, from Ripley County. Named, like Holt County seat *Oregon*, for the western territory, where the American-British boundary dispute was settled in 1846 when the British accepted extension of the international boundary line (49th parallel) from the Rocky Mountains to the Pacific. COUNTY SEAT: *Alton* (elev. 779). POPULATION: 9,470. TOPOGRAPHY (792 sq. mi.): Varies from rolling upland prairie in the south to rugged hills with reliefs of 200–400 feet in the north.

Osage. Organized on January 29, 1841, from Gasconade County. Named for one of its principal rivers, whose name came from an Indian tribal name, possibly Wazha-zhe, that was first recorded in 1673 by the French as Ouchage. The more popular spelling Osage (O'sage) came later. Local Missouri variants include Hoozaw, Huzzah, Hussah, and Whosau, which probably reflect pioneers' attempt at, or good humor with, phonetic pronunciation of the French Ouchage (locally pronounced Hoo'za). COUNTY SEAT: *Linn* (elev. 706). POPULATION: 12,018. TOPOGRAPHY (606 sq. mi.): Sharply hilly with deeply entrenched streams.

Ozark. Organized on January 29, 1841, from Taney County. Named, like Christian County seat *Ozark*, for the Ozark Mountains. Briefly renamed Decatur County in 1843–1845, possibly due to large settlements by Georgians, who transferred the name here. Captain Stephen Decatur (1779–1820) won his early fame during a successful 1804 Tripoli expedition, enhancing it later during the *War of 1812.* He is best remembered for his coined phrase, "our county, right or wrong." COUNTY SEAT: *Gainesville* (elev. 759). POPULATION: 8,598. TOPOGRAPHY (731 sq. mi.): Rugged forested hills with long ridges, *balds, and knobs.*

Pemiscot. Organized on February 19, 1851, from New Madrid County. Named for the principal bayou, the meaning of whose Fox name is uncertain but could translate as runs-alongside-of (a side-channel) or long-rock-at (a location). COUNTY SEAT: *Caruthersville* (elev. 225). POPULATION: 21,921. TOPOGRAPHY (517 sq. mi.): Broad alluvial lowlands.

Perry. Organized on November 16, 1820 (effective January 1, 1821), from Ste. Genevieve County. Named, like its county seat, for Com. Oliver Hazzard Perry. COUNTY SEAT: *Perryville* (elev. 570). POPULATION: 16,648. TOPOGRAPHY (473 sq. mi.): Lowlands in the extreme east-northeast; remainder hilly with reliefs of 200–300 feet.

Pettis. Organized on January 26, 1833, from Saline and Cooper Counties. Named for Spencer Darwin Pettis (1802–1831) of St. Louis, a popular U.S. congressman (1829–1831) who was killed by Maj. Thomas Biddle in a duel on a sandbar opposite St. Louis. COUNTY SEAT: *Sedalia* (elev. 909). POPULATION: 35,437.

TOPOGRAPHY (686 sq. mi.): High rolling prairies; hillier in the north.

Phelps. Organized on November 13, 1857, from Crawford County. Named for John S. Phelps of Springfield (1814–1886), a popular U.S. congressman (1845–1863) and governor (1877–1881) with many ties to Missouri history; he successfully defended Wild Bill Hickok *(Springfield: Park Central Square),* and his wife, Mary, buried Federal general Nathaniel Lyon's body in her garden until it could be transferred for permanent burial *(Springfield: Wilson's Creek).* COUNTY SEAT: *Rolla* (elev. 1,119). POPULATION: 35,248. TOPOGRAPHY (674 sq. mi.): Steeply rolling hills with steeply forested slopes.

Pike. Organized on December 14, 1818 (effective February 1, 1819), from St. Charles County. Named for Zebulon M. Pike (1779–1813), known for his 1805 exploration of the Mississippi River headwaters and his 1806–1807 exploration of the Missouri, Osage, and Arkansas Rivers to today's Pueblo, Colo., where he recorded the peak named for him. Killed in the *War of 1812* at Toronto. COUNTY SEAT: *Bowling Green* (elev. 899). POPULATION: 15,969. TOPOGRAPHY (673 sq. mi.): Gently rolling to steep with reliefs of 200–300 feet *(Lincoln Hills Area).*

Platte. Organized on December 31, 1838, from the *Platte Purchase.* Named for its principal river, whose name, according to "American Place-Names," derives from French, "plat(e)," meaning flat. Omaha Indians referred to the Nebraska portion of the Platte as "Nebraska," meaning a stream not running between high banks but widely spread out, which is a better description than flat. COUNTY SEAT: *Platte City* (elev. 805). POPULATION: 57,867. TOPOGRAPHY (421 sq. mi.): Rolling upland; rugged near major streams.

Polk. Organized on January 5, 1835, from Greene County. Named by Tennessee settlers for Tennessee U.S. congressman James K. Polk (1795–1849), who was speaker of the house in 1835, a staunch supporter of Andrew Jackson (above), and later president (1845–1849) during the *Mexican War.* COUNTY SEAT: *Bolivar* (elev. 1,056). POPULATION: 21,826. TOPOGRAPHY (636 sq. mi.): Rolling upland and prairie.

Pulaski. Organized on January 19, 1833, from Crawford County. Named for Polish patriot Count Casimir Pulaski (c. 1748–1779), who, following a failed 1768 revolt against Russia and exile to Turkey c. 1772, volunteered as a soldier in the American Revolution. After distinguishing himself at the 1777 battle of Brandywine, he was promoted to general; he died of wounds received at the 1779 battle of Savannah. COUNTY SEAT: *Waynesville* (elev. 807). POPULATION: 41,307. TOPOGRAPHY (550 sq. mi.): Sharply hilly to steeply rolling hills; some uplands and lowlands.

Putnam. Organized on February 28, 1845, from Adair and Sullivan Counties; reduced in size, along with its western neighbor Dodge County, after the 1851 settlement of the Iowa–Missouri *boundary* dispute. Dodge (organized December 18, 1846) was incorporated into Putnam in 1853 to comply with minimum size standards for counties. Dodge's namesake is uncertain, although a reasonable assumption is Henry Dodge (1782–1867), who was sheriff in the District of Ste. Genevieve in 1806, a *War of 1812* Missouri militia general, and an 1820 Missouri constitutional convention delegate. He emigrated to Wisconsin Territory in 1827, was a commander during the *Black Hawk War,* Wisconsin's first territorial governor, and its first U.S. senator. Fort Dodge, Iowa, honors him. Putnam County was named for Israel Putnam (1718–1790), who helped organize the Sons of Liberty, a radical colonial secret organization that first appeared openly in 1765 at the time of the Stamp Act. A veteran of the 1754–1763 French and Indian Wars, an explorer in 1766–1767 of the Mississippi River, and a member of the Connecticut general assembly, Putnam is best known as a Revolutionary War general who helped organize the 1775 defense of Bunker Hill, which incidentally was actually nearby Breed's Hill in Charlestown, Mass. COUNTY SEAT: *Unionville* (elev. 1,067). POPULATION: 5,079. TOPOGRAPHY (520 sq. mi.): Steep-sided and closely spaced hills in the east; remainder gently rolling upland.

Ralls. Organized on November 16, 1820 (effective January 1, 1821), from Pike County. Named for Daniel Ralls (1785–1820), a Pike County state legislator who is best known for casting the deciding vote to elect Thomas Hart Benton (above) to the U.S. senate. Ralls died shortly after the vote, and the county was named for him a few weeks later. COUNTY SEAT: *New London* (elev. 577). POPULATION: 8,476. TOPOGRAPHY (482 sq. mi.): Gently rolling prairie with some reliefs of 200–300 feet *(Lincoln Hills Area).*

Randolph. Organized on January 22, 1829, from Chariton and Ralls Counties. Settled mostly by Kentucky, Tennessee, North Carolina, and Virginia immigrants, it was named for John Randolph (1773–1833) of the powerful Randolph family of Virginia. A member of the U.S. congress from 1799 to 1829 (except in 1813–1815), he was a strict constitutionalist who championed states' rights. Although his 1821 will provided for freeing his 400 slaves, he defended slaveholders' rights. COUNTY SEAT: *Huntsville* (elev. 808). POPULATION: 24,370. TOPOGRAPHY (477 sq. mi.): Wide flat tablelands.

Ray. Organized on November 16, 1820 (effective January 1, 1821), from Howard County. Named for John Ray, a Revolutionary War soldier who also served in Illinois in 1780–1782 with George Rogers Clark *(Clarksville)* and worked with Daniel Boone in Kentucky and Missouri. Ray, a Howard County delegate to the 1820 constitutional convention, died shortly afterward. COUNTY SEAT: *Richmond* (elev. 826). POPULATION: 21,971. TOPOGRAPHY (568 sq. mi.): Rolling hills with broad floodplains.

Reynolds. Organized on February 25, 1845, from Shannon County. Named for Thomas Reynolds (1796–1844), a politician and Missouri governor (1840–1844) who was best known for his successful 1842–1843 lobbying to abolish debtors' prisons. Reportedly physically and mentally ill, he fatally shot himself in 1844, leaving a note that referred to "the abuse and slanders of his enemies." COUNTY SEAT: *Centerville* (elev. 774). POPULATION: 6,661. TOPOGRAPHY (809 sq. mi.): Ruggedly hilly (reliefs of 200–300 feet) to mountainous; cherty to thin soil with some limestone outcroppings.

Ripley. Organized on January 5, 1833, from Wayne County. Named for Eleazar W. Ripley (1782–1839), a soldier (highest rank, general), lawyer, and politician who served in the Massachusetts legislature (1807–1809) and fought in the *War of 1812,* receiving a congressional gold medal for his services. A supporter of Andrew Jackson (above), Ripley was an 1832 member of the Louisiana senate and a U.S. congressman from 1835 to 1839. COUNTY SEAT: *Doniphan* (elev. 476). POPULATION: 12,303. TOPOGRAPHY (631 sq. mi.): Varies from rolling upland prairies to sharply hilly forested areas.

St. Charles. Organized on October 1, 1812, as one of five districts that later became the original Missouri Territory counties (County, above). Named, like its county seat, for San Carlos Borromeo, archbishop of Milan and patron saint of Charles IV (1748–1819). COUNTY SEAT: *St. Charles* (elev. 614). POPULATION: 212,907. TOPOGRAPHY (558 sq. mi.): Steeply rolling to steeply hilly with some uplands and lowlands.

St. Clair. Organized on January 29, 1841, from Rives County (Henry, above). Named for Arthur St. Clair (1736–1818), a Scotsman who served with the British in Canada in 1757–1762 before resigning his commission to settle in Pennsylvania. A Revolutionary War general, he served in a 1775 expedition to Canada, fought under George Washington in 1776 at Trenton and Priceton, and took command in 1777 of Fort Ticonderoga. In 1787 he was president of the Continental Congress, and he served as first governor (1787–1802) of the Northwest Territories. COUNTY SEAT: *Osceola* (elev. 763). POPULATION: 8,457. TOPOGRAPHY (699 sq. mi.): Rolling prairie with some limestone and sandstone buttes in the west; remainder sharply hilly with deeply entrenched streams and some heavy forests.

Ste. Genevieve. Organized on October 1, 1812, as one of five districts that later became the original Missouri Territory counties (County, above). Named, like its county seat, for the patron saint of Paris, France, Sainte Geneviève, who reportedly twice saved Paris from its enemies. COUNTY SEAT: *Ste. Genevieve* (elev. 401). POPULATION: 16,037. TOPOGRAPHY (504 sq. mi.): Hilly with steep slopes; some reliefs of 200–300 feet.

St. Francois. Organized on December 19, 1821, from Jefferson, Washington, and Ste. Genevieve Counties. Named for Saint Francis of Assisi (c. 1181–1226; canonized 1228), whose example of attempting to pattern his life after the Gospels inspired the founding of the Order of Friars Minor (Franciscans). COUNTY SEAT: *Farmington* (elev. 918). POPULATION: 48,904. TOPOGRAPHY (451 sq. mi.): Mostly mountainous with knobs *(Balds and Knobs)*, upland valleys, plateaus, and dense forests; hilly with reliefs of 200–300 feet in the east.

St. Louis. Organized on October 1, 1812, as one of five districts that later became the original Missouri Territory counties (County, above). Named like the city of *St. Louis* for Louis IX. COUNTY SEAT: *Clayton* (elev. 616). POPULATION: 993,529. TOPOGRAPHY (506 sq. mi.): Rolling hills; heavily urbanized.

Saline. Organized on November 25, 1820 (effective January 1, 1821), from Cooper County. Its American French name, meaning salt springs, salt lick, saltworks, etc., honors the county's many salt springs. (Salt was a valuable commodity in 1820; it is the origin of the word "salary.") COUNTY SEAT: *Marshall* (elev. 787). POPULATION: 23,523. TOPOGRAPHY (755 sq. mi.): High rolling prairie; broad floodplains.

Schuyler. Organized on February 14, 1845, from Adair County. Named for soldier-politician Philip Schuyler (1733–1804) of New York, the father-in-law of Alexander Hamilton. Schuyler fought in the 1754–1763 French and Indian Wars, was a 1775 delegate to the Continental Congress, helped George Washington formulate army regulations, served as a general during the Revolution, was elected to the New York senate, and was one of that state's first U.S. senators (1789–1791 and 1797–1798). COUNTY SEAT: *Lancaster* (elev. 979). POPULATION: 4,236. TOPOGRAPHY (309 sq. mi.): Level uplands with prairie soils, hilly near large streams; some steep forested slopes.

Scotland. Organized on January 29, 1841, from Clark, Lewis, and Shelby Counties. Named nostalgically by W. B. Carney *(Edina)* for his native Scotland. COUNTY SEAT: *Memphis* (elev. 801). POPULATION: 4,822. TOPOGRAPHY (438 sq. mi.): Level uplands; hilly with some steep forested slopes near streams.

Scott. Organized on December 28, 1821 (effective March 1, 1822), from New Madrid County. Named for John Scott (1782–1861), Missouri's first U.S. congress-

man (1821–1829). COUNTY SEAT: *Benton* (elev. 440). POPULATION: 39,376. TOPOGRAPHY (423 sq. mi.): Hilly in the northeast with reliefs of 200–300 feet; remainder broad alluvial lowlands.

Shannon. Organized on January 29, 1841, from Ripley County. Named for Judge George "Pegleg" Shannon *(Palmyra: Shannon Grave Site).* COUNTY SEAT: *Eminence* (elev. 677). POPULATION: 7,613. TOPOGRAPHY (1,004 sq. mi.): Mainly forested rugged hills with reliefs of 200–400 feet.

Shelby. Organized on January 2, 1835, from Marion County. Named for Isaac Shelby (1750–1826), a Revolutionary War general who defeated the British in 1780 at the Battle of Kings Mountain and was Kentucky's first and fifth governor (1792–1806, 1812–1816). COUNTY SEAT: *Shelbyville* (elev. 768). POPULATION: 6,942. TOPOGRAPHY (501 sq. mi.): Level prairie with some long rolling ridges; bluffs along streams.

Stoddard. Organized on January 2, 1835, from New Madrid County. Named for Amos Stoddard (1762–1813), who was acting governor of the newly created Upper Louisiana Territory in 1804–1805 (County, above). COUNTY SEAT: *Bloomfield* (elev. 497). POPULATION: 28,895. TOPOGRAPHY (815 sq. mi.): *Crowley's Ridge* runs through the center from north to south; remainder lowlands.

Stone. Organized on February 10, 1851, from Taney County. Named for John W. Stone (d. 1849), who immigrated c. 1833 from Tennessee, was a pioneer judge of Taney County, and served under Andrew Jackson at the Battle of New Orleans *(War of 1812);* his property adjoined today's county seat. COUNTY SEAT: *Galena* (elev. 985). POPULATION: 19,078. TOPOGRAPHY (451 sq. mi.): Heavily forested rugged hills, long ridges, cedar glades, and *balds and knobs* in the south; remainder rolling tableland with some steep forested slopes.

Sullivan. Organized on February 14, 1845, from Linn County. Named for New Hampshire soldier-statesman John Sullivan (1740–1795), a member of the first and second continental congresses (1774, 1775), a Revolutionary War general who defeated the Iroquois (British allies) in 1778–1779, president (1786–1788) of New Hampshire, and chairman of his state's convention to ratify the U.S. constitution in 1788. COUNTY SEAT: *Milan* (elev. 969). POPULATION: 6,326. TOPOGRAPHY (651 sq. mi.): Steep-sided and closely spaced hills in the north and east; remainder gently rolling uplands, rugged near streams.

Taney. Organized on January 6, 1837, from Greene County. Named for Roger Brooke Taney (1777–1864) of Maryland. An 1824 supporter of Andrew Jackson (above), Taney helped establish the modern Democratic Party in 1828 and as U.S. attorney general helped Jackson draft his 1832 veto of the federal charter for the privately owned Second Bank of the United States (Wright, below). Appointed by Jackson to the U.S. Supreme Court (served 1836–1864), he was elected chief justice in 1837 and in 1857 wrote the majority opinion in the Dred Scott decision (*St. Louis: Market Street Area Sights*). COUNTY SEAT: *Forsyth* (elev. 947). POPULATION: 25,561. TOPOGRAPHY (608 sq. mi.): Heavily forested rugged hills, long ridges, cedar glades, *balds, and knobs*.

Texas. Organized on February 14, 1845, from Shannon and Wright Counties. Named because of enthusiasm generated by the Republic of Texas, which gained independence from Mexico in 1836 and applied for U.S. annexation and statehood in 1845, becoming the 28th state on December 29, 1845. Another possible factor is its status as Missouri's largest county (larger than Rhode Island). The name—an Angelina and upper Niches valley Hosinai Indian term meaning friend or ally—was recorded as Teyas in Spanish c. 1541 and mistakenly used as the name for those Indians. COUNTY SEAT: *Houston* (elev. 1,180). POPULATION: 21,476. TOPOGRAPHY (1,183 sq. mi.): Varies from rolling upland prairie to sharply hilly with forested slopes.

Vernon. Organized on February 27, 1855, from Bates County. An 1851 organizational act, declared unconstitutional, intended to create Vernon from Cass and Bates, with Vernon encompassing the area of present-day Bates and Bates assuming the area now encompassed by Vernon. Named for Col. Miles Vernon (1786–1866), a state senator from Laclede County and veteran of the Battle of New Orleans (*War of 1812*). COUNTY SEAT: *Nevada* (elev. 880). POPULATION: 19,041. TOPOGRAPHY (837 sq. mi.): Rolling prairie; some hills with steep faces on one side.

Warren. Organized on January 5, 1833, from Montgomery County. Named for physician and patriot Joseph Warren (1741–1775) of Massachusetts, who after the 1770 Boston Massacre was a member of the committee informing the colonial governor that British troops must be recalled, and who dispatched Paul Revere, William Davis, and Samuel Prescott on their famous 1775 ride. Although a general, he fought in the ranks at Bunker Hill (Putnam, above) and was killed while rallying retreating militia. COUNTY SEAT: *Warrenton* (elev. 828). POPULATION: 19,534. TOPOGRAPHY (429 sq. mi.): High rolling prairie in the north; remainder gently to steeply rolling hills with some reliefs of 200–300 feet and karst landforms (*Collapsed Cave Systems*).

Washington. Organized on August 21, 1813, from Ste. Genevieve County. Named for George Washington, whose 1754 skirmish near Fort Duquesne (today's Pittsburgh) precipitated the 1754–1763 French and Indian War during which he attained the rank of colonel and his military reputation; he was the unsolicited unanimous choice for commander of the Continental Army (1775–1783) and America's first president (1789–1797). COUNTY SEAT: *Potosi* (elev. 1,047). POPULATION: 20,380. TOPOGRAPHY (762 sq. mi.): Heavily forested rugged hills with reliefs of 200–400 feet; some tableland and rolling hills in the east.

Wayne. Organized on December 11, 1818, from Cape Girardeau County. Named for Revolutionary War general Anthony Wayne (1745–1796), who earned the nickname Mad Anthony during his 1776–1778 campaigns in Canada, near Philadelphia, at Brandywine, and elsewhere and for his 1779 successful surprise night attack at Stony Point. He helped prevent Benedict Arnold's 1780 treasonous plot (Greene, above) and later aided the 1781 Yorktown victory. Returning to the army in 1792, he negotiated the 1794 treaty that opened the Northwest Territory. COUNTY SEAT: *Greenville* (elev. 406). POPULATION: 11,543. TOPOGRAPHY (762 sq. mi.): Forested rugged hills with reliefs of 200–400 feet; mountainous in the northwest.

Webster. Organized on March 3, 1855, from Greene County. Named for Daniel Webster (1782–1852), who was a U.S. congressman and senator from New Hampshire and then Massachusetts (*Marshfield*) and secretary of state under presidents William H. Harrison (1841), John Tyler (1841–1843), and Millard Filmore (1850–1852). The perennial rival of Henry Clay (above), Webster attained folk hero status as a public speaker after his death. COUNTY SEAT: *Marshfield* (elev. 1,494). POPULATION: 23,753. TOPOGRAPHY (594 sq. mi.): Varies from rolling prairie to forested and sharply hilly, with the highest average elevation of any Missouri county (extremes: 1,690–1,092).

Worth. Organized on February 8, 1861, from Gentry County. Named for American soldier Gen. William Jenkins Worth (1794–1849), who fought in the *Seminole Wars*; as second in command under Zachary Taylor during the *Mexican War*, he captured Monterey in 1846 and fought at Vera Cruz and Mexico City. This is Missouri's smallest county. COUNTY SEAT: *Grant City* (elev. 1,136). POPULATION: 2,440. TOPOGRAPHY (266 sq. mi.): High long-rolling prairie hills with deep-set streams.

Wright. Organized on January 29, 1841, from Pulaski County. Named for Silas Wright (1795–1847), who as a U.S. senator (1833–1844) and staunch supporter of Martin Van Buren (Camden, above) introduced an 1837 bill to establish the Independent Treasury, a federal banking system to replace the so-called Pet Banks (favored institutions used for federal banking) that developed after Andrew Jackson's veto of the Second Bank (Taney, above). He was later governor of New

Unidentified covered bridge. (CHARLES TREFTS PHOTOGRAPH)

York (1845–1846). COUNTY SEAT: *Hartville* (elev. 1,170). POPULATION: 16,758. TOPOGRAPHY (682 sq. mi.): Varies from rolling prairie to forested and sharply hilly.

1. Formerly McCredie (Kingdom City was the railroad station name); George P. McCredie platted the town; p.o. McCredie 1872–1970; Kingdom City 1970–now.
2. Once near *Arrow Rock (New Franklin: Santa Fe Trail)*.

COVERED BRIDGES

Of Missouri's estimated 30 covered bridges in use from the 1820s to c. 1900, only four remain (*Hillsboro, Jackson, Laclede, Paris*). Two types of engineering were used. Howe-Truss construction, patented in 1840 by William Howe, used vertical rods between the upper and lower wooden supports to add strength to the wooden trusses; Burr-arch construction, patented in 1804 by Theodore Burr, used wooden arches to reinforce the trusses (*Paris*). Covering bridges helped to shelter, and thereby preserve, the iron and timber supports and to prevent lifting and sagging. American ingenuity suggested other benefits: the coverings provided an emergency shelter, a romantic meeting place, a landmark, and a signboard.

CRAIG
Population: 346   Map B-1

During the 1840s–1860s, a stagecoach stop and trading post community a half-mile east of here on the Council Bluff, Iowa & St. Joseph *Road* was called Big Spring but designated on maps by its post office name, Tarkio.[1] When the St. Joseph & Council Bluff *Railroad* arrived in 1868, a town was platted along the tracks and the post office was moved there. Named for the president of the line, Gen. James Craig. Post offices: Tarkio 1843–1845, 1849–1856, 1863–1864, 1866–1869; Craig 1869–now.

Craig Reunion. Since 1895. Carnival, entertainment. Late July.

Grundel Mastodon Site. Mastodon bones dating back to 21,100 B.C. were excavated in 1963 (Mastodon *State Park*). Private; 4 m. NW; inquire locally.

Guilliams Mill. Vernacular, 1849. Remnants of this saw/*gristmill* can be seen. I-29 at Big Tarkio River, N approx. 4 m. upstream.

The Summit. Reportedly used as a lookout during the *Civil War*, today the site affords a ten-mile view of the Missouri River valley and the bluffs of Nebraska. E of town; inquire locally.

Thurnau Wildlife Area. *Wildlife Areas.*

1. *Rock Port: Tarkio.*

CRESTWOOD
Population: 11,229 Map St. Louis Area

Platted in 1947 along *Route 66* (now SR 366) as a subdivision of *St. Louis* to avoid annexation by adjacent Oakland, the town was originally settled c. 1805 by the John Sappington family (Thomas Sappington House, below) and later grew as a post office community, Sappington.[1] The town was reportedly renamed by the new subdivision residents for a tree standing at the crest of a hill by a street called Crestwood. *Post office:* Crestwood as a station of the St. Louis post office since 1947.

Architecture. National Historic Register: William Long House (Log, c. 1820), 9385 Pardee. Zephaniah Sappington House (c. 1815), 11145 Gravois Rd.

Father Dickson Cemetery. The cemetery was established in 1903 to honor Rev. Father Moses Dickson. In 1848 Dickson, with 12 other black men, organized the Knights of Liberty "to prepare for an armed struggle to end slavery." After fighting in the Civil War, he became an ordained minister and successfully lobbied for "separate but equal" schools for blacks in Missouri, including Lincoln University *(Jefferson City: Architecture)*. In 1878, as president of the Refugee Relief Board in St. Louis, he helped relocate about 16,000 former slaves. A monument erected in 1915 by The International Order of Twelve, Knights and Daughters of Tabor (established in 1872 to honor Dickson) commemorates the relocation effort by listing states that received black refugees. 845 S. Sappington. *(Cemeteries)*

Parks. LAUMEIER PARK: 96 acres. This is reportedly one of two parks in America to exhibit contemporary, site-specific sculpture. Many of the works are enormous; "The Way," 100 feet long and 50 feet high, consists of former underground storage tanks welded together and painted red. Tours, indoor gallery, picnic area, wooded hiking trails. SR 366 at US 61; SR 366, W 0.5 m. to Geyer, S to Rott. WHITECLIFF: 80 acres. Walking paths to a former quarry site, picnic area. SR 366, S on Grant, S on Pardee.

Thomas Sappington House. Adam, 1808; National Historic Register. Reportedly the oldest residence still standing in St. Louis County, this two-story brick house is structurally unchanged. It was built by the son of Dr. John Sappington *(Arrow Rock);* he used wooden pegs for the framework and handmade bricks, mantels, and molding. Today's colors, ranging from whitewash to flat carbon, match the originals. Period furnishings include Staffordshire china and a canopied bed; flower and herb gardens. Tours. Midtown at SR 366; N 0.25 on S. Sappington (1015).

1. Family name; p.o. 1837–1902, 1904–1907, 1914–1937.

CROCKER
Population: 1,077   Map F-5

The site was platted in 1869 by the Atlantic & Pacific *Railroad* when its route arced north of *Waynesville* before dropping south just east of Humboldt,[1] which was abandoned in 1870–1871 by its residents, who helped to establish this new depot town. Named for railroad stockholder Eurilis J. Crocker, whose family later founded the Crocker bank of San Francisco, the town was one of Pulaski County's first shipping points, serving towns as large as Waynesville. Post offices: Humboldt 1854–1861, 1863–1872; Tallent City[2] 1868–1870; Crocker 1872–now.

Crocker Depot / Museum. Railroad, 1869; restored. This board-and-batten structure displays period furnishings and historical items. Downtown.

Dixon, Mo. Platted in 1869 along the Atlantic & Pacific *Railroad* and named by railroad surveyor Milton Santee, whose hometown was Dixon, Ill., after first settler Father John Dixon. Post office: 1869–now. SR 133, E 10 m.; SR C, E 1.6 m. CLIFTY CREEK NATURAL AREA: 230 acres. Features a natural bridge (40 feet long, 13 feet high, 25–30 feet wide), a limestone glade, cliffs, and oak-hickory bottomland forest. South of a picnic area by the highway is Clifty Spring; 100 yards upstream is a wet-weather waterfall. The bridge, created by *stream piracy,* was carved out by a branch of Clifty Creek (1 m. upstream, bear right; no markers) *(Collapsed Cave Systems)*. Box 509, Rolla 65401. SR 28, N 4 m.; SR W, E 5.6 m. (partly an unmarked road). STICKNEY, Mo. Established c. 1903, this post office community was named for the Stickney family. A general store (c. 1918) and its c. 1926 gas pump add to the nostalgic setting. SR 28, N 6 m.; SR E, E 6.2 m.; or from Clifty Creek Natural Area (above): GR, N approx. 2.3 m.; SR E, W 0.5 m.

Richland, Mo. Platted in 1869 along the Atlantic & Pacific *Railroad* by Milton Santee (Dixon, above), the town was first named Lyon,[3] then changed because of an existing Lyon post office to honor G. W. Rich, a director of the railroad. Post office: 1869–now. SR 133, W 13 m. ARCHITECTURE: Some 1880s commercial buildings. Nearby (inquire locally) is Manes-Calloway House: Greek Revival, 1840; remodeled, additions; National Historic Register. *FLOAT STREAM:* Gasconade River.

Tunnel Cave. In a classic example of subterranean *stream piracy,* water flows into a 1,000-foot natural tunnel from a sinkhole east of SR 17, channeling through a ridge and under the highway to drain into the Gasconade River. SR 17, S approx. 4 m. near a gravel road.

1. Baron Alexander von Humboldt, German writer and traveler; stock name.
2. Postmaster David G. Talents.
3. Federal general Nathaniel Lyon (*Civil War; Springfield: Wilson's Creek*); no p.o.

CROWLEY'S RIDGE

This ridge is an erosional remnant, a highland between two valleys formed by the Mississippi River to the west and the Ohio to the east. Diversion of the Mississippi and Ohio to their present riverbeds may have been caused by a tectonic uplift in southeast Missouri about 18,000 years ago (*New Madrid*). *Loess*, varying in consistency from clay to fine sand on top of the ridge, either accumulated as silt during the ridge's early stages or was windblown and trapped by the already existing ridge. Adding to the uniqueness of this ridge is its forest vegetation, which is more like plants found in hardwood forests east of the Mississippi River. Varying in width from a half mile to 12 miles and extending into Arkansas as far south as Helena, this crescent-shaped landmark has been an overland trail through the river bottoms since prehistoric times.

CUBA
Population: 2,616   Map G-5

When M. W. Trask and W. H. Ferguson platted Cuba in 1857 on Simpson's *Prairie* along the surveyed route of the Pacific *Railroad*, the closest house was a half-mile west, where G. W. Jamison had a post office, Amanda.[1] After the tracks were laid, Jamison moved the post office to Cuba in 1860, changing Amanda's name to Cuba (*La Plata*), the Caribbean island held by Spain that had made emotional and political newspaper headlines during the 1840s and 1850s, which included proposals for annexation. Post offices: Amanda 1857–1860; Cuba 1860–now. (*Route 66*)

The Abbey Winery. Various Missouri wines, rose garden, picnic site; tour and tasting. I-44 at SR UU exit.

Bourbon, Mo. Tradition claims the town was named for the whiskey. In 1853, during construction of the Pacific *Railroad*, store owner Richard Turner established a post office named Bourbon at the proposed townsite of St. Cloud,[2] which was later established further west at its present location (I-44, E 1.7 m.). Turner sold merchandise, including the popular New West liquor, bourbon. Reportedly the name came in two stages; railroad workers first talked of going to the "bourbon

store," later calling it the store at Bourbon. Arguments against this version note that the 1853 Bourbon post office predates any significant railroad construction, lending credence to the assumption that the town was named for the French royal family who supported the American Revolution.[3] St. Cloud, France, was the site of royal mansions, including one owned by the brother of King Louis XIV (1638–1715), the most prominent of the French Bourbon kings. Today's town watertower has its name in bold letters. Post office: 1853–now. I-44, E 7 m. BRAZIL CREEK TRAIL CAMP (*National Forests*): Tables, vault toilets, fireplaces; part of Berryman *Trail*. *ROUTE 66* SIGHTS: below.

Leasburg, Mo. Reportedly a post office community, the site was known as Harrison Station.[4] It was renamed Leasburg in 1859 for Samuel Lea, who built the first residence (a log house) and later established a post office. Platted along the Pacific *Railroad* in 1869. Post office: 1860–now. I-44, N 6 m.; SR H, S 2.3 m. RECREATION: Huzzah *State Forest*; Onondaga Cave *State Park* (SR MM, S 3.5 m.). SNAKE PIT CAVE: Actually a sink (*Collapsed Cave Systems*), the cave has been reported to be about 25 feet deep with a nearly circular 50-by-60-foot rim. Below the rim is an oblong 50-by-25-foot underground lake. Caution: the pit's namesakes can be seen sunning themselves among the ferns. E 0.3 m.; inquire locally.

Route 66 Sights. ARCHITECTURE: Old 66 Cafe, Route 66 Lounge, and Wagon Wheel Motel. In town, SR ZZ. SCENIC DRIVE / PARK: Exit 214. SR ZZ and Old U.S. 66 on S side of I-44, E to Bourbon (above); Oak Grove Wayside Park en route. (*Route 66*)

1. Postmaster G. W. Jamison's wife; p.o. 1857–1860.
2. Saint Clodoald, whose grandfather established a monastery in France during the 6th century at the site of St. Cloud, now a suburb of Paris; no p.o.
3. Bourbonton post office (1849–1857) in Boone County (*Centralia: Sturgeon*) was named for Bourbon County, Ky., which honors the French royal family.
4. William Harrison; p.o. 1830–unknown, probably a substation at a mail road (established Sept. 30, 1830).

DANVILLE
Estimated population: 69   Map G-4

The town was platted along the *Boonslick Trail* as the third county seat of Montgomery County, replacing Lewiston (*High Hill*) when the county's size was reduced in 1834. Named for Danville, Va., which was named for Dan Beckwith, an 1824 trader, Danville prospered as an educational, religious, and political center until burned in 1864 by *Civil War* bushwhacker Bill Anderson (*Centralia*). Nearby *Montgomery City*, located along the North Missouri *Railroad,* continued to gain in importance as a trading center and finally won selection as the county seat in 1924, leaving Danville to decline. Post offices: Loutre Lick *(Mineola)* 1818–1823, 1827–1834; Danville 1834–1942.

Danville Female Academy. Greek Revival, 1859. All that remains of this successful women's college, chartered in 1857, is this structure, which was later used as a Methodist church; private. In town.

Davault Tavern. A red granite marker notes the site of this 1828 tavern, one of many along the historic *Boonslick Trail.* I-70 at SR 19; S. Outer Rd., E 0.2 m.

Graham Cave State Park. I-70 N. Outer Rd. (SR TT), W approx. 2 m. *(State Parks)*

Graham Rock. A popular picnic site for motorists on old US 40, this sandstone outcropping (now between the lanes of I-70) is 11–20 feet high and 50 feet in diameter. I-70, W 2.2 m.

Natural Areas. DANVILLE GLADE: 48 acres. Part of Danville *Wildlife Area.* Features about six acres of limestone glades with plants like little bluestem, pale coneflower, and false pennyroyal; dominant trees are 90–120 years old. Box 2, Williamsburg 63388. I-70; S. Outer Rd., E approx. 2 m.; SR RB, S 2.7 m. GRAHAM CAVE GLADES: 82 acres. Features sandstone and limestone glades and a small headwater valley surrounded by sandstone cliffs and rocky hills. HCR Box 138, Montgomery City 63361. In Graham Cave *State Park* (above).

Sylvester Marion Baker House. Greek Revival, c. 1853–1855. This two-story red-brick house with a wide central hallway survived Anderson's raid (Danville history, above), as did its owner S. M. Baker, a Union sympathizer and U.S. marshall. The county's first fair was held on the grounds. Private. I-70, E approx. 2 m. on N. Outer Rd.

Williamsburg, Mo. Established in 1835 by B. G. D. Moxley, it reportedly was named for Harvey Williams, but there is no supporting evidence of why. Because the post office originally spelled its named Williamsburgh, and because the first settlers, including Alexander Fruit (p.o., below), were Kentuckians, there is good cause to suppose the namesake was transferred from 1819 Williamsburg(h), Whitley County, Ky., which was named for Col. William Whitley (1749–1813), who died of wounds during the Battle of the Thames, an American victory that secured the Detroit frontier; Indian confederacy leader Tecumseh *(County Profiles: Johnson; Gainesville: Tecumseh)* also died there. Post offices: Fruits[1] 1824–1835; Williamsburg(h) 1835–now. *(Boonslick Trails).* CRANES GENERAL STORE: General Store, early 1900s. Woodstove, wooden floors, collections (toys, arrowheads, pipes). In town. WHETSTONE CREEK NATURAL AREA: 1.75 miles of creek,

100 yards along either side. A small highly productive stream with short riffles and long deep pools. Features 34 species of fish (including the endangered blacknose shiner), water willows, and spike rushes. Nearly treeless banks are bordered on one side by steep wooded bluffs. Box 2, Williamsburg 63388. Access: walking from parking lot 0.5 m. S of area at NW side of Whetstone Creek *Wildlife Area;* GR, NW approx. 5 m.; inquire locally.

1. Postmaster Alexander Fruite, who was the first postmaster in this part of the county.

DEFIANCE
Estimated population: 100   Map H-4

Two farming communities began a rivalry for a depot and support services for the Missouri, Kansas & Eastern *Railroad.* The winner would become a town and the area's trading center. Matson[1] (SR 94, W 1.8 m.), already negotiating with the railroad, had the advantage, but W. L. Parsons and James P. Craig quickly organized local farmers to meet railroad depot requirements by building a farm-to-market road to the outlying area (today's county road, S of Main). The competition was a draw. Matson was awarded a depot and water stop; Defiance gained a depot, stockyard, and sidetrack. The town was platted in 1893 by Jessie Ann Silvey on her property. Its name, as celebrated in Craig's 1894 poem "Defiance," commemorates defying the odds against gaining railroad services and becoming a town, as well as defying its rival, Matson. Post office: 1893–now.

Boone Country Winery. Vernacular, c. 1900. Features fruit-flavored wines. Overlooks the Missouri River; tours, tasting, picnics. SR 94, W 2 m.

Boone Fort and Cabin Site / Shobe House. Greek Revival, 1848. This two-story brick house with a full-height entry porch, built by the grandfather of Matson's town founder, is set at the site of Daniel Boone's 1812 fort and near the site of Daniel Morgan Boone's log cabin, where Daniel and Rebecca lived (Boone Home, below). Private. SR 94 S to Matson; GR, W 0.1 m. to bridge; private gravel drive, N 0.1 m. *(Boonslick Trails)*

Boone Home. Georgian, 1803–1810 (possibly 1808–1813); National Historic Register. This two-story limestone house with basement and attic is set on a gentle rise above the Femme Osage Creek. The house was built on property owned by Daniel Boone's son, Nathan. Daniel died here in 1820 at age 86 *(Marthasville: Boone Burial Site);* Nathan lived here until moving to Greene County *(Ash Grove)* in 1836. Boone, the legendary explorer, made his last cross-country trip from here in 1818. Inspired by the descriptions of Wyoming's Yellowstone by John Colter *(Washington: Dundee)*, Boone walked there and back at age 84. Furnished and restored; tours. Grounds: an elm with a 17.5-foot circumference, which is near the site of a log cabin built in 1805 by Daniel for his wife, Rebecca, and himself. SR 94, N 2 m.; SR F, W 5 m. *(Boonville: Daniel Boon[e])*

Cottleville, Mo. Platted in 1839 by Lorenzo Cottle on his 1803 Spanish land grant along the *Boonslick Trail* near the sites of several earlier post office communities. Post offices: McConnell's[2] 1827–c. 1829; Dardenne Bridge[3] 1827–1833; Stockland[4] 1833–1839; Relief[5] 1836–1839; Cottleville 1843–now. SR 94, E 12.6 m.; SR N, NW 1.8 m.

Daniel Boone Historic Area. A 150-square-mile portion of southwestern St. Charles County has been designated a historic area for its late 18th- and early 19th-century Boone and Boone-related settlements. This area, a small portion of the 1799–1820 Boone Settlement, was settled by Daniel Boone and his family after Daniel was recruited in 1798 from Kentucky by Spanish Lt. Gov. Zenon Trudeau as civil administrator and commandant of a large area called the Femme Osage District. Boone's son Daniel Morgan came here first in 1797, but it was Daniel Boone's 1799 arrival that helped encourage immigration of American frontier families *(Cape Girardeau)*. Bounded by SR T, SR N *(Boonslick Trails)*, US 61/40, SR DD, Weldon Spring *Wildlife Area*, and the Missouri River.

Katy Trail State Park. In Defiance and Matson on SR 94. *(State Parks)*

Missouri / Missouriton, Mo. In 1818 the "Missouri Gazette" advertised a sale of lots by Daniel Morgan Boone in the town of Missouri, which was platted on part of Daniel Boone's original Spanish land grant near the river. The Boones sold their interest in 1819. Later the town's name was given as Missouriton (possibly changed to avoid confusion with the state's name). By the early 1870s the Missouri River had washed away all but the post office. From Weldon Spring *Wildlife Area* south to SR 94 at the river, county maps show land grant survey lines. Post offices: Femme Osage *(Augusta: Femme Osage)* 1816–1818, 1828–1833; Missouriton 1833–1880. Defiance Rd., E and S to end of road, or due E of Matson. No remnants.

Missouri Territory Village. Begun in 1974, this private project to restore and reconstruct exemplary 19th-century structures includes many from the early 1800s. All are authentic and most were moved here to prevent their destruction. BORGMAN MILL: 1840s; possibly America's only surviving example of an animal-powered *gristmill*; all-wooden gears. CALLAWAY HOUSE: c. 1811; home of Daniel Boone's daughter

Jemima and her husband, Flanders Callaway *(County Profiles: Callaway)*; Rebecca Boone (Daniel's wife) died in this two-story, double-room, log house in 1813 *(Marthasville: Boone Burial Site)*. FUCHS-WESSLER MILL: 1840s; 40-foot-tall yellow-limestone *gristmill*. LOG STRUCTURES: Among many are these one-room structures: two churches (1840, 1850), a school (mid-1800s), a tobacco barn (mid-1800s), a blacksmith shop (mid-1800s), and a house (1810–1815). NEWTON HOWELL HOUSE: c. 1814; two-story, two-room log. SQUIRE BOONE HOUSE: Daniel Boone's brother began building what was one of the first stone houses west of the Mississippi in 1800–1802 *(Troy: Monroe / Old Monroe)*. The village is not yet (1994) open to the public. Some structures can be seen from the road. Permission to visit: stamped self-addressed envelope, 935 Terrill Farms Rd., St. Louis 63124. SR 94, N 2 m.; SR F, W 6.2 m.

Parsons Cemetery. Among those buried here is Z. Moore, a Revolutionary War soldier who lived in this area from 1810 to 1825. Main, E 2.5 blocks on Lee. *(Cemeteries)*

Pleasant Hill Cemetery. Formerly part of David Darst's c. 1795 Spanish land grant, the site was originally known as Darst Cemetery. Renamed for an 1856 church that burned in the early 1900s. The Darsts and Nathan Boone's son Benjamin Howard are buried here. S 0.5 m.; inquire locally. *(Cemeteries)*

Schluersburg, Mo. Settled by 1840s German immigrants beside a wagon road from *Augusta* to today's SR F, the town was possibly named for its location: at a creek surrounded by hills ("schlucht," German for ravine). ARCHITECTURE: Two log houses. Post office: 1862–1908. SR 94, N 2 m.; SR F, W 4 m.; GR, W 1.8 m.

Thomas Parsons House. Georgian, 1841–1842. Three stories, with 14-inch brick walls, this seven-room house is located in the town's second addition. The original townsite boarders the west side of Main and the north side of SR 94. Main, E to Lee at 3d.

Weldon Spring, Mo. Founded in 1849 along the *Marthasville* Road and named for early settler John Weldon via the spring. Post office: 1875–1957. SR 94, E 10 m. ARCHITECTURE: Two churches: Emmanual Evangelical (two-story brick, Gothic Revival, 1874) and St. John's, which bought property in 1867, merged with a free Protestant group in 1871, and then acquired and remodeled a saloon and dance hall; its doors are from St. Joseph parish in Cottleville (above). KATY TRAIL *STATE PARK:* NE of town off SR 94. WELDON SPRING: Still flows. E side of junction of I-64 (US 40) and SR 94. WELDON SPRING HOLLOW NATURAL AREA: 385 acres. Part of Weldon Spring *Wildlife Area*. Features limestone cliffs, intermittent streams, and rugged river-brake topography. Canadian geese nest in the cliffs. SR 94, E 2 m. Access: trail. Rt. 2, Box 223, St. Charles 63301. *WILDLIFE AREAS:* Busch, Weldon Spring.

1. Family name; p.o. 1893–1971.
2. Personal name; origin unknown.
3. Bridge at Dardenne Creek from family name.
4. Origin unknown but usually from the personal name.
5. Origin unknown but usually from a pioneer-period incident, e.g. Relief Valley, Calif., where an 1850s wagon train was aided by area settlements.

DENVER
Population: 53   Map C-1

Reportedly the first trading center in Worth County, Denver was settled c. 1843 at O. Swaim's *gristmill* and platted in 1851 by William McKnight as Fairview.[1] Due to an existing Fair View post office, this office was named Grant's Hill.[2] When the town was incorporated in 1871, its name and the post office's were consolidated as Denver, a common American place-name that in this case has no recorded derivation.[3] Post offices: Grant's Hill 1854–1871; Denver 1872–now.

Cast Concrete Blocks. Concrete, early 1900s. After downtown businesses were destroyed by fire, new structures were built using individually formed concrete blocks that were cured at the construction site. Typically, the blocks have a distinctive design. The 1913 town bandstand at the city park is a good example.

Denver Bathhouse. Springwater, first judged in 1875 as not fit for drinking or cooking because of its "slight laxative properties," precipitated an 1881 spa boom when the properties of its water were found to match those at Eureka Springs, Ark., a famous health resort town. Remnant; inquire locally.

Seat Wildlife Area. *Wildlife Areas.*

1. Descriptive location.
2. Origin unknown; p.o. 1854–1871.
3. J. W. Denver, governor 1857–1858 of Kansas Territory (then including eastern Colorado), is the namesake of Denver, Colo. Denver is usually from a personal name.

DESLOGE
Population: 4,150   Map H-5

The town was established c. 1887 as Slab Town[1] on the west side of the St. Louis, Iron Mountain & Southern *Railroad* tracks when Firmin Des Loge II of *Bonne Terre* sold his company c. 1886 to the St. Joseph Lead Co. and formed the Desloge Consolidated Lead Co. here. A Desloge post office was established in 1892, but the town was not platted as Desloge until 1930, after the St.

Joseph Lead Co. bought the mining rights (and the town). Together with adjacent Leadville[2] and Three Town (below), Desloge was incorporated in 1941. Post office: 1892–1963. *(Flat River)*

Mining Remnants. Some evidence of mining remains in the form of chat dumps (bald mountains of refuse separated as residue) and a few buildings at Desloge at Doss Streets. Inquire locally.

Nativity of the Virgin Mary. Russian Orthodox Church, c. 1910. This red-brick church with a copper cupola and three-bar crosses had 500 members during the 1920s. Today it serves one of two active Russian Orthodox congregations in Missouri. Visitors welcome. 400 Tyler.

St. Joe State Park. *State Parks.*

Sam Doss House. Vernacular, prior to 1900. Built using clay from a nearby field, this one-story red-brick house has an ornamental black eagle on the roof, which reportedly was taken from the National Lead Company's flagpole by Sam Doss, who later served as county sheriff. In 1926 Doss was gunned down in the kitchen. Private. 411 N. Main.

Three Town. Named for the No. 3 mining shaft and settled by Slavic immigrants recruited as miners, the town is identified today by two-story frame houses built two-rooms-down-and-one-up at the west end of town. The immigrants kept their customs, as is evidenced by Greek and Russian Orthodox churches (Nativity of the Virgin Mary, above) and separate cemeteries. W of US 67B, between SR 8 and SR Z.

1. Because of the slab houses, built from the irregular outside leavings of a squared log; no p.o.
2. A National Lead Co. town on the east side of the tracks previously acquired by St. Joe; no p.o.

DEXTER
Population: 7,559   Map I-7

The site was platted in 1873 by the Cairo, Arkansas & Texas *Railroad*, which built a depot, cut trees out of the proposed streets, and drained the land, which was mostly underwater due to large beaver dams in the area. Tradition claims the town was named for a racehorse. A man named Webb, whose farm was near Dex Creek (origin of name unknown), named his horse Dexter after the creek. Later the horse became regionally famous for winning races at a track in nearby St. Luke.[1] Although it became the county's largest town, and despite its central location, industries, and railroad, Dexter was unsuccessful at securing the county seat from nearby *Bloomington*. Post offices: Dexter City 1873–1887; Dexter 1887–now. (For unknown reasons the federal government occasionally addresses letters to "Dexter City.")

Dexter Heritage House. Vernacular, 1873. This two-room-and-an-attic house, moved from its original location, is Dexter's oldest. SR 114, S on 1 Mile Rd.; E on Market; N 1 block on Cooper.

Natural Areas. BEECH SPRINGS: *Bloomfield.* BRADY-VILLE: 139 acres. Part of Otter Slough *Wildlife Area.* Features a bottomland forest and swamp that support oak, sweet gum, tupelo, cypress, cooper iris, and spider lily. Rt. 3, Box 388B, Dexter 63841. SR 25, S 4.3 m.; SR H, W 6.7 m. HOLLY RIDGE: *Bloomfield.* OTTER SLOUGH: 20 acres. An aquatic area of Otter Slough *Wildlife Area.* Features a shallow winding slough that supports swamp tupelo, buttonbush, the endangered pugnose minnow, and the rare bantam sunfish. Address, directions: Bradyville, above.

Otter Slough Wildlife Area. *Wildlife Areas.*

1. The apostle; no p.o.

DONIPHAN
Population: 1,713   Map H-7

Lemeul Kittrell, Ripley County's first settler (1819), built a house and a *gristmill* at the Current River near the future townsite. In 1847, after reductions in the size of the county, the townsite's first settler (with an 1837 land patent), George Lee, donated about 21 acres for a more centrally located county seat to replace *Van Buren.* Platted in 1847, the town was named for Missouri statesman and long-time lawyer Alexander William Doniphan (1808–1887), who led Missouri troops into Mexico during the 1846–1848 *Mexican War* and whose other namesakes include a WWI Oklahoma training camp, a WWII ship, a city in Nebraska, and a county and a city in Kansas. The town's location at a ford of the Current River and at a *road* between *Potosi* and Little Rock, Ark., helped it grow as a trading center. Post office: 1847–now. Home of Current River Area Vo-Tech.

Architecture. DOWNTOWN: good examples of 19th-century commercial styles.

Barrett House. Queen Anne, 1881; National Historic Register. Features Eastlake detailing, an authentic color pattern, a projecting two-story entrance, bracketed cornices, and balustrades. 209 Plum.

Current River Heritage Museum. Established in 1922, this 7,000-square-foot museum exhibits historical items, e.g. arts and crafts, school mementos, and military memorabilia; extensive historical records. E side of square.

Doniphan Cemetery. This carefully maintained cemetery was established c. 1840. S 1 block from courthouse. *(Cemeteries)*

Grandin, Mo. Established c. 1885 by the Missouri Lumber and Mining Company. Reportedly, this mining company was once the site of Missouri's largest yellow pine sawmill. The peak population before the mill closed in 1909 was 2,000 *(Bunker).* Named for E. B. and George Grandin, major company stockholders. Post offices: Lee[1] 1878–1887; Grandin 1887–now. US 160, W 2 m.; SR 21, N 18 m. MISSOURI LUMBER AND MINING COMPANY: Vernacular, c. 1888; National Historic Register. Office and bank. In town.

Heritage Park. Set in a triangular block of historic downtown: gazebo, benches, fountain, memorial stone. Washington, 1 block E of square.

The Narrows. About three-fourths of a highway lane wide, 100 feet high, and flanked by steep bluffs, this narrow ridge divides the Eleven Point River and Fredrick Creek. Springs, karst formations *(Collapsed Cave Systems).* US 160, W 2 m.; SR 142, W 21 m. to Eleven Point River bridge.

Natural Areas. CUPOLA POND: 160 acres, National Natural Landmark. Part of Mark Twain *National Forest.* Features a 2.5-acre sinkhole pond *(Collapsed Cave Systems)* ringed by tupelo gum trees surrounded by an Ozark upland forest. 1105 Jackson, Doniphan 63935. US 160, W 20 m.; SR J, N approx. 9.3 m.; FR 3224, E approx. 1.2 m.; FR 4823, N approx. 1.5 m. RED MAPLE: 84 acres. One of Missouri's three pond swamps, this is the only one dominated by red maples; two varieties of sedge. 1105 Jackson, Doniphan 63935. US 160, W 11 m.; SR C, N approx. 10.8 m. (approx. 1.8 m. N of cemetery at Barren Creek bridge). SAND PONDS: 68 acres. Two sections of Sand Pond Natural History Area feature an upland sand forest, a bottomland forest, and small sand dunes associated with shallow depressions. Federal endangered species include pondberry, corkwood, and mud snake. 1207 N. 1 Mile Rd., Dexter 63841. SR 142, E 16 m. through Oxly[2] to Naylor;[3] continue SR 142, S 0.5 m.; SR W, S 4 m. WELLS BRANCH FEN: 2 acres. Bedrock underlies this open *prairie* fen with scatter trees and small shrubs that protect the endangered yellow-eyed grass and false loosestrife. 1105 Jackson, Doniphan 63935. US 160, W approx. 3 m.; GR and FR 4811, N approx. 3 m.; walk W 200 feet.

Old Ripley County Jail. Vernacular, 1898–1899; National Historic Register. This two-story brick structure served as a jail and sheriff's residence until about 1960; it is now an office building. S side of square.

Recreation. BUFFALO CREEK CAMPGROUND *(National Forests):* Picnic, no fee, water, pit toilets, fire ring, creek fishing; RV limit: 22 feet. DEER LEAP CAMPGROUND *(National Forests):* Water, pit toilets,

Current River fishing. FLOAT CAMP CAMP-
GROUND / PICNIC AREA *(National Forests)*: White
Oak Forest and Woodchuck *Trails*, water, tables, toilets,
grills, Current River fishing, swimming, waterskiing.
FLOAT STREAMS: Current and Jacks Fork Rivers.
FOURCHE LAKE: 49 acres. Bass, sunfish, catfish. SR
21, S 6 m.; SR CC, W 2.2 m.; GR, S 1.9 m. RIPLEY LAKE
PICNIC AREA *(National Forests)*: Water, boat ramp,
tables, grills, toilets, fishing in Ripley Lake (20 acres;
bass, sunfish, catfish). *STATE FORESTS*: Fourche
Creek (SR 142, W 12 m.; SR P, S 2.7 m. to main tract;
others along and bounded by SR 142, SR Z, and GR)
and Little Black. *TRAILS*: White Oak Forest /
WoodChuck.

Ripley County Courthouse. Second Empire, 1898 –
1899; National Historic Register. Set on a cut-stone
basement and foundation, this two-story brick courthouse, the county's third, has a dominant central tower
with arched and oval windows, dormers and a cupola,
a mansard roof, and four corner pavilions with dormers and metal cresting. Cost: $20,000 (extensive remod-
eling and central air/heat 1976, $325,000). Downtown.
(County Profiles)

SR 142 Road Cut. Remaining layers of about 60 feet of
sandstone, chert, and clay graphically demonstrate the
dissolving powers of percolating groundwater on
limestone and dolomite *(Collapsed Cave Systems)*. US
160, S 2 m.; SR 142, S approx. 1 m.

    1. Doniphan merchant Daniel Lee.
    2. Wood products businessman F. G. Oxly of Cincinnati, Ohio;
p.o. Varner, the townsite owner Daniel Varner, 1883–1900; Oxly
1900–now.
    3. Local lumber land surveyor William A. Naylor; p.o. Barfield,
O. F. Barfield who donated townsite, 1883–1892; Naylor 1892–now.

DORENA
Estimated population: 400   Map J-7

This turn-of-the-century community is set at a
Mississippi River landing across from Hickman, Ky.
Reportedly, its name was coined by the postmaster,
who altered the 1890s slang for money, doreen, thinking it would be a lucky name. However, the story is
questionable because doreen's derivative, dough (c.
1850 slang), was used in the sense of bribe money or
money obtained unethically, and a Dorena post office
(1898 only) had been established previously in Ripley
County. Dorena, Ore., was named in 1901 for two
women, Dora and Rena. Post office: 1899–1915,
1919–1973.

Big Oak Tree Natural Area. 940 acres. Part of Big Oak
Tree *State Park*. Features a bottomland swamp, presettlement forest, and over 146 species of birds. It is

Missouri's only known location of the western chicken
turtle. Self-guiding trail, half-mile boardwalk. Rt. 2,
Box 343, East Prairie 63845. SR PP, W 2.1 m.; SR 102, N
1.9 m.

Frontline Levee Road. A short gravel road on the
levee's crown leads past borrow pits (areas from which
dirt was taken for the levee) that now are filled with
water and support wildlife like blue herons, eagles,
Mississippi kite, Canadian geese, cardinals, and blue-
birds. SR 77, S 2 m.; SR A, west. BIRDS POINT–NEW
MADRID FLOODWAY: *East Prairie*.

Nearby Points of Interest. BELMONT BATTLEFIELD:
SR 77N, N 13 m.; SR 80, E 6 m. *(East Prairie)*. 34 COR-
NER BLUE HOLE: SR 77, N 13 m. WOLF ISLAND: SR
77N, N 10 m.; SR 77 spur, E 0.6 m.

Recreation. BIG OAK TREE *STATE PARK*: Big Oak
Tree Natural Area, above. SEVEN ISLAND *WILDLIFE
AREA*.

Towosahgy State Historic Site. These Mississippian
period mounds *(Indians)*, dating from 1000–1400 A.D.,
were set inside a fortified village of about 75 houses.
The largest mound is 180 feet wide, 250 feet long, and
16 feet tall. Those who lived here were part of a sophisticated culture that probably traded with nearby
Cahokia *(Kahoka)* and other Nodena Phase Mississippian groups like the temple-mound builders in
West Tennessee and Mississippi, whose successors
were the Chickasaw *Indians*. Located on otherwise
level farmland, today's mounds appear to be small
hills covered with vegetation. Undeveloped. SR 77, N
5.5 m.; GR (at Mt. Zion Church), W 1.9 m.

DOWNING
Population: 359   Map F-1

Formerly a post office community named Cherry
Grove,[1] the town was platted in 1872 along the tracks
of the Iowa & Nebraska *Railroad* by the Missouri Town
Company and named for its president, H. H. Downing.
Post office: 1873 – now.

Architecture. BUCHANAN HOUSE: Queen Anne, c.
1895; fish-scale shingles, bracketed tower. SR A, S end
of town. CUMBERLAND PRESBYTERIAN CHURCH:
Carpenter Gothic, 1893; two-story central bell tower.
SR A, N on Cook. TOWN: Good examples of 19th-
century architecture.

Downing City Lake. Fishing: bass, bluegill, catfish. SR
N, N approx. 2 m.

Downing Depot Museum. Railroad, 1872; National
Historic Register. Board-and-batten with pressed metal
shingles, bracketed eaves, and tall narrow windows,
the building was moved here from its original location.

Interior features include plaster walls, beaded paneling, and a ticket window. Displays: local items, quilts, tools, military memorabilia. The former one-room stucco city jail (1930s) is adjacent. SR A, S end of town at city park.
Grand Divide. *Grand Divide.*

1. A cherry grove; p.o. 1848–1873.

DUTZOW
Estimated population: 100   Map H-4

Founded in 1832 and platted in 1835 by William Bock, Dutzow was reportedly named for his estate in Germany. This site is supposedly the first (1824) recorded land in Missouri settled by a European-born German (Gottfried Duden, below). Always a farming community, today it has a small downtown (post office and general store) and some well-preserved 19th-century architecture. Post office: 1869–now.
Blumenhof Vineyards. The vineyards specialize in dry table wines but offer a wide variety from American and European grapes. Tours, tasting, picnics. SR 94, E 0.5 m.; signs.
Gottfried Duden. Born in the Rhine province of Germany in 1785, Duden spent 1824–1827 at today's Dutzow, returning to Germany to write an account of his observations. His 1829 best-selling book, today known as "The Duden Book," described Missouri as paradise, which contributed greatly (along with Germany's political, economic, and religious turmoil) to 19th-century German immigration to Missouri. A hill near town bears his name. MUENCH STONE BARN: Stone, mid-1800s. Marks Duden's farmsite. SR TT, N approx. 2 m.; private road, E 0.1 m.; inquire locally.
Katy Trail State Park. SR 94 S of town. *(State Parks)*
St. Vincent De Paul. Gothic Revival, 1874. This impressive landmark, brick with a tall spire and arched stained-glass windows, set on a ridge high above the Missouri River bottomland, can be seen from SR 47. The adjacent *cemetery* has ornate markers. SR 94, S 1 m.

EAST PRAIRIE
Population: 3,416   Map J-7

Called Belgrade or Bell's Grade[1] when graded in 1881 as a railroad right-of-way, the townsite was platted in 1883 as Hibbard[2] by a St. Louis–based corporation, the Southwestern Improvement Association, along the tracks of the Texas, Arkansas & St. Louis *Railroad.* That same year, Dr. S. P. Martin moved the East Prairie post office one mile south from his farm on the eastern edge

The Battle of Belmont, November 7, 1861.

A Knox County farm, c. 1900. (FROM WILLIAMS, "THE STATE OF MISSOURI")

of a large *prairie* to this location, buying the first lot and erecting a building. Exactly when the town name was changed is uncertain. One source claims the city council changed it in 1890 (probably complying with *post office* regulations), after which legal descriptions for city property read: "City of East Prairie, formerly Hibbard." However, county records of July 26 and September 25, 1900, are notarized City of Hibbard. Also, the 1895 newspaper, the city's first, was the *Hibbard Banner*, which, with a short lapse, operated until 1900. The next newspaper was the 1901 *Leader*, followed by the 1905 *East Prairie Eagle*. Post office: 1872, 1879–now.

Battlefield / Belmont, Mo. Reportedly platted in 1853 by a stock company, the town was named for New Yorker John Belmont. Once the terminus for a branch of the St. Louis, Iron Mountain & Southern *Railroad*, it is now defunct. Post offices: Belmont Landing 1867–1868; Belmont 1869–1923. BATTLE OF BELMONT: November 7, 1861. This was reportedly U. S. Grant's first battle. He was poised to attack Fort De Russey at Columbus, Ky., which was held by about 10,000 Confederates. Grant intended this battle at Belmont, across the river from Fort De Russey, to be a demonstration of the Federal strength massed at Cairo, Ill. Using ships in an amphibious assault, he attacked Belmont from the Mississippi River, forcing the Confederates to retreat after four hours of sharp fighting. Overconfident, the Federals set no defenses and were counterattacked that same day by a reinforced Confederate command that drove them back onto their transports. Losses: Federal, 607; Confederate, 642. SR 80, E 16 m. No signs; undeveloped.

Birds Point–New Madrid Floodway. East Prairie sits nearly midway along a large floodplain that is protected from the Mississippi and Ohio Rivers by three levee systems: (1) Mainline Levee from *Birds Point* north to Commerce;[3] (2) Setback Levee running diagonally southeast from Birds Point to *New Madrid*; and (3) Frontline Levee along the Mississippi River *(Dorena: Frontline Levee Road; Cape Girardeau: Little River Drainage District;* Lakes: 34 Corner Blue Hole, below).

Lakes. 34 CORNER BLUE HOLE: 9 acres. Formed when the levee failed, this small circular lake surrounded by shade trees still receives river overflow (Birds Point, above). Stocked with bass, sunfish, crappie, catfish, and carp. SR 80, E 12 m. UPPER BIG LAKE: 110 acres. Same as 34 Corner but no carp. Nearby; inquire locally.

Nearby Points of Interest. BIG OAK TREE *STATE PARK:* SR 102, S 11 m. TEN MILE POND *WILDLIFE AREA.* TOWOSAHGY STATE ARCHAEOLOGICAL SITE: *Dorena;* SR 80, E 10 m.; SR 77, S 7.5 m.; GR (at Mt. Zion Church), W 1.9 m.

Wolf Island, Mo. This c. 1846 post office community was named for nearby Wolf Island (below), which received its name in 1792 for the wolves seen on it. Post office: 1846–1860, 1868–now. (This post office building, about the size of a storage shed, is probably Missouri's smallest.) SR 80, E 10 m.; SR 77, S 2.7 m. THONG TREE: Located in the center of a group of trees; points northeast *(Thong Tree).* SR 77, N past Story Farm headquarters; near E side of SR 77. WOLF ISLAND NO. 5: While this island and the ones north of it appear to be part of Missouri, they are owned by Kentucky. In 1901, Wolf Island was reportedly the largest Mississippi River island (approx. 5,000 acres). SR 77 spur, E 0.6 m.

1. The grade contractor Bell; no p.o.
2. The railroad surveyor Hibbard; p.o. East Prairie.
3. Commendatory; p.o. 1834–now.

EDINA
Population: 1,283   Map F-2

Anticipating the 1845 organization of Knox County, William J. Smallwood bought land here in 1839 at an assumed central location, setting aside four blocks for a county seat site that Steven W. B. Carnegy, formerly of Edinburgh, Scotland, then surveyed and named Edina, which is a coined name popularized by previous Edinburgh immigrants. Carnegy also named the adjacent Scotland County and, in it, a town, Edinburgh.[1] Edina was designated county seat in 1845. Post office: 1841–now.

Architecture. The town square has some good examples of 19th-century commercial buildings. The south side burned in 1881, was rebuilt by 1886, and mostly retains that period's style.

Historical Museum. Features local historical items and photographs. Lower level of courthouse.

Knox County Courthouse. Italian Renaissance, 1934–1935. The county's second, this two-story brick courthouse has a pseudo-rusticated first level, a different window treatment on each floor, a pedimented entry, projecting wings, and a roofline parapet. After the former courthouse burned (suspected arson) on Christmas Eve of 1885, offices were rented for 50 years. Cost: $80,000 *WPA* grant. Downtown. *(County Profiles)*

Knox County Sever Lake. SR 15, S 1 m.; SR 6, W 6 m.; SR A, S 3 m. *(Newark: Sever Wildlife Area / Lake)*

The Missouri Giantess. *South Gorin.*

Novelty, Mo. Two stories try to explain this name: (1) Dr. Tom Pendry, an eccentric who built the first store, placed a flagpole on it as a guide. He named the place for the store's assortment of merchandise. (2) Pendry built a store, house, and office. To make the office easier to find, he raised a flag over it. His wife said the flag was a novel idea. Usually applied to villages as an unusual name, the name is not novel. Post office: 1854–now. SR 15, S 11 m.; SR 156, W 1 m.

St. Joseph's Catholic Church. Gothic Revival affinities, 1872–1875; remodeled. This 137-by-67-foot church, set on a rock foundation, has red brick trimmed with green Warsaw sandstone. The 1894 steeple appears to be twice as tall as the city watertower. The original mosaic slate roof was replaced by copper in the 1970s. The adjacent 1837 *cemetery* has ornate markers. Main at Marion.

1. P.o. 1840–1845.

ELDON

Population: 4,419   Map F-5

Platted in 1882 along a branchline of the Missouri-Pacific *Railroad* two miles north of a popular spa, Aurora Springs (below), the town according to one story was to be named Almira for founder George Weeks's wife, but the name was changed to Eldon (sup-

posedly for the British Lord Eldon) because of an existing Almira. Other sources state the town was named for a railroad surveyor but list no specifics. In fact, the Eldon post office (the first postmaster was John Weeks, George's brother) was named before the town was platted, and there is no Almira (or close spelling) in Missouri postal records from 1804 to 1886, although there was an Elmira post office from 1887 to 1959. To add to the confusion, historical accounts spell Mrs. Weeks's name as Elmira, although her family spells it with an "A." Another Eldon (Wapello County, Iowa) about 220 miles north, also platted as a railroad town (1870), claims to be named for John Scott Eldon, Lord of Eldon (1751–1838), who was a member of parliament, Lord Chancellor for much of 1801–1827, and reportedly visited the area, remarking that it was beautiful (no records confirm his travel). Missouri's Eldon claims that Weeks, who immigrated in 1865 from New England, traced his ancestry back to England. Most historians agree that Lord Eldon, an extreme conservative, had no interest in America. Construction of the Lake of the Ozarks (below) helped the town prosper. Post office: 1881–now. Home of Tri-County Technical School.

Aurora Springs, Mo. Billed as "The Great Sanitarium of the West," the town had an 1881 population of 700, a Western Union telegraph office, daily stage service to Jefferson City, and daily mail. Its classical name translates from Latin as dawn and also refers to the goddess of dawn, an allusion to new beginnings. A decline in the belief in the curative powers of water and the growth of nearby Eldon reduced it to weeds and trees. Post office: 1882–1912. SR 54B/52 at Eldon S city limits, E 0.7 m.; CR 52-10, S approx. 0.2 m.; GR, W; turn to cross creek, then left. SPRINGS: Still flow; derelict.

Eldon Caboose. Set at the original location of the depot was the spot where trains came to rest after rolling backward down a slight grade, this caboose marks the spot around which the town grew. Downtown; 2d and Maple.

Fantasy World Caverns. Large underground lake, flowstone, petrified algae, complex formations, guided tours. US 54B/54, S 3.25 m.

Fred E. Shane Mural. 1940–1941. This 5-by-15-foot mural, commissioned by the Treasury Department under its fine arts competition during the Depression *(WPA)*, depicts a picnic in the Ozarks. The artist included himself in the mural as the man holding his plate out for food. Downtown; post office.

Park. Shade trees, picnic shelters, swings. SR 54B, near S city limits.

Recreation. LAKE OF THE OZARKS. LAKE OF THE OZARKS *STATE PARK.* SALINE VALLEY *WILDLIFE AREA.*

Saline Valley Wildlife Area. *Wildlife Areas.*

EL DORADO SPRINGS
Population: 3,830   Map D-5

Local tradition claims that Mrs. Joshua Hightower, on her way to Eureka Springs, Ark., in 1881 "to take the cure," was forced by ill health to stop here. After drinking the water for two weeks, she was able to return home. Her cure was so widely publicized that a town—complete with a post office, hotel, store, and other buildings—was platted and incorporated that same year by brothers N. H. and W. P. Cruse. The stock name is derived from Dorado (Spanish for gilded), stemming from the legend of the "gilded man," which was later applied to a place of fabulous wealth, especially in gold. Post offices: El Dorado Springs 1881–1894, 1940–now; Eldorado Springs 1894–1940.

Natural Areas. SCHELL-OSAGE *PRAIRIE* RELICTS: Five separate tracts, totaling 41.5 acres. Small and hard to find, these tracts contain 41.5 acres of high-quality prairies in the Schell-Osage Wildlife Area. Box 137, Shell City 64783. SR 82, N 3 m.; SR H, N 6.2 m.; SR Y, W approx. 1.3 m. SCHELL-OSAGE *WILDLIFE AREA*. TABERVILLE PRAIRIE: 1,360 acres. A National Natural Landmark and Missouri's largest *prairie* natural area (a remnant of about 28,000 square miles) features upland prairie, sandstone outcroppings, prairie mounds, a headwater stream, wildflowers, native tallgrasses, and one of Missouri largest populations of prairie chickens. Rt. 2, Box 93, Lockwood 65682. SR 82, N 3 m.; SR H, N 7.9 to Taberville,[1] SR H, N approx. 2.5 m.

Spring Park. This inviting park is situated in a natural bowl landscaped in three tiers and lined with benches. At the bottom is a springhouse flanked by a presettlement stone washbasin. A nearby fishpond grotto and a bandstand (the site of weekend concerts) are accented by folk-art rockwork. A community building, picnic area, playground, and pool are adjacent. The original spring (50 feet SW of present bandstand) was channeled in 1890 to the springhouse, around which today's park grew. Bring a jug. SR 82, downtown.

1. The first settler, Taber; p.o. 1866–1968.

ELLINGTON
Population: 994   Map H-6

Ellington's early history involves three families and three town names. About 1835, Thomas Barnes bought land along Logan's Creek and built a *gristmill* and distillery on the north side, around which grew the community of Barnesville/Logan's Creek.[1] James and Sina Huff Ellington lived nearby; Landon Copeland settled 10 miles east c. 1839. In 1845 the Logan's Creek post office was established, but Barnesville was selected as the town's name in 1848, resulting in the community being called both Barnesville and Logan's Creek. James Ellington left for the California gold fields c. 1849. Sina stayed, buying land in 1856 (with her own money) that would later become Ellington's townsite. During the *Civil War*, Barnesville was mostly destroyed by partisan fighting and by flooding. About 1868, William Copeland (who had married an Ellington) returned to Logan's Creek. He built a saw/*gristmill* c. 1870 on the south side; after his death ("soon after" mill construction), his sons M. L. and W. A. cleared farmland and platted a town, Barnesville, that was later replatted when the Missouri Southern *Railroad* arrived in 1896 and renamed Ellington for postmaster M. L. Copeland's grandmother, Sina Ellington. The Logan's Creek post office had already been renamed Ellington in 1895 in line with 1892 *post office* directives; Barnesville was not available as a post office name because it was already in use (Macon County 1878–1904). Post offices: Logan's Creek 1845–1863, 1867–1895; Ellington 1895–now. (*Centerville: Reynolds County Courthouse*)

Spring Park, El Dorado Springs.

Garwood, Mo. Garwood was platted in 1914 along the tracks of the Missouri Southern *Railroad*. Its remaining architecture is typical of rural railroad towns that sprang up in Reynolds County during the lumber boom *(Buckner)*. The origin of its name is not known. Post office: 1907–1959. SR 21, S 16 m.; SR 34, E 2 m. GENERAL STORE: Vernacular, c. 1887. Still in business. Elevated covered porch; new advertising signs have replaced older ones. RAILROAD HOUSE: Vernacular, c. 1887. Built for the section foreman by the Missouri Southern. Weathered clapboard, tin roof. Next to general store. SCHOOLHOUSE: *WPA*, 1939. Two rooms, cement and small-rock walls.

Gravel Spring. Part of Ozark National Scenic Riverways *(National Parks)*. The subtle outlet from a small gravel bar belies the 11-million-gallon daily flow of 58°F water. SR 21, S 8 m.; SR D, S 1 m.; GR, W 4 m. to colorful Paint Rock at the Current River (E side, just downstream).

Recreation. CLEARWATER LAKE AND DAM: *Lakes: Corps of Engineers*. CORPS OF ENGINEERS RECREATION AREA: Swimming, camping, fishing. SR K, E 18 m. to bridge at Black River. OZARK NATIONAL SCENIC RIVERWAYS *(National Parks)*: Beal Landing, Logyard, and Paint Rock river access. STATE FORESTS: Reynolds County is one of three Missouri counties (along with adjacent Carter and Shannon) that has over 80 percent of its land in forests, which have recovered from being nearly stripped bare during the lumber boom of c. 1885–1915 *(Bunker)*. Ellington, except to the east-northeast, is nearly ringed by state forests: Bloom Creek, Cardareva, Carr Creek, Clearwater, Deer Run (site of Missouri's first fire tower, 1926), Dickens Valley, Logan Creek (4 tracts from SR 106 / SR B and between SR B and SR F), Paint Rock, Powder Mill, and Webb Creek.

1. The creek via Thomas Logan.

EMINENCE
Population: 582   Map G-6

Little recorded history remains due to four courthouse fires. Eminence has had two locations. The first, on the north bank of the Current River about two miles below Round Spring (Ozark National Scenic Riverways, below), was selected in 1841 as a central location for the county seat of Shannon County by settlers from Kentucky and Tennessee. A post office was established in 1844, and a log courthouse was built in 1845. Loss of its central location, due to reductions in the county's size in 1845 and 1859, and the destruction of the town during the *Civil War* resulted in the county court's selection of a new site. County judge and site selection commissioner Thomas J. Chilton, after finding no suitable land with clear titles, deeded 50 acres for the new county seat along the Jacks Fork River, where today's town was platted in 1868. While some histories refer to the first Eminence as being on a bluff, it was actually located in the Current River valley on a narrow terrace at the base of a steep hill. The original Eminence was named for the Kentucky hometown of Shannon County namesake Judge George "Pegleg" Shannon and county surveyor Robert M. Shannon. Post office: 1844–now. (Maps of 1847, 1848, and 1861 show Nimrod,[1] Chilton,[2] and Chiltonsville, respectively, as the county seat, with no Eminence listed at all; no evidence supports these cartographers' anomalies.)

Architecture. National Historic Register: Chilton-Williams Farm Complex and Rhinehart Ranch (Spring Valley Ranch); inquire locally.

Forty-Acre Sinkhole. About 11–15 acres; 180 feet deep, 300 yards in diameter. The hole appears to have been caused by a massive explosion but really was slowly eroded by groundwater *(Collapsed Cave Systems)*. SR 106, W 12.5 m. (0.5 m. E of junction with SR D), look for country lane, turn E, 0.1 m. Or from Flat Rock Lookout Tower at junction of SR 106 and SR D, look SE.

Ink, Mo. When postmaster George Shedd applied for a *post office*, he complied with a recommendation from the postmaster general's office (in anticipation of the January 1886 Postal Guide's official suggestion) to keep the name short. Shedd sent a number of three-letter names to Washington, one of which was Ink. His inspiration for the name is still debated *(Bunker: Rat)*. Post office: 1885–1954. SR D, N 11.3 m.; SR N, N 3.1. m.

Natural Areas. BLUE SPRING: Ozark National Scenic Riverways, below. CURRENT RIVER: 10 acres. Old-growth oak forest (white oaks more than 300 years old); difficult to locate, inquire locally. Box G (SR 19N), Eminence 65466. MILL MOUNTAIN: Ozark National Scenic Riverways, below. PIONEER: 6 acres. Features a stand of eastern red cedars and associated hardwoods. Difficult to locate. Access: by water or 4-wheel drive; inquire locally. Box G (SR 19N), Eminence 65466. PRAIRIE HOLLOW GORGE: Ozark National Scenic Riverways, below.

Ozark National Scenic Riverways. Many of this national park's attractions are located near Eminence *(Ellington: Gravel Spring; Van Buren: Big Spring)*. ALLEY SPRING / MILL / CAMPGROUND: Named for an early settler, prominent farmer John Alley, who probably had no direct connection with the *gristmill* first established here in 1869. Today's mill (Vernacular, 1894) used part of the spring's 81-million-gallons-per-day flow that surges from beneath a 100-foot dolomite bluff, collects in a one-acre pool, then cascades down a half-mile branch to a 32-foot-deep pool. A 1992 archaeological dig uncovered a Clovis projectile point used for hunting by Paleolithic *Indians* about 9,500 years ago. SR 106, W 6 m. to Alley Spring;[3] signs. BLUE SPRING: 17-acre natural area. Part of Carr Creek *State Forest.* Of Missouri's nine Blue Springs, this one reportedly sets the standard for blue. At 256 feet deep, it is Missouri's deepest spring (90 million gallons daily). Large, scenic, undisturbed; small park. Note: wading, swimming, boating, and fishing are prohibited in the spring and branch. Rt. 1, Box 1, Piedmont 63957. SR 106, E approx. 12 m. to Current River; SR 106, E approx. 2.8 m.; steep GR, W approx. 2.3 m. at Current River. JACKS FORK AND CURRENT RIVERS: *Float Streams.* MILL MOUNTAIN: 180-acre natural area. Part of Mule Mountain *State Forest.* Features an upland pine-oak-cedar forest, igneous rocks and glades, and a *shut-in* on Rocky Creek at nearby Rocky Falls (below). Box 490, Van Buren. SR 106, E 7 m., SR H, S 3.9 m.; SR NN, E approx. 3.4 m. OZARK *TRAIL.* PRAIRIE HOLLOW GORGE: 74-acre natural area. A classic example of an igneous gorge with sheer canyon walls, *shut-ins,* talus slopes, and igneous glades. Features highbrush and lowbrush blueberry and thick carpets of lichen and mosses. Box 490, Van Buren 63965. SR 106, W 4 m.; SR V, N approx. 2.1 m. ROCKY FALLS SHUT-IN: Wet weather is the best time to see this primeval setting that includes Rocky Creek's *shut-ins* and a waterfall cascading 40 feet to pink-to-purple rocks. Nearby is Mill Mountain Natural Area (above). SR 106, E 7 m.; SR H, S 3.9 m.; SR NN, E 2 m.; GR (appears to be country lane), S 0.75 m. (bear left at 0.3 m., continue straight). ROUND SPRING / CAVERN / CAMPGROUND: The spring's daily flow of 26 million gallons comes from beneath part of a *collapsed cave* roof that today forms a natural arch. The nearby cavern was explored in 1931 by developers interested in its proximity to newly acquired Round Spring State Park (now part of the national park). Strange and beautiful formations are illuminated by handheld lights used to preserve the cave's atmosphere. Summer tours for small groups; one-mile gravel path. SR 19, N 13 m. to just N of Round Spring, Mo.;[4] signs. OTHER FACILITIES (*National Parks):* Bay Creek, Blue Spring Current River, Horse Camp, Jerktail Landing, Keatons, Roberts Field, Rocky Falls, and Shawnee Creek river access.

Recreation. OZARK NATIONAL SCENIC RIVERWAYS: above. *STATE FORESTS:* Alley Spring, Beal, Blair Creek, Bloom Creek, Carr Creek, Clow, Indian Creek, Mule Mountain, Rocky Creek, Shannondale.

Shannon County Courthouse. Moderne, 1939–1941. The county's fifth, this two-story (with a basement) brick-veneer courthouse contains what records remain after fires destroyed three previous ones (Civil War, 1871, and 1938). Cost: $77,500. Grounds: small log cabin. Downtown. (*County Profiles*)

The Sinks Natural Tunnel. 200 feet long, 12 feet high. What is reportedly Missouri's only navigable natural tunnel was formed by the channel's cutting through a meander loop of Sinking Creek. The abandoned meander loop has been dammed and is now a lake. Small park, picnicking, boating, fishing. SR 19, N 19 m., SR A, E 0.5 m., SR CC, S 1.9 m.; GR, E approx. 1.3 m.

1. Biblical, the first potentate on earth (Gen. 10:8); no p.o.
2. Family name, possibly Thomas J. Chilton; no p.o.
3. P.o. Alley 1884–1950; Alley Spring 1950–1974.
4. Descriptive; p.o. 1871–1894, 1927–1980.

EUREKA
Population: 4,683   Map H-4

Platted in 1858 along the Pacific *Railroad,* the town was named by the railroad's construction engineer, who was looking for a way to avoid extensive grading beyond *Kirkwood.* When he saw this narrow valley near the Meramec River, he supposedly shouted "Eureka!" The name was given to a railroad camp established here in 1853, and then passed to the town when it was platted. The place-name, made popular by the famous story about Archimedes, was in vogue during the 19th century (e.g. California's 1849 motto: The Eureka State; Eureka, Calif., 1850; Eureka Springs, Ark., 1879) and is derived from Greek, "heureka," which roughly translates as "I've found it." Post office: 1860–now.

Babler Southwoods Hollow Natural Area. 17 acres. Part of Dr. Edmund A. Babler Memorial *State Park.* Features old-growth white oak and sugar maple in a narrow east-facing valley. 800 Guy Park Dr., Chesterfield 63017. SR 109, N 9 m.

Black Madonna Shrine and Grottoes. This remarkable work of folk art took one man, without machinery, 22 years to complete. A hillside landscaped by hand is the setting for large complicated grottoes built of barite (often found as diamond-shaped crystals) highlighted by seashells, costume jewelry, statues, crosses, and imaginative rockwork. Franciscan brother Bronislaus Luszca, who immigrated from Poland in 1927, began the grottoes in 1938 as a tribute to Our Lady of Czestochowa, the patron saint of Poland. The painting of the Black Madonna that inspired him has been described as "a strange painting depicting Christ's mother as a black woman." Like the origin of the painting (reportedly brought from the East to Poland 1382), the Madonna and Child's coloring is a mystery, although art historians agree that Florentine features for religious works were not popular until the Renaissance (1300s–1600s). A 1960 rendering of the original is at the Grottoes' chapel. SR W, S to SR FF, S (8 m. total).

Pacific, Mo. The town was platted in 1852 as Franklin and first named for its county. Due to an existing Franklin *(New Franklin)* in Howard County, it was renamed Pacific when incorporated in 1859 for its post office, which honors the Missouri-Pacific *Railroad*. Post office: Pacific 1854–now. I-44, W 7 m. PACIFIC FILLED SINKS: Deep road cuts between Pacific and Eureka show where extensive vertical and horizontal fractures have created large fissures now filled with weak shale and clay that often crumble, causing intensive maintenance *(Collapsed Cave Systems)*. ROBERTSVILLE *STATE PARK:* SR N, S 9.3 m. *WILDLIFE AREAS:* Catawissa, Pacific Palisades, Swiftwater Bend.

The Palisades. Created by erosional centrifugal force of the river, sheer 200-foot limestone bluffs, dotted by cedars, rise above this meander loop on the Meramec floodplain. I-44, E 2.5 m.; Exit N (E Meramec River bridge), W to Lewis Rd.; Lewis Rd., N 1.7 m. to Crescent;[1] cross railroad tracks; W on Allen Rd., N 1.5 m. to end.

Recreation. HILDA J. YOUNG *STATE FOREST.* ROCK-WOODS RESERVATION *TRAILS / STATE FOREST.*

Six Flags / Eureka Stream Piracy. Originally, Fox Creek ran east near a meander loop of the Meramec River just south of Six Flags, then paralleled I-44 to join the Meramec northeast of Eureka. Either because of erosion or by breaking through a divide, Fox Creek took a shortcut to the Meramec, eliminating the meander loop and draining the land, which provided dry ground for an interstate, two sets of railroad tracks, and Six Flags, one of America's largest amusement parks. I-44 to Six Flags.

Times Beach, Mo. The town was established in 1925 by the "St. Louis Times" and promoted as a working-man's resort. Its name links the newspaper's with the idea of a vacation by the water. The paper offered 20-by-100-foot lots along the Meramec River in return for a six-month subscription at $67.50, with terms of $10 down and $2.50 per month; 6,000 lots were sold. When the Great Depression provoked massive St. Louis home foreclosures, many Times Beach property owners were forced to permanently resettle here. The community was never successful. Its unpaved roads precipitated a fog of dust during the summer, a condition alleviated in 1972 by spraying them with an oily waste product of a medical cleanser, hexachlorophene, mixed with other oils. This waste product, dioxin, was applied every summer through 1976, after which federal funds were used for road improvements. By 1982, dioxin was confirmed to be carcinogenic and 14 confirmed and 41 suspected toxic sites in Missouri were identified. Times Beach, a suspected site, became

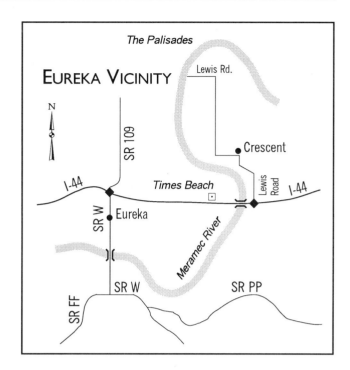

nationally known in 1982 when the Missouri Department of Health and the Centers for Disease Control announced that the town (pop. 2,242) should be evacuated. It was disincorporated in 1985 and razed in 1991; defunct, possibly dangerous. Post office: none. I-44, E 2.4 m. (formerly NW of the Meramec River bridge, defined by I-44, the river, and the railroad).

1. Descriptive location at Meramec River; p.o. 1884–1964.

EXCELSIOR SPRINGS
Population: 10,354   Map D-3

In a familiar boomtown spa story, the town was platted and named Excelsior in 1880 when water once said to be unfit to drink was found to contain "medicinal properties" similar to those fueling a nationwide fad for mineral water. "Excelsior" was denied for *post office* use due to an existing one, so the post office was established in 1881 as Viginti.[1] When the town was incorporated in 1883, both the town's and the post office's name were changed to Excelsior Springs in keeping with both the source of the town's income and its aspirations as epitomized by Longfellow's sentimental poem of unflinching resolve, "Excelsior" (Latin for ever upward). With the help of the Chicago, Milwaukee & St. Paul *Railroad*, which arrived in 1887, and $500,000 from the Excelsior Springs Company, the town grew from a tin-cup spring into a sophisticated resort, supporting hotels like the Elms (below). The decline in popularity of mineral water during the late 1930s ended the town's reputation as a health resort. Post offices: Viginti 1881–1883; Excelsior Springs 1883–now. Home of Excelsior Springs Area Vo-Tech. Maps: chamber of commerce, 101 E. Broadway (Hall of Waters, below).

Adjoining Towns. MOSBY: Established c. 1887 by the railroad (Excelsior Springs history, above) as a cattle shipping point and named for the landowners, the Mosby brothers. Post office: 1887–now. US 69/SR 10; US 69, W 2 m. PRATHERSVILLE: Established c. 1874 by minister, cattleman, miller, and farmer L. J. A. Prather, the town was derisively nicknamed Shoo Fly due to its size and perceived insignificance. Post office: 1876–1904. SR H/SR 10; SR H, S 3.1 m.

The Elms Hotel. Tudor, 1912; National Historic Register. This limestone and concrete structure, built on 23 acres, is the third Elms at this site (the first was built in 1888). Al Capone played all-night poker here, and Harry S. Truman *(Independence)* woke up here in 1948 as America's 33d president, defeating Thomas E. Dewey in America's biggest political upset. Downtown; SR 10 at Regent and Elms.

Excelsior Springs Golf Club. Completed in 1915; first 9 holes, 1910. The 15th tee of this English-type course (no bunkers or traps) has a monument to the Battle of Fredricksburgh,[2] a *Civil War* skirmish fought on the southwest sector of the course. The clubhouse (Neo-Tudor, 1969) is built around a walnut log cabin (c. 1825). Public. SR 10, E edge of town near airport (1201 Golf Hill Dr.).

Excelsior Springs Historical Museum. Housed in the former Clay County State Bank building (1906; remodeled 1920, 1950), the museum features local historical items, e.g. two large murals, a c. 1865 working loom, lead soldiers, and vintage town photographs. Downtown; SR 10, N on Marietta to Broadway (101 E).

Hall of Waters. Art Deco, 1938; National Historic Register. This three-story stone and concrete building with an 85-foot tower of structural glass has a recessed entrance accented by elaborate bronze grilles and Mayan-motif bas-reliefs. The interior has inlaid variegated tiles on the walls. Set in Siloam Park near Siloam Spring and Fishing River, this million-dollar structure, built by *WPA* funds, features the world's longest water bar (47 ft. 4 in.), where four varieties of mineral water can be sampled. CALCIUM BICARBONATE: Reportedly appetizing as table water and helpful in kidney and bladder disorders. IRON MANGANESE: Supposedly "a potent blood builder by adding iron to the bloodstream." Reportedly this is America's only natural supply of this water and one of only five sources for it in the world. SODIUM BICARBONATE: "A stabilizing agent . . . used extensively in anti-acid

therapy." SULPHO-SALINE: A mild laxative also used for bathing. The Hall of Waters also features a 25-meter indoor pool, mineral-water steam baths and showers, and massages. Grounds: walking trail and two pagodas. City-owned (also houses city offices). Downtown; SR 10, N 2 blocks on Marietta.

Isley Park Woods Natural Area. 15 acres. Features an old-growth forest (oak, walnut, maple) and migrating birds (e.g. warblers). 112 Thompson, Excelsior Springs 64024. SR 10 at SR Y.

Tryst Falls. Reportedly this former mill site was named for its use by lovers. The limestone-base falls of Williams Creek have a maximum height of 10–12 feet. The romantic setting features a 60-foot pool, eroded watercourse, *glacial erratic* pink boulders, and a concrete arched bridge. An abandoned quarry serves as a picnic area; tennis, fishing, restrooms. SR 10, W 1 m.; US 69, N 2.6; SR 92, W 2.2.

Watkins Mill State Park / Historic Site. US 69, N 3 m.; SR 92, W 1.5 m.; SR RA, N 1 m.; signs at Greenville.[3] *(State Parks)*

1. Latin for 20, presumably the number of local springs; p.o. 1881–1883.
2. For Fredericksburgh, Va. (for the Prince of Wales, son of George II); p.o. 1836–1842.
3. *Greenville;* p.o. Claytonville, Clay County namesake *(County Profiles),* 1870–1893.

FARBER
Population: 418   Map G-3

Platted in 1872 as a station for the Louisiana & Missouri River *Railroad* by landowner Finas W. Farber, the town grew as a shipping point later aided by a coal, then a firebrick, industry *(Mexico)*. Post office: 1872–now.

Laddonia, Mo. The town was platted in 1871 along the Louisiana & Missouri River *Railroad* by Amos Ladd and J. J. Haden, whose wife's name was Donia. Another example of a place named for two people is nearby: Rush Hill.[1] Post office: 1871–now. US 54, W 7 m. DIGGS WHITE OAK NATURAL AREA: 3 acres. Part of the 1,015-acre Diggs *Wildlife Area*. Features a small stand of white oaks over 100 years old. SR 19, S 9.7 m. to Martinsburg;[2] GR, S 1.9 m.; inquire locally. VANDALIA COMMUNITY LAKE: 44 acres. Bass, sunfish, crappie, catfish. SR K, E 3.8 m.; GR, E 2 m.

Railroad Museum. Railroad, 1874. Reportedly one of two *(Higginsville)* of its style left in Missouri, the two-story depot was relocated to the city park and restored by community ingenuity, including an aluminum-can drive that drew nationwide publicity. It now houses railroad memorabilia, e.g. telegraph equipment, porcelain advertising signs, and a desk. In town.

1. Landowners Rush and Hill; SR KK, W 4.1 m.; SR B, S 2 m.; p.o. 1881–now.

2. 1859 town founder W. R. Martin; p.o. Shy Post, origin unknown, 1849–1858; Loutre, the township via French for "the otter"; Martinsburg(h) 1870–now.

FARMINGTON
Population: 11,598   Map H-5

Settled c. 1800 by the Murphy family from Tennessee, it was known as Murphy's Settlement until platted as St. Francois Court House, the county seat of newly organized St. Francois County, on 52 acres donated in 1822 by David Murphy. The name Farmington was selected in 1825. A stock name, it presumably honors the agricultural economy, but, ironically, the town grew into a shipping, trading, and financial center for the area's mining industry *(Bonne Terre)*. After Farmington was narrowly bypassed by three railroads, businessmen formed a trunk line, the St. Francois Electric Railway Co. (1901–1940s). Post offices: Murphy's Settlement 1817–1823; St. Francois c. 1823–1825; Farmington 1825–now.

Architecture. COLUMBIA ST. HOUSES (SR W, W side of downtown): Brodsky House (1904), 628 W.; Cozean House (1834), a former Presbyterian manse, 503 W.; McCormick House (1874), 324 W.; Roberts House (1863–1865), 502 W.; Wright House (c. 1900), 604 W. LONG HOUSE: 1834; Ste. Genevieve at Long. MUNICIPAL SWIMMING POOL BUILDING: 1935, Art Moderne; SR W, E of downtown.

Doe Run, Mo. Named for the nearby creek that was named for its deer population. A lead-mining boom in 1885–1895 helped create one of Missouri's fastest growing (and then declining) towns. Post office: 1887–now. SR W, W 4 m.

Hawn State Park / Natural Areas. *Ste. Genevieve: Hawn State Park / Natural Areas.*

Knob Lick, Mo. Platted in 1865 as a farming town near good springs, Knob Lick was helped to become a shipping point for area mines by the 1871 arrival of the St. Louis & Iron Mountain *Railroad.* The town was named for the nearby knob (below) and the animals (deer and buffalo mentioned most) that used its salt licks *(Licking).* Post office: 1870–now. US 67, S 8 m. THE KNOB: Long views, picnic table, fire tower. SR DD, W 0.2 m.; US 67, S 0.5 m.; SR DD, W 1.3 m. *(Balds and Knobs).* UNION CHURCH: Vernacular, 1894. Now called the Church on the Hill, this typical rural clapboard church served four denominations; derelict. *Cemetery* adjacent. SR DD, W near US 67.

Knob Lick Vista Trail. *Trails.*

Libertyville, Mo. Settled c. 1810 by Capt. Samuel Kinkead and known as Kinkead, it was renamed Libertyville c. 1863, presumably for the American ideal. Post offices: Kinkead 1846–1857; Locust Grove[1] 1857–1862; Liberty Meeting House 1862–1863; Libertyville 1863, 1866–1919. SR OO, S 7.6 m.; SR DD, E 1 m. CHURCH: Vernacular, 1858. The church's Sunday school was established in 1822. This brick building, which replaced an earlier structure, has two front doors: the men's on the right and the women's on the left (the seating corresponds with the entrances); *cemetery* adjacent. In town. MASONIC HALL: Vernacular 1865–1866. Chartered 1864. In town.

St. Francois County Courthouse. Italian Renaissance, 1926–1927. The county's fourth courthouse on this site since 1826, today's three-story *Carthage* marble and Bedford limestone building has roofline balustrades, two-story columns, and four full-height central projecting entrances with recessed porches and Corinthian columns. Cost: $250,000. Downtown. *(County Profiles)*

St. Joe Mine #25 Headframe. Except for one at St. Joe *State Park,* this is the only remaining headframe (structure over a mine shaft to support a chain and pulley for hoisting sheaves) in the lead belt *(Flat River).* This one, ironically, was bolted together so it could be moved. US 67, W on Liberty to Bray, S 0.6 m. to Pineville Rd., W 2 m.

Sarah Barton Murphy / Masonic Cemetery. The wife of town patriarch Rev. William Murphy is credited with establishing the first Sunday school west of the Mississippi in 1805. A white marble shaft at the *cemetery* commemorates the site of the log church (her grave is a few yards south). Ste. Genevieve St., approx. 5 blocks S of square. *(Cemeteries)*

State Hospital #4. Vernacular, 1903. Built for the treatment of "mental and nervous diseases," these brick and stone buildings reportedly were America's first cottage-plan grouping. Originally designed for 1,500 patients, some of them today are used to confine about 1,700 medium-security prisoners. W end of Columbia.

Syenite, Mo. Established in 1881 by Scottish immigrant and quarry owner John W. Milne, who named it for syenite, a feldspar mined at Syene, the ancient Upper Egyptian town and quarry (now Aswan) once revered as the site that signaled the arrival of the Nile flood. Although syenite generally resembles granite, it lacks quartz. No syenite was found here, but the granite was made into cobblestones. Post office: 1881–1914. US 67, S 8 m.; SR DD, W 1.5 m. MILNE HOUSE: Vernacular, 1880s. This two-story house has 24-inch granite walls, three fireplaces, a basement, and large double front doors. S side of road, W of remaining houses.

1. Descriptive location.

FARRAR
Estimated population: 90   Map I-5

Growing from a German settlement later known as Salem that was centered around the 1859 Salem Lutheran Church, this community began when R. P. Farrar opened a general store here c. 1890 and established a post office in 1892. Another general store and two blacksmiths followed shortly. Due to an existing *Salem*, postmaster Farrar suggested his name as a temporary solution. Post office: 1892–now. *(Perryville: Longtown)* **Brazeau, Mo.** Settled in 1817 by English and Scotch-Irish mainly from North Carolina, it was named for the nearby creek, which was named for a 1790s French merchant/settler, possibly Joseph Brazeau, from St. Louis or Kaskaskia, Ill. *(Ste. Genevieve: Kaskaskia).* Brazeau Presbyterian Church (below) has been the community's buttress since 1819. Post office: 1879–now. SR C, S 4.2 m. ARCHITECTURE: Grouped around the post office are typical 19th- and 20th-century community structures, including a late 1800s general store (2d floor removed), a 1906 white frame schoolhouse (museum inside), a c. 1869 one-story brick house, and the 1944 Brazeau Hall, a one-story frame community center. BRAZEAU PRESBYTERIAN CHURCH: Vernacular, 1852–1854; belfry added 1892; organized 1819. Today's large brick structure replaced an 1833 frame church at this site. The original c. 1819 log church (1.5 m. W) burned c. 1832. Features original pews, hurricane bolts, and adjacent early 1800s *cemetery* and 1906 manse. SR C, in town.
Crosstown, Mo. Never platted, it is typical of Missouri farming communities. The area was settled in the late 1840s, but this community had no name until establishment of its post office, which was reportedly named for its crossroads location. Post office: 1886–1954. SR C, N 3.9 m. BELGIQUE, MO.: French was the official language of Belgium (Belgique in French) from 1830 to 1921. Ironically, this community of immigrants from Belgium is situated between predominately French *(Ste. Genevieve)* and German *(Altenburg)* settlements. Post office: 1889–1971. SR C, N 8.3 m. CORSE'S GENERAL STORE: Vernacular, c. 1900. Built of brick, trimmed with ornamental iron, and set on a cut-stone foundation, the store displays 19th-century farm and home items, Indian artifacts, and fossils. The c. 1895 house beside it is open for informal tours. JONES PLANTATION: Built by Francis Jones c. 1856 near Grand Eddy boat landing, the house and its brick outbuildings are among the area's oldest. SR C, N 0.25 m.; CR 350, E 3 m.
Farrar General Store. General Store, c. 1900. With large windows and ornamental cast iron, the store is typical turn-of-the-century Americana. SR C, in town.

Kassel Cave Natural Bridges. In what is reportedly Missouri's most compact example of a *collapsed cave system*, four natural bridges are contained in an area about 100 feet in diameter, creating the impression of a ruined city. Inquire locally.

FAYETTE
Population: 2,888   Map E-3

After Howard County was reduced in size, Fayette was platted in 1823 as the second county seat, replacing Franklin *(New Franklin)*. It was named for Revolutionary War hero Marie Joseph Paul Yeves Roch Gilbert du Motier, Marquis de La Fayette (or Lafayette) in anticipation of this French national's 1824 visit to America, his first since the Revolution.[1] The historical architecture (below) and the choice of this town as a residence by four governors—John Miller (1825–1832), Thomas Reynolds (1840–1844), Sterling Price (1852–1856), and Claiborne Jackson (1861; below)—indicate Fayette's rapid growth as a political and cultural center. Post office: 1824–now. Home of Central Methodist College (below).
Architectural Tour. Eleven structures, ranging from c. 1828 to 1888, are within five blocks of the Howard County Courthouse (Davis at Church; below). BOONE-WATTS-CARSON HOME: Greek Revival, c. 1834. Built by Daniel Boone's great-nephew, Hampton L. Boone. Two-story brick, with a recessed doorway, carved stone steps, a wrought-iron fence, and stone lintels. 404 N. Church. COLEMAN HALL: Early Classical Revival, c. 1874; National Historic Register. Two-story brick, bracketed, with brick arches over the windows and functional wooden shutters. 502 N. Linn. CREWS HOME: Picturesque, c. 1830–1840. Two-story brick, with bracketed and boxed shallow eaves, tall narrow windows, stone lintels, a one-story porch with brackets, six narrow columns supporting flattened arch woodwork, and an upper-level door with a rectangular full transom light. 310 S. Main. DAVIS HOME: Second Empire, c. 1880–1884. Three-story brick, with a mansard roof with a tower, a porch with stick woodwork, patterned brick window arches, and Venetian red-glass window frames in the front doors. 301 W. Spring. DR. WRIGHT'S OFFICE: Adamesque, c. 1828–1832. Plain two-story brick, with a bull's-eye and fluting above windows and doors and flattened arch brickwork above windows. Originally a hatter's shop; bought in 1882 by Wright. 120 N. Church. FERGUSON HOME: Queen Anne (Patterned Masonry), c. 1883. Three-story brick, with a pyramidal roof with patterned slate, cross gables, stone lintels, stone trim,

stained glass, the original wrought-iron fence, and hidden gutters. 312 S. Main. HUNTING HALL. Gothic Revival, c. 1851. Two-story handmade brick, with sharply peaked gables and a flattened-arch porch support. 105 Lucky. ST. MARY'S EPISCOPAL CHURCH: Gothic Revival, c. 1848; 1960 annex; National Historic Register. One-story Carpenter Gothic vertical board and batten, with a red door to keep the Devil out, lancet windows, and wooden hoodmolds. Reportedly this is the oldest frame church in the West Missouri Diocese; it was moved here in 1920 from Davis at Church. 104 W. Davis. SEARS-CLARK HOME: Greek Revival, c. 1835. Two-story frame, with a two-story portico with an upper level door and ornate brick on the chimneys. 408 N. Church. SHEPARD-DAVIS HOME: Adamesque, c. 1826; south addition, 1850s (original part between the two chimneys). One-story brick, with a standing-seam tin roof, Doric columns, wooden lintels, and a brick foundation. 208 S. Main.

Architecture. Many well-preserved 19th-century structures. OUTSIDE TOWN (all National Historic Register): Jackson Homeplace (late 1850s), SR DD, just E of SR 5. Lilac Hill (Adam, 1828–1832), SR 5, S approx. 0.5 m. Oakwood (Adam, 1836), SR 5, E on Morrison to Leonard. OTHERS: above.

Central Methodist College. National Historic District: the campus roughly bounded by Elm, Church, College, and Mulberry. The college grew from Howard High School, founded in 1844 by Rev. William Lucky. It was operated in 1846 by the Missouri Methodist Episcopal Church, chartered in 1854 as Central College, and finally absorbed in 1961 by other Methodist colleges, adopting today's name. Ten buildings are on the National Historic Register, including: BRANNOCK HALL (Italianate, 1856), CUPPLES HALL (Richardsonian Romanesque, 1899), and GIVINS HALL (Greek Revival, c. 1845–1850). SR 5, E on Elm to Main.

Claiborne F. Jackson House. Greek Revival, c. 1847. The home of the pro-Southern Missouri governor (1861 only). SR 5, N 1.5 m. *(Arrow Rock: Sappington Cemetery)*

Fishing Lakes. Missouri and Fayette city licenses are required for these lakes (channel catfish, crappie, bass, bluegill). CITY LAKE 1: 16 acres. SR 5, S side of city, W 1 m. on Shields. CITY LAKE 2: 60 acres. W. Davis (SR E), W 3 m. ROGERS: 180 acres. Picnic, camping, restrooms; W. Davis (SR E), W 1 m.

Howard County Courthouse. Second Empire, 1887; remodeled 1968 and 1975. The county's third courthouse was gutted in 1975

by fire, but the exterior is still a fine example of its style, which includes elaborate corner towers and a massive central clock tower. Original cost: $32,940; 1968 remodeling: $375,000; 1974 remodeling: not available. Grounds: Gazebo-style bandstand where during the summer the Five Star Cornet Band (organized in the late 1870s) plays. Downtown. *(County Profiles)*

Hungry Mother Wildlife Area. *Wildlife Areas.*

Morrison Observatory. When built in 1875 at Prichett College in *Glasgow*, this was the largest astronomical observatory west of Chicago. The Great Red Spot of Jupiter was first observed in 1878 at Prichett. The dome, equipment, and telescopes were moved to Fayette in 1936 (Prichett closed in 1907). Summer star gazing. City Park (picnicking, swimming, tennis, playground); SR 5, W on Lucky, N on Park.

Stephens Museum. Missouri's third-oldest museum features historical, archaeological, biological, and geological collections, including a painting by George Caleb Bingham and Daniel and Rebecca Boone's original tombstones *(Marthasville: Boone Burial Site)*, which spell their names "Boon" *(Boonville: Daniel Boon[e])*. Central College Campus; SR 5, E on Elm to Main; 2d floor of T. Berry Smith Hall.

1. Not until his 1824–1825 visit was the longer version (Lafayette) used as a place-name.

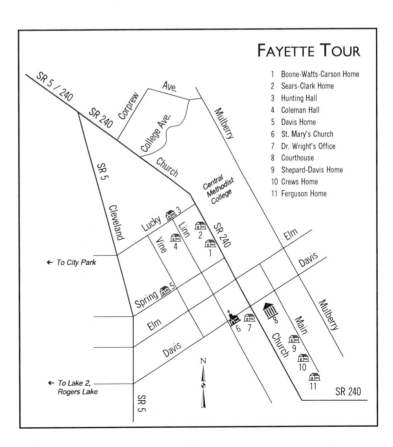

FAYETTE TOUR

1. Boone-Watts-Carson Home
2. Sears-Clark Home
3. Hunting Hall
4. Coleman Hall
5. Davis Home
6. St. Mary's Church
7. Dr. Wright's Office
8. Courthouse
9. Shepard-Davis Home
10. Crews Home
11. Ferguson Home

FERRYBOATS

Besides saving driving time, ferries offer a scenic side trip. The ones listed below are privately owned and inspected by the Coast Guard. Fares vary according to crossing time. Schedules vary according to the season (generally the boats run during daylight hours). The listings are by the nearest Missouri town. Note: like any small business, ferries can close temporarily or permanently; call before planning a route.

Akers Ferry. Current River. SR K and SR KK; crosses to SR K at *Akers.* All year; 5 minutes; 2 cars.

Canton Ferry. Mississippi River. *Canton,* at Front St.; crosses to Meyer. Ill. March 15–December 15, weather permitting; 6 minutes; 6 cars.

Fredricksburg Ferry. Gasconade River. SR N or SR J, S of *Gasconade;* crosses to SR J at Fredricksburg. All year, weather permitting; 2 minutes; 2 cars.

Golden Eagle Ferry. Mississippi River. SR B, E of Kampville, Mo. (N of *St. Charles);* crosses to Golden Eagle, Ill.; March–December, weather permitting; 6 minutes; 16 cars.

Winfield Ferry. Mississippi River. SR N, 2.4 m. E of Winfield to Cap Au Gris *(Troy)* at *Lock and Dam #25;* crosses to Ferry Rd., 2 m. SW of Batchtown, Ill. All year, weather permitting; 5 minutes; 8 cars.

The ferry "Mabelle" crossing the Missouri River at Glasgow, c. 1917.

FLAT RIVER
Population: 4,823   Map H-5

Until lead mining ceased in this area in 1971, Flat River was the center of a collection of former 18th-century mining camps, now towns, that were later collectively referred to as the lead belt. For over 100 years they provided nearly 80 percent of the nation's mined lead. As early as 1720 the French operated small-scale surface mines, worked by men who farmed in the summer and mined in the winter. The lead rush began c. 1800 with mining camps like New Diggings, also known as Flat Camp (named Flat River in 1821). Although Joseph Bogy recorded the first mine in 1765, it was not until the late 1880s that lead companies such as Federal, Doe Run, and St. Joseph began large-scale production. The first mining venture here (1870) failed, but during another attempt in 1889–1891 a deeply buried lead bonanza was struck and the town boomed. The town was incorporated in 1895 as Flat River, its mining camp

name that located the camp at a stream called Platte River by the French (meaning flat, shallow, level). Post offices: 1867–1876, 1886–now. Home of Mineral Area College (junior college). *(Bonne Terre; Desloge)*

Bismarck, Mo. Platted in 1868 two miles north of Dents Station[1] at the Belmont *Railroad* and the main branch of the St. Louis, Iron Mountain & Southern, it was named for Prince Otto von Bismarck (1815–1898), the first chancellor (1871) of the German empire that he was unifying at the time *(Clinton: Urich).* Post offices: Dents Station 1860–1868; Bismarck 1868–now. SR 32, S 9 m. BISMARCK LAKE / *WILDLIFE AREA.*

Chat Dumps. Commonplace in the area, these enormous bald mountains are tailings, refuse separated as residue during lead mining. General vicinity.

Columbia Park. Pool, picnic pavilions, WWII tank. SR 32, W on Woodlawn, W on E. Main.

Flat River Grand Prix. This annual motorcycle race has been featured in "Dirt Bike Magazine." Late September.

Missouri Mines State Historic Site. Federal Mill #3 (Vernacular, 1906–1907) was built by the Federal Lead Co. as a lead ore concentrating plant, then bought c. 1923 by St. Joe Lead Co., which donated it in 1976 to the state. Shaft #27, the only one of its kind in the old lead belt, was dug c. 1927 from the bottom up to provide a means to hoist ore from an underground collection point. A museum features mining equipment, samples of ore, minerals of Missouri and the world, a 1950 company movie of mining here, and mining history and technology; tours. Main, S 1 m. on Federal Mill Drive. ST. JOE *STATE PARK:* SR 32, S 2 m.

Swinging Foot Bridge. Recently replacing its 75-year-old predecessor, used by miners as a shortcut to work, this 70-foot-long *suspension bridge* with a wooden deck crosses Flat River Creek. US 67, N on Crane, W on Maple, N on Haney (W side of Haney).

1. RR station; probably Dent County namesake (*County Profiles*).

FLORISSANT
Population: 51,083   Map H-4

The town was platted in 1794 along Cold Water Creek. Creole French exploring this valley c. 1770 reportedly described the area as prosperous, flourishing (fleurissant) because of its rich soil. The residents of this Spanish possession (*Louisiana Purchase*) were mostly French, and they called the community here Florissant (the traditional French spelling), which it remained until 1786 when the town's first commandant, François Dunnegant, changed the name to San Fernando.[1] Later, French residents changed the spelling to St. Ferdinand. Although a Florissant post office was established in 1818, the community's name remained officially St. Ferdinand until changed by the 1939 city council to Florissant, which despite the other names is what residents had always called it (19th- and 20th-century mapmakers also listed it as Florissant). Slow to grow (from about 300 in 1799 to 3,737 in 1950), it boomed to 39,000 by 1960 as a suburb of St. Louis and is now one of Missouri's larger towns. Post office: Florissant 1818–1901, 1904–now.

Architecture. The old portion of town is bounded by Cold Water Creek, St. Denis, New Florissant, and Washington. Often remodeled extensively, the architecture reflects the influence of French and later (1850s) German, Irish, and American settlers. Map: chamber of commerce; I-270, N on New Florissant, W on St. Catherine (1060). ARCHAMBAULT HOUSE: Greek Revival (with Italianate affinities), c. 1850; National Historic Register. Reportedly built by Auguste Archambault, who worked as a trapper, hunter, and guide for Kit Carson, Jim Bridger, and John C. Frémont, the house is noteworthy for its intact outbuildings. 603 St. Denis. CASA ALVAREZ: Creole French (*Ste. Genevieve*), 1790; National Historic Register. Built for the king's military storekeeper. The house's horizontal logs are covered with clapboard, but the long sweep of the roof, ending at the front gallery, reveals its characteristic French Colonial design. 289 St. Denis. COLD WATER COMMONS PARK: The area was left as a public open space at the western edge of the original plat, as was *Ste. Genevieve*'s Big Field. Between Cold Water and Fountain Creeks. NARROW GAUGE RAILROAD STATION: Railroad, 1878. Moved here in 1969 from Washington at St. Ferdinand, this board-and-batten

structure served the 16-mile narrow gauge railroad that made four daily round-trips to St. Louis; service ended in 1931. Chamber of commerce, 1060 St. Catherine. OLD SAINT FERDINAND'S SHRINE: Brick, 1821 (original facade altered to Gothic Revival c. 1880). Replacing an adjacent 1789 log church, this is America's oldest Catholic church dedicated to the Sacred Heart, the first novitiate of the Sacred Heart in the Western Hemisphere, and America's first Indian school for girls. It ceased being an active parish in 1955. #1 St. Francois. SPANISH LAND GRANT PARK: A gift to residents from the King of Spain. Some early settlers are buried here in unmarked graves. St. Denis at St. Ferdinand.

Creve Coeur Park / Lake. *Kirkwood.*

Myers House. Greek Revival, Bracketed, c. 1868; National Historic Register. The two-story masonry house has a full-height two-story entry porch and bracketed eaves. I-270, N on Graham, W on Dunn (180).

Pelican Island Natural Area. 2,260 acres. White pelicans once rested at and near this island during migration. An excellent example of islands that have disappeared because of channelization, it features a bottomland forest, riverine chute, sloughs, sandbars, and mudflats. Access: footbridge at eastern edge; parking adjacent. 2360 Hwy. D, St. Charles 63304. US 67; SR AC (New Halls Ferry Rd.), N 2.6 m.; Douglas Rd., E approx. 2 m. (part gravel).

St. Stanislaus Seminary. Multiple buildings, 1840–1849; National Historic Register. This complex is grouped around a four-story stone building with Classical Revival trim. Reportedly the world's oldest existing Jesuit novitiate, it was established in 1831 by Father Theodore Mary De Theux as a result of the 1824 failure of the St. Regis Seminary, America's first school for Indian boys, who, if possible, were even more disdainful of classrooms than their white peers. I-270; US 67, N 1.7 m.; Charbonier Rd., W 1.2 m.; Howdershell, S 0.5 m.

Sinks Road. Appropriately named, the road winds around craters as large as 30 to 50 feet deep that appear to have been caused by heavy bombing. US 67, E of SR AC 1.2 m. (just E of Old Halls Ferry Rd.), N on

							HISTORIC FLORISSANT		
← To SR 67	St. Charles	St. Ferdinand	St. Pierre	St. Jean	St. Jacques	Jefferson	Lafayette	St. Denis	Brown	New Florissant
								St. Louis		↑ To SR 67
								St. Francois		
← To SR 67								St. Catherine		To I-270
								Washington		↓

Sinks Rd. (to near the Missouri River, approx. 2.5 m.). *(Collapsed Cave Systems)*

Sioux Passage County Park. 188 acres. Set on a gentle slope to the river: picnicking, hiking, fishing, archaeological sites (National Historic Register). SE corner of Pelican Island (above).

Taille de Noyer. Originally log, now French Colonial style, 1790; National Historic Register. Built as a fur-trading post, the three-room log cabin is named for the French term meaning "clearing in a walnut grove." It was bought in 1805 as a hunting lodge by St. Louis's first millionaire, John Mullanphy, who gave it to his daughter and husband in 1817. They enlarged it and continued expanding it, along with their family (they had 17 children). Today's 22-room French Colonial–style mansion with a fireplace in each room was in the family for 140 years. Bought in 1960 by the Florissant Historical Society, it has been restored and fully furnished. Tours, museum, country store. I-270, S on New Florissant, E on Taille de Noyer to McCluer High School campus.

1. King Ferdinand III (1199–1252); canonized 1671.

FOREST CITY
Population: 380   Map B-2

The town was platted in 1857 four miles northeast of an 1844 ferry crossing known as Iowa Point,[1] formerly Jeffrey's Point.[2] Forest City, a Missouri River steamboat port reportedly named for the area's once extensive forests, grew quickly into an important trading center, only to be abandoned in 1868 by the Missouri River when floodwaters receded, leaving the town two miles inland *(Weston)*. Arrival that year of the Kansas City, St. Joseph & Council Bluffs *Railroad* helped maintain some commercial trade, but loss of the river stunted the town's growth. Post office: 1857–now.

Architecture. Downtown: good examples of c. 1857–1870 styles.

City Hall. Richardsonian Romanesque, 1900; restored; National Historic Register. This red-brick building, built as an opera house, is reportedly the first opera house owned by an American municipality. Downtown.

Fortescue, Mo. Established c. 1884 and named for a family that originally spelled its name Fortesque. Post office: 1884–c. 1973. SR 111, N 5.4 m.; US 159, W 4.1 m.; SR P, N 0.7 m. BIG LAKE *STATE PARK*: US 159, W 1.5 m. SCHOOLHOUSES / MUSEUM: Two school buildings show the change in Missouri's concept of education during the early 20th century: (1) A small two-story brick structure built in 1909 for elementary grades and two years of high school. (2) A large three-story brick building built in 1916 after formation of a consolidated high school district. The 1916 school (closed in 1958) is now the Holt County Museum, featuring uniforms, historical items, and a furnished period bedroom and kitchen. In town.

McCormack Loess Mounds Natural Area. 112 acres. Features *prairie* and forest on rugged *loess* mounds, as well as plants typical of the Great Plains but uncommon in Missouri, e.g. downy painted cup and hairy gamma grass. Also found here are the endangered skeleton plant and low milk vetch. 3408 Ashland, St. Joseph 64506. SR 111, N 5 m.; US 159, N 0.5 m.

Recreation. BIG LAKE *STATE PARK:* Fortescue (above). RIVERBREAKS *STATE FOREST.* SQUAW CREEK *NATIONAL WILDLIFE REFUGE. WILDLIFE AREAS:* Brown, Monkey Mountain.

1. For Iowa Territory; no p.o.
2. Jeffrey Dorways's point of land that extended into what was then Indian Territory; no p.o.

FORSYTH
Population: 1,175   Map E-7

Early records for the town's history were destroyed by an 1885 courthouse fire. Reportedly platted in 1836 along the c. 1835 Carrollton, Ark., to Springfield *Road* on property donated by postmaster, merchant, and county official John W. Danforth, the town was selected as county seat for newly organized Taney County and named for John Forsyth, governor (1827–1829) of Georgia and U.S. secretary of state (1834–1841) under presidents Andrew Jackson and Martin Van Buren. Forsyth grew as a transfer point for commerce between *Springfield* and the White River. Post office: 1837–1863; 1866–now.

Recreation. BULL SHOALS *LAKE: Lakes: Corps of Engineers. FLOAT STREAMS:* Beaver and Swan Creeks. HERCULES GLADES WILDERNESS *TRAIL.* LAKE TANEYCOMO: adjacent *(Branson: Recreation).*

Shadow Rock Park / Civil War. CIVIL WAR: Two engagements were fought here. (1) After the 1861 Battle of Pea Ridge, Ark., Confederates routed Gen. T. W. Seeny's troops. (2) After the 1863 battle of Prairie Grove, Ark., the town and courthouse were fortified for three months by Federals and then destroyed by them when they left. PARK: The original townsite (Taney County Courthouse, below) by the bluffs of the White River at the mouth of Swan Creek, is marked by a stone monument beside the former Carrollton, Ark., to Springfield Road. Grounds: two relocated restored log structures (an 1886 cabin and a smokehouse) and a folk-art rock sculpture that features sliced polish rock and mineral blossom quartz. Facilities: restrooms, picnic tables and pavilions, bank fishing, boat docks, tennis. US 160 at SR 76.

Swan Creek, Mo. Named for the site's creek, which was possibly named for the bird, the community has a pastoral setting of gentle hills with several log cabins and a large cut-stone building that was formerly the post office and general store. Post offices: Swan 1841–1844, 1860–1864, 1867–1868, 1880–1957; Burt Head[1] 1880 only; Swan Fork 1850–1851; Swan Creek 1856. US 160, E 4 m.; SR 76, N 4.5 m.; SR AA, N 4.6 m. JOURNEY'S END: Log Cabin, c. 1860. This large one-story house once provided lodging for travelers, including turn-of-the-century guests like the Wright brothers' father, when he was here to dedicate the Lone Star Church, and a young Herbert Hoover (U.S. president, 1929–1933), who was surveying for the St. Louis & San Francisco *Railroad*. Just S of Swan.

Taney County Courthouse. Fifties Modern, 1950–1951. After the 1837 court met in a private house at the mouth of Swan Creek in recently platted Forsyth, the court ordered the county seat removed to the mouth of Bull Creek; in 1845 it was recalled to the Forsyth location by popular vote. An 1855 brick courthouse was gutted by Federal soldiers, rebuilt, then destroyed by fire in 1885. After five years of wrangling, a cut-stone courthouse was built in 1891 and then dismantled in 1950–1952 due to the rising waters of recently constructed Bull Shoals Lake (*Lakes: Corps of Engineers*). Today's building, the fifth (possibly the sixth) courthouse, is a stucco-on-cinder-block building reportedly inspired by South American architecture and designed by an engineer. It once featured an interior 42-foot-square courtyard within a 116-foot-square building and a heating system utilizing hot water in copper tubes, but 1990 remodeling included filling in the courtyard with a two-story addition to double the size of the building and adding a square two-story tower reminiscent of its predecessor's. Costs (1950): federal compensation of $75,000 for having to relocate. US 160 at SR Y. (*County Profiles*)

1. Personal name.

FREDERICKTOWN
Population: 3,950   Map I-6

Fredericktown grew from St. Michaels,[1] which was originally settled c. 1799 by French Canadian miners from *Ste. Genevieve* who were working at nearby Mine La Motte (below), the first lead mine west of the Mississippi. After a severe 1814 flood, some residents built houses on higher ground south of Saline Creek, where Fredericktown was platted in 1819 as county seat of newly organized Madison County. Slow to grow, it finally absorbed St. Michaels in 1827, which now is locally called North Town. Arrival of the St. Louis, Iron Mountain & Southern *Railroad* in 1869 helped establish it as a trading center. The town's namesake is contested. Possibilities include: (1) early Bollinger County settler George Frederick Bollinger (*County Profiles: Bollinger*), a friend of state surveyor and fellow territorial general assemblyman Nathaniel Cook, who owned the townsite; (2) Frederick Bates (*County Profiles: Bates*), secretary of the territory at the time; and (3) Frederick the Great (1712–1786), king of Prussia, a hero to a large number of German Americans who had recently settled in Madison County. Post offices: St. Michael's 1816–1827; Fredericktown 1827–now.

Chimney Rock Bluff / Trail. Situated on Rock Pile Mountain, which was named for a circle of stacked rocks reported in 1904 as being four feet high (now rubble), Chimney Rock, according to Thomas Beveridge, is the most pinnacled rock in the area. However, he was so overwhelmed by the other geological wonders here (pinnacles, tunnels, fractures, weathering, bluffs, and knobs, as well as the sweeping vistas of the St. Francis River valley) that he nearly overlooked it and forgot to take any dimensions. Directions: Rock Pile Mountain Wilderness *Trail*.

Madison County Courthouse. Italianate, 1899. The county's second (the first was also at this site), this two-story red-brick courthouse features an impressive square tower with paired arched windows, a pyramidal roof, wide bracketed eaves, first-story paired arched windows, and a rusticated stone foundation. Set snugly in the town square, it is surrounded by sidewalks and streets, leaving little room for a lawn. Cost: $22,000; 1993 exterior and interior renovations $1.1 million. (*County Profiles*)

Mine La Motte, Mo. The town's name probably honors French adventurer and soldier Antoine de la Mothe Cadillac, founder of Detroit in 1701 and colonial governor of Louisiana from 1713 to 1716, who reportedly visited here c. 1715. By 1725 Phillip Renault was producing 1,500 pounds of lead per day at the first lead mine in Missouri, opened in 1715. A road built from here to the Mississippi River (by the 1740s to *Ste. Genevieve*) was probably Missouri's first European *road*, the Three Notch Road that was marked by three notches on a tree. Evidence of mining can be seen along SR OO; marker. Post offices: Mine La Motte 1840–1862, 1867–1911; Mine Lamotte 1911–c. 1931. SR OO, N 3.4 m.

Mines. Legend claims that when God finished creating

the heaven and the earth, he pitched what was left over into Madison County. Fredericktown was surrounded by mines: MINE LA MOTTE: North; lead mine (above). NORTH AMERICAN: East; one of three cobalt mines in North America; inquire locally. PARK CITY: South; lead mine; inquire locally. SILVER: West; silver mine (Shut-Ins, below).

Recreation. CAMPING / PICNIC AREA: Shut-Ins (below). FREDERICKTOWN CITY LAKE: 140 acres. Fishing. N of town; inquire locally. MILLSTREAM GARDENS *STATE FOREST. TRAILS:* Audubon, Rock Pile Mountain.

St. Francis River Natural Area. A 1.2-mile section of the St. Francis River. Part of Millstream Gardens *State Forest.* Features include a spectacular *shut-in,* an adjoining slough, and a variety of river life, e.g. the rare eastern slim minnow and several species of crayfish. Box 152 (West Hwy. T), Perryville 63775. Access: Millstream Gardens *State Forest.*

St. Michael's Church. Romanesque-style, 1927; organized 1827. This structure has rusticated stone with a steeply pitched roof, a square central bell tower, and turrets at either end. Inside is "Baptism of Our Lord," a mosaic made from small bits of colored glass. Visitors welcome. US 72, 3 blocks W of courthouse.

Shut-Ins. BLACK MOUNTAIN: Nearly a mile-long stretch of the St. Francis River with scenic cascades and jointed rocks. US 67B, S 0.9 m.; SR E, S approx. 12 m. (3 m. S of bridge). DURAND: Two miles downstream from Marble Creek (below). Accessible by jeep trail. LITTLE ROCK CREEK: Drops about 80 feet in half a mile. US 67B, S 0.9 m.; SR E, S approx. 13 m. (4.3 m. S of bridge). MARBLE CREEK: Eroded crystalline rock, wading, picnic area, camping *(National Forests).* US 67B, S 0.9 m.; SR E, W approx. 19 m. SILVER MINES: Shallow pools, white water, sculpted rocks, sheer jointed bluffs, pink-tinted rocks masked by lichen. This area has some of the Mississippi valley's oldest rocks (600 millions years old), many of which contain silver, lead, and tungsten embedded in quartz veins (over 20 kinds of minerals have been identified). Silver mines were established in 1877 just south of the dam by the Einstine Silver Company, and a dam was built to drive a turbine wheel. About 0.5 miles southwest of the mine was Silvermine, Mo.[2] (peak pop. 600); no remnants. Silver Mines *Trail* leads to a low cut-stone dam, former mine, and now-defunct town, then back to Silver Mines Campground / Picnic Area at the St. Francis River *(National Forests:* Water, toilets, fishing, swimming; 22-foot RV limit). US 72, W 5.9 m.; SR D, S 4 m. TIEMANN: At one time owned by Elmer Tiemann, a landscape architect who began developing the site by laying out trails and planting trees and flowers (now Millstream Gardens *State Forest).* Trail (2.5 m. one

way), St. Francis River shut-ins (granite bluffs, polished and carved rocks, potholes, rapids). SR 72, W 9 m.; GR, S 0.5 m.

SR 72 Guardrails. *Arcadia.*

1. The archangel; p.o. 1816–1827.
2. The mine; p.o. Einstine Silver Mine 1879–1892; Silver Mine 1892–1955.

FREEBURG
Population: 446   Map F-5

Settled in 1850 by Adam Wieberg, this German community grew slowly as a rest stop beside a north–south road from *Linn* via Rich Fountain (below) to *Vienna.* The name changed several times, beginning in 1879 as Englebert.[1] Today's name was originally spelled Frieberg (from the German "Frie," meaning free) and was later altered to match the post office's English spelling. Platted in 1903 after the 1902 arrival of the St. Louis, Kansas City & Colorado *Railroad,* the town grew as a shipping point. Post offices: Englebert 1886–1888; Frankberg[2] 1888–1892; Freeburg 1893–now.

The Church of the Holy Family. Gothic-style, 1920. Massive twin spires dominate the skyline; parsonage, school, *cemetery.*

Gasconade River. *Float Streams.*

Railroad Tunnel. This is one of two places in Missouri *(Gray Summit)* where the railroad tunneled underneath a town rather than building up the grade to it. The tunnel passes east–west under the south side of the post office and is about 200 yards long with a concrete barrel-vaulted ceiling. US 63, N 1 block from church; Gilbert, 0.2 m. E to MFA depot; walk W on tracks about 300 paces. Note the former railroad depot.

Rich Fountain, Mo. This community grew around John Strumpf's c. 1839 *gristmill.* Father Helias D'huddeghem *(Taos: St. Francis Xavier Church;* Westphalia, below), who established a parish here in 1838, reportedly named the area for its clear springs, which presumably inspired the metaphor, Rich Fountain. Post office: 1854–1872. US 63, N 5 m.; SR E, E 3 m. THE CHURCH OF THE SACRED HEART: Vernacular, 1879; National Historic Register. Built on the area's highest hill (Meander Loop, below); huge stone blocks, tile roof. Parsonage, school, and nun's residence adjacent. US 63, N 5 m.; SR E, E 3 m. MEANDER LOOP, ABANDONED: In what is reportedly Missouri's most impressive example of this phenomenon, the Gasconade River once flowed west from today's bridge (SR E, E 3.2 m.) to the edge of town, then flowed north and east, completing the loop just downstream of the bridge. Most likely a neck of land near today's bridge was breached, leaving the loop (8.5 m. long by 0.25 m. wide). View: overlook, E of Church of the Sacred Heart (above). THETA ROCK: This massive white sandstone rock (50 feet high, 150 wide) is part of the northeast bluff of the abandoned meander loop (above). It has two caves: one with a six-foot diameter and one with a three-foot diameter that has a circular opening crossed by a sandstone bar to form the Greek letter theta. SR 89/SR E; SR 89, N 0.5; GR, W 1.9.

Westphalia, Mo. The town was settled in 1835 at a bend of the Maries River by a colony of Catholic Germans from Westphalia (German meaning west plains), a district in northwest Germany. Father Helias (Rich Fountain, above) platted it after establishing a Jesuit mission in 1838 that helped found seven area churches. Post office: 1848–now. US 63, N 11 m. ANVIL ROCK NATURAL TUNNEL: Shaped like an anvil, this 41-foot-long natural tunnel in the west bluff of the Maries River is 16 feet wide with a 7-foot ceiling. US 63, S 2.6 m.; SR T, S 1.5 m. to bridge, look at west bluff (*Collapsed Cave Systems*). ARCHITECTURE: The one-street downtown, built on a bluff above US 63, has well-maintained brick and frame structures set close to the street. Good examples include St. Joseph's Church (Romanesque, 1848; tower added 1883; additions 1905; Main) and Burns House (clapboard over log, 1840s; E end of Main). NEW HELVETIA, MO.: This nearby 1844 utopian society collapsed, reportedly because of "greed, egotism and laziness" after founder Andres Dietsch's 1846 death; defunct. Helvetia is the Latin name for Switzerland. No post office.

1. Early settler and first postmaster Englebert Franke; p.o. 1886–1888; changed in 1888 to Frankberg.

2. Changed from first postmaster Englebert Franke's first name to his last name by popular vote.

FROHNA
Population: 246   Map I-6

Founded in 1839 by 29 German families from the congregation of Trinity Lutheran Church (*Altenburg*), Frohna is one of the first settlements in Missouri established solely for religious reasons. The community's name was shortened from the German town of Nieder-Frohna, the immigrants' starting point. Post office: 1870–now.

Architecture. Good examples of 19th-century vernacular commercial structures include a former flour mill (1860s; now a feed store; SR C), a general store (c. 1865; SR C at SR A), and a former winery (1882; now bowling lanes; SR C at SR A).

Concordia Lutheran Church. Vernacular, 1874. This large but simply designed white frame church replaced two predecessors (1844, 1855); *cemetery* adjacent. SR C, in town.

Die Kleine Schule. Vernacular, 1898. The name means The Little School in German. This 26-by-48-foot one-story brick building mostly served the primary grades until replaced in 1969 (the community added English to the school curriculum in 1883). Restored and furnished with a woodstove, abacus, schoolbooks in German, and desks. SR C, in town.

Saxon Lutheran Memorial. National Historic Register. Established in 1961 by the Concordia Historical Institute (*Altenburg: Log Cabin College*), the memorial preserves the original homestead of C. A. Bergt, who bought land and a log cabin in 1839. Grounds: a pond, two log cabins (1820, 1842), and a log barn. Museum: displays include household items, tools, and farming equipment. Visitor center, restrooms, camping, picnicking. SR C, in town.

FULTON
Population: 10,033   Map F-4

Platted in 1825 on land owned by George Nichols as county seat of Callaway County, replacing Elizabeth,[1] Fulton was first named Volney, for French Count Constantin Volney, a close friend of Thomas Jefferson. Jefferson was the first choice as namesake, but *Jefferson City* was already established. Residents could forgive Jefferson's deism (religion based on human reason and morality, a basis of the Declaration of Independence),[2] but not the atheism of his friend, whom they branded an infidel. The town name was changed the same year to Fulton for Robert Fulton, whose use of steam to power ships helped establish daily commerce on the Mississippi and Missouri Rivers. Post office: 1825–now. Chamber of commerce: US 54B, W on 2d, N on Court (409). Home of Westminster College and William Woods University (below).

Architecture. Good examples of late 19th-century styles, including a historic district. National Historic Register: HOCKADAY HOUSE: S side; US 54, E on Schultze, N on Hockaday (105). WESTMINSTER COLLEGE: gymnasium, historic district, memorial (below). WILLING HOUSE: US 54, W on 2d, N on Jefferson (211).

Callaway County Courthouse. Moderne, 1938. This 134-by-80-foot three-story brick and stone courthouse is the county's third. Cost: $250,000 ($102,273 federal grant). US 54B. (*County Profiles*)

Callaway Plant (Nuclear). The most visible structure at Union Electric's nuclear power plant is its 553-foot concrete cooling tower, which serves about the same purpose as a car radiator except it circulates 585,000 gallons of water per minute. Steam, rising from the tower, is the result of a process that begins when heat is produced by a controlled nuclear chain reaction that turns water into steam pressure, which drives turbines connected to a generator. A video presentation at the visitor center explains the process. Tours: advance notice required. No notice is required for the viewing area (E 1 m.); covered pavilion, displays. US 54B; SR O, E 11.1 m.

Fulton State Hospital. Established in 1847 as the State Lunatic Asylum, this was the first hospital for the mentally ill west of the Mississippi. US 54B, E on 5th.

The Kingdom of Callaway. *County Profiles: Callaway.*

Lovers' Leap. This impressive 60-foot chert and sandstone bluff has an overhanging south-facing crest at Stinson Creek. US 54, E 0.15 m. to S on a lane between Grand and Bluff.

Missouri School for the Deaf. Founded in 1851, the school provides a tuition-free education for elementary, junior high, and high school students. A small museum on the 90-acre campus depicts the history of education for the deaf. US 54B, E on 6th.

Recreation. CARRINGTON PITS PICNIC AREA *(National Forests)*: Vault toilets, fishing at pits. PINE RIDGE CAMPING / PICNIC AREA *(National Forests)*: Water, vault toilets, Cedar Creek *Trail. WILDLIFE AREAS:* Little Dixie, Reform, Whetstone Creek.

Tuttle House Museum. Queen Anne, 1890. Displays in this county historical museum include local items and a fashion collection; furnished house. US 54B, W on 7th (331).

Westminster College. Chartered in 1851 by the Presbyterian Church as Fulton, the school was rechartered in 1853 as Westminster. In 1946, this four-year nonsectarian liberal arts college was the setting for then former British prime minister Winston Churchill's Iron Curtain speech (actually titled "Sinews of Peace"), warning the world of Soviet expansionism. In 1992, from the same lectern, the former president of the former USSR, Mikhail Gorbachev, spoke about the end of the Cold War. CHURCH OF ST. MARY THE VIRGIN: National Historic Register. This 12th-century church survived the 1666 Great Fire of London (the remodeling was completed by Christopher Wren in 1677), only to be gutted by a 1940 German incendiary bomb. The remaining exterior was dismantled in 1965 and moved stone by stone to this location and reassembled, wherever possible, according to Wren's plans (a 12th-century circular stone staircase remains intact). Relocation of the 1.4-million-pound structure was privately financed at a cost of about $3 million. The building was dedicated in 1969. COLUMNS: Six

freestanding Corinthian columns are the only remnants of a 1909 fire that destroyed the original Westminster Hall. US 54B, W on 7th. WINSTON CHURCHILL MEMORIAL AND LIBRARY: The memorial includes the Church of St. Mary the Virgin, above. Displays include oil paintings by Churchill, family personal items, manuscripts, letters, photographs, a scale model of Blenheim Palace, a rare-map collection. Eight concrete sections of the Berlin Wall incorporated in a 10-by-18-foot sculpture, "Breakthrough," by Churchill's granddaughter Edwina Sandys symbolize the crumbling of the Iron Curtain.

William Woods University. Founded in 1870 at Camden Point *(Platte City)* as a school for orphan girls, it was relocated to Fulton after being destroyed by fire in 1889 and later renamed Daughter's College. Today's name was adopted in 1900 after the school received financial aid from Kansas City banker and physician Dr. William C. Woods. It established the world's first four-year equestrian science baccalaureate program. US 54B, W on Campus.

1. Pioneer settler Henry Brite's wife; p.o. Elizabethtown 1822–1825; defunct.

2. Concepts set forth by Immanuel Kant (1724–1804): natural law (all men are created equal), inviolable rights, and government by consent. Jefferson was also convinced that philanthropy and education were essential for democracy.

GAINESVILLE
Population: 659   Map F-7

Destruction of county records by four courthouse fires (Ozark County Courthouse, below) obscures the town's early history. After Ozark County was reduced in size in 1857, Gainesville was selected as a central location for county seat, replacing Rockbridge (Mills, below). Gainesville's town records begin in 1859, but reportedly the site was platted in 1860 on land donated by Isaac Workman. Primarily settled by Georgians, it was named for Gainesville, Ga., which was named for Gen. Edmund P. Gaines, who arrested Aaron Burr on suspicion of treason and who commanded Fort Erie during the *War of 1812*. Gainesville, like its county, was mostly abandoned during the *Civil War* and grew slowly afterward (1960 pop. 266). Ozark County is one of the few Missouri counties bypassed by railroads. Post office: 1860–1863, 1867–now.

Caney Mountain Natural Area. 1,330 acres. Features an upland forest. SR 181, N 5 m.; NW corner; inquire locally.

Hoerman Park. Playground, tennis, picnic. SR 160, E city limits.

Mills. A mill usually precipitated the growth of a small community of the same name. The mills listed below are authentic and offer romantic settings. Directions are from Gainesville. AID-HODGSON: Built in 1897 by Alva Hodgson (at this 1870s mill site) at Bryant Creek, the three-story frame building is located at a spring that reportedly flows at a rate of 12 million gallons per hour; some grinding done. Camping, canoe rentals (*Float Streams:* Bryant Creek, North Fork White River). No community or p.o. SR 181; N 12 m. to Sycamore,[1] then E 0.5 m. to the creek. DAWT, MO.: Today's mill, built in 1900 by Alva Hodgson (who built his first mill in 1892) at the North Fork of the White River, is a three-story frame building featuring a stone millrace; some milling is still done. Camping, canoeing. The source of the place-name is not known. Post office: 1907–1934. US 160, E 10 m.; SR PP, N 1.2 m.; GR, W 0.7 m. HAMMOND, MO.: Named by the first postmaster for the store's landowners, today's mill, built in 1907 by J. W. Grudier at the Little North Fork (of the White River), is a three-story stone and frame structure that was the center of a prosperous community, including a bank (general-store-style architecture) that was closed after being robbed in 1945. The bank's vault, a cut-stone addition barred by heavy iron doors and an ornamental cast-iron surround, is still intact. The mill and a log structure are in good repair; private property. Not on the map. Post office: 1894–1895, 1906–1975. US 160, W 18 m.; SR 95, N 10 m.; SR D, S 1.9 m.; CR 855, E approx. 1.6 m. Bank: CR 855, S approx. 200 yds. at the junction with CR 850. ROCKBRIDGE, MO.: The 1841 former county seat town (Gainesville history, above) was reportedly relocated here c. 1883 after the mill burned twice. This c. 1883 three-story frame structure was remodeled or rebuilt by B. V. Morris; additions continued until the early 1900s. No longer in operation, it is part of a trout and game complex that utilizes several of the former community's buildings, including a restored 1903 bank and an 1894 general store. Reportedly named for a rock bridge crossing Spring Creek. Post office: 1842–1862, 1869–1880, 1883–now. SR 181, N 6 m.; SR N, N 7.2 m.; GR at Spring Creek, W 0.2 m. (signs 1.8 m. N of SR 95). TOPAZ: *Mountain Grove.* ZANONI, MO.: Named for Bulwer-Lytton's 1842 novel of the same name and built in 1906 near a spring close to Pine Creek by A. P. Morrison (the first, built in 1905, burned), the two-story frame mill has an overshot wheel. Derelict; general store nearby; private, view from road. Post office: 1898–1927, 1930–now. SR 181, N 9.6 m. (*Gristmills*)

Ozark County Courthouse. Moderne, 1939. Of five courthouses, four have been destroyed by fire: one in Rockbridge (1858/1859; above) and the others in Gainesville (c. 1863, 1934, and 1937, the last being a converted Christian church). Built using a *WPA* grant,

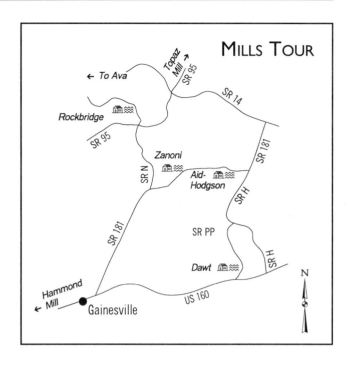

today's three-story structure cost $43,000. Grounds: small log cabin. SR 160, W on SR U. (*County Profiles*)

Recreation. BULL SHOALS LAKE: US 160, W 16 m. to Theodosia[2] (*Lakes: Corps of Engineers*). *FLOAT STREAMS:* Bryant Creek, North Fork White River. GLADE TOP FRACTURES / TRAIL: SR 5 N to SR A, or US 160, W; SR 95, N to Longrun[3] (*Ava*). NORFORK LAKE: Tecumseh (below). NORTH FORK CAMPGROUND / PICNIC AREA (*National Forests*): Trailhead for Ridge Runner and Blue Springs *Trails;* adjacent to Devils Backbone Wilderness. Water, pit toilets, boat launch, North Fork of White River fishing.

Tecumseh, Mo. Named for the Shawnee chief (1768–1813; *Black Hawk War; War of 1812*) who denounced all treaties ceding *Indian* land by claiming it was owned in common for hunting. He organized an Indian confederation stretching from New York to Arkansas whose purpose was to reclaim Indian land. After his death, Tecumseh was romanticized by Americans, who commemorated him with place-names (usually at great distances from the events of his life). Post office: 1898–now. US 160, E 11 m. PATRICK BRIDGE ACCESS: Camping, fishing, canoe put-in for North Fork of White River, and Althea Spring (remnants of a plant to generate electricity). US 160, E 1.5 m.; SR PP, N 5.3 m.; SR H, S 1.9 m. RECREATION: Norfork Lake (*Lakes: Corps of Engineers*).

1. The tree; p.o. 1891–c. 1973.
2. The first postmaster's wife; p.o. 1896–1951, 1960–now. Also served by Lutie, a female member of B. B. Jones's family; p.o. 1893–1917, 1925–1960.
3. Nearby creek, because of its length; p.o. 1898–1980.

GALENA
Population: 401   Map D-7

Records for the sparsely populated Stone County are scarce. In 1851 the newly organized county court, meeting at John B. Williams's house in Cape Fair, ordered a county seat named James Town or Jamestown[1] (Cape Fair, below) to be platted at the James River. In 1853 the name was changed to Galena (for the area's lead ore), probably because of the existence of another Jamestown post office in Moniteau County. The town was slow to grow; maps as late as 1858 listed Cape Fare [sic] without showing Galena or Jamestown. Arrival of the White River *Railroad* in 1904 helped establish it as a trading center. Post office: 1853–now.

Cape Fair, Mo. This 1830s mill town *(Gristmills)* was named for its location near Flat Creek and the James River, which presents a picturesque point of land jutting into the water when viewed from the backbone ridges above. According to oral tradition, the town was ironically known as Cape Fear because this picturesque view was seen when descending by wagon. Located near here at Flat Creek was the first town named Jamestown (Galena history, above), which was destroyed by an 1844 flood. Post office: 1847–1858, 1878–1879, 1886–1887, 1889–now. SR 248, W 5 m.; SR 173, S 7 m.

Dewey J. Short Memorial Building. Vernacular, 1904. This former bank of Galena features memorabilia of town native Dewey Short (1898–1979), a U.S. congressman (with one lapse in terms) from 1928 to 1956, who was instrumental in establishing the Table Rock Lake project *(Lakes: Corps of Engineers)*. Original tile floors, ornamental tin ceiling, teller's cage, 1904 spherical manganese safe *(Centerville: Victor Safe)*. NE side of square.

Stone County Courthouse. Italian Renaissance, 1920; National Historic Register. The county's three courthouses progressed from log to frame to this 65-by-70-foot brick structure that has modest accents like quoins, lintels, a pseudo-rusticated first floor, and a pedimented entry. Cost: $47,600. Downtown. *(County Profiles)*

Wire Road Wildlife Area. *Wildlife Areas.*

Y Bridge / Park. This 1928 concrete bridge, supported by concrete arches, is reportedly one of America's few Y-style bridges: the east end forks, intersecting the highway with two separate ramps, one northbound, one southbound. Now closed to traffic. Adjacent park: restrooms, picnic pavilion, fishing. E end of 4th at river.

1. The river via the apostle James; no. p.o.

GALLATIN
Population: 1,864   Map D-2

Platted in 1837 (with lots sold in 1838) on the south side of the Grand River as county seat of newly organized Daviess County *(Platte Purchase)*, the town was named for Albert Gallatin (1761–1849), one of the most effective secretaries of the U.S. treasury (1801–1814), architect of the Treaty of Ghent *(War of 1812)*, minister to France and Great Britain, and cofounder of New York University. It drew its original population, businesses, and Compton's Store[1] post office from nearby Millport.[2] With a population of about 400, Gallatin was incorporated in 1857 as the county's only chartered town. The arrival of the Chicago, Rock Island & Pacific *Railroad* c. 1871 helped establish it as a trading center. Post offices: Compton's Store 1837–1838; Gallatin 1838–now.

Adam-Ondi-Ahman. Mormon Church Elder Lyman Wright established a ferry in 1837 at the Grand River near Cravensville.[3] Mormon Prophet Joseph Smith arrived in 1838, selecting the site as a "stake" (a territorial and political unit of the church), claiming that God revealed its name as Adam-Ondi-Ahman, which translated from Smith's "reformed Egyptian language" as "Adam's Consecrated Land." Smith further claimed that Adam, three years before his death, gathered all the patriarchs here at Tower Hill to give them his final blessing and that Christ would appear here on Judgment Day. Today, the Church of Jesus Christ of Latter Day Saints *(Independence: Mormon Sites)* has acquired hundreds of acres, crisscrossed by graded and named gravel roads, in this ruggedly beautiful area overlooking a sharp bend of the river. Visitors welcome. SR 13, N 5 m. *(Mormons)*

Architecture. Good examples of late 19th-century styles include: COURTHOUSE (below). DOWNTOWN COMMERCIAL BUILDINGS: SR 13. PLACE HOUSE: Queen Anne, National Historic Register. SR 13, W on Van Buren (212).

Daviess County Courthouse. Italian Renaissance, 1907–1908; National Historic Register. The county's second, this three-story stone courthouse features a rusticated first story, a domed cupola with four clocks, bracketed eaves, a different window treatment on each floor, and four pedimented projecting central entries with Romanesque arches and second-story Ionic columns. Cost: $69,650. Grounds: Civil War (1862) 3-inch ordnance gun. Architect P. H. Weathers also designed early 20th-century courthouses in Cape Girardeau and Stoddard Counties. Downtown; SR 13. *(County Profiles)*

Dockery Park. 20 acres. Tennis, picnic areas, fishing pond. N side; SR 13, E on Lee.

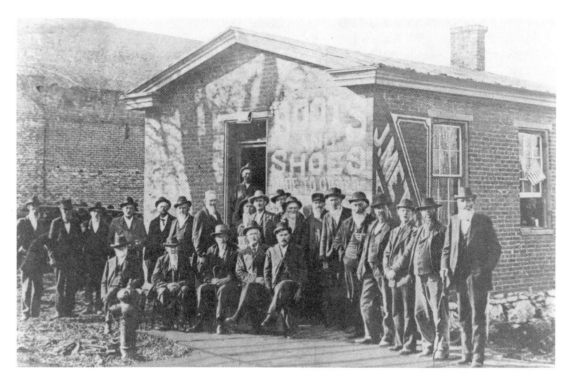

The Daviess County Savings Association robbed in 1869 by Jesse and Frank James.

Gallatin Wildlife Area. *Wildlife Areas.*

James Brothers. Reportedly the first reward for arresting Jesse and Frank James was posted after they robbed the Daviess County Savings Association in 1869, killing Capt. John Sheets (Lyle Cemetery, below).[4] Ironically, one of the James brothers' last robberies occurred at nearby Winston (below). Downtown; SR 13 at North. *(Kearney; Liberty)*

Lewis Mill Site. In 1989 archaeologists unearthed lumber from a *gristmill* that evolved c. 1850–1878 from two wooden waterwheels to metal paddles that were used horizontally to function at double the rate of the standard vertical stream-powered types (water poured from a reservoir above). Reportedly the walnut waterwheel is the oldest of its kind found in Missouri. The mill collapsed into the Grand River in 1899; remnants. SR 6, E 2 m.; SR 13, N 6 m.; SR OO, W 3 m. (part GR) to bridge at the river.

Lyle Cemetery. Here, among other 19th-century tombstones, is a tall shaft marking the family plot of Capt. John Sheets, who was murdered by the James brothers because of a *Civil War* vendetta (James Brothers, above) in what is now thought to have been a case of mistaken identity. In town; inquire locally. *(Cemeteries)*

McDonald's Tea Room. White frame and stucco, looking a lot like a wedding cake with shingle icing, the restaurant was built by Sam and Virginia McDonald after she phased out her husband's grocery-lunchroom. Opened in 1931 when the county had only two

paved highways, it was discovered in 1936 by Duncan Hines, listed in his guide for 27 years, selected by Betty Crocker to introduce her new radio series ("Most Interesting U.S. Restaurants"), and chosen in 1964 by "Better Homes and Gardens" as one of the 90 best restaurants in America. Still serving. SR 13 at courthouse; SR 6B, W 2 blocks.

Rotary Jail. Octagon, 1888. Enclosed in this brick structure attached to a two-story 1888 Italianate brick house, and operating like a lazy Susan, this circular jail with a lavatory at the center had pie-slice-shaped cells with steel ceilings, floors, and walls. Using an 1881 design patented by W. H. Brown of Indianapolis, the jail was built on a hand-cranked steel turntable that the jailer could rotate to a single exit. It served the county intact until remodeled in 1964 as a two-pen stationary jail; abandoned in 1975. One of three known still standing, this one is missing its turntable and cells. SR 13 at courthouse, W on Jackson to dead end.

Winston, Mo. The town was established in 1871 along the Chicago & Southwestern *Railroad*, halfway between Gallatin and *Cameron*, and named Crofton's Depot.[5] Its name was changed in 1872 to Winstonville, honoring F. K. Winston, the 1871 president of the railroad, and incorporated in 1878 as Winston. Post offices: Winstonville 1872–1878; Emporia[6] 1878–1885; Winston 1885–now. SR 6, W 8 m. to Altamont;[7] continue SR 6, W 1 m.; US 69, W 2 m. DEPOT MUSEUM / JESSE JAMES: Railroad, 1871; restored. Displays include railroad memorabilia, furniture, and historical items highlighting the July 15, 1881, train robbery led by Jesse and Frank James, which reportedly was one of their last *(Piedmont: Gads Hill)*. Boarding the train from this depot, they stopped it where getaway horses were tied near today's stone culvert, which was being built at that time (N side US 69, E of town near the cemetery). Arrested in 1882 for robbery, including $4,000–$10,000 from here, and for the deaths of the conductor and a passenger, Frank James was tried at Gallatin, where a jury of his peers (Southern sympathizers) acquitted him *(Kearney: Jesse James Farm)*. The depot's 1,044-foot altitude affords long views, including Gallatin on a clear day. US 69, in town.

1. Store owner; p.o. 1837–1838.
2. Mill at river; p.o. Compton's Store.
3. Early settler Cravens; p.o. 1841–1860.
4. On December 24, 1869, Gov. Joseph W. McClurg requested "30 or more" men formed as a militia to aid the Clay County sheriff in capturing or killing Jesse and Frank James; a reward of $500 for each was offered *(Kearney: Jesse James Farm)*.
5. Frederick Croft, who, among others, donated land for a depot; no p.o.
6. Conflicted with an existing Winston in Dent County; Graeco-Latin meaning market/place of business.
7. Descriptive of the 1002–foot elevation, taken to mean high mountain; p.o. 1890–now.

GASCONADE
Population: 253   Map G-4

Platted in 1821 as Gasconade City at the confluence of the Gasconade and Missouri Rivers as county seat of newly organized Gasconade County, the town was named for the river, which reportedly was named prior to 1800 by "arrogant St. Louis Frenchmen" for the area's "boastful people," who were said to be reminiscent of residents of France's Gascony region, then noted for their rowdy bragging. The town declined after severe flooding precipitated removal in 1825 of the county seat to Bartonville[1] *(Mount Sterling)*. In 1857 Robert J. and Sara A. Heath platted Gasconade City again, this time along the tracks of the Pacific *Railroad*, which had arrived in 1855. Sometime after 1882 (the records are not specific), the town name was shortened, possibly to conform to the post office's. Post offices: Gasconade 1823–1825, 1882–c. 1973; Gasconade City 1865–1882.

Boatyard. Established in 1892 by the Army Corps of Engineers; closed in 1969. Four turn-of-the-century two-story brick houses stand in a row near a cornfield and the former repair shops. SR 100, N on 2d; GR to site.
Ferry / Fredricksburg, Mo. The community was settled c. 1849 by first postmaster William Geiser. The

origin of its name is uncertain but could be for Frederick the Great *(Fredericktown)*. Post office: 1849–1922. Optional routes: (1) SR 100, W 4 m.; SR N, S approx. 4.8 m. (2) SR 100, E 4 m.; SR J, S 8.2 m. FREDRICKSBURG FERRY: Located at the Gasconade River just below a two-story 19th-century limestone house, it connects SR N and SR J. *(Ferryboats)*
Gasconade Park. Bluffs, restrooms, no picnic facilities, camping, fishing, river access, view of Pacific Railroad Bridge (below). N of SR 100 at W riverbank.
Morrison, Mo. A. J. Morrison moved a depot here c. 1858 from nearby Dresden[2] and built a store and later a brewery. Post office: 1860–now. SR 100, W 6 m. ARCHITECTURE: About a dozen late 19th- and early 20th-century buildings. Nearby is A. J. Morrison's two-story antebellum house (weatherboard log; National Historic Register; SR 100, W of town). *FLOAT STREAM:* Gasconade River. PARK: Picnic facilities, ball field, restrooms. E side. ST. JOHN'S CHURCH: Gothic Revival, 1885 (limestone); organized 1855; *cemetery* adjacent. SR 100, E 2 m.; SR N, S 5.9 m.; SR J, E 1.3 to junction with SR OO (just S of ferry, above).
Pacific Railroad Bridge. Truss, 1855. The first bridge here, supported by a temporary trestle, collapsed under the speed and weight of the first train to Jefferson City, killing 34 passengers. SR 100 at river.

1. Origin unknown; p.o. Simpsons, personal name, 1824–c. 1828.
2. Town in Germany; no p.o.; defunct.

GENTRYVILLE
Estimated population: 23   Map C-2

This is reportedly Gentry County's oldest town; the first cabin at the site was built in 1838. Gentryville was platted in 1848 along the Grand River by Charles Gay, who built a sawmill here in 1841. While the town was growing (1874 pop. c. 300), the c. 1880 completion of two railroads (St. Joseph & Des Moines and St. Louis, Kansas City & Northern) helped create new towns that drained Gentryville's population and commerce. Named for the county. Post office: 1846–1938.
Elam Bend Wildlife Area. *Wildlife Areas.*
Gentryville Hotel. The construction date of this two-story nine-room frame structure is not known, but it was operated in 1882 as a hotel (six rooms upstairs). In town.
Gentryville Picnic. A tradition since 1887. August 3.
Mt. Zion Church / Cemetery. Vernacular, 1891; addition c. 1912; organized 1842. This white clapboard structure is the third Presbyterian church at this site. Abandoned in 1952, it remains beside a well-kept cemetery (established in 1842) with interesting markers,

including ones for the county's first settler, Isaac Miller (1813–1899), and Sarah Ann Patton (d. 1864), which is embellished by carved fern and ivy and shaped like a tree trunk (a stone inscription scroll hangs from a branch). SR T, E 2.2 m.; SR A, N 0.6 m.; GR, W 1.2 m. (*Cemeteries*)

GERALD
Population: 888   Map G-4

In 1848 Washington Fitzgerald built a log cabin beside the main east–west *road* south of the Missouri River between St. Louis and Westport (*Kansas City*). His children and grandchildren helped establish a town that was platted in 1901 along the St. Louis, Kansas City & Colorado *Railroad*. The town was named for the Fitzgerald family. Post office: 1901–now.

Bourbeuse River. *Float Streams.*

Folk Art / Cemetery. Eleven graves of the old Cave Springs Cemetery feature late 19th- and 20th-century markers with embellishments: e.g. rock baskets with seashells, petrified wood, stars, hearts, crosses, diamonds, a rock-art 48-star red-white-and-blue American flag, native rock, blossom quartz, foam geodes. The centerpiece is a nine-foot pedestal supporting a four-foot angel made of rocks and crystals. SR H, S 8.8 m.; SR AC, E 3.4 m. (*Cemeteries*)

Gerald Depot / Park. Railroad, 1910; restored. Moved here in 1985. Railroad memorabilia, restrooms, picnic facilities, shade trees. W side; SR 50.

Noser Mill, Mo. This *gristmill* was built in the early 1850s at an 1822 mill site along the Bourbeuse River; it was bought by John J. Noser in 1878. Closed c. 1928, the mill was a headquarters for recreation (boating, camping, fishing) and had a pool hall, tavern, and general store until c. 1974. Derelict (pop. 4); a log dam was replaced c. 1910 by a concrete one. Post offices: Luther[1] 1872, 1896–1902; Noser Mill 1902–1908. US 50, E 6 m. to Beaufort;[2] SR 185, S 2 m.

1. First postmaster Martin Luther Green Crowe.
2. Beaufort, S.C., via the Duke of Beaufort, one of about seven Lord Proprietors of the Carolinas; p.o. 1849–now.

GLACIAL ERRATICS

About a million years ago, four great sheets of ice spread in successive waves southward from the Arctic region. The last wave ended c. 15,000 to 10,000 B.C. Two, the Nebraskan and Kansas glaciers, are known to have reached the Missouri River and further south in some isolated areas (Mastodon *State Park*). Ranging from 100 to 1,000 feet thick, these glaciers ground northern Missouri into today's topography of gently rolling *prairies* and wide shallow valleys. After retreating, they left behind rich drift soil *(loess)* and sometimes strangely isolated boulders called glacial erratics that vary in composition according to their origin (none are from less than 300 miles away).

GLADSTONE
Population: 26,243
Maps C-3 and Kansas City Area

Now part of the greater *Kansas City* area, today's town combines two 1880s Hannibal & St. Joseph *Railroad* communities separated by two miles: to the north, Gash,[1] and to the south, Linden.[2] The two incorporated in 1952 as Gladstone. Named for William E. Gladstone (1809–1898), four-time Liberal prime minister of England. Post office: 1957–1959.

Dan Hughes House. Log, c. 1821–1826; enlarged, weatherboard. Originally a 16-foot-square cabin with a loft, today's two-story L-shaped frame house represents a typical transition from pioneer shelter to permanent dwelling. Rafters and joists are held together by pegs. SR 1 at SR 152; SR 1, S 1 m.

Heritage Village. A reconstructed pre-1850 village: buildings, crafts, demonstrations. SR 1, N to SR 152, E to I-435, N to Barry (7000).

Maple Woods Nature Preserve. 38.7 acres, National Natural Landmark. Wildlife habitat, virgin maple forest, nature trails. Prospect at NE 72d.

Riverside, Mo. Once famous for horse racing (now stock car racing), Platte County's newest (incorporated in 1951) and largest (pop. 3,206) city was named for its location: it is bounded on the west and east by the Missouri River. Post office: none. US 169 at I-29; I-29, W 1.4 m.; I-635, S 2 m. LINE CREEK PARK: A former Hopewell Indian site with a museum, a buffalo and elk compound, trails, picnic areas. I-635, N 2 m., I-29, E 0.5 m.; SR AA (Waukomis Dr.), N 3 m.

1. Landowner's wife's maiden name; p.o. 1899–1959.
2. The tree; p.o 1889–1957.

GLASGOW
Population: 1,295   Map E-3

Platted in 1836 by 13 men (including James Glasgow), the town was established as a shipping and retail point for the area's hemp and tobacco production, replacing three other nearby towns (now defunct) founded at sites plagued by malaria and other diseases: Chariton[1] (founded in 1818; *Keytesville),* Monticello[2] (founded in 1829), and Thorntonburg[3] (founded in 1832). Aided by Irish and German immigrants after 1860, Glasgow continued to grow as a steamboat port, making what appeared to be a successful transition to a *railroad* shipping point during the 1870s with the arrival of the St. Louis, Kansas City & Northern and Chicago & Alton. However, increased competition from other railroad towns eroded its prosperity (Railroad Bridge, below). Post office: 1837–now.

Architecture. Over 50 structures, nearly half of them antebellum, offer examples of Greek Revival, Italianate, Gothic Revival, and Queen Anne styles. At the Missouri River between 1st, Saline, 5th, and Boone are 30 examples. Along SR 5/240 (Randolph) are 10.

Battle of Glasgow. October 5, 1864. Seeking supplies, Gen. Sterling Price's Confederates *(Pilot Knob: Battle of Pilot Knob)* assaulted this Federal-occupied town, forcing a surrender, but only after outnumbered Federals burned the stockpile of munitions stored in city hall, resulting in destruction of a half-block of downtown (losses: Federal, 11 killed, 32 wounded; Confederate, about double that). A week later, bushwhacker Bill Anderson rode into town to collect a bounty of $6,000 for his own capture, dead or alive, that had been offered by Col. W. B. Lewis (Glasgow Public Library, below) because of Anderson's murders in *Centralia* the previous month. After beating and torturing Lewis, Anderson collected $1,000 from him and $5,000 from a family friend. Battle site: second city hall (c. 1867, Romanesque), 2d at Market.

Glasgow Community Museum. Gothic Revival, 1861; National Historic Register. This former Presbyterian church (built by Baptists and sold in 1866) displays local historical items, paintings by regional artist Cornelia Kuemmel (1863–1938), and a 19th-century-era furnished room. Downtown; 4th at Commerce (402).

Glasgow Public Library. Italianate, 1866; National Historic Register. Millionaire tobacco merchant Col. W. B. Lewis (Battle of Glasgow, above) bequeathed $10,000 to begin what is reportedly Missouri's first library founded by private endowment and Missouri's oldest library building in continuous use. Features include a curved iron staircase, walnut bookcases, desks, chairs, a Glasgow Civil War battle flag, local historical items, and a 12-pound bronze howitzer (1863, range 5 miles). Downtown; 4th at Market.

Railroad Bridge. Steel, 1878–1879; the world's first all-steel railroad bridge. Although Chicago & Alton Railroad engineer Gen. Sooy Smith was warned that A. F. Hay's new steel alloy (to replace iron in construction) would cause the bridge to collapse on the first

frosty day, Smith spent $500,000 to build this new type of bridge, which connected Chicago and Kansas City by rail. About 800 tons of steel were used for five 314-foot truss spans and 1,140 feet of approach spans. Replaced in 1899 by today's bridge (built on the former's stone piers) because of increasing weights and speeds of trains, it had not showed signs of weakness. N side of SR 240 highway bridge.

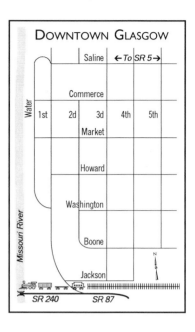

DOWNTOWN GLASGOW

Stump Island Park. Overlooks river; boat ramp, restrooms, picnic shelters, tennis, camping. SR 87, S on old SR 87, then S on Stump Island Dr. (two mid-1850s houses are on this road).

Tour Homes. JACKSON: Queen Anne Free Classic, late 1890s; some additions. Mostly intact, built of oak. 1800s furnishings; inquire locally. VAUGHAN: Italianate, 1857. The relatively simple detailing of this two-story brick house, as opposed to later (1860–1870s) high Victorian, is blurred by elements of Gothic Revival (the upper porch spindles and lower supports). Period furnishings, wine cellar, coal-burning fireplaces. In town; 701 Randolph (SR 5/240).

1. Chariton County's namesake; p.o. 1818–1845.
2. Thomas Jefferson's home; no p.o. of its own.
3. R. B. Thornton; also known as Louisville-on-Missouri River as named by Thomas Joyce of Louisville, part owner of the townsite; no p.o. of its own.

GLENWOOD

Population: 195   Map F-1

Platted in 1868 along the grade of the North Missouri *Railroad* by brothers Stiles and Alexander Forsha, the town was incorporated in 1869 as a rival of nearby county seat *Lancaster,* which was recovering from the *Civil War* and being bypassed by the railroad. Glenwood quickly grew into the county's leading trading center, assuming the nickname Industrial Hollow for its more than 20 businesses, including a hub and spoke factory, mills (saw, *grist,* woolen), and a foundry. Lancaster regained its strength in 1872 with the arrival of the Missouri, Iowa & Nebraska Railroad, which bypassed Glenwood and thereby defeated a proposal to remove the county seat to Glenwood. Ironically, although Glenwood continued to grow, railroads continued to bring cheaper goods to the county, which eroded the town's economic base and eventually caused its decline. The town was named for its township; Glen, made familiar by writer Sir Walter Scott, is derived from Gaelic and used romantically without regard to the original meaning of valley or narrow valley. Post office: 1869–now.

Architecture. The few remaining downtown buildings were some of the first built (1869) and can be recognized by cast-metal columns, corbeled cornices, dentils and sawtooth courses, keystone lintels, and arched headers. Old town.

Coatsville, Mo. Platted in 1868 along the North Missouri *Railroad* and named for railroad land agent N. B. Coates, Coatsville was a modestly prosperous shipping point for nearby coalfields. It never recovered from the Great Depression and today is a bedroom community of 55; most of its 19th-century vernacular-style commercial and residential structures have been abandoned. Post office: 1869–now. SR 202, N 7 m.

Grand Divide. US 63, N and S. *(Grand Divide)*

Rebel's Cove Wildlife Area. SR 202 and SR Z, W 6.5 m. *(Wildlife Areas)*

GRAHAM

Population: 204   Map C-1

The town was first platted in 1856 by saw/*gristmill* owner Andrew Brown at Elkhorn Creek as Jacksonville.[1] After Brown added a second addition in 1858, the name was changed in 1859 to conform to the post office's, which had been established a half-mile north in 1852 by Col. Amos Graham *(Maryville).* Post office: 1852–now.

Nodaway River Shut-Ins. These *shut-ins* were formed by a narrowing of the river valley from three miles to as little as a quarter-mile approximately one mile north and three miles south of nearby Maitland.[2]

Simpson's College / Museum. Vernacular, 1843. This three-room clapboard schoolhouse, set on a low stone foundation, has a brick root cellar and a nearby hand-dug well. Also on the grounds is a late 1890s one-cell brick and stucco jailhouse, an irony some students might appreciate. In town.

1. Origin unknown; common place-name, usually for Andrew Jackson; p.o. Graham.

2. RR employee; p.o. Whig Valley, origin unknown; The Whigs were members of antislavery faction of the Republican Party; p.o. 1861–1864, 1869–1880; Maitland 1880–now.

GRAND DIVIDE

This 19th-century geographical term describes the watershed along a ridge that nearly follows US 63 from the Iowa line to *Moberly,* separating drainage from the Chariton and Little Chariton Rivers to the west and the Fabius and Salt River basin to the east. The west side drains to the Missouri; the east, to the Mississippi above Louisiana, Mo.

GRANDVIEW

Population: 24,963   Map C-4

Settled c. 1840 as a farming community, the town was destroyed during the *Civil War* as a result of *Order No. 11,* then rebuilt and platted in 1889. Grandview is a stock place-name (generally American and particularly western); this town was reportedly named by settlers for the view from the general store. Since the 1873 survey of its first *railroad* (Kansas City, Memphis & Mobile), the town, now a suburb of *Kansas City,* has developed an industrial base. Post office: 1889–now. Maps and guides: chamber of commerce, 1200 Main.

Depot Museum. Railroad, 1912. Built by the Kansas City & Southern and restored by the Grandview Historical Society, the building displays local historical items; the exhibits are rotated every three months. Waiting room, agent's and station master's office, sorting desk. Grounds: caboose. N side; US 71, W on Main, N on 13th to W on Jones (1205).

Longview Park and Lake. *Lakes: Corps of Engineers.*

Truman Farm Home. Folk Victorian, 1894; National Historic Site; *National Park;* National Historic Register. This two-story clapboard home of former president Harry S. Truman is a good example of its style, which includes a three-ranked hipped-roof I-house with bracketed eaves and modest spindlework porch detailing. Truman *(Belton; Independence; Lamar)* lived and worked here at the 600-acre farm of his grandfather, Solomon Young, and also served as a postmaster and school board member from 1906 until leaving in 1917 to serve in WWI at the age of 32. His brother Vivian lived here until his death in 1965. Early 1900 furnishings, some Truman memorabilia, tours. Nearby Blue Ridge Baptist *Cemetery* was established in 1853 by Solomon Young (inquire locally). Incidentally, Truman, the "working class president" and the last president without a college education, was the first recipient (on January 20, 1966) of a Medicare I.D. card. US 71, Blue Ridge exit to 12301 Blue Ridge.

GRANT CITY
Population: 998   Map C-1

Platted in 1863 and named for then Gen. U. S. Grant, commander of *Civil War* Federal forces (later U.S. president, 1869–1877), the town was selected by petition as a central location for county seat of Worth County, replacing Smithton,[1] also known as Worthville.[2] Post office: 1864–now.

Allendale, Mo. Allendale was platted in 1855 as Allenville by brothers William C. and Joel Allen; reportedly the name was changed to Allendale in 1856 due to an existing Allenville. Although the townsite was selected for its location as a rest stop on the road between *Albany* and Mt. Ayr, Iowa, ironically the first business was a saloon, not a hotel; its site today is occupied by a Baptist church (built in 1891). Post office: 1856–now. SR 46, E 6 m. NATION SCHOOL / MUSEUM: Vernacular, 1865. This frame schoolhouse is now a doll museum. Officially called Adams School, its name was changed during a heated debate at a school meeting, when someone remarked, after seeing more people arriving, "here comes the whole damn nation." GR, 2.9 m.; inquire locally.

GAR Monument. Commissioned by the Grand Army of the Republic, "The Returning Soldier" is a sculpture of a tree trunk from which hangs a soldier's rifle, canteen, field jacket, and backpack. It was created in 1896 by Dell Eighmy Sr. from what was reportedly the heaviest single object ever shipped to town, a rough armodite stone (8 tons, 3 feet square, 11.4 feet long) from Bedford, Ind. In town.

Glen Miller Marker. Erected in 1989, the marker notes that big-band leader Miller was a shoe-shine boy for Grant City bandmaster and cleaning parlor operator John Mosbarger, who taught him how to play his first instrument, a trombone. In town.

Worth County Community Lake. 20 acres. Bass, sunfish, crappie, catfish. US 169, S 4.4 m.; SR YY, W 3.3 m.; SR W, W 2 m.; GR, S 1.2 m.

Worth County Courthouse. Richardsonian Romanesque, 1898; National Historic Register. The county's third (the first, built in 1863, burned during its third year), this massive 71-by-80-foot courthouse features a domed clock tower, square corner towers, a busy roof of dormers, and arched windows and doorways. Cost: $21,289. In town. (*County Profiles*)

1. Town founder Eli Smith; p.o. 1861–1867, 1869–1870; defunct.
2. Worth County namesake (*County Profiles*).

GRAVOIS MILLS
Population: 101   Map E-5

Platted in 1884 to include Gravois Creek settlements that had gathered around local mills (a c. 1835 *gristmill* and an 1870 woolen mill), the town was named for the creek's mills (gravois was the American French term for gravel). Today it relies on Lake of the Ozarks tourism (*Camdenton: Bagnell Dam*). Post office: 1860–now.

Natural Bridge. Actually a footpath across a natural arch, the bridge has a 25-foot span and is about 16 feet high and 4 feet wide. SR 5, N 2 m.; SR J, S 0.3 m.; GR, N 0.5 m.; park at sharp turn; look S. (*Collapsed Cave Systems*)

Old St. Patrick's Church. Vernacular, 1868–1879; addition 1936; restored 1968; National Historic Register. Small and rectangular, this stone church was built by Irish immigrants who used locally quarried stone and lumber hewn from trees. Last Mass, 1952; *cemetery* adjacent. SR 5, S 8.5 m. to Laurie;[1] SR O, E 1 m.

1. Origin unknown; no p.o.

GRAY SUMMIT
Estimated population: 300   Map H-4

Post offices trace the town's early history. The 1824 post office community of Point Labaddie,[1] set on a point, traded on the Missouri River. Later it was moved inland to trade on both the river and the St. Louis–Jefferson City *Road*, and the name was changed c. 1838 to Port William.[2] After Port William was narrowly bypassed to the east in the early 1850s by the Pacific *Railroad*, its residents, like many townspeople dependent on the river, underestimated the economic threat from the railroad (*Boonville*). In 1855, a railroad town named for local hotel owner Daniel Gray was platted as Gray's Summit on one of the highest points of the Pacific Railroad's line (Railroad Tunnel, below). Post offices: Port William 1838–1859; Gray's Summit 1859–1892; Gray Summit 1892–now. (*Route 66*)

Labadie, Mo. Platted in 1855 as a Pacific *Railroad* town, Labadie and its nearby predecessor Point Labaddie (Gray Summit history, above) are named for Sylvestre L'Abaddie, an associate of the American Fur Company of St. Louis and the son and namesake of a prominent 18th-century St. Louis merchant who in 1776 married into the Chouteau family that helped found *St. Louis*. Today the town caters to tourists. Post office: 1855–now. SR MM, N 4.1 m. ENGELMANN WOODS NATURAL AREA: 145 acres. Located in rugged river hills, it features weathered limestone cliffs, a mature and old-growth forest (oak, basswood, ash, and sugar maple), small creeks, ferns, celandine poppy, and spring wildflowers. Box 248, Sullivan 63080. SR T, E approx. 5 m.; signs. MT. PLEASANT WINERY: Wine tasting. In town *(Augusta)*. TAVERN ROCK CAVE: National Historic Register. Described in *Lewis and Clark*'s 1804 journals as about 120 feet wide, 40 feet deep, and 20 feet high, the cave now has debris dumped at the mouth by the railroad. While the "many different images" Clark observed painted on the rock have yet to be found, evidence, mostly pits, indicates prehistoric habitation. SR T, E 6 m. to St. Albans.[3] Inquire locally, or park near p.o. and walk the railroad track NE 1.75 m. to the first deep cut in the limestone cliff; at SW edge of cut descend to the river (to the left).

Purina Farms. Established in 1926 by the St. Louis–based 1894 Ralston Purina Company as a research site to develop food for domestic and farm animals, the farm today is 820 acres and offers tours that include a presentation on the relationship between people and animals, hands-on exhibits (i.e. weighing yourself in units of hogs), and the chance to hold kittens, puppies, sheep, rabbits, and piglets. Special events: April–November. SR MM, W 1 m.

Railroad Tunnel. This is one of two places in Missouri towns *(Freeburg)* where the railroad tunneled underneath the town rather than building up the grade to it. The tunnel is 1,580 feet long, 28.5 feet wide, and 25 feet tall. Inquire locally.

Robertsville State Park. I-44, S 7 m.; SR O, E 5.9 m. *(State Parks)*

Route 66. *St. Louis: Route 66.*

Shaw Arboretum. The original 1,300-acre tract on the north side of the Meramec River was bought in 1925 as a relocation site for the Missouri Botanical Garden *(St. Louis)* because of the effects on the horticultural collection of increasing amounts of air pollution. It was extensively landscaped and planted before the relocation plan was abandoned in the late 1930s when St. Louis's air quality improved. However, the horticultural work continued here, and today the nearly four square miles of Ozark Plateau feature an eleven-mile trail system divided into seven different walks. Visitor center, guidebooks, tours, picnic area, cross-country skiing, bird-watching. I-44; SR 100, W; signs. BRUSH CREEK TRAIL: 0.75 miles. Labeled examples of native Missouri trees; meadow. OVERLOOK TRAIL: 0.75 miles. Upland hickory forest, dogwoods, overlook of

the valley from limestone bluffs. PINETUM TRAIL: 0.5 miles. The Midwest's most extensive conifer collection, Pinetum Lake, some native woodland. PRAIRIE TRAIL: 1 mile. Native tallgrass *prairie* (up to 10 feet tall), observation deck, 130 species of wildflowers that bloom May to October, small lake. RIVER TRAIL: 2 miles. Parallels the Meramec River through five distinct Ozark region natural communities; access to river gravel bar. WILDFLOWER TRAIL: 0.75 miles. Spring wildflowers, large dolomite glade, herbaceous plants that bloom in early summer. WOLF RUN TRAIL: 1 mile. Open meadow with a panoramic overview of the countryside, Wolf Run Lake.

1. Location, misspelled family name (Labadie, Mo., below); defunct; p.o. 1824–1838.
2. Postmaster William North; p.o. 1838–1859.
3. English town named for first Christian martyr in England, a Roman soldier; p.o. Becker, origin unknown, 1892–1898, 1922–1943; St. Albans, 1898–1907, 1943–now. The first St. Albans, settled in 1837, was flooded away in 1844.

GREEN CITY
Population: 671   Map E-1

Platted in 1880 along the Quincy, Missouri & Pacific *Railroad* and named for the line's president, Amos Green, the town siphoned off the population, structures, and post office of nearby Kiddville,[1] built a railroad station, and incorporated in 1882. Post offices: Kiddville 1857–1881; Green City, 1881–now.

Dark Hollow Natural Area. 308 acres. Part of Union Ridge *State Forest*. Features an upland forest with, for northern Missouri, many unusually old and large trees and diverse flora, including orchids, yellow lady slipper, bloodroot, and goldenseal. 2500 S. Halliburton, Kirksville 63501. SR 129, N 1.9 m.; GR, N 2 m.; unimproved county road, N 0.8 m. (0.9 m. trail leads to Spring Creek).

Green Castle, Mo. Platted in 1857, this is one of Sullivan County's oldest towns. Tradition claims the town was first called Castle, with Green added later to honor railroad executive Amos Green (Green City history, above), but the railroad did not arrive until c. 1880 and maps of the 1850s carry the name Green Castle, the town's only post office name. Probably the name Greencastle was transplanted and then separated; possible sources include Greencastle, Ind., and the 1782 Greencastle, Pa., named for Greencastle, Ireland, which romanticized the castle's location. Post office: Green Castle 1856–now. SR 6, E 4 m. GREEN CASTLE *CEMETERY:* Established in 1857; the first burial, in 1858, was the 21-year-old daughter of a couple passing through town. A 1922 bronze statue of a WWI soldier stands at the ready with rifle and pack. SR 6, E approx. 1 m.

Green City Depot / Museum. Railroad, 1880. Although board-and-batten, the building is more stylish than the typical farm town depot: a steeply pitched roof slightly flared at the eaves, central bay, and abbreviated tower. Grounds: an 1883 caboose with wooden siding. MUSEUM: Railroad items, e.g. jacks, telegraph equipment, and a baggage truck. Town square.

Mystic, Mo. All that remains of this ghost town is the romantic name that was probably borrowed from Mystic, Conn., which derives its name from the Algonquian for big-tidal-river. Post office: 1898–1903. SR 129, S 7.8 m.

1. Origin unknown; p.o. 1857–1881; defunct.

GREENFIELD

Population: 1,416   Map D-6

The town was platted in 1841 as county seat of newly organized Dade County (Everton, below). Greenfield's stock place-name is descriptive of the area. As the county's most prominent town and most important trading center, it suffered during the *Civil War* from Confederate raids on Union garrisons here. Despite being bypassed in 1881 by the *railroad* (South Greenfield, below), today it is the county's largest town. Post offices: Dade Court House[1] 1842–1850; Greenfield 1850–now.

Architecture. The downtown area has good examples of 19th-century styles. Walking tour maps: historical society (Washington Hotel, below).

Dade County Courthouse. Italian Renaissance, 1934–1935. Although the courthouse was designed in 1921, the financing was rejected by voters until 1934, when $110,000 was contributed by the *WPA*. The country's fourth, this 70-by-70-foot three-story *Carthage* marble courthouse has modest elements of its style: four full-height projecting central entries, a pseudo-rusticated first story, and a roofline parapet. Cost: $135,000. US 160, E on College. (*County Profiles*)

Everton, Mo. Established in 1881 along the tracks of the Kansas City, Ft. Scott & Gulf *Railroad*, Everton was reportedly named for a railroad employee named Everett. Post offices: Rock Prairie[2] 1843–1845, 1847–1863, 1866–1867, 1869–1881; Everton 1881–now. SR 39, S 7 m.; SR K, E 7.3 m. COMET MILL: Vernacular, 1882; collapsed. Until 1947 various mills (*Gristmills*) used this c. 1850 site at the Sac River in Comet.[3] SR 160, E 2.5 m.; SR FF, N 4.5 m.; GR, E 1 m. FIRST DADE COUNTY COURTHOUSE: Log, 1837. Formerly located on

Pennsylvania *Prairie,* this log cabin of William Penn (grandnephew of Pennsylvania founder William Penn) was the 1841 temporary county seat. Moved during the 1930s to Dye Park; in town.

Greenfield Opera House. Beaux Arts, 1888; restored 1986. The words "Drama, Comedy, Opera" are chiseled along the frieze of this ornate three-story brick building. It served as a theater, ballroom, and recital/lecture hall until 1920. The first floor provided commercial space until 1986; today it is a community theater with a capacity of 200. Town square; US 160, E on College.

Hulston Mill / Park. Vernacular, c. 1880; restored. This two-story frame mill (*Gristmills*), the last of several mills built at the same 1838 site, was moved here from the Sac River c. 1968 before being flooded by Stockton Lake (*Lakes: Corps of Engineers*). Picnic facilities, restored log cabins, restrooms. US 160, E 7 m.; SR EE, N 2 m.; GR, E 0.9 m.

Lockwood, Mo. Established in 1880 along the Kansas City, Ft. Scott & Gulf *Railroad*, Lockwood was named for the general passenger agent. Post office: 1881–now. US 160, W 8 m. NIAWATHE PRAIRIE: SR 97, N 9 m.; SR E, W 1 m. (Natural Areas, below). PARKS: Three parks; picnicking, pools, tennis, golf. In town. SINNERS UNION CHURCH: Vernacular, early 1880s. Now owned by the county historical society, the building served all denominations. Its name was suggested by area resident Thomas Gentry, about whom it was said: "like all of us, he had his peculiarities." SR 97, N 6.5 m.; GR, E 1 m.

Natural Areas. BONA GLADE: 20 acres. Part of Stockton Lake (*Lakes: Corps of Engineers*). Features a sandstone glade with characteristic plants and animals. Corps of Engineers, Stockton 65785. US 160, E 9 m.; SR 245, N 8 m. to Bona;[4] SR 215, W 1 m. NIAWATHE PRAIRIE: 240 acres. Features an upland tallgrass *prairie* with exposed sandstone rocks whose fauna and flora include northern harriers, prairie chickens, Henslow's sparrows, short-eared owls (winter), fringed poppy mallow, false blue indigo, royal catchfly, and Mead's milkweed. SR BB, W 8.6 m.; SR 97, N 2.5 m.; SR E, W 1 m.

Park. Community building, picnic shelters, pool, tennis, basketball, playground, restrooms. S side; US 160, E on High or 4th.

Pennsboro, Mo. Established in 1895 along the Kansas City, Ft. Scott & Memphis *Railroad*, Pennsboro was named for the Penn family (Everton, above); defunct. Post office: 1895–1931. SR 39, S 5 m. DILDAY MILL: Vernacular, 1867; collapsed; National Historic Register. Built by John D. Dilday. Until 1943 various mills used this 1840 site at Turnback Creek in Turnback, Mo. (now defunct).[5] SR K, E 3 m.

South Greenfield, Mo. The town was established in 1881 along the Kansas City, Ft. Scott & Gulf *Railroad* when the railroad, following easier terrain, bypassed Greenfield three miles to the south. Ambitions of gaining the county seat were squelched when T. A. Miller organized Greenfield businessmen c. 1886 to form a subscription railroad (the Greenfield & Northern) to connect the towns. Post offices: Watkins[6] 1881–1891; South Greenfield 1891–now. SR 39, S 3 m.

Stockton Lake. *Lakes: Corps of Engineers.*

Washington Hotel / Museum. Italianate, 1867; restored. This 20-room three-story brick hotel, now the county historical museum, displays local historical items and period furniture. Features include a hip roof, wide bracketed eaves, and arched windows. Town square; US 160, E on College.

1. County's name; another Greenfield p.o. was in Shelby County, 1838–1850.
2. Descriptive *(prairies)*.
3. Origin unknown, possibly for the "Comet," the 1813 steamer that was the first to navigate the Monongahela, Ohio, and Mississippi Rivers; p.o. 1896–1907; defunct.
4. Origin unknown; p.o. 1892–1911.
5. An incident: Tennessee immigrants, after traveling over rough land during cold weather, camped at this creek in 1831; discouraged, most turned back, returning to an abandoned Indian camp near Springfield; p.o. 1848–1905.
6. Reportedly a RR man.

GREENTOP

Population: 425   Map F-1

The early history of this town is confusing. Its post office spent some time in a different county, Adair (25 percent of today's population is there), its plat dates are disputed, its place-name is uncertain, and for a while it had a fictitious town attached to it for use by the North Missouri *Railroad* as a depot site (Colorado City, below). One of Schulyer County's oldest towns, it was established c. 1849 on a major north–south road as a trading center. The first plat of record is 1852; it was filed in 1853 by William Landsdale and Oliver Towles, who owned the property, part of which is actually in today's town. The second plat (dated in 1857, filed in 1868), prepared by surveyor Stephen Caywood and landowner G. W. Gatlin, is accepted as the correct one since it, unlike the first, specifies the boundaries. The town name, a stock one, is descriptive. Local tradition offers three explanations: (1) Oliver Towles's wife suggested it, reportedly as a variation of her Kentucky hometown of Greenup; (2) it is a direct transfer from a Kentucky church, Greentop; and (3) it was suggested by the color of the landscape and the town's location at the top of the county. The latter is unlikely, since "top

of the county" could refer only to Adair County, which was not the post office location when the town was named. The arrival in 1868 of the North Missouri *Railroad* helped establish the town. Post offices: Green Top (Schuyler County) 1849–1857, c. 1866–1895; Green Top (Adair County) 1857–c. 1866; Greentop (Schuyler County) 1895–now.

Colorado City, Mo. Because of a steep incline at the intended depot site at Greentop's square *(Eldon: Eldon Caboose)*, Colorado City (origin unknown) was platted in 1869 at a level spot and a depot was built west of today's Main Street, between 6th and 7th, where most of today's interesting architecture is located. Judged obsolete in 1870, Colorado City was replatted as South Addition to Greentop. Post office: none.

Grand Divide. *Grand Divide.*

Lost Creek Bridge. Truss, c. 1900. This one-lane bridge with wooden decking crosses Lost Creek. To the north of the creek is flat valley land; to the south are bluffs and dense timber. NW side; CR, N 1 m. toward SR Y, or US 63, N 1.3 m.; SR Y, W 1 m.; CR, S 0.2 m.

GREENVILLE

Population: 437   Map H-6

Two courthouse fires destroyed county records. When the town was platted in 1819 in a cornfield along the St. Francis River as county seat of newly organized Wayne County, the survey was supposedly made by counting rows of corn. The townsite, formerly Bettis Ferry,[1] was renamed Greenville by county site commissioners to honor the 1794 Treaty of Greenville that was negotiated by county namesake Gen. Anthony Wayne with Miami *Indians* after the battle of Fallen Timbers (near today's Toledo, Ohio), which opened the Northwest Territory for settlement. Arrival of the Williamsville, Greenville & St. Louis *Railroad* during the lumber boom brought brief prosperity c. 1892–1915 *(Bunker)*, but soon the town returned to a rural county-seat economy as a trading and political center. During the *Civil War*, the town, located at a strategic crossroads, was fought for by both sides, who destroyed nearly half its structures. In 1938 the Corps of Engineers, while building a dam to form nearby Wappapello Lake *(Lakes: Corps of Engineers)*, began relocating the town to its present site on higher ground. In 1942 the residents voted to abandon the old site, platting the new town as an annex. Post offices: St. Francis[2] 1816–1820; Greenville 1820–1862, 1865–now.

Dee Chapel Methodist Church. Vernacular, late 1860s; organized in the early 1800s by Rev. Elijah Dees. In 1905 a flood floated this structure to the opposite bank

Howe's Mill near Salem.

of Otter Creek. The congregation swapped the old land for today's site. The building is original except for the foundation, floor, and roof. US 67, S 3 m.; SR A, S 4.3 m.; SR V, W 1.2 m.

Old Greenville. Original sidewalks and building foundations are identified by a walking tour map that shows old photographs of the structures and explains the history. Maps: Corps of Engineers, Wappapello, Mo., or inquire locally. US 67, S 1 m. at river bridge.

Recreation. COLDWATER *STATE FOREST. STATE PARKS:* Sam A. Baker (US 67, N 4 m.; SR 34, W 4 m.; SR 143, N 3 m.); Lake Wappapello (US 67, S 10 m.; SR 172, E 8 m.). WAPPAPELLO LAKE: *Lakes: Corps of Engineers.* WAPPAPELLO *WILDLIFE AREA.*

Shook General Store. General Store, 1903. Still operating today, this store is also the post office and community center. US 67, S 1 m.; SR D, S 10.6 m. to Shook.[3]

Wayne County Courthouse. Moderne, 1941–1943 (Greenville history, above). Reportedly the county's sixth, today's courthouse replaced a $50,000 building completed in 1926 and condemned in 1941. Cost: about $98,000 (compensation of $70,000 from the federal government; partially funded by the *WPA*). In town. *(County Profiles)*

Wright Cemetery. One of the county's oldest cemeteries has about 20 graves, including several cradle graves that were dug mostly beneath the ground but have stone side walls and tops. Near old town, US 67, S 1 m.; just W of bridge and S of hwy. *(Cemeteries)*

1. Pioneer brothers; p.o. St. Francis 1816–1820 (below).
2. The river via St. Francis of Assisi, founder of the Franciscan Order *(County Profiles: St. Francois).*
3. George Shook; p.o. 1904–1923, 1930–now.

 GRISTMILLS

Before flour and meal could be bought packaged, the local gristmill served the community, using first water, then steam, and finally diesel and electricity to power huge stone wheels for the custom grinding of grains such as wheat, corn, and rye. Early homemade mills used shafts and pulleys hewn from seasoned hickory with burrs (millstones) cut 12–15 inches wide and over three feet in circumference. Belts for the drive shaft were often made from tanned cowhide. These first mills replaced the primitive but effective sweep-and-mortar ones that were fashioned by digging a mortar in a stump to grind grain into husks, grits, and meal with a spring-pole pestle, much the same as a pharmacist or chef would crush ingredients. As centers of gossip and tall tales, gristmills preceded the general store. By 1924 even the most isolated farmer could buy packaged grain products cheaper than having his own milled. Tourism has preserved many of these obsolete structures.

 HALLTOWN
Population: 161   Map D-6

Platted in 1887, the town was named for George Hall, who moved here c. 1870 and built a general store. Construction of *Route 66* (below) through the town during the late 1920s helped its economy, which today depends on the nostalgia of the road and a few antique stores. Post offices: Hall Town 1879–1894; Halltown 1894–now.

Chesapeake Fault. This fault arcs 90 miles through Missouri (from southwest Christian County to southwest Vernon County). Escarpments produced by higher displaced sides on the southwest portion of the fault can be seen along I-44. The road cut at the SR N overpass reveals Mississippian era rocks on one side (southwest) and Ordovician on the other (southeast). I-44 exit, S 4.7 m.

Jones Memorial. Sixties Modern, 1963. L. E. Jones, a

realtor from Philadelphia, Pa., bequeathed $300,000 for the construction of this memorial and its maintenance in honor of his mother and his wife. Chapel, meeting rooms, county museum. SR Z, N 5.4 m. ADAMSON CABIN: One-story log dogtrot cabin, 1845. Moved here from three miles west of Lawrenceburg.[1] Adjacent.

Rock Prairie Cemetery. Interesting 19th-century markers. SR Z, S across I-44 to 1st E turn. (*Cemeteries*)

Route 66 to Carthage, Mo. SR 266 (*Springfield: Route 66*) and SR 96 to *Carthage* form Missouri's longest remnant of *Route 66* that does not shadow I-44 or dissolve into a large city (*St. Louis: Route 66*). The following is a good sightseeing excursion: HALLTOWN: Nostalgic structures include the Las Vegas Restaurant / Halltown Hotel and Whitehall Mercantile. SR 266 west from Halltown to stop sign, then continue straight ahead (do not turn toward SR 96). Follow road through the former health spa. PARIS SPRINGS (also Gay Partia; origin unknown), which was first known as Johnson's Mills in the 1850s for co-owner J. R Johnson; it was named Paris possibly for the exotic feeling of Paris, France (*La Plata*), whose name was derived from the original Gallic tribe, Parisii. Post offices: Chalybeate Springs[2] 1872–1874; Paris Springs 1874–1920. Site: Turnback Mill (below). Follow road SW to junction with SR 96, then south on SR N to W at first turn. Site: original curbs along road to the former *gristmill* town of SPENCER (namesake unknown; post office: 1868–1907). Site: grocery store. Continue W 1 m. to junction of SR 96, then W on SR 96 to Carthage through the following towns. HEATONVILLE: Named for founder Daniel Heaton. Post offices: Heaton 1872–1881; Heatonville 1888–1891. ALBATROSS: Probably named for the web-footed seabird; a bus stop for nearby Miller[3] (SR 39, N 2 m.). Post office: none. Site: Miller's Station and Wayside Park at SR 96 and SR 39. PHELPS: Possibly named for Phelps County's namesake (*County Profiles: Phelps*). Post offices: Stalls Creek[4] 1854–1857; Phelps 1857–1864, 1869–1922. Site: white gas station at SR 96 and BB. RESCUE: Namesake uncertain, possibly an incident. Post office: 1897–1904. Site: cabins. AVILLA: For Avilla, Ind., a name coined by Edwin Randall by adding "A" to villa, which local Indiana historians claim is French, meaning town, but linguistically is more properly Mexican Spanish or possibly Italian for residence. Post office: 1860–1863, 1866–now. Site: buildings and stone motel just before Kellog Lake Park.

Turnback Mill. Vernacular, 1857; derelict. Built by M. Sims, this two-story frame *gristmill* introduced self-rising flour to the area in 1914; it closed in 1944. Remnants of the antebellum house of William Likins, who owned the mill in 1858, overlook it. SR 266, 3.5 m. W through Paris Springs (Route 66, above) to near

bridge at Goose Creek; unmarked road, S approx. 0.5 m. to Turnback Creek.[5]

1. Lawrence County; p.o. Dunkle's Store, for the store owner, 1854–1863, 1865–1876; Lawrenceburg(h) 1876–1914.
2. Iron salts in the water.
3. RR employee; p.o. 1891–now.
4. Nearby Dry Fork of Stahl Creek after a family name; the spelling probably came from poor handwriting on the application or a misspelling by the postmaster general.
5. *Greenfield: Pennsboro.*

HAMILTON
Population: 1,737   Map D-2

The town was platted in 1855 by a town company headed by A. G. Davis along the surveyed route of the Hannibal & St. Joseph *Railroad* (which arrived in 1859). It was first intended to be called *Prairie* City for its location, but Davis named the town for Alexander Hamilton, the U.S. treasury secretary (1789–1795), and, according to local tradition, for Joseph Hamilton, an attorney and soldier killed during the *War of 1812* at the battle of the Thames in Canada. Post office: 1858–now.

Architecture. Downtown: 19th- and 20th-century styles.

Breckenridge, Mo. Although the name was misspelled, the town was named for John C. Breckinridge, the U.S. vice president under James Buchanan (1857–1861), the 1860 presidential nominee of the southern Democrats against Abraham Lincoln, and a Confederate general. Post offices: Grandriver[1] 1850–1852, 1854–1860; Breckenridge 1860–now. SR 13 at US 36; US 36, E 7 m.; SR M, N 1.7 m. MILLSTONE: This *gristmill* stone commemorates the 1838 *Mormon* massacre by Lexington County militia at Haun's Mill (mill site: SR M and SR A, S 6.1 m. to Shoal Creek; GR, W 2.5 m.; marker). In town, city park. SCANLON HOTEL: Vernacular, late 1850s. The two-story stone hotel, with two-foot-thick walls, was built by Irish immigrant and railroad section boss John Scanlon for train passengers. Derelict. 5th, off Broadway.

J. C. Penny Boyhood Home. Recently moved to town (formerly 2.5 m. E), the building is now an information center. Doll collection, period furniture. SR 13, in town.

J. C. Penny Museum. Born at Hamilton, the world-famous retail merchant James Cash Penny (1875–1971) visited his hometown frequently, sharing his good fortune with it through substantial donations for building projects, e.g. a library, a high school, and a nursing home. Built with funds from retired Penny's executives, the museum houses memorabilia about the man and his company. (Penny named his first store after his lifelong axiom, The Golden Rule.) SR 13, in town.

The Tom and Huck statue in downtown Hannibal. (MASSIE PHOTOGRAPH)

Kidder, Mo. Platted and named in 1860 for H. P. Kidder by the Kidder Land Company of Boston, the town replaced nearby Emmett,[2] a post office and whistle-stop depot/store along the Hannibal & St. Joseph *Railroad.* A railroad depot was built, and the town became a shipping point. Post offices: Emmett 1860; Kidder 1860–now. US 36, W 6 m.; SR J, N 2.4 m. KIDDER INSTITUTE: Vernacular, 1871. Founded in 1871 as Thayer College by Kidder Institute, the college was closed in 1876 and then reopened in 1884 under the auspices of the Congregational Churches of Missouri as Kidder Institute, which closed in 1934. The building was used as a public school from 1934 to 1981. In town.

Show-Me Llamas. Llamas and other exotic animals are raised here. Also, since 1920, the farm has bred Shorthorn cattle, one of which, Dividend (1973–1982), bought in Ireland, was awarded Sire of the Year for four consecutive years—an American record. His grave is guarded by two stone dogs. Visitors welcome. SR 13, N 7 m.

Spillway / Conservation Park. Next to the Hammon Reservoir; picnicking, grills, shade trees, restrooms, fishing, boat ramp (no gas motors). SR 36B, W 2.1 m.

---

1. The river, descriptive (i.e. big).
2. Origin unknown; probably like Emmett County, Iowa, for Irish patriot Robert Emmet (1778–1803), but misspelled.

HANNIBAL
Population: 18,004   Map G-2

Moses D. Bates, a former chain-bearer for a U.S. surveyor who platted this area in 1818 for the government, returned here to plat a town in 1819 with the help of Thomson Bird, whose father, Abraham Bird *(Birds Point),* had acquired the property via *New Madrid Earthquake* certificates. The town was undisputedly named for the Carthaginian general Hannibal (247–182 B.C.), but the inspiration for its naming is disputed. Some sources credit the town's location near the Fabius River (named for the Roman general who opposed the Carthaginians), but the river was not named Fabius until after the town was founded, and earlier maps show the river's name as variations of French family names, Ferbien and Fabiane. The consensus is that both Hannibal's and *Palmyra's* names were inspired by the post-Revolution fashion of choosing classical names (e.g. Hannibal, N.Y., 1790). The town grew slowly (1830 pop. 30) until rival river town Marion City *(Palmyra)* began to flounder, then it boomed (1840 pop. 1,000; Marion County Courthouse, below). Aided by steamboats and the 1856 arrival of the Hannibal & St. Joseph *Railroad,* it became a prosperous trading center, building Missouri's second Mississippi River bridge in 1871, Missouri's first city-owned power and light company in 1886, and Missouri's first tax-supported library in 1889. Post office: 1820–now. Home of Hannibal-LaGrange College and Hannibal Area Vo-Tech. Maps and information: visitor bureau, 320 Broadway.

Architecture. Over 17 structures are on the National Historic Register, in addition to the following National Historic districts: BROADWAY: S. Main, Broadway, and S. 3d. CENTRAL PARK: 4th, 7th, North, and Lyon. MARK TWAIN: Bird, Main, and Hill. NORTH MAIN STREET: Bird, N. Main, and Hill. STANDARD PRINTING: Center and N 3d.

Cameron Cave. National Natural Landmark. This maze-type cave is one of Missouri newest show caves; lantern tours. SR 79, S 1 m.

Garth Woodside Mansion. Second Empire, 1871; National Historic Register. Features a gray green hexagonal slate roof, four porches, elaborate and ornate trim, and a rare three-story wall-supported (flying) staircase. Original furniture; tours. US 61S, E on Warren Barrett; signs.

Glacial Gravel. Especially noticeable between 2500 and 2900 Market (US 61B) are deposits of gravel approximately 75 feet deep that were swept down the Mississippi in glacial meltwater from as far north as Lake Superior. *(Glacial Erratics)*

Lover's Leap. Along with familiar legends of Indian lovers leaping to their deaths, there is a documented story of a Protestant sect, led by William Miller, who abandoned their crops and stores on October 22, 1844, put on long white robes, and gathered here to wait for the coming of Christ. Overlooks Jackson's Island. SR 79, S approx. 5 m.; Fulton, E; signs.

Marion County Courthouse. Neoclassical with Beaux Arts affinities, 1900–1901. Although Hannibal is not a county seat, its 1840 population of 1,000 created a need for a convenient location for county business. A Court of Common Pleas (*Cape Girardeau*) was established in 1844, to which were added probate matters in 1845 and appeals from city court proceedings in 1847. Today's courthouse maintains a separate circuit court division, county treasurer's office, and other county offices. The 124-by-80-foot two-story masonry courthouse, the second, is ornate, featuring a full-height pedimented entry supported by Corinthian columns, pedimented second-story windows, a roofline balustrade, a rusticated first story, and an elaborate cupola. Cost: $43,500. Downtown; 906 Broadway. (*County Profiles*)

Mark Twain. This legendary American writer was born Samuel Langhorne Clemens during the 1835 appearance of Halley's Comet and died when it next returned in 1910. His family moved here in 1839 from Twain's nearby birthplace, Florida, Mo. (Mark Twain *State Park*). Beginning at age 13, he worked for local newspapers until leaving in 1853 for St. Louis as a journeyman printer. Clemens first used the name Mark Twain as a reporter in 1862–1863 for the "Territorial Enterprise" in Virginia City, Nev. This pen name comes from riverboat slang: the leadsman at the ship's bow would shout back to the steersman what the river's depth measured as marked in fathoms (one fathom equals six feet). Mark (measures) Twain (two) refers to two fathoms of water underneath the ship, which traditionally meant safe water ahead. The characters and settings of Twain's two most important books, "Tom Sawyer" and "Huckleberry Finn" (hereafter "TS" and "HF"), drew heavily from Hannibal. Today the town is the caretaker of these and other settings from the books. BOYHOOD HOME: Built by Twain's father in 1843–1844, the vernacular two-story frame house was restored in 1990–1991. Tom Sawyer (a combination of Twain and two friends, Will Bowen and John Briggs) and Aunt Polly (Twain's mother) lived here. Nearby are a print shop and period schoolhouse. 208 Hill. CARDIFF HILL: Actually Holliday Hill, for the Hollidays (Widow Douglas) who lived on top of it. Twain played here as a boy and used it as a setting in "TS," renaming it for similar hills he had seen in Cardiff, South Wales. GRANT'S DRUG STORE: Greek Revival, 1839; restored as a drugstore museum. The Clemens family, insolvent, lived

here in 1846–1847 with Dr. Grant and his wife. Twain's father died here in 1847. 327 N. Main. J. M. CLEMENS LAW OFFICE: Vernacular, 1840; extensively remodeled; two-story frame; moved in 1955 from 113 Bird. Twain's father, not a successful lawyer, worked in this office, described in "Innocents Abroad." 207 Hill. LAURA HAWKINS HOME: Vernacular, 1840; two-story frame. Laura was the model for Becky Thatcher ("TS" and "HF") and reportedly Twain's childhood sweetheart. Museum. 211 Hill (Rensselaer: Big Creek Cemetery, below). MARK TWAIN CAVE: National Natural Landmark; Missouri's first show cave. Tom and Becky were lost in this cave (McDougal's in "TS"). Here, Injun Joe buried treasure and later died. SR 79, S 1 m. SITE OF HUCK FINN'S HOME: A two-story frame house now occupies the site of Tom Blankenship's house; Tom was a childhood friend of Twain's and the model for Huck Finn. Blankenship's father was the model for Pap Finn ("TS" and "HF"). 213 North. THE WELCHMAN'S HOUSE: Vernacular, c. 1824; rectangular, one-story stone. This was the house of John Davies, a bookseller ("TS"). 509 N. 3d.

Mark Twain Museum. Vernacular, 1937. The two-story stone structure was built to exhibit Twain memorabilia, including the desk used to write "Tom Sawyer" and 16 Norman Rockwell illustrations for "Tom Sawyer" and "Huckleberry Finn." 208 Hill.

Memorial Lighthouse. The first lighthouse on this site was built in 1935 on Cardiff Hill (Mark Twain, above) for the celebration of the centennial of Twain's birth and was lighted at the appropriate moment by a telegraphed message from Pres. Franklin D. Roosevelt. It was destroyed by a storm in 1960. Today's was lighted the same way in 1963 by Pres. John F. Kennedy. Panoramic views.

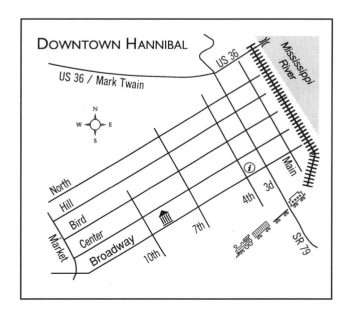

Missouri Tourist Information Center. Maps, information, restrooms. US 61S; signs.

Rensselaer, Mo. This community grew around Big Creek Presbyterian Church (organized in 1832). Its name honors the Van Rensselaer family of New York, whose offer of $200 for the first academy named Van Rensselaer was accepted by the church (below). The academy name, shortened, was adopted by the post office and a depot for the Hannibal & Missouri Central *Railroad* (although the railroad misspelled it Rennselaer). Post office: 1871–1953. US 36, W 10 m.; SR H, S 1.2 m. BIG CREEK *CEMETERY:* Laura Hawkins Frazier, reportedly Mark Twain's childhood sweetheart and the model for Becky Thatcher, is buried in this well-kept cemetery (Mark Twain, above). Across the road and just S of Big Creek Presbyterian Church. FIRST VAN RENSSELAER ACADEMY: Vernacular, 1852. This two-story building was built from brick made across the road by the Megown family. The girls' classes were held upstairs, the boys' downstairs. SECOND VAN RENSSELAER ACADEMY / CHURCH: Vernacular, 1866. The two-story limestone building provided space for the church upstairs and for the school downstairs. The third academy (brick), later a public school (and now a feed store), is across from the second.

Riverview Park. 400 acres. River overlooks, picnic facilities, restrooms, playground. US 36, N on Harrison Hill; signs.

Rockcliff Mansion. Neo-Classical (interior, Art Nouveau influence), 1898–1900; vacant 43 years; restored; National Historic Register. The owner, lumber baron John Cruikshank, wanted the finest woods and furnishings money could buy. Overlooking the town and river, this 30-room mansion is massive and lavish. Costs: landscaping, $75,000; house, $125,000; furnishings, $50,000. Tours. 1000 Bird.

South River Fort / Museum. Log, c. 1861. The building was moved here from South River Crossing, where it housed Union troops guarding the bridge and railroad station. Today it houses historical items, e.g. one of the largest collections of spurs in America, cavalry equipment, Indian artifacts. US 36, N on US 61; signs.

Tom and Huck Statue. Reportedly America's first statue commemorating literary characters, it was erected in 1926 at the base of Cardiff Hill (Mark Twain, above), just N of SR 36 bridge.

Tom Sawyer Days. Since 1956. Arts and crafts, fireworks, food, entertainment, events including the National Fence Painting Contest, the National Frog Jumping Contest, and the Tom and Becky Contest. Fourth of July.

US 61. *New London: US 61 / Red Ball Road.*

HARRISONVILLE
Population: 7,683			Map C-4

The town was platted in 1837 as county seat of newly organized Van Buren County (later Cass County) by a commission that was directed to locate a site in 1835. Named for *Fulton* politician Albert G. Harrison (U.S. congressman 1835–1839), the town grew as a trading center on a major north–south road that branched into a hub of roads by the 1850s. This pro-Union town, situated in The Burnt District[1] during the *Kansas Border War,* was occupied by Union troops during the *Civil War* (Tarkington-Mockbee Home, below). The arrival c. 1871 of the Missouri, Kansas & Texas *Railroad* aided its growth as a shipping point; by 1895 it had four different railroads. Post office: 1837–now. Home of Cass County Area Vo-Tech. Information Center: 400 E. Mechanic.

Amarugia Highlands Wildlife Area. *Wildlife Areas.*

Architecture. TOWN SQUARE: Mostly unaltered examples of late 19th- and early 20th-century commercial buildings. WALL STREET: Noteworthy structures include St. Peter's Episcopal Church (Gothic Revival, 1895; National Historic Register; 25 stained-glass windows), 400 Wall; Deane House (Hexagon, 1867; reportedly tornado-proof), 702 Wall.

Brown House. Early Classical Revival style, 1849; National Historic Register. The two-story brick house has a full-height entry porch, eight fireplaces, and walnut exterior doors. Col. R. A. Brown, an 1842 pioneer of the area, owned 2,000 acres and forty slaves, whom he freed in 1860. Although a Southern sympathizer, as an 1861 Missouri secession convention delegate he voted against seceding. The four-foot-high half-mile-long stone fence was built c. 1849. Brick slave quarters. US 71, N approx. 3 m. to Pettyman Rd.; inquire locally.

Cass County Courthouse. Italian Renaissance, 1897. Possibly the county's third (records are unclear), this 93-by-78-foot three-story yellow brick asymmetrical courthouse is the centerpiece of the town's square. It features a dominant square clock tower that extends far above the roofline, a rusticated first level, a different window treatment on each floor, and a first-story projecting entry with Ionic columns. Cost: $40,000. Wall St., downtown. *(County Profiles)*

Natural Areas. BITTERN BOTTOMS NATURAL AREA. 67 acres. Mostly marsh with some open water and forest. Popular with bird-watchers because of nesters, e.g. least bittern, wood duck, blue-winged teal, mallard, prothonotary warbler, tree swallow. US 71; SR 2, W 2.1 m.; SR DD, S 6.5 m.; GR, E 0.2 m. DORSETT HILL PRAIRIE: 79 acres; 17 percent *prairie.* Features a prairie knoll surrounded by upland shrubs and hardwood. Both areas: Box 180, Jefferson City

65102. US 71; SR 2, W 2.1 m.; SR DD, S 6.5 m.; GR, W 1.75 m.; SR W, S 3 m.; GR E 0.5 m.

Pleasant Hill, Mo. Platted in 1836 by Thomas Henry and descriptively named for its location on a hill, the town was relocated c. 1865 about two miles northeast to the Pacific *Railroad*. Post office: 1839–now. SR 7, N 11 m. ARCHITECTURE: Among many 19th-century structures are eight antebellum houses, including a two-story 16-room brick house built in 1860 and remodeled in 1871 by George Kellog, a regionally known gardener and florist (1209 Independence).

Sharp-Hopper Cabin / Museum. Log Cabin, 1835. Features include a shake roof, dovetail joints, front and back porches, and two fireplaces. Built by Samuel Sharp and bought in 1883 by Thomas Hopper, the cabin was donated in 1974 to the historical society by his grandson and moved here (from 3.5 m. NW of town). Furnishings (c. 1850–1860), local memorabilia. 400 Mechanic.

Tarkington-Mockbee Home. Early Classical Revival style, c. 1847. Originally six rooms, the house has 18-inch-thick brick walls. Col. H. W. Younger, a pro-Union local businessman, was murdered in 1862 by *Civil War* Jayhawkers as a suspected Southern sympathizer because his son Cole Younger (*Lee's Summit*) joined William C. Quantrill's guerrillas after an 1861 fist fight with a Federal officer at a party here. The fight, over the attentions of a young woman, resulted in a warrant for Younger's arrest. 105 N. Price.

1. Named for the destruction caused by the Kansas Border War (*Kansas City: Westport; Lamar; Nevada*). The same area was subject to *Order No. 11* during the *Civil War,* when Harrisonville was known as Fort Harrisonville because of the Federal garrison established there to protect its pro-Union residents (*Nevada*).

HARTVILLE
Population: 539   Map F-6

Court records were destroyed by a courthouse fire in 1896. The townsite was settled in 1832 at Wood's Fork of the Gasconade River by a colony of 16 people, was selected and presumably platted in 1841 as county seat of newly organized Wright County. Hartville was named for early settler Isaac Hart, who donated property for the site. This politically divided town was destroyed in 1863 by a *Civil War* pro-Northern faction during a brief battle. Recovering by 1874, it has continued as the political center of the county. Post office: 1842–1863, 1865–now.

Needle's Eye Natural Arch. One of the most photogenic of Missouri's arches forms a flying buttress against a bluff, rather than being parallel to it.

Extending 40 feet from the bluff, with a 20-foot span and a 10-foot height, the arch's opening has about 35 feet of rock above it. SR 38, E 7.2 m.; GR, SW 0.8 m., then bear right uphill 0.25 m.; walk to river bluff (or wade downstream 0.25 m. from river road access).

Recreation. ALLEN MEMORIAL *WILDLIFE AREA. FLOAT STREAM:* Gasconade River.

Stairstep Swimming Hole. While not as romantic looking as its name suggests, the stairstep sandstone ledges at the banks of this inviting swimming hole are interesting. Swimming, picnicking. SR 38, E 6 m.; SR N, S 4.5 m. to Owens;[1] GR, E 1.1 m.; GR, S to 2d low-water bridge (0.3 m.); park, walk SW 100 yds.

Wright County Courthouse. Sixties Modern, 1964–1965. The county's fourth courthouse, possibly the fifth or sixth (records have been destroyed; Hartville history, above), this two-story glass-and-brick structure was partially financed by the federally sponsored Community Facilities Administration. Cost: $279,950. Downtown. (*County Profiles*)

1. Origin unknown; no p.o.

HERCULANEUM
Population: 2,263   Map H-5

Platted in 1808 by Moses Austin at the Mississippi River and the mouth of Joachim Creek as a shipping point for the area's lead smelting operations (*Potosi*), the town in 1809 was the site of the first shot tower west of the Mississippi (below). Herculaneum was named for the Roman town buried in 79 A.D. by Mount Vesuvius, which after excavation of its treasures in the mid-18th century received wide publicity. Austin imagined the smoke from the lead smelters to be like Mount Vesuvius's and the local limestone strata to be like a Roman amphitheater. The town prospered as the only trading center and post office between *St. Louis* and *Ste. Genevieve* and after 1819 as the first county seat of Jefferson County. It declined after the establishment of *Hillsboro* as county seat in 1836 and became defunct after being bypassed by the Iron Mountain *Railroad*, which helped build nearby Pevely.[1] In 1890 the St. Joseph Lead Company reestablished the post office and lead-smelting operations. Today Doe Run, which bought the operation from St. Joseph in 1981, is America's largest lead smelter (rated at 225,000 tons of refined lead annually). US 61/US 67 at Pevely, Mo., follow signs to Doe Run Co. Post office: 1811–1858, 1890–now.

Architecture. Downtown and residential area: some good examples of late 19th-century styles.

Festus, Mo. The town was first called Tanglefoot c. 1878, because of the liquor sold here and its effects on walking; the name was later considered vulgar and was changed to Limitville, because the town's eastern growth was limited by Crystal City.[2] Finally the name was changed to Festus (namesake uncertain), which local tradition claims was selected by randomly opening the Bible and choosing the first proper name, which, as a stroke of bad luck for this Christian community, was from Acts 25:22, wherein Porcius Festus delivers Paul to Agrippa (Herod) for death or imprisonment as an appeasement to the Jews. Possibly Festus, a common 19th-century first name, honors a person, e.g. St. Louis banker Festus J. Wade (1859–1927). Post office: 1883–now. I-55, S 3 m.

Fletcher Memorial Park. Set aside by the 1808 plat, the park was later named for Thomas C. Fletcher (born here 1827; d. 1899), the state's first Missouri-born governor (1865–1869) and first Republican governor *(Hillsboro).* It overlooks the Mississippi River and the broad expanse of the Doe Run smelting operations. Benches; historic marker. Downtown at Doe Run Co.; Main, N 0.5 m.

Gov. Daniel Dunklin Grave. State Historic Site. Dunklin, Missouri's fifth governor (1832–1836) and Dunklin County's namesake *(County Profiles),* is credited with founding the state's first public school system. Limestone walls surround this grave site on bluffs overlooking the Mississippi. Downtown; Main, N 0.9 m.; Dunklin, E 0.6 m.

Shot Tower Site. Three shot towers were built here by 1819, the first in 1809 (Herculaneum history, above). Molten lead was dripped through a copper sieve into a cistern below, retrieved, and then turned through cylinders to smooth and round the pellets. As a testament to the economic importance of lead, the "Geographical, Statistical and Historical Map of Missouri," c. 1820, reported that "the most remarkable feature in Missouri is its lead mines, which are the most extensive on the globe." Estimates of the production of lead were 300 million pounds annually (worth $120,000 in 1820 dollars), and Ste. Genevieve and Herculaneum were the only ports of trade for that product *(Fredericktown; Potosi).* Railroad station, S 0.5 m. down tracks by foot. Bronze tablet.

Truman Memorial Park. Bordered on three sides by the Mississippi River. Boat ramp, picnic facilities, low-water beaches, sandbar, camping by permit. US 61/ US 67, S 10 m.; SR AA, E then S on Drury approx. 1 m. to E on Big Hollow approx. 3 m. to river.

---

1. Origin unknown; p.o. taken from Herculaneum, 1858–now.
2. Established by American Plate Glass Co. c. 1872; descriptive, i.e. glass clear as crystal; p.o. 1872–now.

HERMANN
Population: 2,754   Map G-4

The German Settlement Society of Philadelphia, Pa., organized in 1836, sent scouts west to states like Indiana, Illinois, and Missouri in 1837 to find a townsite where they could live according to German ideals. This site, set in an amphitheater of hills, was chosen partly because of "The Duden Book" *(Dutzow)* and partly because of its nostalgic location; the first settlers arrived in December 1837. Platted in Philadelphia (Architecture, below), the town was named for the 1st-century German hero Arminius (reportedly a Latinized version of Hermann), who annihilated three Roman legions of about 20,000 men at Teutoburg Forest in A.D. 9, thereby fixing the Roman Empire's sphere of influence (and boundary line) at the Rhine River. In an 1842 county election, notable because women voted (78 years before the 19th Amendment enfranchised them), Hermann was selected as the fourth county seat of Gasconade County, replacing *Mt. Sterling.* In 1855 it secured its prosperity as a trading center by making a successful transition from river traffic to the railroad when the Pacific *Railroad* was completed through here to Jefferson City. Post office: 1838–now.

Architecture. Over 108 structures are on the National Historic Register. Excellent examples of 19th-century frame and brick structures along and beside hills overlooking the Missouri River are set close to the streets, leaving room for gardens and fruit trees in the back. Streets ignore hills, continuing straight ahead as when platted in Philadelphia, Pa.; twice they become stairways: on Mozart between 4th and 5th and on Franklin between 1st and 2d. Two National Historic Districts: HERMANN: 5th St., north to the river. OLD STONE HILL: W. 12th at Goethe, SE to SR 100. Notable structures (also below) include: CITY HALL: 1906; SR 19 at 2d. CONCERT HALL: 1876; 1st St., E of Schiller. EITZEN HOUSE: 1855; Wharf St., N on Schiller to river (Gasconade County Courthouse, below).

Deutschheim State Historic Site. This State Historic Site, whose name is German for "home of the Germans," interprets 19th-century German culture through architecture and exhibits. By 1860, 55 percent of Missouri's foreign-born residents were German *(Altenburg).* 131 W. 2d. POMMER-GENTNER HOUSE: Adamesque, 1840. The two-story brick house, with a projecting center pedimented gable with a fanlight and six-over-six windows with flat lintels that mark its style, was built for Caroline Pommer and her family. It was owned in the 1880s by G. Henry Gentner, one of 17 original Hermann settlers. 108 Market. STREHLY HOUSE: Vernacular, 1842; three-story brick addition before 1869 for commercial wine production. The building housed the town's first print shop and the abolitionist newspaper "Licht Freund" (Friend of Light). Tours: residence, winery, and print shop. 131 W. 2d.

Frene Creek Valley. Along this creek southeast of town are rock houses built by early settlers, some of whose descendants still own them. SR 19/SR 100, SR 100 S approx. 2.5 m.; GR (Puchta Winery sign), E 2.5 m.; joins SR 19 2.2 m. S of Hermann.

Gasconade County Courthouse. Italian Renaissance, 1896–1898; National Historic Register. The county's third (the second at this site), this two-story red-brick courthouse has its style's hallmarks: quoins, balustrades, a rusticated first level, a different window treatment on each floor, a pedimented and colonnaded projecting central entry, and corner towers like projecting wings. Set high on a bluff by the river, this gift to the county from C. D. Eitzen (Architecture, above)

was damaged in 1905 by a fire and remodeled; the slate steps, wrought-iron stair risers, banisters, and mosaic floor are original. Self-taught architect J. B. Legg designed similar courthouses in Mississippi and St. Charles Counties. Cost: $41,5000. SR 19, E on SR 100. *(County Profiles)*

The German School / Museum. Vernacular, 1870. The building combined German and English schools. Exhibits of the early settlement include Indian artifacts, riverboat history, 1890s toys and dolls, 1870 pottery, wood cloth printing blocks, a winepress, and early farm and kitchen tools; small garden. Schiller at 4th.

Katy Trail State Park. SR 19, N 1.3 m. to *McKittrick*. *(State Parks)*

New Haven, Mo. *Washington.*

Octoberfest. Sponsored by the wineries, this event features tours and wine tasting, arts and crafts, antiques, German bands, dancing. October weekends.

Overlooks / Cemeteries. Two of the best views of the

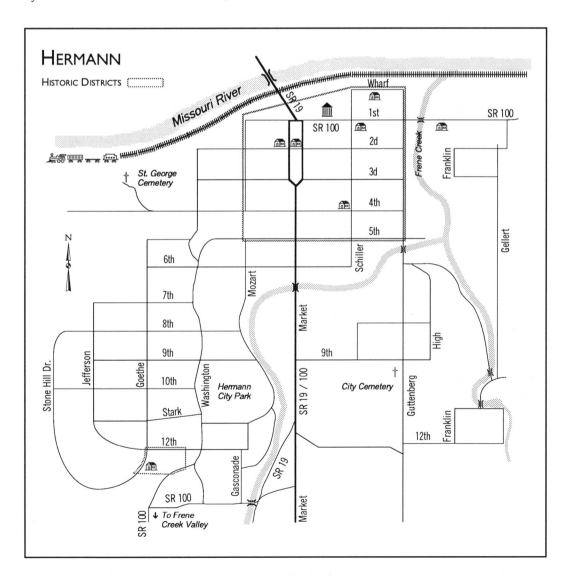

HERMANN

HISTORIC DISTRICTS

river, the truss bridge, and the town are from cemeteries. CITY CEMETERY: Markers range from polished new ones to the city's oldest (G. A. Bayer, sent to buy the land, is buried at the top SE corner). From here Hermann's plat design is obvious, and the viewer is rewarded by a sweeping panorama of the hills and river that enclose the original townsite. SR 19 (Market), E on 9th. ST. GEORGE CEMETERY: Lined with cedars and old tombstones. SR 19 (Market), W on 4th; sign. (*Cemeteries*)

Park. Originally a county fairgrounds. Grounds: the 1864 Rotunda, a hexagonal brick structure for exhibiting grapes, apples, and grains. Nearby: natural amphitheater, picnic facilities, pool. SR 19, W on 6th, S on Washington.

Wineries. ADAM PUCHTA: Reestablished in 1990 by the sixth generation of Puchta vintners, the winery's romantic location in Frene valley (above) includes a limestone remnant of the 1858 family house and the 1882 brick family house. The original 1854 cellar features a barrel-vaulted ceiling and limestone construction. Specialties are Norton and Vignoles grapes; tours, tasting, picnic area. SR 100, S approx. 2.5 m.; low-water bridge; signs. BIAS: 1980. It produces estate-bottled wines from its 1843 vineyard (600 feet away). Tours, tasting, picnic area. SR 100, E 5 m.; SR B, N 2 m. through Berger;[1] E 1 m. (Berger has several good examples of 19th-century residential architecture and three large 1870s–1900 brick churches with spires.) HERMANNHOF: National Historic Register. Founded 1852. Features include a large two-story stone building and the world's largest wine hall. Ten stone cellars stock wines from nearby Hermannhof vineyards that produce French and American hybrids and champagne (Brut, Extra Dry, and Blanc De Blanc). Tours, tasting, a working smokehouse (German sausage), picnics overlooking the river. SR 100, E past Guttenberg; signs. STONE HILL: National Historic Register. Established in 1847 on a hilltop overlooking town, it grew to be America's second largest winery (the world's third largest), producing 1.25 million gallons annually by c. 1900 and winning international gold medals. When it was closed by the 18th Amendment (National Prohibition, 1920–1933), the owners grew mushrooms (65,000 tons annually by 1940) in 20 cellars of this massive red-brick building (some cellars measure 200 by 100 feet, America's largest). The winery reopened in 1965. Wines include Catawba, Villard-Noir, Norton, Chelois, Missouri Riesling, and champagne. Tours, tasting, museum, picnic area, panoramic view. SR 19, W on 8th to Stone Hill Dr.

1. For the creek, via Frenchman Joseph or Pierre Berger; p.o. 1856–now.

HERMITAGE
Population: 512   Map E-5

Courthouse fires destroyed many of the county's records. In 1846 the state legislature directed that a site for the county seat of recently organized Hickory County be located at the Pomme de Terre River as close to the county's geographical center as practical, and that it be named for home of "Old Hickory" Andrew Jackson in Nashville, Tenn. Jackson's choice of that name followed the Southern tradition of a bachelor naming his plantation Hermitage, which was loosely accepted as meaning monastery. Platted in 1847 along the river, the town today is the county's largest, barely (Weaubleau, below). Post office: 1848–now.

Cross Timbers, Mo. Reportedly first known as Garden City,[1] the town was platted in 1871 and named for its 1847 post office, which was named for its location on a road that ran crosswise to a timber belt dividing *prairies* to the north and south. Post office: 1847–now. US 54, E 6 m.; US 65, N 6 m. ANVIL ROCK / MASTODON SKELETON: This rock, about 12 feet long and 5 feet wide, appears to be supported by a 20-foot rock bench. Nearby, in the mid-1800s, bones of an Ice Age mastodon were found in a bog. Reportedly the best specimen ever assembled, it still stands on display at London's British Museum. US 65, N 8 m. near Fristoe;[2] inquire locally. OAK GROVE SCHOOL: Vernacular, 1900. This one-story one-room frame schoolhouse is a good example of its type. SR U, S 3 m. Private.

Hickory County Courthouse. Folk Victorian, 1896. From 1847 until the present structure was built, county residents agitated for removal of the county seat (no alternate location was specified). Fires c. 1860 and 1881 destroyed two previous courthouses and many of the county's records. There might have been an earlier courthouse from 1847 that also was destroyed by fire in 1852, but no records verify its existence. This two-story brick building, possibly the fourth courthouse, has a moderately steep hip roof, an ornate bell tower, and tall narrow windows. Cost: $5,350. Downtown. (*County Profiles*)

Hickory County Fair. Exhibits, special events. Late June.

Hickory County Jail. Vernacular, 1871; truncated. Built of cotton rock, the 21-foot-square building originally had a second story. Used until 1974; steel cells added in 1899. NW corner of square.

Hickory County Museum. The former house of J. S. Williams (National Historic Register), built in 1847 on a terrace overlooking the river valley, today exhibits county memorabilia. Inquire locally.

Pittsburg, Mo. Never platted, Pittsburg was settled in 1839 mostly by the Pitts family from the Nashville, Tenn., and Logan County, Ky., area. Major Burwell Pitts, a veteran of the *War of 1812* and the *Seminole Wars*, is buried in the *cemetery* at Missionary Baptist Church (CR 306). Meekin Pitts's house, Pittsburg's first post office, a derelict log structure, is on CR 305. Post office: 1846–now. SR 254, S 3 m.; SR 64, S 8 m. RECREATION: Pomme de Terre *State Park* and Lake *(Lakes: Corps of Engineers)*. SR D, N 1.7 m.; SR 64B, N 3.3 m.

Pomme de Terre Bridge. Steel, 1890–1891. Built for $5,699, it was the first steel bridge across this river. Replaced in 1925 at its original location, the bridge was disassembled c. 1929, hauled by wagon to Rough Hollow Ford, and reassembled to again bridge the Pomme de Terre River. Still used today. US 54, E 1.2 m.; SR U, N approx. 2 m.; CR 281 (gravel), W approx. 1 m. (CR 281 joins SR Y 0.6 m. W). Caution! Steep inclines.

Quincy, Mo. Established c. 1845 at the site of Samuel Judy's blacksmith shop at a main road through a gap between Hogle's Creek *Prairie* and Twenty-Five-Mile Prairie, the town was first known as Judy's Gap until platted (probably in 1848) and renamed for John Quincy Adams (U.S. president 1825–1829), who died in 1848 *(Palmyra: West Quincy)*. Post offices: Salem[3] 1847; Judy's Gap 1847–1850; Quincy 1850–now. US 54, W 5 m. to Wheatland;[4] continue US 54, W 4 m.; SR 83, N 5 m. *OVERLAND MAIL COMPANY:* marker. SR 83, E side, in town.

Recreation. POMME DE TERRE LAKE: *Lakes: Corps of Engineers.* POMME DE TERRE *STATE PARK:* SR 254, S approx. 5 m.

Weaubleau, Mo. The post office community of Weaubleau City (pronounced Wah'blow) was platted in 1880 as Haran,[5] then changed again to simply Weaubleau, a name derived from the nearby creek, whose name was possibly an Indian term later Americanized via the French ("eau bleue," blue water). The arrival in 1898 of the Kansas City, Osceola & Southern *Railroad* made it the county's only depot town and helped it become today's second largest town in the county (pop. 436). Post offices: Weaubleau City 1876–1880; Haran 1880–1881; Weaubleau 1881–now. US 54, W 15 m.

1. Origin unknown; a common commendatory place-name; no p.o.
2. This is the second Fristoe *(Warsaw)*. Markham Fristoe; p.o. Mount View, location, 1848–1895; p.o. Shaver, origin unknown, 1885 only; Fristoe 1895–1978.
3. *Salem.*
4. President (1857–1861) James Buchanan's house near Lancaster, Pa.; p.o. Bledsoe, for postmaster Bledsoe Montgomery, 1852–1867; Wheatland 1867–now.
5. Prominent biblical name (Gen. 11:27–31): brother of Abraham and father of Lot; important trading center just NW of Mesopotamia; p.o. 1880–1881.

HIGGINSVILLE
Population: 4,693   Map D-3

After the town was platted in 1869 along the grade of the Lexington & St. Louis *Railroad* by landowner Harvey J. Higgins, its population quadrupled by 1879, aided by the arrival of the Chicago & Alton *Railroad* and the local coal-mining industry. Later the town depended on agriculture, as the self-proclaimed "Seed Corn Capital of the U.S.A.," and today it combines agriculture with light industry like ACE Radio Control, Inc., America's only manufacturer of radio control units for model aircraft and model boats. Post office: 1870–now.

Chicago & Alton Depot. Railroad, 1888; National Historic Register. Replacing one destroyed by fire in 1879, this two-story frame depot, set on a stone foundation, is atypically ornate with prominent gables, decorative molding, and eleven-over-one windows for the second-floor employees' quarters. 2109 Main. *(Farber: Railroad Museum)*

Confederate Memorial. National Historic Register; State Historic Site. The Confederate Home of Missouri was established in 1891 by former Confederate soldiers to house needy veterans and their dependents. It was deeded to the state in 1897, and the last veteran died here in 1950 at the age of 107. The structure was razed in 1956 to make way for the State School for Retarded Children. Today this 113-acre park is a memorial to the estimated 40,000 Missourians who fought for the Confederacy. SR 13B, N 1 m. CHAPEL: Vernacular, 1892. This white clapboard chapel with a corner tower is reportedly the only one dedicated to Confederate veterans west of the Mississippi and one of three in America. FACILITIES: Several small fishing lakes, picnic sites. MEMORIAL *CEMETERY:* Plain stones mark the graves of 603 Confederate veterans and 225 of their wives. Adjacent is a 20-foot monument sculpted in Italy in 1906 for $10,000.

Park. RV campsites, restrooms, picnic facilities, tennis, horseshoes, walking track. In town.

HIGH HILL
Population: 204   Map G-4

A wandering post office and two courthouse fires *(Montgomery City)* have obscured this town's early history. An 1837 High Hill post office was located about four miles east of here at the *Boonslick Trail* near today's Jonesburg.[1] Reportedly, today's High Hill was platted in 1851 along the trail at the site of a *gristmill*, taking the name of the post office, which was presumably named for its former location. Whether the town was originally named High Hill or later adopted that name is not clear. Proximity to the Montgomery County seat of *Danville* and the arrival here in 1857 of the North Missouri *Railroad* led to a modest prosperity. Post office: 1837–now.

High Hill Academy. Classical style, 1866; National Historic Register. Built as an exact copy of its 1860 predecessor, which burned, this two-story frame building with five-rank windows and a bell tower is now used as a community center. In town.

Lewiston, Mo. Montgomery County's second county seat, now defunct, Lewiston was located just south of today's New Florence (below). Its predecessor, Pinckney,[2] situated at the Missouri River southwest of *Warrenton* and later washed away, was replaced in 1826 by Lewiston, which was platted in 1825 for that purpose along the *Boonslick Trail,* at a fork to Côte sans Dessein, and named for Meriwether Lewis *(Lewis and Clark Expedition).* Lewiston was replaced in 1834 by *Danville.* Marker. Post office: c. 1825–1837. I-70 Outer Rd. (old US 40), W 1 m.

New Florence, Mo. Platted in 1857 as Florence along the North Missouri *Railroad* by Judge E. A. Lewis and named for his only daughter, the town was renamed New Florence in 1859 due to an already existing Florence[3] in Morgan County. In 1876 the town tried and failed to gain the county seat from *Danville.* Post office: 1858–now. I-70, W 5 m. STONE HILL WINE COMPANY: The *Hermann* parent company's champagne is produced and bottled here. Tours, tasting; other wines available. I-70 at SR 19.

Pinnacle Rock. Sandstone capped by dolomite, this historic county landmark was probably formed by a stream channel. It once rose nearly 100 feet above the floor of a small valley and had a base of about an acre. Today, still distinctive, it is an island mountain, rising 50 feet above an impounded lake created for Pinnacle Lake Estates. I-70 exit; S Service Road, W 2.1 m.; GR, S 4.2. m.

7-Up Formula. Charles Leeper Griggs (1868–1940) invented the formula for 7-Up at his brother's store in Price's Branch,[4] later (1920) establishing the St. Louis–based Howdy Company, which produced orange soda. It changed names in 1936 to 7-Up. SR F, N 5 m.; SR JJ, E 2 m.

1. Pioneer James Jones; p.o. Green Hill, for the location, 1858–1868; Jonesburgh 1868–1893, Jonesburg 1893–now.
2. Miss Attossa Pinckney Sharp, daughter of first county clerk; p.o. Montgomery Court House, Montgomery County namesake *(County Profiles)*, 1819–1824; Pinckney 1824–1893.
3. Origin unknown; p.o. 1839–now.
4. Origin unknown; p.o. 1855–1908.

HILLSBORO
Population: 1,625   Map H-5

An 1832 proposal to relocate the Jefferson County seat from *Herculaneum* to a central location met with opposition not overcome until 1838, when Samuel Merry and Hugh O'Neil donated 50 acres that were officially designated for the county seat by an 1839 act of the legislature. Platted in 1839 by the county surveyor, the town was originally named *Monticello.* Because that name was already in use, Hillsboro, a name said to approximate Monticello, was then chosen. Bypassed in 1857 by the St. Louis & Iron Mountain *Railroad,* Hillsboro has remained about the same size, serving as a political center and farming community. Post offices: Hillsborough 1838–1892; Hillsboro 1892– now. Home of Jefferson College (junior college).

De Soto, Mo. Nicknamed Fountain City because of the large number of artesian wells, De Soto was platted in 1857 by Thomas Fletcher (below) along the tracks of the St. Louis & Iron Mountain *Railroad.* The official name honors the first European to explore the Mississippi River valley, 16th-century Spanish explorer Hernando de Soto. The first newspaper published by soldiers in the field was printed here during the *Civil War,* on May 21, 1861 *(Bloomfield; Macon).* Post offices: Napton[1] 1857–1858; De Soto 1858–now. SR 21, S 4 m.; SR 110, S 2 m. CITY PARK: Follows a tree-lined stream and SR H. In town. FORMER U.S.A. POPULATION CENTER: 1980–1990 *(Steelville).* WASHINGTON *STATE PARK:* SR 21, S 13 m.

Fletcher House. Vernacular, 1851; additions; National Historic Register. The two-story two-room log house was built by Thomas Fletcher *(Herculaneum)* for his bride. Subsequent 19th-century additions (one by Fletcher c. 1853) have resulted in four structures melded into the present house. Elm at 1st.

Jefferson County Courthouse. Vernacular, 1863–1865; additions and enlargements, 1892–1976. Although organized in 1818, the county had no courthouse until 1839. This one, the county's second, was originally a 40-by-60-foot brick building ($4,000). An addition with a connecting walkway was built beside it in 1892 ($5,000) and was merged with it in 1953 ($233,700 plus $62,250 for heating/plumbing). Renovation and expansion in 1975–1976 added a circuit courtroom and law enforcement facilities ($950,000). Downtown. *(County Profiles)*

Jefferson County Parks. Supported by county taxes, the county Parks and Recreation Department (Box 100, Hillsboro 63050) provides a variety of recreational areas, including the following. BALL MEMORIAL PARK: 2.16 acres. Shade trees, bluffs, river, picnic facilities, boat ramp, innertubing. SR B, N 6.5 m. to Big River at Morse Mill.[2] SUNRIDGE: 6 acres. 100-foot fire tower, physical fitness course, playground, picnic facilities, trail. SR 21, N approx. 6 m. from junction of SR A; Tower Rd., W 0.5 m.

Natural Areas. VALLEY VIEW GLADES: 227 acres. Features a large scenic glade complex, a hickory forest, small creeks, and interesting fauna and flora, e.g. Fremont's leather flower and Missouri evening primrose. Topography much like that at Victoria Glades (below). Rt. 1, Box 1599, Glencoe 63038. SR B, N 4.9 m. VICTORIA GLADES: A band 2–4 miles wide from Big River to Ste. Genevieve County. Principally Ordovician-age dolomite, the glades are like those of southern Missouri's White River Hills section, often extending to the tops of *balds and knobs.* Those here are usually found on south- and southwest-facing slopes. Features include thin soil and bedrock supporting flowering plants, grasses (e.g. bluestem, grama, prairie dropseed), and small pockets of trees, especially blackjack oak. District Forester, Rt. 1, Box 1599, Glencoe 63038. Hillsboro-Victoria Rd. (inquire locally), S approx. 1.75 m. to parking lot.

Sandy Creek Covered Bridge. Howe-Truss (Wooden), 1886; restored 1984; National Historic Register; State Historic Site. First built in 1872 to span Sandy Creek, this was one of six *covered bridges* along the Hillsboro–Lemay Ferry *Road* through the mining areas to St. Louis. Destroyed in 1886 by a flood, it was rebuilt using the same specifications (74.5 feet long and 18 feet, 10 inches wide). In 1984 a flood caused extensive damage. Picnic areas. SR 21, N 4.2 m. to Sandy Rd.; E 0.2 m. to Goldman.[3]

1. Used because of existing De Soto post offices 1849–1858 in Jasper and Barton Counties; for Missouri Supreme Court judge William B. Napton.

2. Owner J. H. Morse; p.o. Morse's Mill 1859–1891; Morse Mill 1891–now.

3. Origin unknown; p.o. 1895–1905.

HOLLISTER
Population: 2,628   Map E-7

Platted in 1906 by W. H. Johnson along at the tracks of the White River *Railroad,* the town assumed the name of the railroad station, which took its name from the 1904 post office established by first store owner Reuben F. Kirkham, who thought that Turkey Creek valley looked like the San Benito River valley at Hollister, Calif., where his daughter was born. After the town was incorporated in 1910, Johnson, dissatisfied with the types of structures being built and eager to find a way to promote the town, helped pass an ordinance requiring all buildings in the business district to conform to Tudor style architecture (below). After the White River was impounded in 1913, Hollister became a waterfront resort widely publicized by the railroad, which ran special excursions to town. Still a tourist town, today it emphasizes its location next to *Branson,* shopping, and lake recreation. Post office: 1904–now. Maps and information: American House (below).

American House. Tudor style, c. 1906. Hollister's oldest building, at one time a boardinghouse catering to railroad workers and salesmen, today houses the chamber of commerce. Picnic area, playground. US 65B, W on 4th.

Architecture. Downing Street Historical District (National Historic Register): early 20th-century Tudor-style buildings notable for steeply pitched roofs, prominent side gables, massive chimneys, and decorative half-timbering. Downing (originally Front) between 3d and 4th.

Ashe Juniper Natural Area / Wildlife Area. 31 acres. Located on a knob *(Balds and Knobs),* this dolomite forest dominated by Ozark white cedar features Ashe juniper (a variety native only to the Ozarks) and the rare Trelease's larkspur. 2630 N. Mayfair, Springfield 65803. *(Wildlife Areas)*

Depot / City Hall. Railroad, 1910. The depot closed in 1960; today the building, with a red-tile roof, creek-rock walls, and oak timbers, serves as the city hall. A caboose serves as the police station. US 65 B, W on 3d to Downing.

Murder Rocks. Set beside the former 1830s road between *Forsyth* and Carrollton, Ark., this isolated mass of sandstone contains vertical fractures enlarged by erosion to form 15-foot pinnacles. Said to look like an ambush scene from a western movie, this geological phenomenon actually was used for ambushes by *Civil War* bushwhacker Alf Bolin, who was so despised that when he was killed, his head was cut off and exhibited on a pole in *Ozark.* SR 76, E 4 m.; SR J, S 2.9 m.; SR JJ, S 1.9 m.; NW side of highway. (The Civil War road ran between the rocks and SR JJ.)

Presbyterian Hill. The 365 steps used to reach the top of this panoramic overlook were auctioned one at a time in the early 1920s to pay for their construction. Of the 160 cabins owned by church members, only a few derelict ones remain. US 65, Taneycomo bridge to *Branson.*

Recreation. BULL SHOALS LAKE: *Lakes: Corps of Engineers.* LAKE TANEYCOMO: adjacent *(Branson: Recreation).* SHEPHERD OF THE HILLS *WILDLIFE AREA.* TABLE ROCK LAKE / STATE PARK / DAM: US 65, S 2.6 m.; SR 165, W 5.7 m. *(Lakes: Corps of Engineers).*

Steel Bridge. *Suspension Bridge,* 1912. Approximately 60 feet long, this bridge replaced a swinging footbridge over Turkey Creek (the pillars are still visible). The wooden decking was replaced in 1976 by concrete. 3d St. (connects US 65B and SR BB).

HOUSTON
Population: 2,118   Map F-6

Platted in 1846 as county seat of Missouri's largest county, Texas, the town was named for Sam Houston (1793–1863), hero of the 1836 Battle of San Jacinto that secured Texas's independence from Mexico *(Mexican War).* He served twice as president of the Republic of Texas (1836–1838, 1841–1844), as its first U.S. senator (1846–1859), and as its sixth governor (1859–1861) before being deposed for refusing to swear allegiance to the Confederacy. The town grew slowly as a political and trading center before being destroyed twice during the *Civil War,* which resulted in a population of zero until after the war. Rebuilt but bypassed by railroads, it maintained the seat of justice, remaining the center of county politics. Post office: 1846–1863, 1865–now.

Emmett Kelly. The childhood hometown (ages 6–19) of internationally known clown Emmett Kelly (1898–1979), Houston sponsors a commemorative festival in early May featuring a kiddie carnival, parades, contests, arts and crafts, entertainment, and food.

Natural Areas. HORSESHOE BEND: 69 acres. Part of a public-use area fronts a two-mile horseshoe bend of the Big Piney River. Features include a high dolomite bluff and mixed oak-pine-hickory bottomland forest. 2.5 m. NW; inquire locally. PINEY RIVER NARROWS: 50 acres. One of Missouri's most scenic narrows features a hogback ridge and spectacular pinnacles formed by the Big Piney River and Piney Creek, which would sideswipe each other if they were not divided by this narrow limestone formation. Southeast end: Balancing Rock, trails. Part of a public-use area. Both areas: Box 138 (Hwy. 160W), West Plains 65775. SR 17, W 2.8 m. (at parking lot, wade Big Piney), or turn S on SR Z just past Big Piney bridge (no parking lot).

Paddy Creek Natural Arch. The main part of this double arch is 11 feet high, 20 feet long, and 12 feet wide. To the right is a slot arch 10 feet long and 3 feet wide. To the west is a shelter cave. Access requires wading a shallow creek and some climbing (slippery but not dangerous). SR 17, N 22 m. through Success (below) to Roby,[1] continue SR 17, N approx. 2 m., FR 78, E approx. 4.2 m.; FR 220, S approx. 2.2 m. to Paddy Creek Campground / Picnic Area (Recreation, below). *(Collapsed Cave Systems)*

Recreation. BARNES *WILDLIFE AREA. FLOAT STREAM:* Big Piney River. MIDVALE *STATE FOREST.* OZARK NATIONAL SCENIC RIVERWAYS *(National Parks):* Cedargrove river access. PADDY CREEK CAMPGROUND / PICNIC AREA / *TRAIL (National Forests):* Swimming, pit toilets, water, playing field, natural arch (Paddy Creek Natural Arch, above), trail, Paddy Creek and Big Piney River fishing. ROBY LAKE PICNIC AREA *(National Forests):* Water, pit toilet, trailhead for Paddy Creek and Big Piney *Trails,* Paddy Creek Wilderness Area, fishing in 9-acre Roby Lake.

Success, Mo. Success is a good example of many wandering Missouri communities. Settled in 1880 as Hastings,[2] the community was renamed to honor the American ideal, Success, which was enlarged to Success Springs, probably for advertising purposes, when the community was relocated as a resort to nearby Ebbing Spring, whose name was changed to suit the new enterprise. After Success Spring was moved to today's location and platted in 1933 as Wye,[3] the town succeeded in regaining the original version of its name, Success, c. 1938 (probably because of *post office* regulations). Post office: Success 1880–now. SR 17, N 15 m.

Texas County Courthouse. Moderne, 1931–1932. From 1847 to 1932 Texas County built six courthouses. In 1930 fire destroyed the fifth. Today's courthouse, partially funded by insurance proceeds of $23,000, was built in stages on the former's foundation. Cost: first $20,148, second $25,000 (total cost to the county: about $22, 148). US 63, W on Main. *(County Profiles)*

1. C. H. Roby, merchant; p.o. 1883–now.
2. Local merchant; p.o. Success.
3. At a Y-shaped junction; p.o. Success.

HUNTSVILLE
Population: 1,567   Map F-3

Selected in 1829 as the temporary county seat of newly organized Randolph County, this settlement, probably known as Huntsville, was designated permanent county seat in 1831, at which time it was platted and named for Daniel Hunt, the town's first settler (he arrived in 1819) and one of four men to donate land for the site. Bypassed in 1858 by the North Missouri *Railroad's* northern route, the town was included in 1868 on the western route, which should have helped it prosper, but nearby *Moberly* was established at the intersection of the two routes. Although Moberly outgrew Huntsville, it narrowly lost its attempt to gain the county seat. Today Huntsville, still the county seat, is primarily a residential community. Post offices: Randolph Court House 1829–1831; Huntsville 1831–now.

Architecture. N. MAIN: 1840–1850s commercial buildings near the courthouse. OTHERS: Little Dixie (1832), end of N. Main. Burckhardt House (1840s), Holman Heights, NE city limits.

Hall Cemetery. Buried at this rural family plot are former Maine resident John H. Hall (1781–1840), inventor of the breech-loading rifle c. 1812, and his son W. A. Hall, who helped found the Missouri Bar Association.[1] SR C, 10.1 m. to Darksville;[2] continue SR C, N 1.1 m.; GR, E 0.6 m. to junction at creek; NE side. *(Cemeteries)*

Mayo House / Museum. Log, c. 1818. This one-room cabin was built by the county's first permanent settler, Thomas Mayo. HISTORICAL SOCIETY MUSEUM: Local historical items. Both: courthouse grounds (below).

Mount Airy, Mo. Established c. 1831, Mount Airy has a stock place-name. "Mount" is not specific (no mountain or high ground need be present), and "Airy" is complimentary about the climate *(Arrow Rock)*. Defunct (one 19th-century church). Post office: 1831–1854, 1865– 1902. US 24, W 4 m.; SR 3, S 4 m. HURT *CEMETERY:* The burial site of two Revolutionary War veterans. SR BB, E 0.5 m.; GR, S 1.5 m.

Randolph County Courthouse. Formerly Neoclassical, 1883–1884; truncated 1910; reduced to Vernacular 1973. This structure, the county's third, was reduced to its present shape from a two-story brick building with a massive cupola, two-story pilasters, a full-height entry with pediment and dentils, quoins, and arched windows. Several remodelings and a 1955 fire left only the first floor and the original (but shortened) pilasters, quoins, and arched windows. The metal roof cresting was added in 1973. Cost: originally $35,000. Grounds: Mayo House, above. Main St. *(County Profiles)*

Thomas Hill Wildlife Area / Reservoir. Reservoir: SR C, N 10.1 m. *(Wildlife Areas)*

1. W. A. Hall's son, W. P. Hall, was governor in 1864–1865, finishing the term of H. R. Gamble (1861–1864).

2. Via Dark Creek: reportedly William Elliot camped here in 1821, calling the night the darkest he ever saw; p.o. 1858–1907.

IBERIA

Population: 650 . Map F-5

The first record of an "Iberia" in Miller County was the area post office named Iberia at Rabbit Head Creek about a mile southwest of today's townsite. The town of Iberia was platted in 1859 (the plat was filed in 1860) by landowner H. M. Dickerson, and the Iberia post office was moved to it. In the Iberian language, which predates the Roman era, the word "Iberia" is a rough equivalent of "Spain." Local tradition claims the town was named by an early resident who emigrated from

New Iberia, La., which is the seat of justice of Iberia Parish, settled in 1765 by the French and Spanish. Another possibility that does not discount local tradition is the fashion of the time that favored exotic names *(La Plata)*. Either because of the bare rocks around Missouri's Iberia or because of a legendary mid-19th-century rock fight, it was also known as Rock Town or Rocktown. Iberia was stunted by the *Civil War,* and the post office closed in 1861, reopening in 1862 as Oakhurst.[1] The town was slow to grow; its 1870 population of 100 was mostly former slaves. The population base shifted from black to white by the 1880s, and by c. 1890 Iberia was characterized as the toughest town in the mountains, where women smoked corncob pipes and grown men played marbles and fought. Today, as the second largest town in Miller County *(Eldon)*, it serves a primarily agricultural economy. Post offices: Iberia 1838–1861, 1871–now; Oakhurst 1862–1871.

Bray's Mill. Vernacular, c. 1885. Built by Thomas Bray of Pay Down Mill *(Belle)*, this two-and-a-half-story *gristmill,* powered by a 10-foot metal wheel, has also served Brays community as a woolen mill, post office, way station, and dentist office. Post office: Brays 1894–1923. SR 42, E 2.7 m.; SR 42/54N, N 0.5.

Iberia Academy. Vernacular, c. 1910–1920; National Historic Register. Four buildings (administration, dormitory, gym, and house) remain from a private school established in 1890 by G. Byron Smith. It grew from a class of 1 to a class of 118 by 1940. The school closed in 1951, a year after Smith's death. Private. SR 42 at Normal.

Old City Jail. Vernacular, early 1900s. Looking like an aboveground root cellar, this 10-by-10-foot concrete structure has a strap-iron door, a barrel-vault ceiling, narrow slit windows, a cement floor, and no electricity or water. Closed c. 1947; now used for storage. SR 42, N on Main 2 blocks; adjacent to the red granite Church of Nazarene. Private.

St. Anthony, Mo. / Bridges. Platted in 1906, the town was named for the St. Anthony of Padua Church and School, whose name honors a Portuguese friar and priest (1195–1231) who is most remembered for his devotion to the poor and who is called upon as the finder of lost articles. Post office: 1907–1929. SR 42, E 5 m.; SR A, N 4.2 m. BRUMLEY BRIDGE (KLIETHERMES): *Suspension Bridge,* 1920s. Across Tavern Creek; 304 feet long, 12 feet wide; 2-ton limit. GR, W 3.9 m. to bridge, then CR A, W 0.8 m. to join SR A just W of SR PP; inquire locally. BUECHTER BRIDGE: *Suspension Bridge,* late 1920s. Across Tavern Creek; about 128 feet long, 12 feet wide; 2-ton limit. GR, S (past church and small park) 1.7 m.; inquire locally.

1. Origin unknown, usually a family name; p.o. 1862–1871.

INDEPENDENCE
Population: 112,301
Maps C-3 and Kansas City Area

Platted in 1827 three miles south of the Missouri River as county seat of newly organized Jackson County, Independence dominated the outfitting business for Far West trade from 1828 to 1845, serving as a rendezvous point for three major trails to the Pacific coast (National Frontier Trails Center, below) until nearby rival Westport *(Kansas City)* began gaining importance in the early 1840s. *Civil War* battles (below), *Order No. 11,* and repeated guerrilla fighting substantially damaged its economic growth. During the 1870s–1880s, Kansas City boomed as the Midwest's major livestock and packing center, reducing Independence's former regional importance. Independence continued to grow as a trading, manufacturing, and political center of the county, and today it is Missouri's fourth largest city. It was named for the patriotic ideal. Post offices: Jackson Court House 1827; Independence 1827–now. Home of Fort Osage Area Vo-Tech. Self-guided tours: chamber of commerce, I-70, N on Noland, W on Truman to Maple (111 E.). Truman Home tickets and information: 223 N. Main.

Architecture. GENERAL: Some of the best examples of 19th-century styles and historic sites are near the square in an area bounded by Spring, White Oak, Memorial, and Walnut. I-70, N on Noland to W on Truman Rd. NATIONAL HISTORIC REGISTER: Historic district (Truman, below) and over 14 structures.

Battle of Independence. August 11, 1862; October 21–22, 1864. The first battle here followed the capture of the arsenal at nearby *Liberty* Landing. Confederate Col. Upton Hayes captured the federal garrison here and then turned toward *Lone Jack.* Five markers trace the 1864 battle lines that eventually led to the Battle of Westport *(Kansas City),* which marked the end of organized fighting in Missouri during the *Civil War.* Begin at US 24, just east of the Little Blue River.

Bingham-Waggoner Estate. Vernacular, c. 1860; extensively remodeled 1899; National Historic Register. This large elaborate house with outbuildings on 19 acres was built by John Lewis, a pioneer and saddle maker, and owned in 1864–1870 by Missouri artist George Caleb Bingham *(Arrow Rock: George Caleb Bingham House);* W. H. Waggoner (National Frontier Trails Center, below) bought it in 1879. Some original fixtures and furnishings; tours. 313 W. Pacific (see map).

Jackson County Courthouses. INDEPENDENCE: Adam, 1836; extensively remodeled and enlarged 1852, 1872, 1905; remodeled and expanded to Neoclassical, 1932–1933; National Historic Register. This structure,

technically the county's second courthouse (Log Courthouse, below), provides space for the Jackson County election board and historical exhibits (Truman, below). Daily county business is conducted at 708 W. Kansas, where annexes were built during the 1950s and 1960s. Cost (1932 remodeling and expansion): $143,351. Truman Rd., S on Main. KANSAS CITY: Art Deco, 1933–1934. Although Kansas City is not a county seat, daily county business is also conducted here *(Kansas City: Jackson County Courthouse). (County Profiles)*

La Benite Park / Riverboat. PARK: Picnic and camping area along Missouri River bottomland, river access, athletic fields, hiking trails, restrooms. WILLIAM S. MITCHELL RIVERBOAT: Steam-driven side-wheeler, 1934; National Historic Register. This 277-foot river dredge, permanently moored here after its 1982 retirement, features a 40-man bunk room, pilothouse, dining hall, and wooden paddle wheels. At Sugar Creek, Mo.:[1] SR 291 at SR 78; SR 291, N 7.6 m. at the river.

Log Courthouse. Log, 1827–1828; restored. This two-room 15-by-36-foot log building was used twice as a temporary courthouse. After serving as Jackson County's first courthouse, it was a private structure until donated to the city and moved c. 1916 from Lynn and Lexington to today's site, where in 1932 the presiding county judge, Harry S. Truman, used it as a temporary courthouse while the present one was being remodeled. Its use by the law firm of Gilbert and Whitney makes it important in *Mormon* history. Truman Rd., S on Main to 117 W. Kansas.

Marshal's Home / Jail / Museum. Behind the restored Greek Revival–style (1859) marshal's house and office is the original county jail, with two-foot-thick limestone walls and strap-iron doors (Frank James was held here; *Kearney).* Both: National Historic Register; period furnishings and fixtures. The 1901 annex is now an interpretive museum, exhibiting local historical items. Grounds: 1860s ornamental garden and one-room schoolhouse. 217 N. Main near Truman.

Mormon Sites / Joseph Smith Historic Area. After the death in 1844 at Nauvoo, Ill., of church founder and prophet Joseph Smith, the Church of Jesus Christ of Latter Day Saints (LDS) split into sects, none of which rivals the membership of the original LDS church. MORMON VISITOR CENTER (LDS): Exhibits feature church beliefs, especially regarding Jesus and his second coming, the life and mission of Joseph Smith, westward migration, and the historic and religious significance of Independence. Displays: log cabin, 30-foot painting ("Second Coming of Christ"). 937 W. Walnut near River. RLDS AUDITORIUM: Modern, 1926–1962. The Reorganized Church of Jesus Christ of Latter Day Saints (RLDS) broke with the LDS after 1844, rejecting polygamy and the idea that

Smith endorsed it (LDS continued polygamy until 1890). This 65,648-square-foot world headquarters of the RLDS was completed in 1962 after financial setbacks that began during the Depression. It features over 100 reinforced-concrete columns supporting an elliptical dome, as well as an Aeolian-Skinner organ (6,000 pipes) that reportedly is one of America's finest (30-minute recitals on Sundays). Tours. 1001 W. Walnut near River. TEMPLE LOT: National Historic Register. The Church of Christ (Temple Lot), a continuation of a Bloomington, Ill., group, believes that this temple site, dedicated in 1831 by Joseph Smith as the City of Zion, is where Jesus was to establish the New Jerusalem. Marker, cornerstone. Walnut at River. *(Mormons)*

National Frontier Trails Center. Vernacular, 1875; restored. Located in the Waggoner-Gates flour mill

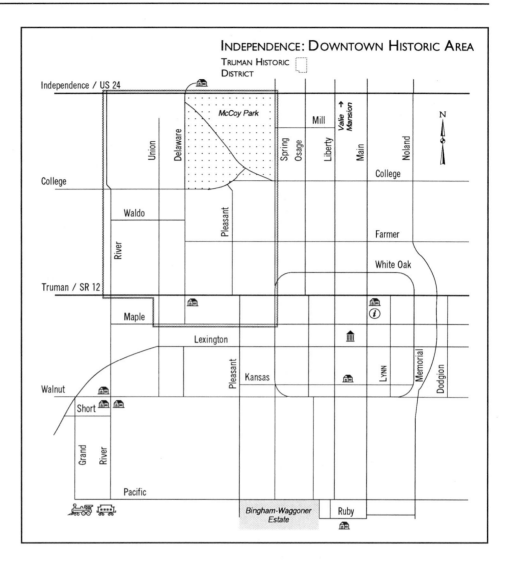

INDEPENDENCE: DOWNTOWN HISTORIC AREA

building (home of Queen of the Pantry Flour) at the site of the *Santa Fe, Oregon,* and California Trails, this is America's only interpretive museum for these three trails. Features include a model freight wagon, tools, quilts, 1840s ladies' apparel, and a 14-minute film on the history of the opening of the West, as well as a library and archives related to western exploration and expansion, e.g. the Mormon Trail, *Lewis and Clark,* Zebulon Pike *(County Profiles: Pike),* and the West's mountain men. S of square; Osage S at Pacific (318 W).

Truman Historic District / Truman Sites. National Historic Register, National Landmark. The district includes sites connected with Harry S. Truman (1884–1972), U.S. president from 1945 to 1953 *(Belton; Grandview; Lamar).* Incidentally, Truman's middle initial is only an initial, reportedly because his parents could not decide which grandfather to name him for, Anderson Shippe Truman or Solomon Young.[2] The Trumans moved here in 1890. After he graduated from high school in 1901, Truman worked at various jobs

until returning in 1906 to his grandparents' farm at *Grandview.* COURTROOM AND OFFICE: The courtroom is restored to the era when county judge Truman presided here; the office is restored to its 1930s appearance when Truman launched his national political career as a senator. A sound-and-light show focuses on Truman's early years and retirement here. Lexington at Liberty (Jackson County Courthouse, above). MCCOY PARK: 16 acres. Picnic shelters and tables, ball field, tennis, restrooms, playground, water fountains. US 24 and Delaware. TRUMAN DEPOT: Railroad, 1913; National Historic Register. Exhibited are photographs of Truman's 1948 whistle-stop campaign when as a dark-horse presidential candidate against Thomas E. Dewey *(Excelsior Springs)* he took his campaign to the people. Amtrak stop. Pacific at Grand. TRUMAN HOME: Gothic Revival, 1865; remodeled 1880s; National Historic Site; *National Park.* Built by Mrs. Harry S. (Bess) Truman's grandfather, G. P. Gates, owner of Waggoner-Gates flour mill (National Frontier

Trails Center, above), this two-story clapboard house (the "Summer White House") with art-glass windows was the Trumans' home from 1919, when they married, until their deaths (Truman Library, below). It contains their furnishings and possessions; tours. 219 N. Delaware at Truman Rd. Tickets: 223 N. Main at Truman Rd. TRUMAN LIBRARY / MUSEUM: National Historic Site. Exhibits include a Thomas Hart Benton (Neosho) mural depicting the town's role in opening the West, Truman memorabilia, gifts, and a replica of the presidential office, the Trumans' graves (Bess d. 1982). Truman's marker is notable because the presidency is only one of many offices listed on the stone. US 24 at Delaware. OTHER SITES: Bess Wallace (Truman) birthplace (117 W. Ruby) and Trinity Episcopal Church, where the Trumans were married (409 N. Liberty).

Vaile Mansion. High Victorian Second Empire, c. 1881–1882; National Historic Register. Built by Harvey M. Vaile, founder of the Star Mail Route and stage lines, this was called the most princely house in the West. The three-story brick house has elaborate detailing, including a five-story central tower with two tiers of paired dormer windows, extensive cresting, broad Italianate eaves with brackets, Gothic Revival–style drip molding, steeply pitched dormer roofs with cross bracing, and one-story porches decorated by complicated spindlework. The interior of this 31-room mansion is equally elaborate, including nine marble fireplaces and intricately turned molding. Tours. Truman Rd. to Liberty (1500 N.).

1. Sugar maples via the creek; p.o. 1904–1951.
2. Because the "S" is only an initial, there is controversy about using a period afterward. Truman used a period, saying he didn't care whether people did or not; his tombstone has a period (Truman Library / Museum, below). Like arguments over pronunciation of Missouri, there is no right or wrong in this situation.

 # INDIANS

Because Christopher Columbus mistakenly believed he landed in eastern Asia, rather than the West Indies, the people he encountered in 1492 were described as Indians, a misnomer still used to describe Native Americans, who like all Americans are a culturally and racially varied people with different customs, belief systems, and languages. Although Columbus was the quintessential newcomer, the people he first met were also "not from here." About 20,000 B.C. an initial migration across a land bridge between Siberia and Alaska, and by boat down the Pacific west coast, brought the first indigenous peoples to North America. Through

10,000 years of experimentation and adaptation, their descendants developed diverse and highly sophisticated cultures totally unrelated, but at least equal, to those of the Old World. The very concept of the North and South American continents being referred to as the New World is enough explanation for the ensuing culture shock experienced by both sides.

Paleo-Indian Period. 12,000–8000 B.C. Little evidence remains of these people other than fluted projectile points used in darts and spears for hunting large, now mostly extinct, animals (Mastodon State Park). These so-called Clovis points, found near Clovis, N.Mex., are the earliest evidence of human habitation in America. While these points are dated c. 12,000 B.C., a larger quantity dated c. 9500 B.C. were recently found in the Missouri-Mississippi River valley, which confirms that toolmakers were in Missouri no later than c. 9500 B.C. and raises the question of whether earlier evidence will be found.

Dalton Period. 8000–7000 B.C. As evidenced by Graham Cave (State Parks), this period in Missouri at the end of the Ice Age (Glacial Erratics) marked a transition from big-game hunting to a relatively more settled society whose members hunted smaller game, foraged for edible wild plants, and lived in caves and other natural shelters. Artifacts of this period (bone needles, mortars, pestles, drills, and other tools) imply that these people made clothes, worked wood, ground meal or flour, and stored food for the winter. Cupstones (pieces of sandstone with indentations ground or pecked in them) have been found filled with paint, which indicates ceremonies were part of their culture. A ring of stones at Graham Cave suggests some type of hierarchy, and a burial underground with special attention to the deceased implies a rudimentary belief in life after death.

Archaic Period. 7000–1000 B.C. This period encompassed an amalgamation of old forms of technology and social organization with new ones. Adjusting to a warmer climate, these hunter-gatherers established temporary communities overlooking rivers, increased their diets to include fish and more wild vegetables, wove baskets and cloth, manufactured more complicated tools such as axes and adzes, and adopted a new hunting device, the atlatl, which was a spear launched by a separate but parallel stick, giving the thrust a slingshot effect. Along with technological advances, belief systems also became more complicated, as is evidenced by the Cuivre River Ceremonial Complex, where a cemetery area indicates elaborate burials sponsored by the group rather than the individual. Special tools and goods were buried with the deceased, indicating a more sophisticated belief in an afterlife.

Woodland Period. 1000 B.C.–A.D. 900. Clay tools, vessels, and utensils from the beginning of this period were the precursors of semipermanent camps and villages that included large ceremonial earthworks. The people engaged in agriculture mixed with foraging, cooperative fishing and hunting, trade, and the manufacturing of nonutilitarian ornaments made from then-exotic materials such as copper, mica, obsidian, and seashells. Characteristic of this period are burial mounds (literally mounds of earth used strictly for burial and becoming increasingly larger over the years) that included nonutilitarian objects indicating a basic idea of religion (Van Meter *State Park)*. While not as elaborate as the mounds at Cahokia in East St. Louis, Ill. *(Kahoka)*, those in Missouri are indicative of the westward spread of cultural influences through a burgeoning trade system that reached even the remotest communities and accelerated the exchange of ideas, e.g. the radically new c. 700 A.D. invention of the bow and arrow.

Mississippian Period. A.D. 900–1700. The *St. Louis* area offers examples of the vigorous expansion from small villages to large towns of both the Indian and the later Euro-American cultures. The Indian campsites gave way to villages, to towns, and then to a metropolis, St. Louis–Cahokia *(Kahoka)*, which served as a trading point for new ideas and technology that precipitated the dependence of a large population on agriculture (corn, beans, squash), division of labor, and commerce, including trade with small towns for raw materials and staples like salt, paint, skins, bow wood, jewelry, and pottery. As evidenced at Towosahgy Historic Site *(Dorena)*, small town farmers also built temple mound complexes that featured wooden houses with center poles, thatched roofs, and wattle-and-daub walls. A ring of palisaded earthworks surrounded by a ditch enclosed the town, whose houses were usually concentrated around a flat-topped temple mound that was often paired with a chief's mound. Town cemeteries contain graves 18–42 inches deep. The deceased was always buried whole, sometimes in the flesh and sometimes after being exposed outdoors until the bones were picked clean. If the burial was of a skeleton, the custom was to place the skull and crossed leg bones on top of the grave. While the symbolism of this arrangement is not known, its shock value to Europeans was not lost on Spanish pirates, who adopted the skull and crossbones as their emblem. Other symbolism of this period—as seen today in petroglyphs (Washington *State Park)* such as crosses, weeping eyes, and sunbursts—is not understood either.

Historic Period. A.D. 1700–1835. When the first Europeans, led by Hernando de Soto, crossed the Mississippi River in 1541, they found a complex society of people joined by loose confederations. Journals kept by the men of De Soto's expedition noted frequent encounters with people who were mostly farmers living in communities grouped around large mounds. However, when the next explorers, Marquette and Jolliet, arrived 131 years later, in 1673, these temple mound builders had vanished. The first reported meeting with Historic Period Indians in Missouri was probably at the Pinnacles (Van Meter *State Park)* in 1714 by Étienne Venyard de Bourgmont, a French explorer-adventurer who ascended the Missouri River to the mouth of the Platte River in southwestern Nebraska. In 1723 he established Fort d'Orleans on the north bank of the Missouri River just west of its confluence with the Grand River near today's Brunswick *(Keytesville)*. The Missouri Indians, induced by a flourishing fur and hide trading business, moved their village a few miles upstream to the south bank of the river opposite the fort and there were joined by the Little Osage, who were persuaded by Bourgmont to break from the main group of Osage. While the Missouri and Osage were clearly the dominant Indians of historic Missouri, other groups foraged and hunted

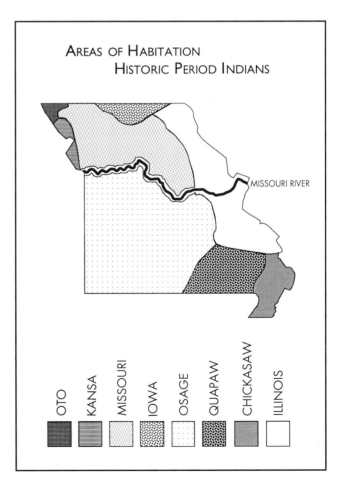

AREAS OF HABITATION
HISTORIC PERIOD INDIANS

MISSOURI RIVER

OTO KANSA MISSOURI IOWA OSAGE QUAPAW CHICKASAW ILLINOIS

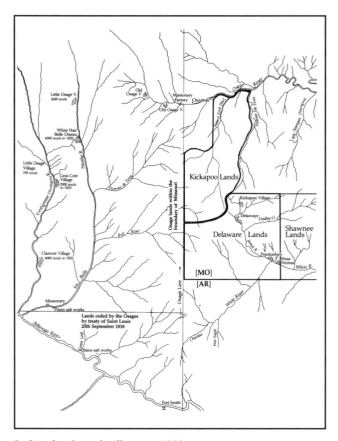

Indian lands and villages c. 1820. (FROM CHAPMAN AND CHAPMAN, "INDIANS AND ARCHAEOLOGY OF MISSOURI")

in the area but mostly maintained permanent villages in areas adjacent to Missouri's present boundaries. CHICKASAW: From West Tennessee and Mississippi the Chickasaw exerted cultural influence in the Missouri Bootheel (*Dorena: Towosahgy*) but probably did not make permanent villages. Muskogean-speaking, they were part of a highly civilized mound-building culture of the Southeast; they were linguistically related to the Apalachee, Alabama, Mobile, Choctaw, Creek, Hichiti, *Seminole,* Tuskegee, and Yamasee. ILLINOIS: The Illinois (or Iliniwek; *Athens*) hunted and foraged in Missouri and established some villages here. They were part of the Illinois Confederacy, an Algonquian-speaking people that included the Kaskaskia (*Ste. Genevieve*), Michigamea, Monigwena, Peoria, Tamaroa, and various subtribes like the *Miami.* IOWA: The Iowa lived in the general area of today's Iowa and hunted in Missouri, especially along the upper portions of the Grand River; they were linguistically related to the Missouri (below). KANSA (KAW): The Kansa lived along the Kansas River and probably established a village on King Hill in *St. Joseph;* they were linguistically related to the Osage (below). MISSOURI: Linguistically related to the Oto, Iowa, and

Winnebago, the Missouri spoke Chiwere Sioux. When they left the state in the late 18th century, they joined the Oto in Nebraska. Culturally, the Missouri were typically Oneota, a group of prehistoric Indians greatly influenced by the Cahokia mound-builder culture (*Kahoka*). They lived in large villages (some covering 150–300 acres), hunted, fished, grew squash, beans, and corn, foraged for edible plants like the American lotus, engaged in commerce and manufacturing, and lived in prairie-style lodge houses built of poles covered with woven mats. Because the Missouri were amalgamated with the Oto after leaving the state, little is known about their specific culture before contact with Euro-Americans. OSAGE: The Osage might have been in southwest Missouri before 1673 and could have been the Indians described to Marquette and Jolliet by other tribes. They were in Vernon County, Mo. (*Nevada*), by 1700 and were first recorded as a group in 1719 by French trader Charles Claude du Tisné. Although they share some Oneota cultural traits with the Missouri, their southwest Missouri ancestors from the three-corners area (*Noel: South West City*) have been difficult to identify. Linguistically they are related to the Kansa (or Kaw), Omaha, Quapaw, and Ponca of the Dhegiha group of Souian-speaking people. The Osage built villages organized in a circle on top of a high *prairie* or terrace that overlooked lower ground. They grouped themselves by blood-related clans that interacted with the whole in a complex social, political, and ceremonial matrix so interwoven that even marriages were arranged for the clan's best advantage. They built houses, gardened, hunted, manufactured tools, and lived similarly to the Missouri. Nonetheless, as a cultural unit, like other tribes of Native Americans, the Osage were unique. In 1808 they relinquished by treaty all Missouri land east of a line drawn due south from Fort Osage (*Sibley*). In another treaty in 1825, five years after Missouri statehood, the Osage relinquished all their land in Missouri. OTO: Originally from Nebraska, the Oto made a minor enclave in Missouri, returning to Nebraska with the Missouri (above) at the end of the 18th century. QUAPAW: The Quapaw ranged north from the mouth of the Arkansas River into Missouri; they were linguistically related to the Osage (above).

Other Missouri Indians. Other Indians associated with Missouri history include the following. DELAWARE AND SHAWNEE: These Algonquian-speaking tribes were recruited from the East by the Spanish in the late 18th century to help control the Osage (above), who were successfully raiding Spanish colonies. The Delaware and Shawnee lived along Apple and Shawnee Creeks near *Cape Girardeau;* the Shawnee also lived at the mouth of the Bourbeuse River and Huzzah

Creek *(Float Streams)*. By 1819 both tribes had been relocated south of the Kickapoo reservation (below). They were removed from Missouri in 1829. KICKAPOO: An Algonquian-speaking people originally from the southwest side of Lake Michigan, the Kickapoo were moved to a reservation in 1819 defined by the Osage north–south line (above) and the Osage and Pomme de Terre Rivers. A major village was located at today's Springfield. They were removed from Missouri in 1832. SAUK (SAC) AND FOX: An Algonquian-speaking people originally from the midwestern area of Lake Michigan, and later located near the Des Moines and Mississippi Rivers north of Missouri, the Sauk and the Fox merged before moving to northeastern Missouri c. 1812. Because of their vigorous claim on their land and the resulting friction with Missouri settlers, they are prominent in state history and legend *(Arcadia: Taum Sauk Mountain State Park; Black Hawk War)*. They were removed from Missouri c. 1837 after the *Platte Purchase*. SOUTHWESTERN MISSOURI INDIANS: The Piankashaw (Miami subtribe), Peoria (part of the Illinois Confederacy; above), and Wea (Miami subtribe) lived briefly in southwest Missouri.

IRONTON

Population: 1,539   Map H-6

One of three mining towns *(Arcadia; Pilot Knob)* joined together today by their city limits along SR 21, Ironton was first settled c. 1853 and platted in 1857 by H. N. Tong and David Carson, mercantile businessmen from the eastern edge of nearby Shepherd Mountain, who bought land here to compete in a general election with Arcadia and Middlebook[1] for county seat of newly organized Iron County. Ironton, selected as county seat in 1857, was named for the area's iron ore. While the town benefited in 1853–1858 from the Plank Road *(Farmington)* and the Iron Mountain *Railroad* (which arrived c. 1871), it has mostly prospered as a county seat. Post offices: Pilot Knob 1858; Ironton 1858–now. Home of Arcadia Valley Area Vocational School. See the map at Arcadia and other nearby attractions at *Arcadia* and *Pilot Knob*.

Architecture. Good examples of 19th-century folk and pattern-book architecture, especially along Main, Russell, and Shepherd Streets. Several downtown buildings use red granite to good advantage.

Battle of Pilot Knob. Skirmishes at Ironton after this battle left scars on the courthouse (below). *(Pilot Knob)*

County Historical Museum. Displays include historical photographs, a mineral collection, railroad memorabilia, furniture, and books; archives. SR 21, W on Russell to Main, 2 blocks N of courthouse.

Emerson Park / Grant's Statue. First landscaped for the 1867 Lindsay-Emerson home, then as a park, this is now a part of the Ste. Marie du Lac Catholic Church. An 1886 bronze statue of a Union soldier was erected by veterans of the 21st Illinois "to commemorate the spot where their colonel, Ulysses S. Grant, received his commission as general" in 1861. After his promotion, Grant was put in charge of the District of Southeast Missouri (which included southern Illinois). He moved his headquarters to Cape Girardeau, then to Cairo, Ill. *(East Prairie: Battlefield)*. Main, 1 block S. of courthouse.

Goulding-Chomyk House. Postmedieval English style with English Queen Anne affinities, c. 1872. Reportedly reminiscent of structures in Dr. R. T. Goulding's native England, the two-story stone house is asymmetrical with a square tower and prominent chimneys. Its grounds feature six-foot-tall 6,000-pound statues of Minerva, Diana, and Venus. Now owned by Chanticleer Ceramics; visitors welcome. SR 21, W on Russell (711).

Iron County Courthouse. Italianate, 1858–1860; enlarged 1964; National Historic Register. Iron County's first and only courthouse, this two-story redbrick structure has Italianate influences that include a center gable with pediment, overhanging eaves, a wide band of trim accented by dentils, paired doors with a transom, an octagonal cupola, quoins, a belt course, and tall second-story arched windows with decorative full-arch drip moldings. Over the entrance is a framed pair of arched windows. During the Civil War *(Pilot Knob: Battle)* each side occupied the courthouse twice. Bullet scars are still visible in the brick. Cost: original (50 by 65 feet) $14,000; enlargement (45 feet added to length) $113,000. Grounds: 1899 gazebo. SR 21, W on Russell to Main. *(County Profiles)*

St. Paul's Episcopal Church. Gothic Revival, 1870; National Historic Register. An excellent example of its style, this wooden church has leaded stained glass, lancet windows, a steeply pitched roof, red and turquoise shingles, cross gables, and a square bell tower rising above the roofline. SR 21, W on Russell, N on Knob (106).

Sheriff's House and Jail. Vernacular, 1886. Still in use, this two-story limestone building housed the sheriff, his family, and prisoners. SR 21, W on Russell to Shepherd.

Stouts Creek Shut-Ins (Upper). About a half-mile long, the shut-ins feature waterfalls carved in dark purple porphyry and a homemade concrete dam (at E end). SR 21 at SR M, SR M, W approx. 3.5 m. to end of state maintenance; continue W on GR 0.2 m. *(Shut-Ins)*

---

1. Origin unknown; p.o. 1858–now.

JACKSON

Population: 9,256　　　　Map I-6

In 1814 the Cape Girardeau County court selected a county seat site located on a broad low hill at an improved plantation that was served by a community post office, Jackson. A town was platted in 1815 and named for the post office, which honored Andrew Jackson, then a folk military hero of the *War of 1812*, who had defeated the Creek Nation in 1812–1814. When the county was organized in 1812, the assumption was that county namesake Cape Girardeau, then the seat of government for the territorial district, would become the county seat, but the federal government had rejected Louis Lorimier's Spanish land grants *(Cape Girardeau)*, invalidating titles to all city lots. Despite an 1849 cholera epidemic, division of loyalties during the *Civil War,* and no *railroad* until the late 1880s when the St. Louis, Iron Mountain & Southern arrived, Jackson grew as a political, milling, and trading center. Post office: 1813–now.

Architecture. CRIDDLE HOUSE: Vernacular, 1817; remodeled, additions. This was the first two-story house built in Jackson. The center-gable entry (four columns on each floor) was replaced by a Queen Anne porch, and a two-story addition replaced the original kitchen in 1915; 22-inch-thick limestone walls; private. Midtown; US 61, E on Main to N. Missouri (119). FRIZEL-WELLING HOUSE: Vernacular, 1817; second story 1838. This two-story frame house has been owned by the same family since 1838; private. Midtown; US 61, to 209 W. Main. OLIVER HOUSE: Greek Revival style, c. 1847; remodeled and restored; National Historic Register. Parts of this two-story brick house were lived in prior to 1847. Features include nine furnished rooms (1850–1900), original coal oil light fixtures, replica wallpaper, and other authentic details; tours. Midtown; US 61, W on Adams to Ohio.

Bollinger Mill / Burfordville Covered Bridge. Both: National Historic Register, State Historic Site. BOLLINGER MILL: *Gristmill,* c. 1867. First built c. 1800, the mill was burned during the *Civil War* then rebuilt c. 1867 as a three-story brick and stone mill, using the original stone first floor. Closed in 1953, it is operated today for visitors. Guided tours, exhibits, picnic sites, hiking trail to Bollinger family *cemetery*. SR 34, W 7 m.; SR HH, E 0.3 m. to Burfordville.[1] BURFORDVILLE COVERED BRIDGE: Howe-Truss, 1858–1868; restored. Completed after the Civil War, this is Missouri's oldest surviving *covered bridge*. Spanning the Whitewater River at the site of a former toll *road* (below) between Burfordville, Jackson, and *Cape*

Girardeau, it measures 140 feet long, 14 feet high, and 12 feet wide. At Bollinger Mill.

Cape Girardeau County Courthouse. Italian Renaissance, 1908. Reportedly the county's fourth, this 81-by-108-foot courthouse was designed as a fireproof structure. It features roofline balustrades, a rusticated first story, four full-height pedimented entries with dentils and Corinthian columns, and a domed cupola. Architect P. H. Weathers also designed early 20th-century courthouses in Daviess and Stoddard Counties. Cost: $125,000. Midtown; US 61, W on Main to Court. *(County Profiles)*

City Cemetery. Platted in 1814–1815, the cemetery has some good examples of 19th-century markers, a few aboveground tombs, and a tall limestone obelisk honoring *Mexican War* and Confederate veteran Col. William Jeffers (1827–1903). US 61, W on Monroe to High. *(Cemeteries)*

Little River Drainage District. *Cape Girardeau.*

Old McKendree Chapel. Log, 1819; restored; oldest standing Protestant church house west of the Mississippi (Bethel Baptist, defunct, was the first in 1806); National Historic Register. The congregation that built this one-story church, one of ten historic shrines of American Methodism, was organized in 1806, just three years after the *Louisiana Purchase* nullified the Spanish order for "no preacher other than Catholic." Services were held here for 83 years. The simple interior has straight-back pews and a wooden floor. Protected by a 1930s steel canopy. E side; US 61, N on Shawnee, E on old Cape, N on Bainbridge; signs.

Park. 125 acres. Pool, tennis, band shell, small lake, hiking trail, picnic facilities, croquet field, creek, playground. N side; US 61, W on Parkview; signs.

Recreation. LAKE GIRARDEAU *WILDLIFE AREA.* TRAIL OF TEARS *STATE PARK.* US 61, N 4 m.; SR 177, E and S 11.1 m.

Steam Train. Built in 1946, this coal-fired steam engine weighs about 115,000 pounds and pulls open-style passenger cars built in the 1920s. A nine-mile tourist ride travels across farmland once served by the Belmont Branch of its namesake St. Louis, Iron Mountain & Southern *Railroad.* US 61 at SR 72.

Toll Roads / House. Folk Victorian, 1890. This is the area's only remaining tollhouse (US 61, E on Main, S on Georgia to 816 Old Cape Road). From c. 1818 until the establishment in 1907 of the State Highway Department, stock companies were formed to build *roads*.[2] Tolls charged for people and animals varied from 1 cent per mile for sheep or hogs to 25 cents per mile for four-horse vehicles. Some exemptions included funerals, church traffic, and parades. A 1920 statewide bond issue initiated construction of all-weather public roads.

1. S. R. Burford; p.o. Gravel Road, for the road surface, 1858–1862, 1865–1869; Burfordville 1869–now.

2. Tolls were collected for about 30 years, after which the county collected the fees.

JAMESPORT
Population: 570   Map D-2

Thomas N. Auberry homesteaded in 1834 what is now the north part of Jamesport, later establishing it as the area's first settlement, Auberry Grove.[1] James Gillilan bought a farm at today's townsite in 1853 and filed a plat in 1857 for a town called James Port. The town is reportedly named for landowner and first postmaster James Gillilan, although two other men named James could conceivably share the honor: Dr. James T. Allen, who supposedly helped survey the property, and pioneer James Callison, who bought land west of the site in 1839 and married Gillilan's sister, Rebecca, in 1852. No records explain this landlocked town's suffix, port, but the term can refer to a shipping and receiving point. The arrival in 1871 of the Chicago, Rock Island & Pacific *Railroad* helped establish the town as a trading center. It was incorporated in 1872 as Jamesport. Today it is known for antique shops and Amish stores. Post office: Jamesport 1857–now.

Amish Community. What is reportedly Missouri's largest settlement of Amish was formed in 1953 when groups from Iowa, Delaware, and Kansas moved near here. The Amish, formerly known as the Old Order Amish Mennonites, are a conservative Protestant sect established c. 1693–1697 when Jacob Ammann, a bishop of the Mennonite Church, left it after a controversy about his strict shunning of excommunicated church members. Amish believe in the supremacy of the Bible, the simplicity of life, an agrarian economy, large families, and separation from the world. Still adhering to a 17th-century lifestyle, they drive buggies, farm with draft animals, and do not use electricity (The Home Place, below). Amish men are easily recognized by their hats, beards without mustaches, and coats without collars. The women wear cloth prayer hats, high-neck dresses, and no makeup; none of the clothes have zippers, a relatively new invention patented in 1913. Please do not take pictures of the Amish; it is against their religious beliefs.

Architecture. DOWNTOWN: good examples of 19th-century commercial architecture. PRAIRIE SCHOOL ARCHITECTURE: Prairie, c. 1910. Unusual for a rural area, this Frank Lloyd Wright style was used mostly between 1905 and 1915. This two-story house features a low-pitch roof, wide overhanging eaves, mixed tile, brick and stucco, marble stairs, and massive square

posts. SR F, E 2 m.

Harris Cabin / Park. Log, 1830–1836; reconstructed. Built by Jesse and Polly Harris four miles east of town and moved here in 1985 for display, this 18-by-18-foot one-room log cabin has period furnishings, e.g. a plank table and benches, a rope bed, and corn-shuck pillows. Picnic facilities, playground, restrooms, RV parking. SR 190 at 4-way stop sign, S 4 blocks.

The Home Place. This self-proclaimed "nonelectric horse-powered farm" is run on gasoline, kerosene, and wood. The owner, nearly as self-sufficient as his Amish neighbors, has no electricity, drives a buggy, gardens, preserves and cans food, and has no telephone. Tours. 12 blocks SW of downtown; inquire locally.

Recreation. JAMESPORT COMMUNITY LAKE: 30 acres. Bass, sunfish, crappie, catfish. SR 190, N 1.6 m.; SR RA, W 2.2 m. POOSEY *STATE FOREST* / LAKE: 192 acres. Bass, sunfish, crappie, catfish. SR F, E 2.9 m.; SR U, S 4.1 m.; SR A, E 1 m.

1. No p.o.; defunct.

JAMESTOWN
Population: 298   Map F-4

The settlement was established c. 1837 between Moniteau Creek and the Missouri River along a main east–west *road*. The post office name was changed from Moniteau[1] by S. L. and E. H. James, who established a mercantile business here in 1846. A mill was built in 1862, and a town was surveyed and incorporated in 1873 with a population of 300. Post offices: Moniteau 1830–unknown, unknown–1850; Jamestown 1850–now.

Lupus, Mo. Reportedly first named Wolf's Point, this Missouri River community changed its name to Lupus (Latin for "wolf") for simplicity when the Missouri-Pacific *Railroad* arrived c. 1884. Post office: 1884–1955. SR 179, N 5.2 m.; SR P, N 4 m. PIONEER *CEMETERIES* / INDIAN MOUNDS: Hickam and Copps Chapel cemeteries are located at Indian mounds. GR W of town, S 1 m. and N 3 m., respectively.

Recreation. BUCKHORN *TRAIL*. PRAIRIE HOME *WILDLIFE AREA*.

St. Mary's Assumption Catholic Church. Gothic Revival, 1867–1872; enlarged 1903; organized 1841. Originally known as Becker's Church, it was later called St. Mary's Assumption Church of Moniteau, an ironic and probably unintentional blending of cultural deities' names (Jamestown history, above). Today it is known as the Cedron Church after the Cedron post office.[2] One of its early priests was Father Helias *(Taos)*.

SR U, W 3.3 m.; SR D, N 0.5 m.; GR, W 1 m. (E edge of Prairie Home *Wildlife Area*).

Sandy Hook, Mo. The community was settled c. 1846 as a Missouri River landing. According to "American Place-Names," the first version of Sandy Hook appeared on a 1656 Dutch map as Sant Punt (Sand Point), but "hoek" was commonly used instead of "punt," with the same general meaning. In this case the sand point is in the river. Post office: Sandyhook 1902–1953. SR AA, E 5 m.

Wooldridge, Mo. The town was established in 1902 along the Missouri-Pacific *Railroad* when descendants of 1820s settlers named Wooldridge donated land for a townsite. Post office: 1902–now. SR 179, N 11 m. WOOLDRIDGE HOUSE: Vernacular, antebellum; original rock foundation and logs. Inquire locally.

1. From the creek via Algonquian term (variously spelled) roughly meaning spirit, implying holy or uncanny; preternatural.

2. Origin unknown, possibly from Spanish "cedro," meaning cedar; 1896–1907.

JEFFERSON CITY
Population: 35,517   Map F-4

The first Missouri Legislature, meeting in St. Louis in 1820, appointed five commissioners to locate the state capital at the Missouri River within forty miles of the mouth of the Osage River. They were directed to meet in May 1821 and proceed with their work at Côte sans Dessein (below), the only place resembling a village in the area. Two sites were recommended: (1) four sections of land at a Missouri River landing (Jefferson Landing, below) that had assumed the ambitious name City of Jefferson in honor of Thomas Jefferson; and (2) Côte sans Dessein. Because the latter's land titles could not be verified and possibly because the former offered twice as much public land, Jefferson City was approved as the state capital on December 31, 1821. The town was platted and named in 1822, and construction began in 1823 for a capitol/governor's residence (below), but no state business was conducted here until 1826 because the temporary location at *St. Charles* had been authorized to conduct business until October 1, 1826 (Temporary State Capital Contenders, below). The new state capital and later county seat (selected in 1829, replacing Marion, below) was the crudest of frontier villages, lacking graded streets and other services until, in an attempt to secure a financial base, the state prison was built here in 1833–1834 (Missouri State Penitentiary, below). The following year the capitol burned, destroying a large portion of the state records. Incorporated in 1839 with 1,174 residents, Jefferson

City prospered for about 10 years, but then misfortune plagued it for the next 50 years. In 1849 the *Mormon* ship "Monroe" docked and disembarked cholera-infected passengers who initiated an epidemic that depressed the economy for two years. In 1855 the Missouri-Pacific *Railroad*, recently completed from St. Louis to Jefferson City, collapsed a bridge at *Gasconade*, delaying traffic for one year. The 1861–1865 *Civil War* stymied all business. While no military fighting took place here, as the state's political center Jefferson City suffered through the war and Reconstruction (1865–c. 1874). Despite light industries like printing and shoe manufacturing established during the 1880s, Jefferson City's economy appeared so weak that *Sedalia* petitioned in 1895 to become the state capital, but Jefferson City rallied to build a drawbridge across the Missouri for easy access from northern counties and built a new courthouse (Cole County Courthouse, below), which persuaded voters to leave the capital here. Today light manufacturing continues, but politics is still the major business. Post office: 1823–now. Home of Lincoln University (Architecture, below; *Crestwood: Father Dickson Cemetery*). Maps and guides: chamber of commerce, US 54 to N on Jackson, W on High to Adams (213); Capitol Visitor Center, Jefferson Landing (below); Department of Conservation (below); Truman Building/State Parks and Recreation (below).

Architecture. Ridges and valleys parallel the Missouri River, giving surprising views of houses and buildings. NATIONAL HISTORIC REGISTER: Missouri State Capitol Historic District (roughly bounded by Adams, McCarty, Mulberry, and the river). Lincoln University Hilltop Campus Historic District (Capitol, E to 820 Chestnut). WALKING TOUR: below.

Cedar City, Mo. Supposedly named for the trees on a nearby bluff when platted in 1870 along the Chicago & Alton *Railroad*, Cedar City reportedly replaced the river town Hibernia[1] as a shipping point. Although annexed by Jefferson City in 1989, Cedar City kept its post office name (as a substation of Jefferson City), contrary to *post office* regulations, because of local sentiment. The flood of 1993 swept away most of the community's structures. Today, locals refer to the area as North Jefferson City. Post offices: Hibernia 1825–1871; Cedar City 1870–1994; Jefferson City 1994–now. US 54, N side of Missouri River. KATY TRAIL *STATE PARK:* US 54 at SR 94; SR 94, W to Oil Well, E on Katy Rd. to sign.

Christmas Caroling. This 50-year tradition takes place at the State Capitol (Walking Tour, below) on the second Tuesday in December.

Cole County Courthouse. Richardsonian Romanesque, 1896; National Historic Register. The county's third courthouse (Jefferson City history, above), built and touted as "nearly fireproof," sustained extensive fire damage in 1913. Regardless, this imposing stone structure remains a good example of its style. Features include a 126-foot clock tower, a rusticated first floor, tall arched windows, spring-arch doorways, parapeted wall dormers, and a hip roof. Cost: $60,000. US 54, N on Monroe to High. *(County Profiles)*

Cole County Fair. Arts and crafts, rides, shows, livestock. Last week in July.

Côte sans Dessein, Mo. In 1808 Jean Baptiste Roi (or Roy) established a trading and shipping point on a long narrow ridge along and in the Missouri River near the confluence of the Osage River. Its name is descriptive American French: côte, a line of hills or bluffs along a stream; sans, without; dessein, design. Despite recent quarrying, this hill, probably an ero-

sional remnant of the Ice Age *(Glacial Erratics)*, remains about 150 feet high, a mile long, and 200 yards wide; it is still clearly visible across the river from *Bonnot's Mill*, a town closely associated with Côte sans Dessein's early history (Jefferson City history, above; *Sibley*). Post office: 1818–1825, 1826–1829, 1838–1876, 1882–1907. US 54, N 0.5 m.; SR 94, E 10.1 m. to junction with SR AA; GR, S 1.3 m. to river. *(Boonslick Trails)*

Department of Conservation. Maps, books, and information about Missouri's natural areas, wildlife, and outdoor recreation are available from the department's offices. An adjacent trail leads through an area of wildflowers, native trees and shrubs, wildlife, and *prairie* plantings. W side; US 50 to N on SR 179; W on Truman; W on Ten Mile Dr. (2901).

Marion, Mo. Platted near the confluence of Moniteau

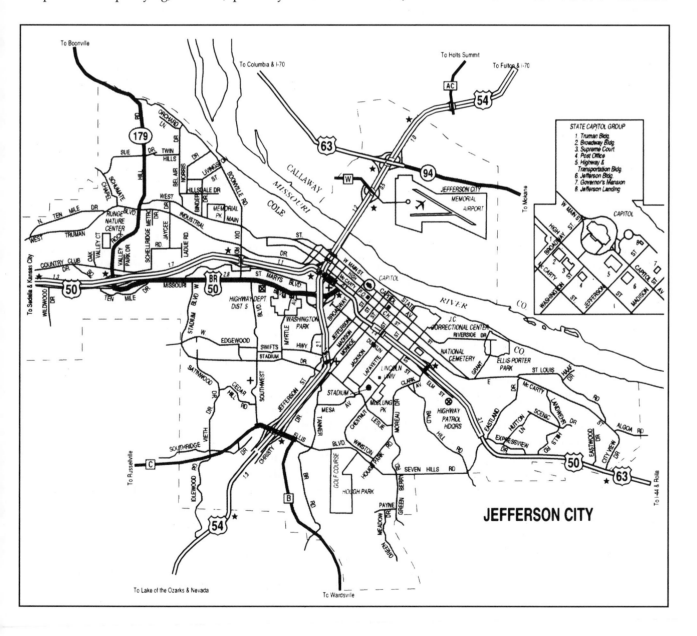

JEFFERSON CITY

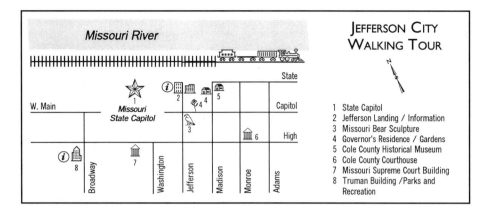

JEFFERSON CITY WALKING TOUR

1 State Capitol
2 Jefferson Landing / Information
3 Missouri Bear Sculpture
4 Governor's Residence / Gardens
5 Cole County Historical Museum
6 Cole County Courthouse
7 Missouri Supreme Court Building
8 Truman Building /Parks and
   Recreation

Creek and the Missouri River as the first county seat of Cole County (1821–1829), the town was named for Revolutionary War hero Gen. Francis Marion, the Swamp Fox. It declined after losing the seat of justice (Jefferson City history, above), becoming nearly defunct after the 1845 formation of Moniteau County left it at Cole County's western edge. Post office: 1823–1953. SR 179, W 14 m.

Missouri State Highway Patrol. Historical exhibits date from 1931 when the patrol was organized and include five patrol cars (dating from a 1931 Model A Ford Roadster to a 1978 Mercury), memorabilia about George R. "Machine Gun" Kelly, a 1950s jail cell, handcuffs, guns, and various weapons. Other displays concern bicycle safety, drunk driving, the use of a Breathalyzer, and drug abuse. Safety Education Center; E side; US 50/63 E. to Elm (1510).

Missouri State Penitentiary. Approved for construction 1834; last addition 1982. The first penitentiary west of the Mississippi housed its first prisoner in 1836, 22-year-old Wilson Eidson, who was sentenced to 2 years and 45 days for grand larceny. Four years later the population was overcrowded at 77, and new cells were built. NATIONAL HISTORIC REGISTER: The oldest remaining building was built in 1868. N on Madison, E on State to Lafayette.

National / Woodland Cemeteries. After National Cemetery was bought in 1867 by the government, some of the first veterans to be buried here were 78 Union soldiers killed after the *Centralia* Massacre. Adjacent Woodland has plots allotted to the state; its burials include two governors: Thomas Reynolds (1840–1844; *County Profiles: Reynolds)* and John S. Marmaduke (1885–1887; *Arrow Rock: Sappington Cemetery).* E side; Capitol, E to Chestnut, S to McCarty (1042). *(Cemeteries)*

Recreation. BINDER COMMUNITY LAKE: Bass, sunfish, crappie, catfish, carp, tiger muskie. US 50, W 8 m. KATY TRAIL *STATE PARK:* Cedar City, above. SCRIVNER ROAD *WILDLIFE AREA.*

Temporary State Capital Contenders. While Jefferson City and Côte sans Dessein were the only choices for the permanent capital (Jefferson City history, above), contenders for a temporary site were abundant. After 66 days of wrangling in the state legislature, *St. Charles* was selected, reportedly because it offered free lodging. Towns voted on for temporary capital were Côte sans Dessein, *Potosi, St. Charles,* and Franklin *(New Franklin),* with the Senate repeatedly voting for Côte sans Dessein until compromising for St. Charles. Others suggested were *St. Louis, Florissant, Boonville, Ste. Genevieve,* and *Herculaneum.*

Truman Building / State Parks and Recreation. Eighties Modern, 1984. Free maps, books, and information about Missouri travel and recreation are available at this department in the Truman Building, which houses over 2,300 state employees. Broadway at High, SW of state capitol.

Walking Tour. Maps: visitor center in the Lohman building, Jefferson Landing (below). COLE COUNTY COURTHOUSE: above. COLE COUNTY HISTORICAL MUSEUM: Italianate style, 1871; National Historic Register. Construction of this two-story (with a basement) building was supervised by Gov. G. Gratz Brown (1871–1873). It was restored in 1948 by the historical society. Features include quoins, a belt course, cornice brackets, and tall narrow two-over-two windows with curved pediments. Displays include Victorian-era furnishings, inaugural ball gowns of former first ladies, and historical items and toys. The adjacent Upschulte house (German style, c. 1867; two stories, red brick) is a good example of its kind. Madison, across from the Governor's Residence (below). GOVERNOR'S RESIDENCE / GARDEN: Second Empire, 1871; National Historic Register. The third governor's residence was built at the site of the first state capitol, which also contained the executive family's apartments. The three-story 27-room brick-and-stone house features a mansard roof, a granite columned portico donated by Gov. G. Gratz Brown (Cole County Historical Museum, above), an interior winding staircase, and marble fireplaces in each room. Tours. E on Capitol, N on Madison. The garden, established by the wife of Gov. Lloyd C. Stark (1937–1941), features seasonal plants and flowers, occasional band concerts, and brown-bag picnics. Jefferson at Capitol. JEFFERSON LANDING: State Historic Site (Jefferson City history, above); tours. Three restored structures remain from the city's commercial river district. The three-story brick Lohman building (mid-1830s, National Historic Register), the city's oldest building, served as an inn, store, and warehouse during the 1850s–1870s. It now serves as a visitor center for the capitol complex, a public meeting room, and a museum. The Union Hotel (1850s), formerly the Missouri Hotel, was renamed after the Civil War by owner Charles Maus, who built the 1854 red-brick house to the south of it. N end of Jefferson. MISSOURI BEAR SCULPTURE: Dominating the 1822 Missouri State Seal are two grizzly bears that symbolize the state's strength and its citizens' bravery. This huge bear (8 feet, 10 inches) was carved in 1952–1953 on location from a single 24-ton block of *Carthage* marble. Sculptor J. E. Frazier also carved a 13-foot statue of Jefferson outside the capitol (above). Jefferson and Capitol. STATE CAPITOL: Neoclassical, 1913–1917; National Historic Register, State Historic Site. Both the first (1826–1837) and second (1840–1911) capitols were destroyed by fire. This massive structure (437 by 300 feet, four stories and basement), with a full-height entry porch supported by classical columns, has 500,000 square feet of floor space. The top of the dome is 262 feet above the basement floor and 400 feet above the river. Built at a cost of $3.5 million, the building is primarily *Carthage* and Phenix marble (*Ash Grove: Walnut Grove*). The surplus from the building fund was used to buy artworks by, among others, Frank Brangwyn, N. C. Wyeth, J. E. Fraser, Alexander Sterling Calder, and Thomas Hart Benton (*Neosho*), whose 1936 commissioned mural "A Social History of the State of Missouri" painted on four walls of the third-floor House Lounge depicts, among many subjects, a country kitchen, Jesse and Frank James, Huck Finn, the song characters Frankie and Johnny, and political boss Thomas J. Pendergast. The "WPA Guide to 1930s Missouri" said Benton "dipped boldly into the historic stuff of Missouri . . . [its] ugliness and simplicity, dignity and corruption" (contemporary comments about the mural included "deliberate insult" and "a painting lie"). The first-floor Missouri State Museum (State Historic Site) features state history (prehistoric to WWII) and natural resources (human and natural effects on the state's development). Overlooking the river are ornate fountains, one of which was created by Karl Bitter for the 1904 St. Louis World's Fair. Tours (30 minutes); Senate and House galleries open to the public. Jefferson at High. SUPREME COURT BUILDING: Italian Renaissance, 1905–1906. On the site of the mansion of T. L. Price, the city's first mayor, today's three-story brick structure provides offices for the attorney general and state supreme court. Across from capitol.

1. Latin and poetic name of Ireland; p.o. 1825–1871.

JOPLIN
Population: 40,866   Map C-7

A post office community known as Blytheville[1] was established here in 1840 by pioneer John C. Cox, who arrived in 1838 and was later Joplin's cofounder. Reportedly, Joplin was named for a creek that divides it east–west, which began at a spring on the farm of 1839 settler Rev. Harris G. Joplin (Parks, below), a Methodist missionary, founder of the county's first Methodist church c. 1840, and a close friend of John Cox. The city of Joplin began as a collection of mining camps that sprung up during the mid-1800s after lead was discovered northwest of the present townsite and at the banks of Joplin Creek. Large-scale mining, at first delayed by the *Kansas Border War* and the *Civil War*, began when a lead bonanza was struck in 1870 near today's Broadway viaduct. Two towns were platted in 1871 on either side of Joplin Creek: Joplin City[2] on the east side by John Cox and Murphysburg[3] on the west side by Patrick Murphy of Carthage. Rivalry between these towns dominated by miners and saloons was immediate and violent. The first attempt to incorporate the two as Union City (1872) briefly succeeded, then failed miserably. In 1873 a second incorporation using Patrick Murphy's suggestion of Joplin as the town name was successful mainly because the previous winter, known as the Reign of Terror, proved that consolidation was needed to prevent anarchy. The 1875 Joplin *Railroad* Company, bought by the St. Louis & San Francisco Railroad in 1879, was followed by other railroads that brought more efficient transportation of lead and precipitated the development of zinc mining. By 1880 the production of zinc was double that of lead, and it eventually reached a six-to-one superiority. From 1899 to 1938 an estimated $827 million of lead and zinc ore was shipped from the Tri-State mining district (below). Ore production peaked in 1926 and then gradually declined until operations ceased in 1970. Joplin's wide-based population (1890 pop. 9,943; 1900 pop. 26,023; 1940 pop. 37,144) helped establish a diversified economy. Today it is the self-proclaimed Motor Freight Capital of America with 33 truck terminals and has over 200 manufacturing companies. Post offices: Blytheville 1840–1871; Leadville[4] 1859; Joplin 1871–1872, 1877–now; Murphysburg 1872–1877; Joplin City 1872–1877. Home of Franklin Technical School and Missouri Southern State College. Maps: chamber of commerce, US 71B, E on 3d (303). (*Route 66*) **Adjacent Joplin Towns.** The following towns share, or are narrowly separated from, Joplin's city limits (pop. 80,000 within 10 miles of downtown). CARL JUNCTION: The only adjacent town not founded on a mining claim was established c. 1878 by Charles Carl at the junction of the St. Louis & San Francisco and Joplin & Girand *Railroads.* Post office: 1878–now. NW side; SR 171, N 3.1 m.; SR Z, W 0.5 m. LONE ELM: This mining community of about 2,500 located c. 1875–1879 at Granby Furnace was named for a single landmark elm tree. Post office: none. N side; US 71B, W on E St., N on Sheridan. ORONOGO, MO. / MINE: This town was formerly known as Leadville Hollow,[5] Minersville,[6] and Centre Creek P.O.[7] Oronogo, a spelling variation of a South American river, is not an uncommon place-name, e.g. Oronoco, Minn. *(La Plata).* Local tradition claims that at a meeting to rename the town because of confusion over mail addressed to Minersville, Centre Creek P.O., a drunk miner quashed other suggestions by jumping to his feet and shouting, "Boys, by God, it's Ore or no go." Supposedly Ore was changed to Oro for euphony with no go. The 300-foot-deep Oronogo Circle Mine reportedly earned $30 million. It closed in the late 1940s and is now filled with water. Scuba diving. SR D; inquire locally. Post offices: Minersville 1858–1859; Centre Creek 1868–1874; Oronogo 1874–now. US 71, N 3.6 m.; SR D, N 3.6 m. WEBB CITY / CARTERVILLE: After plowing up lead in his cornfield in 1873, John C. Webb established a town c. 1875. Lead-rush miners and promoters established an adjacent town in 1875 (reportedly on property owned by a man named Carter). After ore prices dropped, Webb City diversified its economy (1990 pop. 7,309). At SR D and US 71, the city's King Jack Park ("Jack" is dated slang for zinc ore) has reminders of its past: the tracks and barn of the SW Missouri

Electric Railway Company that served the area from 1889 to 1939 and a larger-than-life statue, "Hardrock Miner" (a nearby knoll supports the approximately ten-foot-tall concrete monument "Hands in Prayer"). Carterville, unlike Webb City, sought no new income after ore prices dropped. Its estimated peak population of 12,000 declined (1990 pop. 1,973). Evidence of mining includes tailing piles, millponds, massive concrete foundations for mills, and crushing equipment. Post offices: Webb City 1876–now; Carterville 1875–now. N side; US 71. *(Route 66)*

Architecture. GENERAL: Downtown has good examples of late 19th- and early 20th-century commercial architecture, showing its past as a wealthy boomtown. NATIONAL HISTORIC REGISTER: Elks Club Lodge (318–320 W. 4th), Union Depot (Broadway and Main), Carnegie Library (9th and Wall).

Dorothea B. Hoover Museum. Six furnished rooms give a view of upper-middle-class Victorian life. Also featured are a Colonial-era tavern, an outstanding collection of dolls, an arrowhead collection, an animated miniature circus with music and narrator, demonstrations of 18th-century musical instruments, and local historical photographs. NW side, at Schifferdecker Park (Tri-State Mineral Museum, below); SR 43 (Main), W on SR 66 (7th); signs.

George Washington Carver National Monument. Authorized 1943, dedicated 1953. This *National Park* was the first federal monument to an African American. Born a slave in 1864 at Diamond, Mo., Carver died in 1943 at Tuskegee, Ala., with national and international honors, most notably for research at the Tuskegee Institute, where he introduced the previously ignored peanut plant to the South's one-crop (cotton) agricultural economy. At his death, his efforts had resulted in over 5 million acres of peanut crops with an annual value of $200 million. Carver found 300 useful by-products of the peanut plant, which include the familiar (peanut butter) as well as many surprises (face creams, paints, quinine, axle grease, plastics). A 0.75-mile trail leads to the site of his birthplace,

The mines at Orongo.

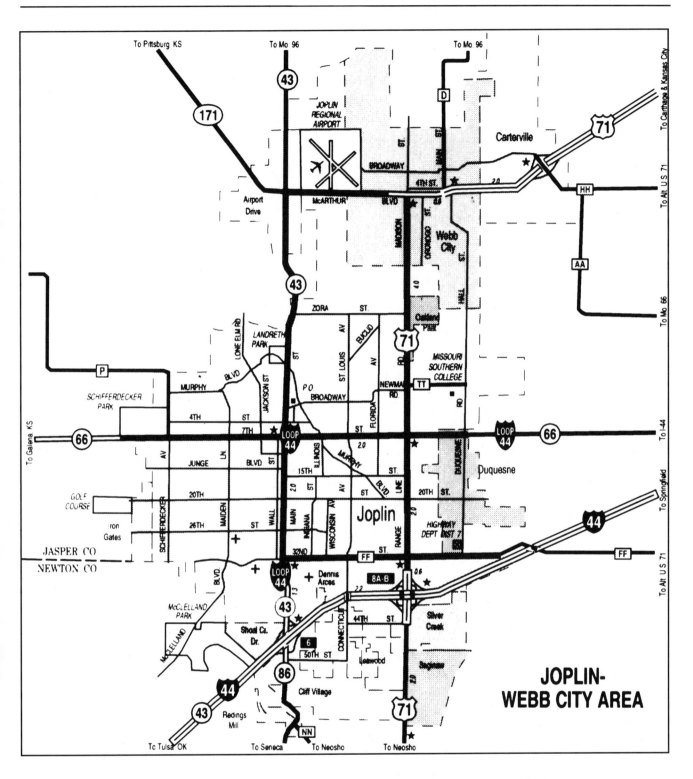

JOPLIN-
WEBB CITY AREA

the "Boy Carver Statue" by Robert Amendola, Carver Spring, Williams Spring, the Moses Carver House, (Vernacular, 1881), and Carver *Cemetery* (George is buried in Tuskegee). Sightseeing, museum, trail, picnicking. Superintendent: Box 38, Diamond 64840. Unmarked road paralleling Kansas City Southern *Railroad* (inquire locally), S to SR V, E 3.7 m.; signs. Or

US 71 and SR V at Diamond;[8] SR V, W 2.5 m.

Grand Falls. With falls ranging from 15 to 25 feet, this is reportedly Missouri's highest continuous waterfall. Formed by outcropping chert, it has deep potholes, benches, and a natural spillway. I-44/SR 86; SR 86, S 1.4 m. across bridge and turn W on unmarked road; W along Shoal Creek approx. 3 m.

Grand Falls, c. 1900.

Natural Areas. DIAMOND GROVE: 515 acres. This large upland tallgrass *prairie* on level and gently rolling land features plants such as royal catchfly, Barbara's buttons, blue star, and fringed poppy mallow. Rt. 2, Box 93, Lockwood 65682. SR V, W 4 m. from Diamond, Mo. (George Washington Carver National Monument, above); GR, N 1.3 m. WAH-SHA-SHE PRAIRIE: 160 acres. This nearly level upland prairie has diverse plant life established on the area's only claypan soil (silt loam). A 10-acre pond and shallow marsh attract reptiles, amphibians, and migrating birds. Rt. 2, Box 93, Lockwood 65682. SR 171, N 13.3 m.; SR M, E 0.5 m. WILDCAT GLADE: 15 acres. Reportedly one of the largest and best examples of its type, this colorful (especially in spring) glade is formed on beds of chert; vegetation ranges from lichen-covered rocks to gnarled stunted oaks and plants including prickly pear cactus, wild onion, rock pink, and Barbara's buttons. 212 W. 8th, Joplin 64802. SR 43, SW to city limits; west edge of Wildcat Park.

Parks. Of 20 parks, 14 were privately donated. The following are closely tied to Joplin's early history. LANDRETH: 160 acres. The site where lead was first discovered c. 1849 and of the 1870 bonanza that began the rush. Markers, picnicking, jogging, playground, tennis. N side; SR 43 (Main), N to Murphy Blvd.; sign. McCLELLAND: 166 acres. The site of Joplin's first fair (1878). Located on a high bluff above Shoal Creek. Picnicking, playground, camping. SW side; I-44, W on Shoal Creek. SCHIFFERDECKER: Tri-State Mineral Museum, below. SPRING: About 2.5 acres. The possible site of Joplin Creek's headwater and the

cabin of Joplin's namesake (Joplin history, above). Undeveloped; trail markers. N side; SR 43 (Main), E on 4th to High.

Post Memorial Art Reference Library. The interior architecture is Tudor, featuring artwork and furniture of the 16th and 17th centuries. The library has art-related periodicals and books, including career information for artists. At Joplin Library, N side; US 71B at 3d.

Route 66 Sights. Nostalgic structures. US 66 at US 71; US 66 (7th St.), W to Kansas state line and a sign, "Old Route 66 next right," and its sights: Stateline Bar & Grill and a gas station. *(Route 66)*

Spook Light. Despite 19th- and 20th-century legends and recent scientific studies, there is no satisfactory explanation for the almost nightly appearance of a glowing orange ball that approaches observers near the same spot on a dark county road. Often close enough to touch, it moves if approached. Explanations include (1) a romantic legend of the intertwined spirits of young Quapaw lovers who killed themselves to avoid separation by their parents; (2) a tale of a heartbroken miner still searching for his children, who were kidnapped by Indians; (3) lantern stories, featuring a decapitated *Civil War* soldier looking for his head; (4) religious theories about the Devil's omen or a sign of God's benevolence; and (5) scientific rationalizations of a will-o'-the-wisp (decayed organic matter that produces glowing gas) or the refraction of car headlights (the spook light predates automobiles). All of these explanations are irrelevant when standing in the dark of night on this deserted county road. I-44 at SR 43, W 2.6 m.; SR 43, S 6 m.; SR BB (or a continued road W from SR BB at SR 43), W 2.5 m. (to Okla. border); GR, N approx. 1 m. to defunct Spook Light Museum; park and wait.

Thomas Hart Benton Mural. This 5.5-by-14-foot mural, titled "Joplin at the Turn of the Century, 1896–1906," is typical of Benton's work, recording all aspects of the contemporary life and look of the city. N side; US 71B, E to 3d (303) at chamber of commerce. *(Neosho)*

Tri-State Mineral Museum / Park. MUSEUM: Established 1930. Exhibits include the area's mining history, machinery, tools, historical items, photographs, and outstanding specimens of regional minerals. Mining camps mostly concentrated near Joplin and the state line ranged from east of Springfield to

Miami, Okla. (including a small portion of Kansas). From 1890 to 1943 this 2,500-square-mile tri-state district mined 50–80 percent of America's zinc and lead, producing over $1 billion of ore during that period. NW side; US 71B, W on 7th; signs. SCHIFFERDECKER PARK: 160 acres. Donated in 1913 by its namesake. Playground, pool, tennis, picnic shelters, golf, horseshoes. Adjacent. (Dorothea B. Hoover Museum, above).

1. Billy Blythe, a wealthy Cherokee who lived at Shoal Creek.
2. 1872–1877.
3. Founder Patrick Murphy; p.o. 1872–1877.
4. The ore.
5. Lead discovered in a hollow; no p.o.
6. Mine workers' town.
7. Via the creek and its relative location among the six rivers or creeks of this area.
8. Formerly Diamond Grove, for a diamond-shaped grove of trees, later Diamond Mill, for a *gristmill*; Diamond p.o. 1883–now.

KAHOKA
Population: 2,195   Map G-1

The early history of this town is confusing and illogical, in that it was surveyed in December 1856 and platted in 1858 around a park (Architecture, below) about three miles southwest of the main road, a good water supply, and the Clark County seat, Waterloo (below). In 1858 Kahoka had just a tavern and by c. 1861 only one store. In 1865, immediately after the *Civil War,* the town was promoted as a central location for county seat by land speculators, particularly self-styled Colonel William Muldrow *(Palmyra: Marion City),* the townsite's recent owner-in-fee. A petition to move the county seat here was approved in 1865. Possibly because Muldrow had no clear land titles, a second 1865 petition requested a new location, and Clark City[1] was established in 1866 two miles to the east. A four-year dispute ended with Kahoka gaining the seat of justice in 1870 (Clark County Courthouse, below). Apparently Waterloo continued to function as county seat until 1870. For unrecorded reasons the town was platted as Cahoka to honor Cahokia *Indians,* an early historic Algonquian-speaking subtribe of the Illini (or Illiniwek) whose predecessor's mounds near East St. Louis, Ill., indicate an extremely large (six square miles) and sophisticated Mississippian era (A.D. 850–1350) city that had a peak population c. A.D. 1050 of at least 20,000 *(St. Louis).* Also unexplained is the change of spelling to Kahoka when the city was incorporated in 1869 (Cahokia is the accepted version). The arrival in 1871 of the Missouri, Iowa & Nebraska *Railroad* helped the town grow, but agriculture and politics remained, as now, the economic base. Post

offices: Cahoka 1858–1882; Kahoka 1882–now.
Alexandria, Mo. The town was platted in 1833 at the confluence of the Des Moines and Mississippi Rivers as Churchville by Francis Church. Its name was changed by popular vote because of Church's "alleged improper domestic relations." The name, a stock one for people and places, comes from Alexandria, Egypt, a seaport west of the Nile River founded in 331 B.C. by Alexander the Great. Although the town lost the county seat in 1854 (Waterloo, below) because of repeated flooding, it continued to challenge St. Louis and Chicago as a pork-packing center (peak 1869–1870). Post office: Alexander 1841–now. SR 136, E 14 m. *NATIONAL WILDLIFE REFUGE:* Gregory Landing Division, part of Clarence Cannon, was set aside for the public in 1989 and consists of a half-mile-wide, three-mile-long tract adjacent to the Mississippi River. Inquire locally.
Anti–Horse Thief Association. A memorial tombstone in the Kahoka *Cemetery* honors Maj. David McKee (1823–1896), one of the 1854 founders of this organization whose motto, "Protect the Innocent and Bring the Guilty to Justice," still attracted 50,000 members c. 1940. Inquire locally.
Architecture. NATIONAL HISTORIC REGISTER: Kahoka Depot (Railroad, 1896), the town's second; derelict. Montgomery Opera House (1890), identified by a large carved sunburst. This was the focus of social life, at times serving simultaneously as a bank, opera house, movie theater, basketball court, and lodge meeting hall. TOWN SQUARE: A park with huge trees, picnic tables, a bandstand, and benches (Clark County Courthouse, below); some good examples of late 19th-century commercial styles.
Battle of Athens State Historic Site. SR 81, N 11 m.; SR CC, E 4.2 m. *(Athens)*
Clark County Courthouse. Italianate style, 1871; stucco-on-brick, 1934; National Historic Register. This courthouse, the county's third, is one of Missouri's few remaining 1870s county structures. Originally brick with quoins, it has elaborately bracketed eaves, tall arched windows, and an octagonal cupola. Because the park around which the commercial businesses were built was donated for park use only, and probably because of uncertain land titles (Kahoka history, above), the courthouse was built outside the commercial district in an 1870 plat addition. Although businesses were encouraged to build around the courthouse, the town hub has always been the park. (The city gained title to the park in 1883, but no proposal for relocating the courthouse is on record.) SR 81, N of downtown. *(County Profiles)*
Clark County Fair. Since 1882. Last weekend of July; fairgrounds, E of town.

Clark County Historical Museum. Local historical items, newspapers, photographs. Morgan at Chestnut.
Clark County Old Settlers Celebration. Since 1883. Contests, a parade, food, music. Late September. Downtown.
Hiller House. Folk Victorian, 1876; National Historic Register. Built by one of the town founders and still occupied by the same family, the house features beveled posts with decorative spandrels, a second-story iron railing, and a bay window; tours by arrangement. 570 N. Washington.
Recreation. FOX VALLEY *STATE FOREST. WILDLIFE AREAS:* Heath Memorial, Neeper.
Waterloo, Mo. The town was platted in 1837 along the Fox River as county seat of newly organized Clark County. Its stock name refers to the 1815 battle near Waterloo, Belgium, where Napoleon Bonaparte's attempt at regaining his empire was crushed by the British (under the Duke of Wellington) and their allies. Never very successful in a sparsely populated county, the town lost the county seat in 1847 to Alexandria (above), declined, then regained the seat of justice in 1854 only to flounder and be replaced by Kahoka (Kahoka history, above). The *cemetery* that once overlooked the town marks the townsite; markers from 1817. Post office: 1837–1876. SR EE, E 2.5 m.; GR, N 2 m. at and N of Fox River bridge (joins SR C, 2.7 m. N).

1. For the county *(County Profiles);* SR EE, E 2 m.; p.o. 1870–1903.

KANSAS BORDER WAR, 1856–1858

The 1854 Kansas-Nebraska Act served as a catalyst for this war. The act organized Kansas and Nebraska as territories and at the same time repealed the *Missouri Compromise,* an 1820 act prohibiting slavery in the *Louisiana Purchase* Territories above 36°30' north latitude, and in its place providing residents the right to vote on the slavery issue themselves. Kansas, whose western territorial border was then defined as the summit of the Rocky Mountains, became a focal point of the national slavery issue. Immediately pro-slavery and free-state advocates rushed like-minded settlers to Kansas Territory to establish their claims and vote for their cause, a situation resulting in Bleeding Kansas, as the violence of this particularly vicious civilian war of 1856–1858 was called. Border Ruffians (pro-slavery Missourians) attacked Lawrence, Kans., and free-state advocates, led by John Brown, murdered five men in retaliation. For nearly two years Border Ruffians rode to join Kansas partisans in opposition to free-state

advocates, and Kansas Redlegs attacked towns and settlements in western Missouri. A joint effort by state governments and federal authorities ended these paramilitary operations that had resulted in the deaths of 200 people and the destruction of property worth $2 million. Although the slavery question dominated the headlines, Kansas's admittance to the Union as a free state, first proposed in 1855 and known as the Kansas Question, was also a complicated economic and political issue that centered on western expansion, the building of the Pacific *Railroad,* and renunciation of the Democratic Party by Illinois U.S. senator Stephen A. Douglas. In 1860 Douglas was defeated for U.S. president by Abraham Lincoln, who advocated admitting Kansas as a free state. Lincoln's victory resolved the Kansas Question (it was admitted as a free state in 1861), but it also helped set in motion America's bloodiest war, the American *Civil War.*

KANSAS CITY
Population: 435,146
Maps C-3 and Kansas City Area

In 1821, near the confluence of the Kansas and Missouri Rivers, American Fur Company agent François Chouteau, whose uncle founded *St. Louis,* established a trading post that was to act as a clearinghouse for other company posts. Flooded out in 1830, the post was moved a few miles east to an established 1828 ferry site (at the foot of today's Grand Ave.), which a few years later was called Westport Landing (Westport, below) because Westport's *Santa Fe Trail* merchants received goods from steamboats docking at Chouteau's post. The Kansas Town Company bought the property in 1838 and in 1839 platted the Town of Kansas, named for the river, which derived its name (via the 1601 Spanish "Escansaque" and the 1673 French "Kansa") from the Kansa Indian tribe that is related to the Osage, Omaha, Ponca, and Quapaw who lived along the river (the "s" in Kansas is the plural of Kansa). After the town was incorporated in 1853 as the City of Kansas, the name was changed to Kansas City in 1889 to distinguish it from the state of Kansas. Although prospering as both a fur trading center and a port for Westport's Santa Fe and *Oregon Trail* outfitters, it had continuing problems with the legality of the site's title that caused the Kansas Town Company to reorganize in 1846 and to again file a plat and sell lots. An 1847 cholera epidemic that continued during the California gold rush years was followed by the *Kansas Border War* and the *Civil War,* which stymied its development. With the 1865 arrival of the Missouri-Pacific

A 1930s band.

Railroad, the pack train and steamboat era ended and Kansas City began to boom, building its economy on transportation, stockyards, grain milling, and commerce, including the founding in 1877 of a stock exchange. Today Kansas City is Missouri's largest city, but its rival, St. Louis, has a larger metropolitan area population. Relying economically on distribution and manufacturing, it ranks first nationally in foreign trade-zone space, underground storage space, and greeting card publishing, as well as second in wheat flour production, auto and truck production, and as a rail center. Post offices: Kansas 1846–1861; Kansas City 1861–now. Home of University of Missouri–Kansas City, Avila College, Cleveland Chiropractic College, DeVry Institute of Technology, Kansas City Art Institute, Metropolitan Community Colleges (Longview, Maple Woods, and Penn Valley), Rockhurst College, University of Health Sciences, and Park College (in Parkville, below).

Note: Kansas City is the center of a complex metropolitan area encompassing about 316 square miles and 1.5 million people (North Kansas City, below). The following points of interest, covered in the broadest and briefest terms, are only highlights. For detailed information, maps, and literature, contact the Convention and Visitor Bureau, 1100 Main, Suite 2550, Kansas City 64105 (downtown near the river; I-70, S on Main). Pedestrians have the right-of-way at crosswalks but must obey traffic lights. Main Street (north–south) divides the city's cross-streets east to west; named streets run north–south. Numbered streets run east–west and begin at the river, increasing toward the south. Streets north of the river begin with N and increase toward the

north. The Metro serves both residents and tourists with area bus stops. Trolleys operate along the Main Street area between 10th and 47th, which includes the Central Business District, Crown Center, Westport, and County Club Plaza.

Architecture. Kansas City is not flat. The altitude ranges from 721 to 1,054 feet, providing interesting perspectives architecturally. Said to have more miles of boulevards than Paris and more fountains than any city except Rome, Kansas City has over 100 structures on the National Historic Register that are not included in its 13 Historic Districts.

Board of Trade. About 6 billion bushels of winter wheat futures are traded here annually, the most in the world. 4800 Main.

City Hall / Observation Deck. Art Deco, completed 1937. Above the sixth floor is a frieze of 16 panels showing the city's historical highlights. The 30th-floor observation deck provides an orientation to the town. 414 E. 12th.

City Market. Covered stalls (since 1888) offer meats, cheeses, spices, flowers, vegetables, potted plants, live poultry, fresh eggs, etc.; open 6 A.M. 5th at Walnut.

Country Club Plaza. When Kansas City merchants refused to deliver goods to real estate developer J. C. Nichols's growing 1905 subdivision (51st and Grand), he built a shopping center at 51st and Oak in 1912 and then in 1922 extended the concept to a shopping city, creating the world's first shopping center in a suburban business area. Extensively landscaping flat land and a marsh, Nichols developed an urban environment dominated by Mission and Spanish Eclectic architecture bisected by boulevards and open spaces that reportedly have a million dollars' worth of fountains and sculptures. The lighting of 156,000 Christmas lights on Thanksgiving eve has drawn crowds since 1925. Nichols Road is billed as the Rodeo Drive of the Midwest. Bounded by 46th, 50th, Belleview, and Main. **Crown Center.** A subsidiary of adjacent Hallmark Cards (exhibits, including original work by Norman

Rockwell and Grandma Moses), this $500 million early 1970s development covers 85 acres. A 10-acre landscaped square offers ice-skating in the winter and free concerts in the summer featuring various headliners. Designed as a living and working environment, the center includes two hotels, an indoor retail area, restaurants, office complexes, a children's creative workshop, a meeting/conference facility, condominiums, apartments, and a five-story waterfall. Grand and Pershing.

Green Mill Candy Factory. Since 1914. The facility offers a 40-minute tour of how candy, including chocolate and peanut brittle, is made; samples. 2020 Washington.

Heritage Village. This reconstructed pre-1850 village includes buildings, crafts, and demonstrations. I-435 at SR 152; 7000 N.E. Barry.

Jackson County Courthouse. Art Deco, 1933–1934. While *Independence* is the official seat of justice for Jackson County, Kansas City also functions as one. The third courthouse since 1871, this 28-story building has vertical bands of windows that emphasize its striking perpendicular lines. Cost: $2,245,000 contract, $1,000,000 site. 415 E. 12th. *(County Profiles)*

Lewis and Clark Point (Lookout Point). This 1806 *Lewis and Clark* campsite overlooks the city, the confluence of the Kansas and Missouri Rivers, and the country to the north. 8th and Jefferson.

Liberty Memorial. Classical with Deco elements, 1923–1926. In 10 days 83,000 residents donated over $2 million to build this memorial commemorating veterans of WWI. A series of integrated structures with a central tower, it consists of five elements: FRIEZE: 1935, 18 by 148 feet; depicts the progress of civilization from war toward peace. 100 W. 26th. MEMORY HALL: The painting "Pantheon de la Guerre" and murals. MUSEUM: America's only museum specializing in WWI; exhibits, weapons, uniforms, a research library, archives. SPHINXES: Two 32-foot sphinxes symbolizing memory and the future; one has its face covered to forget, the other because of the unknown ahead. TORCH OF LIBERTY: It rises 217 feet from a terrace on top of the 143-foot Liberty Memorial, giving a panoramic view of the city. Located at PENN VALLEY PARK, which also includes scenic drives, a lake, and two bronze sculptures: "Pioneer Mother Monument" (1927; *Lexington: Pioneer Mother Monument)* and the city's trademark "The Scout" (1917), an Indian sentinel on horseback.

Museums. ALEXANDER MAJORS HOUSE: Greek Revival, 1856. This two-story house was

KANSAS CITY

built by Majors, a *Santa Fe Trail* trader and co-founder of the Pony Express; limited tours. 8201 Stateline Rd. (Union Cemetery, below). BLACK ARCHIVES: This is the largest collection west of the Mississippi of African American documents, records, and memorabilia, e.g. marriage records from 1860 to the 1930s, jazz history, art photography. E. 18th to Vine (2033). HISPANIC CULTURAL: Exhibits illustrate the cultural heritage of various countries; folk art, pottery, wall hangings. 922 W. 24th. JOHN WORNALL HOUSE: Greek Revival, 1858. The house served as a hospital for both sides during the Battle of Westport (below). Period furniture, herb garden, fireplace cooking demonstration, *Civil War* encampments. 146 W. 61st Terrace at Wornall Rd. KANSAS CITY: The R. A. Long home (Beaux Arts, 1909; National Historic Register), overlooking the Missouri River valley, provides exhibits on regional and natural history, a planetarium, and a replica of a 1910 drugstore. Independence (US 24) at Chestnut; US 24, E to Gladstone (3218). LIBERTY MEMORIAL: above. NATIONAL ARCHIVES: This is one of 11 national field branches; genealogy data, Federal Census data (1790–1920), war documents (Revolution to WWI), other resources. US 71S; 2312 E. Bannister. NELSON-ATKINS FINE ARTS: Neoclassical, 1933. Four facades have bas-reliefs showing "the conquest of the American West"; the central hall features 12 black marble columns; the collection is comprehensive and critically acclaimed, with more than 50,000 works of Oriental, European, and American art. Outdoors is a fine collection of sculpture, including the Moore Sculpture Garden. 4525 Oak. TOY AND MINIATURE: Exhibits include antique toys and exact-scale miniatures and over 70 antique dollhouses from Germany, England, and America. 5235 Oak.

Mutual Musicians Foundation. National Historic Landmark. Kansas City's jazz continues here in the 18th and Vine Historic District where nightclubs once featured stars like Count Basie, Ella Fitzgerald, and Charlie Parker. Jam sessions. E. 18th to Highland (1823).

North Kansas City, Mo. An 1891 post office community established directly across the Missouri River from Kansas City was platted and named in 1912 by the North Kansas City Development Company, which built commercial buildings and residential houses (mostly one- and two-story frame houses for factory workers). Now part of the Kansas City metroplex. Post offices: Harlem[1] 1866–1913; North Kansas City 1891–1897, 1913–1925 (now substation of Kansas City).

Original Plat. The original plat of Kansas City roughly contained an area extending from the river to either

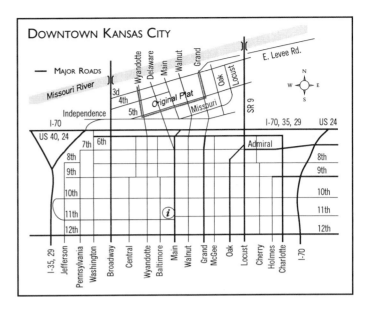

side of today's Grand, 5th, and Wyandotte Streets. A "Public Squair" [*sic*] was bounded by 4th, Walnut, 5th, and Main (the south side of today's city market, above), with a spring located in the southeast corner.

Parkville, Mo. This 1838 Missouri River port known as English Landing[2] was renamed by its founder and first postmaster, George S. Park, who secured a 99-year lease in 1840 for the property from David English and filed a town plat in 1844. Before the Civil War and the arrival of the railroads, it was an economic rival of Kansas City. Post office: 1841–1962 (substation of Kansas City). US 24 at SR 9; SR 9, N 8.6 m. ARCHITECTURE: The original downtown has cobblestone sidewalks and good examples of restored antebellum structures. DOLL MUSEUM: Exhibits include thousands of dolls and a doll hospital. Main. PARK COLLEGE: The school was founded by Park in 1875 and built by student labor during the 1880s. Mackay Hall, the administration building, is Gothic Revival style, 1893; National Historic Register. Park House (Vernacular, c. 1839), now Park College Museum, displays family and faculty memorabilia. Bluffs provide river overlooks.

Performing Arts. ACTOR'S ENSEMBLE: Off-Broadway comedies. 320 Southwest Blvd. AMERICAN HEARTLAND: Broadway plays, musicals. Crown Center (above). THE COTERIE: Plays for children. Crown Center (above). LYRIC: Opera, Kansas City Symphony, Kansas City Ballet. 11th and Central. MARBLE PLAYHOUSE: Off-Broadway musicals and comedies. 100 E. 43d. MIDLAND CENTER PERFORMING ARTS: Theater League productions and concerts. 1228 Main. MISSOURI REPERTORY: Fully professional, seven plays per season (July–March). 4949 Cherry. MUSIC HALL: A variety of fine-arts programs.

Municipal Auditorium, 13th and Central. NEW DIRECTIONS: Classical, new, foreign plays. 210 Wyandotte. QUALITY HILL: Plays, musicals. 10 and Central. STARLIGHT THEATER: Broadway musicals, concerts; 7,800-seat amphitheater. Swope Park, below. UNICORN: Contemporary, original plays. 3820 Main.

Sports Complex / American Royal. AMERICAN ROYAL ARENA: Although the city's legendary stockyards are now closed, the American Royal, originating in 1899 as a cattle show, now hosts a two-week rodeo and a livestock and horse show each November. Adjacent to Kemper Arena (below). KEMPER ARENA: 16,300 seats. Soccer (the Comets), basketball, tournaments (Big 8, NAIA, BMA), track and field. I-670 near state line; signs. TRUMAN: America's only twin stadiums: baseball (Royals), 40,000 seats; football (Chiefs), 78,000 seats. I-70 at Blue Ridge Cut-Off.

Swope Park / Zoo. 1,700 acres. The land was donated in 1896 by realtor T. H. Swope. NATURE CENTER: Tours along the marsh, wildflower garden. RECREATION: Picnics, boating, swimming, fishing. SPORTS: Baseball, football, rugby, soccer, basketball, tennis, archery, jogging, golf, and flof (frisbee-golf, with baskets instead of holes). ZOO: 80 acres. 700 animals (apes to zebras), miniature train. I-435 and Gregory; signs.

Thomas Hart Benton Home / Studio. Eclectic, 1903–1904. State Historic Site, National Historic Register. Benton lived in this two-and-a-half-story house from 1939 to 1975 and converted the carriage house into a studio, where he died while working. The house is furnished with family possessions, and the studio has much of his equipment. Tours. I-35, S on Southwest Trafficway, W on Valentine, N on Belleview (3616). (*Neosho*)

Union Cemetery. 27 acres. The cemetery was platted in 1857 and named for its location halfway between Kansas City and Westport. Its 55,000 burials include a remarkable cross section of the towns' early population, e.g. the first policeman, artist George Caleb Bingham, town founder John Calvin McCoy, and Alexander Majors, co-founder of the Pony Express (Museums, above). Walking tours. Main, E on 30th; signs. (*Cemeteries*)

Union Station. Italian Renaissance, 1914. The lobby of this limestone and granite building, America's third largest railroad station, has a 94-foot ceiling. 2400 Main.

Unity Village. *Lee's Summit.*

Westport, Mo. Directly responsible for Kansas City's early growth, the town was platted in 1833 (with the plat filed in 1835) about four miles south of Kansas City at the *Santa Fe* and *Oregon Trails* by John Calvin McCoy (Union Cemetery, above), later a member of the Kansas Town Company (Kansas City history, above), who had built a store in 1832 on the west side of the Big Blue River to compete with outfitters on the east side at *Independence*. Reportedly this common place-name (e.g. 1797 Westport, Ky.) refers to the town's being the port of entry to the West, but another interpretation could be its location as a port west of Independence and the Big Blue. Using Chouteau's ferry site (now Kansas City) as a steamboat landing, McCoy's Westport was easily stocked. It not only intercepted returning Santa Fe Trail pack trains, it also siphoned outfitting trade from Independence by eliminating the difficult crossing at the Big Blue for westbound traffic. By 1845 it dominated the outfitting business. An 1847 cholera epidemic, the expansion of steamboat traffic (*St. Joseph*), and the extension of the railroads after the Civil War precipitated its decline, and it was merged with Kansas City in 1899. Today the area is known for its historic district, shopping, and tourism. Post offices: Shawnee[3] 1832–1834; Westport 1834–1902. Marker: Broadway just N of Westport Rd. BATTLE OF WESTPORT: October 21–23, 1864. The final battle of Price's Raid (*Civil War*) and the last significant military action in Missouri was fought here. After Gen. Sterling Price was turned back from the outskirts of St. Louis and Jefferson City, he marched north to *Glasgow* for supplies. Federals believed his next attack would be on Kansas City, followed by one on Fort Leavenworth, Kans. Gen. S. R. Curtis, commanding the Department of Kansas and Indian Territory, began raising a militia that grew to 24 regiments poised on the Kansas border. Generals Alfred Pleasanton and A. J. Smith were pursuing Price from Jefferson City and St. Louis. Federal general James S. Blunt, commanding the department of South Kansas, took up a position at Lexington to delay Price so Pleasanton and Smith could attack from the rear. On October 20, Price and Blunt engaged south of Lexington, and Blunt fell back to east of Independence at the Little Blue River. On October 21, Blunt was pushed west of Independence to the Big Blue River where a line of battle was drawn that positioned Curtis and the Kansas militia between Kansas City and Westport. Their intention was to hold Price east of the Big Blue and wait for Pleasanton and Smith to trap him. On October 22, Curtis was about to be driven off his battle line when Pleasanton's cavalry attacked Price from the rear, routing Price's troops. That night Price camped south of Westport, west of the Big Blue. On October 23, Curtis moved south and Pleasanton moved west, confronting Price with two armies. The battle covered five or six square miles with ferocious all-day fighting that finally broke Price's lines. He and his army retreated, pursued south along the Kansas border into Arkansas. Of the approximately 25,000 Federals and Confederates actively engaged, the casualties were nearly equal: an estimated 500

Federals and about 492 Confederates. Marker: 63d at The Paseo.

Worlds / Oceans of Fun. One of America's largest amusement parks. I-435, N of river; signs.

1. Origin unknown; in N.Y. for the Dutch city with later English spelling.
2. Brothers David and Stephen English; no p.o.
3. For the Indians adjacent to the site.

KEARNEY
Population: 2,260   Map C-3

The community of Centerville, established in 1856 near the center of Clay County, used nearby Kendall post office.[1] Its 20 families were reduced to 2 after the *Civil War,* and they were narrowly bypassed in 1867 by the Hannibal & St. Joseph *Railroad.* Kearney, platted in 1867 along the tracks by John Lawrence, absorbed Centerville when incorporated in 1869. The town's namesake is disputed. County histories insist Lawrence named it, despite the spelling, for his former residence, Fort Kearny, Nebr., whose namesake is Gen. S. W. Kearny, commander of the Army of the West (mostly Missourians) during the 1846–1848 *Mexican War.* Others claim the namesake is Charles E. Kearney, a railroad official. The town's livestock and agricultural economy has declined. Today it is a bedroom community of Kansas City. Post offices: Kendall 1837– 1842, 1857–1864, 1866–1868; Kearney 1868–now.

Jesse James Farm. Vernacular; original log portion 1822 (bought by the Jameses in 1845), front addition 1893; National Historic Register. Born in 1847 at this farm, Jesse Woodson James grew up here with his older brother, Alexander Frank James (born in 1843). The family were Southern sympathizers *(Kansas Border War).* At the beginning of the Civil War, Frank joined William Quantrill. A year later, Jesse went with Quantrill lieutenant Bill Anderson *(Centralia).* After the war, the brothers, along with the Younger brothers *(Lee's Summit: City Cemetery / Cole Younger),* formed the gang that became a legend when contemporary writers romanticized their bank and train robberies despite the deaths of innocent people *(Gallatin: Winston; Liberty).* In 1881 Gov. T. T. Crittenden posted a reward for the capture of Jesse and Frank ($5,000 each). The next year, posing as Thomas Howard at *St. Joseph,* Jesse was shot through the back of the head by gang member Bob Ford *(Richmond: Cemeteries),* who was accompanied by his brother Charlie (Mt.

Olivet Cemetery, below). Because they killed rather than captured Jesse, the Fords only collected a few hundred dollars *(St. Joseph: Museums).* A few months later Frank gave himself up and was tried and acquitted for several robberies *(Gallatin: Winston).* After living in Nevada, Mo. *(Nevada: Architecture),* Frank retired to this farm in 1891, dying in 1915 as a model citizen. CLAYBROOK: Greek Revival, mid-1800s; National Historic Register. Once occupied by Jesse's daughter, Mary. Furnished, tours. MUSEUM: Reportedly the only authentic collection of Jesse's guns and possessions. PLAY: The farmhouse, bought by Jesse's father, Rev. Robert James, was owned by the family until sold by Jesse's grandsons to Clay County in 1978. Now restored, it contains the original furnishings and serves as a backdrop for the late summer weekend play "The Life and Times of Jesse James." VISITOR CENTER: Audiovisual presentation. I-35; SR 92, E approx. 3 m. to James Farm Rd.; signs.

Mt. Gilead Church / Academy. Both structures have replaced early ones. ACADEMY: This two-story frame building's lower floor has been restored; original

From left to right: Jesse James with Charles Fletcher Taylor, a member of William C. Quantrill's guerrillas, and Frank James.

desks, stove, chalkboard. CHURCH: Vernacular, 1873. The site of this brick church, with a shake roof and two front entrances, has been used for worship since 1830. The adjacent *cemetery* dates from the 1830s. SR 92 at SR 33; SR 92, E 2.7 m.; unmarked road, N 1 m.

Mt. Olivet Cemetery / James Grave. Buried in 1882 at the farm because the family feared his grave would be vandalized, Jesse James was reburied here in 1902 beside his wife, Zerelda Mimms (his first cousin), who died in 1900. Their joint marker is unadorned and modern. Zerelda's inscription is commonplace (Born and Died); Jesse's reads Born and Assassinated. Buried nearby are his mother, Zerelda (Cole) James-Sims-Samuels; his stepfather, Dr. Rubin Samuels; and his young half-brother, Archie Peyton Samuels, who was killed in 1875 when detectives surrounded the Samuels house and, thinking the James brothers were there, threw an explosive device inside. Jesse's mother lost her right arm. In town. I-35; SR 92, E 0.5 m. W end of cemetery. *(Cemeteries)*

Native Rock Museum. Begun in 1938 by Claude Melton, this folk-art collection of rocks from across America includes Bible scenes and encompasses about an acre. By appointment. 107 W. Major St.; inquire locally.

Smithville, Mo. The town was established in 1822 along the Little Platte River by New Jersey immigrant Humphrey Smith. Around his 1824 *gristmill* grew a community known as Smith's Mill. His son Calvin bought government land in 1836 on which the town was built (it was incorporated in 1867). Post offices: Owensville[2] 1839–1844; Smithville 1844–now. SR 92, W 12 m.; SR 169, N 1.3 m. AKERS *CEMETERY*: National Historic Register. Markers for some of Smithville's first pioneers. Little Platte Park (Woodhenge, below). HONKER COVE WATERFOWL REFUGE: Undeveloped, called a bird-watchers' paradise, this federally owned refuge also allows hunting, fishing, and trapping except for October 15–February 20. SR F, N 4.9 m.; SR W, E 2.6 m.; SR J, N 1.2 m. (N end of Smithville Lake); signs. SMITHVILLE LAKE: SR DD, N of town *(Lakes: Corps of Engineers)*. WOODHENGE: This replica of a c. A.D. 800 Mississippian culture sun calendar that was flooded by the lake consists of a 45-foot square with wooden poles arranged to chart daily sunrises and sunsets, as well as to mark the solstices and equinoxes. Little Platte Park at the lake; inquire at visitor center (SR DD at lake).

Tryst Falls. SR 92, E 5 m. *(Excelsior Springs)*

Watkins Mill State Park / State Historic Site. SR 92, E 5.6 m.; SR RA, N 1 m.; signs at Greenville.[3] *(State Parks)*

1. Origin unknown; usually personal; p.o. 1837–1842, 1857–1864, 1866–1868.

2. Origin unknown.

3. *Greenville*; p.o. Claytonville, Clay County namesake *(County Profiles)*, 1870–1893.

KENNETT
Population: 10,941   Map I-8

The town's early history is obscured by an 1872 courthouse fire that destroyed all records. Platted in 1846 as county seat of newly organized Dunklin County, it was first named Chillitecaux (or Chilliticoux) for the nearby village and the leader of the last remaining Delaware tribe in this area. It was briefly named Butler in 1849, the year that adjacent Butler County was organized. The name was changed to Kennett c. 1850–1951, honoring, for no recorded reason, Luther Kennett, the 1849–1852 mayor of St. Louis and a railroad promoter. While maps from 1852 to the late 1860s show proposed routes of the St. Louis & Iron Mountain *Railroad* extending south from Pilot Knob to sites at and to the west of Kennett, this landlocked town had no railroad to ship the area's cotton until the 1890s, when the St. Louis, Kennett & Southern built branches east to the Mississippi River and north to join the St. Louis Southwestern Railroad. Its county, Dunklin, is Missouri's leading cotton producer. Post offices: Dunklin Court House 1845–1846; Chillitecaux 1846–1859; Kennett 1860–1863, 1867–now. Home of Kennett Vo-Tech.

Campbell, Mo. Established c. 1882 along the Texas & St. Louis *Railroad* and named for Judge Alexander Campbell, the town replaced the older Four Mile

Cash Swamp Natural Area near Kennett.

(below), which was bypassed about two miles to the east by the railroad. Post offices: Four Mile, below; Campbell 1882–now. SR 25, N 12 m. to Holcomb.[1] SR 53, N 7 m. DOWNTOWN: Turn-of-the-century architecture, e.g. 1906 city hall. FOUR MILE, MO.: The town was established c. 1855 at a former Indian trail (*Roads and Traces*) later called Chalk Bluff Road and the Military Road. The road ran northeast–southwest through the county, crossing the St. Francis River at the Chalk Bluff, Ark., ferry, which was four miles from this post office community initially called Possum Trot.[2] Today the site is marked by a *cemetery* and the Taylor-Owen House (Vernacular, 1860). On May 1–2, 1863, Confederate general John S. Marmaduke, leading a force of 5,000, swept across the state line into Arkansas at the Chalk Bluff ferry intending to recruit and generate enthusiasm to aid in the capture of Missouri, but he was turned back by 8,000 Federals. Marmaduke lost 130 men; contemporary Federal reports called their losses "disastrous." Post office: 1855–1863, 1867–1882. SR 53 at SR OO; SR 53, N 1.1 m.; GR, S 0.3 m. WALKER PARK: Picnic area, large shade trees, ball fields, playground. US 62 at SR OO. WILHELMINA *STATE FOREST.*

Cardwell, Mo. The town was established in 1896 as a timber shipping center by the Burtig brothers of Paragould, Ark., who named it for Bank of Paragould cashier Frank Cardwell. Post offices: Hasty[3] 1894–1895; Cardwell 1895–now. US 412, S 10 m. to Senath;[4] continue US 412, S 11 m. HORNERSVILLE SWAMP *WILDLIFE AREA.* LOWEST POINT IN MISSOURI: Two places claim this distinction; both are 230 feet above sea level and near the state line. (1) US 412, W 3 m.; SR AC, S 1.7 m.; SR F, S 1.7 m. to state line; GR, W 1.75 m. (2) SR 164, E 11 m. to Hornersville;[5] S of town in Hornersville Swamp *Wildlife Area;* inquire locally.

Cash Swamp Natural Area / Wildlife Area. 310 acres. Part of the southern end of Cash *Wildlife Area.* Features include a high-quality remnant of tupelo-cypress bottomland forest, river otter, and swamp rabbits. Wet and low, it can be reached only by boat from the northeastern end. Rt. 3, Box 388B, Dexter 63841. SR 25, S 2.9 m.; SR A, W 2.1 m.; GR, W 1.5 m.

Dunklin County Courthouse. Moderne, 1937–1940. The first two courthouses burned. The third, built in 1892 after 20 years without a courthouse, was razed in 1937 as unsafe. This two-story 116-by-75-foot brick-and-concrete structure has a terrazzo floor with patterns that form a map of Dunklin County. Cost: $178,000 (WPA assistance, $150,000). (*County Profiles*)

Dunklin County Museum. Displays include area historical items, a record-size alligator gar, and the Birthright Letters (correspondence between slaves and former owners). In town, 122 College.

1. County sheriff Lewis Holcomb; p.o. 1882–now.
2. A popular place-name, usually derogatory but sometimes self-depreciating, indicating an out-of-the-way location so sparsely populated that opossums established unmolested trails.
3. Origin unknown; usually a personal name, e.g. Hasty, N.C.; occasionally for circumstances, e.g. Hasty, Ark., due to the community's rapid growth.
4. Town founder A. W. Douglass's wife; p.o. 1881–now.
5. 1840s storekeeper William H. Horner; p.o. 1875–now.

KEYTESVILLE
Population: 564   Map E-3

The town was platted in 1832 by 1831 settler John Keytes, a Methodist minister from England who donated the land, stipulating that it replace Chariton (*Glasgow*) as Chariton county seat. Selected as county seat in 1833, it prospered as a trading center by using Keytesville Landing, about six miles south at the Missouri River. In the 1860s the town suffered a series of setbacks that resulted in its decline: its courthouse was burned during the *Civil War,* the river shifted a mile and a half south of its landing, and the Western Branch of the North Missouri *Railroad* bypassed it (Brunswick, below). Post office: 1831–now.

Architecture. FIRST PRESBYTERIAN CHURCH: Early Classical Revival, 1853; addition, remodeling, 1900; National Historic Register. Originally the rectangular frame structure was one story; the 45-foot steeple, semi-octagonal tower, and stained glass were added in 1900. US 24, N on East to Hill. REDDING-HILL HOUSE: Originally Georgian, 1832; additions, remodeling, 1866 and 1872 to conform to Romantic with Italianate affinities; National Historic Register.

Brunswick, Mo. / Fort d'Orleans. The town was platted in 1836 as a Missouri River port by Keytesville's founder (Keytesville history, above); he built a mill and general store, was postmaster, and died here in 1844. Reportedly he named the site for his former English home, Brunswick Terrace. Post office: 1836–now. US 24, W 11 m. FORT: Built near the confluence of the Grand and Missouri Rivers to defend against Spanish expeditions from today's New Mexico, this 1723 French fort, the first European fort in the Missouri River valley, reportedly had four cannons at each corner and a chapel; no remnants (*Indians: Historic Period*). Two separate DAR markers approximate its location. US 24, W 6 m. (small park), and US 24, just E of town; inquire locally.

Chariton County Courthouse. Seventies Modern, 1974–1975. The county's first courthouse was destroyed during the *Civil War,* and the second (1867–1973) burned during renovations. This one, a one-story brick structure resembling a modern Protestant church, was mostly funded by fire insurance, revenue

A prairie near Salisbury.

sharing, and a grant. Cost: $725,000. Downtown. (*County Profiles*)

Corinth Presbyterian Church / Cemetery. Vernacular, 1854; derelict. The c. 1837 *cemetery* predates the one-story frame church; it has markers for veterans of the Civil War and both world wars. US 24/SR 5; SR 5, N 5 m.; GR, N 1.3; GR, W 0.4 m. to abandoned farm; walk small road, S and W 0.25 m. (former Stevenson Farm). (*Cemeteries*)

Mendon, Mo. First known as Salt Creek[1] c. 1865, this successful business center changed names after being platted in 1871 and moved 1.25 miles north in 1888 after being bypassed by the Chicago, Santa Fe & California *Railroad*. Its namesake is uncertain, but other Mendons (e.g. 1667 Mendon, Maine) are derived from Mendham, a town in England. Post offices: Salt Creek 1866–1870; Mendon 1872–now. SR 24, W 10 m. to Brunswick (above); SR 11, N 12 m. FLOYD *WILDLIFE AREA.* SWAN LAKE *NATIONAL WILDLIFE REFUGE,* SWAN LAKE, and SILVER LAKE: W of town; signs in town. YELLOW CREEK NATURAL AREA: 617 acres. Part of Yellow Creek Natural History Area. Features a natural creek bordered by an outstanding bottomland forest. Rt. 2, Meadville 64659. Adjacent to SW portion of Swan Lake *National Wildlife Refuge.* Access: on foot or by boat.

Salisbury, Mo. The town was established in 1867 along the Western Branch of the North Missouri *Railroad,* which was initially begun in 1860 at *Moberly* as the Chariton and Randolph Railroad but was delayed, like the establishment of the town, by the *Civil War.* It was named for Lucius Salisbury, one of the three men who

platted it. Post office: 1862–now. US 24, E 9 m. HISTORICAL MUSEUM: Chariton County historical records and items; farming machinery and equipment. 115 E. 2d. POTTS PARK: Picnic shelters, ball fields, walking trails, archery, golf. SR 129, S 1 m. STERLING PRICE COMMUNITY LAKE: 35 acres. Bass, sunfish, catfish. US 24, W approx. 2.6 m.; GR, S 0.8 m. **Sterling Price Monument / Museum.** MONUMENT: A 1915 heroic-style bronze statue honors Confederate major general Sterling Price (1809–1867; *Civil War*). His father, Pugh W., moved one mile south of here in 1831 (inquire locally). Sterling, born in Virginia, also moved here in 1831, married in 1833, and bought a farm four miles south of Dalton[2] (US 24, W 3 m.; SR MM, S 2.6 m.). Before the Civil War, he served as state representative (1836–1838), speaker of the house (1840–1844), U.S. congressman (1844–1846; resigned to fight in the *Mexican War),* and governor (1853–1857). Price Park, downtown. MUSEUM: Local historical items, Price memorabilia. SR 5, W on Bridge (412).

1. Originally located near Salt Creek, a descriptive name.
2. Landowner William Dalton; p.o. 1867–now.

KIMMSWICK
Population: 135   Map H-4

Platted in 1859 by German immigrant Theodore Kimm along the tracks of the St. Louis & Iron Mountain *Railroad,* this small German community prospered as a summer resort for nearby St. Louis and as a shipping point that used rail and Mississippi River transportation. The derivation of "wick" as used here (Kimm's wick) is prehistoric western German via the Latin "vicus," village. Bypassed by federal highways in the early 20th century, the town declined. Preservation efforts beginning in 1969 have resulted in a representative collection of 19th-century architecture, including one- and two-story log structures relocated here. Today's economy relies on tourism. Post office: 1858–c. 1973. Self-guided walking-tour maps at shops and restaurants.

Architecture. Of the 34 structures on the walking tour, 27 are from the 19th century with 9 dating before 1867,

17 from 1867–1896, and 1 two-story log house from c. 1770 with an 1831 addition (Old House). Still bound within its original survey, this river town and its architecture are a nostalgic set piece.

El Camino Real. A marker was erected in 1917 by the DAR. SR K, W approx. 2.5 m. to Rock Creek. *(Roads and Traces)*

Mastodon State Park. I-55 at Kimmswick exit; W Outer Rd., N 0.5 m; sign. *(State Parks)*

Windsor Harbor Road Bridge. Wrought Iron, 1874; National Historic Register. Reportedly the oldest of its kind in Missouri, the bridge was moved here in 1930 from Ivory St. in Carondelet.[1] Spanning Rock Creek; S end of Front.

---

1. Baron de Carondelet, governor-general of Louisiana at the time of naming, 1794; annexed by St. Louis in 1870; p.o. 1826–1873.

KING CITY
Population: 986   Map C-2

The town was settled in 1856 along the St. Joseph–Ottumwa, Iowa, freight trail by blacksmith John Pittsenbarger, who later applied for a post office name, Petersburg, that was rejected due to an existing Petersburg[1] in Boone County. U.S. Postmaster General Rufus King submitted his name, which was approved and applied to the town when it was platted in 1869. The arrival c. 1878 of the St. Joseph & Des Moines *Railroad* helped establish King City as a shipping point. Post office: 1861–1862, 1865–now.

Big Bluestem Grass / Virgin Sod. 300 acres. Harvey-Spiking Farm: US 169, S 2.1 m.; GR E 1 m.; inquire locally.

Depot / Tri-County Museum. Railroad, 1900. Local historical items, large farm equipment, a caboose, special events. In town.

Park. Pool, baseball, tennis, rodeo grounds. In town.

Recreation. KING LAKE *WILDLIFE AREA.* LIMMP COMMUNITY LAKE: 29 acres. Bass, bluegill, catfish. SR Z, W 0.9 m.; SR CC, N 0.6 m.

---

1. Petersburg, Ky.; p.o. 1838–1849.

KINGSTON
Population: 279   Map D-2

The eastern half of today's town (including the square) was bought in 1835 by Abraham Couts, the western half in 1837 by Roswell Stevens. Selected in 1843 as a central location for county seat of Caldwell County,

replacing Far West (below), the town was platted in 1843 along Shoal Creek and named for judge Austin A. King of Richmond, Mo., a prominent judge and later governor (1848–1852). Except for limited service by a branch line of the Hannibal & Kingston *Railroad* during the mid-1890s, it was bypassed by railroads to the north and south. Today Kingston remains the political center of a sparsely populated county. Post office: 1843–now.

Bonanza Wildlife Area. *Wildlife Areas.*

Caldwell County Courthouse / Jail. Richardsonian Romanesque, 1898; National Historic Register. The county's fourth, this two-story 74-by-69-foot brick courthouse with limestone trim has a massive entry porch, twin central towers with conical roofs, and rounded arches above recessed windows. Cost: $24,827. Behind it, the two-story brick county jail (Folk Victorian, 1867) is still in use. It has iron grates bolted across windows and all-steel cells (floors, walls, and ceilings). Downtown. *(County Profiles)*

Christian Church. Gothic Revival, 1858–1865. Frame with lancet windows and a belfry, the building was built by Southern Methodists, who sold it in 1869 to the Christian Church, which has held services here regularly since 1865, the year the building was completed. 2 blocks E of courthouse.

Far West, Mo. National Historic Register. Caldwell County was organized by the state legislature in December 1836 as a sanctuary for *Mormons*. The modifier "Far" in the town name is usually interpreted to indicate a sense of isolation, which is what the Mormons sought. With a few exceptions in the counties they fled from (Jackson, 1833; Clay, 1835), this site was as far west as any contemporary American settlement. The town was platted in 1836 as county seat of Caldwell County by W. W. Phelps and John Whitmer *(Richmond: Cemeteries)*; the survey reflected typical Mormon planning: a 396-foot-wide square with a 100-foot-wide main street and other streets 81.5 feet wide. Its 1838 estimated population of 5,000 was ordered to leave that winter by Governor L. W. Boggs. The 1838 order and subsequent massacre at Haun's Mill *(Hamilton: Breckenridge)* resulted in a ghost town where about 150 houses, a courthouse, and commercial buildings were eventually torn down. Today a landscaped park encloses rough flat boulders, remnants of the temple's foundation cornerstones (the first one was laid by Brigham Young). Markers, restrooms. Post office: 1837–1847. SR HH, W 5.6 m.; SR D, N 2.6 m.

Polo, Mo. Established in 1868 at a crossroads, the town was named, as was 1856 Polo, Ill., for Marco Polo (1254–1324) of Venice, whose book based on 17 years at the court of Kublai Khan reeducated Europe about Asia. Post office: 1868–now. SR 13, S 6 m. METHO-

DIST CHURCH: Vernacular, 1903. One-story brick with a large and detailed stained-glass window.

Wright House / Museum. Greek Revival, c. 1865. The town lot for this pink-brick two-story house was sold in 1846; no exact construction date is known. Architecturally, it features upper-story five-ranked six-over-six windows and first-floor windows with modestly decorated stone lintels. A museum for local historical items is planned. SR HH, 1 block W of courthouse.

KIRKSVILLE
Population: 17,152   Map F-1

Much of the town's early history was lost in an 1865 courthouse fire. Formerly known as both Long Point and Hopkinsville for no recorded reasons, today's townsite was selected and platted in 1842 (with the plat filed in 1847) as a central location for recently organized Adair County. Local tradition insists namesake Jesse Kirk, a nearby tavern owner and later the town's first postmaster, received the honor in exchange for serving the county surveyors a turkey dinner and good whiskey. The town was slow to grow (1850 est. pop. 300; 1860 pop. 659), but the arrival in 1868 of the North Missouri *Railroad* and the establishment of two colleges (below) helped develop today's mixed economy of agriculture, commerce, education, and recreation. Post office: 1843–now. Home of Kirksville Area Vo-Tech, Kirksville College of Osteopathic Medicine (below), and Northeast Missouri State University (below).

Adair County Courthouse. Richardsonian Romanesque, 1897–1898; National Historic Register. There was a 33-year lapse between the destruction of the first courthouse by fire and the construction of the present one. This massive 113-by-85-foot structure was built with contemporary state-of-the-art conveniences and materials, e.g. electricity, steam heat, a limestone foundation, sandstone walls, granite columns, a slate roof, and tile floors supported by steel and concrete foundations. Cost: $46,695. Midtown; US 63B. *(County Profiles)*

Architecture. CABINS HISTORIC DISTRICT: *Novinger.* NATIONAL HISTORIC REGISTER: Dockery Hotel (Elson at McPherson); Grim Building (113–115 Washington); Harris-Parrish House (1308 N. Franklin). TOWN SQUARE: Good examples of late 19th- and early 20th-century commercial styles. Bounded by Jefferson, Elson, Harrison, and Franklin.

Battle of Kirksville / Park. August 6, 1862. About 1,000 Federals commanded by Col. John McNeil routed 2,000 poorly armed Confederates led by Lt. Col. Joseph C. Porter, who had been recruiting in the area. Memorial Park marks the site of Federal fieldpieces that shelled the Confederates at the courthouse (above); 26 Confederates were killed (Forest-Llewellyn Cemetery, below). A 20-foot obelisk raised in 1932 commemorates all the county's veterans. Midtown; US 63B to 400 block of E. Hickory.

Bear Creek Church. Vernacular, 1838; National Historic Register. Small, plain, and rural, the structure and setting are nostalgic. *Cemetery* adjacent. SR B, N 2.5 m.

Farmer's Market. Fish, farm produce, baked goods; Saturday mornings. US 63B at town square.

Forest-Llewellyn Cemetery. The cemetery was begun in 1846 as a public burying ground. Interments include town founder Jesse Kirk (d. 1846), Dr. A. T. Still (Kirksville College of Osteopathic Medicine, below), and 26 Confederates in a mass grave (Battle of Kirksville, above). Midtown; US 63B, W on Washington, N on Osteopathy; signs. *(Cemeteries)*

Fort Matson Site. Selected by Capt. Matson, this 1832 fort had a blockhouse and palisade for defense during the *Black Hawk War (Novinger).* Marked by today's Fort Matson church. US 63, N 8 m.; SR A, E 2.5 m., GR, S 0.75 m.; GR, E 1 m.

Grand Divide. *Grand Divide.*

Kirksville College of Osteopathic Medicine. The world's first osteopathic medical college was founded in 1892 by Dr. A. T. Still (1828–1917), who became the world's first osteopathic physician in 1874. It emphasized the theory that diseases are largely due to loss of structural integrity in the tissues. Treatment relies on manipulation of body parts, as well as surgery, medicine, diet, and other therapies. Today there are 15 American osteopathic medical colleges. This college has about 500 students and 15 buildings (including two hospitals) on over 50 acres. STILL NATIONAL OSTEOPATHIC MUSEUM: Three buildings. (1) An 1820s furnished log cabin where Still was born; (2) the first school, a two-room 1874 vernacular house; and (3) a building displaying osteopathic memorabilia. Midtown; US 63B, W on Jefferson (800). *(Macon: Fredrick Wilhelm Blees)*

Northeast Missouri State University. Established in 1867, today the school has an enrollment of 6,500. MUSEUMS: Three museums include historical items (pioneer, Indian, war), books, and memorabilia concerning Abraham Lincoln, John F. Kennedy, and Mark Twain. S side; US 63B.

Recreation. HAZEL CREEK RESERVOIR: 530 acres. Fishing. US 63, N 4.6 m. *STATE FORESTS:* Big Creek, Montgomery Woods, Sugar Creek. THOUSAND HILLS *STATE PARK:* SR 6, W 2.7 m.; SR 157, S 2.7 m.; signs.

St. Mary's Church. Romanesque, 1904; National Historic Register. Built on high ground for $10,000, this large structure is unusual for its style because of the frame construction and two asymmetrical towers (one square, one octagonal). SR 11, E 11 m.

KIRKWOOD
Population: 27,291
Maps H-4 and St. Louis Area

Today a suburb of *St. Louis*, the town was settled c. 1808 in an area later known as Gravois.[1] Anticipating the arrival of the Pacific *Railroad*, real estate promoters H. W. Leffingwell and R. S. Elliott in 1852 organized the Kirkwood Association (which was chartered in 1853), bought three small farms on Dry Ridge, and began advertising the site's 640-foot altitude as healthful, which played on the then-justifiable fear of cholera in urban areas around St. Louis. The town was platted in 1852 (with the plat filed in 1853) along the Pacific Railroad at the site of Collins Station[2] and named for 1850 railroad surveyor James P. Kirkwood; the station was renamed for him as well. Post office: 1854–1901. Home of Meramec Community College.

Architecture. NATIONAL HISTORIC REGISTER: Grace Episcopal Church (Taylor at Argonne); Missouri-Pacific Depot (W. Argonne Dr. at US 67). TOWN: Good examples of 19th-century styles.

Castlewood State Park. SR 100 (*Route 66*) at US 67; SR 100, W 8.6 m.; Ballwin Rd., S 2.5 m.; Keifer Creek Rd., E about 1 m. to park office; signs. (*State Parks*)

Chesterfield, Mo. Platted in 1818, the town was probably named, like others, for English statesman and man of letters P. D. Stanhope, fourth Earl of Chesterfield (1694–1773). Post office: 1820–1824, 1895–now. I-270 at I-44; I-270, N 6.1 m.; US 40/61 W 6.6 m. BONHOMME'S OLD STONE CHURCH: Stone, 1841. Organized in 1816, the Presbyterian congregation is the second oldest one west of the Mississippi (*Caledonia: Bellevue Presbyterian Church*). *Cemetery* adjacent. E side; Conway at White. HOWELL ISLAND WILDLIFE AREA: *Wildlife Areas*. ST. LOUIS CAROUSEL: One of 10 existing carousels made in the 1890s–1920s by Philadelphia's Dentzel Company features 60 hand-carved painted wooden horses, four reindeer with real antlers, and two chariots supported by a 40-foot mast; rides. Faust County Park; SR 340 (Olive St. Rd.), E near river; signs. THORNHILL: Log and Weatherboard, c. 1807–1819; National Historic Register. This is Missouri's oldest standing governor's residence. It was the home of Frederick Bates, secretary of Louisiana and Missouri Territories and land claims commissioner, as well as Missouri's second governor (1824–1825). Carved mantels, built-in cupboards, out-

buildings; tours. Faust County Park; SR 340 (Olive St. Rd.), E near river; signs.

Creve Coeur, Mo. Crevecoeur (French for heartbreaker) was the name of a supposedly impregnable 17th-century Dutch fort that was easily captured in 1672 by the French army during a war with Holland. La Salle built a Creve Coeur fort in Illinois in 1689, naming it in honor of that victory (and most likely to taunt the Dutch). Its name was probably transferred here to the creek, lake, and town. Post office: 1851–1959. I-270 at SR 100; I-270, N 3.7 m.; SR AB, E 0.3 m. CREVE COEUR PARK / LAKE: 1,141-acre park. Athletic fields, trails, picnic areas, camping, tennis, playground; 320-acre lake: canoeing, sailing ice-skating, fishing (no swimming or gasoline-powered boats); adjacent marsh with large bird population. I-270 at US 70; I-270, S 2.5 m.; Dorsett, W 1.4 m.

History House. Italianate, c. 1865. The frame house's siding is cut and beveled to resemble stone. Each room is furnished in a different era. Special programs; weekends only. I-44, N on Kirkwood (US 67) to E. Argonne (549).

Magic House. Missouri's only children's museum of its kind features hands-on exhibits focusing on art and science. Divided by age groups: one–seven and five–older. 516 S. Kirkwood Rd. (US 67).

National Museum of Transport. Founded in 1944. While the emphasis is on design and technology, there are 39 acres of locomotives and rolling stock (Civil War to 1940s), automobiles, streetcars, buses, horse-drawn vehicles, aircraft, and other means of transportation, both national and international, as well as pipeline segments, communication devices, and two 1850 railroad tunnels, the first bored west of the Mississippi, that are listed on the National Historic Register. I-270, N to Dougherty Ferry Rd., W to Barretts Station Rd. (3015).

Parks. CREVE COEUR PARK: I-270 at SR 100; I-270, N 6.6 m.; Dorsett Rd., W 1.5 m. (above). GREENTREE PARK: Public boat ramp, fishing, picnic sites, playground, athletic fields. I-270 at SR 100; I-270, S 2.5 m. to Big Bend–Marshall Rd.; Marshall Rd. W to river (approx. 1.6 m.). QUEENY PARK: 569 acres. Indoor-outdoor skating rinks, tennis, playground, hiking trails, pool, St. Louis Symphony's Pops during the summer (*St. Louis: The Arts*). Jarville House (Greek Revival, 1853; National Historic Register) features the Dog Museum (moved here in 1982 from New York City), which exhibits art and literature about canines throughout history. I-270 at SR 100; SR 100, W 1.5 m., then N on Mason (1721).

1. From the French for gravel via the creek; no p.o.
2. Owen Collins, one of the farm owners, via the RR station; no p.o.

LACLEDE

Population: 410   Map E-2

Platted in 1853 along the proposed route of the Hannibal & St. Joseph *Railroad* by businessmen Cross, Eastman, and Worlow, the town was named for *St. Louis* founder Pierre Laclède (1724–1778), namesake of Laclede County. After the railroad was completed in 1859, expected prosperity was stymied by the *Civil War*. The father of John J. Pershing (below) was one of the trustees of the town's 1866 incorporation. Post offices: Meade[1] 1854–1856; Laclede 1856–now.

Locust Creek Covered Bridge. Howe-Truss, Wooden, 1868; National Historic Register, State Historic Site. Spanning Locust Creek (whose channel has moved east) at the main east–west road of northern Missouri, this is, at 151 feet, the longest of Missouri's surviving *covered bridges.* SR 36, W 4 m.; GR, N 1 m.; GR, E 0.3 m.

Natural Areas. For all of the following, contact Pershing State Park, Laclede 64651. CORDGRASS BOTTOMS: 30 acres. This cordgrass marsh area is surrounded by 50 acres of wet bottomland forest. Features cow parsnip, blue flag, arrowleaf, pink weed. SR 36, W 1.9 m. LOCUST CREEK: 330 acres. Part of Pershing *State Park* (Recreation, below). One of the last northern Missouri examples of a meandering river system with associated oxbows, sloughs, and floodplain forest (old-growth shellback hickory, cottonwood, oak); rare ostrich fern. YELLOW CREEK: SR 139, S 10 m. (*Keytesville: Brunswick*).

Pershing Boyhood Home. Gothic Revival, 1860s; restored; National Historic Register, National Landmark, State Historic Site. This two-story white frame house, where John J. Pershing (1860–1948) lived from 1866 to 1882, has late 19th-century furnishings, local historical items, and memorabilia of Pershing, whose military career after West Point began with fighting the Apache and ended during the atomic bomb era. His 1919 promotion to General of the Armies, a title created for him, made him second in all-time rank only to George Washington. A 1932 book about his WWI experiences won the Pulitzer Prize. Grounds: Prairie Mound School, a one-room school where he taught. SR 5, in town.

Recreation. FOUNTAIN GROVE *WILDLIFE AREA.* PERSHING *STATE PARK:* SR 36, W 1.9 m.; SR 130, S; signs. SWAN LAKE *NATIONAL WILDLIFE REFUGE:* SR 139, S 10 m.

Sumner, Mo. The town was platted in 1882 at the junction of the Brunswick & Chillicothe and Burlington & Southwestern *Railroads* and first named by the latter as Crossland.[2] Its name was changed in 1882 to honor a railroad official of the St. Louis, Kansas City & Northern, the parent company of the Brunswick & Chillicothe. Post offices: Crossland 1882–1883; Sumner 1883–now. SR 139, S 12 m. FULBRIGHT MUSEUM: local historical items. Main, downtown. MAXIE: This 40-foot statue of a goose, reportedly the world's largest of its kind, complements the town's self-proclaimed title of Wild Goose Capital of the World. Community Park; in town. RECREATION: Above.

US 36 Completed. On September 20, 1930, the last concrete for construction of this federal highway was poured near Meadville,[3] about five miles west of here.

1. Charles Meade, Hannibal & St. Joseph employee.
2. For the junction of the two railroads.
3. Charles Meade, Hannibal & St. Joseph employee; p.o. Bottsville, for John Botts, 1860–1869; Meadville 1869–now.

LAGRANGE

Population: 1,102   Map G-2

Godfrey Le Seur built a trading post in 1795 at the mouth of the Wyaconda River where the Mississippi narrows, providing deep water close to shore. Two settlements followed: one by John Bozarth in 1819 (about two miles south) and another by John McKinney, who built a mill in 1822 and platted a town, Waconda,[1] near the river's mouth. John S. Marlow, a merchant, settled just south of Waconda in 1828 at a site by both rivers that was surveyed in 1830 by William and Mary Wright, who filed a plat in 1832 for a town they named LaGrange,[2] honoring the French countryseat of American Revolutionary War hero Marquis de La *Fayette*, whose legend spawned over 50 American town names. LaGrange grew quickly as a steamboat port, precipitating Waconda's decline. Incorporated in 1853, it was at the peak of its prosperity when divided loyalties during the *Civil War* paralyzed its economy, a setback from which it never recovered. Post office: La Grange 1832–now.

Architecture. Good examples of 19th-century styles, dating from the 1830s (especially on 3d–7th and on Monroe St.).

Artesian Well. Proof of LaGrange's late 19th-century nickname, City of Mineral Springs, this 600-foot well was drilled in 1887 for a steel mill that failed before even opening. The water was later bottled commercially; bring a jug. SR B, in town.

Le Seur's 1795 Trading Post. A 1928 marker locates the county's first settlement. SR B at S bank of Wyaconda River.

Marshall Home. Greek Revival, 1850s; altered 1959. The plain two-story frame house was the 1858–1860 home of Thomas R. Marshall (1854–1925), whose father, an abolitionist, moved the family to Indiana. Governor of Indiana (1908–1912) and vice president under Woodrow Wilson (1913–1921), Marshall coined the catchphrase "What this country needs is a really good five-cent cigar." Near 3d and Jefferson.

Riverfront Park. Picnic facilities. SR B, at the Mississippi.

State Park / Wildlife Area. UPPER MISSISSIPPI *WILDLIFE AREA.* WAKONDA *STATE PARK:* SR B, S 2.8 m.

Union Soldier's Monument. An 1864 marble shaft commemorates those who died defending their county during the Civil War. Town square.

US 61. *New London: US 61 / Red Ball Road.*

1. Spelled Wahkondah and Wyanconda on 1820–1830 maps; named by way of the river for the variously spelled Siouan term for spirit or sacred; no p.o.

2. The official Missouri state map and the U.S. postmaster spell the name La Grange. The original plat is handwritten but appears to read La Grange. "American Place-Names" offers two variations, La Grange and Lagrange. This town, its post office, and its county use LaGrange. As in the case of Harry S. Truman's initial *(Independence: Truman Historic District),* the owner's preference, in this case the town's, is honored.

LAMAR
Population: 4,168   Map C-6

After two years of disputes, this site was selected and platted in 1857 as a central location for county seat of recently organized Barton County. George E. Ward, an 1852 settler who donated 40 acres for the original plat, named the town for Mirabeau B. Lamar, his Louisiana friend and the second president (1838–1841) of the Republic of Texas. Established during the *Kansas Border War,* the town suffered from the beginning and was, like the county, abandoned during the *Civil War* due to *Order No. 11.* So divided was the town that ill feelings continued until formally set aside in 1910, when veterans met at the square and shook hands, saying "The war is over, everyone is glad." The arrival in 1881 of the Missouri-Pacific *Railroad* helped strengthen its economy as a trading center. Post office: 1858–1863, 1866–now. Home of Lamar Area Vocational School.

Architecture. Good examples (1880s to early 20th century) can be found around the courthouse and north–south of it along Gulf, between 16th and 3d.

Barton County Courthouse. Richardsonian Romanesque (truncated), 1888. The county built four courthouses, two of them temporary. The first permanent structure of 1860 was destroyed in 1862 during the *Civil War,* although most of the records were saved. Today's massive 80-by-120-foot red-brick-and-stone

structure is set on the original 400-foot court square, one of Missouri's largest. Removal of the central clock tower and replacement of corner tower turrets with pyramidal roofs has not measurably changed its characteristic Richardsonian Romanesque design: arch springs, a hip roof with cross gables, a line of arched windows, a heavy post-and-lintel porch support, cushioned capitals, and polychrome stonework. Small museum in basement; large park with benches. Cost: $32,500. US 160, N on Gulf. *(County Profiles)*

Barton County Fair. Reportedly this is Missouri's largest free county fair; first week of September.

Golden City, Mo. Reportedly named for a small amount of gold found here, the town was established in 1870 and today has some good examples of late 19th-century architecture along US 160. Post office: 1869–now. US 160, E 17 m.

Mindenmines, Mo. The town was originally platted in 1883 as Minden, for either Minden, La., or its namesake Minden, Germany. The suffix, referring to its coal-mining operations, was added after mail mixups with Chariton County's Mendon.[1] Post offices: Tusconia[2] 1883–1884; Minden Mines 1884–1895; Mindenmines 1895–now. US 160, W 16 m. DAVIS (LESTER R.) *STATE FOREST.* PRAIRIE *STATE PARK /* NATURAL AREAS: *Liberal.*

Recreation. CITY PARK: 54 acres. Maintained by a full-time caretaker. Tennis, flowers, pool, picnic facilities, playground, free overnight RV parking (hookups available), 45 varieties of trees. SW side; US 160, S on Walnut; signs. LAMAR LAKE: 250 acres. City water supply, fishing (bass, catfish, bluegill, carp, crappie), boating; no swimming or waterskiing. SE side; SR 160, S on Hagney; signs.

Truman Birthplace. Vernacular, c. 1881; National Historic Register, State Historic Site. Harry S. Truman *(Belton; Grandview; Independence)* was born on May 8, 1884, in this frame bungalow bought in 1882 from the builder by his parents, John (age 30) and Martha (age 29). They moved when Harry was 11 months old. Late 19th-century furnishings, Truman memorabilia. Midtown; US 160, N on Truman to 11th.

1. *Keytesville;* p.o. Salt Creek, descriptive, 1866–1870; Mendon 1872–now.

2. Origin unknown; probably of Indian derivation.

LANCASTER
Population: 785   Map F-1

The site was selected in 1845 as a central location (Tippecanoe, below) for county seat of newly organized Schuyler County. The court ordered it platted in

1845, accepting Robert S. Neeley's suggestion for the town's name, which honored his hometown, Lancaster, Ohio (established in 1800). Another source credits Jim Lusk with choosing the name but gives no reason. Regardless, it is a stock place-name derived from Lancaster, England, chartered in 1193 on the ruins of Saxon and Roman towns. Divided loyalties during the *Civil War* stunted the town's initial fast growth because most males left to join the armies. Narrowly bypassed in 1868 by the North Missouri *Railroad*, it recovered with the 1872 arrival of the Missouri, Iowa & Nebraska, defeating a proposal to remove the county seat to *Glenwood*. Post office: 1846–now.

Architecture. Many good examples of 19th-century styles, e.g. Queen Anne, Greek Revival, Italianate.

City Lakes / Park. NEW LAKE: Boat ramp, fishing. US 63, S 0.7 m. OLD LAKE: Boat ramp, restrooms, fishing. US 136 / SR 202; SR 202, W 0.5 m. PARK: Fishing lake, tennis, volleyball, restrooms, picnic facilities. SE side; SR D.

Grand Divide. *Grand Divide.*

Hall House / Historical Museum. Queen Anne Free Classic, c. 1898–1900; National Historic Register. Clapboard with cross gables and a one-story wraparound porch with paired ionic columns, the house was owned by W. P. "Diamond Billy" Hall, who favored tall silk top hats, purple velvet waistcoats, and diamonds (rings, cufflinks, stickpins) and traded and trained circus animals for worldwide export from Lancaster. Reportedly, he housed here one-tenth of America's elephant population. Exhibits: Hall memorabilia, local historical items, a collection of Rupert Hughes's books (Hughes House, below), an 1880s furnished log cabin, a one-room schoolhouse. US 136, 1 block W of courthouse.

Hughes House. Vernacular, 1870s; abandoned. Felix T. Hughes, grandfather of legendary entrepreneur Howard R. Hughes Jr., lived in Lancaster from 1869 to c. 1880 with his sons: Howard Sr., Rupert (a popular 20th-century novelist and biographer; Hall House, above), and Felix Jr. N side of Washington at viaduct.

Rebel's Cove Wildlife Area. *Wildlife Areas.*

Schuyler County Courthouse. Sixties Modern, 1960–1961. The original modern design of the county's fourth courthouse was, by popular request, modified to more traditional lines (Adamesque affinities). Today's building has two stories, red brick, quoins, stone lintels, pilasters, dentils, a center gable, and twelve-over-twelve windows. Cost: $254,351. Downtown. *(County Profiles)*

Tippecanoe, Mo. Established in 1840, the town derived its name from the 1840 presidential campaign slogan of William H. Harrison, "Tippecanoe and Tyler Too" ("Tyler Too" referred to his vice presidential running mate, John Tyler). Incidentally, Harrison, the ninth

president (1841–1841), was the first to die in office, and John Tyler, who served without a vice president, was the first president (1841–1845) not elected to office. "Tippecanoe" called attention to Harrison's 1811 victory over Indian leader Tecumseh's brother *(Gainesville: Tecumseh)* at Tippecanoe, Indiana Territory, while serving as the first (1801–1812) governor of that territory. Harrison, convinced that the British were inciting the Indians, lobbied for the *War of 1812*. Tippecanoe is a corrupted Potawatomi name, ki-tap-i-kon, for the local river. Missouri's Tippecanoe was a prosperous town, the most westerly town in northern Missouri, but declined after losing a political fight for county seat to Lancaster when the county's size was reduced; defunct. Post office: Tippicanoe [*sic*] 1840–1846. SR D, S 2.6 m.; SR V, E 0.3 m.; inquire locally.

LA PLATA
Population: 1,401   Map F-2

The town was platted in 1855 around a city park (below). Its name was reportedly picked from a hat after arguments about preferences deadlocked. A colorful story claims that the winner, La Plata, was suggested by Dr. W. Moore, whose pretentious knowledge of French led him to mistakenly use a Spanish word as a metaphor for his vision of the local countryside: wild prairies of grass as a great river of silver flowing north. La Plata is Spanish for silver only, unless accepted as a shortened version of Argentina's Rio de la Plata,[1] which would corroborate Moore's inadvertent metaphorical use of the Argentine namesake and correspond to an exotic-sounding town name as favored by this era, e.g. *Callao* (18 m. S) and *Cuba*. La Plata is a popular name applied to American towns, mountains, and rivers and a species of dolphin. The arrival in 1868 of the North Missouri *Railroad* helped establish a shipping-based economy. Post office: 1856–now.

Gilbreath-McLorn House. Queen Anne, 1896; National Historic Register. A good example of its style, the house features Eastlake detailing, six gables, an octagonal tower, a wraparound porch, and roofline ornamental urns with ornamental flowers. The builder's daughter, Olive G. McLorn, as an interpreter for the Red Cross, traveled in 1914–1915 from Siberia to St. Petersburg, witnessed the Russian Revolution, contributed articles to *Harpers* and the *Yale Review,* married a British bank director in Shanghai in 1934, and later spent two and a half years as a Japanese prisoner after Japan's invasion of China. McLorn moved back to La Plata and lived in this house until her death in 1981. Oriental and English furnishings; tours. 225 N. Ownesby.

Grand Divide. *Grand Divide.*
Hidden Hollow State Forest. *State Forests.*
Lester Dent House. Under the pen name of Kenneth Robeson, Dent wrote the "Doc Savage" series for pulp magazines during the 1930s. Corner of Ownesby and Colbern.
Parks / Lake. CITY PARK: Landscaped, Korean War jet, benches. Moore, 1 block W of old US 63. HASTINGS: Nine-hole golf course. E side; SR 156; signs. LA PLATA CITY LAKE: 81 acres. Fishing and hunting. SR 156, W 1.6 m. SANTA FE LAKE: Donated to the city by the railroad. Swimming, fishing, picnic facilities. US 63, NE of town; signs.

1. Argentina, which also has a prairie topography, was making newspaper headlines for drafting South America's first representative constitution in 1853–1854.

LEBANON
Population: 9,983   Map E-6

Platted in 1849 as county seat of recently organized Laclede County, the town was briefly called Wyota [*sic*] for a former nearby Indian village, Witoka.[1] County residents, mostly Tennessee immigrants, agreed to rename the town Lebanon, as suggested by Rev. Benjamin Hooker of Lebanon, Tenn. This stock place-name commemorates biblical Lebanon and Mount Lebanon, known for its cedars. When the city council refused c. 1868 to donate land to the Pacific *Railroad* for a depot, the railroad narrowly bypassed the town in 1869, which resulted in a town addition platted in 1869 along the tracks. The courthouse (Laclede County Courthouse, below) was sold in 1870, and businesses moved to the railroad. Today's Commercial Street marks the railroad addition; Main, St. Louis, Broadway, and Hill mark the 1849 town square. Situated on a major 19th-century east–west road (later *Route 66* and I-44) and a railroad, the town prospered as a trading center. Post offices: Witoka 1848–1850; Lebanon 1850–now. Home of Laclede Area Vocational School.
Architecture. Several good examples; National Historic Register structures: Ploger-Moneymaker Place (291 Harwood); Wallace House (230 Harwood).
Bennett Spring Hanging Fern Natural Area. SR 64, W 12 m. *(Buffalo: Hanging Fern Natural Area)*
Boswell Park. Pool, tennis, trails, restrooms, picnic facilities. *Route 66*, between I-44 exits 127 and 129.
County Jail / Museum. Italianate style, 1876; National Historic Register. This two-story red-brick jailhouse with iron bars across the windows was closed in 1955. First floor: local historical items, furniture. Second floor: original cells with graffiti, a dental office, early radio broadcasting equipment. At courthouse.
Harold Bell Wright House. Pastor of the Christian Church here from 1905 to 1907, Wright used the town as a setting in "The Calling of Dan Mathews," which continues the story of old Matt's family from "Shepherd of the Hills" (published the year Wright left Lebanon; *Branson*). The church was razed; the house is on Adams, between *Route 66* and the courthouse; inquire locally.
Laclede County Courthouse. Italian Renaissance, 1924–1925. The first courthouse, built in 1851, was sold in 1870 for $50 when businesses relocated (Lebanon history, above) to the railroad addition, which precipitated a 24-year tug-of-war for the courthouse. The new addition was joined to the original town on paper only and the Missouri Supreme Court upheld a lower court decision allowing the old town to keep the court records. Later, a clause in the 1875 Missouri constitution, stipulating that additions to county seats were legally part of the county seat, resulted in the new town securing the records, but a second courthouse was not built until 1894. It burned in 1920 and was replaced after two bond elections with today's 100-by-63-foot three-story brick building that has modest elements of its style: four full-height pilasters, cornice dentils, a projecting central entry, pseudo–roofline parapet, and belt course. Cost: $72,428. Grounds: elaborate cast-iron statue of R. P. "Silver Dick" Bland, a local lawyer elected 12 times to the U.S. Congress (between 1872 and 1898) who was a free-silver advocate and an 1896 contender for the Democratic Party presidential nomination (William Jennings Bryan won it). I-44 exit 129, W on Jefferson, N on 2d to Adams. *(County Profiles)*
Natural Arches. DECATURVILLE: Described as an igloo perforated at several points around its base, this unusual inverted bowl–shaped arch has an 8-foot ceiling and a circumference of approximately 30 feet. SR 5, N 10 m. to SR E; continue SR 5, N 2.7 m.; GR, E 0.5 to S curve; park, walk E 0.25 m. DEVILS TABLES: Two arches (6-foot spans about 10 feet high) have associated tables formed by resistant limestone over less resistant pedestals. Good view of the Gasconade River valley. SR 32, E 18 m.; SR K, N 3 m.; GR, E 5.5 m. Park at pullout, walk S a few feet. *(Collapsed Cave Systems)*
Oakland, Mo. Reportedly the site was settled in 1830 by Samuel Monholen near the Osage Fork of the Gasconade River and at southern Missouri's major east–west road, later the Military or Wire Road between *Rolla* and Ft. Smith, Ark. Oakland was named for the area's trees. Post offices: Onyx[2] 1836–1841; Oakland 1841–1863, 1865–1953. SR 5, S 0.8 m.; SR 123, E 5 m.; SR B, S 2 m. OAKLAND GENERAL STORE: Vernacular, 1881; second story 1908. Closed 1970;

frame; derelict. OAKLAND METHODIST CHURCH: Gothic Revival, 1883. Built for a Moravian congregation; bought by Methodists in 1913; still maintained.

Orla, Mo. The community was originally called Ball's Mill for the Tennessean who built the mill and a general store at the Osage Fork of the Gasconade River. The name was changed to Orla when Ball named the post office for one of his sons, whose name was also spelled Orle and Orley. Today's mill, built in 1913, is a two-story frame building with a race and wheel. Private. Post office: 1880–1954. SR 5, S 12 m.; SR V, E 3.1 m.

Recreation. BENNETT SPRING *STATE PARK:* SR 64, W 12 m. GOOSE CREEK *STATE FOREST:* Five tracts, all from Phillipsburg (Route 66 Sights, below). (1, 2, 3) SR CC, S 1 m.; railroad track, S 1 m.; GR, S 1 m. (4) SR Y, S 2.5 m.; GR, W 0.6 m. (5) SR M, W 7.4 m.; SR A, N 6 m.; GR, W 1 m. OAK RIDGE *STATE FOREST:* Three tracts, all from Lebanon. (1) SR 5, S 6 m.; SR C, W 1.5 m. (2) SR 5, S 4 m.; SR HH, E 4.8 m.; GR, E 2.2 m.; GR S, 0.5 m. (3) SR 5, S 14 m.; SR J, W 2.6 m.; GR, N 0.5 m.; GR, E 1.5 m. OSAGE FORK *STATE FOREST:* Multiple tracts, all from Lebanon. (1) "C" Road: SR 5, S 6 m.; SR C, W 1.5 m. (2) Davis Mill: SR 5, S 14 m.; SR J, W 2.6 m.; GR, N 0.5 m.; GR, E 1.5 m. (3) Orla: SR 5, S 4 m.; SR HH, E 4.8 m.; GR, E 2.2 m.; GR, S 0.5 m.

Route 66 Sights. ARCHITECTURE: Munger Moss Motor Court, Hall-Moore Stuff Co., Village Oaks, remnants of Camp Joy and other structures. I-44 exit 130, Old *Route 66.* 66 SCENIC DRIVE: From Phillipsburg[3] (I-44, S 11 m. to exit 118); SR CC, W 18.6 m. to *Marshfield;* SR OO, W 13.3 m. to Strafford *(Springfield: Exotic Animal Paradise).*

Sleeper, Mo. Established c. 1869 along the Pacific *Railroad,* the town was first called Sleeper's Switch, after a railroad construction gang foreman named Sleeper. Post offices: Sleeper's Switch 1879; Sleeper 1883–1895. Hazelgreen *(Waynesville: Route 66 Sights)* temporarily served as Sleeper's post office. I-44, E 6 m.; SR F, N 1.4 m. BEAR CREEK *STATE FOREST.*

1. Siouan, reportedly meaning female captive, e.g. 1855 Witoka, Minn., named for a Sioux woman.
2. Origin unknown.
3. Antebellum merchant Rufus Phillips; p.o. Phillipsburg(h) 1871–now.

LEE'S SUMMIT
Population: 46,418   Map C-4

Established in 1865 by William B. Howard as Strother[1] near the surveyed grade of the Pacific *Railroad,* the town was platted in 1868 as Lee's Summit when

Howard donated every other lot to the railroad in exchange for a depot *(Lebanon).* Its namesake is disputed; some sources claim Confederate general Robert E. Lee and others claim Dr. Pleasant Lea, a local physician whose name was supposedly misspelled. Local tradition insists the spelling error occurred when railroad officials wrote the name on the boxcar used as the first depot, but the original post office was named Lee's Summit and the area's first settlers were from Kentucky and other surrounding Southern states, which favors the general as the namesake. Summit refers to the townsite's elevation (1,046 feet), the highest on the railroad between St. Louis and Kansas City *(Gray Summit).* Founded after the Civil War *(Lone Jack),* it prospered as a shipping point. Today a suburb of *Kansas City* and Missouri's third largest city in area (64 square miles), it has some light industry and one of America's larger retirement communities, John Knox Village. Post offices: Lee's Summit 1865–1866, 1868–now; Strother 1866–1868. Home of Longview Community College.

Architecture. Downtown buildings date from the early 1900s; some residential structures date from the mid-1800s.

City Cemetery / Cole Younger. Buried here is Thomas Coleman (Cole) Younger (1844–1916), who rode with Quantrill during the early *Civil War* and in 1864 joined Confederate general Sterling Price *(Pilot Knob: Battle of Pilot Knob).* Along with his brothers *(Roscoe: John Younger Monument),* he joined the James brothers *(Kearney),* riding with them until captured after trying to rob a Northfield, Minn., bank in 1876. Released from prison in 1901, he settled in Lee's Summit, joined a church, and was a model citizen until his 1916 death. Two markers: one erected in 1916, showing his rank as captain; the other from the mid-1950s. US 50 at SR 291; SR 291, N to near 3d. *(Cemeteries; Harrisonville: Tarkington-Mockbee Home)*

Longview Farm. Multiple farm structures, 1912–1916; National Historic Register. This 2,000-acre, partially self-sufficient community (electrical plant, telephones, dairy operations, cottages for employees) was built by lumber magnate R. A. Long. His daughter, Loula Long Combs (d. 1972), was an internationally known equestrian and the only woman elected to the Madison Square Garden Hall of Fame. I-470 at SR 350; I-470, 3.5 m.; Raytown Rd., S approx. 1.5 m. to S.W. Longview Rd. (11,700 & 850).

Recreation. LAKES: Blue Springs *(Lakes: Corps of Engineers),* Jacomo *(Blue Springs),* Longview *(Lakes: Corps of Engineers).* REED *WILDLIFE AREA.*

Unity Village, Mo. Multiple structures, Italian Renaissance style; since 1889. Incorporated in 1953 as a village, this 1,400-acre community was founded in 1889 by Charles and Myrtle Fillmore as The Unity School of

Christianity, where "I am the child of God, and therefore I do not inherit sickness." Now called the Unity School for Religious Studies (with about 1,300 students), it has a large TV and radio ministry and runs one of the Midwest's largest religious publishing houses. Landscaped gardens, fountains, woods; free guided tours. Post office: none. I-470 at SR 350; SR 350, N 1 m. to Bannister/Colbern Rd.; signs. UNITY VILLAGE NATURAL BRIDGE: About 125 feet long, the bridge tapers from the lower end (12 feet high, 40 feet wide) to the upper end (8 feet high, 25 feet wide). At Unity Village (above). *(Collapsed Cave Systems)*

1. Howard's wife's maiden name; p.o. 1866–1868.

LEWIS AND CLARK EXPEDITION, 1804–1806

This historic and well-documented expedition explored the Missouri and Columbia River valleys while mapping a route from St. Louis to the Pacific Ocean. In January of 1804 president Thomas Jefferson, with the approval of Congress, authorized Meriwether Lewis *(County Profiles: Lewis)* and Capt. William Clark *(Clarksville)* to explore the American territory acquired by the 1803 *Louisiana Purchase,* specifically directing the party to find a route to the Pacific Ocean (which would also open new areas for fur trading). Lewis and Clark left St. Louis on May 14, 1804, ascending the Missouri River to the present site of Bismarck, N.D., where they wintered. Continuing along the Missouri in April 1805, the expedition reached the Columbia River and descended to within sight of the Pacific Ocean in November 1805. They returned after wintering on the coast until May 1806, arriving in St. Louis in September 1806. As a reward for their services, Lewis, the expedition leader, was appointed governor of Louisiana Territory (1807–1809) and Clark was promoted to brigadier of Missouri Militia and later appointed governor of Missouri Territory (1813–1820). (Lewis, Clark, and Jefferson grew up on neighboring plantations in Virginia.) *(Old Mines: Richwoods; Palmyra: Shannon Grave Site; Washington: Dundee)*

LEXINGTON
Population: 4,860   Map D-3

Settled mostly by Kentucky, Tennessee, and Virginia immigrants, Lexington was platted in 1822 by county commissioners James Bounds, John Duston, and James Lillard near an 1819 Missouri River ferry landing two years after the first steamboat, "The Western Engineer," ascended the river. This stock place-name, here honoring 1775 Lexington, Ky., is derived from the Revolutionary War battle at Lexington, Mass.[1] Selected county seat in 1823 of Lillard (later Lafayette) County, Missouri's Lexington replaced Mount Vernon.[2] It grew rapidly as a river port, with warehouses and docks for the storage, sale, and shipping of furs and hemp. In 1836, New Town, today's downtown, was platted as a first addition, extending and shifting the city's center west 10 blocks toward the river. With the steamboats came outfitters for the western trails *(Santa Fe Trail),* including Alexander Majors, whose 1848 freight business of six wagons grew into 3,500 wagons as the 1858 company of Russell, Majors and Waddell, which later established the Pony Express *(St. Joseph).* At the peak of the town's prosperity in 1861, the *Civil War* (Battle of Lexington, below) undercut its original economic base; after the war it reestablished itself with an economy based on coal, education, and *railroads* (St. Louis, Kansas City & Northern on the opposite bank, 1868; Lexington & St. Joseph, 1869; St. Louis, Kansas City & Wyandotte, 1877). Although a pontoon bridge was built across the river in 1889, it was too flimsy for bad weather and heavy traffic, and it was not until 1925 that today's bridge (River Bridge, below) reliably connected the town to northern Missouri. Post offices: Lexington Hill[3] 1823–1831; Lexington 1831–now. Home of Lex La-Ray Area Vo-Tech and Wentworth Military Academy (below).

Anderson House. Greek Revival, 1853; restored; National Historic Register, State Historic Site. This L-shaped two-story brick house was occupied by Federals and Confederates for use as a hospital during the Battle of Lexington (below). It still shows the battle scars from attacks by both sides. A controversy about each side's attack on it as uncivilized has been dismissed by contemporary impartial reports because occupation of this strategic site was practical and inevitable. Tours. See map; signs.

Architecture. Reflecting Lexington's enormous early prosperity are over 100 antebellum structures and four different National Historic Register districts. The majority of the structures are along Main, Franklin, and South streets, between the river and 17th St. Along US 24 to the east, between Lexington and Dover, Mo. (below), are over a dozen antebellum houses. Maps: chamber of commerce, 1127 Main (SR 13/224).

Battle of Lexington. September 18–20, 1861. Battle of Lexington State Historic Site, National Historic Register. The Federal strategy of isolating Missouri from Confederate influence *(Civil War)* required control of port towns like Lexington. Federal Col. James A. Mulligan, camped outside Jefferson City, was ordered

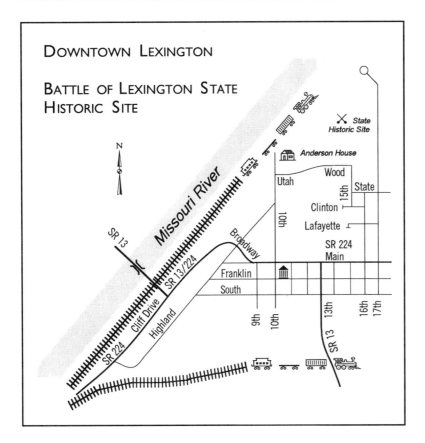

DOWNTOWN LEXINGTON

BATTLE OF LEXINGTON STATE
HISTORIC SITE

on August 30 to proceed to Lexington and hold it at all costs to keep northern Missourians from joining the Missouri state militia *(Carthage;* College Park, below). After the Confederate victory at Wilson's Creek near *Springfield,* Confederate general Sterling Price on August 25 turned toward Lexington, gathering 12,000 troops and arriving on September 12 to encounter a determined federal skirmish line. Resupplied on September 18, Price attacked Mulligan's fortified breastworks defended by about 3,600 men, including Mulligan's 23d Illinois Volunteers, parts of other regiments, and about 350 members of the Missouri Home Guard. Overwhelmed, the Federals were pushed back to interior positions, forced to abandon their water supply. The day ended with the Anderson House (above) changing hands several times and finally being secured by Confederates. On September 19, Federals still occupying the high ground returned futile rifle fire as Confederates began rolling huge hemp bales toward their positions while others covered the advance with supporting fire. Soaked with water, the bales did not catch fire and acted as movable breastworks, absorbing shots. On September 20, with Confederates within 100 yards of his defenses and with no food or water and little ammunition, Mulligan surrendered. Casualties: Confederate, 25 killed, 72 wounded; Federal, 39 killed, 120 wounded, 3,500

captured. Trenches, earthworks, maps, and guided tours. FACILITIES: Picnic area, hiking, river fishing.

Christ Episcopal Church. Gothic Revival, 1848. In continuous use, this church has some of Missouri's oldest stained-glass windows; original pews, vaulted truss ceiling arch. 13th at Franklin.

College Park. The sites of Col. James A. Mulligan's headquarters (Battle, above) and three colleges are located on a landscaped area of the river bluff. Colleges: the world's first Masonic college (1844–1859; *Palmyra: Marion City),* Marvin Female Institute (established 1871); and Central College (1828–1961). Grounds: small-scale reproduction of the 1847 Masonic College Hall that burned in 1934 and a 1797 cannon used on the frigate "Constitution" ("Old Ironsides"), which saw action in Tripoli in 1803 and in the *War of 1812.* N side; 16th, N to State.

Dover, Mo. The town was platted in 1835 by John Duston of Lexington and named for the Dover Christian Church, which was not named for the cliffs in England but for the 1832 report of the Dover Association of Virginia. This report was greatly influenced by Alexander Cambell (1788–1866), whose separation from the Baptist Church led to the founding of the Christian Church, an event that gave this stock place-name a special meaning for both sects: it marked the birth of the latter and the purification of the former. Post offices: Tabo Grove[4] 1832–1835; Dover 1835–now. US 24, E 11 m. DOVER CHRISTIAN CHURCH: Vernacular, 1848–1849. First organized in the 1820s as New Light Church and later (c. 1832) identified with the Christian Church. The one-story brick structure has a square tower and tall narrow windows.

Lafayette County Courthouse. Greek Revival, 1847–1849; additions 1854, 1886 (two-story Italianate), 1939; National Historic Register. The oldest continuously used county seat courthouse in Missouri, the main building now has storm windows and doors; the clock tower was added in 1886. The most easterly of four Ionic columns has a small cannonball embedded near the top, a dud fired during the Battle of Lexington (above). The county's third courthouse, it replaced the one in Old Town (Lexington history, above) after Lexington was incorporated in 1845. Original cost: $12,000. Grounds: bronze miniature of the Statue of Liberty. SR 13, court square. *(County Profiles)*

Lexington Historical Museum. Italianate, first floor 1840, second floor 1846; National Historic Register.

This two-story brick building with an elaborate and bracketed bell tower and octagonal cupola has served as a church, school, and library. Displays include local historical items, photographs, Pony Express memorabilia, and Civil War relics. 112 S. 13th.

Lindwood Lawn. Italianate, 1850; National Historic Register. An excellent example of its style, the 26-room two-story pink-brick house has stilted arches with elaborate window crowns, quoins, and a hip roof with bracketed eaves. Cost: $85,000. Private. S. 24th, 2.5 m. S of US 24.

Machpelah Cemetery. Established in 1849, this tree-lined cemetery with cast-iron fences contains graves of early settlers (including Gilead Rupe, the county's first settler in 1815) and Confederate soldiers. Also buried here are victims of the "Saluda" steamboat disaster; on Good Friday of 1852 possibly 200 Mormons (accounts vary) were killed when the captain of the "Saluda" ordered excessive steam pressure in an attempt to drive the boat against a stiff current. About 30 feet from shore, the ship exploded, blowing pieces of passengers over the river and banks; there were few survivors. S side; 20th at Jefferson. *(Cemeteries)*

Napoleon, Waterloo, Wellington, Mo. These towns, set close together in a row, have no oral or recorded explanation for their ironic grouping except for the latecomer Waterloo, whose founder reportedly said, "Napoleon and Wellington are both dead, but Waterloo still flourishes"—a premature metaphor comparing his town to the battle site and the others to the two dead men. Except for Waterloo the towns were established along a major east–west road and grew as river landings until the river shifted *(Camden)*. All three were shipping points on the Missouri-Pacific *Railroad*. NAPOLEON: Originally called Poston's Landing,[5] the town was platted in 1836 as Napoleon, then abandoned during the financial panic of 1837; it was platted again in 1857 as Lisbon,[6] changing names to Napoleon c. 1869. Post offices: Napoleon City 1858–1861; Lisbon 1861–1863, 1865–1869; Napoleon 1869–now. US 24, W 11 m. WATERLOO: Platted in 1905 along the tracks of the Missouri-Pacific *Railroad*, the town was overshadowed by its two neighbors and rapidly declined. Post office: 1877–1909 *(Kahoka: Waterloo)*. US 24 W 9 m. WELLINGTON: Platted in 1837 near Pleasant Grove[7] as Wellington, possibly as a counterpoint to its neighbor Napoleon, this was a mill town. Post offices: Pleasant Grove 1831–1840, defunct; Wellington 1840–now. US 24, W 6 m.

Old Town. The original center of town. Street names have been changed, but the 1822 plat shape is the same. Bounded by Main, 23d, Monroe, and 24th. Marker at the former courthouse square; S side between 23d and 24th.

Pioneer Mother Monument ("Madonna of the Trail"). DAR Statue, 1928. Designed by Fredrick Hibbard to commemorate the women who helped settle the West, this 18-foot-tall cast-stone statue depicts a woman wearing boots, a long dress, and a bonnet and holding a child. Similar ones were erected along the National Old Trails Road; this one was dedicated by then county judge Harry S. Truman *(Independence)*. SR 13, W at river (Highland and Broadway).

River Bridge. Truss, 1925. Bright blue-green, about a half-mile long and dramatically situated, the bridge is more impressive than the river it crosses. Cost: $1,246,000. SR 13.

Wentworth Military Academy. Multiple structures; Headquarters, Italianate; National Historic Register; founded 1880. Classes range from seventh grade through junior college. ROTC graduates are eligible for commissions as army second lieutenants. Some historic buildings, a Vietnam War monument with a mounted HU-1E helicopter, a nature trail named for Wentworth graduate Marlin Perkins, full-dress parades on Sundays. N side; 18th and Washington.

1. Named in 1713 for Laxton, England, probably an alternate spelling of Lord Lexington (1661–1723).
2. For George Washington's home; about 0.5 m. E of Tabo Creek on the river bluff; p.o. 1820–c. 1823; defunct.
3. Location; the name Lexington was denied due to another in Boone County.
4. Via the creek, Americanized from French for either Francis Thibaut/Tableau or C. B. Thibeault.
5. J. A. Poston; no p.o.
6. Capital of Portugal; exotic name, e.g. *La Plata*.
7. Commendatory location; p.o. 1831–1840.

LIBERAL
Population: 684   Map C-6

Platted in 1880 by G. H. Wasler (1834–1910), a disciple of prominent agnostic humanistic rationalist Robert G. Ingersoll (1833–1899), Liberal, a *utopian society*, was named for Ingersoll's Gospel of Humanity, wherein happiness is the only good and the only way to be happy is to make others happy. The ideal was to judge others as people, not by religious or political beliefs, which had the effect of drawing agnostics, deists, and spiritualists to the community. The c. 1883 intersection of two *railroads* (the Kansas City, Ft. Scott & Gulf and a branch of the Missouri-Pacific) precipitated the simultaneous platting in 1884 of two towns named Dension[1] (North and South) at either side of Liberal (today, the north and south sides of town). A few years later their depot was designated Pedro[2] by the railroads, and they were noted as "growing and enterprising Christian communities." Liberal was incorporated in

1884, and the two Densions were incorporated with Liberal in 1894, assuming its name. Veering steadily toward spiritualism, Wasler's influence waned after a séance c. 1887 was exposed as a fake. The town became remarkably less liberal after his 1910 death but continued to prosper as a shipping point. Post offices: Liberal 1880– now; Denison 1885–1886; Pedro 1886–1900.

Natural Areas. The following natural areas (and Prairie *State Park,* below) are remnants of Missouri's presettlement tallgrass *prairies.* EAST DRYWOOD CREEK: 50 acres. One mile of high-quality prairie headwater stream with rock-bottom riffles, deep pools, and scenic sandstone ledges. Fauna includes those of Tzi-Sho (below) plus the Mississippi kite and yellow-headed blackbird. In Prairie *State Park* (below). HUNKAH PRAIRIE: 160 acres. Similar to Tzi-Sho (below) but flat. Rt. 2, Box 93, Lockwood 65682. W of Tzi-Sho, 0.5 m. REGAL PRAIRIE: 240 acres. Part of Prairie *State Park* (below). Features fauna similar to that in the other areas, with the addition of scissor-tail flycatcher, burrowing crayfish, bull snake, and regal fritillary butterfly. W of Tzi-Sho, 1.5 m. TZI-SHO PRAIRIE: 240 acres. Sandy and silt loam soils; habitat for northern harriers, short-eared owls, upland sandpipers, prairie chickens, and Henslow's sparrows. All except Hunkah: Box 97, Liberal 64762. SR NN, S 5.1 m.; GR, W 0.4 m.

Recreation. BUSHWHACKER *WILDLIFE AREA.* PRAIRIE *STATE PARK:* SR K, W 2 m.; SR P, S and W 2.1 m.

---

1. Probably for Denison, Tex., a regular destination shipping point.
2. Origin unknown.

LIBERTY
Population: 20,459
Maps C-3 and Kansas City Area

Liberty was platted in 1822 at an artesian spring on land donated by Charles McGee and the area's first (1819) settler, John Owen, as the county seat of recently organized Clay County. The town's name, derived from the American ideal, was also given to its Missouri River port four miles south, Liberty Landing (below). Liberty's location north of the Missouri River and at the western edge of a new nation left it virtually an outpost until after the 1837 *Platte Purchase,* when it served as a supply outlet for towns and communities resulting from the newly acquired territory. Despite the turmoil of the 1830s to the 1860s—the *Black Hawk War,* Mormon War, *Mexican War,* California gold rush, *Kansas Border War, Civil War* (William Jewell College,

below), guerrilla raids, and postwar outlaws (Jesse James Bank Museum, below)—Liberty continued to grow. The arrival of the Kansas City & Cameron *Railroad* c. 1867 helped secure the town's economic future, which was based on agriculture and politics. Today it has some light industry and is part of the Kansas City metropolitan area. Post offices: Clay Court House 1822–1829; Liberty 1829–now. Home of William Jewell College (below).

Architecture. Good examples of 19th-century styles, with the highest concentrations along Franklin and the square.

Clay County Courthouse. Art Deco affinities, 1935–1936; 1970s addition. Although restrained, the geometric friezes around the top of the original 117-by-87-foot white limestone building and the vertical emphasis of its stairs, windows, doors, and structural design suggest the Art Deco style. This is the county's third courthouse; its predecessor (1857–1934) was razed as obsolete. Original cost: $263,410 (partially funded by a $75,000 *WPA* grant; reportedly Missouri's first project of the kind). I-35; SR 152, E 2 m. to square. (*County Profiles*)

Clay County Museum. Vernacular, 1865; remodeled Italianate-style facade, 1877. Built as a drugstore and doctor's office, the museum's exhibits include patent medicines, herbs, a doctor's office (occupied by only two doctors, 1865–1963), furnished rooms, clothing, china, Indian artifacts, guns, toys, and dolls. I-35; SR 152, E 2 m. to square to N. Main (14).

Jesse James Bank Museum. Vernacular, Greek Revival affinities, 1858; restored, addition. The robbery of the Clay County Savings Association on February 13, 1866, reportedly the world's first successful daylight bank robbery during peacetime, is attributed to a 12-member gang, including Jesse James (*Kearney*). A Jewell College student was killed and about $60,000 was taken. Restored bank office, vault, photographs, historical items. I-35; SR 152, E 2 m. at square.

LDS Visitor Center / Liberty Jail. Reconstructed in 1963 inside the Church of Jesus Christ of Latter-Day Saints visitor center is the Clay County jail (1833–1856) where LDS prophet Joseph Smith and five other church leaders were held during the winter of 1838–1839 while 12,000 to 15,000 church members were forced to leave the state (*Mormons*). Also available are exhibits and audiovisual presentations about the events, church history, and LDS doctrine and a replica of the plates, later published as the "Book of Mormon," translated by Smith from "writings of ancient prophets who lived on the American continents." I-35; SR 152, E 2 m. to square to N. Main (216). (*Independence*)

Liberty Landing, Mo. Established in 1830 by Shubael

Allen as a port for Liberty, it initially prospered as a shipping point for interior towns. Liberty Landing was first known as Allen's Landing; the name was changed to Baxter's Landing[1] in the early 1850s, then to Liberty Landing, although it was known briefly c. 1865 as Arthurton.[2] The port's importance declined with the arrival of the railroad after the Civil War. Post office: 1871–1873. At the river; private; inquire locally. U.S. ARSENAL: Isolated and insecure because of bitter disputes with Indian nations (*Black Hawk War*), Clay County residents petitioned the federal government for an arsenal, which was built at Liberty Landing in 1837. Comprising 12 buildings, it remained active until 1869 and was captured by *Civil War* pro-Southern forces in 1861. Defunct; inquire locally.

Lightburne Hall. Greek Revival, 1852. Home of a prominent hemp farmer, the two-story brick 26-room mansion is furnished with 19th-century antiques; orchards, tours. I-35; SR 152, E 2 m. to square to N on Water (301).

M. L. Thompson Nature Sanctuary. 100 acres. This habitat for over 600 species of plants and 160 species of birds also features a hardwood forest, meadow, limestone glen, marsh, pond, creek, restored *prairie*, and a trail system that includes an abandoned 1920 interurban railroad line. Visitor center, exhibits. Adjacent to Rush Creek Natural History Area. SR 33 at SR 152; Kansas, E to Jewell, S to Richfield, E to 407 N. LaFrenz.

Missouri City, Mo. Shrewbury Williams established Williams' Landing in 1834. It was later called Richfield[3] and in the 1840s was joined by adjacent towns St. Bernard[4] and Atchison.[5] The three towns incorporated in 1859 as Missouri City. Post offices: St. Bernard 1853–1857; Missouri City 1867–now. SR 210, E 6 m. COOLEY LAKE / *WILDLIFE AREA.*

Ole Bill's Museum. This 30-year collection of 16th-to-20th-century Americana claims to include 20,000 items. 801 SR 291N.

William Jewell College / Civil War. Founded in 1849, this liberal arts college has an enrollment of about 2,000. JEWELL HALL: Greek Revival, 1850–1858; National Historic Register. After a skirmish at nearby Blue Mill Ferry (September 16, 1861; historical marker), Union troops retreated here, digging trenches and using the building as a hospital and stables. Like many Missouri towns settled mostly by southerners, Liberty suffered more from pro-South guerrilla raids on Federals than from military engagements. Ill feelings continued long after the war, and reportedly the courthouse here did not fly the Stars and Stripes until 1912. SR 291 at SR 33; SR 33 N to E. Franklin at N. Jewell.

1. Stephen Baxter, landowner.
2. Michael Arthur, hemp manufacturer.
3. Usually in honor of good soil; p.o. 1836–1837.

4. Probably the influential 12th-century monk who vastly expanded the Cistercian Order and organized the Order of Templars, knights who fought in the Crusades.
5. *County Profiles: Atchison;* no p.o.

LICKING

Population: 1,328   Map G-6

Settled in 1826 near a salt lick, the site was known locally as Buffalo Lick or The Lick. After a community formed c. 1831, it was later listed as Lick Settlement and then Licking, the name used when the town was platted in 1857.[1] Like nearby *Houston,* this town suffered during the *Civil War* and recovered slowly. Today's economy depends on some light manufacturing. Post office: 1844–1845, 1847–1863, 1866–now.

Contorted Sandstone. The sharp folds, deep dips, and slumping of this reddish brown sandstone mixed with chert and clays are not the result of geological mountain-building. As in most karst areas (*Collapsed Cave Systems*), dissolving limestone left insoluble material at the whim of gravity. US 63, N; intermittently beside the road for 6 m. (best examples: 0.9 m. N and 0.3 m. S of SR CC).

Montauk State Park. SR 137, S 2 m.; SR VV, E 9.8 m. to Montauk.[2] (*State Parks*)

Natural Arches. PADDY CREEK ARCH / CAMPGROUND / PICNIC AREA (*National Forests*): Houston. From Slabtown Arch (below): SR AF (changes to GR after bridge), W approx. 4.2 m.; GR, S approx. 2.2 m. SLABTOWN NATURAL ARCH: Set 200 feet above the base of a limestone bluff, 15 feet long and averaging 8 feet wide, the arch spans a deep ravine. Green lichen, pine, and juniper cling to the rocks above it. It can be viewed from the east bank of Big Piney River by following the bank and a footpath along the bluff; to reach it, cross the river and climb the ravine. SR 32, W 3.9 m.; SR N, W 2.2 m.; SR AF, W 5.8 m.; fishing access road, W 0.2 m. (*Collapsed Cave Systems*)

Quercus Flatwoods Natural Area. 48 acres. Part of the White *State Forest* Nursery. Features old-growth post, black, and blackjack oak (the dominant post oaks average more than 200 years old). Rt. 2, Licking 65542. Old US 63, N approx. 0.7 to nursery; GR from nursery, N approx. 3.5 m.

Recreation. BIG PINEY TRAIL CAMP (*National Forests*): Camping, picnics, tables, fireplaces, toilets, stock watering pond, hitching post. *FLOAT STREAM:* Big Piney River. PADDY CREEK CAMPGROUND / PICNIC AREA: Natural Arches, above; *Houston.* SLABTOWN PICNIC AREA (*National Forests*): Pit toilets, tables, fireplaces, Slabtown Bluff Trail, Big Piney River fishing and access. *TRAILS:* Big Piney, Paddy Creek,

Slabtown Bluff. WHITE *STATE FOREST* NURSERY.
Reis Winery. Established 1978. Located at 1,350 feet, it produces 30 varieties of French hybrid and American grapes. Tasting room, picnic area, views. US 63, N 6 m.; SR CC, E 4 m.; just W of Maples.[3]

1. "Licking" is a participle normally used in place-names as an adjective to modify a particular place or thing, e.g. Kentucky's Licking River. Evidently, in the case of Licking, Mo., the name developed from "where the buffalo lick" (Buffalo Lick).
2. Algonquian meaning Fort-at, e.g. Montauk point at the extreme eastern end of Long Island in N.Y.; p.o. 1844–1974.
3. J. J. Maples, postmaster/merchant; p.o. 1891–1901, 1903–1967.

LINCOLN HILLS AREA

Between US 61 and SR 79, from *Troy* to *Hannibal*, this broken hilly area's rocks are folded in an arch trending toward the northwest and ranging in age from 440 million to 235 million years old. Mostly bypassed by the last ice age *(Glacial Erratics),* the hills retained their original flora, thereby botanically corresponding with the Ozarks south of the Missouri River.

LINN
Population: 1,148   Map G-4

Platted in 1843 as county seat of recently organized Osage County, the town was briefly called Lin(n)ville until the name was shortened, supposedly to specify its namesake as Lewis F. Linn, U.S. senator from 1833 to 1843, and thereby eliminate the assumption of the more commonplace derivation, the linden tree. Before its selection as seat of justice, courts were held in houses at nearby locations, including Loose Creek (below) and Van Buren,[1] both of which were considered for selection as county seat. Landlocked and bypassed by railroads, Linn developed an economy based on county politics. The name of today's local paper, "The Unterrified Democrat," established in 1866, typifies post–Civil War attitudes: the editor declared his paper would remain Democratic despite threats provoked by his politics. Post office: 1844–now. Home of Linn Technical College.
Architecture. NEARBY (unmarked roads; inquire locally): David Mantle House (Weatherboard Log, 1865), 5 m. NE; Flora School (Weatherboard Log, 1867–1868), 6 m. NE at Flora.[2] TOWN: Good examples of 19th-century styles.
Ben Branch Lake. 44 acres. Fishing, hunting.
Hope, Mo. The community of Boerger's Store grew around Simon Boerger's 1859 store (p.o., below) and

was named Hope for unknown reasons. Post offices: Boerger's Store 1871–1897; Boergers 1897; Hope 1897–1974. US 50, E 7 m.; SR N, N 6.3 m. FREDRICKSBURG FERRY: SR N, N 5.6 m.; SR J, W 2.1 m. *(Ferryboats).* SALEM-HOPE UNITED PRESBYTERIAN CHURCH: Vernacular, 1860; frame. Services were conducted in German from 1908 to 1935; *cemetery* adjacent. SR N, N 0.3 m.; SR KK, E 0.5 m.; GR, N (and E past N junction) 0.5 m. SIMON BOERGER STORE: Vernacular, 1859; stone with a 1930 addition. The town's original store. In town. STONY POINT CHURCH: Log, 1857. Originally deeded to Methodist Episcopal Church, later for all denominations. Vacant, private, *cemetery* adjacent. SR N, S 5.8 m. near junction with GR.
Loose Creek, Mo. In 1841 the first Osage County court meet at Thomas Robinson's house (below). August Pickineaud bought the future townsite in 1843. Named for the nearby creek, it is a corruption of the French L'Ourse Creek, or Bear Creek. Post office: 1849–now. US 50, W 6 m. ROBINSON'S HOUSE: Weatherboard Log, 1841. The first county court was held here on January 20, 1841; private.
Natural Tunnel / Waterfall. Crossed by a county road, the tunnel, 190 feet long and about 7 feet high, is a result of *stream piracy*. The waterfall, close to the road at the west end, has about a 30-foot vertical fall flanked by steep walls and junipers. SR U, S 3.2 m.; SR DD, W approx. 1 m.; GR, N approx. 0.4 m.
Osage County Courthouse. Italian Renaissance, 1923–1925. The county's third permanent one, this three-story brick courthouse features a different window treatment on each floor, a balustraded and full-height projecting central entry, second-story arched windows, a pseudo-roofline parapet (with a lighter-colored belt course), and paired square brick columns with stylized Corinthian capitals. Although it departs from the mainstream of its style, the hallmarks are kept intact. Architect H. H. Hohenschild designed a similarly esoteric adaptation for Pulaski County. Cost: $85,000. Downtown. *(County Profiles)*

1. *Van Buren;* p.o. Goodman's Mills, for the mill owner, 1849–1850; defunct.
2. Origin unknown, usually personal or for rich vegetation; p.o. 1881–1898; defunct.

LINN CREEK
Population: 232   Map E-5

One of Missouri's newer towns, its history features change. In 1843, the county court changed Kinderhook County's 1841 name to Camden County, selecting the

The junction of the Osage and Niangua Rivers at Old Linn Creek.

c. 1838 Osage River community of Oregon[1] as county seat; its name was changed in 1843 to Erie[2] for no recorded reason. By 1845 the majority of Osage River traffic had been attracted to a nearby c. 1837 settlement at the mouth of Linn Creek where a town by that name was platted in 1845 and named via the creek for the basswood or linden tree (also known as linn, bee tree, or whittlewood). An 1845 court-approved petition to relocate the county seat to Linn Creek was delayed due to protests from outlying areas, and it was not until after an 1854 cholera epidemic at Erie that the seat of justice was moved in 1855 to Linn Creek. On February 4, 1931, the county court adjourned at Linn Creek and workmen began to raze the town, making way for the impoundment of the Lake of the Ozarks by Bagnell Dam (*Camdenton*). The court later reconvened at the new county seat of Camdenton, but some former Linn Creek residents moved three miles south up the creek (with some structures) to the town of Estherville,[3] which had been platted in 1930 and was renamed Linn Creek (Old Linn Creek, below). As in *Forsyth* and *Greenville*, the emotions and litigation involved in condemning the former Linn Creek for the hydroelectric project were poignant and complex (a U.S. Supreme Court decision finally settled the legal issue). Ironically, water is again threatening today's Linn Creek. Several miles downstream, a gravel company dug a 15-foot hole in the creek, and the water is trying to seek that level, resulting in decay of the creek banks that has toppled nine homes and two buildings. Post offices: Erie 1843–1854; Linn Creek 1844–now.

Camden County Museum. Exhibits include a c. 1900 schoolroom, an 1853 post office, weaving demonstrations, a blacksmith's shop, period furniture, historical photographs, information on Ha Ha Tonka (*State Parks*), and vehicles such as a surrey. SR V, W.

Coakley Hollow Fen Natural Area. 4 acres. Features a swampy spring-fed meadow and boglike seeps that are sites for northern glacial relics like Riddell's goldenrod; trail, boardwalk. Lake of the Ozarks *State Park*, Kaiser 65047. US 54, E 1.3 m., SR A, E 7 m. to Freedom (Passover, below); inquire locally.

Indian Burial Cave. Reportedly, prehistoric Indians were buried here; includes a boat tour of an underground lake. In town.

Old Linn Creek, Mo. When forced to leave, residents had three options: leave the area altogether, resettle in *Camdenton*, or try to relocate the town. Enough houses and businesses relocated uphill, above the lake level, to form this small lakeside community. Others moved to the town of Estherville (Linn Creek history, above), renaming it Linn Creek. US 54, N 2.9 m.; SR Y, 2.2 m.; GR, S 1.1 m.

Osage Beach, Mo. Platted in 1928 as one of the first real estate developments surveyed when the Bagnell Dam project was proposed (*Camdenton*), the town was named for promotional purposes, combining the name of the Indian nation (*County Profiles: Osage*) with an attraction, a man-made beach. It is now one of the largest tourist towns at the Lake of the Ozarks. Post offices: Zebra[4] 1886–1935; Osage Beach 1935–now. US 54, N 9 m. RECREATION: Among many tourist-oriented attractions are the Lake of the Ozarks (*Camdenton: Bagnell Dam*) and Lake of the Ozarks *State Park*; both adjacent.

Ozark Caverns. Features handheld lanterns, tours by state park naturalists, and Angel's Shower, a stream of water flowing from stalactites. Visitor center, nature trails, picnic facilities. US 54, E 1.3 m., SR A, E approx. 8 m.

Passover, Mo. The town was most likely not named for the Jewish feast but by corrupting a family name like Passaeur. Post office: 1901–1931. US 54, E 1.3 m., SR A, E 7 m. to Freedom;[5] GR, N approx. 3.2 m. SCHOOLHOUSE: Log, c. 1887; restored. This one-room log school, in use until 1940, predates the post office. In town.

Recreation. LAKE OF THE OZARKS: Adjacent. LAKE OF THE OZARKS *STATE PARK:* Osage Beach, above.

Woodland Scenics, Inc. For model-train enthusiasts

worldwide, this small company manufactures and ships miniature buildings and landscapes. In town.

1. For Oregon country, a popular western expansion destination; a disputed and complicated place-name *(Oregon)*. Post office: none; derelict.

2. A tribal Indian name first applied by the French to one of the Great Lakes; a stock place-name.

3. Origin unknown; no p.o.

4. According to R. L. Ramsey, possibly a corruption of the personal name Zieberer; or for colorful stripes on cliffs facing the creek.

5. Stock name, the ideal; no p.o.

LINNEUS
Population: 364   Map E-2

Platted in 1839 as county seat of newly organized Linn County on a 50-acre site donated in 1839 by first townsite settler John Holland, the town was originally named Linnville, honoring the county namesake. In 1840 the name was changed to Linneus due to an existing Linnville in Jefferson County, a choice influenced by local attorney John U. Parsons, who meant to honor Swedish botanist Carl Linnaeus, called the father of modern systematic botany, but a clerk misspelled the name. An 1857 legislative act corrected the spelling, but tradition has preserved the name as Linneus. The town grew slowly as a political and trading center aided by the c. 1872 arrival of the Linneus Branch of the Burlington & Southwestern *Railroad*. Post offices: Locust Creek[1] 1838–1840; Linneus 1840–now.

Historical Jail Museum. Vernacular, 1869; renovated and expanded in 1935 by the *WPA*. Local historical items. Across from the courthouse.

Linn County Courthouse. Italian Renaissance, 1913–1914. This is the county's third courthouse; the second, expensively repaired beginning in 1857, was partially abandoned in 1879. Today's three-story gray-brick 55-by-80-foot building, while severe, has most of its style's main characteristics: a belt course, balustrades, a rusticated first level, a projecting central entry, and a second-story porch with pilasters and an arched window. Cost: $60,000. Downtown. *(County Profiles)*

Nearby Attractions. *Laclede:* SR 5, S 6 m.

1. The area was known as Locust Creek Country after nearby locust-lined Locust Creek; also the township's name.

LOCKS AND DAMS

Construction of locks and dams was a result of the U.S. Corps of Engineers' 1824 mission to clear snags and sandbars from the Ohio and Mississippi Rivers. U.S.

waterborne commerce totals over 2 billion tons annually, with fuel-related commodities (petroleum, coal, coke) accounting for 68 percent. As directed by 1930 congressional legislation (the Nine-Foot Channel Navigation Project), the Upper Mississippi River is maintained at a minimum depth of 9 feet and width of 400 feet by 29 locks and dams from Minneapolis, Minn., to St. Louis, after which it is free-flowing (ocean-going vessels can sail as far north as Baton Rouge, La.). The Missouri River has no locks or dams and is navigable from St. Louis to Sioux City, Iowa. The water level inside a lock can be raised or lowered to allow boats to move up- or downstream in a stairstep fashion. Although the breaking up and reforming of tow barges at locks appears to be inefficient, one barge can carry the equivalent of 15 railroad cars or 58 trucks. The following locks and dams are on Missouri's section of the Mississippi (some access only via Illinois). (Lock and dam #23, part of the master plan, was deleted, leaving a break in the sequence.)

Lock and Dam #20. *Canton.*
Lock and Dam #21. *Palmyra: West Quincy.*
Lock and Dam #22. *Saverton.*
Lock and Dam #24. *Clarksville.*
Lock and Dam #25. *Troy: Winfield.*
Lock and Dam #26. *St. Charles: Portage Des Sioux.* Also known as Melvin Price Lock and Dam.
Lock and Dam #27. *St. Louis: Chain of Rocks.*

LOESS

These buff-to-yellowish-brown unstratified deposits of loam range in consistency from clay to sand. Believed to be mainly deposited by wind, loess (pronounced lo'ess) in Missouri tends to stand in vertical bluffs that were created between and after glaciation *(Glacial Erratics)*. It is chiefly calcareous and usually contains shells, bones, teeth of mammals, calcium carbonate, and iron oxide. When mixed with water (rain), it makes an excellent soil. With exceptions like *Crowley's Ridge* and the Pinnacles at Van Meter *State Park*, this topography is most prominent in the northwest along the east side of the Missouri River where the westerly winds blew off the floodplains.

LONE JACK
Population: 392   Map D-4

The town was platted in 1841 along a main north–south road and named, like its previously established post office, for the area and its landmark, a solitary blackjack oak tree. Because Lone Jack is landlocked and bypassed by railroads, its rural-based economy and population have changed little since the 1860s. Post office: 1839–1902, 1904–now (minor lapses 1894, 1966).

Battle of Lone Jack. August 16, 1862. This fiercely fought five-hour battle included hand-to-hand combat and was the result of Confederate Upton Hayes's August 11 capture of the Federal garrison at Independence and his subsequent search for recruits as reinforcements. Federal Maj. Emory Forest attempted but failed to deny Hayes further support. The sides sustained about 110 casualties each.

Civil War Museum. The museum features an electronic map, diorama, and exhibits explaining the Battle of Lone Jack and other area engagements. The adjacent *cemetery* has a mass grave of Confederates marked by a 26-foot shaft and a former mass grave for Federals (they were exhumed in 1867 and reburied at Leavenworth, Kans.) marked by an 8-foot pillar of concrete blocks built c. 1917. At the battlefield; US 50, S 0.3 m. on SR E to SR 150.

Lone Jack Wildlife Area. *Wildlife Areas.*

LOUISIANA

Population: 3,967   Map H-3

While the area was settled earlier (Buffalo Fort, below), the townsite was settled in 1816 just north of Noix Creek and south of Salt River at the Mississippi. One of Missouri's older towns, it was platted in 1818 and selected county seat of newly organized Pike County in 1819. Its name is popularly acknowledged as honoring Louisiana Bayse, reportedly the first child born in St. Louis after (and named for) the *Louisiana Purchase.* Her father, J. W. Bayse, who later helped establish *Bowling Green,* moved his family here in 1818 when his daughter was 14 years old. Whether this story is accurate or the intended namesake was the Louisiana Purchase, the derivation is from Louisiane, the name given in 1682 by La Salle to the New World territory he claimed for King Louis XIV. The Spanish changed the name to Luisiana, and Americans mixed them together as Louisiana. The town lost the seat of justice to *Bowling Green* in 1822 but continued to prosper from river trade and then from the *railroads* with the c. 1871 arrival of the Clarksville & Western and from interstate trucking with the completion of the Mississippi River bridge in 1928. Today its economy is based on large companies, including the historic Stark Bros. Nurseries (below). Post office: 1820–now.

Architecture. DOWNTOWN: This is a substantial river town of brick homes and buildings, with good examples of 19th-century architecture. NATIONAL HISTORIC DISTRICT: Along Georgia between Main and 7th.

Buffalo Fort / Cemetery. Near old Buffalo Cemetery is a granite boulder designating the site of this 1811–1815 fort used to defend early settlers, especially during the *War of 1812,* from Sauk and Fox Indians allied with the British. Robert Jordon and his sons, farming close to the fort, were killed in 1813 by Indians and were later buried where they fell, which became the site of the cemetery. US 79, S 1 m.; SR D, S 1.5 m.; GR, W 1.2 m. *(Cemeteries)*

Dover Baptist Church. Vernacular, c. 1863–1866. The one-story frame building has two front entrances that divide the congregation by sex, with corresponding seating in the one-room sanctuary *(Lexington: Dover).* US 79, S 1 m.; SR D, S 7.8 m. to SR N at Calumet.[1]

Natural Areas. BUR-REED SLOUGH: 20 acres. Part of the Shanks *Wildlife Area.* Features a natural marsh that supports giant bur reed, great bulrush, associated marsh plants, and a variety of birds. Access: wildlife headquarters at Ashburn. DUPONT UPLAND FOREST: 80 acres. Part of DuPont Reservation *Wildlife Area.* Features a mixed upland hardwood forest known for its fall colors (basswood, oaks, and sugar maple) and a small limestone glade with springtime flora. Located along the Mississippi. Access: scenic overlook road. OVAL LAKE: 20 acres. Part of Shanks *Wildlife Area.* Features a five-acre floodplain pond unchanged since 1816 that is surrounded by a marsh and bottomland forest; supports typical marsh plants and wildlife. Access: wildlife headquarters at Ashburn. All: Box 13, Ashburn 63433. SR 79, N 14 m. to Ashburn.[2]

Phillips Museum. Barn, 1917. Indian artifacts, animal-horn collection, toys, dolls. Inquire locally.

Riverfront Walk / Park. Benches and a walkway with a low stone wall along the river. E end of Georgia near the railroad depot at the river.

Riverview Cemetery / Lincoln Hills. Set on a high bluff, the cemetery gives a broad view of the Mississippi River and, to the south and west, an excellent view of the *Lincoln Hills* area. N side; US 79; signs. *(Cemeteries)*

Stark Cabin / Nurseries. Log, c. 1830; restored. Built by nursery founder James Stark, the two-room cabin was moved here in 1951 from the nursery's original 1817 site (SR NN, S 2.5 m.). Owned today by the sixth generation of Starks, the nursery is Missouri's oldest and one of America's oldest and largest nurseries, providing fruit trees and ornamental plants. Reportedly, it was begun from the contents of Stark's saddlebags. Cabin displays: memorabilia of Luther Burbank

(1849–1926), from whom the nursery inherited its plant breeding program. US 54, W 1 m. *(Newtonia: Stark City)*

Wildlife Areas. DuPont Reservation, Shanks. *(Wildlife Areas)*

1. From the nearby creek; French for the ceremonial Indian pipe used in counsel; p.o. 1872–1907.
2. Origin unknown; p.o. 1857–now.

 # LOUISIANA PURCHASE

French territory until 1763, most of the land included in this purchase changed hands three times during the next 53 years: it was ceded in 1763 to Spain by the Treaty of Paris ending the French and Indian War, returned in 1800 to France as required by Napoleon's Treaty of San Ildefonso, then sold to America on April 30, 1803, by France during a brief May 1802–May 1803 truce with Great Britain during the Napoleonic War *(War of 1812)*. The price for these approximately 565,166,080 acres was $15 million, or about three cents an acre. Formal transfer of the property took place at St. Louis on March 9, 1804. Initially, President Thomas Jefferson only knew that Napoleon was badly in need of money to finance military campaigns and that it was in America's best interest to secure the Mississippi River for shipping. Jefferson's envoys at Paris, R. L. Livingston and James Monroe (U.S. president from 1817 to 1825), while attempting to buy New Orleans and West Florida as directed, were surprised when Napoleon offered all of Louisiana. Napoleon privately reasoned that (1) the British might take the land anyway, (2) he needed money, and (3) strengthening America would weaken the British. Exceeding their instructions, Livingston and Monroe bought this vast uncharted wilderness, a virtual pig in a poke. Although we now know it includes land ranging from the Mississippi River to the Pacific Ocean, ten years after the purchase no survey had been made of even the limited areas explored by *Lewis and Clark* and by Zebulon Pike. Moreover, it was not until 1818 and 1819 that Great Britain and Spain, respectively, signed treaties assigning America title to all the land defined by the purchase. For Missouri, as for the other states created by this purchase, the subsequent legal process of validating land titles, especially the Spanish land grants, was a serious problem *(Cape Girardeau; Jefferson City)*. Regardless, the Louisiana Purchase was the single most important territorial acquisition in American history, securing free navigation of the Mississippi River and access to the Caribbean, eliminating the

LOUISIANA PURCHASE 1803

Missouri R. / Mississippi R. / Arkansas R.

French as competitors in North America, acquiring the land for the majority of today's west-central states, and joining both coasts under one united government.

 # MCKITTRICK

Population: 66   Map G-4

Records for this town are sketchy. McKittrick's 1897 plat (filed in 1971) reads "platted as Loutre," but no records show a plat for any town named Loutre (Loutre Island, below). An 1894 post office was established at the Missouri, Kansas & Texas *Railroad* and named McKittrick for the 1893 railroad station, which was reportedly named for a "drummer" at the mercantile store. The community probably changed names from Loutre to McKittrick after it was platted to conform to *post office* regulations. A water and coal station for the railroad, the town prospered until modern highways changed freighting routes. The depot was closed in 1958. Post office: 1894–1967. Note: a nearby Loutre post office was established in 1902 and closed in 1904. *(Boonslick Trails)*

Architecture. NEARBY: Several antebellum houses about a mile east. TOWN: Two 19th-century two-story derelict brick buildings; at the highway.

Loutre Island, Mo. This area post office wandered between Montgomery and Warren Counties and was probably the namesake of a community preceding McKittrick (McKittrick history, above), although its later township was named Loutre (French for otter). In

1807, Loutre Island was the site of the second westward expansion of the Daniel Boone settlement *(Defiance: Daniel Boone Historic Area)*. Fairly large by 1810, it was harassed by Indians, especially during the *War of 1812*, when four forts were built. In 1810 the Lindsay Carson family, including their one-year-old son, Kit, lived here *(New Franklin)*. The settlement site became an island in 1807 when Loutre Creek's channel formed a horseshoe bend at today's SR 94, isolating this land. Post offices: 1818–1852, 1864–1894 (in Montgomery County), 1852–1864 (in Warren County), removed 1894 to McKittrick. SR 94, S to river, about 6 m. (from just W of McKittrick to 5.7 m. E); the settlements were south of today's Bridgeport (Old Brick Church, below) and Case.[1]

Old Brick Church. Vernacular, Greek Revival affinities, 1841. Built in 1836 by the M. E. Loutre Island Church, the building's distinctive red brick is due to the local clay (fired here on the grounds), and the foundation rocks came from a nearby hill. Two front doors divided the congregation by sex, with corresponding sanctuary seating. SR 94, E 2.9 m.; Daniel Boone *State Forest* road, N 0.6 m. to just S of Bridgeport.[2]

Recreation. DANIEL BOONE *STATE FOREST*. KATY TRAIL *STATE PARK:* In town.

St. Peter Pinnacle. Composed of St. Peter sandstone, its many fissures and impressive bulk (about 50 yards in diameter, 30–75 feet high) make this unusually shaped pinnacle interesting. SR 94, E 5 m.; junction SR B, E 0.15 m. on SR 94 (S side).

---

1. Origin unknown, possible corruption of 1850 store owner Joseph Kosse; p.o. Bridgeport (below); Case 1893–1946.
2. Origin unknown; there was no town of that name, but there were a township and a landing; this popular place-name is often not associated with a bridge or port; p.o. 1833–1847, 1864–1893.

MACON
Population: 5,571   Map F-2

Macon's prosperity is directly due to the 1859 junction of two *railroads* (the North Missouri and the Hannibal & St. Joseph) and Bloomington's (below) choice of sides during the *Civil War*. Settled in 1852 by J. T. Haley, it was platted in 1856 as Macon City, honoring Macon County's namesake. In 1857, an adjacent rival town, Hudson,[1] was platted. Macon City, as a strategic northwest Missouri town during the Civil War, was occupied by Federals whose First Iowa Infantry commandeered "The Macon Register" and on June 15, 1861, published "The Whole Union," the second newspaper published by soldiers at the front *(Bloomfield; Hillsboro: De Soto)*. When the town was selected as

county seat in 1863, Macon City and Hudson incorporated, adopting the name Macon. Post offices: Macon City 1856–1892; Macon 1892–now. Home of Macon Area Vo-Tech.

Architecture. GENERAL: Good examples of 19th-century styles, particularly Victorian era. NATIONAL HISTORIC REGISTER: Wardell House (Queen Anne Free Classic, 1890), 1 Wardell Rd.

Bloomington, Mo. The townsite was settled in 1832 as Owensby Settlement by Joseph Owensby and Clemens Hutchison. In 1837 the first store was built by D. C. Garth and a Garthsville post office was established, so it was also known as Garthsville until 1838. When it was selected in 1837 as county seat of newly organized Macon County and platted in 1838, the court intended to call it *Bloomfield*, but the name was taken, so the court accepted Bloomington, an equally popular commendatory or descriptive name usually applied in admiration of nature. In its early years the community was also known as Box Ancle, Ankle, or Angle.[2] During the *Civil War*, Federal general Lewis Merill ordered Maj. Thomas Moody to burn the town because of its use as a pro-Southern rendezvous and shelter. Legend claims that Moody, a Macon County resident, proposed running for the legislature with Federal government support and, when elected, having the county seat moved to Macon City, which would effectively destroy the town without violence. His plan worked. No longer county seat and later bypassed by railroads, the town had fewer than 100 residents by 1899. Post offices: Garthsville 1837–1838; Bloomington 1838–1904. US 36, W 5 m.; SR O, N 2.6 m. COURTHOUSE MARKER: A large rock with a plaque dedicated in 1928 by the DAR commemorates the site of the county's first courthouse.

City of Maples. This nickname stems from an 1872 tax debt of $116 owed by J. W. Beaumont, who bartered 10,000 maples and elms for cash. The city gave each resident 6–10 trees to plant.

Excello, Mo. This 1869 post office community grew from an 1853 wood yard that supplied fuel for the North Missouri *Railroad*. After the railroad changed to coal fuel, a short line, Emerson Coal Switch, was built to a nearby coal mine. The community continued to grow under the name Emerson until platted in 1878 and named for its post office, Excello (Latin for I excel), whose name is assumed to be for commendatory reasons. Post office: 1869–now. US 63, S 5 m. ARDMORE, MO. / GHOST TOWN: This 1884 coal-mining camp had a boomtown population of 1,500 by 1902 after the Central Coal & Coke Company gained control of the mines. A company-store town, it adopted an early form of socialized medicine. For a monthly fee (75 cents for single men, $1.50 for families) all medical charges were covered. When the mines played out in the early 1900s, the town folded. This common American place-name probably traveled from Ardmore, Pa., which took its name from a town in Ireland. Post office: 1889–1929. SR T, W 3 m. COAL HILLS: Rounded hills covered with tall grass and seasonal sweet clover are evidence of local coal mines. Along SR Y and T.

Flywheel Museum. Most conspicuous on a steam engine, a flywheel operates to moderate fluctuations of speed in the machinery with which it revolves. This museum displays all kinds of engines, including a 1890 Bates Corlis engine with a 14-foot flywheel (with a 20-inch bore) that weighs 11 tons. Also displayed are tools, license plates from 42 states (Missouri's from 1912 to 1987), service-station items, and household objects. S side; US 63 at the fairgrounds (built by the *WPA*); signs.

Fredrick Wilhelm Blees / Academy. Romanesque affinities, 1898–1900; National Historic Register. Formerly Blees Military Academy, these buildings— massive brick with crenellated towers, ribbon windows, and arched entrances—were bought in 1912 by Still-Hildredth Sanitarium for patients suffering from nervous and mental disorders (the co-owners were sons of Dr. A. T. Still; *Kirksville);* it closed in 1968 because of the buildings' overhead. F. W. Blees was an 1881 German immigrant of a Prussian aristocratic family that was suing the legendary German industrialist Krupp family. Unsure of recovering the family fortune, Blees worked in America as a drugstore clerk, musical instrument salesman, schoolteacher, and musician, marrying a woman from Macon, where he moved in 1892, establishing a boys' school. His family won a settlement from Krupp, part of which Blees inherited c. 1896 and from which Macon benefited. Before his 1906 death, he had underwritten paved streets, electric lights, waterworks, sewers, landscaped parks, factories, and the half-million-dollar academy. Today the buildings are used by the National Guard and as housing for the elderly. S side; US 63.

Grand Divide. *Grand Divide.*

Macon County Courthouse. Italianate, 1865; annex 1895; National Historic Register. The county's third, and one of Missouri's oldest, this two-story red-brick courthouse is the only one built in Macon. Its features include bracketed eaves, an elaborate cornice design repeated over the doors, and tall arched windows. Cost: about $30,000; annex about $8,500. Downtown. *(County Profiles)*

Recreation. LONG BRANCH LAKE / *STATE PARK:* US 36, E 2.2 m. MACON LAKE: Fishing, picnics, playground; the nearby *WPA* pool is reportedly Missouri's largest city pool. US 36, W of junction with US 63. THOMAS HILL RESERVOIR: 4,500 acres. Built by

Associated Electric Cooperative Incorporated as a cooling source for the company's coal-fired electrical power plant (in service 1966). Surrounded by grassland and farms, the reservoir provides water recreation, including fishing (bass, catfish, crappie). Macon and other towns like *Bevier* provide food, lodging, and supplies. US 63, S 5 m.; SR T, W 9.1 m. *WILDLIFE AREAS:* Atlanta, Thomas Hill.

1. Origin unknown; no p.o.
2. Reason unknown; box usually refers to "hemmed in" or a geographical shape; Angle, e.g. Angle Lake, Wash., to a bend.

MALTA BEND
Population: 289   Map E-3

Malta Bend was platted in 1867 by J. R. Lumbeck. In 1841 the steamboat "Malta" sank near a bend two miles north of the townsite, which was then named Malta Bend. The name passed from the bend to a landing to a post office to this town on the bluffs. It was formerly part of the area's hemp industry *(Lexington);* the arrival of the Missouri-Pacific *Railroad* helped it become a shipping point. Post office: 1860–1861, 1866–now.

Grand Pass, Mo. Named for the nearby narrow pass (100–500 yards wide) that divides the Salt Fork and Missouri River valleys, the town originally catered to travelers on the *Santa Fe Trail* (marker in town). Post office: 1831–1849, 1888–now. US 65, W 4 m.

Malta Bend Community Lake. 25 acres. Boating, picnic, fishing (bass, sunfish, catfish); no camping. US 65, W 1.5 m.; SR 127, S 1.3 m.

Recreation. GRAND PASS *WILDLIFE AREA.* VAN METER *STATE PARK:* US 65, E 3 m.; SR N, N 3 m.; GR, E 2.5 m.; SR 122, N 2 m.

'Tit Saw Bottoms. The broad lowlands extending north to the river from about midway between Malta Bend and Grand Pass were called Les Plains des Petites Osage, the plains of the Little Osage *(Indians),* by the French. Petite (Pe'teet) was often corrupted to 'tit (teet) and when joined with Osage (o'saje) eventually produced today's colloquial name.

MANSFIELD
Population: 1,429   Map F-7

Platted in 1882 along the grade of the Kansas City, Springfield & Memphis *Railroad,* Mansfield was named for one of the town founders, F. M. Mansfield. The town's economy is still based on agriculture, which seems odd considering the area's prairie-like rolling hills and nearby Lead Hill's status (below) as one of the highest elevations in the state. Post office: 1882–now.

Laura Ingalls Wilder Home / Museum. Vernacular, c. 1895; National Historic Register. The nine "Little House" books written by Wilder (1867–1957), including "Little House on the Prairie," have been published in 40 languages. Reared in the Midwest, she married Almanzo Wilder and moved here to Rocky Ridge Farm from the Dakotas in 1894 with their daughter, Rose.[1] Almanzo built this house and Laura spent the rest of her life here. She planted many of today's apple, dogwood, and walnut trees. Laura, Almanzo, and Rose (also a popular writer) are buried in the *Mansfield Cemetery.* MUSEUM: Original manuscripts, first editions, objects

A fiddler sits in front of one of the oldest houses in the area, near Seymour. (PHOTO BY JOE STANDARD, FROM "OZARKS MOUNTAINEER")

mentioned in the books, e.g. Pa's fiddle, Mary's Braille slate; a special section for Rose's works. SR A, E 1 m.

Lead Hill / Seymore Ridge. At 1,744 and 1,740–1,760 feet, respectively, the hill and the ridge are stiff competition for Missouri's highest point, Taum Sauk Mountain at 1,772 feet. (*Arcadia: Taum Sauk Mountain State Park; Caledonia: Buford Mountain).* Lead Hill: SR 60, W 4 m. (between the railroad and the highway). Seymore Ridge: SR 60, E 11 m.; 7 m. NE of Seymour.[2]

---

1. In his biography of Rose, "The Ghost in the Little House," William Holtz argues convincingly that Rose is the one who gave her mother's books their final form.

2. Origin unknown; despite the different spellings of the town and the ridge (Seymour and Seymore) the pun, intentional or coincidental, is wonderful; p.o. 1881–now.

MARBLE HILL
Population: 1,447   Map I-6

Although some highway maps have not taken note, Marble Hill and Lutesville (below) were consolidated and named Marble Hill in 1986 by popular vote, marking one of the few instances in which a town kept its location and identity after being narrowly bypassed by a railroad. Selected as a central location for county seat of newly organized Bollinger County, the town was platted in 1851 on land that included an earlier platted town, New California.[1] The site commissioners designated the newer town Dallas (*County Profiles: Dallas*), but an already existing Dallas in Greene County resulted in the post office name Greene,[2] which proved confusing: the town was known variously as "Dallas (P.O. Greene)" or "Greene, Village of Dallas"; some cartographers listed the town as Green. The county court, before incorporating the town in 1868, ordered the name changed to Marble Hill, which had been selected by popular vote at a town meeting where someone with a little geological knowledge spoke for the name, mistakenly identifying the Kimmswick limestone rocks of the area as marble. Narrowly bypassed in 1867 by the St. Louis, Iron Mountain & Southern *Railroad* (Lutesville, below), the town was still close enough to take advantage of rail service, but it depended mostly, as now, on the surrounding agricultural community and on county politics. Post offices: Greene 1851–1868; Marble Hill 1868–now.

Architecture / Downtown Marble Hill. Some intact 1939 *WPA* concrete sidewalks and unpretentious late 19th- and early 20th-century structures, including the Wisecarver building (two-story brick, 1893, across from the courthouse, below); the Conrad House (two-story red granite, c. 1900), W of courthouse; and Will Mayfield College (1884–1930), which has several campus buildings remaining (Mayfield Dr., top of the hill; private). A small town park with picnic facilities is set by Crooked Creek at SR 34.

Artesian Well. The well flows like a fountain (about 27 gallons per minute), forming a stream along which grow watercress and flowers. SR 34, W 2 m.

Bollinger County Courthouse. Colonial Revival, 1885; enlarged 1912; extensive repairs 1960s–1970s. The county's third, this 50-by-60-foot two-story brick courthouse, built when Lutesville (below) attempted to gain the county seat, is front-gabled with a triangular pedimented dormer, an elaborate cupola, a hip roof, a decorative cornice, and paired double-hung windows. Costs: $9,000; 1912 enlargement $7,000. Downtown. *(County Profiles)*

Castle Rock Bluff. This dolomite bluff has been weathered to a pinnacled surface. The castellated profile extends, with breaks, about a half-mile from the bluff's north end. SR 34, W 16 m. to junction of SR MM at Sitzke Store;[3] continue SR 34 past second bridge (approx. 0.3 m.); GR, S 1.2 m.; look west.

Cowan Cemetery. First used by Indians (probably Shawnee) and then by the R. D. Cowan family c. 1819, this cemetery features a tall, handsomely carved 1870 shaft that marks the grave of seven Confederate soldiers who were shot by Federals on May 28, 1865, after surrendering. SR 34, W 18 m.; SR OO, S 5.5 m. *(Cemeteries)*

Dinosaur Fossil Site. In 1942 the state's first (and only to date) dinosaur fossils were found one mile north of Glenallen.[4] They were originally thought to be from the Upper Cretaceous period (c. 60 million years ago), but recent findings suggest they are late Jurassic, or twice as old. SR 34, W 3 m.; inquire locally.

Dolle's Mills. Vernacular, c. 1815–1828 (operating no later than 1828). This two-story frame structure, mortised and pinned, is still sound. The race, dug by slaves, is five feet wide and about three miles long. The site is named for 1868 mill owner J. H. Dolle. Post office: Dolle's Mills 1877–1895. SR 34, E 2 m.; SR B and SR K, N 15.5 m. to Sedgewickville;[5] SR EE, E 3.9 m.

Joined Oaks. Widely separated, these two large white oaks are joined by a thick common branch (about six inches in diameter and seven feet above the ground) to form the letter H. No apparent junction can be found. SR 34, W 9 m.; SR DD, N approx. 1 m. (readily visible from the road in winter).

Leopold, Mo. Settled in 1856 by immigrants from Germany and Holland, it was first known as Vinemount[6] for the nearby mountain. In 1887 it was renamed Leopold, honoring Pope Leo XIII, which is in keeping with the spiritual inspiration that was required for the community effort of building St. John's Church (below). Originally an agricultural, nearly all-Catholic community, it remains so today. Post offices: Vinemount 1870–1871; Laflin[7] 1871–1954; Leopold 1887–now. SR 51, S 3 m.; SR N, E 3.5 m.; SR N

spur, N 0.6 m. LEOPOLD PICNIC: Since 1890. Food, dining facilities, a fishpond. Last Saturday in July. ST. JOHN'S CHURCH: Gothic Revival, completed 1901. This massive structure, built from locally quarried limestone, using donations and labor from the community, has all the details of its style, including lancet windows, a towering steeple, and flying buttresses. The interior (completed in 1915) is decorated and furnished in elaborate detail. An adjacent rock-art shrine was dedicated in 1944 to armed forces personnel; the *cemetery* dates from c. 1856.

Lutesville, Mo. Jacob and Sophia Lutes (Sophia was born here in 1808) were among the original landowners of Marble Hill's site. Their son, Eli Lutes, owned land at the old military road's ford of Crooked Creek (on the west side of the creek, approx. 0.5 m. from Marble Hill), where Eli platted a town in 1869, donating 10 acres for a depot and every other city lot to the St. Louis & Iron Mountain *Railroad*. An active shipping point with a larger population than Marble Hill, Lutesville lost an 1884 election to gain the county seat (Bollinger County Courthouse, above); in 1986 it was consolidated with Marble Hill as Marble Hill, even though its population was larger (865 v. 601). Post office: 1872–1991.

Massey Log House / Museum. Four-Pin Log, 1860; rebuilt 1984. Furnished, period rooms, 19th-century items, handwork. Grounds: replica of log smokehouse. SE of courthouse.

Zalma, Mo. Established c. 1877 as Bollinger Mills,[8] a post office and milling community along the Castor River, it changed names after the c. 1889 arrival of the Cape Girardeau Southwestern *Railroad*. Reportedly railroad owner Louis Houck *(Cape Girardeau)* named the town for his friend Zalma Block, owner of Cape Girardeau's St. Charles Hotel. Post offices: Bollinger Mills 1877–1890; Zalma 1890–now. SR 51, S 11 m. to Dongola;[9] continue SR 51, S 8 m. BLUE POND NATURAL AREA: 15 acres. This part of Castor River *State Forest* contains Missouri's deepest natural pond (about 66 feet). Its origin is not certain. The depth and sheer sides are not consistent with sinkhole formations *(Collapsed Cave Systems)*. Possibly the pond was a result of the *New Madrid Earthquake*. Closed to camping; no swimming, boating, or other water activities. Box 152 (SR T), Perryville 63775. SR H, N 1.8 m.; GR, W 3 m. MINGO *NATIONAL WILDLIFE REFUGE*. *STATE FORESTS:* Castor River, Clubb. *WILDLIFE AREAS:* Dark Cypress Swamp, Duck Creek.

1. Name inspired by the *California* gold rush excitement; no p.o.
2. Nearby 1834–1851 area post office in Cape Girardeau County; probably same namesake as Greene County; discontinued when absorbed by Bollinger County, then reopened as Dallas's p.o.
3. Origin unknown; probably the store owner; no p.o.

4. Origin unknown; p.o. Glen Allen 1872–1894; Glenallen 1894–now (*Post Offices*).

5. For Federal general John Sedgwick, like the Linn County town of Sedgwick, but misspelled; p.o. 1867–1869, 1875–now.

6. Popular name, usually pertaining to wild or cultivated grapes.

7. Origin unknown.

8. The mill owner and a prominent regional family name (*County Profiles: Bollinger*).

9. Contemporary news about the Sudanese Muslim–British war during the 1890s; e.g. Dongola, Ill.; p.o. 1899–1923.

MARCELINE
Population: 2,645   Map E-2

Platted in 1887 along the Chicago, Santa Fe & California *Railroad* and later a division point for the Atchison, Topeka & Santa Fe, the town first relied on the area's coal industry, shipping, and agriculture for its economic base. Today, it is the home of Walsworth, one of the world's largest school yearbook publishers. Originally the town was thought to have been named for the wife of a railroad official, although no proof exists, but recent research suggests its namesake was an early French settler, Marceline Silvadon, whose name appears on land records from the time of the town's incorporation in 1888. Incidentally, one of the town's three newspapers was named the "New Deal" in 1900, predating President F. D. Roosevelt's 1933 New Deal agenda, which included the *WPA*. Post office: 1887–now.

Brookfield, Mo. Platted in 1859 at the Hannibal & St. Joseph *Railroad* by J. W. Brooks, the town's namesake. ARCHITECTURE: Good examples of late 19th-century commercial styles. SR 5, N 3 m.; US 36, W 8 m.

Nehai Tonkayea Prairie Natural Area. 90 acres. One of the few *prairies* on the Kansas glacial till plain; big and little bluestem tallgrass, Indian grass. Rt. 2, Marceline 64658. SR 5, S 8 m.; SR D, E 5.2 m.; SR DD, S 0.5 m.

Recreation. MARCELINE CITY LAKE: 156 acres. Fishing, hunting. SR 5, S 3 m.; SR E, W 1.6 m.; GR, N 0.8 m. MUSSEL FORK *WILDLIFE AREA*.

Ripley Park. Railroad engine and caboose, fountain, pond with ducks, gazebo, 130 American Flags honoring the 1991 United Nations war against Iraq.

Walt Disney. Walter Elias Disney (1901–1966) lived here from 1905 to 1910, attended art school in *Kansas City* and Chicago, served as an ambulance driver during WWI, and in 1920 became a cartoonist in Hollywood, where in 1928 he created Mickey Mouse in the cartoon "Steamboat Willie" (his first popular character was Oswald the Rabbit). Disney Elementary School has a mural featuring Pluto, Bambi, and others that was painted in 1960 by Disney Studio artists under Disney's direction. In town.

MARSHALL
Population: 12,711   Map E-3

Selected and platted in 1839 as a central location for Saline County's third county seat (Former County Seats, below), the town was named by the county court for John Marshall (1755–1835), U.S. Supreme Court justice from 1801 to 1835. The arrival in 1874 of the Chicago & Alton *Railroad* helped establish it as an agricultural shipping center that grew dramatically after WWII to include food packaging and processing as well as light manufacturing. Post office: 1840–now. Home of Missouri Valley College, Saline County Career Center (vo-tech training), and the Marshall Habilitation Center.

Architecture. National Historic Register: Baity Hall, Missouri Valley College (500 E. College); Buckner House (125 N. Brunswick); C & A Depot (Sebree St.); Courthouse (below); First Presbyterian Church (212 E. North).

Former County Seats. Besides Marshall and *Arrow Rock* (which served as a temporary county seat in 1839), Saline County had two other county seats. JEFFERSON: Named for president Thomas Jefferson, this Missouri River town, also known as Old Jefferson, served from 1820 to 1831; defunct. Today's Cambridge[1] is near the former courthouse site (marked; inquire at Gilliam, below). Post offices: Walnut Farm[2] 1826–1838; Old Jefferson 1838–1845. SR 240, N 17 m. to Gilliam;[3] SR PP, E 3.3 m.; GR, E 0.5 m. JONESBORO: Around an 1821 mill known as Gilbraith's Mill[4] grew a community known as Jonesboro[5] that served from 1831 to 1839 as a more available county seat location than Jefferson. Jonesboro was initially a successful *Santa Fe Trail* outfitting center, but by 1881 it was described as a wreck of its former greatness. The town was revived in the 1880s as Napton, or Naptonville,[6] by the arrival of the Missouri-Pacific *Railroad*. Post offices: Jonesboro 1828–1840, 1843–1866, 1872–1873; Rocktens Mills[7] 1840–1843. SR 41, E 6 m.; SR E, S 4.1 m. (inquire locally for marked courthouse site).

Indian Foothills Park. 240 acres. Pool, picnic facilities, tennis, croquet, shuffleboard, archery, golf, two fishing lakes, baseball. Midtown, E side; US 65B, E on Eastwood; signs.

Marshall Philharmonic Orchestra. Marshall is reportedly the smallest American city with a full-size symphony orchestra (about 60 players). Its philharmonic was founded in 1963 by W. C. Gordon Jr. and still utilizes local musicians, mostly amateurs, whose ages range from 13 to 80 and whose occupations range from goat farmer to librarian. The philharmonic won two TV Emmy awards (1985 and 1986) and has been featured in newspapers like the "New York Times" and on shows like Roger Mudd's "American Almanac." Free concerts; various times. Box 97, Marshall 65340.

Recreation. *ARROW ROCK* STATE HISTORIC SITE: SR 41, E 14 m. VAN METER *STATE PARK:* SR 41 and 122, N 13 m. *WILDLIFE AREAS:* Blind Pony, Grand Pass, Marshall Junction.

Saline County Courthouse. Italianate, 1882; National Historic Register. The county's sixth courthouse, the third in Marshall (Former County Seats, above), today's structure was built when Marshall was challenged for county seat by nearby Slater.[8] This two-story brick courthouse features a small entry porch with columns, tall narrow arched windows with stone hoods, a fanlight above the front and rear doors, a hip roof with bracketed pediments, an elaborate square central clock tower, and broad bracketed eaves. The interior has maintained its 19th-century appearance. Cost: $56,752. Grounds: two iron fountains, a red granite *Santa Fe Trail* marker, a WWI doughboy statue, and a memorial to all veterans who died during a war. Court square; US 65 B, N side. *(County Profiles)*

1. Township name, possibly from English county Cambridgeshire at the Cam River via Cambridge, Mass.; p.o. 1845–1903.
2. The tree.
3. W. T. Gilliam; p.o. 1879–now.
4. Mill owner Alexander Gilbraith.
5. For 1828 mill co-owner John A. Jones. Originally spelled Jonesborough.
6. Missouri Supreme Court judge W. B. Napton; p.o. 1880–now.
7. Origin unknown.
8. Col. J. F. Slater, director of the Chicago & Alton RR; SR 240, N 14 m.; p.o. Petra, origin unknown, 1842–1878; Slater 1878–now.

MARSHFIELD
Population: 4,374   E-6

Platted in 1856 as county seat of newly organized Webster County, the town was named by the court for county namesake Daniel Webster's Massachusetts hometown, which took its name c. 1640 from the area's marshes. Both the town and the county are sparsely populated. Until the recent establishment of light industry, Marshfield's economy depended largely on providing shipping for the area's agricultural products (the Atlantic & Pacific *Railroad* arrived c. 1872), which were mainly grown between Marshfield and Stafford, where the land drops from the highlands to the Springfield Plateau, in an area known first as Osage Country and then as the Kickapoo Prairie because of the *Indians* who lived here, respectively, before and after the *War of 1812*. Post office: 1856–now. Incidentally, at 1,494 feet this is reportedly the highest town on

I-44 east of the Rocky Mountains. *(Route 66)*

Diggins, Mo. Diggins was platted in 1887 along the Kansas City, Springfield & Memphis *Railroad* by C. H and Sallie L. Patterson. The derivation of its name is not known. Post offices: Diggins 1886–1890, 1904–now; Livingston[1] 1890–1904. SR A, S 12.5 m. FINLEY FALLS: The falls (50 yards long, 7 feet high) and a precarious ford were formed by water eroding dolomite and scouring potholes in sandstone that then resulted in serrated edges. Finley Creek's flow over large sandstone fingers and broken boulders mimics a *shut-in* but is open, not constricted. Easily accessible. Junction of railroad track and SR NN; SR NN, S 2.1 m.; GR, E 0.9 m.; GR (sharp turn), S 0.2 m.

Fordland, Mo. In 1882 the town was platted along the Kansas City, Springfield & Memphis *Railroad* by Joseph Ford and S. B. Dugger. Post office: 1882–now. SR A, S 8 m.; SR FF, S 8.3 m. DEVIL'S DEN: A classic example of an elongated sink (*Collapsed Cave Systems*) formed by an enlargement of a fracture, this eerie 20-yard-wide and 100-yard-long chasm is situated by an oak grove. About halfway down its nearly vertical drop, on a rock ledge above 70-foot-deep water, brass bands reportedly gave concerts c. 1900. Caution! Climbing is dangerous. Junction US 60 and SR PP; SR PP, E 3.7 m. to a stile (S side of road); follow fence trail S approx. 400 feet.

Niangua, Mo. This 1870 Atlantic & Pacific *Railroad* town, formerly Miteomah,[2] was named for the river and the county (*County Profiles: Dallas*). Post office: 1870–now. SR CC, N 6.3 m.; SR M, E 1.4 m. CEDAR BLUFF NATURAL BRIDGE: The bridge (18-foot span, c. 10-foot ceiling) is set on a scenic bluff overlooking a popular fishing spot at Cantrell Creek; it can be reached by a short walk and easy climb (*Collapsed Cave Systems*). SR F, E 5.6 m. (0.3 past bridge); GR, S 0.2 m to low-water bridge; park, follow creek upstream (path) approx. 0.25 m. to rising bluff; climb, follow path to overhang. *ROUTE 66* SIGHTS: Abbylee Court (in town) and scenic drive (*Lebanon: Route 66 sights*).

Niangua State Forest. *State Forests.*

Route 66 Sights. Niangua, above.

Webster County Courthouse. Moderne, 1939–1941. The county's third, this two-story *Carthage* marble courthouse was built using *WPA* funds. The first courthouse was destroyed during the *Civil War;* the second, damaged by an 1880 tornado, was condemned in 1930 and razed in 1939. Cost: $150,000. Downtown. *(County Profiles)*

1. Origin unknown, possibly from the county.
2. Origin unknown, possibly based on the biblical parable of the widow's mite, e.g. Luke 21:2, wherein her donation of what could have been her last two copper coins was a greater sacrifice than others' lavish gifts; no p.o.

MARTHASVILLE
Population: 674   Map H-4

In 1817 Dr. John Young advertised lots for sale in a town named for his wife Martha. Young described the town as being on a ridge by "the river road, leading from St. Louis," which placed it about half a mile east of the 1767 French village of La Charrette.[1] Young noted that a mill was being built, that he had opened a general store, and that he planned to add a tavern and, with his associate Dr. Jones, establish a practice in "Physic [sic], Surgery, etc." Marthasville, a shipping and trading point, was slow to grow. In 1833 there were about 6 houses; German immigration from 1834 to the 1850s brought the 1860 population to 100. The arrival in 1892 of the Missouri, Kansas & Eastern *Railroad* influenced the relocation of the downtown to today's site at the tracks and helped the town continue as an area trading center. Post office: 1818–now. *(Boonslick Trails)*

Architecture. Good examples of 19th-century structures. Augustus Grabs House (log, 1830s; enlarged 1844), weatherboard, derelict; used as a residence, general store, post office, and c. 1865 school. Harvey Griswold House (Vernacular, 1859), two-story red brick. Both: E side of town.

Boone Burial Site. Both Daniel (1735–1820) and his wife, Rebecca (1737–1813), were buried here. Daniel choose this site, a low hill overlooking the Missouri River on land belonging to his nephew, David Bryan, whom he reared. Also buried here are Jemima, their daughter, and her husband, Flanders Callaway *(Defiance: Missouri Territory Village)*, as well as David and Mary Bryan and Augustus Grabs (Architecture, above). Granite boulders mark the Boones' graves *(Fayette: Stephens Museum)*. Junction SR 47 and SR D; SR D, E 1.8 m.; unmarked road, E approx. 0.5 m.; N side. *(Defiance: Boone Home)*

Emmaus Home. Vernacular, 1851–1858. These two-story stone buildings were first used by Marthasville Seminary, which was founded in 1849 by the German Evangelical and Reformed Church of Missouri and relocated as Eden Theological Seminary in 1883 to near St. Louis. Emmaus Home for the handicapped was established here in 1892 by the Evangelical Synod of North America. SR D, E 4.5 m.

Hopewell, Holstein, and Treloar, Mo. Three towns settled by German immigrants and well-kept 19th-century farmhouses set among rolling hills make a nostalgic drive: SR 47, N to SR N; SR N, S to SR 94. HOPEWELL, MO.: Settled c. 1880, its commendatory name comes from Hopewell Academy (a two-story brick building later used as a general store), which

predates the town. Nearby New Boston *(Warrenton)* was considered for county seat in 1833. Post office: Hopewell Academy 1863–1906. SR 47, N 7 m. at junction with SR N. HOLSTEIN, MO.: Settled c. 1855, it was named for a district in Germany at the Danish border that passed to the counts of Holstein in 1386 as a fief of the Holy Roman Empire. The Holstein Mill (three-story frame, 1870) is located one block east of SR N. TRELOAR, MO.: Settled in 1896 along the tracks of the Missouri, Kansas & Eastern *Railroad*, the community was named for W. M. Treloar, professor of music at Hardin College in *Mexico*, Mo. St. John's United Church of Christ (Gothic Revival, 1870), a frame church, has lancet windows and a wooden spire with a bell tower; parsonage and *cemetery* adjacent (W of town: SR 94, W 6 m.). KATY TRAIL *STATE PARK:* In Treloar.

Katy Trail State Park. SR 94 S of town; N on first; W on Depot to sign. *(State Parks)*

Marthasville Record. Vernacular, 1896. This two-story tin-clad frame building has always housed a newspaper: first the "News" and later the "Record." The interior and exterior are little changed, as is the c. 1928 Mergenthaler Linotype, a nearly 2,000-pound machine (invented 1896, now obsolete) that casts 600°F lead into a line of type used for printing. The newspaper, the last letterpress weekly in Missouri, is published 52 weeks a year. Incidentally, proofreading linotype copy before printing requires reading it upside down and backward. Public welcome; in town.

1. Via the local creek, possibly for Joseph Chorette, a St. Louis fur trader. Also the site of a Spanish fort, San Juan de Misuri, the town was known as Charrette or St. Johns and was noted by the 1804–1806 *Lewis and Clark Expedition.*

MARYVILLE
Population: 10,663   Map C-1

The townsite, situated just west of the One Hundred and Two River (below), was selected and platted in 1845 as county seat of newly organized Nodaway County *(Platte Purchase)* and named for Mary Graham, the wife of the town's first resident, Amos Graham (Architecture, below). According to the "The WPA Guide to 1930s Missouri," an 1846 visitor to Maryville said that Graham was "county clerk, collector, assessor, and 'everything but the judge'" (he was also the postmaster). An early area trading center, Maryville was aided by the c. 1869 arrival of the Kansas City, St. Joseph & Council Bluffs *Railroad*, about the same time the town was finally incorporated in 1869. Post office: 1846–now. Home of Northwest State Missouri

University (Architecture, below) and Northwest Missouri Area Vo-Tech. Information: chamber of commerce, Main on N side of courthouse square.

Architecture. CONTEMPORARY: Geodesic Dome House; SW of town on N. Dewey Ave. GOVERNORS' HOUSE: Italianate, 1884; remodeled. This was the home of two Missouri governors: A. P. Morehouse (governor 1887–1889; served the remaining term of John S. Marmaduke), a law partner of Amos Graham (Maryville history, above), and F. C. Donnell (governor 1941–1945). SR 46/US 136, N on Vine (605). GRAHAM-ROSE HOUSE: National Folk, 1868; addition. After her husband's death, town namesake Mary Graham built this house, living here until her death in 1903. US 71S, W on Edwards, N on Buchanan (422). IN TOWN: A large group of 19th- and early 20th-century styles can be seen in areas bounded by US 71/SR 36 (N. Main), E. 6th, Oak, and E. 3d, as well as US 71/SR 36 (N. Main), W. 3d, Frederick, and 1st. NEARBY TOWNS: Good examples of styles can be seen in the following towns. Clearmont, Mo.:[1] Weber-Vansickle House (Queen Anne, late 19th century), with elaborate spindlework and detailing; US 71, N 18 m. Hopkins, Mo.:[2] a row of mostly derelict Italianate buildings with ornate bracketing, decorative hood molding, and cast-iron columns; US 71, N 3 m.; SR 148, N 12 m. Pickering, Mo.:[3] 1970s Concrete Cloverleaf House; US 71, N 3 m.; SR 148, N 5 m. Skidmore, Mo.:[4] Marteny Skidmore house (Queen Anne Free Classic, 1880s), with cross gables, towers, a tall chimney, columns, patterned shingles, and a projecting bay. SR V, W 13.6 m. NWMSU CAMPUS: Founded in 1905 as a teachers college, the school became a four-year college in 1919. Landmarks include the Administration Building (Tudor Gothic, 1907–1910); Presidents' House (Classicism, 1873; National Historic Register), with altered porches; and Hickory Grove School (Vernacular, 1883), with a furnished 19th-century classroom. ST. FRANCIS HOSPITAL: International, 1970. This $2.8 million building is locally referred to as "ship of the plains" because of enormous oval windows that resemble portholes; 1802 S. Main.

Arkoe, Mo. Platted in 1874 along the tracks of the Chicago, Burlington & Quincy *Railroad*, Arkoe was named by town founder Dr. P. H. Talbot, who granted the railroad a right-of-way through his property. "Arkoe" is a name from Robert Paltock's "Peter Wilkins and the Flying Indians"; in the book's fictitious language it designated "a smooth stretch of water" that the flying Indians, like seaplanes, could use for landings. Talbot imagined the adjacent One

Arkoe Methodist Church, built c. 1885. (PHOTO BY SHIRLEY CORROUGH LUSK)

Hundred and Two River to be an arkoe. A busy shipping point (1917 pop. 250), the town declined after the Depression (1990 pop. 63). Post offices: Bridgewater[5] 1871–1877; Arkoe 1877–1953. US 71, S 6.4 m.; SR U, E 2 m. to the river. DR. P. H. TALBOT'S MURDER: In 1880 Talbot was shot and fatally wounded at his nearby country home. His two sons, Albert and Charles (ages 21 and 16, respectively), were convicted of the crime; although they maintained their innocence, they were hanged in 1881 despite a plea for clemency to Gov. John S. Phelps. They are buried near their father in a private *cemetery* on the Talbot farm. Their markers read: "We Died Innocent." Inquire locally. ONE HUNDRED AND TWO RIVER SHUT-INS: The river's name, first explained as a distance (between a site and the river or as its actual length), has been best described as a phonetic error in the translation of an unnamed Indian tribe's location at the river's headwaters, çondse ("upland forest" or "hillside forest"), to French as Cent Deux, which was translated to English exactly. The *shut-ins* narrow from two miles wide at Maryville to a quarter-mile at Arkoe. To follow the river to Maryville: SR U at river, W 0.7 m.; GR, N 6 m.; US 136, W 0.5 m. (a dirt road, closer but less dependable, does the same: river bridge, E 0.1 m., then N 6 m. to US 136; W 1.6 m.).

The Big Pump. Art Deco, c. 1937; National Historic Register. Initially painted black and white, designed locally to look like an electric gas pump, this small service station has been moved from its original location on US 71S to US 71N at the edge of town; derelict.

Maryville Cemetery (Old). Platted in 1845 outside the city limits; most burials here are prior to 1865; none were after 1875. SR 46/US 136; 1st, E to Water St. *(Cemeteries)*

Nodaway County Courthouse. Second Empire, 1881–1882; National Historic Register. An excellent example of its style, this 111-by-76-foot two-story red-brick courthouse with sandstone trim is the county's third. Its features include a mansard roof with metal cresting, cornice brackets, paired windows, a massive and elaborate central tower with dormers, and hooded windows. Few alterations have been made. Cost: $60,000; 1950 renovation $15,000. US 71/136, N to 3d. *(County Profiles)*

Nodaway County Museum / House. Greek Revival, 1846; National Historic Register. The house, with a few exceptions, is still as originally built. Front-gabled and unassuming, the two-story frame structure houses local historical items, including quilts and clothing. N Main, N to W. 2d (422).

Possum Walk, Mo. Reportedly there are over 15 Possum place-names in Missouri (Walks, Trots, or Hollows) that honor this largely nocturnal marsupial whose full name, opossum, is reportedly derived from Algonquian via the French "apasum" *(Kennett: Campbell)*. This town had no post office and little history, but its hotel is listed on the National Historic Register. US 71, N 18 m. to Clearmont (Architecture, above); SR C, W 3 m.; GR, S 0.8 m.

Recreation. BILBY RANCH *WILDLIFE AREA*. NODAWAY COMMUNITY LAKE: 73 acres. Bass, sunfish, crappie, tiger muskie. SR 46, W 12 m.; SR PP, N 3.7 m.; GR, W 1.6 m.

St. Patrick's Day Parade. In what is reportedly the world's shortest parade, marching bands and floats travel about a half-block down Buchanan Street. The route is shortened a few inches each year to retain the record. March 17; in town.

Weather Vane. 37 feet tall, 15 feet wide. This is reportedly the world's largest pheasant weather vane; the bird is as colorful as the weather vane is large. Robbins Lighting, downtown.

1. Origin unknown, usually variously spelled (e.g. clare- and clair-), commendatory of clear mountains and popularized by Robert Fulton's c. 1810 steamboat "Clermont"; p.o. Claremont 1871–1881; Clearmont 1881–now.
2. A. L. Hopkins, 1817 superintendent of the Kansas City, St. Joseph & Council Bluffs RR; p.o. 1871–now.
3. Pickering Clark, RR official; p.o. 1871–now.
4. Landowner Marteny Skidmore; p.o. Union Valley, patriotic,

descriptive, 1873–1880; Skidmore 1880–now.
5. Former early mill town's location near three bridges that crossed the One Hundred and Two River; p.o. 1871–1877; defunct.

MAYSVILLE
Population: 1,176   Map D-3

Most of the county's early records were destroyed in 1878 by a courthouse fire. Selected and platted in 1845 near Lost Creek (Amity, below) as a central location for county seat of recently organized De Kalb County, Maysville was named by the court, but its namesake is now not known. It could be for Maysville, Ky.,[1] for a personal name (first or last), for some significant event in May, or sentimentality for the month. One of the county's few early towns, it prospered as a political and agricultural trading center aided by the 1885 arrival of the Chicago, Rock Island & Pacific *Railroad*. Today's economic base remains agricultural, as witnessed by about 55 farms that have been in the same family for over 100 years. Post office: 1846–now.

Amity, Mo. Founded in 1865 along the previously abandoned 1824 postal and military trail that ran nearly due north–south between *Liberty* and Council Bluffs, Iowa, Amity was given a popular commendatory name that reportedly honors the 1871 Amity Congregational Church. The town (1885 pop. c. 200) was moved in 1885 from its original site, located by Amity *Cemetery* (some ornate markers; SR J, S 0.5 m.), to the now-defunct Chicago, Rock Island & Pacific *Railroad*. During a harsh 1824–1825 winter, three soldiers carrying mail from *Liberty* became lost (wandering to near today's Maysville) and almost died. The incident gave Lost Creek its name. Post office: 1872–now.

Architecture. COMMERCIAL: Mostly late 19th-century; early 1900s brick streets join at the square. RESIDENTIAL: Black's House (Vernacular Romantic, c. 1854), with dormers, porch added; the town's oldest; 400 W. Main. Miller's House (Italianate, c. 1870; addition), 211 W. Main. Christian Church (Gothic Revival, 1870), the town's oldest; SW corner of square. J. T. Blair Jr.'s Birthplace (Prairie Box, c. 1900); Blair was governor from 1957 to 1961; SR 33S at S. Polk (409).

De Kalb County Courthouse. Moderne (some Art Deco affinities), 1938–1939. The county's third, this 110-by-55-foot elevated two-story brick courthouse is trimmed in stone, has symmetrical vertical windows, and features geometric designs and fluting along its main entry. Cost: $59,000 (part from a federal grant). Downtown. *(County Profiles)*

Jumpin'-Off Days. This self-proclaimed largest "motorless" parade in the Midwest features craft demonstrations, an 1860s military ball, an art show, and a melodrama. Second week of June.

Museums. COUNTY: Local historical items and displays, e.g. quilts, newspapers, and a replica of a turn-of-the-century schoolroom. E side of square. PONY EXPRESS RANCH: A working ranch that displays local historical items, especially farm machinery; camping. SR 33, S 2 m.

Recreation. PONY EXPRESS *WILDLIFE AREA* / LAKE: 240-acre lake; bass, sunfish, crappie, catfish, tiger muskie.

---

1. Formerly called Limestone, renamed c. 1790 for federal surveyor John May.

MEMPHIS
Population: 2,094   Map F-1

The townsite, located near the North Fabius River, was selected and platted in 1843 as permanent county seat of recently organized Scotland County *(South Gorin: Sand Hill)*. The town reportedly took the name of a nearby 1837–1840 postal substation, Memphis, which was supposedly named for Memphis, Tenn.[1] Other sources claim that former Tennessee resident Lilly Cecil, who with her husband, Samuel, donated the townsite, named it for Memphis. The town grew as an agricultural and political center, and the arrival c. 1871 of the Missouri, Iowa & Nebraska *Railroad* helped strengthen its economy. Post office: 1841–now.

Bible Grove, Mo. Reportedly the community was named for its 1858 post office, Bible Grove. Jesse Stice, Scotland County's first settler and second *gristmill* owner, organized the county's first church c. 1835. The congregation in 1858 built Bible Grove Christian Church, a vernacular frame structure still standing (remodeled 1882; *cemetery* adjacent). Possibly early church members met at a nearby grove, inspiring the name later applied to the post office and community. Post offices: Hard Scrabble[2] 1858; Bible Grove 1858–1895; Biblegrove 1895–1908. US 136, W 0.9 m.; SR 15, S 7.8 m.; SR T, W 5.2 m. INDIAN HILLS *WILDLIFE AREA.* MAGGARD HOUSE: Greek Revival, c. 1840s–1850s. This two-story red-brick house was used as a field hospital after a *Civil War* skirmish, the Battle of Vassar Hill, in July 1863. Private. GR (keep left after bridge), N 3.8 m.

Lakes. LAKE SHOW ME: 250 acres. Small boats, fishing, camping, picnicking, shooting range. US 136, W 2.3 m.; GR, S 0.9 m. OLD MEMPHIS LAKE: Fishing, picnicking. US 136, W 0.9 m.; SR 15, S 0.5 m.; GR, W 0.6 m.

Scotland County Courthouse. Italian Renaissance, 1907–1908. The county's third, this two-story 107-by-77-foot stone-veneer courthouse with a slate roof and an elaborate copper-covered dome has a rusticated first level, a two-story pedimented and projecting central entry flanked by two-story Corinthian columns, and a widely overhanging cornice that hints at a roofline parapet. Cost: $50,000. Downtown. *(County Profiles)*

Scotland County Museums. BOYER HOUSE: Prairie Box, c. 1900, also called American Foursquare, a subtype designed by the Prairie School of Chicago architects. The house was originally built onto the Downing House (below) when it was used as a hotel. Relocated in 1917, it now displays local items, including a size 24 shoe associated with Ella Ewing, the Missouri Giantess *(South Gorin)*. 303 S Main. DOWNING HOUSE: Italianate, 1858–1860; remodeled; National Historic Register. Later used as a hotel, the building is still a good example of the style, with a three-story square tower, bracketed eaves, arched windows, quoins, classical columns, and a balustrade. Local historical items; furnished. 311 S. Main. MEMPHIS DEPOT: Railroad, 1871. Railroad memorabilia. Downtown.

Tom Horn House. Vernacular, date unknown. This was the childhood residence of Horn (1860–1903), the legendary Indian scout and cowboy who was hanged for murder at Cheyenne, Wyo. A Hollywood film starring Steve McQueen tells the story of his life. Private. US 136, E 12 m. to junction with SR F near Granger;[3] GR, S 1 m.

---

1. 1819 namesake of the c. 2,850 B.C. royal residence at Memphis, Egypt, whose Sixth Dynasty name Men-nefer was transcribed by Greeks as Memphis.
2. Stock frontier humor, usually meaning hard to make a living, especially by farming.
3. For a farmers' organization, The Grange; p.o. 1875–1967.

MENNONITES

The members of this Protestant denomination founded in 1525 at Zürich, Switzerland, believe they are the true heirs and consummators of the Reformation begun (and they say betrayed) by Luther, Zwingli, and Calvin (who established state-church Protestantism). Although the members of this sect originally referred to themselves simply as Brethren, in Germany they were called Anabaptists because they rejected infant baptism, requiring instead consenting adult baptism. The Mennonites were named for Menno Simons (1492–1559), a Dutch leader who joined the movement in 1536. Their beliefs in radical New Testament Christianity can be superficially stated as renewal of the Apostolic Christian faith and practice, separation of church and state, voluntary church membership, and a literal following of Christ's teachings, including rejection of war and violence and avocation of love and nonresistance.

MEXICAN WAR, 1846–1848

Westward expansion during the 1840s, along with the 1836 independence of Texas from Mexico and its 1845 American annexation and statehood, precipitated resentment between Mexico and America that eventually led to war. In April 1846, Gen. Zachary Taylor, refusing to withdraw from disputed Texas territory just east of the Rio Grande, was attacked by Mexican forces. Gen. Stephen S. Kearny (*Kearney*) led troops from Missouri that first captured Santa Fe, then advanced on California. They were joined there by Commodore Robert F. *Stockton*, and the region was secured. Taylor, Gen. Winfield Scott, and then Col. A. W. *Doniphan* invaded the Mexican interior, capturing Mexico City in September 1847. In accordance with the February 1848 treaty of Guadalupe Hidalgo, Mexico ceded half its territory to the United States, an area stretching from Oklahoma's panhandle to the Pacific Ocean, which included that part of today's Colorado south and west of the Arkansas River and all of New Mexico, Utah, Arizona, Nevada, and California. U.S. troops killed, c. 11,300.

MEXICO
Population: 11,290   Map F-3

Platted on April 23, 1836, at the south fork of the Salt River nearly eight months before the organization of Audrain County, the town was selected county seat after landowners R. C. Mansfield and J. H. Smith offered the county court every other town lot and a public square. Reportedly the court named the town "New Mexico," and it was called that for the first two terms of the court, but other sources claim the name was an error by the commissioners and that the intended town name was Mexico. Exotic place-names (*La Plata*) were popular in the 19th century; this one was probably inspired by the romance and wealth of the *Santa Fe Trail* and the exciting publicity of the 1821–1835 U.S. colonization of Mexico's Texas. Ironically, when the town was named, American Texans were at war with Mexico, fighting for independence (March 2–April 21, 1836). The town's agriculture-dependent economy was strengthened by saddle-

horse breeding (Graceland, below), the c. 1858 arrival of the North Missouri *Railroad*, and the establishment of a female seminary (1858), later Hardin College (1873–1932), and the Missouri Military Academy (below). Today Mexico's economy largely depends on the clay deposits discovered here c. 1900 (Fire Clay, below). Post office: 1837–now. Home of Davis H. Hart Mexico Area Vo-Tech and Missouri Military Academy.

Architecture. Good examples of 19th- and early 20th-century styles, especially in the courthouse area (below).

Audrain County Courthouse. Italian Renaissance, 1950–1951. The county's fourth, this three-story brick-with-stone-trim courthouse, first proposed and designed in 1938, then redesigned again in 1947, was stripped to its basic elements in 1950 to meet the budget. It has two-story pilasters, two-story first-story square columns, pedimented entries, wings, belt courses, and a flat roof. Cost: $527,300. Downtown; US 54, W on Jackson. (*County Profiles*)

Fire Clay / A. P. Green. The discovery here c. 1900 of fire clay (refractory clay, for nonmetallic ceramics resistant to heat and corrosion) resulted in the establishment of companies like A. P. Green, founded in 1910. By 1935 it was the world's largest fire clay plant, producing 60 million bricks annually that were used during the 1940s in steel mills, ship's boilers, and America's first synthetic rubber factory. Today A. P. Green, an international corporation with 17 plants in three countries, manufactures a multifaceted line of fire clay products. Headquarters (Neo-Classical architecture), E side; US 54, E on Green Blvd.

Graceland / Saddle Horse Museum. Greek Revival (Bracketed), 1857; National Historic Register. Set on 11 acres, this two-story 10-room frame house features furnished rooms, including a typical Victorian parlor, an 1860s bedroom, and a children's room with toys, doll furniture, and the Creasey collection of 400 dolls; research material, genealogist. W side; US 54, W on Green Blvd. to N on Muldrow (501 S.) at Glenn Memorial Park. AMERICAN SADDLE HORSE MUSEUM: Graceland's second owner (1867), C. T. Quisenberry, brought the area's first blooded horses from Kentucky. Rex McDonald, Champion Saddle Horse of America (1904 St. Louis World's Fair), earned the town its title of Saddle Horse Capital of the World. Horse-related memorabilia, publications, exhibits, Rex McDonald's grave, a furnished 1904 schoolhouse. Adjacent to Graceland.

Missouri Military Academy. Founded in 1889 by C. H. Hardin (governor from 1875 to 1877), who also founded Hardin College here in 1873, this private high school has been rated as an Honor School by the U.S. Army since 1930. Since 1947, 87 percent of its graduates have entered college. E side; US 54, E on Jackson.

Parks. Both Lakeview (S side of town) and Plunkett (N side of town) have picnic facilities, playgrounds, fishing lakes, and nature trails. Lakeview has camping facilities.

Wildlife Areas. Northcuff, White (R. M.). *(Wildlife Areas)*

MIAMI

Population: 142   Map E-3

Henry Farrell bought land here in 1833, established a ferry in 1836, and in 1838 platted a town called Greenville.[1] In 1843 it was renamed Miami, possibly to avoid confusion with Wayne County's *Greenville*. It is usually difficult to verify the source of Miami as a place-name because of the tendency of like-sounding names to assume that spelling, but in this instance it honors the Miami *Indians*, a mid-American tribe related linguistically to the Algonquian, formerly of Ohio, who were here at the nearby bluffs before 1810. Decline of the hemp industry and river trade after the Civil War *(Lexington)* ruined the town's economy. Post office: Miami 1838–now.

Recreation. GRAND PASS *WILDLIFE AREA*. VAN METER FOREST NATURAL AREA: 114 acres. Part of Van Meter *State Park*. Geologically and botanically interesting, the Pinnacles consist of extremely rugged serrated ridges of dunelike *loess*; Devil's Backbone (south part of Pinnacles) features steep slopes, ridges, and ravines with a rich forest that has a diverse and undisturbed understory. Van Meter State Park, Miami 64344. SR 41, S 6 m.; SR 122, N 5 m. VAN METER *STATE PARK*: SR 41 and SR 122 S and N 11 m.

Riverfront Park. 3 acres. Camping, boating, ramp, picnicking, restrooms. SR 41 at Missouri River.

1. Origin unknown; usually commendatory, for the color green, but probably for Treaty of *Greenville*.

MILAN

Population: 1,767   Map E-1

Selected in 1845 as county seat of newly organized Sullivan County, the town was platted twice at the same site, which was first been settled in 1840 by A. C. Hill and known as Hill Settlement. Reportedly, the first court-ordered plat (by Esom Hanant, 1846) was never filed because the paper was worn out during the selling of the lots. In 1850, the court ordered Abner

Gilstrap to survey another plat. Local tradition, relying on a 1905 obituary of prominent 1844–1905 resident M. B. Whitter (who died at age 102), claims Whitter named the town Milan (locally pronounced My'lun) because of "having read the noted Milan Decree," which was one of a series of British and French trade embargoes from 1806 to 1810 *(War of 1812)*.[1] A stock place-name used for 13 American towns, Milan usually reflects, like this site's first post office, Pharsalia,[2] the 19th-century fashion of selecting exotic or famous foreign cities for namesakes *(La Plata)*. Extremely slow to grow, this Milan was not shown on some maps from 1846 to 1852 (the city was not incorporated until 1867; an 1859 attempt failed). The arrival c. 1872 of the Burlington & Southwestern *Railroad*, which was crossed in 1879 by the Quincy, Missouri & Pacific, helped establish it as a trading center (as it is today) for a sparsely populated county. Post offices: Pharsalia 1845–1847; Milan 1847–now.

Architecture. NATIONAL HISTORIC REGISTER: Campground Church and *Cemetery*; west of town, inquire locally. TOWN SQUARE: Late 19th-century styles, including the Stanley Hotel (1891), still in business.

Bairdstown Erratic. Reportedly the largest and most perfectly preserved of its kind in northern Missouri, this pink granite boulder has an exposed surface measuring 20 by 20 feet (8 feet high) and an estimated age of 1.7–2.5 billion years. Junction SR 6 and SR OO; SR OO, N approx. 7 m. (0.2 m. S of junction with SR BB) to Bairdstown.[3] From Bairdstown Methodist Church (Vernacular, 1885; *cemetery* adjacent): private road (permission: first house past church), NE 0.3 m.; look 250 yards SE. *(Glacial Erratics)*

Browning, Mo. Platted in 1872 along the Burlington & Southwestern *Railroad*, the town was named by Justin Clark, a railroad company officer, who honored the sister-in-law of Judge O. H. Browning, a resident of Burlington, Iowa. Post office: 1873–now. SR 5, S 12 m. ROCKY FORD: Public fishing area and a swimming hole formed by an unusual (for this area) exposure of limestone. Rapids, picnicking. SR 5, N 1.3 m.; GR, W 0.5 m. to concrete low-water bridge at Locust Creek.

Humphreys, Mo. The town was platted in 1881 as Haley City[4] around a town park and along the Quincy, Missouri & Pacific *Railroad*. When the first addition was added in 1882, the name was changed to Humphreys, possibly to match the post office name, which honors a pioneer family. Like many small Missouri towns, it declined after the railroad discontinued service here; derelict. Small park, picnic shelter. Post office: 1881–now. SR 5/SR 6, S 5 m.; SR 6, W 9 m.

Museums. DEPOT: Railroad, 1882; restored. More elaborate than most, this dark red structure with a copper roof served the town from 1879 to 1980. Railroad memorabilia, related items, caboose adjacent. E. 3d. SULLIVAN COUNTY HISTORICAL: Vernacular, c. 1879–1880. Built as division headquarters for the railroad, the building was later used as a temporary courthouse, then a jail. Period rooms, local historical items, a doll collection, and a locally painted mural depicting the area c. 1900. Square; Water at 2d.

Recreation. LAKES: (1) Sears Community. About 20 acres. Fishing (bass, bluegill, crappie, channel catfish), restrooms, boat ramp; easy access; no gas motors. SR 6, E 1 m.; SR Y, E 1.9 m.; SR RA, N 2.4 m. (2) Elmwood. 190 acres. Fishing (bass, bluegill, crappie, channel catfish), restrooms, boat ramp; camping; 5 h.p. motors. SR 5, N approx. 1.9 m. (3) Others: two small lakes east of town (bass and crappie). LOCUST CREEK *WILDLIFE AREA.*

Sullivan County Courthouse. Moderne, 1939. The county's fourth, this 110-by-66-foot three-story brick and limestone courthouse was designed by a favorite son, 23-year-old L. V. DeWitt. Courthouse square is set on a leveled Indian mound (V-shaped, c. 15 feet high, pointing NW); three skeletons were found during excavation. The county's third courthouse (1908–1938) was a former railroad building (Museums, above) that was bought for $6,000 as a temporary replacement after the second one burned. Cost: $25,500 (*WPA* assistance). Downtown. (*County Profiles*)

1. As a suspicious coincidence, Whitter's two previous residences at Unionville, Ohio, and St. Albans, Vt., were both relatively close to towns named Milan.
2. Classical 19th-century name from Lucan's mediocre epic poem "On the Civil War," often mistakenly called Pharsalia, where Caesar defeated Pompey in 48 B.C. at Pharsalus, today's Farsala, Greece.
3. M. B. Baird; p.o. 1858–1884, 1893–1903.
4. Pioneer family, no p.o.

MILL SPRING
Population: 252   Map H-7

Platted in 1871 along the Black River by the St. Louis & Iron Mountain *Railroad* as a water stop for its wood-burning locomotives, the town was named by the railroad for the nearby spring that powered a sawmill (inquire locally). Clarkson Company's narrow-gauge railroad, the Mill Spring, Current River & Barnesville, was chartered in 1884 and later acquired by the Missouri Southern. It hauled yellow pine to lumber mills from Reynolds County (Leeper, below) to here. Like this area's other 1885–1915 lumber boomtowns (*Bunker*), Mill Spring declined after the timber was cut. Post offices: Otter Creek[1] 1853–1876, 1885–1888; Mill Spring 1874–now.

Architecture. Testifying to former prosperity are about

eight vernacular Greek Revival and Italianate houses

The Gulf. Also known as Blue Grotto, this water-filled sinkhole's exposed portion is about 100 feet long, 20 feet wide, and 40 feet to the water level. A flooded cave is reported to extend about 500 feet further with a depth of nearly 200 feet. This exposed oval of luminescent blue water creates an optical illusion, reflecting sky and land in a confusion of which way is up or down. SR 49 at railroad tracks, S 2 m. to stop sign at Carson Hills Cemetery; GR (stay right), E 1.8 m. to narrow trail, right 0.3 m. (*Collapsed Cave Systems*)

Leeper, Mo. A Clarkson Company town established c. 1884 about a mile north of the mills at Mill Spring, Leeper was also headquarters for Clarkson's railroad (Mill Spring history, above). First called Leeper Station, it was named for Capt. William T. Leeper, an early resident (c. 1868) at Otter Creek. Post office: 1885–1967. SR 49, N 2 m. ARCHITECTURE: The Methodist Episcopal Church South (c. 1914) is weathered gray but still displays its Romantic design. Missouri Southern's headquarters' building is a two-story frame structure. The Ozark Hotel (c. 1930) reportedly was once Wayne County's most elaborate resort. VICTORY HORSE *TRAIL.*

Recreation. *FLOAT STREAM:* Black River. MARKHAM SPRING CAMPGROUND / PICNIC AREA (*National Forests*): Tent and RV camping, tables, fireplaces, flush toilets, water hydrants, dump station, boat ramp, Black River access, trails.

1. Via the creek for the animal.

MINEOLA
Estimated population: 70   Map G-4

The town was platted in 1879 by H. E. Scanland (with the plat filed in 1880) as Mineral Springs (Spring, below) along the Loutre River at the former site of Loutre Lick (below). In 1881, when the Mineola post office was established, Scanland paid the legal fees for a petition to change the town's name to Mineola (no reason was given). Local sources claim the federal post office dropped an "n" from the proposed "Minneola" and the town's spelling conformed. The name could have either of two popular derivations, or both: (1) from the Souian word "minneola" meaning "water much" (e.g. Minneola, Minn., and Mineola, Ga.), and (2) from the personal names Minnie and Ola, in this case Scanland's daughter Minnie Maude and her friend Ola Gregory (e.g. Mineola, Kans., also spelled Minneola, and Mineola, Tex.). Derelict. Post office: 1881–1967. (*Boonslick Trails*)

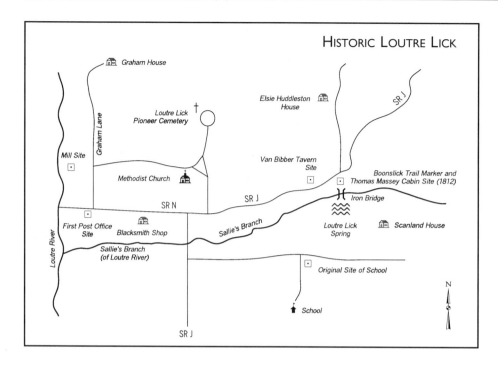

HISTORIC LOUTRE LICK

Loutre Lick, Mo. The community grew around a tavern built in 1821 by Isaac Van Bibber, the adopted son of Daniel Boone. Van Bibber bought the property in 1815 from Nathan Boone *(Defiance: Boone Home)*, who received this site and the area around Graham Cave (Recreation, below) as a Spanish land grant c. 1800. Salt manufacturing at the spring failed, but the slightly salty water was widely acclaimed as medicinal, especially for stomach and bowel ailments. A popular rest stop on the *Boonslick Trail*, probably because of the Boone reputation and Van Bibber's garrulous personality, Loutre Lick declined after the trail's importance waned; Van Bibber died in 1836 (Spring, below). Loutre is French (L'outre) meaning "the otter," but "otter" is the intended meaning here, with lick being a salt source for animals. Post offices: 1818–1823, 1827–1834; passed to *Danville*. (Architecture / Remnants, above)

Recreation. DANVILLE *WILDLIFE AREA* / NATURAL AREAS: SR J, S 0.9 m.; GR, E; signs *(Danville: Recreation)*. GRAHAM CAVE *STATE PARK*: SR J, E 3 m. to I-270 N. Outer Rd. / SR TT, then W approx. 2 m.

Spring. In 1824 U.S. politicians Henry Clay, Daniel Webster, John Calhoun, and Thomas Hart Benton praised the site and Loutre Lick Spring, as did writer Washington Irving (1832). An 1893 bottling plant and spa development failed. In 1916 the site was referred to as a Eureka[1] for visitors of moderate income. The water, first controlled in 1880 by a hollow sycamore tree, was later contained by a concrete form and covered by a frame gazebo. Private. (Mineola history, above; map of Historic Loutre Lick, above)

1. Eureka Springs, Ark., a stylish spa.

Architecture / Remnants. All are located at or just off the former *Boonslick Trail*; see the map of Historic Loutre Lick. BLACKSMITH SHOP: Vernacular, c. 1884; second-story addition. Originally one-story stone. ELSIE HUDDLESTON HOUSE: Vernacular, early 1880s. The front two rooms are from Scanland's house (below); moved here in the early 1880s. GRAHAM HOUSE: Vernacular, begun in 1829 by Robert Graham; successive additions (Graham Cave *State Park*). Private. IRON BRIDGE: Early 1900s. Built with stone pilings from *Danville's* courthouse. METHODIST CHURCH: Vernacular, c. 1917. MILL SITE: Remnants of an 1883 mill. MT. HOREB BAPTIST CHURCH: Vernacular, 1897; National Historic Register. Organized in 1833 in the home of Samuel Boone, Daniel's nephew. Out of town; inquire locally. SCANLAND HOUSE: Folk (Front Gable and Wing), late 1890s. Named Cliffbrook for nearby cliffs and Sallie's Branch; two-story frame; private. SCHOOL: Vernacular, 1892; closed 1952. One-story frame; moved from the road south to higher ground to avoid flooding; private. TAVERN: site of Van Bibber's tavern (Loutre Lick, below).

Callaway Grave Site. In 1815 Callaway County namesake Capt. James Callaway, the son of Jemima Boone *(Defiance: Missouri Territory Village)*, and three rangers were killed by Indians (possibly Sauk) during the *War of 1812*. The rangers' graves have three stone markers (west side of road, a possible alternate route of the *Boonslick Trail*). Callaway's site: NE of road, over the hill at Loutre River and a branch. SR N, W 0.8 m. (past bridge); GR, due S (keep left) approx. 4.7 m. (site: approx. 0.3 m. S of a W junction).

MISSOURI COMPROMISE, 1820

The Missouri Compromise ended U.S. congressional debate over Missouri's admission to the Union by framing legislation admitting Missouri as a slave state and Maine as a free state and excluding slavery in the

Louisiana Purchase territories north of 36°30' north latitude (the Mason-Dixon Line).[1] The practice of pairing slave and free states remained in effect until the repeal of the Missouri Compromise by the 1854 Kansas-Nebraska Act *(Kansas Border War)* and the 1857 divided U.S. Supreme Court's Dred Scott v. Sanford decision that affirmed the repeal by declaring the compromise unconstitutional *(County Profiles: Douglas; Noel: South West City; St. Louis: Market Street Area Sights).*

1. Named for 1763–1767 surveyors who divided Pennsylvania and Maryland.

MOBERLY

Population: 12,839   Map F-3

Platted in 1858 by the recently chartered Chariton & Randolph *Railroad* at its planned junction west from the North Missouri *Railroad,* the town had a population of one person until 1866. In 1861, residents of nearby Allen[1] were offered the same amount of property they currently owned in exchange for moving their houses and buildings to Moberly. Only Patrick Lynch accepted the offer, becoming the town's only resident from 1861 to 1866. The *Civil War* and restructuring of the railroad (sold to the North Missouri Railroad in 1864) delayed rail construction until 1866, when town lots were advertised for sale by the North Missouri Railroad. Named for the first president of the Chariton & Randolph Railroad, William Moberly, the town earned the nickname Magic City by growing from a *prairie* devoid of water and trees to a major shipping and railroad division point with railroad shops by 1872. The 1896 population of 12,000 also reflected development of local and area coal mines in the 1880s and 1890s (Historical and Railroad Museum, below). Moberly is still an important railroad town, with an economy that also relies on light manufacturing, education, and the Missouri Training Center for Men, a medium-security penal institution. Post offices: Allen 1857–1869; Moberly 1869–now. Home of Moberly Area Junior College and Moberly Area Vocational School.

Contemporary Folk Art. Accented by a quarter-mile-long wrought-iron fence is an imposing yellow brick entrance gate guarded by seated and standing lions and capped by an American eagle. Set in the brick are colorful windmill turbines. Inside the fence are clothed statues as well as life-size sculptures of a horse and a moose. US 63, N of town; N 1.1 m. from airport.

Ginkgo Tree. This tree, transplanted here from the 1904 St. Louis World's Fair, has a 139-inch circumference as measured four and a half feet above the ground. 114 S. Williams; inquire locally.

Grand Divide. *Grand Divide.*

Higbee, Mo. Originally Bournesburg,[2] the town was renamed for James Higbee, who gave land c. 1872 to the Missouri Kansas & Texas *Railroad* for a depot. Post office: 1873–now. SR A, S 6 m. BRADLEY HOUSES: The area has two childhood homes of WWII five-star general and army chief of staff Omar Bradley *(Trails: Moniteau Wilderness),* whose parents operated the Mutual Telephone Co. switchboard and whose father was also a rural schoolteacher. (1) Vernacular, early 1900s. E end of Grand (SR BB). (2) Vernacular, two-story frame. Railroad and Cross Streets in Clark.[3] SR B, E 10 m.

Historical and Railroad Museum. Housed in a railroad express building just south of the working depot (Italianate affinities, 1889), the museum displays railroad memorabilia and local historical items, including those related to former residents Omar Bradley (Higbee, above) and Jack Conroy, who won a Pulitzer Prize for "The Disinherited," a novel about the local coal mines (the site of his Monkey Nest Mining Camp: SR JJ, N 1 m.; private; inquire locally). Midtown; US 63B, W on Reed to N. Sturgeon (100).

Oakland Cemetery / Lincoln Statue. Platted in 1871, the cemetery now has more residents than Moberly. The first interment was former slave Abe Doughty. A 1915 Italian marble statue of Abraham Lincoln, believed to be Missouri's only life-size sculpture of him, faces south toward a 1901 Confederate statue. US 63, W 2 blocks to SR EE (Rollins). *(Cemeteries)*

Parks. Moberly's many parks include the following. LIONS / BEUTH: 25 acres. Site of a former clay quarry; picnic facilities, fishing, restrooms. Features a bridge made from a double-deck rail car carrier. E side; US 63, E on McKinsey. ROTHWELL: 350 acres. Ball fields, pool, tennis, picnic facilities, campground (hookups, tents), trails (bikers, hikers, horses), and lake (a 1907 reservoir for the railroad) with 15 m. of shoreline, swimming, boating (trolling motors only), fishing. W of US 24 at US 63.

Recreation. BENNITT *WILDLIFE AREA.* MONITEAU WILDERNESS *TRAIL.* SUGAR CREEK LAKE: Also known as Moberly Lake. The city's water supply; boating (10 h.p.), fishing, hunting, picnicking, camping. SR DD, N 2.2 m.

1. Origin unknown; p.o. 1857–1869; defunct; a shipping point for Randolph County seat *Huntsville.*
2. Early settler; p.o. 1838–1842.
3. Originally Clark's Switch; both Clark origins unknown; p.o. Perche, for the nearby creek locally pronounced pur'shi and probably twisted etymologically from French "roche perceé," meaning rock or cliff with a hole, via Osage "paçi," or hilltop, 1877–1887; Clark 1887–now.

Musicians picnicking near Billings. (FROM "BILLINGS CENTENNIAL, 1871-1971")

MONETT
Population: 6,529   Map D-7

Platted in 1887 by the Monett Town Company as a division point for the St. Louis & San Francisco *Railroad* on the north side of the tracks and named for a railroad employee, the town was incorporated in 1888, absorbing nearby Plymouth,[1] whose post office was Gonten.[2] Plymouth was originally named Billings[3] before it was platted in 1871 as Plymouth along the south side of the then Atlantic & Pacific *Railroad* by G. A. Purdy, an agent for the line.[4] After Purdy vacated the railroad's Plymouth in 1876, Martha and Samuel Withers platted another Plymouth in 1881 (p.o. Gonten). To add to the confusion of town and post office names, Billings was the name of the first Plymouth's post office because of an existing Plymouth post office along the railroad in Christian County. In 1871, the Billings post office moved up the railroad line and into Christian County to absorb the Plymouth post office there and become the town of Billings (p.o. Billings). Monett's situation as a division point resulted in its dominance, and the town grew as a shipping point for area berry growers. Today its economy combines shipping with light manufacturing and processing companies. Post offices: Gonten 1881–1887; Monett 1887–now. Home of Monett Area Vocational School.

Butterfield Stage Stop. The site of J. D. Crouch's *Overland Mail Company* stage station is marked. US 60, E 4 m.; SR Z, E 4 m.; GR, continue E 2.5 m.

Calton Mill, Mo. Founded at a mill (derelict; c. 1840) at Little Flat Creek, the community was also known as Tom Town for the son of Morgan Calton, the mill owner and builder. US 60, E 4 m.; SR Z, E 3.5 m.; GR, S 2.3 m. (keep left).

Courdin House / Waldenses. Italian Folk, 1875; National Historic Register. This stucco one-story house with few windows and thick walls was built by David W. Courdin, a member of the Protestant Waldensian Colony that immigrated here in 1874 from near the French–Italian border. The Waldenses, a relatively small religious sect, was founded by 12th-century Lyons merchant Peter Waldo, who adopted a life of apostolic poverty. In 1535 the group prepared a new French version of the Bible that included two prefaces by John Calvin, the first of his Protestant writings. Few Waldenses immigrated to America. This site was Missouri's only colony. Unmarked blacktop, SE 1.7 m.; inquire locally.

Pierce City, Mo. Platted in 1870 along the Atlantic & Pacific *Railroad*, the town was named for railroad president Andrew Pierce. The name was misspelled Peirce on the original plat, and some maps list the town as Peirce City. Post office: 1870–now. SR 37, N 6 m. ARCHITECTURE: Downtown has unrestored 19th-century commercial structures. A 1922 stone band-stand with a conical tile roof is set in the center of the street, dividing traffic left and right (Commercial at Walnut, downtown).

1. Origin unknown; popular name from 1620 Mass. Pilgrims of the Plymouth Co., Plymouth, England.
2. Origin unknown.
3. John Billings, RR official; p.o. (in Barry County) 1870–1871; (in Christian County) 1871–now.
4. G. A. Purdy is the namesake for Purdy, Mo. (p.o. 1880–now), which was also known as Winslow for 1881 St. Louis & San Francisco RR president E. F. Winslow; p.o. 1880–now.

MONROE CITY
Population: 2,701   Map G-2

The town was platted in 1857 along the grade of the Hannibal & St. Joseph *Railroad* as a shipping point by E. B. Tallcott, a building contractor for the railroad who anticipated the need at this location for a station. Named for Monroe County, it developed into a grain, livestock, and poultry market. Today two federal high-ways help the town serve as a gateway to nearby Mark Twain Lake *(Lakes: Corps of Engineers)*. Post office: 1860–now.

Elmslie State Forest Natural Area. 100 acres. Part of Elmslie *State Forest* along the south fork of the North River. Features a great diversity of plants in hills and draws; the dominant tree is oak (post, white, and red). Box 324, Hannibal 63401. SR Z, N 3.1 m.; SR CC, W 1.5 m.; GR, N 3 m.

Gray Ghost Museum. Highlights the *Civil War* in northeast Missouri. SR W, E 4 m.; SR J, S approx. 5.6 m.

Recreation. MARK TWAIN LAKE / CLARENCE CANNON DAM and MARK TWAIN *STATE PARK* / MARK TWAIN BIRTHPLACE STATE HISTORIC SITE: SR 24, W 8 m.; SR 107, S 6 m. *(Lakes: Corps of Engineers)*

St. Jude's Episcopal Church. Gothic Revival, 1866–1867; tower added early 1900s. Limestone with lancet stained-glass windows, this L-shaped structure was designed by a civil engineer of the railroad. N. Main (311).

MONTGOMERY CITY
Population: 2,281   Map G-3

The town was platted in 1853 by Benjamin P. Curd, who correctly speculated that the North Missouri *Railroad* would tailor its route and locate a depot here in exchange for town lots (the railroad was graded in 1856, with tracks laid in 1857). It was named for

Montgomery County. As the county's principal trad-ing center, it eventually won a long political and legal battle (1888–1924) with *Danville* for county seat, mak-ing it Missouri's newest seat of justice (Montgomery County Courthouse, below). Post office: 1857–now.

Architecture. DOWNTOWN: 19th- and 20th-century styles. NEW PROVIDENCE METHODIST CHURCH: Vernacular, 1857; remodeled 1907. A second-story lodge was removed in 1907 from this frame structure. Two front entrances divided the congregation by sex, with corresponding sanctuary seating. *Cemetery* adja-cent. SR 161, N 3.8 m.; SR V, E 4.6 m. to S of Bellflower;[1] SR E, E 1.6 m.; GR, S 1.2 m.; GR, E 0.5 m.

Historical Museum. Vernacular, mid-1880s. Originally the Farmers and Traders Bank, this two-story brick building now features local historical items and period rooms. 112 W. 2d.

Middletown, Mo. Growing from the nearby 1817 set-tlement of Charley Wells, Middletown was platted in 1834 along a main road approximately midway between *Louisiana* and *Fulton*. Post offices: Middle-town 1832–1835, 1837–now; West Fork[2] 1833–1835. SR 161, N 7 m. to Buell;[3] continue SR 161, N 6 m. METHODIST EPISCOPAL CHURCH: Gothic Revival, 1870–1871; rebuilt 1889; addition 1956; organized 1848. Services are still held here. SR BB, in town.

Montgomery County Courthouse. Moderne, 1953–1955. The county's fifth courthouse for its four county seats,[4] this two-story structure with classical affinities was designed by E. T. Friton and is reminiscent of his *WPA* design for Dunklin County. In 1889, Montgomery City built a courthouse to accommodate some county offices. After *Danville's* courthouse burned in 1901, no vote could be mustered to build a new one there (Montgomery City history, above). Cost: $383,599. Downtown. *(County Profiles)*

Wellsville, Mo. The town was platted in 1856 by Carty Wells, the town namesake and a *Mexican War* veteran, on his government land grant for army service. Wells donated five acres for a North Missouri *Railroad* depot (the railroad arrived in 1861). Post offices: Little Loutre[5] 1853–1857; Wellsville 1857–now. SR 19, N 8 m. DEPOT MUSEUM: Railroad, 1907. Built by the Chicago, Burlington & Quincy; moved here in 1981. Furnished, railroad memorabilia, caboose. SR 19, in town. DIGGS WHITE OAK NATURAL AREA: SR ZZ, W 2.6 m.; SR RA, W 2.7 m. *(Farber: Laddonia)*. WILD-LIFE AREAS: Diggs, Wellsville Lake.

1. The plant; p.o. 1887.
2. West Fork of the Cuivre River.
3. 1903 businessman Buell Hensley; p.o. 1904–1978.
4. Pinckney, 1819–1826 *(High Hill)*; Lewiston, 1826–1834 *(High Hill)*; Danville, 1834–1924; and Montgomery City, 1924–now.
5. Nearby Little Loutre Creek; *Mineola: Loutre Lick.*

MONTICELLO

Population: 106   Map G-2

Missouri's smallest county seat was platted in 1833 as a central location for newly organized Lewis County and named for former U.S. president Thomas Jefferson's Virginia home (in Italian, Monticello means little mountain). Initially prosperous as a trading center situated on major roads, it was eventually isolated from major transportation routes (steamboat, railroad, and federal highway). Post office: 1834–now.

Deer Ridge Wildlife Area. *Wildlife Areas.*

La Belle, Mo. The town was established in 1856 by storekeeper and first postmaster William Triplett. The name he chose, which translates as "The Beautiful," probably refers to the countryside. Post office: 1856–now. SR 16, W 7 m. to Lewistown (below); SR 6, W 7 m. LA BELLE CITY LAKE: 335 acres. Fishing, boat ramp, and hunting; handicapped accessible. SR D, S approx. 3 m.; sign.

Lewis County Courthouse. Second Empire, 1875; additions. The county's second permanent courthouse, this two-story brick structure (originally 75 by 50 by 30 feet) with a patterned mansard roof, bracketed eaves, and a cupola is one of Missouri's few remaining 1870s courthouses. Cost: $10,000. Downtown. *(County Profiles)*

Lewistown, Mo. First called Primrose[1] in 1858 (or Primrose Stage Station), the town was platted in 1871 along the Quincy, Missouri & Pacific *Railroad* as Lewiston, honoring Meriwether Lewis *(Lewis and Clark Expedition).* In 1897, it broadened its name to Lewistown, possibly to make clear the intended namesake. Today's industries include America's only TomBoy Lawn Mower Manufacturing Company and Mark Twain Media Dura-Clad Books, one of America's five largest jobbers of educational books. Post offices: Primrose 1858–1860, 1862–1872; Lewiston 1872–1897; Lewistown 1897–now. SR 16, W 7 m. QUINCY, MISSOURI & PACIFIC DEPOT: Railroad, 1871; National Historic Register. The town's first depot; some original furnishings. In town.

1. Origin unknown, usually a personal name.

MORMONS

Properly called Latter Day Saints or Saints, the Mormons are members of the Church (and Reorganized Church) of Jesus Christ of Latter Day Saints *(Independence).* The church was organized in 1830 at Fayette, N.Y., by Joseph Smith; its theology and law are based on the Bible, the Book of Mormon, "Doctrine and Covenants" (Smith's revelations, published in 1835), and "The Pearl of Great Price" (Smith's visions, lost and revised scriptures, and 13 articles of faith, published in 1851 after Smith's death). All of these books are reportedly divinely inspired. The Book of Mormon (published in 1829) sets forth Smith's religious experiences, including his first vision in 1820 of the Father and Son promising further revelations; it is purportedly "by the gift and power of God," whereby in 1823 the angel Moroni revealed the existence of gold plates on which were written "the fullness of the everlasting Gospel" *(Richmond: Cemeteries).* In 1827, with the aid of magic stones or spectacles called Urim and Thummin by Smith, he translated the word of God from "reformed Egyptian hieroglyphs" on the plates that had been kept by "ancient Americans" (600 B.C.–A.D. 400) who escaped to America from Jerusalem to avoid Babylonian captivity. This eclectic religion agitated nonbelievers, a situation compounded by the theocracy and the communality of the Mormons, whose industry and like-mindedness enabled them to form successful and competitive economic and political communities that outsiders found threatening. Pressured to leave New York in 1831, Smith chose Kirkland, Ohio, but nevertheless began plans that same year for a temple lot in *Independence,* from which Mormons were forced to move in 1833. Attempting to settle in Clay County *(Liberty),* they were forced to move again in 1835 to Daviess and Caldwell Counties *(Gallatin; Kingston).* In 1838 Gov. Lillburn W. Boggs, declaring that the more than 2,000 Mormons in the state were seditious, ordered the state militia to either exterminate or remove them from Missouri. The ensuing Mormon War resulted in the deaths of approximately 20 Mormons and 1 militia soldier. Joseph Smith and other leaders were arrested and jailed *(Liberty),* and by 1839 Smith and the Mormons had left Missouri, establishing themselves at Nauvoo, Ill.

MOUND CITY

Population: 1,263   Map B-2

Blacksmith Peter Forbes, who built a shop in 1852 at the future townsite, was followed by Galen Crow in 1855, who moved the post office from Jackson's Point (below) to here, changing its name to North Point.[1] Crow and others formed a town company and platted Mound City in 1857 along Davis Creek, naming it for the local *loess* mounds (Recreation, below). Its location by the road from St. Joseph to Council Bluffs, Iowa, the development during the 1870s–1880s of the Kansas City, St. Joseph & Council Bluffs *Railroad*, and today's I-29 have helped make it Holt County's largest town. Post offices: North Point 1855–1871; Mound City 1871–now.

Baldwin Cemetery. This is the county's oldest verified cemetery, established c. 1840 after the 1839 arrival of Jeremiah and Daniel Baldwin. Set on a bluff; ornate markers. SR E, S approx. 2 m. *(Cemeteries)*

Depot Museum. Railroad, 1921; National Historic Register. One of Missouri's few two-and-a-half-story railroad depots, this stucco and tile structure features early post office items, 19th-century clothing, and period rooms (e.g. a 1930s kitchen and a country store). 311 State.

Griffith Park. 60 acres. Golf, tennis, pool, picnic shelters, community building, horseshoes, restrooms, playground, restaurant, lounge. N end of Nebraska.

Jackson's Point, Mo. Settled at the south fork of Davis Creek along the road between St. Joseph and Council Bluffs, Iowa, the town was named for the post office, whose first postmaster, A. P. Jackson, bought Thomas Ferguson's 1840 wayside tavern here. Post offices: Bluff[2] 1846–1850; Jackson's Point 1850–1854. Defunct.

Recreation. BIG LAKE *STATE PARK:* SR 118, W 6.3 m.; SR 111, S 2.2. m. MCCORMACK LOESS MOUNDS NATURAL AREA: SR E, S 6.6 m. *(Forest City).* SQUAW CREEK *NATIONAL WILDLIFE REFUGE.*

1. Origin unknown, possibly for the location on the north side of Davis Creek.
2. Descriptive.

MOUNTAIN GROVE
Population: 4,182   Map F-6

Today's town is a collection of closely spaced communities from both sides of the Wright–Texas County line that were consolidated in 1882 when the Kansas City, Springfield & Memphis *Railroad* was being built. In 1857 old Mountain Grove (below) was platted along the Springfield Road (now 9th St.) near the intersection of a road from Lebanon and named for its location. In 1859 Mountain Store, a general-store community on a mountain top, was established near these same roads in Texas County; in 1860, along with the Hickory Spring post office,[1] it was moved closer to the crossroads in Wright County. About 1860, the community of Fyan[2] was established. When the railroad began

The State Fruit Experimental Station at Mountain Grove.

surveying a grade c. 1880, Mountain Store was moved south to Mountain Grove, anticipating the grade's construction there, but the railroad track was laid c. 1882 to the north of nearby Fyan. In 1882, Joseph Fisher bought land on the south side of the railroad, donated a depot, and platted a town named Fyan (along today's Front St.). Dr. Isaac Lane bought land in 1882 on the north side of the railroad, donated land for a square (Town Square, below), and petitioned the court for the name Mountain Grove, which was approved in 1882. The rivalry was settled in 1886 when the two towns incorporated as Mountain Grove, which grew as a trading center that today is Wright County's largest town. Incidentally, the three former communities are within nine blocks of each other (9th to Front). Post offices: Hickory Spring 1853–1875; Mountain Grove 1875–now. Home of Mountain Grove Area Vocational School.

Architecture. National Historic Register: Faurot Hall (Queen Anne, 1901), now State Fruit Experimental Station; SR 95, 0.25 m. N of US 60.

Cabool, Mo. Reportedly, the real estate promoters who platted this Kansas City, Ft. Scott & Memphis *Railroad* town in 1882 liked the sound of the name. Although it is not close in spelling to their intention, Kabul, the capital of Afghanistan, it does sound the same. Post office: Cedar Bluff[3] 1857–1863, 1871–1882; Cabool 1882–now. SR 60, W 9 m. *FLOAT STREAM:* North Fork White River. NOBLETT LAKE CAMPGROUND / PICNIC AREA / *TRAIL (National Forests):* 80-acre lake, fishing (bass, sunfish, catfish), small springs, water, pit toilets, fire rings, boat launch. RIDGE RUNNER *TRAIL.*

Old Mountain Grove. Surrounded by houses, this parcel of land (Mountain Grove history, above) is still owned by the city; today it is marked only by the remnants of the town's first well. US 60B, N on Main, E on 9th, S on Water to Poe.

Parks. The city's nine parks include the following. ALUMNI MEMORIAL: Granite wall with names of school graduates since 1888, picnic shelter, restrooms, springhouse, courtyard. N end of Green's Park; Wall, N of US 60. WOODLAND: Pool, picnicking, archery. NW side; US 60B, N on Bush, E on 13th.

Topaz Mill / Area Mills. Vernacular, c. 1893. Topaz Mill is reportedly the area's oldest. It was built by a Choctaw woman and her husband on a land grant acquired in 1830 from an Indian agent. Set at the North Fork of the White River, today's unrestored three-story *gristmill* has an idyllic setting. Other area mills can be seen in a 120-mile round-trip tour *(Gainesville)*. SR 95, S 10 m.; SR 76, E 1.5 m.; SR EE, S 2.6 m.; GR, E 1.5 m. to Topaz.[4] Tour maps: Mountain Grove chamber of commerce.

Town Square / Bandstand. Part of the original 1882 plat, the square is still the center of town life. Its bandstand (Craftsman, 1915; restored 1987) was dedicated in 1915 by U.S. Vice President T. R. Marshall (he served from 1913 to 1921 under Woodrow Wilson) and dedicated again by Vice President George Bush after its restoration. The square includes a bronze statue of a Civil War soldier facing south, an Italian marble statue of a WWII soldier, and a triangular shaft honoring Korean and Vietnam veterans. US 60B, S on Main.

1. Set in a hickory grove at a spring; 1853–1875.
2. County judge R. W. Fyan; no p.o.
3. Descriptive location.
4. Topaz, Calif., which was named for the occurrence of the gem; p.o. 1893–1943.

MOUNTAIN VIEW
Population: 2,036   Map G-7

Platted in 1888 by the Kansas City, Ft. Scott & Memphis *Railroad* in Goldsberry Township on land donated by Frank Pollock, the town was named for its 1879 post office, which was located in the Campbell-Goldsberry store (the first postmaster was John Campbell). This general-store community, set on a slight elevation with a broad view, served the local lumber industry. Post office: 1879–now.

Natural Areas. Both are part of Ozark National Scenic Riverways (below). BARN HOLLOW: 160 acres. Features narrow, steep-walled dolomite cliffs and ledges, *caves,* a headwater stream, and associated plants and animals. Barn Hollow Creek is clear with small deep pools, shallow riffles, and beaver ponds. Bear Cave is managed by the National Park Service. Box 490, Van Buren 63935. SR Y, N 1.3 m.; GR, N 1.5 m.; GR, E 1.3 m. JAM UP CAVE: 148 acres. Contains a variety of *collapsed cave* features, e.g. an enormous cave entrance, a swallow hole, a subterranean waterfall, a steep-walled sinkhole, and a karst window. The cave (about 80 feet high and 100 feet wide) opens into a dolomite cliff capped by sandstone; it supports rare plants and mosses from the glacial period. Access: by canoe from Jacks Fork or by foot (requires topographical map); inquire locally. Box 490, Van Buren 63965.

Parks. GLENN SMITH MEMORIAL: Frisco caboose, playground, horseshoes, pool, restrooms, and a small homestead best described as Folk Log Deco (with half-round logs, cross gables, an arched doorway, tapering walls, and a split-rail fence). SR 60, E city limits. VETERANS MEMORIAL: Folk Art stone entrance, Korean War–era jet plane, amphitheater (music Saturday nights). SR 17, S; 5th St., E 0.2 m.

Recreation. *FLOAT STREAMS:* Jacks Fork and Current Rivers. NATURAL AREAS: Above. OZARK NATIONAL SCENIC RIVERWAYS *(National Parks):* Blue Spring of Jacks Fork, Bluff View, Buck Hollow, and Rymers river access. SIMS VALLEY LAKE. 38 acres. Bass, sunfish, catfish. US 60, W 7 m.; SR RA, N 2.3 m.

MOUNT STERLING
Population: 70   Map G-4

The Shockley's Bluff community at the Gasconade River was selected in 1828 as the third county seat of Gasconade County *(Gasconade)* and was reportedly platted as Mount Sterling in 1832 on land donated by Isaac Perkins and Shockley. Its namesake is uncertain, but coincidence suggests Mount Sterling, Ky., which was founded in 1792 and became a county seat in 1797; its 1801 post office was called Montgomery Court House and its postmaster was Joseph Simpson (p.o., below). Kentucky's Mount Sterling was intended to honor an Indian mound located in town and Stirling, Scotland, but the spelling was corrupted and never changed. Mount Sterling, Mo., lost the county seat to *Hermann* in 1842 and declined during the Civil War. Post offices: Simpsons[1] 1824–c. 1828; Gasconade Court House 1828–1843; Mount Sterling 1843–1864, 1893–1965.

Architecture. DALLMEYER-LANGENBERG STORE: Vernacular, 1858, annex 1925. Near the steamboat landing; served as a store and post office with a second-story residence. SR A, S 2 m.; SR D, W 1.3 m. to Cooper Hill.[2] NEESE HOUSE: Vernacular, 1850; restored, German tradition. Stone cottage with a sharply peaked roof and small dormers. US 50, E 7 m. RAUSCHEN-BUSCH HOUSE: Vernacular, 1847; additions. One-story frame; derelict. US 50, E 5 m.; GR, N 1.25 m. REHMERT BLACKSMITH SHOP: Vernacular, 1860. Small frame building, a blacksmith shop for 95 years; derelict. US 50, E 6 m. (1.2 m. E of SR K); SR P (alternate) or old Jeff City State Rd., S 0.25 m. STONY POINT CHURCH: Log, 1857. All denominations. US 50, W 4 m.; SR N, N 2.5 m. to Ryors;[3] formerly Stony Point community.[4]

Drake, Mo. Formerly Lee's Cross Roads,[5] the community grew at the intersection of two main roads: an east–west road between St. Louis and Jefferson City and a north–south one between St. James and Hermann, along which iron blooms were hauled from the Maramec Iron Works near *St. James.* It was named for Sen. C. B. Drake. Post office: 1868–1938. US 50, E 11 m. ARCHITECTURE: Dr. H. A. Grosse house (he married Lee's daughter), built 1861; two-story frame; enlarged. US 50, in town. Ruskaup House, National Historic Register. US 50, W of town; inquire locally.

Filled Sinks. Road cuts show clay, shale, and sandstone in vertical fissures. US 50, E 3.5–4.5 m. (*Collapsed Cave Systems*)

Pilot Knob. US 50, E 5 m. (*Balds and Knobs*)

1. Personal name.
2. Personal name; p.o. Cooper's Hill 1860–1893; Cooper Hill 1893–1957.
3. Origin unknown; p.o. 1905–1934; defunct.
4. Descriptive location; no p.o.
5. 1835 settler Greenberry Lee; p.o. 1846 only.

MOUNT VERNON

Population: 3,638   Map D-7

When the town was platted in 1845 as a central location for newly organized Lawrence County, the court reportedly considered two names, Lawrenceburg and Mount Vernon, choosing the latter in honor of George Washington's home, which conveniently coincided with a previously established post office name. Aided by the 1891 arrival of the Greenville & Northern *Railroad* connecting it to Aurora (below) and the completion of I-44 through the county in 1965, it continues to prosper as a trading and political center. Post office: 1837–now.

Architecture. COUNTY JAIL: Vernacular, 1874. The 1877 site of Lawrence County's only public hanging; private. N side of square. DOWNTOWN: 19th- and 20th-century styles. MISSOURI REHABILITATION CENTER: Colonial Revival, 1907. Built as Missouri Tuberculosis Sanatorium. Main at SR CC.

Apple Butter Makin' Days. Since 1966. Contests, live entertainment, games, melodrama, cooking demonstrations. 2d weekend, October.

Aurora, Mo. The town was platted in 1870 as a depot town for the Atlantic & Pacific *Railroad,* which arrived in 1872. Its classical name (Latin for dawn, alluding to new beginnings) was justified when shallow deposits of pure galena ore were accidentally discovered in 1885 (*Eldon: Aurora Springs*). Post offices: Elk Horn[1] 1870–1871; Aurora 1871–now. SR 39, S 13 m.

Big Spring. The spring has an estimated daily flow of 12 million gallons. This former public picnic area is now owned by Baptist Hill Assembly; permission required. SR V, W 3.5 m.; inquire locally.

Chesapeake State Fish Hatchery. Missouri's oldest state fish hatchery, dating from 1926, completed a $5.3 million renovation in 1988, including hatchery buildings, computers (to monitor equipment and water quality), and a four-acre solar pond to preheat water. Two deep wells and Chesapeake Spring's million-gallon-per-day flow combine to deliver 450 gallons per minute (average temperature 55–58°F). Species in the 24 ponds include channel catfish, walleye, and bass (white, largemouth, and hybrid striped). I-44, E 3 m.; SR 174, E 5 m. to Chesapeake.[2]

Lawrence County Courthouse. Richardsonian Romanesque, 1901–1902; National Historic Register. The county's third, this 84-by-104-foot three-story stone courthouse has spring arches, arched windows, ornate square corner towers, and a domed tower supporting a statue of Justice. On the polished red granite cornerstone (northeast corner) is inscribed: "Be sure your sins will find you out" (Num. 32:23). Architect G. E. McDonald designed nearly identical courthouses for Andrew, Bates, and Johnson Counties. Cost: $48,875. Downtown. (*County Profiles*)

Natural Area / Wildlife Area. MOUNT VERNON *PRAIRIE:* 40 acres. Features a remnant of upland tallgrass *prairie* and interesting plants like porcupine grass and fringed poppy mallow. Rt. 2, Box 93, Lockwood 65682. SR Y, N 0.8 m.; SR CC, E 1.8 m.; GR, N 0.5 m. TALBOT *WILDLIFE AREA.*

Park / Cemetery. OLD CITY *CEMETERY:* Markers date from c. 1845. N. McCanse, NE of square. SPIRIT OF '76 PARK: Olympic-size pool, tennis, picnic area along creek, community building. Main, N of square.

1. Elks shed their horns annually. The finding of some fine specimens on or by a natural formation often resulted in its being named Elkhorn, which occasionally was transferred to a nearby habitation as a place-name.
2. U.S. frigate "Chesapeake" commanded by Lawrence County's namesake (*County Profiles*); p.o. 1850–1853, 1865–1914.

NEOSHO

Population: 9,254   Map C-7

The town was platted in 1839 south of the confluence of Shoal and Hickory Creeks as a central location for the county seat of newly organized Newton County. Its name, a Souian word ("ne" meaning water, "osho" probably meaning main, i.e. main water), comes from the 460-mile-long Neosho River, which flows through eastern Kansas and Oklahoma to the Arkansas (fed by, among others, Missouri's Spring and Elk Rivers) and which was first explored by François Chouteau c. 1800 (*Kansas City*). The town prospered, aided by a regional lead-mining boom (Granby, below), as a trade and political center but was destroyed during the *Civil War* (Newton County Courthouse, below). On October 21, 1861, pro-Southern state assembly members met here, adopting an act to secede from the Union. Approaching Federal troops caused them to retreat to *Cassville*. The town was reincorporated in 1866, and the arrival in 1870 of the Atlantic & Pacific *Railroad* helped reestablish it as a trading center. Post offices: Newton Court House 1839; Neosho 1839–now. Home of Crowder College (junior college; Camp Crowder, below).

Big Spring Park. Formerly an Indian campground, the site was used as a water source by settlers beginning in 1839 and as a tanyard during the 1850s. A park since the 1890s, today it is extensively landscaped; ornate flower gardens, picnic sites. The spring still flows. Town square; Spring, W 3 blocks.

Camp Crowder / College. Established in 1941 as an army signal school training base (some original barracks remain) and named for Enoch H. Crowder (*Trenton: Edinburg*), this was also a German POW camp in 1943–1945; closed in 1954. Today it is the location of Crowder College and a National Guard training site. Memorabilia, displays at Crowder College. 3006 Laclede; signs.

County Jail / Museum. Vernacular, 1887. Brick and frame, this 12-cell jail and sheriff's residence (closed in 1936) is now the county historical society. Features include replicas (e.g. a Victorian parlor, an 1880s kitchen), toys, clothing, farm tools, mining items, and war memorabilia (Civil War, WWI, WWII). McCord at Washington (121).

Flower Boxes. This self-proclaimed Flower Box City holds annual contests judging business and residential flower-box arrangements.

Fort Crowder Wildlife Area. *Wildlife Areas.*

George Washington Carver National Monument. *National Parks.*

Granby, Mo. The site of Southwest Missouri's oldest lead and zinc mines, Granby was established when Cornish miner William Foster discovered lead here in 1853, precipitating the "Granby Stampede" that resulted in a population of about 2,500 in 1874 (*Joplin*). Its stock place-name is from Granby, Mass., founded in 1768 and named for the Marquis of Granby, a member of the British cabinet. Post office: 1856–1863, 1865–now. US 60, E 7.7 m.

Neosho National Fish Hatchery. Established in 1888, this is the oldest of the 65 U.S. fish hatcheries and one of the few inside a city limits. Four gravity-flow springs provide 1,800 gallons per minute of 58°F water for rearing rainbow trout (about 70,000 pounds annually). Parklike setting (15.6 acres), picnic sites, aquariums, visitor center. Incidentally, the sea horse on the flagpole was made by an early-1900s employee. SR 86, S on Freeman, W on Park.

Newton County Courthouse. Moderne with Art Deco affinities, 1936. The county's fifth, this 112-by-90-foot four-story stone courthouse echoes Art Deco with a decorated frieze, subdued stylized motifs, and an emphasis on vertical lines, e.g. tall narrow windows in groups of three, a projecting two-story central entrance flanked by one-story wings, and the smaller fourth-story rooftop structure (the jail). Cost: $173,837. Downtown. (*County Profiles*)

Spook Light. *Joplin.*

Thomas Hart Benton. Born here in 1889, the great-nephew of his namesake, the Missouri politician (*County Profiles: Benton*), Benton left when a teenager, was hired by the "Joplin American" as a sketch artist (although untrained), later attended art school in Chicago, studied in France, and returned to the United States in 1913 as a nationally recognized painter. Two of his best-known works are at the state capitol (*Jefferson City: Walking Tour*) and the Truman Library (*Independence*). Some of his lithographs are here at the high school library (downtown, 511 Neosho Blvd.). Called an interpreter of midwestern America, he died in 1975. In town. (*Kansas City*)

NEVADA

Population: 8,597   Map C-5

Platted in 1855 (the first houses were built in 1856) as a central location for the county seat of newly organized Vernon County, the town was named Nevada City for Nevada City, Calif., as reportedly suggested by DeWitt C. Hunter, who had recently returned from the California goldfields. "City" was dropped after its 1869 incorporation. Nevada's stock place-name is derived from Spanish (snowed upon, snowy, especially mountains seen at a distance); the California town's namesake is the Nevada Mountains (named c. 1776). Known as the Bushwhacker Capital (*Kansas Border War*) because it served as headquarters for various Confederate detachments during the *Civil War*, Nevada was destroyed in 1863 by Federals who gave residents 10 minutes to pack and leave, then burned the town (*Order No. 11*). The town was rebuilt after the war, and the arrival of the Missouri, Kansas & Texas and the Missouri-Pacific *Railroads* (in 1869 and 1879 respectively) helped it prosper as a trading center. Post office: 1856–1861, 1863, 1866–now. Home of Cottey College (below) and Nevada Area Vo-Tech.

Architecture. FRANK JAMES HOUSE: Vernacular, late 1870s–early 1880s. James lived here with his family from 1885 to 1891 (*Kearney*). Incidentally, this frame house was paid for by W. C. Bronaugh, a rancher and the founder of Bronaugh, Mo.,[1] who was inspired to write "The Youngers' Fight for Freedom" after Cole Younger (supposedly) saved his life during the *Civil War* battle of Pea Ridge, Ark. US 54, S on Cedar (520). WALKING TOUR: Over half of the town's 19th-century structures are located around the courthouse square, bounded by Hunter, Washington, US 54, and Ash. Maps: chamber of commerce, 110 S. Adams, or at the Bushwhacker Museum (below). WILLIAM JOEL STONE HOUSE: Vernacular, 1877. This stone house is reportedly the town's oldest. William Stone (Vernon County Courthouse, below) was a U.S. congressman (1885–1891), governor (1893–1897), and U.S. senator (1903–1918). US 54, S on Cedar (527).

Bushwhacker Museum / Jail. Vernacular with Italianate affinities; 1860–c. 1871 (either built on the site of its unfinished and war-damaged predecessor or incorporated into the 1860 original building and completed in 1871); National Historic Register. Reportedly designed by itinerant English architect C. M. Libby, this two-story side-gabled sandstone building has wide unbracketed eaves and trim and a gabled and pedimented central projection that contains two narrow matching windows with segmental arched drip moldings. It was used as the county jail until 1960; the cells are original, which for 20th-century prisoners confirmed its reputation as the state's worse jail (*Gallatin: Rotary Jail*). Exhibits focus on cells, outlaws, bushwhackers, the Civil War, Victorian furnishings, clothing, guns, county historical items, and archaeology. Courthouse square; Main, N 1 block.

Cottey College. This women's junior college was founded in 1884 by Virginia A. Cottey and donated in 1927 to the P.E.O. Sisterhood (a private organization since 1869 that awards college scholarships to women). Enrollment: 350 (from 35 states and 12 countries). W side; US 54 at College.

Deepwood Cemetery. Among those buried here are town founders and Civil War veterans, including soldiers primarily from Wisconsin and Illinois in a 21-grave plot. US 54, S on Washington to Barr. (*Cemeteries*)

Montevallo, Mo. Settled c. 1854, the town was abandoned after being completely destroyed during the *Civil War*. A new Montevallo was built c. 1867 at a new location, which slightly affected the intent of the original's descriptive place-name, a pseudo-Italian word (meaning mountain and valley) intended to describe its location. Post office: 1854–1865, 1867–1968. US 71, S 5 m.; SR E, E 12.3 m. OLD MONTEVALLO: A derelict *cemetery* marks the site. SR E, W 0.9 m.; GR, W 0.3 m.

Natural Areas. LITTLE OSAGE *PRAIRIE*: 80 acres. This remnant of an upland tallgrass prairie has diversified plants. Rt. 2, Box 93, Lockwood 65682. US 71, S 5 m. to junction with SR E; GR, W 1.5 m. MARMATON RIVER BOTTOMS: 260 acres. A relatively flat area underlain by sandstone, it features a bottomland forest, *prairie*, and savanna. Slough grass dominates the wet prairie parts, and pecan trees are found in the forest. 2800 S. Brentwood Blvd., St. Louis 63144. US 71, N 10 m.; SR D, W 2.5 m.; SR O, S 2.9 m.; GR, E 1 m.; GR, S 1.4 m. OSAGE PRAIRIE: 1,506 acres. The area features a large remnant of tall grass *prairie* with diversified plants, prairie chickens, northern harriers, short-eared owls, Henslow's sparrows, badgers, and coyotes. Rt. 2, Box 93, Lockwood 65682. US 71, S 5 m. to junction with SR E; GR, W 0.6 m.; GR, S 1.2 m.

Nevada Habitation Center. Multiple structures, 1885–1887; extensively remodeled. The center provides services for persons with mental retardation and developmental disabilities from a 21-county area. N city limits.

Osage Village. State Historic Site. A self-guided walking tour loops through the earliest known site of an Osage *Indian* village in western Missouri. Archaeologists today believe the village, first described in 1719 by French fur trader Charles Claude du Tisné, was the home of 2,000–3,000 people who hunted, planted crops, and traded with Europeans. The houses, always facing east, were 30–50 feet long and 15–20 feet wide. Among the 10 marked points of interest are Blue Mound (a 200-foot landmark reportedly used as a burial ground), the site of an 1802 trading post, and Harmony Mission (*Butler: Papinsville*). US 54, E 6 m.; SR C, N 5.8 m.; GR, W 3.1 m.

Parks. DAVIS: Picnic shelters, overnight camping. Adjacent to Katy Allen Lake, a county park and fishing lake. US 54, E city limits. WALTON: Pool, fishing lake, trail. N side; SR W (Ash), W on Atlantic.

Radio Springs. Sulfur water was struck during drilling for oil in 1888, and its geyser created this lake. Speculation about the unusual name includes: (1) the recent invention of radio transmission (1888–1889) spawned "radio" as a buzzword, and (2) European radioactive spring spas were in vogue. Fishing lake, picnic area, trail, replica of original gazebo on island. W side; US 54, S on College.

Recreation. FLIGHT LAKE: 40 acres. Marshes, hunting, fishing. PRAIRIEWOODS *STATE FOREST. WILDLIFE AREAS:* Bushwhacker, Osage Prairie (Natural Areas, above), Schell-Osage.

Vernon County Courthouse. Richardsonian Romanesque, 1906–1908. This three-story *Carthage* stone courthouse (80 by 100 feet), the county's third, has all the characteristics of its style, e.g. spring arches, corner towers, arched windows, rusticated stone, and a massive central clock tower with a total height of 126 feet. Cost: $80,000. Architect R. G. Kirsch also designed courthouses for Adair, Johnson, and Polk Counties. Grounds: William Joel Stone (Architecture, above) memorial, erected in 1935 by the state; a heroic-style eight-foot bronze statue of Stone accented by Missouri red granite. US 54, N on Main. *(County Profiles)*

W. F. Norman Company. Established 1897. Called a museum in operation, the company has a drop-hammer press for making pressed-tin ceilings that is the type used since c. 1789. Tours by appointment. Cedar, 1 block N of square.

1. P.o. 1886–now.

NEWARK

Population: 82   Map F-2

Knox County's oldest town was platted in 1836 as a trading point at the South Fabius River and a main road. It failed to grow when the river did not provide consistent waterpower for manufacturing and it was bypassed by railroads. The place-name is usually derived from 1666 Newark, N.J., which was named for a town in England. While the English name reportedly has a religious connotation, reinforced here by the former common spelling New Ark, the plat and order of incorporation specify Newark. Sacked by Confederates after an 1862 battle in the streets (Odd Fellow's Cemetery, below) and damaged by two fires (1936, 1938), the town, built around an open square, is mostly derelict. Post office: 1836–now.

Odd Fellow's Cemetery. Ironically, a statue here honors Confederates killed during the battle at this town (Newark history, above). Inquire locally. *(Cemeteries)*

Plevna, Mo. The townsite was settled c. 1872 as Owl Creek.[1] When the town was platted in 1877, the name was changed to honor a successful 1877 Russian siege

(143 days) of Plevna, Bulgaria. Reportedly, Owl Creek's first postmaster, John Naylor, who named the new town, was, for unexplained reasons, nicknamed Plevna. Post offices: Owl Creek 1872–1877; Plevna 1877–now. SR 156, W 5.3 m.; SR 15, S 1.1 m.

Sever Wildlife Area / Lake. Lake: 158 acres. Primitive campsites, fishing, hunting, picnic tables, shelter houses. *(Wildlife Areas)*

1. The bird via the nearby creek.

NEWBURG

Population: 589   Map F-5

The town was platted in 1883 along Little Piney Creek by Capt. C. W. Rogers of the St. Louis & San Francisco *Railroad* as the second choice for a division point (the first choice, *Rolla,* declined to donate land because past railroad operations like this were not permanent). It was surveyed and named Newburgh by William Painter. When the town was incorporated in 1888, the spelling of this stock place-name, commonly accepted as meaning new town, village, etc., was changed to that of the *post office.* Some of its early population and structures came from nearby Ozark Iron Works (Iron Furnaces, below). Post offices: Frisco[1] 1884; Newburg 1884–now.

Doolittle, Mo. The community was established in 1944 on farmland along *Route 66* and named for WWII general Jimmy Doolittle. Its streets are named for famous military leaders. No post office. SR T, N 3.1 m. *ROUTE 66* SIGHTS: Aaron's Radiator and Malone's Service Station. Eisenhower St. TEMPLE *CEMETERY:* A pioneer cemetery also known as Lucky Cemetery. In town, just off Route 66.

Houston House. Vernacular, 1883; galleries removed 1920s; annex. First called the Railroad Hotel and Eating House, serving railroad passengers and crews, this large three-story frame building is still open for business. In town.

Iron Furnaces / Alhambra Grotto. About 1873, a community named for its foundry, Ozark Iron Works,[2] was established. The ironworks filled orders for the floundering Meramec Iron Works *(St. James),* but an 1883 financial panic precipitated the operation's failure; two furnaces remain (National Historic Register). During the early 1930s, the Alhambra Grotto of St. Louis (a degree of the Masonic Lodge) remodeled the ironworks' brick administration building for use as a deluxe resort for its members. It burned in 1970; standing ruins. SR P, W 1.5 m.; GR, N 0.5 m.; inquire locally.

Natural Tunnel / Arch. KANINTUCK HOLLOW

NATURAL TUNNEL: A result of *stream piracy;* remote, scenic location. SR T, S 6.3 m. (0.2 m. past church); GR, W 0.7 m. to access trail; right at springhouse remnants to head of east-draining hollow. PROTO ARCH: 4 feet wide, 8–10 feet long, 2–3 feet high. Small and relatively recently formed. 0.3 m. from springhouse (above) in steep NE draining tributary.

Newburg Museum. Railroad memorabilia, caboose. Water St., N of Houston House (above).

Recreation. MILL CREEK CAMPGROUND AND PICNIC AREA *(National Forests):* Water, trout fishing in creek, cave, natural arch, Mill Creek Interpretative *Trail.*

1. Nickname of the St. Louis & San Francisco RR company via the colloquial name for San Francisco *(Carrollton: Coloma).*
2. Descriptive; p.o. Ozark Iron Works 1873–1882; Knotwell, for the iron works founder, 1882–1884.

NEW FRANKLIN
Population: 1,107   Map E-3

The 19th-century history of New Franklin involves three towns: (1) Franklin, the original townsite and one of the largest towns west of St. Louis, now referred to as Old Franklin; (2) New Franklin, the relocated town of Old Franklin; (3) and Franklin, an 1894 railroad junction just west of New Franklin. Old Franklin, named for Benjamin Franklin, was platted in 1816 along the Missouri River and the *Boonslick Trail* as county seat of newly organized Howard County (Old Franklin, below). Its businesses focused mostly on land speculation (a U.S. Land Office was here from 1818 to 1824) and trading, especially after Henry Becknell *(Arrow Rock)* organized the first regular *Santa Fe Trail* expeditions here in 1821 (Santa Fe Trail, below). While competition from nearby *Boonville,* loss of the county seat to *Fayette* in 1823, and loss of the Santa Fe Trail trade to *Independence* c. 1828 undermined its economy, Missouri River flooding beginning in 1826 effected its decline. In 1827–1828 the town was relocated two miles north as New Franklin, which was platted in 1828 and named by the New Franklin Land Company just as the original site was destroyed by the river (later the river current rebuilt the former townsite's land). Although many Old Franklin residents moved structures to New Franklin and built new ones, a greater number moved elsewhere. New Franklin grew slowly (1883 est. pop. 250) until the 1894 construction of the Missouri, Kansas & Eastern *Railroad,* which ran west through town to form a junction one mile southwest with its north–south tracks. This is the site at which Franklin[1] was incorporated in 1894. Post offices:

Howard Court House[2] 1817–1821; Franklin 1821–1892; New Franklin 1892–now. Incidentally, laborers during this era were often orphans and dependents bound out by courts and families. Kit Carson (1809–1868; *McKittrick),* bound at age 15 to an Old Franklin saddle maker by his brother, left within the year on a Santa Fe wagon train. His employer offered a one-cent bounty for the boy, who later became the hunter, trapper, and scout who was part of John C. Frémont's expeditions during 1842–1846 *(Stockton).* Kit Carson's granddaughter, a lifelong resident here, operated the Kit Carson Motel. Information: Howard County Museum and Visitor Center; Missouri at Broadway.

Architecture. The town and surrounding area have good examples of 19th-century styles, including the following. AGNEW HOUSE: C. 1857. Two-story brick, L-shaped, painted gray; SR P, E 1.3 m. AMICK-KINGSBURY HOUSES (CEDAR GROVE): Two houses side-by-side; both National Historic Register. (1) Georgian, c. 1825. Small one-story brick with five glass panes in the door. (2) Greek Revival, 1856. Two-story brick with a full transom. SR 87/SR Z; SR Z, W approx. 0.8 m.; inquire locally. CLARK'S CHAPEL: Vernacular, 1879; remodeled Gothic Revival windows. One-story brick; 1824 *cemetery.* SR 87/SR Z; SR 87, N 0.2 m. DISCIPLES OF CHRIST CHURCH: Vernacular, 1883; towers, stained glass added 1902. SR 5, in town. EDWARDS HOUSE: Antebellum. Two-story brick, rear addition. E of SR 5, 311 Edwards. HARRIS-CHILTON HOUSE: Adam, 1832; front porch added; National Historic Register. Two-story brick with a fanlight and 18-inch-thick walls. N of SR 5, 108 Missouri. HICKMAN HOUSE: English-influenced Dutch Colonial, 1819. One-story brick with an attic, built by an Old Franklin merchant; fanlight. University of Missouri Farms, west edge of city (John Hardeman Garden, below). RIVERSCENE: Second Empire, 1869; National Historic Register. Built by riverboat captain Joseph Kinney; three-story brick with a mansard roof, cresting, Italian marble fireplace mantels, black walnut throughout, and a cypress exterior. Tours. US 40/SR 5; SR 5, S 1.2 m.; GR (at junction of SR 87), E approx. 100 yds. SCOTT-KINGSBURY: Adam, c. 1832; additions, extensive remodeling, porches added 1890s. Two-story brick across the road from c. 1830s Mt. Pleasant *Cemetery;* apple trees planted c. 1872. SR 5, N 1.6 m. THE SEMINARY: Vernacular, c. 1832. Two-story brick; a school until 1882; now a private residence. N of SR 5, 110 Market.

Boon's Lick State Historic Site. *Boonesboro.*

John Hardeman Garden. In 1820 Hardeman planted a 10-acre maze-type garden 10 miles west of Old Franklin, gathering plants worldwide to test them in this climate. Reportedly, visitor Henry Shaw used some of Hardeman's ideas for his now-famous botanical garden in *St. Louis*. Destroyed by an 1826 flood. A two-acre replica, without the maze, is being constructed at the University of Missouri Horticultural Center; visitors welcome. West edge of city.

Old Franklin / Marker. A marker commemorates the "Missouri Intelligencer and Boon's Lick Advertiser," Missouri's first newspaper west of St. Louis, founded April 23, 1819. About 500 feet west is Old Franklin's townsite (New Franklin history, above), the starting point of the *Santa Fe Trail* (below). US 40 at SR 87, N end of bridge.

Recreation. KATY TRAIL *STATE PARK:* Old Franklin (above); SR P at SR 5; SR P, S 1.3 m.; SR Z, W 0.5 m.; the trail drops SW from here through *Boonville* to *Sedalia*. In town. *WILDLIFE AREAS:* Davisdale, Franklin Island.

Salt Creek Cemetery. This was the site from 1817 to 1850 of a Disciples of Christ Church. DAR marker. SR P, E approx. 6.1 m. at GR. *(Cemeteries)*

Santa Fe Trail. The initial 1821 route traces the former *Boonslick Trail* and the Old Franklin–*Arrow Rock* Ferry Road. A marker locates the site of Col. B. A. Cooper's Fort *(County Profiles: Cooper)* during the *War of 1812* (at 0.9 m. W on GR, below). SR 87/US 40; SR 87, W 2.7 m.; SR Z, W 7.2 m. to Petersburg;[3] GR, W 1.5 m.; walk 0.5 m. W to river site of former Arrow Rock ferry. *(Santa Fe Trail)*

1. P.o. 1900–now.
2. For the county *(County Profiles)*.
3. Origin unknown, possibly for Petersburg, Va., named in 1733 for former Peter's Point; no p.o.

NEW LONDON
Population: 988   Map G-2

The town was platted in 1819 just south of the Salt River by William Jamieson and selected in 1821 as county seat of newly organized Ralls County. Although its namesake is uncertain, towns in Ohio and Wisconsin honor New London, Conn., named in 1658 for London, England.[1] Its location at the Salt River Country Road (US 61 / Red Ball Road, below) and an extension of the St. Louis, Hannibal & Keokuk *Railroad* in the late 1870s helped the town grow as a trading and political center. Post office: 1820–now.

Anderson Wildlife Area. *Wildlife Areas.*

Architecture. Good examples of 19th-century residential and commercial styles.

Cemeteries. BARKLEY: Professionally landscaped in 1890, it has a small chapel, winding walks, flowers, trees, some markers moved here from older cemeter-

ies, ornate iron fences, a long rock with rungs for hitching horses. NE side; inquire locally. SALT RIVER CHRISTIAN CHURCH CEMETERY: 150-year-old cast-metal cenotaphs in pink, blue, and white. SR V, E 4.5 m.; SR T, S 0.4 m.; GR, E 0.9 m. *(Cemeteries)*

Lincoln Hills. *Lincoln Hills Area.*

Ralls County Courthouse. Greek Revival, 1858; two-story addition 1935; National Historic Register. The county's third, this two-story temple-style courthouse features a two-story full-facade colonnaded porch with a bracketed pediment, an impressive cupola, and a full transom entry with simple entablature; the interior is mostly original. A replica of the front facade was built for the entrance to the Missouri buildings in the 1939 New York World's Fair and San Francisco Golden Gate International Exhibition. Cost: $18,000; addition $25,000 ($15,490 from federal funds). Town square, Ralls and 3d. *(County Profiles)*

Ralls County Jail. Vernacular, 1867–1869. National Historic Register. Two-story limestone with a frame addition for the jailer; used until the 1980s. Town square; Ralls and 3d.

US 61 / Red Ball Road. The historic Salt River Country Road, extending from St. Louis to here (and later to Iowa), was improved during the early 20th century as the Red Ball Road, which was named for the signs along its route: a red ball painted on a white square attached to a telephone pole. These signs were maintained by merchants to guide motorists to the next town offering gasoline and supplies. US 61 overlays and approximates these two roads. *(Roads and Traces)*

1. From Londinum, founded by invading Romans in 43 B.C.; the name was recorded by Tacitus c. 115–117; "lond" is Old Irish meaning wild.

NEW MADRID
Population: 3,350   Map J-7

First platted in 1789 one mile from today's site at the north end of a horseshoe bend in the Mississippi River, the town not only survived after nearby sites were destroyed by the river, it also persevered despite the worst earthquake in recorded history (New Madrid Earthquake, below). Today's site is set in the confines of a levee (New Madrid Museum, below). County records prior to 1816 are missing. Historical documents claim French Canadian brothers François and Joseph LeSieur, commissioned by St. Louis merchant Gabriel Cerrè, located a trading post in 1786–1787 at a Delaware Indian village near here *(Cape Girardeau)*. American Col. George Morgan, who noted the site as a promising location for an American colony and acquired a conditional land grant c. 1786 from the Spanish colonial governor, Esteban R. Miro. Morgan published a prospectus and arrived at the land grant in 1789 with about 60 colonists to settle approximately one mile south of today's town, where Morgan platted Nuevo Madrid, the name honoring Madrid, the capital of Spain. Political intrigue, typical of the period, influenced Miro to rescind Morgan's grant but allow the settlers to keep their property. A short-lived Spanish military post of little consequence, Celeste,[1] was established. After the *Louisiana Purchase,* settlement in the area increased, resulting in the 1805 District of New Madrid, followed by the organization of New Madrid County in 1812 with New Madrid as temporary county seat. Following two permanent county seats in the Sikeston area *(Benton)*—Rossville[2] (1814–c. 1817) and Winchester[3] (c. 1817–1822)—and after reduction of the county's size *(County Profiles: Scott),* New Madrid was selected county seat in 1822. The town was slow to grow (1874 est. pop. 700), but the arrival in 1878 of the Little River Valley & Arkansas *Railroad* helped broaden its commercial base as a trading center. Post office: 1805–now. Home of New Madrid County Area Vo-Tech. Tour maps: New Madrid Museum, below; Missouri Information Center: I-55 at junction with US 61.

Architecture. The downtown area has some good examples of 19th-century styles.

Donaldson Point State Forest. *State Forests.*

El Camino Real. *Roads and Traces.*

Hunter-Dawson Home. Italianate (predominately), 1859; remodeled; National Historic Register, State Historic Site. Built by William Hunter, an 1830 Virginia immigrant to New Madrid and later a successful businessman, the 15-room 9-fireplace house reflects the affluence of antebellum southern Missouri gentry. This centered-gable two-story yellow-cypress house is a rare subtype, with its paired columns, low hip roof, and wide bracketed eaves. Reportedly it served as the headquarters for Federal general John Pope (Island No. 10 / Siege of New Madrid, below). Furnished, tours, picnic area. US 61 at SR U; SR U (Dawson), SE to just E of 1st.

Island No. 10 / Siege of New Madrid. March 3–April 8, 1862. Island No. 10, about two miles long and a half-mile wide, was situated at the first sharp bend of a double bend in the Mississippi River just south of New Madrid. Heavily fortified and reinforced by a floating battery of nine guns and a shore battery on the Tennessee side, it blocked all river traffic while remaining protected on the north and east by swamps and on the west by New

Madrid, whose guns complemented the island's. In keeping with Federal *Civil War* policy to gain control of the Mississippi River, Gen. John Pope and Flag Officer A. H. Foote were ordered to attack Island No. 10, but first New Madrid had to be captured. On March 3, Pope was in place, north of town with about 20,000 men. He began an artillery duel with the forts to the east and west of town and with the gunboats in the river. Pope quickly learned that bigger guns were needed to drive back the gunboats, so he sent a request to Cairo, Ill., that was not filled until March 12. On March 13 the newly arrived 128-pound siege guns pounded New Madrid and the gunboats so severely that the fort's defenders evacuated their positions during the night. Foote, after vainly attempting on March 15 and 16 to take the island by river, waited while 600 engineers, about ten miles above the island, worked 19 days to cut a 12-mile channel west from the river to join a slough to bayous emptying into the river at New Madrid. Meanwhile, two Federal gunboats slipped past the island at night and were set at New Madrid to protect troop transports using the new channel to carry part of Pope's army downstream to a point below the island, allowing them to approach on dry land to attack from the rear on the Tennessee side. The island garrison and shore battery were then trapped by what had protected them, and on April 8 they surrendered. N 6 m.; no longer exists.

Levee Road. The town's levee was built in 1915 by the Corps of Engineers, then repaired and heightened in 1928 after a disastrous flood. SR WW continues east as

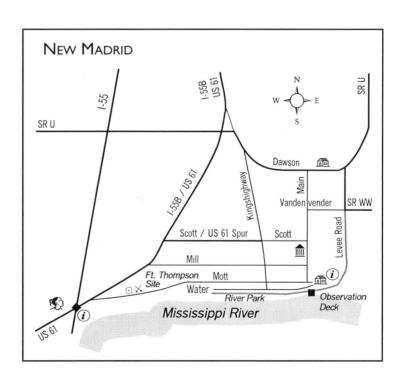

CR 520, connecting with SR A south of Big Oak Tree *State Park* and just west of *Dorena*. Optional gravel roads provide access for driving on top of the levee. BIRDS POINT–NEW MADRID FLOODWAY: *East Prairie*.

New Madrid County Courthouse. Neoclassical, 1915–1919. The county's fifth, this 107-by-75-foot two-story brick front-gabled courthouse is located north of the original town to avoid flooding. It has a raised first level, a pedimented projecting central entry with two-story Ionic columns, dentils, a pedimented side entry, and two-story pilasters with stylistic Corinthian cushions. Cost: $100,000. Downtown; Main St. *(County Profiles)*

New Madrid Earthquake. The worst earthquake in recorded history struck New Madrid at 3 A.M. on December 16, 1811, with a speculated magnitude of 8+ on the Richter Scale. On January 23 and February 7, 1812, two others of 7+ followed. The effects of these shocks were felt in Washington, D.C. Eyewitnesses said the land sank 50 feet in some areas, gases spewed from cracks in the earth, and the Mississippi River, dammed by an uplift, flowed backward for two days. During major events, "the earth was in continual agitation, visibly waving as a gentle sea." Over the next year there were more than 1,800 quakes, with periodic ones for several years. The federal government initiated its first disaster relief fund by issuing New Madrid Certificates, entitling displaced landowners to new acreage in *Louisiana Purchase* territory. Bounty Certificates (payment in land in lieu of cash to veterans of the *War of 1812*) located in the damaged area were also exchanged for New Madrid Certificates that offered land elsewhere, a practice that encouraged speculators to manipulate the two types of government land grants. Evidence of the quake can still be seen (New Madrid Museum, below).

New Madrid Museum. Vernacular, 1886; at one time the Kendall Saloon. Exhibits include local historical items, Civil War relics, and information about the New Madrid Earthquake, the town's historic *cemeteries*, and nearby Indian mounds, including a 1,000-year-old mound (adjacent to the south interchange of I-55 and US 61). SR U; Main, S to river.

Observation Deck. Eight-mile views of the river can be seen from the boardwalk. Incidentally, the land enclosed by the river's meander loop (on the south side of the river) belongs to Fulton County, Ky., although the residents' only land access is from Tennessee. SR U; Main, S to river.

Park. River view, picnic facilities, benches. SR U; Kingshighway, S to river.

Portageville, Mo. In an area of swamps, bays, bayous, and rivers, the town's location was evidently appealing as a portage site (the French term means to carry a canoe, etc., from one body of water to the next). While some historians place the name here as early as 1807, the first store was reportedly built in 1848 at Portage Bayou, now called Portage Open Bay Ditch *(Cape Girardeau: Little River Drainage District)*. Post office: 1873–now. I-55, S 12 m.

1. Wife of Miro; no p.o.
2. Origin unknown; no p.o.
3. Col. Henderson Winchester; p.o. 1813–1822.

NEWTONIA
Population: 207   Map D-7

Newton County's first settler, Lunsford Oliver in 1830, was followed in 1832 by M. H. Ritchey, who, along with two other men, donated land in 1857 for an academy and a townsite, which was platted at a major north–south road on Oliver's Prairie as Newtonia (for Newton County's namesake; *County Profiles*). The previous community, Prairie City,[1] was listed on 1840s–1850s maps by its post office name, Olivers Prairie. Mostly destroyed during the *Civil War* and by a subsequent 1868 fire, and bypassed in 1870 to the north by the Atlantic & Pacific *Railroad* (Ritchey, below), the town grew slowly (1874 est. pop. 400). Post offices: Olivers Prairie 1841–1858; Newtonia 1858–c. 1973.

Harmony Methodist Churches. WANDA COMMUNITY BUILDING: Vernacular, 1860; room added 1890–1893. Built by the congregation and used for services until 1893, when it was moved 300 feet south of the present church; used as a school until 1950. In town. WEEMS LOG CABIN: Log, pre-1837; enlarged, remodeled. Used for services from 1837 to 1860. SR M, S 3 m.; SR O, S 4.3 m. to Wanda;[2] GR, E 1 m.

Jolly Mill / Community. Vernacular, 1837; National Historic Register. The original hand-hewn-log brewery was incorporated into a later frame two-and-a-half-story *gristmill* with a cupola. The community, now defunct, first known as Isbel's Mill,[3] was later called Jolly Mill and Jollification either for the subsequent owner, presumably a man named Jolly, or for the good times associated with the site, or both. Post office: Jolly 1898–1903. SR EE, E 4.7 m.; GR, N 1.8 m.; junction with GR, E 0.8 m. to Capp's Creek.

Ritchey, Mo. The town was platted in 1870 along the Atlantic & Pacific *Railroad* on land donated by M. H. and Mary E. Ritchey. Post office: 1871–1974. SR M, N 3 m.; SR W, N 1.9 m. RITCHEY MILL: Vernacular, 1910, using part of an 1874 foundation on a mill site in use since the 1830s. Closed 1961; private. At Shoal Creek.

Ritchey House / Battle of Newtonia. Built by M. H.

Ritchey c. 1840s; enlarged from four rooms to six rooms with an outside kitchen; National Historic Register. This brick house is also known as Mansion House and Belle Starr House because of this legendary outlaw's visits here (*Carthage*). Damage is still evident from its use as headquarters and a hospital for Federals and Confederates during an 1862 *Civil War* battle. BATTLE: September 30, 1862. A nearby marker at rock-wall breastworks identifies the area as Newtonia Battlefield. A good example of an accidental battle, the engagement here began as a skirmish, a test of strength, and ended as a full-scale battle. Although the Confederates' strength had been siphoned east of the Mississippi after the Battle of Pea Ridge (*Civil War*), they still controlled the important roads in northwest Arkansas and parts of southwest Missouri, enabling them to quickly mass an army large enough to cause Federal general Samuel R. Curtis concern for his head-quarters and supply depot at Springfield. A skirmish on September 29, initiated by Federals, was turned back by Confederates, who did not think much of the action until the next day when they were attacked in force by 3,500 Federals who apparently believed the Confederates' objective was the nearby Granby lead mines (*Neosho*) but who underestimated their enemy's strength (about 4,000). Reinforcements from both sides charged the sound of the guns. The Confederates pos-sessed the field at the end of the day, making this tech-nically a Confederate victory, but they were forced to withdraw by October 4 in the face of Federal general John M. Schofield's advancing 18,000 men and 52 pieces of artillery. By mid-November Confederate positions had been forced from southwest Missouri and the prairies of northwest Arkansas to south of the Arkansas Boston Mountains. Casualties: Federal, 50 killed, 80 wounded, 115 missing; Confederate, 220 killed, 280 wounded. In town, 1 block N and 2 blocks E of SR 86.

Stark City, Mo. Established in 1907, the town was named for William P. Stark of the historic Stark Bros. Nursery family (*Louisiana*) when he began a nursery here, which today operates under a different name. Post offices: Chester[4] 1898–1905, 1908–1912; Stark City 1912–now. SR 86, S 1 m. STELLA, MO. / MUSEUM: Reportedly established about 1870 at Indian Creek. The community's namesake, supposedly a local woman, is unknown. Museum: city history, artifacts; 473 Ozark. *Float Streams:* Big Maple and Indian Creeks, Elk River. Post office: 1884–now. SR O, S 8 m.

1. Location; p.o. Olivers Prairie, 1841–1858.
2. Origin unknown, usually a woman's name; also known as Old Harmony; p.o. 1886–1908.
3. Original mill owner George Isbel.
4. Origin unknown.

NOEL
Population: 1,169   Map C-7

In 1891 postmaster and merchant Thomas Marshall moved his store and the Noel post office about a mile north, platting a town named Noel by the Elk River at the grade of the Kansas City, Pittsburg & Gulf *Railroad*. Locally pronounced No'-ul, the name honors a local pioneer family, although some sources specify family member Uncle Bridge Noel. Aided by the railroad and then the automobile, the town grew as an Ozark resort. Post office: 1886–now.

Bluff Dweller's Cave / Museum. Operated as a show cave since 1927, the cave has evidence of early human habitation, which is explained during guided tours that also include interesting formations, e.g. Balanced Rock (a 10-ton rock that could be moved by pressure from one finger), Rimstone Dam (a shallow 200-foot-wide lake and 1-by-12-inch rock dam), Musical Chimes (formations that produce a tone when tapped), and the Lobby (science fiction–style natural architecture). MUSEUM: Crystal fossils, arrowheads, historical items. Picnicking, rock garden. SR 59, S 2 m.

Christmas City. Despite the pronunciation of the town's name as No'-ul (the French word for Christmas, Noel, is pronounced nuh-ell'), it inspired the nickname Christmas City, which inspired a 1930s promotion fea-turing Christmas cards postmarked here. During the 1940s, coverage by radio/TV personality Kate Smith of this Christmastime novelty brought nationwide atten-tion. Today about 100,000 cards are received annually. Send a stamped addressed card enclosed in an enve-lope to Christmas City Postmaster, Noel 64854; the card will be mailed with the postmark Noel. Post office. (*St. Patrick: St. Patrick's Day Postmark*)

Elk River. *Float Streams.*

Elk River Bluffs. Formed when the relatively nonre-sistant Chattanooga shale underlying the Lower Mississippian limestone was cut away by the Elk River, the bluffs are scenic and dramatic, forming roofs that nearly cover some sections of the highway. Along SR 59 to Lanagan, Mo. (*Truitt's Cave, below*)

Ozark Wonder Cave. Discovered in 1862 by Civil War soldiers and open since 1916, this seven-room *cave* had evidence of early human habitation and today features colorful and interesting rock formations. SR 59, N 4 m. to Ginger Blue;[1] cave located 0.5 m. E at Elk Springs.[2]

South West City, Mo. The town was platted in 1870 just north of Honey Creek post office.[3] "South West" describes its location in the county and the state. Post offices: Honey Creek 1843–unknown, unknown–1863; South West City 1871–now. SR 90, W 6.7 m.; SR 43, S 2.2 m. CITY *CEMETERY:* Buried here are Civil War

Hanging Rock Drive, underneath the Elk River bluffs.

veterans and Millie S. S. Sprouse (1840–1914), the granddaughter of George Washington's sister. The vacant area is an Indian burial ground. In town. MISSOURI-ARKANSAS-OKLAHOMA MARKER: Stacked one on top of the other are state-line markers erected between 1821 and the 1960s. On top, shaped like a headstone, is the original marker with "Mis. 1821" (the date of statehood) on the north side and "Ark." (no date; it was still a territory) on the south. Oklahoma, at the time, was Indian Territory. This stone is reportedly the western survey for the 1820 *Missouri Compromise*. Below it, a marble pedestal erected by the Ozark Culture Club in 1915 identifies all three states along with their dates of admission to the Union (Ark., 1836; Mo., 1821; Okla., 1907). At the bottom is a 10-foot cement circle with three bronze state lines erected by the Lions Club in the 1960s. Only Four Corners (Utah., Colo., N.M., Ariz.) has more converging state lines. Had the Kansas boundary been extended about 35 miles further south, this spot would have shared that distinction. SR 43, across from convenience store.
Truitt's Cave. Opened in 1929 by J. A. Truitt (the Cave Man of the Ozarks), who also developed several other area *caves*, including Ozark Wonder Cave (above), this cave has over 220 yards of lighted walks, as well as an outdoor junkyard flea market of such excess as to be an art form. SR 59, N 5 m. to Lanagan.[4]

1. Coined name for the local resort; no p.o.
2. *Pineville: Rutledge.*
3. Via the creek, whose namesake is not known. Various Honey-modified place-names are not necessarily associated with honey or bees, e.g. Honey Creek, Ore., named in 1864 for a sweet substance on the stream's willow leaves.
4. For an Irish RR official via Lanagan's Addition; p.o. 1891–now.

NOVINGER
Population: 542   Map E-1

Platted in 1888, the town was named for an 1879 post office and railroad station that was named for landowner John C. Novinger, who, for that honor, granted right-of-way to the Quincy, Missouri & Pacific *Railroad*. Discovery of coal during the late 19th century precipitated an early 20th-century mining boom. Most of the new arrivals were Pennsylvania Germans and immigrants from southern and eastern Europe (est. peak pop. 5,000). Mining declined after WWII, ceasing entirely in the 1960s. Post office: 1879–now.
Cabins Historic District. Multiple 19th-century structures and sites; National Historic Register. Known as The Cabins of the White Folks or The Cabins, the site was first settled in 1829 after Iowa, Sauk, and Fox *Indians* ceded the land in 1824. It was abandoned after a skirmish with Iowa Indians that resulted in the

deaths of a few whites and Iowas (the Iowas were later exonerated by a jury). The district was reestablished in 1830 by other settlers who remained during the 1832 *Black Hawk War (Kirksville)*. Tours (2.5 hours) by appointment. SR 149 at SR 6; SR 6, E 1.3 m.; GR (E of bridge), S 2 m. ASA COLLETT HOUSE: Vernacular, board and batten, 1830s. This house was built by Asa, the father of Ira (below). COLLETT *CEMETERY:* Burials here include a Revolutionary War soldier, pioneer families, and slaves; overlooking the valley. COLLETT SPRING: This well-known area spring features a sandstone basin and a stone-and-wood springhouse. FORT CLARK: A 1925 DAR plaque on a red granite boulder (a 7-by-6-foot *Glacial Erratic)* marks the site of this 1832 *Black Hawk War* fort. INDIAN MOUNDS: Sauk, Fox, and Sioux mounds reportedly provide evidence of habitation 15,000 years ago. IRA COLLETT HOUSE: Greek Revival affinities, c. 1860s. This two-story frame house has a full-facade colonnaded porch. JOHN CAIN HOUSE: Greek Revival affinities, c. 1835–c. 1840. The two-story frame home of 1830 settler John Cain was the site of the first circuit court of Adair County in 1841. TANNERY: A three-sided shed marks this 1840s–1850s site.

Coal Miners Museum. Exhibits highlighting the community's ethnic and coal-mining heritage include equipment, photos, clothing, and housewares. Just E of Main.

Grand Divide. *Grand Divide.*

Nineveh, Mo. Established in 1849 along the Chariton River as a branch of William Keil's utopian colony at *Bethel* and named for the wicked biblical capital of Assyria, this modestly prosperous town with small shops, stores, and a large steam saw/*gristmill* declined after Keil's death. Post office: 1852–1882. SR 149, N 4 m. to just SE of Connellville;[1] inquire locally.

1. Personal name; p.o. 1902–1937.

OLD APPLETON
Population: 82
Map I-6 (as Appleton)

The townsite was settled c. 1808 along Apple Creek just east of a large Shawnee village (c. 1786–c. 1825; *Cape Girardeau)* and El Camino Real *(Roads and Traces)* by Kentuckians and German immigrants. When platted in 1847, the town adopted the name of its 1818 Apple Creek post office, which was named for the creek and adjacent crab apple trees. In 1856 its name was changed to Appleton, possibly out of pride or to clarify that it was now a town, not a post office community. That name was modified in 1917 to Old Appleton by the postmaster general to remedy delivery confusion with Appleton City *(Roscoe)*. Some contemporary state maps mistakenly list Old Appleton as Appleton. Post offices: Apple Creek 1818–1856; Appleton 1856–1917; Old Appleton 1917–now.

Apple Creek / Sites. A 1982 flood destroyed an 1879 iron truss bridge, and a 1986 flood destroyed the historic mill (a site since the 1820s); restorations are planned. Scenic location, fishing (bass, catfish, sunfish). Main.

Architecture. Some 19th-century structures remain after a 1986 flood (Apple Creek, above).

Our Lady of St. Joseph Shrine. 1973–1975. A statue of Mary overlooks landscaped grounds that include a small rock bluff and a cave with a spring-fed waterfall. US 61, N 1.2 m.; SR F, W 2.2 m. to Apple Creek,[1] an 1830s church community, also known as Schnurbusch community.[2]

Uniontown, Mo. The site, one of seven closely grouped German Lutheran immigrant communities *(Altenburg)*, was settled in 1839 by 15 charter members and known as the Paitzdorf Settlement.[3] Near the end of the Civil War it was named Uniontown, presumably for the belief in united states. Post office: Uniontown 1868–1965. US 61, N 1.3 m. GRACE LUTHERAN CHURCH: Vernacular, 1876. Brick and frame with a tall steeple. Today's name was adopted in 1929, 90 years after the church's founding (Paitzdorf, above). Its first *cemetery* is on a hillside behind the church. In town.

1. The creek (Old Appleton history); p.o. 1901–1909.
2. J. W. Schnurbusch, who donated the first church structure.
3. 1839 community church, Old Lutheran Church of Paitzdorf; no p.o.

OLD MINES
Estimated population: 300   Map H-5

First known as La Vieille Mine[1] after Philippe François Renault organized shallow lead diggings c. 1726, this mining concession was later surveyed into 10,540 acres equally divided by 31 families. They established a village c. 1802 at Old Mines Creek that was later known by its post office name, Old Mines. Never incorporated, the town today is located in the original mining concession, a narrow strip of land paralleling SR 23 and the creek. As late as 1941, Creole customs and language were still prevalent. Reportedly these mines were Missouri's first industry *(Potosi)*. Post office: 1827–1861, 1861–1969.

Etienne Lamarque House. Weatherboard Log, 1818.

French immigrant Lamarque, the son-in-law of Louis Bolduc[2] and owner of this three-room house with a hip roof and a wide front porch, donated most of the money used to build St. Joachim Church (below). W of SR 21; inquire locally.

Log Cabins. These restored 19th-century log structures are chinked with short pieces of split logs and a mixture of clay and straw; outside are two Four-a-Pains (a French name for biblical-era igloo-shaped bread ovens with whitewashed interior walls). Across from St. Joachim cemetery (below).

Murphey's Furnace Chimney. A 40-foot-tall pyramid-shaped rock chimney marks the location of a lead-smelting furnace built c. 1848 by Irish immigrant Thomas R. Murphey. SR 21, N 7.5 m. through Racola[3] to 1 m. W of entrance to Washington *State Park* (below).

Richwoods, Mo. French farmers and lead miners settled here on Spanish land grants during the late 18th century. Its namesake, an 1832 post office, is probably commendatory. Post office: 1832–1841, 1844–now. SR 21, N 5 m.; SR 47, N 8 m., SR A, W 1.2 m. *CEMETERIES:* Two cemeteries in town have ornate and interesting 19th-century makers. (1) Catholic: Local tradition maintains that the Toussaint Charbonneau buried here is the famous trapper, a guide and interpreter for the *Lewis and Clark Expedition* and the husband of Sacajawea (or Sacagawea), a Shoshoni Indian sold to Toussaint in 1804 who accompanied him. Her help on the expedition as a mediator for her people, among other contributions, resulted in her having more monuments built in her honor than any other American woman. (2) Protestant (Horine Cemetery): The hand-carved stone for Augustine Godat (b. 1763 in Neuchâtel, Switzerland; d. 1854) lies flat, covering the entire grave. SUITER'S STORE: Vernacular, c. 1900. The two-story frame structure is still operated as a general store. In town.

St. Joachim Catholic Church. Cruciform, 1828–1830; enlarged 1858–1868; restored 1945. This brick church with windows and a door emphasizing the Cruciform design has its original belfry and spire, stone lintels, and stained-glass windows. The adjacent *cemetery* has iron crosses of various designs with French inscriptions, an iron entrance gate wide enough to accommodate a wagon, and divided sections for Irish, slaves, freedmen, and Indian converts. Nearby picnic area. W on A'Renault Rd.; inquire locally.

State Park / Natural Area. WASHINGTON *STATE PARK:* SR 21, N 7.5 m. WASHINGTON STATE PARK HARDWOODS NATURAL AREA: 68 acres. Dominant trees, some over 150 years old, include the Kentucky Coffee Tree and oaks (northern red, chinquapin, and white). Dense and diverse wildflowers bloom in the spring. Rt. 2, De Soto 63020. In park.

Tiff, Mo. This post office community is presumably named for barite, or tiff, once considered worthless but after the Civil War used as an inert pigment and filler. Post office: 1905–now. SR 47, E 3.3 m.; SR E, N 2.4 m. through the c. 1798 mining community Shibboleth[4] to the 1819 mining community Bellefontaine[5] (note Goff House, weatherboard log, c. 1835); SR E, E 2.2 m.; GR, S 1.9 m. ARCHITECTURE: General store and catholic church.

1. French for The Old Mine; no p.o.
2. A successful lead miner, merchant, and farmer, among the first settlers of *Ste. Genevieve*.
3. Community landowner John Racola Coleman; p.o. 1898–1930.
4. The biblical password used to distinguish Gileadites from Ephraimites based on their pronunciation, Judg. 12:6; no p.o.
5. French for beautiful spring; no p.o.

 # ORDER NO. 11

This Civil War general order of August 25, 1863, required residents in most of Jackson, Cass, and Bates Counties and part of Vernon County to evacuate specified areas within 15 days (*Civil War: 1863 Guerrilla War map*).[1] It was precipitated by continued successful guerrilla warfare and bushwhacker raids, culminating in William Quantrill's 1863 raid on Lawrence, Kans., where 150 townspeople were killed and more than 185 buildings destroyed. The order's rationale was based on the Federals' inability to identify an enemy who could be plowing a field during the day and attacking them at night. In effect, the order depopulated entire counties. In Jackson County, all residents living within one mile of Independence, Kansas City, Blue Springs, Hickman's Mill, and Pleasant Hill were ordered from their homes. Those allowed to remain in these towns were required to give an oath of loyalty, which was taken so seriously that during the previous September in Macon, Mo., 10 Confederate prisoners had been executed for repeatedly violating their oaths. Other towns, like *Nevada*, were considered so recalcitrant that they were evacuated and burned. (*Liberty: William Jewell College*)

1. Some of the larger towns affected were *Lamar, Nevada,* and Westport (*Kansas City*).

 # OREGON
Population: 935   Map B-2

Platted in 1841 as county seat of newly organized Holt County, the town was briefly (from June to October) named Finley.[1] The court ordered the name changed to Oregon, presumably because of enthusiasm over that year's first mass migration (of mostly Midwesterners) along the *Oregon Trail* to an area in the Pacific Northwest known as Oregon. According to "American Place-Names," the name is the result of a 1715 French cartographer's error. First applied to the Wisconsin River, and usually spelled Ouisconsink, it was engraved as Ouariconsint and separated to fit the space, with "sint" below, making the name appear to be Ouaricon. Later documents used variations (Ouargon, Ourgan, Ourigan) to describe the river now known as the Columbia. The name Oregon appeared first in the 1778 work of John Carver and afterward was applied to the river's area, the territory, and finally the state. Missouri's Oregon, although situated between two navigable rivers, the Missouri and the Nodaway, was landlocked and later bypassed by railroads. The town grew as the county political center. Post office: 1843–now. *(Platte Purchase)*

Carroll Stagecoach Inn. Vernacular, c. 1844; porch added 1925; National Historic Register. The main part of this two-story frame structure (log covered by clapboard) was built by Jesse Carroll as a tavern on the historic St. Joseph–Council Bluffs, Iowa, stage *road*. Private. US 59, E. 3.5 m.; SR B, N 1.5 m.; GR, E 1.5 m. to a bend in the road (Oregon is 4.5 m. directly W of here via this road).

Holt County Courthouse. Sixties Modern, 1965–1966. The county's third, this 90-foot-square brick courthouse has a flat roof and tinted windows. The first courthouse (1841–1852; frame) was built by Jesse Carroll (above). The second structure (1852–1965; brick) was remodeled three times, painted twice, then returned to natural brick before being destroyed by fire in 1965. Cost: $194,863. Grounds: on the northwest corner is a large thornless locust, the last of seven that were here before the town was platted. Downtown. *(County Profiles)*

Oregon Cemetery. Large historic section; stones date from 1842. SE side. *(Cemeteries)*

1. One of the site commissioners, Travis Finley.

 # OREGON TRAIL

This legendary route, the longest frontier trail of its era, stretched from its initial jumping-off places of *Independence*, Westport *(Kansas City)*, and *St. Joseph* to Oregon City, a journey of about 2,020 miles that took four to five months. An estimated 300,000 people trav-

eled this route between 1830 and the turn of the century, with the heaviest traffic between the 1840s and c. 1860. Over 30,000 of these emigrants are still buried beside the trail. Unlike the merchants' *Santa Fe Trail,* this one was followed by families who wanted a new life, cheap land, or the thrill of an adventure that promised rewards described only vaguely by their imaginations. Outside events also drove them. Two depressions in 1837 and 1842 helped begin a steady stream of Oregon-bound emigrants that turned into a flood after the 1849 California gold rush *(St. Joseph).* By the 1850s, maps were not necessary because westward travelers could either follow the wagon ruts or their noses, which was a coarse joke told to soften the reality of a perpetual stench from dead animals, garbage, and open latrines lining the entire length of the trail. Women's diaries of the trail's early years are frank about this so-called adventure across 2,000 miles of *prairies*, mountains, deserts, and rivers. Few Indian battles or acts of bravery are recounted. More men were shot by mistake than killed by Indians. More people died from mundane accidents and cholera than from heroic deeds. Women's diaries are also filled with accounts of the tedious, repetitive daily tasks of trying to make or break camp while tending the stock, the children, the sick, and the dying; of cooking in sheets of rain, choking dust storms, and plagues of mosquitoes; of days without water, nights without sleep, and food without taste but plenty of sand. Men, women, and children walked or rode all day through torrential rain, blistering sun, or numbing cold, forded or floated countless rivers and creeks, and witnessed marriages, births, and deaths while keeping the pace of putting one foot in front of the other. In the early years, those who reached Oregon found little comfort. Few arrived with their possessions, money, or food. The rich new land was vast and wild and without home or hearth or hope for any soon. Yet despite all the hardships and losses, the letters sent back East glowed with such exaggerated praise for this new country that true believers kept rolling westbound in what seemed like a never-ending wagon train jammed end-to-end between the Missouri and Columbia Rivers.

Few modern highways parallel the original Oregon Trail, but it is possible to follow nearly all of it exactly by using a complicated web of paved, gravel, and dirt roads that are described in detail in "The Oregon Trail Revisited." Allow ten days for following the general route and four weeks for the exact one. Also, some modern atlases like *AAA* show the route but not the smaller roads. Generally, the trail used rivers as guideposts; the towns and site names used to describe the route here are the modern ones. From the early jumping-off places at *Independence* Landing or Westport

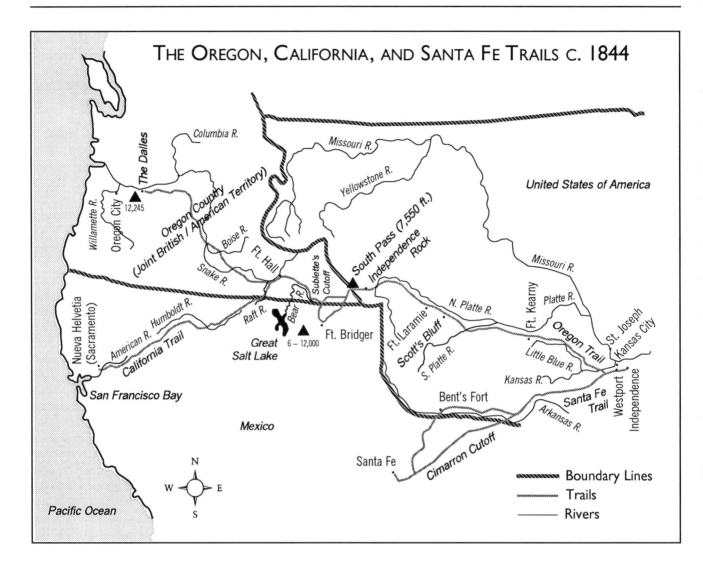

THE OREGON, CALIFORNIA, AND SANTA FE TRAILS C. 1844

Landing *(Kansas City)*, travelers followed the *Santa Fe Trail* west to Gardner, Kans., where the two split. Oregon-bound wagons followed the Kansas River to and through Topeka, Kans., northwest into the Little Blue River valley to follow that river northwest until it bent south near Hastings, Nebr., where the trail then cut directly to the Platte River near Kearney, Nebr. From here, the trail followed the Platte and North Platte Rivers through Scotts Bluff, Nebr., to Casper, Wyo., where the river bends south, flowing down to Alcova, Wyo. From Alcova the trail loosely followed today's SR 220 west to the Sweetwater River at Independence Rock, Wyo., and then on to South Pass at the Continental Divide (altitude 7,550 feet). Here the trail split and later rejoined. Some took Sublette's Cutoff, which headed directly southwest across the Green River to pick up the Bear River. Most followed Pacific and Sandy Creeks (approximating SR 28) to Sneedskadee Wildlife Area, then on southwest to Fort Bridger, Wyo., southwest of which are the Wasatch

Mountains, which marked the way to Salt Lake City via the *Mormon* Trail.[1] The Oregon Trail left Fort Bridger heading northwest to intercept Sublette's Cutoff southwest of Sage, Wyo., at the Bear River, which was followed northwest into Idaho up to Soda Springs, then northwest cross-country to Fort Hall, Idaho, at the Snake River.[2] About 25 miles south of the Snake River's American Falls, the California Trail[3] split off at Raft River, Idaho. The Oregon Trail continued west along the Snake River to Glenns Ferry, Idaho. From there it cut cross-country northwest to Boise at the Boise River before following that river west to its confluence with the Snake at the now defunct Fort Boise (on the Idaho–Oregon border). From the fort, the trail struck out northwest across the dry parts of Oregon to Pendleton, Ore., where it paralleled the Columbia River west, approximating US 30, to The Dalles,[4] where the choice was rafting the river or traveling west through rough country around Mount Hood to eventually arrive 12 miles south of today's Portland, Ore., at Oregon City and the Willamette valley.

1. Originally, in 1847, it departed from Nauvoo, Ill., crossing Iowa to Council Bluffs, Iowa, and Florence, Nebr., where it then followed the north side of the Platte to join the main route of the Oregon Trail at, and sometimes after, Fort Laramie, Wyo. From Salt Lake City it struck southwest to Los Angeles.

2. Between 1857 and 1859, Landers Cutoff, a new road, was constructed from Burnt Ranch near South Pass directly to Fort Hall, which cut off the wide sweep through Fort Bridger, but the immigration along the trail had peaked and it was little used.

3. It followed the Raft River southwest to pick up the Humboldt River, which guided the way southwest through Nevada to the Sierra Nevada Mountains, which were crossed at Lake Tahoe, from which the American River then led the way into Sacramento, Calif.

4. French for flagstone or slab of rock, a quasi-generic term for places where water runs over smooth rocks; The Dalles specifically identifies those of the Columbia River and the town.

OSCEOLA

Population: 755   Map D-5

In 1836 Philip Crow and R. P. Crutchfield built a store at the Osage River where Crow established a ferry. The site, first known as the Crossing on the Osage at Crow and Crutchfield's, was platted as Osceola (the plat was filed March 1, 1839, by George Lewis). The place-name is a stock one, but this town is directly named for Asivaholo, also known as Osceola (1804–1838), who during the Second *Seminole War* (1835–1842) organized resistance against U.S. efforts to force the Seminoles from the Florida Everglades. Osceola, deceived by the promise of a truce, was captured and put in prison, where he died in 1838 (*County Profiles: Dade*). After a bitter political struggle with now-defunct Wyatt's Grove,[1] Osceola was selected county seat in 1841 of newly organized St. Clair County. It prospered as a political center and steamboat port (the first steamboat, the "Flora Jones," arrived in 1844) until destroyed during the *Civil War* by Kansas Jayhawker Jim Lane and about 200 men, who sacked and burned the town in September 1861, reportedly in retaliation for *Kansas Border War* crimes. Bypassed by railroads until the late 1880s, it was slow to recover economically. Post offices: Mouth of Sac[2] 1837–1839; Oseola[3] [*sic*] 1839–1842; Osceola 1842–now.

Architecture. Downtown has 19th-century storefronts.

Birdsong Wildlife Area. *Wildlife Areas.*

Harry S. Truman Reservoir. Although the reservoir is known as the spoonbill capital, it still holds the world's record for a blue catfish (117 lbs.). Lichen Glade Natural Area is adjacent (*Roscoe*). Multiple access. (*Lakes: Corps of Engineers*)

Natural Areas. BRUSH CREEK: 26 acres. Part of Birdsong *Wildlife Area*, this Ozark headwater stream fea-

tures a stable channel with well-defined runs, riffles, and pools that support 41 species of fish and diversified invertebrate life. Also found here are dolomite cliffs and an upland forest. Box 147, Clinton 64735. SR 13, S 12 m. to Collins;[4] US 54, W 5.1 m.; SR J, S 2.2 m. DAVE ROCK: 44 acres. Part of Dave Rock Natural History Area. Features include a sandstone glade, a forest, lichen, moss, little bluestem, and poverty grass. Box 250, Clinton 64735. SR 13, N 8 m. to Lowry City;[5] GR, S approx. 1 m.; inquire locally. LICHEN GLADE: SR 13, N 2 m.; SR B, W approx. 5.7 m. to Salt Creek (*Roscoe*).

Parks. CITY: Swimming, picnic facilities, playground, riverside RV camping, courtesy docks, bathhouse. At the river near downtown; signs. ROADSIDE: Overlooks the confluence of the Sac and Osage Rivers (Osceola history, above); picnic shelters, horseshoes, shuffleboard. SR 82 at SR 13; SR 82, W 2.8 m.

St. Clair County Courthouse. Italian Renaissance, 1916–1923. This two-story yellow-brick structure with white stone trim is the county's fourth or fifth courthouse: a third courthouse could have been destroyed in 1864 after the second was burned by Jayhawkers (Osceola history, above). Although its 1867 predecessor was vacated as unsafe in 1908, the building was not razed until 1916, and work was not completed on this structure until 1923 because of lawsuits against the county (by the heirs of lenders for a failed c. 1876 railroad project). The building has a rusticated first level, two-story Ionic columns, a projecting central entry, and a roofline parapet. Cost: possibly $52,500, but prolonged piecemeal construction and legal fees obscure the calculations. Downtown. (*County Profiles*)

1. Personal name; no p.o.; 1 m. E of *Roscoe*.

2. Confluence of Sac and Osage Rivers; Sac or Sauk *Indians*, whose Algonquian name means river mouth, outlet.

3. Misspelled Oseola when in Rives County (*County Profiles: Henry*).

4. Township named for county judge William Collins; p.o. 1873–now.

5. A merchant named Lowry; p.o. 1871–now.

OTTERVILLE

Population: 507   Map E-4

The town was platted in 1837 as Elkton[1] by G. R. Thompson on land bought from W. R. Wear, who like most of the new residents had left the failing settlement of nearby New Lebanon (below). In 1848 a post office was established and named Otterville (for the area's otters) because another Elkton post office existed in Hickory County. Wear, the first postmaster, then platted the town of Otterville in 1854 to overlay Elkton, naming it for the post office. After the 1860 arrival of the Pacific *Railroad,* the town boomed briefly as a terminal, but it declined when the terminal, along with businesses and some buildings, was moved c. 1861 to *Sedalia.* Post offices: Arator[2] 1835–1862; Otterville 1848–now.

Architecture / Sites. The town and area have good examples of 19th-century structures and historic sites. BANK/HOTEL: Vernacular, 1855–1856. SR A at railroad; in town. CIVIL WAR TRENCHES: SR A, E 1.2 m.; S along Lamine River. JESSE JAMES HILL: Reportedly one of his lookout sites for trains. SR A, E 2 m.; near roadside park. STOCKYARDS: E side; SR A at railroad. OTHERS (in town; inquire locally): 1840 McKnight House; a c. 1880 college building; portions of the c. 1861 Jefferson City–Georgetown *(Sedalia)* Trail; an 1869 schoolhouse; Pleasant Grove *Cemetery;* and a pioneer campground.

Filled Sink. A road cut has exposed a 150-foot-long 30-foot-tall mass of white sandstone (the fill) resting on dolomite bedrock, an excellent example of a sinkhole later filled. SR A, E 2 m.; N side of SR A, near roadside park. *(Collapsed Cave Systems)*

Lamine River Wildlife Area. *Wildlife Areas.*

New Lebanon, Mo. Settled in 1819–1820 by Kentuckians, including the Wear family (Otterville history, above) and Rev. Finis Ewing, who organized the Cumberland Presbyterian Church here in 1820 (below), the community was named for their former Kentucky church, Lebanon Presbyterian *(Lebanon).* Post office: 1887–1906. SR A, E and N 7.3 m. *CEMETERY:* Markers date from 1822; two Revolutionary War soldiers are buried here. SR A, S 0.2 m. CUMBERLAND PRESBYTERIAN CHURCH: Vernacular, 1860; National Historic Register. This brick church replaced an 1821 log one; in town. SCHOOL: Vernacular, 1889. A one-room building; in town.

    1. An abundance of elk; no p.o.
    2. Origin unknown; an area post office due west in Pettis County at the Cooper County line *(Sedalia: Smithton).*

OVERLAND MAIL COMPANY

The Overland Mail Company was organized in 1857 by John Butterfield of New York when he was awarded a six-year U.S. mail contract for $600,000 a year with the rate of 10 cents a letter. The company's route between St. Louis and San Francisco and Memphis and San Francisco used more than 100 Concord coaches, 1,000 horses, 500 mules, and nearly 2,000 employees. St. Louis and Memphis mail and passengers were consolidated at Fort Smith, Ark. (at the Arkansas River and today's Oklahoma border). Although the St. Louis route called for twice-a-week service each way, the Memphis schedule varied because of terrain and conveyances, which included train, boat, stage, and, for mail, horseback. From St. Louis both passengers and mail traveled by train to *Tipton* and thereafter by stage. The 1858 St. Louis run averaged about 120 miles during 24 hours (they ran night and day) for 2,800 total miles with 141 stage stations spaced every 20 miles (Missouri had 17 stage stations). The coaches could carry nine scheduled passengers (40 lbs. of free baggage each) for a fare of $200; wayside passengers were charged 10 cents a mile. An early timetable shows a 165-mile stage trip from *Springfield* to Forth Smith, as departing Wednesday and Saturday at 7:45 A.M. and arriving Friday and Monday at 3:30 A.M. Interrupted by the *Civil War,* the line declined and was never reestablished as a whole.

OZARK
Population: 4,243   Map E-7

In 1837 John Hoover bought Joseph Kimberling's 1833 mill and property. Near Hoover's new mill at Finley Creek grew a settlement known as Hoover's Mill. The Village of Ozark was platted in 1843 (Architecture; Ozark Mill, below) and named for the post office, which was named for the nearby mountains that take their name from the Quapaw *Indians,* who, like the Osage and Kansa, were referred to by early French explorers by a shortened name: Kans, Os, and Arcs. French records of the period reflect hunting or trading "aux [in the] Kans, aux Os and aux Arcs." The town was selected in 1859 as a central location for county seat of newly organized Christian County and has since served as the county's political center. Post offices: Hoover's Mill 1839–1840; Ozark 1840–now.

Architecture. Over 14 19th-century houses are north of the courthouse in an area bounded by Church, 3d, Jackson, and 4th. Two of the oldest are the Weaver house (c. 1855) and the Barron house (1860); both are located at 3d and Jackson, the former town square.

Busiek Wildlife Area / State Forest. *Wildlife Areas; State Forests.*

Christian County Courthouse. Italian Renaissance, 1919–1920. The first courthouse was burned in 1865 by an arsonist (all records were lost). The second was razed in 1914 after state legislation authorized counties to issue bonds for public buildings without a vote on the question. The third and present courthouse is a three-story brick structure with belt courses, balustrades, a rusticated first level, four projecting central entries, a second-story colonnaded porch, and different window treatments on each floor. It was designed by H. H. Hohenschild, who also designed courthouses for Barry, Pemiscot, and Scott Counties. Cost: $90,000. Square, 3d at Church. *(County Profiles)*

Christian County Museum. Indian, pioneer, and Civil War items, historical photographs, and records. 3d, E on Church to 2d (401).

Nixa, Mo. This 1850s crossroads community was platted in 1889 and named for its post office, whose name reportedly was coined from the name of early settler and blacksmith Nicholas (Nick) A. Inman. Post offices: Faught[1] 1878–1881; Nixa 1881–now. SR 14, W 6.3 m. CATHEDRAL CHURCH OF THE PRINCE OF PEACE: This 14-by-17-foot stone church, with a blue onion-dome cupola and a congregation of about 15, is reportedly the world's smallest cathedral. US 160, S 8 m.; SR EE, E 0.2 m. to Highlandville;[2] set in a backyard just N of SR EE. RIVERDALE MILL: The first mill at this site on Finley Creek was built c. 1840. Today's early 1980s mill replaced a 1930 cattle feed grain mill that also drove an electrical generator installed for a planned tourist attraction. The attraction failed, and today's water-powered dynamo produces about 570,000 kilowatts a year, which are sold to an electric company. US 160, S 3 m.; GR, E 1 m. to the steel bridge at Riverdale[3] (derelict).

Ozark Mill. Vernacular, 1939. Since Kimberling's 1833 mill (Ozark history, above), there has been a progression of owners of *gristmills* at Finley Creek. The present water-powered 1939 mill uses a horizontal waterwheel, steel turbines, and movable fins. The brand-name flour produced here included Hawkins Brothers Best and White Swan. Tours. Across from the park (below).

Park. Fishing, swimming, picnicking, large shade trees, playground, boat ramp, Ozark Mill (above). N. 3d at the creek.

Smallin's / Civil War Cave. This cave's natural opening (90 feet high, 200 feet wide) is reportedly one of America's largest and was first reported in 1818. The cave, nearly three miles long, features an underground river, a waterfall, and 19th-century graffiti. Visitors welcome; permission required from caretaker at entrance gate. Grounds: Abraham Lincoln's funeral railway car, picnicking. N 3 m. via Riverside Rd.; pass Riverside Inn, cross a steel bridge, and keep right 1 m.; cave on left.

Tracker Marine. Bass Pro Shop's 100,000-square-foot building houses automated machinery, huge conveyor belts, and programmed robotics to build about 75,000 boat trailers annually. A 14-foot-tall, 100-foot-long window provides viewing. US 65, N approx. 2 m. *(Springfield: Bass Pro Shop)*

1. Early settler and merchant.
2. Commendatory; p.o. 1872–now.
3. Descriptive; p.o. 1889–1907.

PALMYRA
Population: 3,371   Map G-2

After an 1818 survey to subdivide St. Charles County indicated the size and shape of the new counties, four men platted Palmyra in 1819, correctly anticipating the area's growth and need for a new county and county seat. Moses D. Bates, a chain-bearer for the 1818 survey who was not involved in the town's original platting *(Hannibal),* bought land adjoining the original plat and laid it out in 1827 as an addition that included the courthouse square when Palmyra was selected county seat of newly organized Marion County. The town's popular place-name refers to a biblical-era oasis city (now Tadmor) along a desert caravan route between Syria and the upper Euphrates. Called Palmyra (Palm City) by the Greeks and Romans, it was first recorded in 1100 B.C. as Tadmar by Tiglath-Pileser I (King of Assyria) and referred to as Tadmor in 2 Chron. 8:4 of the Old Testament. Stories about Zebonia, Queen of Palmyra, captured by Romans c. 272, helped popularize the name. The Missouri name was partially inspired by the town's location, through a stretch of the imagination that substitutes the Mississippi and Salt Rivers for the Tigris and Euphrates. Mark Twain in "Tom Sawyer" saw humor in the affectation and referred to the town as Constantinople. Palmyra grew quickly, aided by its status as county seat, the location here of a U.S. land office from 1825 to 1858 (it sold over 3 million acres), and the flooding of Marion City (below). The arrival in 1857 of the Hannibal & St. Joseph *Railroad* and in 1860 of the Palmyra & Quincy helped secure its continuing economic growth. Post office: 1820–now. Incidentally, the "Palmyra Spectator," founded in 1839 as the "Missouri Whig" by Jacob Sosey, is one of Missouri's oldest weekly newspapers and was owned by the same family until 1967, making it one of America's oldest continuously owned family newspapers.

Architecture. Called the Handsomest City in North Missouri in 1860, Palmyra has over 200 antebellum structures, including Adam and Greek Revival, as well as other styles, e.g. Italianate, Gothic Revival, Victorian, Romanesque, Prairie School. A sample of these (near the square) is in an area bounded by Bradley, Home, and New. Walking tour maps: visitor center (below). NATIONAL HISTORIC REGISTER: Darwell House (Italianate, 1860), the childhood home of Jane Darwell, the winner in 1940 of an Academy Award for

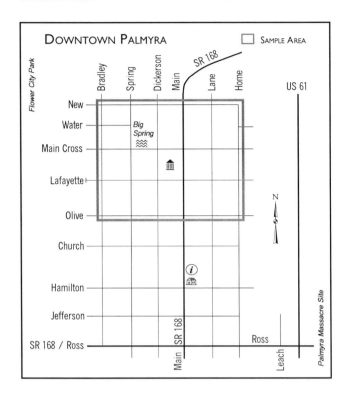

DOWNTOWN PALMYRA   □ SAMPLE AREA

best supporting actress as Ma Joad in "Grapes of Wrath"; Ross (SR 168), S on Main (1425). Dryden-Louthen House (Italianate, 1858), Ross, N approx. 100 ft. on Leach. Spiegel House (Italianate, 1850), SR 168, N 3 blocks on Dickerson.

Big Spring. The 1819 town and 1827 county seat addition (Palmyra history, above) were platted at this spring, a popular Sauk *Indian* campsite as late as 1821. It was the town's only water supply until 1894. Between Spring and Dickerson, NW of courthouse.

Flower City Park. 160 acres. Natural area, ball field, playground, tennis, picnic shelters. SR 168 at Bradley; SR 168, W to Breckenridge, N to park, or W on New/Old Philadelphia; signs.

Marion City, Mo. The town was platted on paper in 1835 by Col. William Muldrow, whose failed schemes inadvertently benefited Missouri by helping to build towns like Palmyra (history, above) and *Kahoka*, as well as establish a college (below). Marion City, grandiosely billed as The Gateway to the Orient, failed because its location, the former Green's Landing,[1] was nearly surrounded by water, including about a mile and a half of the Mississippi. It flooded in 1836, shortly after the first wave of settlers arrived, prompting unfulfilled promises of a levee system. Some refugees from successive floods moved to Palmyra. While Marion City did establish a large hog market and provide a landing for the county and Palmyra, major flooding in 1844 and 1851 finally destroyed the town. Today the Mississippi covers the eastern side and swamps cover the western.

Post office: 1837–1861. SR 168/US 61; SR 168, E 3 m.; SR JJ, E 3 m.; marker. MARION COLLEGE: Muldrow's 1836 promotion of Marion College and Marion City precipitated an immigration from the East, particularly Pennsylvania, that was so large it was locally called The Eastern Run. Despite large donations ($100,000 by E. S. Ely), the college failed, primarily because cattle herded north to subsidize students' tuition arrived in the fall without feed and subsequently died of starvation during the winter. The college had been divided between two locations with an upper branch at Philadelphia, Mo.,[2] and a lower branch southwest of Palmyra. A Masonic order bought the college in 1842, moving it in 1844 to *Lexington: College Park,* where it became the world's first Masonic college.

Marion County Courthouse. Richardsonian Romanesque, 1900–1901. The first courthouse was not completed until 1835. Today's, the county's third (*Hannibal*), is a three-story dark-gray-brick structure (113 by 79 feet) with all the characteristics of its style, including spring-arch doorways, a rusticated first floor, a hipped roof with cross gables, and a massive central tower. Cost: $41,600. Ross (SR 168), N on Main to square. COPPER BALL: This cupola ornament from the second courthouse was used for target practice by Confederates; several bullet holes are evident. Grounds. PALMYRA MASSACRE MONUMENT: A granite monument topped by a Confederate soldier commemorates 10 Confederate prisoners taken from the county jail (below) to the old fairgrounds (see map) on October 18, 1862. Under orders from Union general John McNeil, they were shot by 30 Union riflemen as a reprisal for Confederate Col. J. E. Porter's refusal to return a captured spy. The first volley killed three men, wounded six, and missed one entirely. The remaining seven were then shot with pistols. Grounds. (*County Profiles*)

Marion County Jail / Sheriff's House. Greek Revival style, 1858. This one-story jail, built using massive stone blocks (about 4 feet long, 20 inches high, 20 inches thick), is attached to a two-story brick sheriff's residence. Courthouse (above). PALMYRA MASSACRE: Courthouse (above).

Shannon Grave Site. At sixteen years old, George "Pegleg" Shannon (1787–1836) was the youngest member of the 1804–1806 *Lewis and Clark Expedition.* He was wounded in the leg during an Indian fight near today's Bismarck, N.D., and his leg was later amputated. After completing the expedition, he accompanied Nathaniel Pryor on a western trip, escorting a Mandan chief, then later helped Nicholas Biddle edit the Lewis and Clark journal, served as U.S. district attorney of Missouri, and was elected to the Missouri legislature. Marker; US 61, S of North River bridge; inquire locally. *(County Profiles: Shannon)*

Tour House. Italianate, 1858; National Historic Register. Built by wealthy Virginian P. J. Sower, the house, featuring Ionic columns, stained-glass windows, and an ornate interior, was bought in 1869 by banker John Russell, the son of William Russell, who founded the Pony Express *(St. Joseph)* and died here in 1872 (he is buried at Greenwood *Cemetery*, Dickerson at N city limits; monument). Ross, N 4 blocks on Home.

US 61. *New London: US 61 / Red Ball Road.*

Visitor Center / Museum. Adam and Greek Revival affinities, 1828; National Historic Register. The exhibits at this former stagecoach stop, hotel, tavern, school, and residence include local historical items. Ross (SR 168), N 2 blocks on Main.

West Quincy, Mo. Willard Keyes established here in 1829 the first ferry north of *Louisiana*. Platted in 1874 but never very successful, the town was frequently flooded by the Mississippi and overshadowed by its Illinois namesake, which honors John Quincy Adams, U.S. president from 1825 to 1829. Incidentally, "Quincy" was used rather than "Adams" because "Adams" as a place-name was preempted by J. Q.'s father, John Adams, America's second president (1791–1801). Post office: 1861–1862, 1866–1869. US 61, N 9 m.; SR 24, E 6 m. *LOCK AND DAM* #21: Built 1938. Dam: 2,960 feet long; locks: 600 feet long, 110 feet wide. Launch ramp. S of Quincy, Ill.; follow signs on Ill. 57.

1. Landowner Dr. Green; no p.o.
2. Greek meaning brotherly love, from the New Testament, Rev. 1:11, 3:7, via Philadelphia, Pa.; p.o. Marion College 1833–1844, Masonic College 1844–1847, Philadelphia 1847–now; SR 168, W 14 m.

PARIS

Population: 1,486   Map F-3

The town was platted in 1831 along the Middle Fork of the Salt River as a central location for newly organized Monroe County on land donated by Josephus Fox, the son of Ezra Fox, who in 1820 founded the county's first settlement, Fox's Settlement,[1] east of Middle Grove.[2] Mrs. Josephus Fox named the town for her former hometown, Paris, Ky., which was named for its county, the latter honoring French aid during the American Revolution. Paris prospered as the county's political center and as a major crossroads trading center, aided by the c. 1872 arrival of the Hannibal & Central *Railroad*. Post offices: Monroe Court House 1831–1841; Paris 1841–now.

Architecture. Good examples of 19th-century styles are located near court square in an area bounded by Locust, Walnut, Marion, and Hill. Interesting structures from this area and elsewhere include the following (note that SR 15 is Main). ALLEN HOUSE: Italianate, 1869; remodeled. Made of handmade bricks, the two-story house has paired brackets and tall narrow windows. The small family *cemetery* of George Davis, whose house, burned by Federals, preceded this one, is just south of it. Main, S edge of town; inquire locally. BRACE HOUSE: Greek Revival (Bracketed), c. 1850. The handmade bricks and lumber for this two-story house were floated down the Mississippi from Minnesota; one-story portico with a balustrade; 80-acre farm. Main, W on Locust to end, S 0.25 m. BROUGHTON HOUSE: Greek Revival style, 1831; altered. Reportedly this was the original Bethlehem Baptist Church building. SR 15, E on Marion to N on Hill (last corner before the river). BUCKNER HOUSE: Italianate, 1869; addition 1900. Features of this house include a full-facade porch, paired columns, wide overhanging eaves, and paired brackets. William Buckner (1828–1929) was reportedly the last surviving veteran of the 1846–1848 *Mexican War* and, at age 80, held the longest membership of any American Masonic lodge member. S. Main (526). BUERK HOUSE: Vernacular, late 1850s–early 1860s; remodeled. The house was built by 1853 German immigrant Thomas Buerk, a cobbler. His obituary described him as thrifty and austere but courteous; reportedly he was the county's wealthiest person. Main, E on Caldwell (201). BURGESS HOUSE: Second Empire, c. 1860; porches added later. The house has eight brick rooms, a mansard roof, and a massive hand-cut stone foundation. Main, W on Monroe (319). CONYERS HOUSE: Greek Revival style, 1845; two-story addition 1905. The 1845 portion (one and a half stories, handmade solid brick) was built by Thomas Conyers, a major in the *Black Hawk War*. S. Main (526). GRIMES HOUSE: Queen Anne, 1889. The house features curved porches, a recessed balcony, and cross gables. Main, W on Monroe (330). MALE ACADEMY: Greek Revival style, 1850. A small *cemetery* west of the two-story brick 13-room house was used for 1850s smallpox victims. Main, E on Monroe to just N of Fairgrounds. MALLORY HOUSE: Greek Revival style, c. 1831;

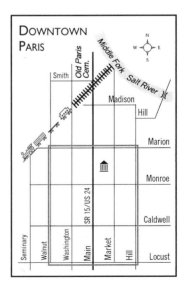

altered. Built by town founder Josephus Fox, this is believed to be the oldest house in town. Main, W on Marion (328). MOSS HOUSE: Queen Anne, 1884. The house has ornamental rooftop cresting, French plate-glass windows, and cross gables. Main, W on Locust (403).

Cemeteries. OLD PARIS: Three wives of D. W. Dulany are buried side-by-side under one long ornately carved tombstone rising to three pinnacles, under which are recorded birth, marriage, and death dates. Two wives died after nearly two years of marriage; one after eight months. Dulany's grave cannot be located. Also inside the iron picket fence are other markers presumed to be children and/or other wives. Another Old Paris marker is engraved with two names, Harry E. Thomas and Ruby Hall, and one birth date, August 1881. Ruby (Rube) Hall, while a young man, thought he had killed a man trying to rob him. Thinking he was wanted for murder, he changed his name. Although 14 years later he learned the man was not dead, he was still known by both names until he died in 1970. N. Main at Smith. WALNUT GROVE: One small stone reads Marr, marking the single grave of Nellie and Chester, man and wife, buried in caskets one on top of the other. The cemetery had run out of space, and they wanted to be buried at the same location. Nearby is a chimney-shaped marker made of brick. B. C. M. (Barney) Farthing built it for his family and himself. Inquire locally. *(Cemeteries)*

Dwarf Redwood Cypress. Also called the Montezuma Cypress, the tree was brought here in 1832 as a seedling from southern California by town founder Josephus Fox, who had traveled to Mexico and California after platting Paris. Approximately 146 feet tall, 9.5 feet in diameter. Main, W on Monroe (406); private.

Monroe County Courthouse. Italian Renaissance, 1912. The county's third, this three-story 108-by-82-foot masonry courthouse has a rusticated first level and four projecting central entries with two-story Corinthian columns. Reportedly its elaborate dome was the last built for a Missouri courthouse. Cost: $83,450. Monroe County Museum: below. Grounds: memorial to the Potawatomi Indians who camped near here in 1838 during their forced removal to *Indian Territory* (Oklahoma). Main at Marion. *(County Profiles)*

Monroe County Museum. Exhibits, some rotating, include WWI, WWII, and Indian items, wooden farm implements, an 1853 sewing machine, artists' proofs of Western paintings by former Paris resident Gordon Snidow, and four murals by local artist Doris Hill that epitomize Paris in fifty-year increments, 1776–1976. Courthouse.

Paris Covered Bridge Remnant. This bridge built in 1857 over the Middle Fork of the Salt River was destroyed by a 1958 flood. Today's modern bridge is partially supported by the 1857 stone foundation. Courthouse; Marion, E to Hill, N to river.

Recreation. MARK TWAIN LAKE / CLARENCE CANNON DAM and MARK TWAIN *STATE PARK* / MARK TWAIN BIRTHPLACE STATE HISTORIC SITE: SR 154, E 11 m.; SR 107, N 3 m. *(Lakes: Corps of Engineers)*. WILLINGHAM *WILDLIFE AREA*.

Union Covered Bridge. Burr Arch, 1870–1871; 120 feet long and 17.5 feet wide with a 12-foot entrance (high enough to accommodate a wagon full of hay); National Historic Register, State Historic Site. Closed to all but foot traffic in 1970, this is the only survivor of five covered bridges built in 1857–1871 by J. C. Elliot and his son in Monroe County (4 were destroyed by flood, 1 was razed). It is Missouri's only surviving example of a Burr arch design. US 24, W 5 m.; SR C, S 3.5 m.; SR C spur, W 0.3 m. to Elk Fork of the Salt River. *(Covered Bridges)*

1. No p.o.

2. Its location in a grove near a *prairie* between *New London* and *Fayette* on an early mail route; p.o. Middle Grove 1829–1894; Middlegrove 1894–1907 *(Post Offices)*.

PERRYVILLE

Population: 6,933   Map I-6

Platted in 1822 as a central location for newly organized Perry County on land donated by Bernard Layton, the town was named for its county, which honors Capt. Oliver Hazzard Perry (1785–1819), who in 1813 won the Battle of Lake Erie *(War of 1812)*, a victory that became famous because it marked the first time that England lost an entire naval squadron by surrender and because of Perry's message afterward: "We have met the enemy and they are ours." Slow to grow (1890 pop. 879), it was the political and trading center of an area settled c. 1801 that was served by El Camino Real (below). Completion of the Chester, Perryville, Ste. Genevieve & Farmington *Railroad* during the early 1890s helped establish a secure economic base. Post office: 1823–now. Home of Perryville Area Vocational School.

El Camino Real. Marker, NW corner of courthouse square. *(Roads and Traces)*

Hill of Peace. The former Peace Lutheran Church, organized in 1844, was known as Frankenburg Hill Church from 1852 until it relocated in 1885 to Friedenberg.[1] Since the congregation disbanded in 1980, this one-story red-brick structure (Classicism, 1885), with tall narrow twelve-over-twelve windows arched at the top, has been used as a "church history book" by its owner, Concordia Historical Institute (*Altenburg: Log Cabin College*). Visitors welcome. US 61, S 1.8 m. to Peace Lutheran *Cemetery* (the former Frankenburg Hill Church location at US 61 and SR P); US 61, S 0.9 m.; CR 300, E 0.1 m.; CR 302, N and E 1.2 m.

Longtown, Mo. Platted in 1871 along the Perryville–*Jackson* Road and possibly named for 1860 settler John Long, the town was formerly an 1821 Methodist church settlement later known as Abernathy. It was settled by, among others, the Abernathys, Rutledges, and Farrars (*Farrar*), who founded the Everlasting Gospel of Jesus Christ Methodist Church, later called York Chapel (still holding services at its 1837 location; N of town). Post offices: Abernathy 1834–1836, 1866–1873; Longtown 1837–1866. US 61, S 7 m. ARCHITECTURE: 19th–century houses and a 1912 Gothic Revival–style Lutheran church.

Museums. The following are owned by the Perry County Historical Society. DUERR HOUSE: Folk Victorian, 1881. Local historical items. City Park (Recreation, below). FAHERTY HOUSE: Vernacular, c. 1827–1831; brick addition 1854; restored. This one-story four-room brick-and-stone house is furnished in two areas to reflect styles c. 1831 and c. 1870s–1880s. 11 Spring.

Perry County Courthouse. Chateauesque, 1904. The county's third, this massive three-story red-brick courthouse (62 by 92 feet) with a rusticated stone foundation has a pinnacle and an elaborate square clock tower, multiple at-the-cornice pinnacled dormers, windows with hood molds, and shallow relief carving. It was designed by J. W. Gaddis of Vincennes, Ind. Cost: $31,819. Grounds: a granite statue of a Union soldier, honoring the 1,800 from Perry County; donated by sons of the veterans. Downtown. (*County Profiles*)

Recreation. CITY PARK: 67 acres. Pool, tennis, playground, ball fields, picnic facilities, historical museum (Museums, above). GOLF: Grass greens, 9 holes. Perryville Country Club; signs. MARK TWAIN *NATIONAL FOREST*: A small pocket of the larger forest to the west; SR T at I-55; SR T, W 8.3 m. to Silver Lake;[2] SR CC, S 2.6 m.; GR, W 3 m. PERRY COUNTY COMMUNITY LAKE: 101 acres. Bass, sunfish, catfish; signs.

St. Mary of the Barrens. CHURCH OF THE ASSUMPTION: Tuscan style, 1827–1837; facade remodeled as Romanesque 1913. Built as a scale model of its mother church in Rome, the Church of Monte Citorio, today's massive structure features a four-story square tower accented by arches and quoins and an enormous rose window set in the brick-and-stone facade of the sanctuary. Inside are murals, high arches, domes, side altars, and ornate detailing. Formerly, a chapel near the alter was reserved for sermons held in French.

COUNTESS ESTELLE DOHNEY, BISHOP SHEEHAN, RARE BOOK MUSEUMS: Displays include books, including the Gospel of St. John from the Gutenberg Bible, paperweights, porcelains, enamels, and Oriental art. NATIONAL SHRINE OF OUR LADY OF THE MIRACULOUS MEDALS: A series of decorated arches under a domed mural highlight the statue and altar of the shrine: "Come to the foot of this alter, here graces will be showered on all." Nearby is a c. 1917 grotto in her honor. On the grounds. ROSATI'S CABIN: Log, 1818; restored. Father Joseph Rosati's one-story log cabin was relocated here in 1936 and protected by a stone canopy. On the grounds. SEMINARY: Founded in 1818 by Venetian missionaries led by Father Rosati, this is the oldest institution of higher learning west of the Mississippi, graduating the first bishops of Buffalo, Galveston, Monterey, New Orleans, Pittsburgh, and St. Louis, as well as missionaries for China. W side; junction SR 51 and SR T.

Yount, Mo. The town was settled in the early 1800s by German families, primarily the Yundts, Hahns, and Bests, whose names were Americanized as Yount, Hawn, and Bess. The town was established by Henry Yount after the Civil War when he opened a post office in his store. Today's community is identified by the Lutheran church (organized in 1852, reorganized in 1868), around which a *cemetery* was platted nearly to the foundations. Post offices: Younts Store 1872–1887; Younts 1887–1954. US 51, S 10 m.; SR J, E 4.6 m. ALLIANCE, MO.: The town was established c. 1873 around a pottery factory. Its commendatory name could refer to a pottery cooperative. Remnants: kiln foundations. Post office: 1889–1953. SR J, E 4.6 m.; US 51, S 4.2 m.; GR (0.2 m. S of bridge), S 1 m. (to join SR EE to Sedgewickville,[3] continue S 0.9 m.; GR junction, N 0.3 m.; second GR junction, E 1.4 m.).

1. German, friede(n) + berg, peace hill; p.o. 1899–1906.
2. Nearby lake, descriptive; p.o. 1869–1954.
3. *Marble Hill: Dolle's Mills.*

PIEDMONT
Population: 2,166   Map H-6

The McKenzie Creek area was settled c. 1851 by family and friends of two brothers from Paint Rock, Ala., James E. and William Daniel. William Daniel owned today's original townsite, a community known as Danielsville until 1871 when the St. Louis & Iron Mountain *Railroad* arrived and railroad builder Thomas Allen platted a town he named Piedmont because he wanted "a more attractive name." The term, a French word meaning lying or formed at the base of mountains, was used in the mid-18th century to describe the area east of the Appalachians and is the French name for a region in northwest Italy. A railroad terminal was established in 1872, and as a trading center Piedmont soon outgrew nearby Patterson (below) and *Greenville*. Post offices: Danielsville 1871–1872; Piedmont 1872–now.

Architecture. DOWNTOWN: Mostly 1890s storefronts. FOLK ART: A fireplace as a picnic area. SR 34, W 1.2 m. MISSOURI-PACIFIC DEPOT: Railroad, 1940; red granite with limestone lintels. N end of 2d. WAYLAND HOUSE: Neoclassical, 1913; brick, tile roof. SR 34, E approx. 0.5 m.

Gads Hill, Mo. Platted in 1871, this sawmill and coke-kiln town, a refueling stop for wood-burning locomotives, was named for English novelist Charles Dickens's house near Chatham, Kent. Dickens, born in 1812 to a poor family, had during 1821–1822 walked on Sundays with his father past Gad's Hill and a house on it, Gad's Hill Place, which he thought of as a palace. In 1857, as a famous writer, he bought Gad's Hill Place. He made it his permanent home in 1860 and died there in 1870. Gad, of the Old Testament, refers to a son of Joseph (Gen. 8:11), one of the 13 tribes of Israel (Num. 1:25) and a prophet who advised King David (e.g. 1 Sam. 22:5). Post offices: Gads Hill 1872–1874, 1879–1887, 1906–1915, 1924–1940; Zeitonia[1] 1887–1906. US 49, N 6 m. FIRST MISSOURI TRAIN ROBBERY: On January 31, 1874, Gads Hill was the site of Missouri's first train robbery (*Roscoe: John Younger Monument*). A contemporary "St. Louis Dispatch" news article accused Jesse and Frank James, Cole and Bud Younger, and Arthur McCoy. Passengers, as well as the mailbags and express safe, were robbed. Estimates of the loss ranged from $2,000 to $22,000. (The James' brothers first train robbery was probably in 1873 at Adair, Iowa.) RIVERSIDE *STATE FOREST*.

Patterson, Mo. This c. 1851 community gained importance as a stagecoach relay station from 1858 to 1872 on the primary north–south road from the Iron Mountain railhead at *Pilot Knob* to Arkansas. It was named for its post office, which reportedly honors G. R. Patterson, a farm-implement dealer. Post offices: Patterson 1851–1862, 1865–now; Virginia Settlement[2] 1862. SR 34, E 10 m. *CIVIL WAR:* The use of the stage road as a military road and the town's location prompted construction of Fort Benton (remnants, south of town on a hill; inquire locally). An 1863 battle resulted in 19 Union casualties (41 missing). A two-room log cabin (later remodeled and enlarged; Main St.; inquire locally) served as a hospital and telegraph office and was the birthplace of Sam A. Baker, Missouri's governor from 1925 to 1929. MOUNT PISGAH CHURCH: Log, 1857; additions include a bell tower. The building was dismantled,

moved here, and reconstructed in 1889 by the congregation from near Clubb.[3] *Cemetery* adjacent. SR 34, E 6 m.; US 67, N 3 m. MUDLICK MOUNTAIN NATURAL AREA: 1,370 acres. Part of Sam A. Baker *State Park*. The area has been called one of the most significant remaining old-growth forests in the Ozark region. Its eastern slope, strewn with igneous boulders, is heavily forested with oak and a well-developed understory of dogwood. At the north end, Big Creek forms one of Missouri's largest and deepest canyon-like gorges, featuring *shut-ins*, igneous glades, slopes, and sheer bluffs. Mudlick Mountain is one of the state's highest igneous knobs (*Balds and Knobs*) and is subject to windstorms, lightning, snow, and ice (interpretive themes at the park). Patterson 63956. SR 143, N 4.9 m.

Recreation. CLEARWATER LAKE: SR HH, W 6 m. *FLOAT STREAM:* Black River. FUNK *WILDLIFE AREA*. SAM A. BAKER *STATE PARK:* SR 143, N 3 m. from Patterson (above). *STATE FORESTS:* Mountain Lake, Riverside.

1. Postmaster Anthony Zeitinger.
2. Possibly in honor of an 1802 settler, Virginian Joseph Parish, who was related to Logan Township's namesakes.
3. Personal name; p.o. 1892–1959; SR 34, E 13 m.

PILOT GROVE
Population: 714			Map E-4

Platted in 1873 by Samuel Roe along the Missouri, Kansas & Texas *Railroad*, the town was named for a nearby area post office that was named for the township (settled c. 1820) that took its name from a tall grove of trees used by early settlers as a guide or pilot while crossing the *prairie* here. The population (in 1919 approx. 800) of this trading center has remained fairly stable. Post office: 1833–now.

Architecture. AREA: Betteridge House (1858), with a lookout on the roof; SR 135, S 5.4 m. at SR E junction. *Suspension bridge*, built by Joe Dice of Warsaw, Mo.; a good example its style; SR 135, S 1 m.; SR N, W 2.8 m. to Clear Creek[1] (notice two mid-1850s *cemeteries*); continue SR N, W 3 m.; GR (second), W 0.5 m. TOWN: Good examples of 19th-century styles, including the old city jail (late 1870s) and Harris lumber company (1893). SR M along railroad tracks.

Katy Trail State Park. At SR HH, between SR M and SR 135. (*State Parks*)

Mt. Vernon Cemetery. Formerly an early settlers' religious campground and the site of Cumberland Presbyterian Church (c. 1833; defunct). SR 135, S 1 m.; GR (E of bridge and junction of SR N), S 0.3 m. (*Cemeteries*)

Pleasant Green, Mo. Named for the Walker family plantation (commendatory; below), the town was platted in 1873 along the Missouri, Kansas & Texas *Railroad*. Post office: 1842–1867, 1869–1871, 1873–1954. SR 135 S 7.2 m. ARCHITECTURE: Grouped together are a Methodist church, organized in 1825, reportedly the second Methodist church west of St. Louis County (present structure, 1868; *cemetery* adjacent); Pleasant Green Plantation House (c. 1818; National Historic Register; tours); and Walker House (antebellum). SR 135, W 1.8 m. KATY TRAIL *STATE PARK:* In town; no facilities.

1. Nearby creek; descriptive; p.o. 1871–1872.

PILOT KNOB
Population: 783   Map H-6

Platted in 1858 at the terminus of the Iron Mountain *Railroad,* Pilot Knob is one of three former mining towns *(Arcadia, Ironton)* joined today by their city limits along SR 21. It began c. 1834 with families mining at the base of town namesake Pilot Knob (below) and developed as both a mining town and a trading center (1890 pop. 757). Post office: 1858–now. See the map at Arcadia and other nearby attractions at *Arcadia* and *Ironton.*

Architecture. Some 19th-century structures, including Immanuel Evangelical Lutheran Church (Vernacular, c. 1862; frame; National Historic Register), which still has its original pipe organ, furnishings, and custom-made 2,000-pound bell; SR 21, 1 block E, Pine at Zielger.

Battle of Pilot Knob. September 27, 1864. This was the first battle of what is now called Price's Raid *(Civil War).* On September 19, 1864, Confederate general Sterling Price *(Keytesville: Sterling Price Monument),* in command of three mounted divisions led by Generals James Fagan, John Marmaduke, and Joseph Shelby, entered southeast Missouri from Arkansas, advancing rapidly in three columns. Camped at Fredericktown on September 26 while detailing plans for an attack on St. Louis, Price, not wanting to leave Federal troops at his rear, sent Shelby to destroy the railroad at Irondale and ordered Fagan, with 9,000 men, to attack Fort Davidson (below), which had been hastily reinforced to 1,000 men. The fort, a hexagonal earthworks surrounded on three sides by high hills, was commanded by Federal general Thomas Ewing, who concentrated cannons and rifles at the only approach, an open level valley. Price's choice of a frontal assault resulted in an estimated 1,200 Confederate casualties in less than an hour (compared to 184 Federal casualties). That night,

Ewing, knowing his situation was desperate (disastrous if Price positioned artillery on the hills), led his troops in a silent retreat through Confederate lines. At dawn, Price, discovering the escape, futilely dispatched Marmaduke to pursue. FORT DAVIDSON: National Historic Register, State Historic Site. Earthwork remnants. SR 21, near S city limits; signs.

Buford State Forest. Large glades. *(State Forests)*

Elephant Rocks Natural Area. 7 acres. Part of Elephant Rocks *State Park.* Features the best-known examples of the park's spectacular and massive spheroidal pink granite boulders, whose shapes suggested the park's name. Braille trail, wheelchair access. Star Route 1, Box 91, Belleview 63623. SR 21, N 3.6 m.; SR RA, W 0.5 m.

Iron Mountain, Mo. This mining town's namesake, a hill about 200 feet high with a 500-acre base, was thought to be solid iron when the Missouri Iron Company was organized in 1836. After an investment of $5 million here and at Pilot Knob (below), the company failed in 1845 and was replaced by the American Iron Mountain Company *(Ste. Genevieve: Felix Valle House, Plank Road),* which employed over 1,200 men and built a plank road (below) during the boomtown years of 1848–1860. Mining activity declined appreciably by 1884, ceased after WWI, then continued intermittently until the 1960s. Post office: 1846–1894, 1906–1978. SR 21, N 3 m. to Graniteville[1] (note red granite structures and walls); SR W, N 3.8 m. PLANK ROAD: Reportedly the longest of its kind in Missouri, this 42-mile *road* was built in 1851–1853 with heavy timber laid lengthwise and oak planks nailed crosswise. Used for hauling iron from Iron Mountain via *Farmington* to *Ste. Genevieve* at the Mississippi, it was abandoned in 1858 when the St. Louis & Iron Mountain *Railroad* reached *Pilot Knob.* Route: SR W, E 17 m. to Farmington; SR 32, E 25 m. to Ste. Genevieve.

Pilot Knob. Reportedly one of the largest masses of its kind in America, this cone-shaped knob, a Precambrian igneous formation and historic area landmark rising 581 feet, was thought to be solid iron until extensive mining produced only surface deposits (Iron Mountain, above). SE of town. *(Balds and Knobs)*

1. The rock; p.o. 1874–1973.

PINEVILLE
Population: 580   Map C-7

Early records for the town were destroyed in 1863 when the courthouse was burned during the *Civil War.* Local tradition claims the town was platted in 1847 at

Elk River and Sugar Creek as Maryville.[1] Because of an already established *Maryville,* it was renamed Pineville. The place-name's common descriptive prefix usually refers to a nearby growth of pine, as opposed to a thicket at the site, and is often used to suggest a cool mountain setting of open forest. Another source claims the name was transferred from Pineville, Ky., but that town, while it might have been known informally as Pineville after c. 1825, was established in 1818 as Cumberland Ford, and the name was not changed to Pineville until it was platted in 1867. In keeping with confusion about the place-name, Pineville and Rutledge (below) were both selected in 1849 as county seat of newly organized McDonald County (Pineville by the county commissioners, Rutledge by a contested popular vote). Both towns had separate county officials and separate meeting places from 1849 until 1858, when the Missouri general assembly chose Pineville as the legal county seat after Rutledge proved too unruly (an 1850 fight resulted in three deaths, and the court building was overturned by a mob in 1856). Landlocked and bypassed by railroads, the town grew as the county political center. Post office: 1849–now.

Jane, Mo. Formerly the site of White Rock Prairie post office,[2] which was moved to Caverna (below), Jane was established c. 1882 and named for the first postmaster's daughter. Local tradition claims the name for the site preceding White Rock was Gotham, a nickname also spelled (as pronounced) Gottem or Gottam, whose namesake is uncertain, but Gotham, England, is best known for the Three Wisemen of Gotham in Mother Goose. Post office: 1882–1966. US 71, S 5 m. CAVERNA, MO.: Established when White Rock Prairie post office was moved here (above), the town was named for the vicinity's many *caves,* one of which includes the last discovery of J. A. Truitt *(Noel: Truitt's Cave),* which collapsed before it could be explored (W side of US 71 at state line next to a spring). Post office: 1876–1906. US 71, S 3 m. *CEMETERY:* Beautifully landscaped with 89 walnut trees and bluegrass; E edge of Jane.

McDonald County Courthouse. Seventies Modern, 1977–1978. Excluding a log building in Rutledge (Pineville history, above), this one-story masonry structure (72 by 84 feet) is the county's fourth courthouse (Old McDonald County Courthouse, below). Cost: $165,000 ($145,000 from a federal grant). N of town square. *(County Profiles)*

Old McDonald County Courthouse. Folk Victorian style, 1870; addition 1905; remodeled 1943, 1969. Originally a red-brick two-story structure (about 42 by 48 feet), the county's third courthouse (McDonald County Courthouse, above) was a centerpiece for the 1938 Hollywood movie "Jesse James," which featured Tyrone Power, Randolph Scott, and Henry Fonda. Today it is used for various government offices. Town square.

Recreation. BIG SUGAR CREEK *STATE PARK:* Currently being developed as a state park; inquire locally or write Box 176, Jefferson City 65102. *FLOAT STREAMS:* Elk River, Big Sugar, and Indian Creeks. HUCKLEBERRY RIDGE *STATE FOREST.*

Rocky Comfort, Mo. This community's name, taken from a wandering post office (below), has two suggested derivations, related in spirit: (1) from its location near rocky hills, comforting springs, and a scenic valley, and (2) from Rocky Comfort, Ark. (via c. 1844 Rocky Comfort Academy), which was reportedly named for a spring flowing from limestone at a tree-shaded creek. Post office: 1860–1876 (Newton County), 1876–now (McDonald County). US 71, N 4 m.; SR 76, E 26 m. ALBERT E. BRUMLEY MEMORIAL PARK: The last full weekend in September, this is the site of a festival emphasizing gospel music, held since c. 1969; picnic facilities; SR 76, S 10 m.; SR E, S 5.3 m. to Powell.[3] FOWLER NATURAL TUNNEL: Testifying to the popularity of this picnic site are two concrete foundations, ruins of an unfinished 1920s resort development. The tunnel, with a 15-foot ceiling at the northwest end, leads south for 150 feet, then turns northeast for 55 feet to the upper mouth. A product of water percolating through limestone *(Collapsed Cave Systems)* and *stream piracy,* it is still developing (eroding) and therefore dangerous in wet weather *(Caves).* From Powell (above), GR (at sign to a campground), follow Big Sugar Creek W 1.8 m. to northwest-flowing tributary crossed by the road; walk 100 yards up the tributary. PINE LOG ELKS: Over 1,000 elk, reportedly the largest herd east of the Rocky Mountains, can be found in these 1,700 acres. SR 76, S 1.7 m. then W 1 m.; GR (Pinelog Rd.), S 3 m.

Rutledge, Mo. The town was named for John Rutledge, a Revolutionary War hero and the first state governor of South Carolina, 1776–1778. The site, at the confluence of Indian Creek and Elk River, is now a field in front of Ozark Wonder Cave *(Noel).* Between 1891 and 1935 there were two other names for the townsite: (1) Madge,[4] when the Kansas City, Pittsburg & Gulf *Railroad* quarried rock here for roadbed ballast, and (2) Elk Springs,[5] when a resort was established. Post office: 1849–1867; defunct.

---

1. Reportedly named for Mary Mosier (or Moser), an unspecified relative of an early settler.
2. Descriptive location; p.o. 1854–1868, 1870–1871, 1873–1876.
3. Local physician or the family name; p.o. 1871–now.
4. Wife of RR president; p.o. 1891–1903.
5. For the animal via the springs and the river; p.o. 1907–1935.

PLATTE CITY
Population: 2,947   Map C-3

Settled in 1828 along the east side of the Platte River by Zaddock (or Zadoc) Martin, who was licensed to operate a ferry here, the town was known as Martinsville (no p.o.) and Platte Falls (no p.o.), the latter being designated temporary county seat of newly organized Platte County *(Platte Purchase)*. Platte City was selected county seat, platted, and named for the river and county *(County Profiles)* in 1839. A successful trading center along the river and the military road between *Liberty* and Fort Leavenworth, Kans., as well as an outfitter for westbound travelers *(Oregon Trail)*, it was destroyed by Federals during the *Civil War*. The arrival in 1870 of the Chicago & Southwestern *Railroad* (Tracy, below) helped reestablish its economy. Post office: 1839–now. Home of Platte County Area Vo-Tech.

Architecture. Good examples of 19th-century structures, including: Fox House (c. 1834; remodeled as apartments), 3d at High; Jenkins House (1842), 100 block of Main; and Pence House, SR J, NE 2.25 m. About 30 structures, ranging from 1839 to 1893, are located in the 100–500 blocks of Ferrel, Main, Paxton, High, 1st, 2d, and 3d.

Basswood Springs / Lake. The water, once shipped worldwide, is still for sale. The scenic lake, now commercial, was once owned by Kansas City millionaire A. J. Stephens; tours of west side. SR HH, E 5 m.; Interurban Rd. (former rail bed for the 1913–1933 Electric Interurban Trains from Kansas City to St. Joseph), S 1 m.

Camden Point, Mo. Established c. 1837, the town was named for British Lord Camden *(County Profiles: Camden)* and its hilltop location. Post office: 1837–1848, 1850–now. I-29 at SR HH; I-29, N 6.2 m.; SR U, E 2.6 m. OLD PLEASANT GROVE *CEMETERY:* Buried here are six Confederate soldiers, part of a detachment ambushed in 1864 while picnicking with locals. Six flat stones, NE corner; monument. SR 371, N 5 m.; SR U, E 3.5 m.; SR EE, N 0.5 m. (W of new cemetery).

New Market, Mo. One of the county's oldest towns *(Platte Purchase)*, it was settled in 1830 and known as Jacksonville[1] until renamed New Market when application for a post office revealed an existing Jacksonville in Randolph County. New Market is a popular American place-name derived from Newmarket, England, a market town located by a 7.5-mile-long Iron Age mound and ditch. Post office: 1839–1959. SR 371 at SR 92; SR 371, N 9 m. INDIAN MOUND: Oval-shaped, about 100 feet long, 25 feet high. SR 371, S approx. 5 m.; 20 yds. off road, W side; no signs.

Platte County Courthouse. Early Classical Revival, 1866–1867; additions; National Historic Register. The county's second courthouse, originally 80 by 100 feet, this two-story center-gabled brick building has three front entrances highlighted by semicircular fanlights that are repeated over recessed windows to approximate traditional twelve-over-twelve sashes. The projecting central entry porch and raised first level give the feeling of a full-facade entry with columns. Cornices with dentils and modillions, stone belt courses, and quoins complete the details. The interior has black-and-white flagstones. Cost: $88,500. SR 92; 3d N to Main. *(County Profiles)*

Platte County Museum. Second Empire, 1882; National Historic Register. Unusual because of its size (only one story; brick with a mansard roof), the asymmetrical building is an excellent example of its style, with quoins, roof cresting, a one-story porch, and bracketed windows. The paired entry doors were replaced. Furnished (1880s style), tours. SR 92; N on 3d to Ferrel.

Recreation. PLATTE FALLS *WILDLIFE AREA.* SMITHVILLE LAKE: SR 92, E 12 m.; US 169, N 2 m. *(Lakes: Corps of Engineers)*. WESTON BEND *STATE PARK:* SR J, W 4 m.

Tracy, Mo. The town was established in 1870 as a depot for Platte City by the Chicago & Southwestern *Railroad*. The name was changed to honor an official of the line. Post office: 1882–now. Adjacent. PLATTE COUNTY FAIR: Since 1863. Reportedly Missouri's oldest continuous county fair *(California: Moniteau County Fair)*. Late July.

1. Pres. Andrew Jackson *(County Profiles: Jackson)*; no p.o.

PLATTE PURCHASE

Immigration to western Missouri *(Liberty)* and westward expansion *(Santa Fe Trail)* helped create pressure on the state government to acquire an approximately 2-million-acre triangular piece of land (bounded on the west by the Missouri River from Iowa to north of Kansas City), even though its acquisition violated the *Missouri Compromise* and necessitated relocation of *Indians* who had been ceded this territory in 1830 by the Prairie Du Chien treaty. Not included in Missouri's original 1821 statehood *boundaries*, this area was added by an 1836 act of the U.S. Congress (signed in 1837 by president Martin Van Buren), under a bill sponsored by Missouri senator Thomas H. Benton that resulted in the organization of six new counties (Platte, Buchanan, Andrew, Holt, Atchison, and Nodaway; *County Profiles)* and the removal of Indians in

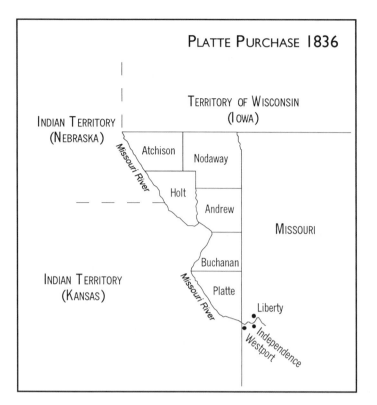

PLATTE PURCHASE 1836

INDIAN TERRITORY
(NEBRASKA)

TERRITORY OF WISCONSIN
(IOWA)

Atchison

Nodaway

Holt

Andrew

MISSOURI

INDIAN TERRITORY
(KANSAS)

Buchanan

Platte

Liberty

Independence
Westport

accordance with an 1836 treaty negotiated by William Clark *(Clarksville)*.

PLATTSBURG
Population: 2,248   Map C-3

Platted in 1833 as county seat of newly organized Clinton County, the town was named Concord[1] by the court, which changed the name in 1834 (for reasons unknown) to Springfield.[2] Because of an existing *Springfield*, the state legislature changed the name in 1835 to Plattsburg(h), honoring Plattsburgh, Clinton County, N.Y., on the Sarnac River, whose name is derived from Dutch (plat, meaning flat or little current). An 1830s crossroads trading center and the location of a U.S. land office from 1843 to 1859, Plattsburg became a railroad center c. 1871 when depots were built by branch lines of the St. Louis, Kansas City & Northern and the Hannibal & St. Joseph *Railroads*. Post offices: Clinton[3] 1834–1835; Plattsburg(h) 1835–now.

Clinton County Courthouse. Seventies Modern, 1975. The county's fourth courthouse, this brick structure was mostly financed by a $700,000 bond. Cost: $827,235. Grounds: 1928 life-size metal statue of David Rice Atchison (below). Downtown. *(County Profiles)*

Clinton County Museum. Queen Anne, early 1880s;

19-century furnishings. Exhibits include a 350-million-year-old fossil (ammonite) and Civil War and local historical items. SR 116, S to Birch (308). **David Rice Atchison.** Atchison, who helped establish this town and the Atchison, Topeka & Santa Fe *Railroad*, and who is the namesake of Atchison County *(County Profiles)* and Atchison, Kans., was, according to some, the 12th U.S. president. President elect Zachary Taylor refused to be inaugurated on a Sunday for religious reasons, thereby leaving no constitutional president or vice president in office. Atchison, then president of the U.S. Senate, was U.S. president pro tempore for 35 hours: from midnight on March 3, 1849, to 11:00 A.M. on March 5. He is buried at Green Lawn *Cemetery*; inquire locally; statue at courthouse.

Ellis House. Folk Victorian, c. 1900. J. Breckenridge Ellis (1870–1950), the author of 26 books and longtime president of the Missouri's Writers Guild, lived in this one-story frame house with bay windows and a cupola. The summerhouse, where he entertained, remains. Clay (500).

Lathrop, Mo. Platted in 1867 along a branch of the Hannibal & St. Joseph *Railroad*, the town was named for railroad company treasurer John L. Lathrop. After the arrival of another branch line (of the St. Louis., Kansas City & Northern) c. 1871, it continued to grow as a shipping point, reaching its peak in 1900–1920 as the world's largest mule stockyard, supplying about 170,000 mules for the Boer War and about 90,000 for WWI *(Auxvasse)*. Post office: 1868–now. SR 116, E 7 m. LATHROP LIBRARY MUSEUM: Exhibits include local historical items associated with the town's role as Mule Capital of the World and with an 1899 factory once called the Midwest's largest sunbonnet factory, which manufactured 500 per day. 713 Oak. WORLD OF CANDY: Over 150 varieties of hand-molded hand-dipped candy are made in imaginative shapes and in all sizes; tours. In town; signs.

O. O. McIntyre Birthplace. Vernacular, date uncertain; two-story frame. McIntyre (1884–1938), a New York syndicated columnist and one of the world's highest-paid journalists, lived here for five years and returned to visit his father during the summers. W. Maple (206).

Perkins Park. One of four parks, it has picnic facilities, a ball field, restrooms, a playground, and access to Smithville Lake *(Lakes: Corps of Engineers)*. In town; E. Clay (SR 116).

1. Commendatory, patriotic; no p.o.
2. Commendatory *(Springfield)*; no p.o.
3. For the county *(County Profiles)*.

POPLAR BLUFF
Population: 16,996　　Map H-7

The town was selected in 1849 as county seat of newly organized Butler County. Its descriptive name is for the townsite's original location near a dense growth of yellow poplars (tulip trees) at a 25-to-50-foot rise on the east side of the Black River that was a well-known landmark called the Poplar Bluff by early travelers. The town was nearly depopulated by the *Civil War*, then grew rapidly as a logging and trading center after the arrival of the St. Louis & Iron Mountain *Railroad* in 1873 and of the Cairo, Arkansas & Texas in 1874. Post office: 1850–now. Home of Three Rivers Community College and Poplar Bluff Area Vocational School.

Architecture. DAVIS HOUSE: Folk Victorian, 1889; 19th-century furnishings. Cherry (522). MARGARET HARWELL ART MUSEUM: Colonial Revival, 1883; remodeled, additions, before 1930s. Exhibits of state and regional art. N. Main (421). SPURLOCK CABIN: Log, 1900. Built at Cane Creek; 1900–1920s furnishings. Hendrickson Park; W. Davis at 13th.

Butler County Courthouse. Italian Renaissance, 1927. The county's fourth, this three-story 100-foot-square Bedford-stone courthouse, a good example of its style, features roofline balustrades, a rusticated first story, different window treatments for each floor, and four full-height central projecting entries with sec-

ond-story Ionic columns. Cost: $265,000. Downtown. *(County Profiles)*

Frisco Depot. Mission, 1927. No longer operating as a depot, the building features yellow brick and a red tile roof; a caboose and baggage car display railroad memorabilia. Moran at Cedar.

Hargrove Pivot Bridge. Truss, 1912; National Historic Register. The bridge was built so that a 120-foot section on wheels at the center pylon can be rotated to allow river traffic to pass. SR 53, S 9.3 m. at the Black River.

Historical Museum. Italian Renaissance, early 20th century; date uncertain. Housed in the former Mark Twain High School are logging-related tools and exhibits, photographs, and local historical items. N. Main at W. Harper.

Natural Areas. ALLRED LAKE: 76 acres. Part of a 160-acre natural history area, cited as one of Missouri's best examples of an undisturbed cypress pond. Features two endangered species (swamp darter and taillight shiner), old cypress and tupelo trees, water locust, sweet gum, pecan, willow, swamp chestnut, and oak, including the rare Nuttal's oak. Wildlife refuge, day use, nonmotorized boats (0.25 m. portage). Rt. 3, Box 388, Dexter 63841. SR 142, S 14 m.; SR HH, E 0.2 m.; SR H, S 1.8 m. through Vastus;[1] GR, S 0.8 m.; signs. POPLAR BLUFF BOTTOMLAND HARDWOODS: 19.5 acres. Part of Poplar Bluff *State Forest*. Features a diverse bottomland forest, e.g. cherry bark, swamp chestnut, varieties of oaks and maples, sweet gum, rock elm, black cherry. Box 631, Poplar Bluff 63901. US 60, N 2.1 m.; SR W, N approx. 2 m. to GR past Hillard;[2] GR, E 1.75 m.

Recreation. COON ISLAND *WILDLIFE AREA*. LAKE WAPPAPELLO *STATE PARK:* SR W, N 14.3 m.; SR 172, E 3.7 m. POPLAR BLUFF *STATE FOREST*. VICTORY HORSE *TRAIL*.

1. Latin for great, presumably because of the community's potential; p.o. 1891–1904, 1912–1927.
2. G. W. Hill's woodyard for the RR, shortened by postal authorities from the suggested Hill's Yard; p.o. Hilbert, origin unknown but probably a form of Hill's name again, 1881–1884; Hillard 1884–1906.

The Green Ridge post office, Pettis County, c. 1910.

POST OFFICES

Prior to 1894 a town, its post office, and its railroad station could have different names, provided the post office name was not already used elsewhere in the state. Some post offices were established later than their respective towns, or they were discontinued for various reasons (the *Civil War* being most prevalent) and later reestablished. During the lapse, a nearby post office usually provided service *(Carthage; Caruthersville)*.

When a new post office began the same year another was discontinued, it usually meant that the latter was absorbed by the former *(Kearney)*. Beginning in 1886, the U.S. postmaster general issued guidelines suggesting that towns and post offices share the same name *(Monett)*, that short names were preferred, and that prefixes (East, Center, etc.) and suffixes (-boro, -burgh, etc.) were objectionable. By 1892 the postmaster general added objections to possessives, hyphens, and compound names, emphasizing that short names were preferred and that the post office, railroad station, and town should share the same name. In 1894 the previous suggestions were issued as an order, with the declaration that new post offices could have only short one-word names, resulting in new towns with limited names—and spawning, at the extreme, names like Ink, Rat, and Not.

POTOSI
Population: 2,683   Map H-5

The town developed from Mine à Breton,[1] which was established c. 1773 in a seasonal lead-mining area (harvesttime until Christmas). In 1797 Moses Austin (1761–1821), reportedly Missouri's first industrialist, acquired the mine and about three square miles of land as a Spanish grant, transforming the mine into a successful year-round operation with an 1804 population of 200, the first reverberatory furnace west of the Alleghenies (providing heat from the roof), a shot tower, a sheet-lead processing plant, mills, and stores. In 1814 Austin and his partner, county judge John R. Jones, donated acreage for a town, Potosi, that was platted at the northwest side of Mine à Breton as the county seat of newly organized Washington County. Potosi (Po'tosi) was named for San Luis Potosí, Mexico,[2] a rich silver-mining town during the Mexican colonial era. Mine à Breton was consolidated with Potosi in 1826 when the latter was incorporated. While lead mining helped establish Potosi, discovery after the Civil War of the many uses of barite *(Old Mines)*, and the town's location near America's largest deposit of it, helped maintain the economy. Post offices: Mine au Burton[3] 1811–1824; Potosi 1824–now. Incidentally, Austin died after returning in 1821 from San Antonio, where he had received permission for 300 American colonists to settle in Texas. His son Stephen F. Austin (1793–1836), called the Father of Texas, renegotiated the agreement in 1821, helping about 8,000 Anglo-Americans to colonize the Lower Brazos in 1825–1832.

Architecture. The Pine Street area has good examples of 19th-century styles. WASHINGTON COUNTY JAIL: Vernacular, 1892; remodeled c. 1990; two-story brick with a stone foundation and iron bars; still in use. SR 8, across from courthouse.

Cresswell Furnace Chimney. Stone, 1838. Part of a Scotch hearth furnace that had a daily capacity of two and a half tons of pig lead. Private. SR F, N 8.9 m. (at bridge over Mineral Point Creek).

Folk Art Cemetery. Enclosed behind a wooden fence at the highway, two life-size plastic bulls and a carved tombstone (with a bull, trailer, and truck) mark the grave of Nicholson Farms owner Daley Nicholson. SR 8/SR 187; SR 187, W 0.5 m. *(Cemeteries)*

Museum / Austin's Grave. Vernacular, 1833. The Washington County historical museum, formerly a Presbyterian church (steeple removed; last service held in 1908), houses local items, including collections pertaining to medicine, music, education, and mining. Moses Austin's tomb, a plain boxlike monument, is in the adjacent *cemetery*. Breton, 1 block NW of courthouse.

Recreation. BERRYMAN TRAIL CAMP *(National Forests; Trails)*: Vault toilets, fireplaces, tables, camping; former CCC *(WPA)* campsite. WASHINGTON *STATE PARK*: SR 21, N 14 m.

Washington County Courthouse. Italian Renaissance, 1908; additions. The county's third, this large brick courthouse with two stories and a basement has a rusticated first floor (the basement), balustrade balconies, arched windows, wide eaves, a hip roof, roofline balustrade, and square central tower with bracketed eaves. There is no town square; the courthouse is set on a corner lot with not much land around it. Cost: $30,000. Downtown; SR 8. *(County Profiles)*

1. For mining operation owner François Azor (or Azau), nicknamed Breton for his Brittany, France, birthplace, who was formerly employed by Philippe François Renault *(Old Mines)*.

2. The Mexican name honors San Luis Potosí, Bolivia (est. 1651 pop. 160,000), set at 13,600 feet in the Andes, where about $2 billion of silver was mined during the 16th–18th centuries; "potosí" is Spanish for great wealth.

3. From the pronunciation of Mine à Breton.

PRAIRIES

Creating an ocean of grass (in the summer an ocean of color), prairie plants are rooted in sod that took thousands of years to form. Missouri, like other tallgrass prairie states, has two general types of prairies that often grow side by side: moist and desert. A moist prairie is like a sponge, collecting water in flat areas, depressions, and low valleys. Its plant life blooms longer and is taller and thicker and consists of differ-

Prairie State Park, August 1994. (PHOTO BY GARY GREEN)

ent species from those of the desert prairies that form on steep hillsides or where sandstone or shale lies close to the surface. Before prairie settlers (sod busters) began farming, fires swept thousands of acres at once, clearing them of plants, living and dead, so sunlight could reach new growth. Buffalo stimulated growth by trampling, grazing, and fertilizing vast areas. The demise of prairies was precipitated by an increase in farmland, which is not susceptible to fire, and a decrease in the buffalo herds. Once estimated in the millions, the buffalo were reduced to 600 by 1889 because of excessive demand for their hides. Missouri tallgrass prairies once totaled 15 million acres. Of the 70,000 remaining acres, only 12,000 are now actively managed through controlled burning, hay harvesting, and grazing. These tallgrass prairies, like Prairie *State Park*, foster flowering plants, insects, fish, animals, birds, and reptiles that once inhabited over 400,000 square miles of North America.

PRINCETON
Population: 1,021   Map D-1

Platted in 1846 as county seat of newly organized Mercer County, the town was named for Princeton, N.J.,[1] where the county's namesake fought during the Revolution and later died of wounds sustained in that 1777 victory. Princeton grew as a political and trading center on a major east–west road, subsequently aided c. 1872 by the arrival of the Chicago, Rock Island & Pacific *Railroad*. Post office: 1846–now. Incidentally, Martha Jane Canary (1852–1903) was born here. She traveled west as a teenager with her parents; after they died, she took up residence in Deadwood, S.D., a mining town of outlaws, whores, cardsharps, and mule skinners, where she earned the name Calamity Jane as a two-fisted drinker and sometimes prostitute who was glorified by 1880s–1890s dime novels and who

c. 1900 appeared in wild-west shows and the 1901 Pan-American Exposition dressed as an Indian scout recklessly driving a six-team wagon. Calamity Jane returned to Deadwood, where she died of pneumonia caused by heavy drinking and was buried next to her hero Wild Bill Hickok (*Springfield: Park Central Square*).

Bagley Natural Area. 20 acres. Features an old-growth hickory-oak forest, including the state-endangered jack oak, a small stream, and wildflowers. Access: trail (about 0.2 m.) through private property. Rt. 2, Box 162, Princeton 64673. Directions: Lake Paho *Wildlife Area*.

Cainsville, Mo. In 1854 Kentuckian Peter Cain built a saw/flour/*gristmill* at Thompson River on the Harrison–Mercer County line, where the town was platted in 1855 and named for him. Primarily an agricultural town, it had an 1899 population of about 1,000 but boomed to over 2,000 during short-lived coal-mining operations (1910–1919) that were abandoned as dangerous and expensive due to the deposits' 500-foot depth. Post offices: Cainesville 1857–1925; Cainsville 1925–now. US 136, W 6 m.; SR B, N 4 m.; SR N, W 4.3 m. BOHEMIAN *CEMETERY:* Late 1890s Czechoslovakian immigrants established farms in the Thompson River valley west of Cainsville. Markers, many in Slovak, are set in a grove of pines overlooking the Thompson River. SR N, W 0.9 m.; SR B, S 3.1 m.; GR, W 0.5 m. STOKLASA FUNERAL HOME: Queen Anne, 1900. A fine example of its style, this three-story house features a conical turret, a wraparound porch, and cross gables. In town.

Lake Paho Wildlife Area. *Wildlife Areas*.

Mercer County Courthouse. Neoclassical, 1912–1913. The county's third, this three-story 65-by-95-foot stone courthouse has a main entrance with a pedimented full-height entry porch with two-story Ionic columns, dentils, and a roofline parapet. It was built on a new square bought by public donations because the county had sold the former location for a city park after its predecessor burned in 1898. Cost: $76,000. Downtown. (*County Profiles*)

1. Its 1724 naming was a general compliment to the British royal family.

QUEEN CITY

Population: 704   Map F-1

Although the plat was filed in 1867 and most histories list 1867 as the plat date, other reliable sources report that the town was laid out in 1862, at least on paper, in anticipation of the arrival of the North Missouri *Railroad,* which was delayed by the *Civil War* (a railroad addition was platted in 1868). Its name reflects the enthusiasm and expectations of the town founders that this would be a preeminent city. Post office: 1866–now.

Architecture. Good examples of late 19th- and early 20th-century styles near the town square include: CHRISTIAN CHURCH: Gothic Revival, c. 1891; truncated tower; Main. COOK HOUSE: Folk Victorian, c. 1895; 10th at Cedar. HIGHT-ROLSTON HOUSE: Queen Anne, c. 1898; Cedar (1 block N of courthouse). JUNIOR HIGH SCHOOL: Vernacular, 1898–1899; remodeled; E end of 6th. WOOD-DEIERLING HOUSE: Queen Anne Free Classic, c. 1900; 10th at Main. ZEIBER-RILEY HOUSE: Folk Victorian, c. 1900; Main at 4th.

Chariton River Bridge. Truss, c. 1900. This one-lane 15-by-95-foot steel bridge was built across the river's old channel. SR W, W 5.5 m.; SR H, N 1.3 m.; GR, W past cemetery near defunct Jimtown;[1] continue W past river's new channel 2.2 m. Note: GR, W 1.1 m., joins SR FF via Lick Skillet.[2]

Germania, Mo. The community was settled largely by German immigrants but also by immigrants from Holland, Switzerland, Prussia, and Austria. Its name (Latin for Germany) predates the post office's. Incidentally, 85 Germans received citizenship in this county, the first in 1848. Post offices: Fabius[3] 1879; Germania 1879–1902. SR O, E 4.2 m.; GR, N 1.8 m. ST. JOHN'S LUTHERAN: Gothic Revival, 1904; organized 1866. Today's structure, large and clapboard with cross gables and a tall tower, is all that remains of the community's buildings, except well-kept farmhouses, barns (mostly 1880s), and a nearby *cemetery* (GR E from church 0.6 m.).

Grand Divide. *Grand Divide*.

Lauer Blacksmith Shop. Vernacular, board and batten, c. 1875. The second floor of this two-story building with a metal roof initially served as the city school. The shop was used by German immigrant George S. Lauer, and later his sons, to repair farm equipment and carriages and to manufacture wagons and buggies in an assembly line–style process. No electric lights; tours. Washington at 7th.

1. Via local tradition, an ironic name due to the town's small size; several local Jameses were called Jim; p.o. 1893–1904; defunct.

2. Humorous, often derogatory, meaning a place so poor that residents even licked their skillets clean; no p.o.

3. The nearby river, formerly spelled Fabiane and Ferbien, probably after a Frenchman.

RAILROADS

Should a heated argument develop over which railroad was where under what name, don't take sides.

Railroads were usually financed through bonds, then bought, sold, leased, consolidated, returned to and retrieved from receivership—and renamed in the process (sometimes merely changing the designation from railroad to railway). Frequently, larger companies operated smaller lines under different corporate names. The eventual 1917 consolidation of the Missouri-Pacific Railroad as the Missouri-Pacific Railway involved no less than 156 separate company names. (To facilitate cross referencing and indexing, this book always uses the designation "Railroad.")

The first steam railroad west of the Mississippi River, the Pacific Railroad, was charted in 1849 to run from St. Louis to Jefferson City, Sedalia, Independence, and Kansas City, where it was to join any line being built east from the Pacific coast. Actual construction began in 1851, resulting in 37 miles of track to Pacific, Mo. *(Eureka)*, by 1852, at which point the tidy history of Missouri railroads ends. For example, an 1852 branch at Eureka (Southwest Branch of the Pacific Railroad), authorized to cut diagonally to Springfield, changed owners and objectives several times, becoming part of the South Pacific Railroad Company in 1868, of the Atlantic & Pacific Railroad Company in 1870, and finally of the St. Louis & San Francisco Railway Company in 1876. The original Pacific Railroad was owned in 1876 by the Missouri-Pacific. The Frisco line's acquisition of the Atlanta & Pacific included franchise rights from all the former owners, giving it 292 miles of track between Pacific, Mo., and Seneca at the western Missouri border, and it also gained trackage rights over the Missouri-Pacific line (formerly the Pacific Railroad) from Pacific, Mo., to St. Louis, thereby securing an important eastern terminus.

Railroad building was enormously expensive, complicated, and political. For the relatively small 1852 Pacific Railroad building project, U.S. senator Thomas Hart Benton lobbied the U.S. Congress to donate over 2.6 million acres of public land to the company, which then secured a state loan of $4.5 million by using the land and railroad as collateral. The 19th century's most audacious and successful manipulator of railroad financing, Jay Gould, owned (with associates) the Missouri Pacific–Iron Mountain systems, which by 1883 encompassed a 9,547-mile empire, stretching from Buffalo, N.Y., to Kansas City and from Chicago to San Antonio and Laredo.

Generally, the federal government offered six sections (one section equals a square mile, or 640 acres) for every mile planned to be built, using the logic that railroad companies could sell the land for townsites and depots, which in turn would raise money for the companies while establishing markets for shipping. This town-building idea worked ideally on paper. By these

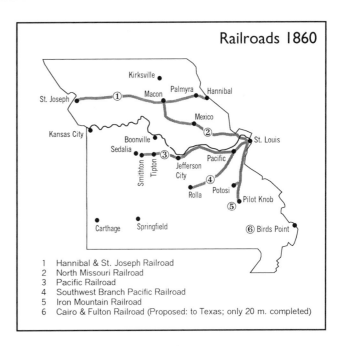

Railroads 1860

1 Hannibal & St. Joseph Railroad
2 North Missouri Railroad
3 Pacific Railroad
4 Southwest Branch Pacific Railroad
5 Iron Mountain Railroad
6 Cairo & Fulton Railroad (Proposed: to Texas; only 20 m. completed)

means railroads made (and broke) Missouri towns from the 1850s through the early 1900s, leaving a poignant footnote to the coming of the railroad: the demise of historic towns. Those bypassed usually faded from maps, their populations absorbed by the new railroad towns that were often named by (and for) the friends, family, or officials of the line.

REEDS SPRING
Population: 411   Map E-7

First established in 1871 as a post office community at a spring named for either a man or brothers named Reed, the area was settled by families from Kentucky and Tennessee who homesteaded near the spring and a major road between Harrison, Ark., and *Springfield*. The Reeds Spring post office was discontinued in 1879 and reestablished in 1884 about two miles away as Ruth,[1] where it remained until the White River *Railroad* was built near the road and the spring. In 1905 the Ruth post office was moved to a 1902 railroad camp and renamed Reeds Spring. The new community grew into a shipping point; it was incorporated in 1947. Post offices: Reeds Spring 1871–1873, 1876–1879, 1905–now; Ruth 1884–1905. Home of Omar Gibson Area Vo-Tech.

Notch, Mo. The community's postmaster, Levi Morrill (Uncle Ike), was made famous by Harold Bell Wright's "Shepherd of the Hills" *(Branson: Shepherd of the Hills Homestead)*. Notch was named for its location in a forest clearing that formed a notch. Post office: 1895–1934.

SR 76/SR 265; SR 76, W 1 m. EVERGREEN *CEME-TERY:* The land was donated by Levi Morrill (1837–1926), whose granite tombstone cites his service in Company 1 of the 7th Kansas Cavalry. SR 76/SR 265; SR 76, 1 block W. NOTCH P.O. / HOMESTEAD: Morrill's post office (small clapboard with steeply pitched roof) and house (Folk Victorian); tours. In Notch; signs.

Railroad Tunnel. This 2,000-foot tunnel was cut through solid rock using steam-powered drills that drew water from the spring (below). Park at lumberyard, walk about 0.25 m. E down the tracks. Caution! Tunnels are like *caves.*

Recreation. SHEPHERD OF THE HILLS *WILDLIFE AREA.* TABLE LAKE / ROCK *STATE PARK* / DAM: SR 76, S 7 m.; SR 265, S 6 m.; SR 165, S 1.3 m. *(Lakes: Corps of Engineers).*

Reeds Spring. The town namesake is covered by a springhouse (vernacular); the water is not suitable for drinking. Downtown; SR 13.

Talking Rocks Cavern. The main chamber (100 by 150 feet) has about 90 formations, including an 85-foot stalactite that provides a natural corridor. Special lighting and sound effects help explain the cavern's history. Trail, lake view, picnic tables, petting zoo. SR 13, S 5 m. via Lakeview.[2]

Waterfalls / Rock Garden. The artificial waterfall, about 200 yards long and 50 feet high, and the rock gardens are accented by an American flag, a 3-foot-tall 400-pound cast-iron eagle, and a bronze eagle with a 12-foot wingspan. SR 13, about 0.3 m. S of p.o.

1. Origin unknown, presumably a personal name with the biblical namesake Ruth (Ruth 1:16).
2. Descriptive; no p.o.

RHINELAND
Population: 157   Map G-4

German farmers from Gasconade County settled the area in 1837–1848, after which merchant Andrew Rincheval platted a town in 1853. The name comes from the common Anglicized spelling of the German River Rhein as a descriptive generalization (e.g. Rhinecliff, N.Y., at the Hudson River, the Rhein of America). Post office: 1853–now. *(Boonslick Trails)*

Bluffton, Mo. Settled c. 1847, the town was later referred to as Stringtown, a common, humorous, and usually derogatory description of a community with no center, i.e. strung out in a line. It was platted in 1866 by 1866 Bluffton Wine Company owner Samuel Miller and named for the impressive local bluffs (below). Post office: 1867–1966. SR 94, W 8 m. BLUFFTON-

RHINELAND BLUFFS: These 400-foot nearly vertical dolomite bluffs line SR 94 for six miles between the two towns. MILLER-GREGORY HOUSE: Vernacular, 1866; moved in 1892 0.25 m. W; addition 1920. Two-story frame with a rock foundation, the house was built using some materials and trim from the steamboat "Clara," which sank near here in 1858. In town. KATY TRAIL *STATE PARK:* In town.

Katy Trail State Park. In town. *(State Parks)*

St. Martins Church. Gothic Revival, 1873–1875; additions; National Historic Register. Rough stone, lancet windows, stained-glass windows, flying buttresses, a 125-foot steeple, and a steeply pitched roof complement the style. St. Martins replaced The Church of the Rising Savior, a log church built for area residents in 1852. When Father George G. Hoehn became the pastor at St. Martins in 1887, he applied for a post office that he named Starkenburg.[1] The community assumed the name of the post office. Next to the church are a large pine imported from Germany and planted in 1890 and a large *cemetery* dating from 1860. St. Martins and Starkenburg are located between Rhineland and Americus.[2] SR 94, W 0.8 m.; SR P, N 2 m. ARCHITECTURE: Various church structures; all National Historic Register. CHAPEL OF OUR LADY OF SORROWS: Romanesque, 1908–1909. Heavy stone, spring arches on Corinthian columns, a square tower with a pyramidal roof, and a large wheel window highlight the style. The main alter has a dome ceiling with frescoes and stained-glass windows (Shrine of Our Lady of Sorrows, below). LOURDES GROTTO: Folk Rock, 1934. On the site of a 1900 predecessor are a statue of the Madonna, a stone well with a bucket, a small stream, and a bridge. MOUNT OLIVET: Folk Art Grotto, 1941. On the site of a 1904 predecessor are life-size statues of a winged angel and Christ depicting the "Agony in the Garden"; nearby stream. THE SEPULCHER: Built in 1950, this underground tomb, reached by stairs and lighted by candles, is designed to give the viewer the feeling of Christ's death. Aboveground is Mount Calvary, with life-size statues depicting Christ crucified flanked by Mary and Saint John. Incidentally, the sepulcher was built to be atom-bomb proof. SHRINE OF OUR LADY OF SORROWS: Folk Log, 1888. This small log shrine, with folk Gothic Revival affinities, opens like a triptych to reveal white beaded-board walls, a cerulean-blue ceiling, altars, and a statue of the Madonna who inspired annual pilgrimages still attended by thousands (the third Sunday in May and the second Sunday in September) by answering prayers in 1891 for fair weather to save farmers' crops. STATIONS OF THE CROSS: These 13-foot-tall solid concrete stations replaced the original 1901 stations of brick with wood crosses.

1. For Starkenburg castle (German for strong fortress) near his former home in Heppenheim, Germany; p.o. 1888–1896, 1898–1918.

2. Reportedly for 1832 Americus, Ga.; Latinized form of Amerigo Vespucci (1454–1512), Italian navigator and the continent's namesake; p.o. 1867–1959.

RICHMOND
Population: 5,738   Map D-3

The town was platted in 1827 as a central location for the permanent county seat of Ray County, replacing Bluffton *(Camden)*. Polly Crowley suggested the name Richmond in honor of the capital of Virginia, near where she and her husband, Jeremiah, once lived. Reportedly, the county commissioners adopted the name out of respect for the Crowleys, who had offered 51 acres for the county seat, an offer that was rejected for unknown reasons in favor of property donated by J. Wollard, W. B. Martin, and W. Thornton. The 1733 name of the Virginia city on the James River was probably inspired by the English town on the Thames River. Missouri's Richmond grew as a political center and crossroads trading center, aided by the c. 1871 completion of the St. Joseph Division of the St. Louis, Kansas City & Northern *Railroad*. Post office: 1828–now.

Architecture. Good examples of 19th-century styles include KEYS-HUGHES HOUSE: 1857; two-story brick; 443 S. Shaw. MASON-TRIGG HOUSE: 1868; two-story frame; 618 E. Lexington. WATKINS HOUSE: National Historic Register; Camden at W. Lexington.

Cemeteries. Buried not in a cemetery but in the middle of a street (W. Lexington) is 1846–1848 *Mexican War* hero Gen. Israel Hendley. PIONEER: Established in 1846, closed in 1878, and first called Public Burial Ground, the cemetery has been maintained by the Mormons since 1945. A large granite memorial dedicated in 1911 by Salt Lake City, Utah, Mormons honors Joseph Smith and the three witnesses to Smith's revelations *(Mormons;* Ray County Museum, below), one of whom, Oliver Cowdery, is buried here. Buried here also are early settlers whose ornate markers have been restored and laid out in a mosaic; Austin A. King, Missouri governor from 1848 to 1852; and Bloody Bill Anderson (Orrick, below). Thornton, 4 blocks N of courthouse. RICHMOND CITY: Buried here are Bob Ford (1841–1892), who killed Jesse James *(Kearney;* Ford's sister, Mrs. Martha Bolton, lived in Richmond); Forrest Smith, Missouri governor from 1949 to 1953; and David Whitmer (1805–1883), one of three witnesses to Joseph Smith's revelations *(Mormons;* Pioneer, above), who helped plat Far West *(Kingston)*. W side, SR 10. *(Cemeteries)*

Farris Theater. Also known as Daughtery Auditorium. Vernacular with Italian Renaissance affinities, 1901; renovated 1930; National Historic Register. Reportedly a copy of the Leadville, Colo., Tabor Opera House, this flat-roofed building with quoins and a second-story colonnaded porch was built by former Colorado gold mine owner S. S. Daughtery. Said to have acoustics sensitive enough to project a whisper, it was closed in 1911, then bought by J. L. Farris and operated as a movie house until 1957, after which it has been used for live performances and community activities. Main (203 W.).

Hardin, Mo. Platted in 1868 along the West Branch of the North Missouri *Railroad* and named for prominent Missouri politician Charles Hardin (later governor, 1875–1877), the town grew from an 1815 settlement at Crooked River called Buffalo.[1] Old Hardin, located near the *cemetery,* was moved to the tracks. Post office: 1858–now. SR 10, E 7.4 m. SEWARD'S GROVE: The city recreational park has a 60-foot-tall chinquapin oak with an 80-foot crown and a 42-foot circumference that is estimated to be over 300 years old. SE side, SR 10; sign.

Henrietta, Mo. Established in 1867 on Charles Allen Watkins's land at the junction of the St. Joseph & St. Louis *Railroad* and the West Branch of the North Missouri, the town was named for Watkins's wife, but the depot was called Lexington Junction, and, due to an existing Henrietta in Franklin County, the post office was named Henry. Incidentally, the Watkins's daughter, Marie Watkins Oliver, helped design the Missouri state flag *(Cape Girardeau)*. Post offices: Henry 1869–1908; Henrietta 1908–now. SR 13, S 3 m. FARMVILLE, MO.: The community was founded just northeast of today's Henrietta in the 1830s (no p.o.) by brothers James and Thomas Allen of Farmville, Va., the uncles of Charles Watkins (above). In 1849 James built a two-car mule-drawn railroad on wooden tracks at a cost of $1,500 per mile. Technically the first railroad west of the Mississippi, it ran five miles from Farmville to the 1819 site of Jacks Ferry across from *Lexington*. No remnants. MAIN STREET STATION: This early 20th-century brick depot with a green tile roof houses railroad memorabilia and Indian artifacts. In Henrietta at viaduct.

Orrick, Mo. The town was platted in 1873 by civil engineer and St. Louis, Kansas City & Northern employee W. W. Orrick along the tracks that bypassed by one mile the older town of Albany.[2] Post office: 1873–now. SR 10, W 2.6 m.; SR EE, S 6.9 m.; SR 210, W 1.6 m., SR O, S 1.4 m. BLOODY BILL ANDERSON: During a 10-minute skirmish in October 1864, Confederate guerrilla Capt. William T. "Bloody Bill" Anderson *(Centralia)* was killed by a Federal advance

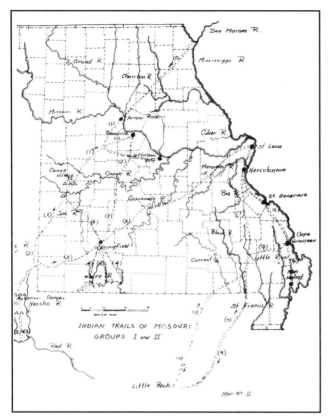

Missouri's Indian trails. (FROM M. M. WOOD, "EARLY ROADS IN MISSOURI," THESIS, 1943)

guard near Albany. Ten of his men died trying to retrieve his body. Anderson was taken to Richmond, set on display, and photographed; the others are buried on a bluff overlooking the battle site between Fishing River and Albany (a mortarless retaining wall marks the townsite). Marker: SR O at SR 210; SR O, N 300 yds. to bluff; or inquire locally.

Ray County Courthouse. Italian Renaissance, 1914–1915; National Historic Register. The county's third, this 75-by-100-foot limestone courthouse has roofline balustrades, a rusticated first story, and four projecting central wings with second-story paired Ionic columns supporting pediments. Cost: $98,000. Grounds: 10-foot-tall bronze statue of Alexander *Doniphan*, Bicentennial Time Capsule (to be opened in 2076), war memorials. Downtown. (*County Profiles*)

Ray County Museum. Vernacular, 1909–1910; National Historic Register. Built as the County Home (Poor Farm), this three-story 54-room structure today contains a large county museum. Exhibits in separate rooms concentrate on themes: e.g. a restored coal mine, toys, WWI and II, Mormons (with one of five U.S. replicas of the gold-plated leaves of the Book of Mormon), a 19th-century bedroom and two parlors, Indian artifacts (reportedly one of the best collections

in Missouri), a school, a post office, costumes, quilts, coverlets, and china. Main, S on Camden, W on Royale; signs.

Recreation. CROOKED RIVER *WILDLIFE AREA.* RAY COUNTY LAKE: 25 acres. Bass, sunfish, catfish. NW of town; inquire locally.

Roadside Park. Overlooks Crooked River: picnic tables, grills, grass, shade trees, short trail to river. SR 13 at SR 10; SR 13, N 5 m.

1. Reportedly prevalent at the time; p.o. Buffalo City 1838.
2. *Albany;* p.o. Ada, town founder Ely Carter's wife, 1864-1873.

ROADS AND TRACES

Topography, large rivers, and animal trails influenced the location of *Indian* trails that were the basis of Missouri's early roads. These early roads today parallel, approximate, or are overlaid by paved highways, the first of which (in the state system) was a 1918 concrete road from Webb City (*Joplin*) to the Kansas border (Federal Project No. 2, also called the Kickapoo Trace, Wire Road and *Route 66* / US 71). Probably Missouri's first road was built c. 1725 to haul lead ore from Mine La Motte (*Fredericktown*) to the Mississippi River near *Ste. Genevieve.* Like a magician's handkerchiefs, roads joined roads joining roads, and so on. When a road was cleared to accommodate heavy traffic, the result was a corridor of stumps made worse by mudholes and erosion churned by hooves and wagon wheels. An 1814 General Assembly law, shifting responsibility for road building to the counties (*Jackson: Toll Roads*), required roads to be cleared of all trees and brush and to be at least twenty feet wide, with the stipulation that "no stump shall exceed twelve inches in height." Because the roads through thick forests were usually marked only by blazed trees, getting lost was not just possible, it was probable.[1] Backtracking to the right road, repairing broken wagon wheels, and struggling through gumbo mud were commonplace, and while some large rivers had irregular ferry service, bridges were nonexistent. Fording countless rivers and creeks presented real dangers of drowning, illness from exposure during cold weather, and loss of possessions, including draft animals and entire wagons. Faced with these conditions, it was generally agreed that poling a flatboat upstream was preferable. Throughout Missouri history, roads and their towns waxed and waned, each dependent on the other, each greatly affected by changing modes of transportation: horses, wagons, steamboats, railroads, paved highways, and, recently, interstates. Today Missouri has over 117,000 miles of roads, streets, and highways.

Two of Missouri's oldest named roads were the 1720s Three Notch Road *(Fredericktown: Mine La Motte)* and El Camino Real (The Royal Road, The King's Trace, The King's Highway; the source of today's Kingshighway place-name). Planned c. 1776 between *St. Louis* and *Ste. Genevieve* and along an Indian trail from *New Madrid* north to the trading post at *Cape Girardeau* toward St. Louis, El Camino Real was reportedly laid out c. 1789 between these four towns. Despite the grand name, it was no more than a path.[2] The first territorial law (June 30, 1808) specifying a road referred to this route as "roads," ordering that they be laid out between the same four towns, which indicates their previous poor and disconnected condition. Approximates today's US 61. Marker, US 61, N 1 m.

1. "I was never lost, but I was bewildered once for three days" (Daniel Boone, 1819).
2. Moses Austin *(Potosi)*, leaving St. Louis for Ste. Genevieve on an inspection tour of lead mines in 1797, chose to travel on the east side of the Mississippi River.

ROCHEPORT
Population: 255   Map F-3

This 1819 Missouri River ferry crossing, the site in 1820 of Arnold's Warehouse, was first known as Mouth of the Moniteau, for the large creek that flows into the Missouri here. When platted in 1825 near the *Boonslick Trail*, it was given another descriptive name, Rocheport (French for rock port). A prosperous and resilient port town, it recovered from three epidemics of cholera (1833–1852), an 1844 flood, and frequent Confederate attacks, including those by bushwhacker Bill Anderson *(Richmond)*. The arrival c. 1894 of the Missouri, Kansas & Eastern *Railroad* helped reduce the economic effects of the loss of river trade. Post office: 1827–now. (Early mail was probably delivered via Lexington,[1] an area post office on Thrail's *Prairie* that was moved to Boonton.[2])

Architecture. The town is on the National Historic Register, with good examples of 19th-century styles.

Boone Cave. Known as *Lewis and Clark* Cave in the 1960s, this cavern, set above the Missouri River and

U.S. 40 in Jackson County, once the main road between Kansas City and St. Louis.

Katy Trail *State Park* (below), reportedly has one of the state's largest openings. Sinking Creek is entirely swallowed here, sucked down into a sinkhole over 100 feet deep (*Collapsed Cave Systems*). SR BB, E 2 m.; Roby Farm Rd., S 1.5 m. (S of I-70); signs.

Boonslick Trail / Fort Head. A marker identifies the former location of this trail and the nearby *War of 1812* Fort Head. SR 240 spur, N 1 m.; US 40, W 0.5 m.; GR, N 1 m. (*Boonslick Trails*)

Katy Trail State Park. SR BB at SR 240; SR BB, E to 3d, S to 1st, E to sign. (*State Parks*)

Les Bourgeois Vineyard. Its specialties are Bordeaux-style table wines produced from the French hybrid Seyval Blanc and Chancellor grapes, as well as native Norton and Catawba grapes. Tours, tasting, picnic sites on top of Missouri River bluffs. SR BB, E 1.5 m.

1. *Lexington;* 1821–1829.
2. *Daniel Boone;* p.o. 1829–1836.

ROCK PORT
Population: 1,438   Map B-1

Platted in 1851 by Nathan Meeks along Rock Creek directly across from his 1843 *gristmill* as a proposed replacement for Linden (below) as Atchison County seat, the town was named for the creek and a boat landing at it. Rock Port, five miles south of Linden, finally won a long political struggle in 1856 when the seat of justice was moved here. While not centrally located geographically (Tarkio, below), it is demographically, which along with proximity to major roads has helped it prosper as a trading and political center. Post offices: Byron[1] 1855–1856; Rockport 1856–now.

Architecture. Some good examples of 19th- and early 20th-century styles, including Dopf Mansion on the National Historic Register (407 Cass, across from courthouse).

Atchison County Courthouse. Second Empire, truncated, 1882–1883. The county's third (the second at Rock Port), this 75-by-91-foot brick courthouse had an imposing square tower that was removed and replaced by decorative brick corbeling; other distinctive features, like the mansard roof and elaborate dormers, remain. Cost: about $35,000. Downtown. (*County Profiles*)

Brickyard Hill Wildlife Area. *Wildlife Areas.*

Linden, Mo. Platted in 1846 as county seat of newly organized Atchison County and reportedly named for the linden tree, the town was replaced by Rock Port as seat of justice after losing its central location when a U.S. Supreme Court decision moved the Iowa–

Missouri *boundary line* 10 miles south. A church, *cemetery,* and several houses mark the former townsite. Post office: 1846–1871. US 136, W 1.2 m.; US 275, N 5 m.; GR, W 0.8 m.

Natural Areas. BRICKYARD HILL LOESS MOUNDS *PRAIRIE:* 125 acres. Part of Brickyard Hill *Wildlife Area.* Features *loess* mounds and plants rare in Missouri but common on the Great Plains, e.g. soapweed, downy painted cup, plains muhly grass, hairy gamma grass, silver scurf pea. 3408 Ashland, St. Joseph 64506. US 136, W 2.7 m.; I-29, N 5 m. to junction with SR A; SR RA, E to Charity Lake; sign. TARKIO *PRAIRIE:* Tarkio, below.

Tarkio, Mo. Platted in 1880, the town, like the Tarkio post office at the Little Tarkio River in Holt County (*Craig),* was named for the river. The derivation of the river's name, while unknown, is guessed to be Indian, appropriately meaning unknown or uncertain. Although this is the county's largest town, with 28 percent of the population, and the most centrally located, it is isolated in miles of cornfields (the self-proclaimed center of the corn belt). Post offices: Taskio [*sic*] 1880; Tarkio 1880–now. US 136, E 8 m. TARKIO COLLEGE: After the town prematurely built a courthouse c. 1882 during a vain attempt to gain the county seat from Rock Port, this embarrassing reminder of failure was turned into a source of civic pride by the 1883 founding of Tarkio Valley College and Normal Institute. NW side. TARKIO *PRAIRIE:* 57 acres. Part of Tarkio Natural History Area. Features part of Long Branch Creek, a small pond, and one of two sites of the western prairie fringed orchid. Rt. 2, Mound City 64470. US 136, E 7.1 m.; SR M, N 3.6 m.; GR, E 1 m., GR, N 0.5 m.

1. Personal name made popular by Romantic poet Lord George Byron (1788–1824), e.g. 1820 Byron, N.Y.

ROLLA
Population: 14,090   Map G-5

In 1855 the Pacific *Railroad* built offices and warehouses at a midway point, now Rolla, between St. Louis and Springfield. After Phelps County was organized in 1857, the court specified that the county seat should be platted along the railroad without regard to a central county location. Former railroad contractor E. W. Bishop offered 50 acres here for a county seat town. John A. Dillon (below), whose house (six miles east of here) was used for early county court meetings, suggested his site. After hard-fought political and legal disputes, Bishop's property was selected in 1858, Rolla was platted in 1859 as county seat, town lots were sold in 1859, the first passenger train arrived in 1861, and the *Civil War* began. One of the few Missouri towns to prosper during the war, Rolla was garrisoned in 1861 by thousands of Federals, who built two massive forts, earthworks, and trenches that nearly surrounded the town (no remnants). The town continued to grow after the war as a trading, educational, and political center. Rolla's disputed place-name has four possible derivations, some of which are entertainingly inventive: (1) Southerners meant to honor 1792 North Carolina capital Raleigh, but they were too ignorant to spell it correctly, or because of Northerners' objections, the spelling was altered to Rolla, with the understanding that it was still Raleigh but pronounced as in "Missour-uh." (2) As compensation for winning the dispute of selecting the townsite, the majority allowed the minority to choose the name; the latter, in spite, chose the name of the most despised dog in the area, Rollo, which was then spelled in accordance with the custom of feminine endings for towns. (3) The name honored a person who is now forgotten. (4) The adaptations by Anglo-Irish dramatist Richard Brinsley Sheridan (1751–1816) of popular German stage writer August Von Kotzebue's works included a popular 1799 Sheridan melodrama, "Pizarro," subtitled "The Death of Rolla." Rolla, a highly romantic hero, was an early 19th-century Missouri favorite, and *Columbia*'s cultural-minded residents sponsored "Pizarro" in 1832 as the town's first play. Using the process of elimination, number 4 is probably the namesake. Place-names derived from literature were fashionable in the 19th century, including esoteric references, e.g. Arkoe (*Maryville*) and Braggadocio (*Caruthersville*). In Polk County, an 1858 Rolla post office predated this one by six months,[1] which eliminates numbers 1 and 2, both colorful but implausible stories. As for number 3, the probability of one or more persons being honored by two post offices during the same year and then forgotten is improbable if not downright poignant. Post office: 1858–now. Home of University of Missouri–Rolla (below) and Rolla Area Vo-Tech. (*Route 66*)

Architecture. Good examples of 19th-century architecture and historic sites are listed on a walking tour map (chamber of commerce: I-44B; E on 9th to Pine). These include the following. CHAMBERLIN HOUSE: Vernacular, 1862. Two-story stone, hip roof. I-44B, E on 6th to Olive. CHANCELLOR'S RESIDENCE: Richardsonian Romanesque, 1889. University of Missouri campus (below). CHRISTIAN SCIENTIST CHURCH: Formerly Catholic. Greek Revival, 1861. I-44B, E on 7th, S on State. OLD PHELPS COUNTY JAIL: Vernacular, 1860. Two-story limestone, two cells on first floor. I-44B, E on 6th, S on Park. OLD PRESBYTERIAN CHURCH: Gothic Revival, 1868. Frame, lancet window and doors. I-44B, E on 6th to Olive. ROLLA

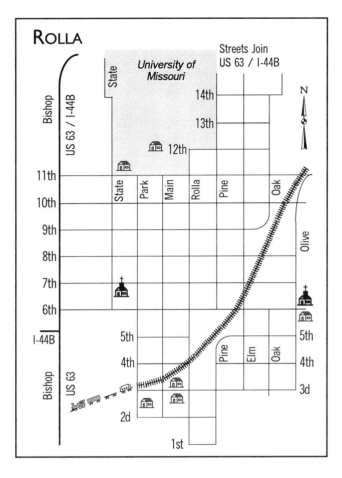

BUILDING: Second Empire, 1871. University of Missouri campus (below).

Arlington, Mo. The town was platted in 1867 by Virginian Thomas Harrison, who with his father, James Harrison, settled near here at the confluence of Little Piney Creek and the Gasconade River c. 1818, where James Harrison established Little Piney,[2] the temporary county seat of Crawford County. Named c. 1867, as was fashionable after the Civil War, for Gen. R. E. Lee's confiscated plantation later designated a national cemetery, Arlington served briefly as the terminus for the Pacific *Railroad*, as did the town directly west of it, John C. Frémont's Jerome.[3] Defunct (bought in 1946 by R. E. Carney). Post office: 1868–1958. I-44, W approx. 12 m. to Sugar Tree Rd.; S across overpass; W on outer road; signs. CRY BABY HOLLOW: Various legends describe the abandonment and death of a baby here. Some stories allege murder, others accident; some involve a young Indian woman, others a young Missouri woman. The result of pronouncing Hollow in Ozark dialect as Holler reinforces the eerie reports of a baby's cry heard when the wind blows. Inquire locally.

Buehler Park. Picnic shelters, trees, historical marker. I-44B just off I-44 at Bridgeschool Rd.

Conical / Slaughter Sinks. Reportedly these are two of

Missouri's most spectacular sinks. I-44, W 13 m. to SR D (exit 172); outer road, W 3 m.; GR (Boiling Spring Rd.), N 0.25 m. Incidentally, Boiling Spring boils from the bed of the Gasconade River at a reported 42 millions gallons per day (W 3.2 m.; E base of bluff). CONICAL: The smaller of the two sinks, separated from the road by a chain-link fence, is 100 feet deep and 300 feet in diameter. Wild orchids grow at the bottom. SLAUGHTER: Across from Conical, 150 yards north of the road, this sink is about 0.25 miles long and 175 feet deep; the floor is nearly flat. Along the east wall of a draw draining north is a steep path ending at a promontory. From there, Chimney Rock can be seen to the west, an isolated pinnacle of fractured dolomite. (*Collapsed Cave Systems*)

Dillon Cabin Museum. Log, c. 1840s–1850s. This two-story log house with gable-end fireplaces was the site of Phelps County's first court meetings (Rolla history, above). Moved here, it displays local historical items; furnished. I-44B, E on 6th, S on Main, E on 3d.

Ed Clark Museum. Features Missouri's minerals and fossils. Missouri Division of Geology and Land Survey. I-44 exit 184, Fairground Rd., E 0.5 m.

Mapping Center. Headquarters for the Mid-Continent Mapping Center, National Mapping Division, U.S. Geological Survey. Tours. Independence Rd. (1400).

Phelps County Courthouse. Greek Revival with Early Classical Revival affinities, 1859–1863; vault and jail added after 1881 and 1921, respectively; cupola removed 1940s. This two-story 45-by-65-foot front-gabled courthouse with tall windows, stone lintels, a front portico, and quoins was Rolla's first brick structure. Confederates made speeches from the cupola, and Federals used it as a storehouse, hospital, and headquarters. In June 1991, voters approved construction of a new structure to replace this one, Phelps County's only courthouse and one of Missouri's only original county courthouses still used for court. Original cost: $5,975 ($2,000 was deducted for poor workmanship). I-44B, E on 6th, S on Main, E on 3d. (*County Profiles*)

Recreation. LANE SPRING CAMPGROUND / PICNIC AREA (*National Forests*): Vault toilets, Little Piney River fishing (including trout), Blossom Rock / Twin Springs *Trails*. LITTLE PRAIRIE LAKE: 100 acres; bass, sunfish, crappie, catfish. I-44, E 3 m.; SR V, N 1.2 m.; GR, E 1 m.

Rolla Cemetery. Among the large cedars, other evergreens, and burial sites of Civil War veterans and townsfolk are two large stones, one marked only Broadway, the other with a ceramic picture of a man and a woman. Broadway, reportedly a Gypsy queen, died in 1964 at a campground beside *Route 66* and is buried here surrounded by great quantities of plastic flowers, carved wooden birds, and other adornments. Other Gypsies have been buried here since, and the graves are visited and decorated each Memorial Day. I-44B, E on 6th, S on Rolla St. past SR 72; sign. (*Cemeteries*)

University of Missouri–Rolla. Formally inaugurated in 1871 at Rolla as the University of Missouri School of Mines and Metallurgy, the school became the University of Missouri at Rolla in 1964, signifying it now offered courses other than engineering and mining. I-44B, E on 11th. EXPERIMENTAL MINE: 19 acres. Begun in 1914 on seven acres and still one of the few like it in the world, today's two underground mines and two small quarries are used primarily for instruction and research. Guided tours. I-44 at Bishop; I-44, W to Bridge School; Bridge School, S approx. 1.5 m.; inquire locally. MINERAL MUSEUM: Established 1904. Features collections donated by the state from its exhibits at the 1893 Chicago World's Fair and the 1904 St. Louis World's Fair, totaling over 3,500 specimens from 92 countries and 47 of the 50 states. McNutt Hall. STONEHENGE: Dedicated in 1984, this is a partial replica of England's megalith that was built in three stages from 2800 to 1100 B.C. The replica has 29.5 sarsen stones (each 1.5 feet high) forming a 50-foot diameter around a horseshoe of five trilithons (two vertical stones capped by a lintel; 13.25 feet in total height). Along with the original's functions, like determining solstices and equinoxes, Rolla's formation includes two new ones: (1) The south-facing trilithon determines the date (the image of the noon sun shining through an opening describes a figure eight on the base of the stones). (2) The north-facing trilithon, equipped with a Polaris window, allows the North Star to be viewed. At the center of this Stonehenge is a triangulation marker used by the North American Triangular Network for mapping and control purposes. I-44B, N of 14th. UMR NUCLEAR REACTOR: Completed in 1961, this heterogeneous thermal pool–style reactor, Missouri's first nuclear reactor, is similar to the first one built during WWII at Oak Ridge, Tenn. Used primarily for instruction and research, it is licensed for 200 kilowatts and is cooled by natural convection. Tours (groups preferred; 20 max.). Behind Parker Hall.

Vichy Road Filled Sink / Altitude Vichy: At 200 feet wide and 40 feet tall, this is one of the largest filled sink exposures along a Missouri highway. North side: blocky sandstone slumps into softer clay; iron oxide produces a purple color. South side: laminated and contorted clay filling. I-44 at Vichy Rd. overpass (W of US 63 overpass) (*Collapsed Cave Systems*). ALTITUDE: In 12 miles, I-44 drops 425 feet between Rolla (alt. 1,120) and Arlington (alt. 695; above), as it crosses the Gasconade River and Little Piney Creek valleys.

1. Reportedly, the U.S. postmaster general required the older Rolla to change its name to Rondo *(Bolivar: Polk County Ghost Towns)*.
2. For trees via the river; p.o. 1829–1868.
3. RR executive; p.o. 1867–1868, 1870–1872, 1910–now.

ROSCOE

Population: 100   Map D-5

Founded in 1839 along the Osage River near the Huffman (or Hoffman) Ferry, the town was moved a quarter-mile south and platted in 1867 at its present location. Its namesake is unknown. This river town prospered at first (pop. 600), then lost half its population in 1870 when the Missouri, Kansas & Texas *Railroad* was completed to Appleton City.[1] Post offices: Roscoe 1840–1860, 1867–now; Howards Mills[2] 1854–1886.

Architecture. Nearby are 1920s log houses built by Kansas City developer F. F. Hoard at the Sac-Osage Heights subdivision (on the south bank of the Osage). Inquire locally.

Harry S. Truman Reservoir. *Osceola.*

John Younger Monument. Cole Younger's brother John (1846–1874) was killed near here by a Pinkerton detective a month and a half after he and his brothers reportedly robbed a train. In 1876, Cole and the other brothers were wounded and captured during an attempted bank robbery at Northfield, Minn. (the James brothers escaped; *Kearney*). Bob (1853–1889) died of TB in prison; after Jim (1850–1902) and Cole *(Lee's Summit: City Cemetery)* were released in 1901, Jim

committed suicide. SR E, N 3 m.; GR, E 0.5 m.; marker.

Lichen Glade Natural Area. 29 acres. This sandstone glade and bluff area bordering Salt Creek features lichens, mosses, ferns, and wildflowers, e.g. blue toad-flax, fame flower, and widow's cross sedum, as well as oak and bottomland forest. SR E, N 6 m.; SR B, E 1.6 m. at Salt Creek.

Monegaw Springs, Mo. Named for Osage *Indian* chief Monegaw, the springs (in 1884 there were 102 within a 200-foot area) were well known by c. 1857 when the spa town of Monegaw was promoted but failed because of the *Civil War*. Reestablished c. 1888 as a spa, Monegaw Springs today is beside Truman Reservoir *(Osceola)*. Post office: 1888–1953. SR E, N 6 m.; SR B, W 2.6 m.; SR YY, S 2.5 m.

Roscoe Museum. Vernacular, early 1900s. Built of hand-hewn stone with ornamental cast-iron trim. Features local historical items, e.g. tools, office equipment, and a telephone switchboard. In town.

1. N.Y. publisher David S. Appleton; p.o. Charlemont, probably for the Earl of Charlemont (related by marriage to Mass. governor Francis Bernard), as were Charlemont, Mass., and Pike County's Charlemont, Mo.; p.o. 1870–1871; Appleton City 1871–now.
2. Mill owner.

 # ROUTE 66

Begun in 1926, this famous federal highway stretched about 2,200 miles from Chicago to Los Angles, from

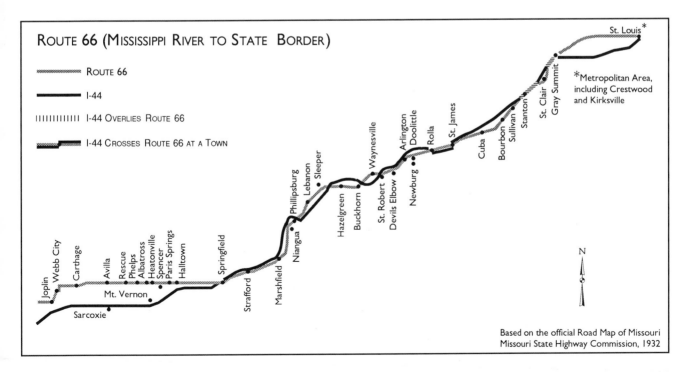

ROUTE 66 (MISSISSIPPI RIVER TO STATE BORDER)

Route 66
I-44
I-44 Overlies Route 66
I-44 Crosses Route 66 at a Town

St. Louis*

*Metropolitan Area, including Crestwood and Kirksville

Based on the official Road Map of Missouri
Missouri State Highway Commission, 1932

Lake Michigan to the Pacific Ocean at Santa Monica. In 1985, just west of Flagstaff, Ariz., the last highway signs for Route 66 were taken down. Despite its bureaucratic death, most of its pavement and some of its attractions survive. In Missouri the route, except through large cities, is uncomplicated: from *St. Louis* it overlays or parallels I-44 to *Springfield;* from there it follows SR 266 through *Halltown* to SR 96, which it follows to Webb City and to *Joplin*. From Joplin it goes into Kansas as SR 66. The route is marked by metal signs. For sites, see, in addition to the towns mentioned above, *Carthage, Crestwood, Gray Summit, Lebanon, Marshfield, Newburg, St. Clair, Sullivan,* and *Waynesville*. For a detailed map, routes, and sight information, write Route 66 Association, Box 8117, St. Louis 63156.

ST. CHARLES
Population: 54,555   Map H-4

The first European settlement along the Missouri River was established in 1769 as a Spanish post by French Canadian fur trader and hunter Louis Blanchette, who, as civil and military commandant, named it Les Petites Cotes.[1] In 1786 Auguste Chouteau *(St. Louis)* surveyed the town. In 1791 the population was 225 and the second Catholic church, replacing Blanchette's first (1769), was dedicated under the invocation to San Carlos Borromeo (1538–1584), archbishop of Milan and patron saint of Charles IV, king of Spain from 1788 until he abdicated in 1808 after the invasion of Napoleon *(Louisiana Purchase)*. On the same day the church was dedicated, the town name was changed to San Carlos, shortened from the church name to also honor King Charles IV. San Carlos was Americanized as Saint Charles in 1804 during the formalization of the Louisiana Purchase, after which it was selected in 1805 as seat of government for St. Charles District of the newly organized Louisiana Territory. The town was incorporated in 1809, designated in 1812 as county seat of newly organized St. Charles County, and selected by the 1820 state general assembly as temporary state capital (First Missouri State Capitol, below). Like St. Louis, it had its population and economic base greatly increased by western expansion, German immigration (beginning in the 1830s), the 1849 California gold rush, and river trade. The 1859 completion of the North Missouri *Railroad* from here to *Macon* and the construction of the 1871 Missouri River railroad bridge and the 1904 highway bridge helped the town make the transition from a river port to a trading center based on agriculture and industry. Much of St. Charles's history is

still evident today in the sites that have helped establish its newest industry, tourism. Post office: 1806–now. Home of Lindenwood College (below), St. Charles Community College, and Lewis and Clark Technical School. Tourism Center: 230 S. Main; parking, shuttle service, guided walking tours, driving and walking tour maps. *(Boonslick Trails)*

Architecture. Numerous examples of 18th- and 19th-century styles are easily located in two districts. (1) FRENCHTOWN NEIGHBORHOOD: Still part of everyday life, it contains 48 notable structures. Within easy walking distance are nine structures on 2d between Franklin and Montgomery. (2) NATIONAL HISTORIC REGISTER DISTRICT: Mostly along Main. This nine-block area roughly bounded by First Capitol, Riverside, Boonslick, and 2d has over 30 structures, brick streets, and gaslights. MARKET / CITY HALL: Vernacular, 1823; remodeled 1876, 1886. Built as a public market and fish house, the building was bought by the city in 1833 and today houses historical society archives and displays. 101 S. Main. NORTHERN WARD OF OLD ST. CHARLES: This area is roughly bounded by Olive, 2d, Clark, and 5th. ST. CHARLES BORROMEO CHURCH: Gothic Revival, 1916. Decatur, between 5th and 4th.

First Missouri State Capitol. Vernacular, c. 1817; National Historic Register, State Historic Site. Three two-story brick buildings, called Peck's Row for bachelor brothers Ruluff and Charles Peck, the owners and builders who offered the space rent-free to Missouri's government, served as Missouri's temporary capitol from 1821 to 1826 *(Jefferson City: Temporary State Capital Contenders)*. The middle building housed the general assembly on the second floor, with the brothers' living quarters and merchandise store on the first. Gov. Alexander McNair's office and a committee room were on the second floor of the northern building, above Chauncey Shepard and his family. At this site on June 4, 1821, the general assembly passed the legislation required by the U.S. Congress for admitting Missouri to the Union; on August 10, 1821, it became the 24th state, the first U.S. state west of the Mississippi. Restored; 1821–1826 furnishings, tours, picnic area. Main at Madison.

Golden Eagle Ferry. SR 94 at the SR 115 bridge; SR 94, N 3.5 m.; SR B, W 4.9 m. *(Ferryboats)*

Great Rivers Museum. Displayed in the 1932 river dredge "Ste. Genevieve" are river-related items and memorabilia. First Capitol at the river.

Katy Trail State Park. I-70 at 5th; N on 5th to Boonslick, S to river. *(State Parks)*

Lindenwood College. Established in 1827 by George C. *Sibley* and his wife, Mary, this was one of the Mississippi valley's first schools for women; it was chartered in 1853. SIBLEY HALL: Vernacular with Italian Renaissance/Classical affinities, 1857; Colonial Revival porch added; National Historic Register. First Capitol, W to Kingshighway.

Parks. 350 acres of parks include the following. BLANCHETTE: 42 acres. Concessions, pool, restrooms, picnicking, playground, tennis, fitness court, horseshoes, formal floral displays, shade trees, ball fields. I-70, N on First Capitol and Kingshighway to N on Randolph (1900). BOONSLICK: 24 acres. Pool, restrooms, picnicking, playground, tennis, ball fields. I-70, N on First Capitol, E on Boonslick to Rosebrae (1000). FRONTIER: 16 acres. Riverside picnicking, floral displays, restored c. 1895 Missouri-Kansas-Texas *Railroad* depot. At river, 1 block S of National Historic Register district (Architecture, above); 500 Riverside. MCNAIR: 98 acres. Concessions, pool, restrooms, picnicking, playground, tennis, fitness court, horseshoes, 11 athletic fields, exercise trail. I-70, N on First Capitol, W on Clay, N on Droste (3400).

Portage Des Sioux, Mo. The town was platted in 1799 by François Saucier, who was appointed commandant when directed by Spanish Lt. Gov. Zenon Trudeau to establish a town at Le Portage des Sioux. Creoles on the American side of the Mississippi River had requested a settlement on this side of the river, and the governor was anxious to protect the area from attacks by the Sauk and Fox *Indians* and to have a settlement to counter an American fort being built opposite this site near the present town of Alton, Ill. The name is derived from the two-mile portage between the Mississippi and Missouri Rivers here that saved about 25 miles of paddling. Reference to the Sioux stems either from their use of the portage or from various legends involving a victory over an enemy through use of it. Post office: 1819–1827, 1833–1847, 1857–1867, 1871–now. SR 94, N 6 m.; SR H, N 7.7 m.; SR J, N 1 m. LADY OF THE RIVERS SHRINE: This 25-foot-tall statue was erected in thanksgiving that no lives were lost during the massive flood of 1951. US 367 at SR 94; just N on US 367. *LOCK AND DAM #26:* Built in 1984–c. 1993, replacing its 1930s counterpart located two miles upstream, this is one of the largest Corps projects (at a cost of $500 million) and one of America's busiest facilities (about 81 million tons of freight pass through here annually). Vegetative Management Area: includes a 1,200-acre wet *prairie* with conditions similar to those of presettlement that features bird-watching, trails, 67-acre Teal Pond (bank fishing), and Ellis Bay Waterfowl Refuge (a 500-acre backwater area). Dam: 1,160 feet long; locks: 1,200 feet long, 110 feet wide (longer than the Panama Canal locks). SR J, S 1 m.; SR 94, E 9 m. to West Alton;[2] US 67, N 2.5 m. ST. FRANCIS CHURCH: Gothic Revival, 1879. In town.

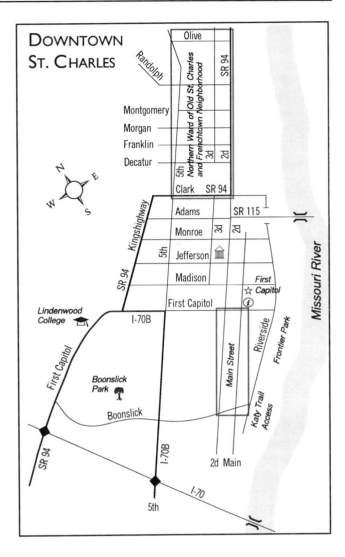

TREATY OF 1815: A marker commemorates this area as the site where an Indian delegation from a confederacy once led by Tecumseh during the *War of 1812* made peace with the U.S. government, which was represented in part by Auguste Chouteau (St. Charles history, above) and William Clark *(Clarksville).* The treaty confirmed the surrender of land on both sides of the Mississippi north of the Missouri and Illinois Rivers *(Black Hawk War).* At the river. *WILDLIFE AREAS:* Marais Temps Clair, Upper Mississippi.

Sacred Heart Academy. Vernacular, 1834; additions 1873, 1886, 1890, 1960. Saint Rose Philippine Duchesne (b. 1769 in Grenoble, France; d. 1852; beatified 1940; canonized 1988) founded here in 1818 the first American convent of the Religious of the Sacred Heart of Jesus Christ and the first free school west of the Mississippi. She is buried here at the Shrine of St. Philippine Duchesne. 619 N. 2d.

St. Charles Borromeo Cemetery. Buried here are a cross section of early St. Charles residents, including

A Boonslick Trail marker in St. Charles County.

town founder Blanchette; Jean Baptiste Point du Sable (1745?–1818), a free black Haitian fur trader around whose c. 1783 trading post Chicago grew; François Duquette (1774–1816), a salt manufacturer at Boon's Lick *(Boonesboro)*; Sir Walter Rice (1799–1858), whose parents named him for Sir Walter Scott, thinking Sir was a first name; and William Dugan (1803–1874), whose wife's constant admonishments about his drinking habits were validated when his mule kicked him to death, after which she had the scene carved on his marker with an explanation. Randolph, W of Blanchette Park (Parks, above). *(Cemeteries)*

St. Charles County Courthouse. Italian Renaissance, 1901–1903. Until the first courthouse was built in 1846, the county rented space, including offices at Peck's Row (First Missouri State Capitol, above). This three-story stone structure, the county's second courthouse, has all the hallmarks of its style: quoins, a first-floor belt course, different window treatments on each floor, pedimented and colonnaded projecting central entries with balustrades, and corner towers (like projecting wings) with arched-top dormers. It was designed by self-taught architect J. B. Legg, who also designed courthouses still standing in Gasconade and Mississippi Counties. Cost: $94,349. 3d and Jefferson. *(County Profiles)*

Wildlife Areas. Bangert, Marais Temps Clair, Upper Mississippi. *(Wildlife Areas)*

Winery of the Little Hills. Since 1860. Champagne and 13 varieties of wine. Tasting. 501 S. Main.

Woolen Mill. Vernacular, 1851; restored after 1966 fire. Built by Gibbs and Broadwater at Blanchette Creek on the site of town-founder Blanchette's 1769 *gristmill* and Pierre Chouteau's 1789 mill, this large three-story brick structure specialized in wool blankets and mittens. During the Civil War it was a Federal hospital and prison. S. Main at Boonslick.

1. French for The Little Hills; no p.o.
2. *Alton;* p.o. Lamotte Place *(Fredericktown: Mine La Motte)* 1874–1895; West Alton (for its location) 1895–now.

ST. CLAIR
Population: 3,917   Map H-4

Platted in 1859 along the Pacific Railroad, the town was named for a resident railroad engineer named St. Clair and not for St. Clair County's namesake *(County Profiles).*[1] The original population mostly came from Travelers Repose,[2] which was established in 1843 a few miles north of here on a major north–south road. Post offices: Travelers Repose 1843–1859; St. Clair 1859–now. *(Route 66)*

Hearst Friendship Park / Museum. Both the park and the museum honor Phoebe Apperson Hearst (1842–1919), a philanthropist and the 1897 cofounder of the National Congress of Parents and Teachers (now known as the PTA), who had married her former Franklin County neighbor, California mining magnate George Hearst (1820–1891). Their only child was publisher William Randolph Hearst (1863–1951), whose "New York Journal" lighted the way for the newspaper genre of yellow journalism, which through sensationalism helped start the 1898 Spanish-American War. The war resulted in American dominance in the Caribbean through the annexation of Puerto Rico and the establishment of a base on Cuba and extended American influence into the South Pacific with the annexation of Guam and the Philippines. MUSEUM: Phoebe Hearst memorabilia. Adjacent is a replica of the one-room log Salem school attended by Phoebe beginning in 1847; furnished. SR PP, S approx. 6 m.; sign.

Moselle, Mo. Established in 1859 along at the Pacific *Railroad* as a shipping point for iron from the Moselle Furnace, the town was named for the furnace company, whose setting at the Meramec River is reportedly reminiscent of the French valley through which the Moselle River flows northeast to the German Rhine. Post offices: Moselle Furnace 1851; Iron Hill[3] 1856–1860; Moselle 1860–1863, 1865–1871. I-44, E 3 m.; SR AH, S 2.3 m. *FLOAT STREAM:* Meramec River. MOSELLE IRON FURNACE: Stone, 1848; 31 feet high; National Historic Register. Built by F. A. Evans and G. L. Nuckolls *(St. James: Maramec Spring Park).* From railroad tracks: GR, E 1 m.

Recreation. LITTLE INDIAN CREEK *STATE FOREST.* RIVER 'ROUND *WILDLIFE AREA.*

Route 66 Sights. Abandoned motels and cabins. SR WW, W to I-44 N. Outer Rd., W 8 m. to Stanton *(Sullivan).*

1. "American Place-Names" credits the Clair County namesake *(County Profiles).*
2. Uncertain but probably, like Travellers Rest in Ky. and S.C., from an inn; p.o. 1843–1859.
3. Descriptive.

STE. GENEVIEVE
Population: 4,411   Map I-5

While earlier histories use founding dates in the mid-1720s and mid-1730s (particularly 1732 and 1735), recent histories argue that the site was probably settled as a village in the late 1740s by French Canadian farmers from Kaskaskia, Ill. (below), with the first land record being from 1749. A 1752 French census reported 23 people: 9 property owners and their families and laborers (indentured and slave). Initially French territory, it changed hands three times in 53 years (*Louisiana Purchase*). Missouri's oldest permanent European settlement, it was successful because of rich farmland (Big Field, below), salt manufacturing at nearby Saline Creek, fur trading, and a lead industry (storage, commerce, and shipping) beginning in the 1740s with Mine La Motte (*Fredericktown*) and increasing to 14 area mines by 1804. Although the town is definitely named for the patron saint of Paris, France, Sainte Genevieve (c. 422–512), there is no historical record of when. The village was also known by the nickname Misère,[1] reflecting French Creoles' mania for nicknames (*St. Louis*). A 1754 property sale refers to the Village of Sainte Genevieve, but at first the town was often called by its earlier parish name, Poste de Sainte Joachim.[2] The first settlement, strung out for about a mile along the Mississippi River near Big Field, had a 1772 population of 691. In 1785 a record flood (the worst until 1973) convinced most settlers to relocate at today's site, about three miles northwest on small hills between the two branches of Gabouri Creek. Relocation was slow, but the old site was essentially abandoned by 1791, and the church was moved in 1794. Laid out during the 1780s–1790s in conformation with Spanish Colonial regulations, the town evolved in grids of survey blocks, with the church and town square in the center and oriented to a western road from the mines (today's Market St.; Plank Road, below) and a northern road toward *St. Louis* (today's Main St.). No formal plat was recorded until the surveys, already allowing for streets, were connected as a whole in 1877 (known today as the Connected Plat of the Town of Ste. Genevieve). After the 1803 *Louisiana Purchase*, a territorial district of Ste. Genevieve was organized in 1812 with the town of Ste. Genevieve as the seat of government. It continued in that role for Ste. Genevieve County after Missouri's 1821 statehood. Ste. Genevieve, like its rival, *St. Louis*, had an 1805 population of about 2,780. By 1838 Ste. Genevieve's population was still about the same, but the population of St. Louis, near the confluence of the Mississippi and Missouri Rivers, gateway to the West, had grown to over 16,000. The decline of Ste. Genevieve

in prominence was also due to losses: by 1819 *Herculaneum* shipped half of Missouri's lead, by 1836 the fur trade had moved west, new salt refining methods were developed, steamboats preferred St. Louis's broad safe harbors, *railroads* bypassed it until the arrival of the St. Louis & San Francisco in 1899, and a modest 1851 iron-shipping boom collapsed (Plank Road, below). During 1825–1845 German immigrants shifted the ethnic population base and expanded the importance of agriculture, which along with county trade and politics helped the town prosper. Post office: 1805–now. Tour maps: Tourist Information Center (former court clerk's office; Italianate, 1876; 3d at the square) and Great River Road Interpretive Center (below).

Architecture / Museums. Within walking distance in this National Landmark and National Historical District town are rare examples of 18th- and 19th-century traditional and Creole French Colonial styles mixed with 19th-century German architecture (brick structures near the street) and pattern-book styles like Adam, Greek Revival, Gothic Revival, and Victorian. The most concentrated area, and easiest to walk, is roughly bounded by Main, S. Gabouri, 4th, and Merchant, but three of the oldest houses are along St. Marys Rd. at the southeast city limits. Creole French Colonial styles are characterized by the use of vertical-log walls that were either set on poles in the ground (set into a trench and backfilled) or set into a sill on a stone foundation. About 80 percent of Ste. Genevieve's early houses were the pole-in-the-ground type, but only three examples remain. Both types usually had massive Norman truss roofs (hipped and double-pitched to carry the weight) and a gallery that shared the roof and surrounded the four sides of the house. A stockade or palisaded fence enclosed the house, outbuildings, and a garden. About 30 French-style houses remain, many remodeled. Following are examples of the vertical-log-wall style open to the public. AMOUREAUX: Creole French Colonial c. 1770 or after 1792 (date disputed). Pole-in-the-ground construction; overlooks Big Field (below). Furnished; antique dolls and toys. St. Marys Rd., approx. 0.3 m. S of S. Gabouri; sign. BEAUVAIS: Creole French Colonial, according to local tradition built in 1770 at old town and moved here prior to 1790. Pole-in-the-ground construction; furnished, demonstrations, garden. S. Main near Merchant. BEQUETTE-RIBAULT: Creole French Colonial, c. 1789 or 1808–1809 (date disputed); fully restored. Pole-in-the-ground construction; overlooks Big Field (below). Living history museum; demonstrations. St. Marys Rd., approx. 0.5 m. S of S. Gabouri; sign. BOLDUC: Creole French Colonial, according to local tradition moved from old town, which would set its probable building date at 1784–1794; fully restored. Sill-on-stone construction;

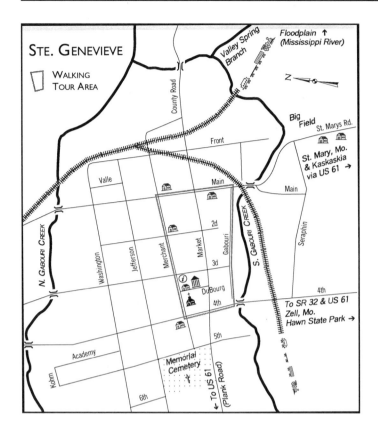

furnished, garden, outbuildings, stockade. S. Main (123) near Market. GREEN TREE TAVERN: Also known as the Janis-Ziegler House. Creole French Colonial, 1791. Sill-on-stone construction; furnished. St. Marys Rd., just S of creek; sign. GUIBOURD-VALLE: Creole French Colonial, sometime from 1799 to 1806–1807 (date disputed). Sill-on-stone construction; furnished, courtyard, garden, well. 4th at Merchant.

Big Field. Also known as Le Grand Champ. National Historic Register. Situated behind the old village that fronted the river, south of Gabouri Creek and east of the bluffs now paralleled by St. Marys Rd., the field was about 3,000 acres of rich river soil. It was given to the town by the king and divided into lots (usually about 192 feet wide and a mile long) that were owned by families who mostly grew cotton, flax, wheat, barley, oats, corn, pumpkins, and tobacco. The field has been greatly reduced by erosion from flooding. *INDI-AN* MOUND: This Mississippian Period mound measures about 16 feet high, now probably far smaller than originally. E side of St. Marys Rd., approx. 2 m. S of creek.

City Museum. Vernacular, 1935. Local French, Spanish, German, and American memorabilia, Indian artifacts, Spanish documents and land grants, a scale model of a railroad transfer boat, equipment from Saline Creek saltworks. At the square, adjacent to courthouse; Merchant and DuBourg.

El Camino Real. *Roads and Traces.*

Felix Valle House. Adamesque, 1818; State Historic Site. Built by Philadelphia merchant Jacob Philipson as a residence and a store for trading manufactured goods for fur and lead, the house was sold in 1824 to the town's last commandant, Jean Baptiste Valle, whose firm controlled Indian trade in Missouri and Arkansas. Valle's son Felix along with James Harrison organized the American Iron Mountain Company (*Pilot Knob: Iron Mountain*) in 1843. This two-story stone house features twelve-over-twelve windows, keystone lintels, dentils, a side-gable roof, and post-medieval-style masonry walls. Merchant at 2d.

Great River Road Interpretive Center. Maps, brochures, information about river towns. Next to City Museum (above).

Kaskaskia, Ill. A four-by-five-mile section of Illinois that includes the town of Kaskaskia was looped c. 1881 to the east by the Mississippi when the river captured the nearby south-flowing Kaskaskia River (*stream piracy*), cutting off access to Illinois and making today's island appear to be part of Missouri. In 1720 the first of three Fort de Chartres[3] was built here near a 1703 Catholic mission and trading town of Kaskaskia Indians (below) and a few French traders (1707 pop. 2,200). Because of the forts (1720, 1727, 1753) and the relocation of the Indians in 1719, a French settlement grew that eventually helped establish Ste. Genevieve. In 1778, during the American Revolution, George Rogers Clark (*Clarksville*) and 175 men traveled over 1,000 miles in two months to capture the fort and town here (*St. Louis*). US 61, S 9 m. to St. Mary (below); signs. CHURCH OF THE IMMACULATE CONCEPTION: Gothic Revival, 1894; established 1703. The bell for this large brick church was cast in 1741 in La Rochelle, France, commissioned by King Louis XV "For the Church of the Illinois, with the compliments of the King from beyond the sea." KASKASKIA *INDIANS*: After being displaced by La Salle's 1683 Fort St. Louis at Starved Rock (east of LaSalle, Ill., on the Illinois River), the Kaskaskias formed and abandoned two villages (one of 18,000), then settled here in 1703 (*St. Louis*). LEVEE ROAD: Graded for driving; good vantage point.

Memorial Cemetery. Part of the land was donated to Ste. Genevieve Catholic Church (below) by the Spanish. This is reportedly Missouri's oldest cemetery; its gate is dated 1787, and the first internment was in 1796. Many graves appear to be aboveground as in New Orleans, but the custom here was to bury the casket six feet deep. Ornate tombstones (stone pylons, crosses, etc.), mausoleums. Many of the tour houses

(Architecture, above) were built or owned by those buried here. Bounded by 5th, Jefferson, 6th, and Market. (Cemeteries)

Natural Areas. The following are all associated with Hawn State Park (Recreation, below). BOTKINS PINE WOODS: 30 acres. A mature pine-oak forest with stands of shortleaf pine at the heads of coves and along slopes. In park. LAMOTTE SANDSTONE BARRENS: 81 acres. Features a sandstone glade, a sandstone forest with shortleaf pine, and Whitlow grass (a rare species). N side of park from SR 144; Bauer Rd., NE 0.8 m. ORCHID VALLEY: 120 acres. Permit required. Steep valleys and sandy-bottomed streams flanked by sandstone ledges, cliffs, and ravines. Seven species of orchids and 17 species of ferns. PICKLE CREEK: 58 acres. A high-quality sandy-bottomed creek in a remote and narrow forested valley. Features crystalline rocks, unusually diverse plant communities with rare species, *shut-ins,* and 21 species of fish (e.g. rainbow darter, striped shiner). In park. PICKLE SPRINGS: 180 acres. National Natural Landmark. Features a sandstone glade, talus, forest, savanna, and cliffs, as well as the white smooth violet, shining nut rush, hay-scent fern, amphipod, and state endangered ground cedar. SR 144, N 3 m.; SR 32, W 5 m.; SR AA, S 1.5 m.; GR, N 0.3 m.

Plank Road. From c. 1853 to c. 1858 this road was used to haul iron ore here from the mines at Iron Mountain (*Pilot Knob*). Today's Market St.

Recreation. HAWN *STATE PARK:* Among other attractions, it features Chimney Rocks Area. Dozens of sandstone shapes (with and without names) have been sculpted by erosion and weathering. Those given names include Devil's Oven, Devil's Fretwork, Pickle Knob, Chimney Rocks (a cluster of columns 80 feet high), and Rattlesnake Rocks (nearby are a natural bridge, a giant stone turtle, and a balancing rock). Inquire at the park. At and near the park are five natural areas (below). Trail, maps: Box 176, Jefferson City 65102. SR 32, W 15 m.; SR 144, S 3 m. to park. MAGNOLIA HOLLOW *STATE FOREST.*

Ste. Genevieve Catholic Church. Gothic Revival, 1876–1880. This is the third church at this site. Its basement foundation has remnants of the first (log, 1754, moved here in 1794) and second (stone, consecrated in 1837). Vertical buttresses, lancet stained-glass windows. DuBourg and Merchant. MEMORIAL CEMETERY: Above.

Ste. Genevieve County Courthouse. Second Empire, 1885–1886; extended 1915. The county's second at this site, today's two-story brick courthouse (originally 26 by 48 feet) shares part of the first's 1820s foundation. Interesting features include roof cresting, a stone foundation with a belt course, a decorative cornice, and a

miniature pyramidal tower extending at and above a roofline pediment. 3d, between Market and Merchant. (*County Profiles*)

Ste. Genevieve Winery. From these vineyards (and a second winery; SR 32, W 12.3 m.; SR C, N 8.4 m.) comes a full range of wines, e.g. sweet and dry reds and whites, a semisweet rosé, and a white dessert wine. Merchant (245).

St. Mary, Mo. Established as a Mississippi River landing c. 1818 and named for the Virgin Mary, the community was later a port for Perryville and Mine La Motte (*Fredericktown*). Its post office names (below) and early nicknames (Camp Rowdy, Yankeetown) help describe its gradual transition to a town, which was incorporated in 1867 as St. Mary. For unknown reasons the town and *post office* continued to use the name St. Marys until 1992, when the error was discovered and corrected. Most locals still refer to the town as St. Marys. Post offices: St. Marys Landing[4] 1831–1853; St. Marys 1853–now. US 61, S 9 m. ARCHITECTURE: Many late 19th-century structures, including Marion Cliff Manor (Italianate style), US 61 at SR M; and St. Marys Catholic Church (1889), with extensive terracing, in town, sign. BURNT MILL: Stone, 1800. Built by François Vallé II at the Three Notch *Road*, the mill was burned in 1864 during the *Civil War*. The walls (approx. 65 feet high) remain; hidden in the summer by foliage. US 61, S 6 m.; SR NN, W 3.8 m.; GR, W 0.1 m.; on bridge look W (approx. 15 yds.). STE. GENEVIEVE FAULT SYSTEM: Exceptionally complex, involving many fractures and extending across Perry and Ste. Genevieve Counties, the fault is visible on Landsat imagery from 500 miles above Earth. At the intersection of I-55 and SR Z the fault is obvious from the crushed and steeply dipping rocks. SR Z, W 4.2 m. to interchange at I-55.

Zell, Mo. Established c. 1845 as part of the German immigration of 1825–1845 (Ste. Genevieve history, above), the community was named for an individual or family, like Zell, S.D. Post office: 1881–1922. SR 32, W 6.1 m., SR A, N 1.8 m. ST. JOSEPH CHURCH: Vernacular Cruciform style, 1845–1847; transepts and sanctuary 1900, bell tower 1909. Stone, stained-glass windows. Adjacent *cemetery* has sunken graves marked by wrought-iron crosses and gray tombstones with German inscriptions. SR A, just S of Zell.

---

1. Misery.
2. The father of Blessed Virgin Mary, according to the 2d-century apocryphal Gospel of James; no p.o.
3. In 1763 Pierre Laclède and his fifteen-year-old stepson Auguste Chouteau (*St. Charles*) used this fort as a base for trading with Indians. In 1764 Laclède sent Chouteau to start work on what Laclède called *St. Louis.* In 1773, the Spanish government awarded Maxent, Laclède and Company an eight-year trading monopoly.
4. River port.

ST. ELIZABETH
Population: 257   Map F-5

St. Elizabeth's early history is confusing and obscured by scant records. The area was settled by Germans from neighboring Osage County in the mid-1850s. St. Elizabeth was platted in 1869 along the east bank of the Osage River by Owen Riggs, who donated land for a port town and for Miller County's first Catholic church (built in 1870). Both the town and the church were probably named in honor of his daughter's namesake, Saint Elizabeth (Elizabeth of Thuringia, 1207–1231), whose relics at one time were buried at St. Elizabeth's Church in Marburg, Germany. In 1872 Riggs, reportedly in financial trouble, sold 6,000 acres (including today's townsite) to Westphalia *(Freeburg)* land speculator Charlie Holtschneider, who c. 1879, at the request of area Catholics wanting a more central location for a church, donated land on a high plateau three miles inland from St. Elizabeth. A new parish, St. Lawrence, was established in 1879, and a plat was filed in 1880 for a town named Charlestown (also known as Charlietown) in Holtschneider's honor. Charlestown and Lawrenceton (St. Lawrence Catholic Church, below) were rejected as post office names because of existing usage in Mississippi and Ste. Genevieve Counties. Sometime after 1880, St. Elizabeth declined (Hoecker, below) and its 1877 post office was moved to Charlestown, keeping its same postal name. Despite federal *post office* directives, the town and post office names remained separate, with St. Elizabeth being listed on maps as the town name until Charlestown was officially changed in 1961 to St. Elizabeth. Today some locals still refer to St. Elizabeth as Charlietown. Post office: St. Elizabeth 1877–now.

Bridges. BOECKMAN: *Suspension bridge;* National Historic Register. Across Tavern Creek; 240 feet long, 14 feet wide, 12-ton limit. Low bluffs, swimming hole. SR 52, S approx. 1 m.; CR 52-54, E 0.8 m.; second GR, S 0.9 m.; GR, E 1.2 m. HOECKER: Truss bridge. Built across Tavern Creek near its confluence with the Osage River; 240 feet long, 12 feet wide, 6-ton limit. Small park with shade trees; site of the first county settler's 1815 homestead (Hoecker, below). SR E, N 3.5 m.; GR (bear left), N approx. 1.8 m. KEMMA: *Suspension bridge.* Across Tavern Creek; renovated with extra steel cables and aluminum decking; 189 feet long, 12 feet wide, 15-ton limit. Small park with picnic table, shade trees; pastoral setting. GR W of church, S 1.5 m.

Hoecker, Mo. This depot and post office community, named for postmaster James Hoecker, was located at the St. Louis, Kansas City & Colorado *Railroad's* Osage River crossing and replaced Brouses Bend.[1] Both

defunct. Post offices: Brouses Bend 1902–1904; Hoecker 1904–1921. From Hoecker Bridge (Bridges, above), GR, N 1.1 m. to railroad. RAILROAD BRIDGE: This turn-of-the-century truss and steel bridge spans the Osage River.

St. Lawrence Catholic Church. Gothic Revival style, 1905–1907. Visible from all parts of town, this large brick church with a tall steeple is set like a courthouse on the town square.

1. Personal name, location.

ST. FRANCISVILLE
Estimated population: 90   Map G-1

Established in the late 1820s as Clark County's first settlement, St. Francisville was platted in 1834 along a major north–south road and the Des Moines River by Francis Church, whose namesake Saint Francis, possibly Francis of Assisi *(County Profiles: St. Francois),* is directly honored by the town name. Bypassed by railroads and later bypassed by what is now US 61 *(New London),* the town's population has not varied greatly since 1899, when it was approximately 125. Post office: 1836–c. 1973.

Fort Pike Marker. The site of an 1832 *Black Hawk War* fort. S of bridge.

St. Francisville Baptist Church. Vernacular, c. 1853; rebuilt 1904. The original church was built using river stone by 1829 settler Jeremiah Wayland, who was the county's first schoolteacher. It was torn down and rebuilt using the same materials in a slightly different design. In town. Incidentally, the Wayland name is honored by Wayland, Mo.[1] (SR B, S 4.9 m.).

Sickles Tavern. Vernacular, 1846; National Historic Register. This two-story frame structure was built as a way station for passengers along the Alexandria *(Kahoka)*–Bloomfield, Iowa, stage road. SR B, S 2.2 m.; SR C, W 1.7 m.

1. P.o. 1874, 1877–now.

ST. JAMES
Population: 3,256   Map G-5

In 1856, anticipating the arrival of the Pacific *Railroad,* John Wood bought part of a 600-acre tract owned by Thomas James, the owner of the Maramec [*sic*] Iron Works for use as a shipping point. The property included today's townsite on Big *Prairie.* Wood possibly intended to plat a town and name it Scioto,[1] but

Thomas James's son William and a son-in-law, James A. Dun (the town's first postmaster), acquired the site from Wood on December 30, 1858, and on October 21, 1859, platted Jamestown, which was renamed St. James (by scratching out Jamestown on the original plat) after the name was rejected for the post office as a duplicate. Considering the number of Jameses involved and the intent of the original town name, the addition of Saint can be viewed as part of the American fashion of creating pseudo-saints, wherein for various reasons individuals were summarily elevated to sainthood, e.g. Joe, Tex., becoming St. Joe, Tex., which lengthened and dignified a short name honoring a person.[2] However, place-name histories identify the apostle James (Matt. 4:21) as the direct namesake and Thomas James or the James family as indirect honorees. Although the first train arrived in 1860, the town grew slowly (1876 pop. 500) along the tracks and a road to Jefferson City (today's Jefferson St.). Post office: 1860–now.

Architecture. Good examples of 19th-century styles include the following. LEWIS JAMES HOUSE: Greek Revival, 1855; brackets and porch trim 1870. Built by this cattleman, the first president of the town board and the son of ironworks owner Thomas James. I-44; SR 68, S approx. 6 blocks to Springfield, W 5 blocks (725). OUSLEY HOUSE: Queen Anne, 1912. Dr. Edward Ousley's wife, Mayme, was elected mayor of St. James in 1921 (by 8 votes), becoming Missouri's first woman mayor. I-44; SR 68, S approx. 9 blocks to Scioto, W 1.5 blocks (214). ST. JAMES CHAPEL: Gothic Revival, 1868; wind-damaged steeple replaced by dome 1890s; National Historic Register. Stained-glass lancet windows, vertical buttresses, and brackets. I-44; SR 68, S approx. 10 blocks to Church, W 1 block.

Boys Town of Missouri. Missouri's first home for underprivileged and homeless boys was established in 1948 by Bill James on 120 acres; 15 buildings, gym, cottages. I-44; SR 68, S approx. 16 blocks to Cartall, E 1 block to Boys Town Rd., E 2 m.

Maramec Iron Works, Mo. This community was established c. 1828 around the 1826 Maramec Iron Works (Maramec Spring Park, below), which was named for the nearby river, using the river's spelling of that time, which varied because of phonetic transcriptions to different European languages from an Algonquian word that in midwestern dialects means catfish and in northeastern dialects probably means deep place. Today the river is spelled Meramec. The community (peak pop. 500) declined after the 1873 depression and new processing techniques contributed to the bankruptcy of the ironworks in 1876 (Newburg). Post offices: Maramec Iron Works 1827–c. 1829; Maramec 1829–c. 1873. Defunct. At Maramec Spring Park (below).

Maramec Spring Park. 1,800 acres. National Historic Register, Missouri's first National Natural Landmark. In 1938 Lucy Wortham James, William James's granddaughter, died, leaving a trust administered since 1941 by the James Foundation that includes the ironworks and surrounding area, all of which is called Maramec Spring Park. SR DD at SR 68/SR 8; SR 8, S 4 m. to Maramec Spring, Mo.;[3] signs. FACILITIES: Rustic camping at the river, showers, fishing (200,000 trout stocked annually), picnic tables and pavilions, tennis, basketball, baseball, volleyball, horseshoes, playground. In park. MARAMEC IRON WORKS: Stone Cold Blast Furnace, 1857; refining furnace stacks, 1843. In 1825 Thomas James recognized the iron-producing ore mineral hematite being used as decorative paint on Shawnee Indians who were camped near his Chillicothe, Ohio, residence. They described the minerals and a large spring, and James sent his business partner, Samuel Massey, back with them to the site where, in 1826, Massey established Missouri's first commercially important ironworks. Today's massive stone remnants formerly helped produce about 14 tons daily (cold air was forced into the furnace to raise the temperature for melting iron ore). In park. MARAMEC SPRING: With a flow of about 96 million gallons per day (a maximum of 231 million), the spring rises 190 feet to form a pool at the base of a bluff overhang; the water flows over a dam to join the Meramec River (Float Streams) one mile away. In park. MUSEUMS: (1) History: exhibits, models, and dioramas depicting the 1860s community, ore refining, transportation, and geology. (2) Agricultural: one of Missouri's largest collections of farm equipment and machinery. (3) Nature Center: exhibits focusing on local wildlife, ecological systems, and the food chain. In park. OBSERVATION TOWERS: One 40-foot tower overlooks the spring area; another, 30 feet tall, overlooks the valley. Automobile trail; in park. WOODS BOTTOMLAND FOREST NATURAL AREA / WILDLIFE AREA: 15 acres. Part of the wildlife area that encompasses Maramec Spring Park. Features include a backwater slough, Meramec river frontage, and an old-growth bottomland forest with oak, hickory, sycamore, persimmon, river birch, and butternut. Box 414, St. James 65559. Trail from the parking lot or by boat. In park.

Meramec River. Float Streams; Maramec Spring Park, above.

Missouri Veterans Home. Gothic Revival (High Victorian Gothic), 1867. Called Dunmoor when built by William James (St. James history, above), the three-story brick house with a mansard roof, turrets, wings, and elaborate detailing is of a style usually reserved for churches and public buildings. It was bought in 1896 by the G.A.R. women's auxiliary as a home for disabled Federal soldiers and their wives and widows.

Financial problems resulted in the state's 1897 acquisition of the home and its acceptance of all veterans. Now jointly owned with the federal government. I-44 at SR 68.

Museums. OLD CITY HALL: Stick, 1892; restored 1976. This small one-story frame structure with a steep gabled roof, front gable ornamentation, brackets, and a bell tower contains the original furnishings of the mayor–city council office in front and a double jail cell (including a ball and chain) at the rear. Local memorabilia. I-44; SR 68 to downtown; sign. OLD GRADE SCHOOL: Richardsonian Romanesque, 1899. Designed by H. H. Hohenschild, who also built several of Missouri's courthouses (e.g. Pemiscot County, *Caruthersville)*, this massive two-story building features arched and segmented-arch windows, spring arches, rusticated stone, belt courses, and a recessed entrance. Inside: high ceilings and yellow-pine floors and walls; fine arts center, historical museum, and community center. I-44; SR 68, S approx. 10 blocks to Church, W 1 block.

Natural Arches. DRY FORK: In a bluff south of Dry Fork Creek; 15-foot span, 12-foot height, 8-foot width. SR DD at SR 68; SR 68, S approx. 3.4 m. to bridge (look up and S from bridge center). PINNACLES BLUFF: Includes a natural arch (6–7 feet high, 15 feet long, 7–10 feet wide), two pinnacles (one tapered from 2 feet at the pedestal to approximately 4 feet at the crown), and a small *cave*. SR DD, E 2 m. to Boys Town (above; note sandstone ledges at 1.2 m.); blacktop and GR, E 1.6 m. to arch at a sharp bend of Dry Fork Creek; continue E 0.1 m. to steep path on the north side (leads to a *cave)*; continue E 0.25 m. to pinnacles. *(Collapsed Cave Systems)*

St. James Park. JAMES MEMORIAL LIBRARY: Ozark history, historic photos; 54,000 volumes; inquire locally. ST. JAMES POOL: Public. I-44; SR 68, S approx. 15 blocks to James; signs. SCIOTO LAKE: 5.5 acres. Picnic area, fishing dock; stocked annually with bass, bluegill, and catfish; inquire locally.

Wineries. FERRIGNO: Nine local wines: dry to semisweet; tour, tasting, wine garden. I-44; SR 68, N to SR B; SR B, E 4.5 m. HEINRICHSHAUS: French hybrid and American varieties: light, dry to semisweet table wines; tasting, picnic area. I-44; SR 68, N to SR B; SR B, E 1 m.; CR 113, E 3.8 m.; SR U, N 3 m. ST. JAMES: Established 1970. Locally grown grapes noted for Sweet Concord, Catawba Niagara, and beer wines. Tours, tasting, picnic area. I-44; SR 68, N to SR B; SR B, E; signs.

1. Specific namesake uncertain; the probable meaning is deer, e.g. Scioto, Ohio, part of a longer Iroquois name.
2. St. Joe, W.Va., honored as many as three local men named Joseph.
3. The spring; no p.o.

ST. JOSEPH
Population: 71,852   Map C-2

St. Joseph's popular 19th-century nickname, St. Joe,[1] reflects its populist roots as a place where traders, buffalo hunters, Indian scouts, merchants, bankers, cattle butchers, railroad workers, cowboys, and westward-bound pioneer families shared the city streets and public houses. The town grew rich fast, epitomizing the opportunities of the American West. In 1826 Joseph Robidoux (1782–1868; locally pronounced Roobidoo), an agent for the American Fur Company, established a trading post in Indian Territory at a deep bend in the Missouri River along the 200-foot-high Blacksnake Hills at Roy's Branch (near today's Waterworks Rd.), then moved a little south to today's townsite at the mouth of Blacksnake Creek (at the foot of today's Julie St.). In 1833, still one of the few white people within a 50-mile radius *(Agency)*, Robidoux bought the company's share, the value of which was greatly enhanced when his Indian trading friends allocated 160 acres for him as part of the 1836 *Platte Purchase*. At what was called Robidoux's Landing (p.o. Blacksnake Hills)[2] he continued building a family trading business that included over 100 trappers and hunters, a *gristmill*, and the area's only ferry. As increased steamboat traffic allowed westward-bound settlers and traders to travel further west than *Independence* and Westport *(Kansas City)* before buying and outfitting slow and cumbersome wagons, Robidoux saw the need for a safe and organized meeting place that could be protected by nearby Fort Leavenworth in Kansas. Three town plats were drawn for him, two with broad streets, one with narrow streets. As is evident today, he choose the latter, which had been named by its draftsman, Fredrick W. Smith, for Robidoux's name-saint, Joseph.[3] From two houses in the 1843 plat, St. Joseph grew to 350 houses by 1846, the same year the Buchanan County seat was moved here from Sparta.[4] From 1846 to c. 1910 St. Joseph boomed, helped by the 1849 California gold rush (of 100,000 westbound travelers to Oregon and California in 1850, half left from St. Joseph via the *Oregon Trail)*, steamboat traffic (20 arrivals per day in 1849), the 1858 Colorado gold rush, the 1859 arrival of the Hannibal & St. Joseph *Railroad* (making it the western terminus of the American railroad system), and a post–Civil War economic boom fueled here by Texas cattle and 14 railroad lines (South St. Joseph, below) that helped increase the population to 77,000 by 1910, making it by 1941 the world's fifth largest livestock market and tenth largest flour producer. Post offices: Blacksnake Hills 1840–1843; St. Joseph 1843–now. Maps and information: chamber of commerce; I-29 exit

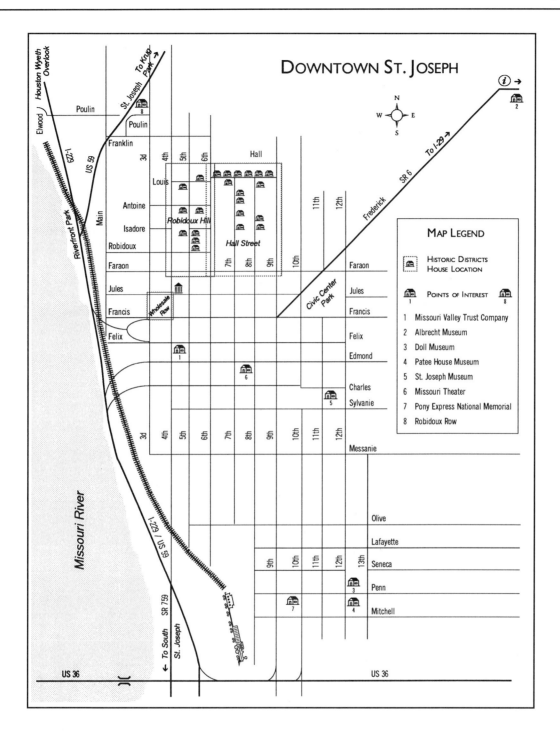

DOWNTOWN ST. JOSEPH

MAP LEGEND

Historic Districts
House Location

Points of Interest

1   Missouri Valley Trust Company
2   Albrecht Museum
3   Doll Museum
4   Patee House Museum
5   St. Joseph Museum
6   Missouri Theater
7   Pony Express National Memorial
8   Robidoux Row

47, W approx. 2 m. on Frederick (3003). Home of Missouri Western State College and N. S. Hillyard Technical School.

Architecture. The town can be divided into three population centers created by transportation: the river city, railroad city (South St. Joseph, below), and automobile city (Parkway, below). The majority of significant 19th-century structures, built during the 1880s–1890s, were heavily influenced by two architects, E. J. Eckel and Harvey Ellis. Eckel, whose career here lasted 65 years,

was trained at L'Ecole des Beaux Arts in Paris. Ellis, who worked for Eckel from 1888 to 1893, studied under H. H. Richardson, a Beaux Arts student and creator of the American architectural style Richardsonian Romanesque. Beaux Arts architecture fit neatly with the rise of America's pre-income-tax capitalists from the 1880s to 1920. The style is prevalent here and easy to identify by its general, but not always inclusive, characteristics: smooth light-colored masonry walls, tall arched hooded windows with keystones, paired columns with Ionic or Corinthian capitals, symmetrical facades, flat or mansard roofs, balustrades (roofline and balcony), quoins, decorative garlands, floral patterns, and pilasters. The list of interesting and significant 19th- and 20th-century architecture is lengthy and includes styles ranging from Adamesque to Prairie School. Over 30 individual structures are on the National Historic Register, not including those in four groups and districts: HALL STREET / ROBIDOUX HILL: Roughly bounded by Hill, Robidoux, 4th, and 9th. MARKET SQUARE: Roughly bounded by Edmond, Felix, N. 3d, and Market Place. MISSOURI VALLEY TRUST COMPANY: 1859–1860. Reportedly the oldest bank building west of the Mississippi continuously used for banking; Felix and 4th. WHOLESALE ROW: Roughly bounded by Jules, 3d, 4th, and Francis.

Buchanan County Courthouse. Beaux Arts, 1885 (original of 1873–1876 gutted by fire in 1885 and vastly remodeled); extensive restoration 1979; National Historic Register. The county's third (the second of two at St. Joseph), this massive three-story courthouse was extensively altered from its original Greek-cross plan (235 by 205 feet, with a 40-foot dome), reflecting E. J. Eckel's influence (Architecture, above), although reconstruction was supervised by R. K. Allen. Among its many Beaux Arts features were painted-white red brick (restored to red in 1979) that simulated smooth light-colored stone, belt courses, a rusticated first floor, quoins, tall arched windows with keystone lintels, pilasters with Corinthian capitals, an elaborately decorated cornice, and full-height bracketed pedimented porticos supported by Corinthian columns. On the main floor of the center hall is a state seal that is reportedly Missouri's largest. Downtown; 4th at Jules. *(County Profiles)*

Krug Park. 162 acres. Established 1936. City parks headquarters: maps and information, outdoor events, one-acre lagoon, circular drive (1.3 m.), castle and children's circus (Italian Renaissance style), buffalo, longhorn cattle, paddleboats, waterfall, landscaping, playgrounds, picnic area. NW city limits; US 59, W on NW Parkway; signs.

Museums. ALBRECHT ART: The permanent collection of about 1,300 items includes paintings by Thomas Hart Benton *(Neosho)* and George Caleb Bingham *(Arrow Rock)*. State, local, and national traveling exhibits; gardens. I-29 exit 47, W 1.5 m. on Frederick (2818). DOLL: Exhibits include antique dolls, dollhouses, toys, furniture, and miniatures. 1115 S. 12th; near Patee House (below). JESSE JAMES HOUSE: Living as Tom Howard with his wife and children in this one-story frame house, Jesse was murdered on April 3, 1882, while he stood on a chair, dusting a pic-

ture *(Kearney)*. Bob Ford, helped by his brother Charlie, shot Jesse in the back of the head. Bob was shot to death in 1892 in Creede, Colo., and Charlie killed himself in 1884 in *Richmond*. Located on the grounds of the Patee House (below); original location, 1318 Lafayette. KEMPER HOME: Queen Anne, 1883. The house offers turn-of-the-century furnishings and 10 stained-glass windows; tours. I-229 downtown; Edmond to 15th, N on Francis; sign. PATEE HOUSE: 1856–1858. This massive four-story brick structure served as a hotel and a college before being converted in 1885 into a factory (South St. Joseph, below). It now houses western and Americana exhibits, e.g. replicas of a train depot, the Pony Express headquarters, and a saloon, as well as fire trucks, a cabbagehead locomotive, and memorabilia. US 36 at I-29; US 36, W to 10th, N to Penn, E to 12th. ST. JOSEPH MUSEUM: below. STATE HOSPITAL PSYCHIATRIC: Exhibits include psychiatric history and equipment and methodology since 1874, patients' artwork, and reproductions of 15th-century cells and treatment devices. I-29 exit 47, W 0.5 m. on Frederick (3400).

Parkway / Parks. The intertwined importance of the automobile and eastward city growth precipitated legislation that resulted in $2 million in 1921 to build a parkway system connecting new parks with others established around the east side. Today the parkway is most evident along Southwest Parkway from SR 752 to just north of US 36 and includes (S to N): HYDE PARK: 93 acres. Swimming, tennis, picnic facilities, restrooms, playground, ball fields, concessions, one-mile drive. Hyde Park Ave. at 4th. OLD HYDE PARK: Formerly tennis courts; botanical garden planned. Alabama at 3d. KING HILL OVERLOOK: 13 acres. Overlooks river, Kansas, and stockyards; former Kansa *Indian* ceremonial grounds, half-mile drive, highest point in city (about 300 feet above the river; South St. Joseph, below). Fleeman to Kinghill Dr. BODCE ICE ARENA: Rentals, concessions, restrooms, locker rooms. Southwest Parkway (2700). FAIRVIEW GOLF COURSE: 137 acres. Southwest Parkway at US 36. BARTLETT: 24 acres. Picnic facilities, restrooms, playground, ball field. Southwest Parkway, between Duncan and Renick. OTHER CITY PARKS: A full list is available from park headquarters at Krug Park (above). Civic Center (10 acres; Pony Express Statue, replica of Statue of Liberty, memorials; downtown, Frederick between 9th and 10th); Corby Grove (105 acres; fishing, picnic, trail, comfort station; Frederick, N on NW Parkway); Huston Wyeth (33 acres on river bluffs; overlook, picnic facilities, restrooms, playground; N of I-229 at US 59; W on Franklin, N on Main, W on Poulin to Elwood, then N; signs); Riverfront (22 acres; at river, picnic tables, concessions; I-229 at US 59).

Performing Arts. For specific information contact the Allied Arts Council, 120 S. 8th (Missouri Theater, Missouri Theater Building; National Historic Register). PERFORMING ARTS ASSOCIATION: Sponsors theater, music, dance, and motion picture events annually at various locations. ROBIDOUX RESIDENT THEATER: Four stage and four experimental plays each season. Missouri Theater. SYMPHONY: Four concerts with international guests each season. Missouri Theater.

Pony Express National Memorial. Vernacular, rebuilt in brick in 1887 by the St. Joseph Transfer Company; National Historic Register. The original frame building of 1858 was used in 1860–1861 as the 200-horse stable for the Central Overland California and Pike's Peak Express Company Offices (the Pony Express). Company partners William H. Russell, William B. Waddell, and Alexander Majors *(Lexington; Kansas City: Museums)* established a private mail service here and based their bid for a federal mail contract on St. Joseph's position as the western-most location of both the telegraph and the railroad, initially charging $5.00 for the first half ounce (later $1.00). An 1860 Pony Express advertisement was a masterpiece of grim reality: "WANTED: Young skinny wiry fellows, not over eighteen. Must be expert riders willing to risk death daily. Orphans preferred. Wages $25 per week." One of the successful applicants was 14-year-old W. F. "Buffalo Bill" Cody (1846–1917). For 79 weeks—from April 3, 1860, to October 26, 1861, two days after the transcontinental telegraph was completed—more than 100 young men, some barely teenagers, raced on horseback nearly 2,000 miles in about ten days between St. Joe and Sacramento, Calif., using more than 120 relay stations for the two-minute horse swaps allotted by the company. Mail service ran in both directions, cutting stagecoach delivery time in half *(Weston: McCormick Distilling Company)*. EXHIBITS: An 80-foot diorama depicting the trail through the plains, prairies, and mountains between St. Joe and California; a life-size statue of the first rider, Johnny Fry, and his horse, Sylph; a replica of a relay station; and hands-on exhibits like a hand-pump well and a mochilla (mail pouch). US 36 at I-29; US 36, W to 10th, N to Penn.

Recreation. BLUFFWOODS *STATE FOREST.* LEWIS AND CLARK *STATE PARK:* SR 752 at US 59; US 59, S 17.2 m.; SR 45, S 1.1 m.; SR 138, W 1.1 m. to Lewis and Clark, Mo.[5] *WILDLIFE AREAS:* Pigeon Hill, Worthwine Island.

Robidoux Row. Vernacular, c. 1850; western third demolished for a 1932 highway; restored 1974–1984 by St. Joseph Historical Society; National Historic Register. These one-story brick row houses, reportedly the first apartments west of the Mississippi, were built as temporary housing for the population boom after the 1849 gold rush by town founder Joseph Robidoux, who lived at the east end after his wife died in 1857 until his own death in 1868. Furnished. I-229 exit 6A to 3d at E. Poulin (219–225).

St. Joseph Museum. Gothic Revival (turrets with battlements), 1879. This two-story stone 43-room landmark was styled after a castle on the Rhine. In 1887 the Tiffany firm of New York redecorated it (possibly the firm's first out-of-state contract), adding today's impressive stained-glass windows. Highlights of the museum (established 1926) include Missouri's largest collection of North American Indian items (5,000 pieces), representing over 300 tribes, ranging from the Iroquois to the Eskimo; displays on midwestern wildlife, from the least shrew to the Alaskan brown bear; and exhibits on St. Joseph history and the town's role in the development of the West, e.g. a fur-trading post, a covered wagon, and local items. US 36 at I-29; US 36, W to 10th, N to Charles, W to 11th.

South St. Joseph, Mo. John Patee first attempted to establish a new business center here by donating land for a Hannibal & St. Joseph *Railroad* depot and by building Patee House (Museums, above), a 140-room luxury hotel. Premature, the venture failed, and the hotel was used for railroad offices and the headquarters of the Pony Express (above). Patee's idea was proven right, however, when postwar railroad traffic stimulated a need for a factory town that was begun by the St. Joseph Stock Yard Company (organized in 1887; bought by Swift & Co. in 1897). Among the giant flour companies established here was R. T. Davis Milling Co., which introduced Aunt Jemima in 1889, the first pancake mix. Annexation by St. Joseph voters was approved in 1972. Post offices: Stockyards[6] 1892–1898; South St. Joseph 1898–1909, 1912–1975. I-29 at US 36; US 36, W to SR 759; SR 759, S 1.6 m. KING HILL: At 300 feet, this is the highest hill in St. Joseph. In 1846 Father De Smet reported finding it covered with human bones. Judging from a nearby line of mounds that looked like fortifications, he concluded that a tribe he called the Blacksnake had been wholly destroyed. Between Cherokee, 1st, Lookout, and Indiana (above).

---

1. Today the nickname is spelled both Joe and Jo, the latter being based on the book "The Story of Old Saint Jo" by Sheridan A. Logan, who chose the spelling used by Eugene Field *(St. Louis: South Broadway Area Sights)* in his sentimental poem "Lover's Lane, Saint Jo." According to "American Place-Names" the spelling is St. Joe.

2. From its previously named hills first listed on early French maps, probably for black garden snakes still in the area.

3. The foster father of Jesus, Matt. 1–2 *(St. James)*.

4. *Sparta;* p.o. 1841–1865; defunct.

5. For the *Lewis and Clark Expedition;* no p.o.

6. For the livestock yards.

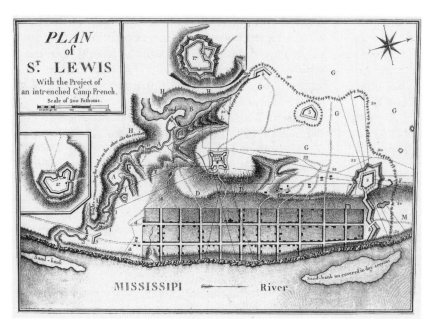

The "Plan of St. Louis," 1796. (DRAWN BY GEORGE DE BOIS ST. LYS FOR GEORGE HENRI VICTOR COLLETT AND PUBLISHED IN PARIS BY A. BERTRAND IN 1826)

ST. LOUIS
Population: 396,685
Maps I-4 and St. Louis Area

From 1700 to 1703 Jesuit Gabriel Marest maintained a mission for Kaskaskia *Indians (Ste. Genevieve)* at the mouth of River Des Peres, near today's southern city limits. Across the Mississippi River was Cahokia *(Kahoka)*, North America's largest prehistoric group of artificial earthen mounds north of Mexico. In 1764 Pierre Laclède[1] and his fifteen-year-old stepson, Auguste Chouteau *(St. Charles)*, established a trading post here to manage Laclède's company's exclusive trading rights in the Missouri River valley *(Ste. Genevieve: Kaskaskia)*. In 1780, Laclède platted the post. The original plat, labeled St. Louis des Illinois, shows seven named streets and a line of fortifications that were successfully used in that year to defend against a combined attack of British, Indians, and Canadian traders during the American Revolution. Two plat blocks, set aside for a church (Gateway Arch Area Sights: Old Cathedral, below) and a public square, were located at the river between today's Market and Walnut Streets by the Gateway Arch. St. Louis was named for Louis IX (1214–1270; canonized 1297), traditionally regarded by the French as the patron and example of the monarchy. The choice was possibly inspired by patriotic bravado in response to the 1763 Treaty of Paris *(Louisiana Purchase)*, which required France to cede its territory west of the Mississippi.

Typical of Creole French mania for nicknames *(Ste. Genevieve)*, the town was also called Pain Court or Paincourt (literally bread-short), a humorous, usually derogatory nickname, like the American pioneers' Lick Skillet *(Queen City: Chariton River Bridge)*. Set at the Mississippi just south of its confluence with the Illinois and Missouri Rivers, the town first thrived (1799 pop. 921; 1840 pop. 16,394) as a trading center and gateway to the West for fur traders, explorers, and settlers. After the 1803 *Louisiana Purchase* (formally authorized here in 1804), St. Louis was the seat of government of various administrative jurisdictions, in 1805 becoming capital of Louisiana Territory and seat of government for St. Louis Territorial District (later an original county seat, 1812) and in 1812 becoming capital of Missouri Territory. At statehood in 1821, *Jefferson City* was chosen state capital, and St. Louis continued as county seat of St. Louis County until 1876, when it was granted home rule, separating it from the county *(Clayton)*. The arrival in 1817 of the steamboat "Zebulon M. Pike" began St. Louis's ascendancy as one of the Mississippi River's most prosperous port towns. With the help of nearly 30,000 German immigrants by 1850, it also became a successful industrial center, with flour mills, distilleries, factories making food products, woolens, lead products, steamboat engines, and ornamental iron (including whole storefronts), and foundries, including those making the *prairie* sod plows that helped settle the Great Plains of "America's Breadbasket." Two 1849 disasters, a 13-block fire followed by a cholera epidemic, changed the physical shape of St. Louis by forcing it off the river to the area of present-day Fourth and Market Streets (Market Street Area Sights, below). Streets were widened and brick structures built just in time for the 1851 construction of the Pacific *Railroad*, which led the way for St. Louis to be the terminus for all westbound lines, except the Hannibal & St. Joseph. With manufacturing and transportation set on a solid base, the town continued its phenomenal growth, fueled by the California and Colorado gold rushes of the 1850s, westward expansion, the *Civil War* (as the Federals' western headquarters; military spending approx. $180 million; pop. 190,500), and the postwar Gilded Age of industry, during which it closed the 19th century with a population exceeding 500,000 people who were to host the 1904 Louisiana Purchase

Exposition, popularly known as the St. Louis World's Fair, celebrating the spectacular growth of the town and the Midwest. Today St. Louis is America's second largest inland port and third largest rail center; it is Missouri's second largest city but has a larger metropolitan area population than rival Kansas City. Post office: 1804–now. Home of St. Louis University (founded in 1818, the oldest university west of the Mississippi), Harris-Stowe State College, University of Missouri–St. Louis, St. Louis and St. Louis County Community Colleges (Florissant Valley, Forest Park, and Meramec), Fontbonne College, Maryville College, Missouri Baptist College, Washington University, Webster University, O'Fallon Technical Center (vo-tech training), Special School District of St. Louis County (vo-tech training), St. Louis College of Pharmacy, and the St. Louis Conservatory and School for the Arts. *(Route 66)*

> Note: Metropolitan St. Louis fans out from the river to the town's semicircular western city limits, encompassing a complex area of about 2.4 million people. The following points of interest are only highlights of the city. For other towns in the metropolitan area, consult the Index under their names. For detailed information, maps, and literature: St. Louis Visitor and Convention Center, Market at Broadway; S on Broadway (10). Missouri Tourism, N side, at the Mississippi; I-270 at Riverside. For air travelers, MetroLink, a light rail system, runs to the downtown.

Architecture. The city's first brick house was built c. 1820, after which thousands were constructed, including a great many characterized as St. Louis Vernacular, a blend of Adamesque and Greek Revival. Hundreds of excellent examples of both brick and frame 19th-century styles are listed on the National Historic Register. Over 30 National Historic Register Districts are located throughout the city, with the tightest concentration being roughly between I-44, Broadway, and Jefferson.

The Arts. AMERICAN THEATER: 1,880 seats; originally built 1917; Broadway hits. Downtown; Market, N on 9th to St. Charles St. ART MUSEUM: Forest Park, below. FABULOUS FOX THEATER: A restored 1929 movie palace in a style characterized as Siamese Byzantine. Las Vegas entertainment, country, rock, jazz. Midtown. I-64 (US 40), N on Grand (527 N. Grand). MUNICIPAL OPERA: Forest Park, below. SYMPHONY: America's second oldest symphony orchestra, formed from the St. Louis Choral Society in 1880, dating in its present form from 1897. National and international artists; classical to popular. Midtown; I-64 (US 40), N on Grand to Delmar (718 N.

Grand) in Powell Hall, a restored vaudeville theater.

Cathedral of St. Louis. Romanesque, 1907–1914. Locally known as the New Cathedral, this massive gray-granite 204-by-305-foot structure features square corner towers, paired arched windows, three domes, and a full-height towered portico with multiple recessed arches below a large rose window. The Byzantine-style interior, reportedly one of the best examples of its type in North America, is awe inspiring: a 21-by-90-foot vestibule 26 feet high with extensive ceiling mosaics by Tiffany and Oerken of Germany depicting the life of Saint Louis, walls banded by yellow marble, two large rose windows, a yellow marble altar dominated by a 57-foot-high domed canopy (baldachin) supported by ten 20-foot-high red, yellow, and green marble columns with golden-black marble bases. Its 83,000 square feet of mosaics form the world's largest collection. A museum, the world's only of its kind, explains how mosaics are made and installed. Initial cost: $3 million. West St. Louis; I-64 (US 40) to Grand, N to Lindell (4431).

Chain of Rocks / Lock and Dam #27. The Mississippi River's Chain of Rocks Reach, along northeastern St. Louis County, contains two separate sections of rock ledges extending underwater from the east bank that act like a dam, resulting in a sharp increase of water velocity that makes navigation difficult and dangerous. Lock and Dam #27, built in 1946–1953 along with the lateral Chain of Rocks Canal (10 miles long, 550 feet wide, with an average depth of 32 feet), allow traffic to bypass this hazard. Dam: 3,000 feet long; main lock: 1,200 feet long, 110 feet wide (longer than the Panama Canal locks). Visitor center, Corps river navigation exhibits. I-270, E over river; Ill. SR 3, S approx. 4 m. to Granite City, Ill.; sign. *(Troy: Monroe)*

Forest Park. This 1,300-acre park, larger than New York's Central Park, was the site of the 1904 World's Fair that, among a large panoply, introduced the ice cream cone, iced tea, the hamburger, and the hot dog. Features, in addition to those listed below, include a conservatory (seasonal flowers), boat rides (paddle, electric, canoe, and row), picnicking, biking, soccer, softball, baseball, handball, running, archery, tennis, ice- and roller-skating, and golf (on a course established in 1912). Western St. Louis; I-64 (US 40), W to Kingshighway, exit N; signs. ART MUSEUM: Housed in the building that was the Fine Arts Palace of the 1904 World's Fair, this art museum is reportedly among America's top 10. The collections include paintings by Rembrandt, Rodin, Renoir, Rubens, El Greco, Titian, and Van Gogh and pre-Columbian, African, Oceanic, and American Indian works. HISTORY MUSEUM: The museum is operated by the 125-year-old Missouri Historical Society at the Neoclassical 1913

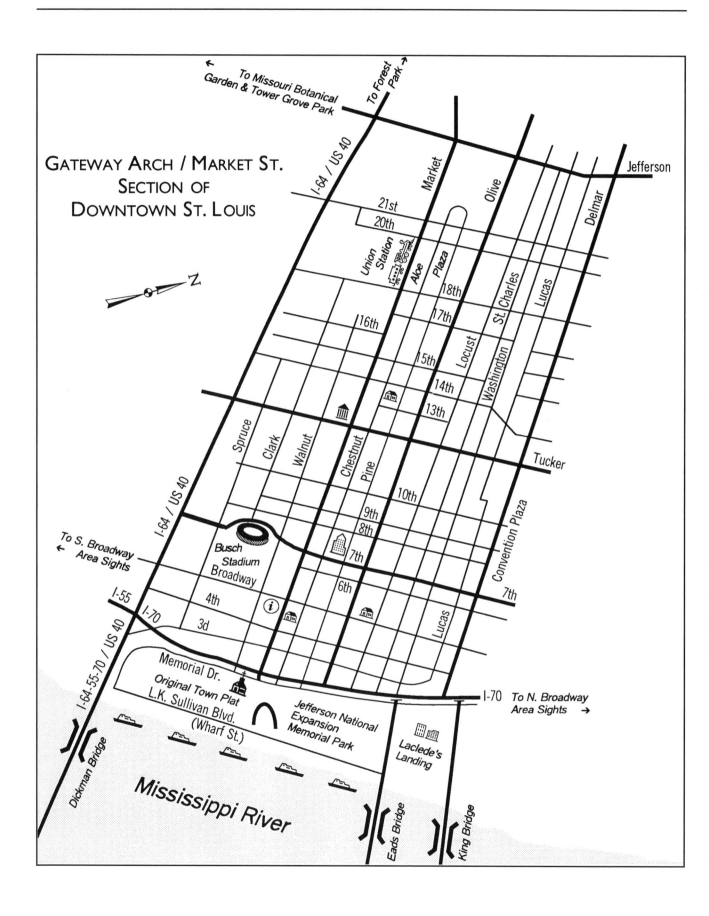

GATEWAY ARCH / MARKET ST.
SECTION OF
DOWNTOWN ST. LOUIS

Jefferson Memorial building (the first national memorial to Jefferson), which was built using excess revenue from the 1904 World's Fair. In 14 galleries, a combination of rotating exhibits, permanent displays, audiovisual aids, and historic film footage examine St. Louis, the state of Missouri, and the West since 1764. Features include an inlaid map of the *Lewis and Clark Expedition,* period costumes, and firearms, as well as exhibits on volunteer fire fighting, the 1904 World's Fair (souvenirs, actual film footage), Charles Lindbergh, music (ragtime to rock 'n' roll), and life from the 1870s to the 1940s (pre-automobile to pre-television). MUNICIPAL OPERA: 12,000 seats. Set in a natural amphitheater, the Muny is America's largest outdoor musical theater, with Broadway productions, operettas, concerts, and musical comedies from mid-June through September. SCIENCE CENTER: This nationally popular museum, with 1.7 million visitors annually, offers hands-on informal science education. Features include a working weather station, a planetarium, a giant level that allows children to lift their families, a color maze, a roller-coaster, and the Star Theater (a multi-image space theater). ZOO: 83 acres. One of the world's largest and finest zoos features thousands of mammals, birds, and reptiles in naturalistic settings, e.g. bluffs, jungles, pampas, woods, lakes, and glades, as well as a 3.5-acre children's zoo and a railroad.

Gateway Arch Area Sights. Roughly bounded by the river, the I-55/70 bridge, Memorial Dr., and the King Bridge. EADS BRIDGE: Truss, 1867–1874; National Landmark. This three-span two-tiered structure (traffic above, trains below) was the first to cross the Mississippi and the world's first arched truss bridge (6,220 feet long, 54 feet wide, 55 feet abovewater). Washington at river. GATEWAY ARCH: Weighted Catenary Curve, completed 1965. Built using 886 tons of stainless steel to commemorate 19th-century westward expansion, this 630-foot arch is America's tallest national monument (twice as tall as the Statue of Liberty). Self-leveling elevators give a four-minute ride to the top for a 30-mile panoramic view. Beneath the arch (underground), the Museum of Westward Expansion has exhibits about the 19th-century West, and Tucker Theater features films about the building of the arch and the settlement of the West. Part of the Jefferson National Expansion Memorial Park *(National Parks).* LACLEDE'S LANDING: This renovated 19th-century warehouse district has cobblestone streets, cast-iron streetlights, and tourist attractions. Memorial, N of Arch. OLD CATHEDRAL: Basilica of St. Louis. Greek Revival, 1831–1836. Built in the same plat block as the city's first church (log, 1770; marker), this large limestone structure with a 40-foot square tower and octagonal spire offers the same indulgences as the

seven basilicas of Rome. A museum (west side) has the original church's c. 1774 bell, paintings presented by King Louis XVIII, and photos. Walnut at Memorial, W of Arch. (Cathedral of St. Louis, above.) WHARF STREET: On display are the USS "Inaugural" (a WWII minesweeper; National Landmark) and various Mississippi River boats, including a barge towboat with a museum and working replicas of steamboats; tours. E of Arch, at the river.

Market Street Area Sights. From the Mississippi River to Jefferson. ALOE PLAZA: Carl Milles's 1940 fountain "Meeting of the Waters" dominates the plaza. This heroic-style sculpture features 14 bronze figures personifying the confluence of the Missouri and Mississippi Rivers: a young man (the Mississippi) rides a catfish and extends a flower to a young woman (the Missouri) who is coyly arranging her hair. The "WPA Guide" describes the couple as attended by "three tritons, a waterman with two great sharks, a waterwoman hauling two urchins along by the scruffs of their necks, figures of leaping fish, and small boys bearing large fish." Across from Union Station (below). BUSCH STADIUM: Circular stadium, seats 53,000. Home of the St. Louis Cardinals baseball team. The Sports Hall of Fame (between gates 5 and 6) has World Series movies, trophies, tours, and displays about local sports teams. Market, S on 7th. NATIONAL BOWLING HALL OF FAME: Films, photographs, and memorabilia depict the history of bowling from 5200 B.C. to the present. Bowling on turn-of-the-century or modern lanes; 50,000 square feet. Across from Busch Stadium, 8th at Walnut. OLD COURTHOUSE: Greek Revival, west wing 1839–1845, rotunda 1839–1844, east wing 1852–1856, south wing 1853–1856, north wing 1857–1861, new dome 1860–1861. Now part of, but not adjacent to, the Jefferson National Expansion Memorial *(National Parks),* this massive three-story mostly limestone cruciform complex with a cast-iron dome and Doric columns was used as a courthouse from 1839 to 1930. Among many historic events at this building (e.g. the first national railroad convention) was the initial lawsuit that provoked the U.S. Supreme Court's 1857 Dred Scott decision that affirmed the Kansas-Nebraska Act's *(Kansas Border War)* repeal of the 1820 *Missouri Compromise.* Scott (North Broadway Area Sights, below), an illiterate slave sponsored by his titleholder's son, sued in 1847 for his freedom on the grounds that he was taken into the territories, which were free, and therefore he was free. The court ruled: (1) his original status remained regardless of location, (2) no slave could be a U.S. citizen, (3) no slave could sue the government, (4) the Missouri Compromise was unconstitutional, and (5) slavery could not be prohibited in the territories. Reportedly this case convinced abolitionists that *civil war* was inevitable *(County Profiles: Taney)*. Exhibits on the history of St. Louis, 30-minute film, observation area at rotunda, restored courtrooms; tours. Market at Broadway. OLD POST OFFICE: Second Empire, 1884; National Landmark. Originally this massive three-story red-and-gray-granite building housed a U.S. courthouse, custom house, and post office. Designed with underground tunnels and vaults (cost: $5 million), it features a four-story interior court with marble staircases and a six-story dome with the sculpture "America at War and Peace" by D. C. French, whose best-known work is the seated Abraham Lincoln in Washington, D.C. W of 8th on Olive. ST. LOUIS CENTRE: When completed in 1985, this was America's largest enclosed downtown shopping mall (1.7 million square feet). Bounded by Olive and Washington, and 6th and 7th. ST. LOUIS CITY HALL: Beaux Arts, 1899–1904. Based on the Paris, France, city hall, the building was designed by Eckel & Mann *(St. Joseph: Architecture)*. Tucker and Market. ST. LOUIS MERCANTILE LIBRARY: Richardsonian Romanesque, 1889. Established in 1846, this is the oldest circulating library west of the Mississippi, and one of 18 remaining private-membership libraries in America. It still serves as a history, business, and humanities library (open to the public for a fee), history and art museum, public forum (First Wednesday Lunch and Lecture series), and research facility that includes the recent (1993) MercSource, an electronic-based information service. Its two predecessors were the 1824 St. Louis Library Association and the 1831 St. Louis Lyceum. Artworks include paintings by George Catlin and George Caleb Bingham and John J. Audubon's 435-plate aquatinted "The Birds of America." The general library's collection is enormous: over 300,000 books, 350,000 historical photographs, and thousands of rare maps and prints about travel and exploration. In addition, special collections include Western Americana, National Inland Waterways, and National Railroads. Locust (510) at Broadway, fifth floor. SCOTT JOPLIN HOUSE: Italianate, late 1860s; National Historic Register, State Historic Site. This second-story flat (2685A) is the only surviving structure associated with Scott Joplin (1868–1917; *Sedalia)*, who helped make ragtime a unique musical genre. Here in 1901–1902, Joplin brought his bride, Belle, and here they conceived a child. Tragically, the child died within a few months, and the couple separated permanently. The flat has been restored to its 1902 appearance, and the building serves as a museum on the life and work of Joplin and St. Louis's ragtime era (including Tom Turpin and others). A player piano features recorded performances of Joplin. N of Jefferson on Delmar (2658). SMITH PARK: Picnic area, benches,

flowers. Market at 4th. SOLDIERS MEMORIAL MILITARY MUSEUM: Moderne, 1935–1938; proposed 1923, dedicated 1936 by president Franklin D. Roosevelt. Flanking the entrance are heroic-style stone sculptures personifying Courage, Sacrifice, Vision, and Loyalty. Inside, a black granite cenotaph, listing 1,075 residents who died in WWI, is surrounded by rose-colored marble walls rising 38 feet to a mosaic tile ceiling describing a large gold star dedicated to the mothers of the honored dead. Two museums exhibit weapons, banners, posters, medals, photos, uniforms, and memorabilia from the early 1800s to the present. E of 14th on Chestnut. UNION STATION: Richardsonian Romanesque, 1893–1894; renovated 1985; National Landmark. This four-story limestone-and-brick structure has corner turrets, a steeply pitched roof, a 230-foot clock tower, and a two-block-long limestone facade on Market St. Extravagant and ornate (original cost: $6.5 million; renovation: $135 million), it once was America's busiest station (approx. 100,000 passengers daily). Features include the Grand Hall's vaulted four-story ceiling, perfect acoustics, and stained-glass windows lighting the south side. Guided and self-guided tours; a tourist attraction as well as a shopping center. Market from 18th to 20th. WAINWRIGHT BUILDING: Skyscraper, 1890–1891; National Landmark. Built by Chicago architect Louis Sullivan, this was one of the world's first skyscrapers, with a 10-story brick-and-stone-over-steel frame, ornately decorated cornices, and terra-cotta trim. Between Chestnut and Pine on 7th (105).

Missouri Botanical Garden. Established c. 1859; 79 acres; National Landmark. Locally known as Shaw's Garden, this is America's oldest botanical garden. With the help of German-born Dr. George Engelmann (a physician, botanist, and scientist), the gardens were begun in the 1850s by English immigrant and wealthy St. Louis businessman Henry Shaw around his county house Tower Grove (Italianate, 1849; tours; Tower Grove Park, below), where he cultivated in greenhouses and outside, for display and for scientific purposes, rare and unusual plants and trees *(Gray Summit: Shaw Arboretum)*. After Shaw's 1889 death, the gardens became part of a self-perpetuating trust. CLIMATRON: The world's first (1960) geodesic greenhouse; year-round climate for over 4,000 tropical plants. JAPANESE GARDENS: 15.5 acres. The largest one of its kind in North America; includes lakes, waterfalls, and a Japanese structure. SCENTED GARDENS: Designed for fragrance. TROPICAL LILY PONDS: Large and exotic lilies, including ones six feet in diameter. I-44, south midtown; exit Shaw to Tower Grove; signs.

North Broadway Area Sights. North St. Louis; use I-70.

BELLEFONTAINE *CEMETERY:* Some of the world's most ornate tombs can reportedly be found here; notables buried among the large trees include William Clark *(Lewis and Clark Expedition)*, Adolphus Busch (South Broadway Area Sights, below), U.S. senator Thomas Hart Benton *(County Profiles: Benton)*, Confederate general and Missouri governor Sterling Price *(Civil War)*, businessman Ellis Wainwright (Market Street Area Sites, above), and James Eads, the designer of the first successful Civil War ironclads and the first arched truss bridge (Gateway Arch Area Sights, above). I-70N, N on W. Florissant to Calvary. CALVARY *CEMETERY:* Large trees shade interesting and ornate markers. Among the notables buried here are city cofounder Auguste Chouteau (St. Louis history, above), Missouri's first governor (1820–1824) Alexander McNair, slavery lawsuit plaintiff Dred Scott (Market Street Area Sights: Old Courthouse, above), Civil War generals D. M. Frost and W. T. Sherman, humanitarian Tom Dooley, and playwright Tennessee Williams. I-70N, N on W. Florissant to Riverview.

Route 66. Among several routes, the late 1920s–early 1930s route crosses the McKinley Bridge from Venice, Ill. (from I-270 use Ill. SR 203 to Madison into Broadway to the bridge). From there, follow Salisbury off the bridge onto Natural Bridge, turn left on Florissant and around the S-curve to Tucker (12th St.) to Gravois (SR 30) to Chippewa (SR 366) to Watson (SR 366) to Lindbergh (US 61/67), north on Lindbergh to Manchester Road (SR 100), west on Manchester Road to *Gray Summit* (west of Clarkson Road, follow Manchester Road whenever possible instead of SR 100). Downtown bypass route: I-270 to Lindbergh (US 67) to west on Manchester (SR 100). *(Route 66)*

South Broadway Area Sights. From I-64 to I-255. ANHEUSER-BUSCH BREWERY: Group of 71 structures, some before 1900; administration building and stable are National Landmarks; established 1857 by Eberhard Anheuser on the site of a bankrupt brewery. With his 1865 junior partner and son-in-law Adolphus Busch, Anheuser formed the 1875 Anheuser-Busch Company, which pioneered pasteurized lager beer, a process lengthening storage life that helped make this the world's largest brewery. Guided one-hour tours include Clydesdales, an 1891 Brewery, the bottling house, tasting. Broadway (S of Russell) at Pestalozzi. EUGENE FIELD HOUSE AND TOY MUSEUM: Greek Revival Row House, c. 1845. This three-story red-brick structure, what remains of a 12-unit row house razed in 1936, is the birthplace of journalist Eugene Field (1850–1895), best known for sentimental poems, e.g. "Little Boy Blue" and "Wynken, Blynken and Nod." Features include early Victorian furnishings, toy and doll collections, and Field memorabilia. Incidentally,

Field's poem "Lover's Lane, Saint Jo" is the basis for today's alternate spelling of *St. Joseph's* nickname as St. Jo. 634 S. Broadway; 2 blocks S of Busch Stadium. JEFFERSON BARRACKS / NATIONAL *CEMETERY:* National Landmarks. This 1826 supply depot for Western troops and training center (historic buildings, museum, cemetery) housed later notable Civil War officers (1826–1861), including Federal generals Grant, Sherman, Buell, Hancock, and Frémont, and Confederate generals Lee, Longstreet, J. E. Johnson, Crittenden, Frost, A. A. Pope, and J. B. Hood, as well as Nathan Boone *(Ash Grove)* and Confederacy president Jefferson Davis. At the river; I-255 at SR 231/Telegraph (10 m. S of town). OLD ST. LOUIS ARSENAL: Group of buildings (limestone, 1830s; brick, 1850s); established 1827 to manufacture ammunition and small arms for Jefferson Barracks (above). After the 1861 fall of Fort Sumter, the arsenal's munitions, including about 60,000 weapons, were kept from Confederates by commandant Capt. Nathaniel Lyon, whose unauthorized removal of these munitions effectively neutralized Missouri Confederates for the rest of the *Civil War (Springfield: Wilson's Creek)*. Across from Anheuser-Busch Brewery (above); Arsenal at 2d (3100 S.), adjacent to Lyon Park. SOULARD FARMERS MARKET: Reportedly one of America's oldest continuous markets, it was established in 1842 as a gift from the widow Julia Soulard with the stipulation it remain only a market. Fresh homegrown produce daily; open 6 A.M. Broadway, W on Lafayette to 7th.

Tower Grove Park. In 1867 Henry Shaw deeded most of this 276-acre park to the city in exchange for money to develop it. Part of his country estate (Missouri Botanical Garden, above), it was designed by Shaw as a Victorian walking garden that still includes thousands of trees, lily ponds, marble busts of famous composers around an ornate gazebo, America's first bronze statue of Christopher Columbus, a Chinese Gazebo, and an 1860 entrance gate flanked by statues of lions, deer, and griffins. Sports fields, tennis, picnic area. Adjacent to S side of Missouri Botanical Garden.

---

1. Laclède often signed his name Pierre Laclède Liguest in order to distinguish himself from his brother.

ST. PATRICK
Estimated population: 53   Map G-1

Settled in c. 1830 by Irish Catholics (Shrine of St. Patrick, below), the town grew south of Barnesview[1] near a road that connected *St. Francisville* at the Des Moines River to *Monticello,* where the road split in all directions. Reportedly first named Marysville[2] (also North Santa Fe or Santa Fe Mission[3]), it was renamed St. Patrick, in honor of Ireland's patron saint, because of the already established Maryville in Nodaway County. Platted in 1854. Post office: 1857–1860, 1867–1869, 1878–now.

Buck and Doe Run Wildlife Area. *Wildlife Areas.*

St. Patrick's Day Postmark. Irish immigrant Father Francis O'Duignan arrived in 1935 at his new parish, saw the condition of the church, and began that year a worldwide letter-writing campaign, asking for help with a building program. The envelopes were marked with a shamrock and the green cachet "St. Patrick, Mo.—the only one in the world" (the only post office in the world named St. Patrick). In 1936, the Associated Press picked up the story. From that initial publicity the town annually receives about 20,000 letters for cancellation, mostly on March 17, St. Patrick's Day. Post office. *(Noel: Christmas City)*

Shrine of St. Patrick. Vernacular, 1957. The fourth Catholic church here (first 1834), reportedly designed by Father Francis O'Duignan (St. Patrick's Day Postmark, above) after the Church of Four Master in Donegal, Ireland, this one-story front-gabled granite-and-stone building has multiple recessed arches at the entrance and a tall circular stone bell tower with a conical roof beside it. The 36 stained-glass windows, patterned after illustrations of the Book of Knells, were designed and built in Dublin, Ireland. The interior has marble from Spain and Italy. Grounds: 1926 statue of St. Patrick. In town.

1. Postmaster G. A. Barnes and location; p.o. 1835–1840; defunct.
2. Although this place-name is usually not religiously significant, the circumstances here suggest the Blessed Virgin Mary.
3. Possibly because of recent enthusiasm for the *Santa Fe Trail*; Spanish meaning Holy Cross.

SALEM
Population: 4,486   Map G-6

The townsite was settled in the 1830s by farmers from Tennessee, Kentucky, and North Carolina and platted in 1851 as county seat for newly organized Dent County. Its popular place-name, honoring Salem, N.C., is commendatory, assumed to mean peace, as well as a shorter name for Jerusalem. Two courthouse fires (during the Civil War and in 1866) destroyed all county records. An 1861 Civil War skirmish here resulted in 16 Federal and 36 Confederate casualties. The arrival in 1872 of the St. Louis, Salem & Little Rock *Railroad* helped Salem prosper as a shipping point in the 1870s for the region's iron mining and timber boom (Iron

Mines, below; *Bunker).* Post offices: Dent[1] 1853–1863, 1866–1869; Salem 1869–now.

Annut, Mo. Established c. 1890, Annut was named for popular schoolteacher Annet Lenox by an admirer who was obviously more enthralled by her than by her teaching (her reaction to this well-intentioned gesture is not known, but the postmaster general accepted the spelling as submitted). Post office: 1890–1963. SR 72, N 7 m.; SR C, W 4.8 m. CLEMENT *STATE FOREST.* CLEMENT *WILDLIFE AREA.*

Dent County Courthouse. Second Empire, 1870; additions 1896–1897, 1911; remodeled 1933; renovated 1976; National Historic Register. Despite additions and remodeling, the county's third courthouse, originally a 42-by-78-foot brick structure, is a good example of its type that features a mansard roof with metal cresting and dormers on the steep slope, decorative brackets, and projecting center-facade tower. Original cost: $17,200. Downtown. *(County Profiles)*

Dent County Museum. Local historical items. 4th at Pershing.

Indian Trail State Fish Hatchery. This warm-water facility built in 1937–1938 by the CCC is basically unchanged since then. Water is supplied by gravity-flow pipes from impounded Blackwell Lake (no water activities allowed). Fish include bass, catfish, bluegill, and redear sunfish. Picnic area; closed weekends and holidays. At Indian Trail *State Forest.* SR 19, N 14 m.; SR 117 and state forest roads (signs), E approx. 4 m. WHITE RIVER TRACE / TRAIL OF TEARS: Surveyed in 1835 by the federal government along a former Indian trail for, ironically, the removal of Indians from North Carolina and Tennessee. Signs.

Iron Mines. Evidence of Dent County iron mining is disappearing. The former Orchard Mine, now flooded, is across from G&W Grocery.

Natural Areas. HYER WOODS: 30 acres. Features an old-growth upland oak-hickory forest with a small spring and stream. Box 509, Rolla 65401. SR 72, N 11 m.; adjacent to Lake Spring;[2] sign. MONTAUK UPLAND FOREST: 40 acres. Part of Montauk *State Park* (Recreation, below). Features an oak-pine forest, steep ravines, and bluffs. Its understory includes dogwood, redbud, red maple, rusty blackhaw, and hawthorn. RR 5, Salem 65560. SR 32 at SR 72; SR 32, S 9.4 m.; SR 119, S 8 m.

Recreation. *FLOAT STREAMS:* Jacks Fork and Current Rivers. INDIAN TRAIL *STATE FOREST:* Indian Trail State Fish Hatchery, above. MONTAUK *STATE PARK:* SR 32, W 12 m.; SR 119, S 10 m. to Montauk.[3] *WILDLIFE AREAS:* Hyer Woods (Natural Areas, above), White River Trace.

Standing Rock. This mass of brown sandstone (40 feet wide, 25 feet high) has parts so naturally cemented together they are quartzitic. Along Gladden Creek is chert resembling huge cabbage heads that is thought to have been formed by reef-building fossils over 520 million years ago. Roadside park: picnic area, wading. SR 19, S 10 m. at bridge; or 2.4 m. S of SR 19 at SR N; or SR 19, 1.6 m. N of Gladden.[4]

1. Dent County namesake *(County Profiles);* another Salem p.o. in Linn County 1855–1869.
2. Spring-fed lake; p.o. 1856–1863, 1867–now.
3. Algonquian meaning fort-at, originally used to describe the point at the eastern extremity of Long Island, N.Y; p.o. 1844–1974.
4. Prominent area family; p.o. Winston, possibly like Winston-Salem, N.C., for Revolutionary War general Joseph Winston, 1852–1867, 1871–1885; Gladden 1885–1972.

SANTA FE TRAIL

This legendary trail, the first organized land route connecting the Midwest to the Far West, was used from 1821 until 1880, after which railroads provided faster and more economical service. In 1821 Mexico gained independence from Spain, which had prohibited trade with America. The trail, composed of former Indian routes, was now open, and the early 17th-century city of Santa Fe, Mexico, became the destination. William Becknell of Franklin *(New Franklin)* placed an 1821 advertisement in the "Missouri Intelligencer and Boon's Lick Advertiser" for 70 men to trade horses and mules, and to "catch wild animals of every description that might be for the benefit of the company." Eleven men applied (a total of 15 filled out the company). This first trip proved that enormous profits could be made not from horses, mules, and wild animals of every description but from American utensils and clothing (and later the wagons themselves). The 1825 survey of the primary 900-mile route for the government by George

C. *Sibley* involved about 100 wagons and took about three months. From Missouri, this route goes through Kansas to Bent, Colo. (which reportedly featured the only billiard table in the Far West), and then south to Santa Fe. A cutoff (southwest from Cimarron, Kans.) reduced the trip to 770 miles, but it ran through 58 miles of desert and 150 miles of hostile Comanche territory. Only about 90 traders used the Santa Fe Trail, but they generated approximately $3 million for Missouri in 1822–1843. Some modern road atlases trace the entire route, e.g. AAA Road Atlas, 1990. *(Oregon Trail)*

SAVANNAH
Population: 4,352   Map C-2

The town was platted in 1841 as a central location for the county seat of newly organized Andrew County. It was first named Union[1] in 1841, but the name was changed to Savannah the same year by the county court, reportedly through the efforts of 1837 settler Samuel Crowley, whose former home was near Savannah, Ga. Another version claims the first white child born here was named Savannah, honoring her parents' former Georgia residence, and the town was named for the child. Popular as a place-name, the word "savanna" or "savannah" is defined as a meadow in the sense of an open and level tropical or subtropical grassland, and it came to 17th-century English from Carib Indian via Spanish. The town grew as an area trading and political center later aided by the c. 1869 arrival of the Kansas City, St. Joseph & Council Bluffs *Railroad.* Post offices: White Hall[2] 1840–1841; Savannah 1841–now.

Andrew County Courthouse. Richardsonian Romanesque, 1899–1900; National Historic Register. The

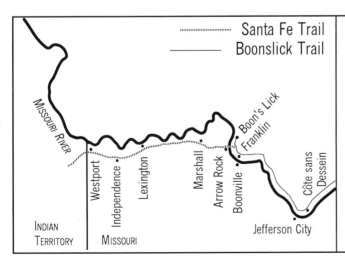

Until c. 1826 caravans left from Franklin heading northwest along the Boonslick Trail to Arrow Rock, west approximating SR 41 to Marshall, west following the Missouri River and approximating US 65 and US 24 through Lexington to Independence and then southwest. After 1828 the trail began at Independence, which dominated the trade until it began shifting to Westport in the early 1840s.

county's third, this 84-by-104-foot brick courthouse with sandstone trim and a slate roof rises 120 feet to the top of its domed central clock tower. Features of the style include a rusticated first floor, spring arches, ornate square corner towers, belt courses, and arched windows. Architect G. E. McDonald designed nearly identical courthouses for Bates, Johnson, and Lawrence Counties. Cost: $37,500. Downtown. *(County Profiles)*

Andrew County Museum. Displays include local items, a replica of a general store, quilts, an antique car collection, a large collection of Kewpie dolls, a Gatling gun, and war memorabilia. Duncan Park (below).

Architecture. Predominately late 19th- and early 20th-century, e.g. Queen Anne and Prairie style.

Duncan Park. 100 acres. Golf, miniature golf, tennis, picnic area, playground, two fishing lakes, volleyball, ball fields, c. 1840 log cabin. US 71 at SR E; SR E, E then 2 blocks N.

Wildlife Areas. Christie, Happy Holler, Honey Creek. *(Wildlife Areas)*

1. Presumably for patriotic reasons.
2. Origin unknown but usually indicates a building named for a person.

SAVERTON
Estimated Population: 150   Map G-2

The town was platted in 1819 along the Mississippi River at the site of a French village established near a salt lick. The name has no recorded explanation, and no local or prominent families or French towns of that name exist. One theory is that it was a French nickname *(Ste. Genevieve)*, perhaps a pun on "saveur" (French for flavor in the sense of savor), referring to the economically important salt source here. Americans also attached humorous nicknames to towns (e.g. Lick Skillet, Paydown), so possibly the name was kept but corrupted to Saver with the suffix -ton added for town. Saverton grew along an important north–south *road* (later branching west) aided by the c. 1879 arrival of the St. Louis, Keokuk & North Western *Railroad*. Post office: 1832–1845, 1851, 1856–now.

Anderson Wildlife Area. *Wildlife Areas.*

Ilasco, Mo. Ilasco was established in 1900 by the United Atlas Cement Company. Its coined name contains the beginning letter of each component of the Portland cement made here at the time: iron, lime, aluminum, silica, calcium, and oxygen. Slavic laborers who immigrated here under contract (Monkey Run, below) helped produce the 4 million barrels of cement used for the 51-mile $380 million Panama Canal. While the canal was being built in 1905–1914 (it formally opened in

1920), this plant was the world's largest. In the 1960s, the community was abandoned because of blasting at newer quarries. It is now owned by a Norwegian firm that uses electric kilns to heat crushed rock and shale to 3,000°F (production is about 650,000 tons of cement annually). The old plant is on the west side of SR 79 with quarries to the east. Post office: 1919–1960. SR 79, N 5 m. **MONKEY RUN, MO.:** The town was established at the Mississippi River during the early 1900s by immigrant Slavic employees of the cement plant (above). Its name has no recorded explanation. The most flattering theory is that dynamiters were traditionally called powder monkeys and after lighting the fuse they were encouraged to run ("run, monkey, run"). The least flattering is that because they were foreigners, their children were harassed and taunted by other children who chased them, yelling "run you monkeys, run." In this theory, the community was then referred to as the place where monkeys run or where the monkey runners live and later the name was shortened to the nickname Monkey Run. No post office. GR, S 1.5 m.

Lincoln Hills. *Lincoln Hills Area.*

Lock and Dam #22. Built in 1934–1938. Dam: 3,080 feet long; locks: 600 feet long, 110 feet wide. Launch ramp. SR E, S 1 m. *(Locks and Dams)*

SEDALIA
Population: 19,800   Map E-4

First platted in 1857, the town was named Sedville by state legislator and Pacific *Railroad* board member George R. Smith, who laid it out on paper while trying to persuade the railroad to build its line along a southern route that included his property (Georgetown, below). In 1860 Smith platted another town along the railroad grade that included the first plat and changed the name to Sedalia, which, like Sedville, honored his daughter Sarah, whom he nicknamed Sed. The suffix -alia was added for euphony (e.g. *Centralia*). Despite the promise of prosperity from the arrival of the first train in 1861, business was delayed by the *Civil War*, but the town, a federal garrison, did not suffer. After the war, it boomed as a shipping point and stockyard for cattle drives from Texas (1866 estimate: 168,000 cattle), which romanticized its name, spawning other Sedalias in eastern and western states. In 1865, the state legislature designated Sedalia county seat of Pettis County, replacing Georgetown (below). By 1870, cattle trails had shifted to more northern routes *(Kansas City; St. Joseph)*, but Sedalia, with three railroads, continued to grow as a regional shipping point and as a political center. Its late 19th-century prosperity was made conspicuous by a failed attempt in 1895 to replace floundering *Jefferson City* as state capital. Post office: 1861–now. Home of State Fair Community College and State Fair Area Vocational School. Tour maps: chamber of commerce, Broadway, N to E 4th (113), or visitor center, US 65 near 20th.

Architecture. Good examples of 19th-century styles dating from Sedalia's boomtown years from the 1870s to the 1890s are located along Main Street, part of the original business district, which along with Broadway and Ohio St. shifted at night to gambling houses and ragtime bars (Scott Joplin, below). NATIONAL HISTORIC REGISTER: Harris House (Queen Anne, 1885), Broadway,

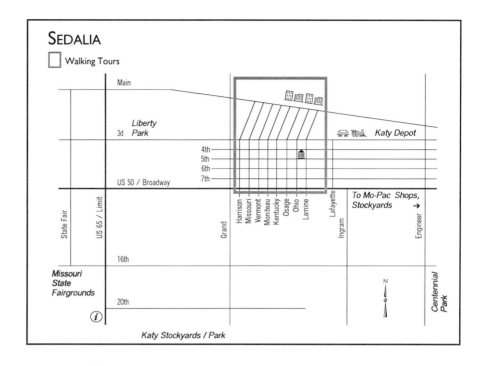

N on Harrison to 6th. Missouri, Kansas & Texas Depot (Railroad), Broadway, N on Lafayette, E on 3d (600). Missouri-Sedalia Trust Company (Richardsonian Romanesque, 1886), Broadway, N on Ohio to 4th. Sedalia Public Library (Italian Renaissance, 1901), terracotta and stone, marble floors; Broadway, N on Kentucky to 3d.

Bothwell Lodge. Tudor, 1897–1928. State Historic Site. Steeply pitched roofs, castellated turrets, cross gables, windows on the main gables, and yellow-stone building material highlight this group of four structures built by John H. Bothwell (lawyer, politician, businessman), whose 1929 22-page testament gradually transferred ownership from his family and friends (for use as a clubhouse) to the state, which accepted it as a state park in 1974. Bothwell, a widower, lived here from 1897 until his death; his wife of four years died in 1887. Reportedly, his "interior decorating lacked a woman's touch," with unpainted plaster walls and mismatched furniture bought for quality and at whim. Original furnishings, tours, trail, picnic area. US 65, N 5.5 m.

Georgetown, Mo. This 1837 county seat established on land owned by county court member James Ramey and his partner Thomas Watson (St. Helena, below) was named by early settler David Thomson either for his former hometown of Georgetown, Ky., which honors George Washington, or to directly honor Washington. Residents' refusal of George Smith's railroad proposal (Sedalia history, above) resulted in the platting of Sedalia and the subsequent loss of the county seat in 1865. Post office: 1837–1921. US 65 at US 50; US 65, N 3.3 m.; SR H, W and N 2 m. ARCHITECTURE: All pri-

vate residences; inquire locally. The Academy (c. 1843–1849), once used by Sedalia town founder Smith as a home and a school for his and local children; SR H. Thomson House (prior to 1840; National Historic Register; also known as Elm Springs), two-story brick with basement, shade trees; SR H, just S of Hughesville.[1]

Katy Trail State Park. NE side; US 50, N on Engineer, E on Griessen Rd.; signs. *(State Parks)*

Liberty Center. Italian Renaissance, 1920s; restored 1981–1983. Originally the New Lona Theater (an opera house, later a movie theater), the building was used for cold storage by Beatrice Foods from 1857 to 1981, then restored as a performing arts theater. Plays, concerts, exhibits. E side; US 50, N on Osage.

McVey School. Vernacular, 1886; restored. This small one-story front-gabled brick structure with arched windows was used for grades one through eight until 1956; typical rural schoolhouse. Broadway, E city limits (E of SR M).

Missouri State Fairgrounds. 396 acres. Sedalia won the 1899 general assembly's competitive bidding for the state fair, which it has hosted at this site since 1901. Most of the brick buildings were built in 1903–1906. Agricultural, commercial, and competitive exhibits, entertainment, rodeo, car races, food, carnival. August (third week; 11 days); other year-round events include sales and rallies. US 65, W on 16th to State Fair Blvd.

Parks. The following are among the city's many. CENTENNIAL: 37 acres. Pool, tennis, picnic area, playground, athletic fields. E side; US 65, E on 16th past Engineer. DAVIS SPORTS COMPLEX: Exercise trail (16 stations), 1.5 m. track. State Fair Community College; US 65; W on 16th (3201). KATY: 18 acres. Picnic area, playground, practice fields. US 50, S on Grand, W on 24th to Clinton. LIBERTY: 32 acres. Pool, tennis, fishing lagoon, ice-skating, rose garden, playground, picnic area, volleyball, horseshoes. US 65, E on 3d; sign.

Pettis County Courthouse. Italian Renaissance, 1923–1925. The county's fourth (the third here), this three-story 136-by-96-foot courthouse has belt courses, eight two-story columns on all sides, a rusticated first floor with pedimented entries and arched windows, and roofline balustrades. Cost $285,500 (without mechanicals). Downtown. *(County Profiles)*

Railroad Stockyards. MISSOURI, KANSAS & TEXAS RAILROAD: Arriving c. 1872, the Katy continued the town's cattle-based economic prosperity after trail drives ended. At Katy Park (above). MISSOURI-PACIFIC RAILROAD: Texas cattle were driven here for shipment east. The railroad shops, built 1904–1905, were some of the largest west of the Mississippi. E side; Broadway, E to Marshall.

St. Helena, Mo. Settled prior to 1820 by *gristmill* owners James Ramey and Thomas Watson, the town was also known as Pin Hook.[2] Its current name comes from the site of Napoleon's last exile, a British island off Africa (Longwood, below). After serving as the temporary county seat of newly formed Pettis County in 1833–1837, it was replaced by Georgetown (above). Remnants: stone pilings for defunct bridge; marker. Post office: St. Helena 1833–1837. US 65, N 2 m.; SR HH, E 2.5 m.; SR EE, N 2.5 m.; access road marked by

Mo. Dept. of Natural Resources sign. LONGWOOD, MO.: First established c. 1825 as Hermantown[3] a mile north on the *Arrow Rock–Georgetown Road*, the town was moved down the road and renamed Longwood for Napoleon's residence at St. Helena. The Presbyterian *cemetery* (S of town) is one of the area's oldest. Post office: 1837–1844, 1856–1957. SR EE, N 5 m.; GR, N 3.2 m.

Scott Joplin. A marker at the site of the Maple Leaf Club commemorates this world-famous ragtime composer and musician (1868–1917), whose c. 1900 "Maple Leaf Rag" sold a million copies (Architecture, above). Joplin, a Sedalia resident from 1893 to 1900, produced his best work here before moving to St. Louis (*Market Street Area Sights*) and then New York. Incidentally, ragtime, although a contemporary of early jazz, was a structured style said to be partly based on march music. US 65, E on E. Main (121). ARCHIVES: Joplin letters, music, memorabilia; stained-glass window from Maple Leaf Club. State Fair Community College; US 65; W on 16th (3201).

Smithton, Mo. Platted in 1859 by William E. Combs along the Pacific *Railroad*, Smithton is reportedly the second town named for Sedalia town founder George Smith. The first, established c. 1858 about three miles west of here, failed because of alleged swindling of the lot owners, and another town was platted by area farmers who named it Farmers City.[4] Bypassed by the railroad, Farmers City declined, losing its population to Smithton. Post offices: Smith City[5] 1860–1871; Smithton 1871–now. US 50, W 6 m. ARCHITECTURE: Interesting structures include Community Church (Vernacular, 1860), moved from Farmers City in 1873, Chestnut at Clay; and Richter and Son Blacksmith Shop (Vernacular, 1890s), now Semkins Service Station, downtown.

Spring Fork Lake. 140 acres. Crappie, bluegill, bass, catfish; boat rentals. US 65, S 9 m.; SR V, E 1.1 m.; sign.

1. R. Hughes, early settler; p.o. Magoffin, either for the Ky. county or its namesake, Gov. Beriah Magoffin, 1872; Hughesville 1872–now.

2. Popular place-name (five in Kentucky) that has various explanations, including fishing with a bent pin, sharp trading practices by merchants, and location, e.g. Sandy Hook (*Jamestown*) with hook meaning point as in land, i.e. a sharp curve at a point.

3. Origin unknown; no p.o.

4. P.o. Arator 1835–1862; origin unknown (*Otterville*); Farmers City 1862–1864.

5. There was an existing Smithton p.o. in Worth County 1858–1867, 1869–1870.

An outing near Longwood.

SEMINOLE WARS

Beginning c. 1800, Seminoles—whose name comes from a Creek word approximately meaning wild man—moved into empty areas of Florida. They comprised an amalgam of runaway slaves and late 18th-century tribes (e.g. Lower Creek, Yuchis, Hitchitis) splintered by European settlements. FIRST SEMINOLE WAR: 1817–1818. Weak Spanish authority and mounting American accusations that Seminoles were harboring runaway slaves precipitated this war, which began when U.S. troops were sent to arrest a Seminole chief. The 1818 invasion by Andrew Jackson *(County Profiles: Jackson)* of Spanish territory to fight the Seminoles resulted in Spain's ceding Florida in 1819. The Seminoles were assigned a reservation; American settlers occupied the vacated land. SECOND SEMINOLE WAR: 1832–1842. The conflict was a direct result of *Osceola*'s refusal to relocate in accordance with the 1830 Indian Removal Bill *(Trail of Tears);* U.S. troops killed: c. 2,000 *(County Profiles: Dade).*

SENECA

Population: 1,885   Map C-7

Settled in 1833 at today's Missouri–Oklahoma border by Ohio settlers, the site was platted in 1868 along Lost Creek, keeping its c. 1833 common place-name honoring the Seneca Indians who were relocated to adjacent Indian Territory. The Seneca were best known to Europeans as members of the c. 1570 Iroquoian league called the Five Nations, a powerful confederation including the Mohawks that ranged south along the Great Lakes from western Ohio through New York. The spelling of Seneca, a Mohegan name for the tribe literally meaning stone, was standardized euphonically in the 18th century to agree with that of the Roman writer Seneca. The arrival in 1871 of the Atlantic & Pacific *Railroad* helped this farming town's economy, which was further aided by the 1871 organization of the Monarch Tripoli Company (Seneca Standard Tripoli, below). Post office: 1869–now. Chamber of commerce: Frisco Caboose behind post office and city hall, downtown.

Architecture. Some late 19th- and early 20th-century styles, e.g. the Mitchell Block downtown and a restored late 19th-century schoolhouse behind the post office.

Lost Creek. Eight-foot walkways on either side of the bridge allow fishing for catfish, bass, shad, and perch. Downtown; SR 43.

Murals. Painted locally, depicting historical scenes of Seneca. State Bank, city hall; downtown.

Quapaw Pow-Wow. Since 1872. The nationwide gathering of this tribe features dancing, competitive dancing with other tribes, concessions. Fourth of July (three days).

Seneca Standard Tripoli. A material discovered here in 1869 was originally thought to be tripoli, siliceous deposits found only in Tripoli, North Africa, but later analysis reclassified it as a different particle structure (the North African substance is now called tripolite). Seneca Standard Tripoli, found only in this vicinity in 325-million-year-old deposits, was first mined in 1871 by the Monarch Tripoli Company, which marketed it as American Bath Brick for scouring and polishing applications. Today it is used as an agent in rubbing compounds, paints, and cement and for viscosity control. Samples are available at the library or mill, downtown.

Spook Light. SR 43, N 7 m.; SR BB (or a road continuing W from SR BB at SR 43), W 2.5 m. to Oklahoma border; GR, N approx. 1 m to defunct Spook Light Museum; park and wait. *(Joplin)*

SHELBYVILLE

Population: 582   Map F-2

Platted in 1835 as a central location for newly organized Shelby County, the town was named by the court for the county's namesake *(County Profiles: Shelby).* Although Shelbyville was initially prosperous as the county's political center, the construction in 1857 of the Hannibal & St. Joseph *Railroad* through Shelbina (below) stunted its growth. Post office: 1836–now.

Bollow State Forest. *State Forests.*

Hager's Grove, Mo. Established c. 1850 east of the Salt River by landowner John Hager, the town was platted in 1859. Derelict except for a vernacular frame church (built 1873, closed 1987); *cemetery* adjacent. Post office: 1851–1864, 1867–1915. SR K, W 10.7 m.

Looney Creek Primitive Baptist Church. Vernacular, c. 1838; organized 1835. This brick church was the second built by this congregation, which, despite its name,[1] was as sane and civilized as any. SR 168, E 6 m.; SR W, N 4 m. to Burksville;[2] GR, E 1 m.

Shelbina, Mo. Platted in 1857 by the railroad, the town was named for the county's namesake. The suffix -ina could be for euphony, although in taxonomy -ina is used to denote a relationship or resemblance within the same group. Post office: 1858–now. SR 15, S 7 m. BENJAMIN HOUSE: Italianate, 1872–1874; National Historic Register. The three-story brick house has a

cupola, brackets, arched windows, and a one-story porch with columns. Shelby St. (322). GEN. U.S. GRANT: Reportedly Grant's first *Civil War* combat assignment *(East Prairie: Battlefield)* was to guard the Salt River railroad bridge being rebuilt after its destruction by Confederates in July 1861. Marker, 2 m. W of Hunnewell.[3] US 36, E 7.9 m. HUNNEWELL *WILDLIFE AREA* / HATCHERY: The warm-water fish hatched here include bass, catfish, walleye, and muskie. US 36, E 10 m. to Hunnewell; SR Z, N 2.5 m.
Shelby County Courthouse. Richardsonian Romanesque, 1891–1893; renovated 1934. The county's second, this two-story 80-by-90-foot brick courthouse rises 85 feet to the top of its dome. Plain for its style, it features a rusticated foundation, a hip roof, and a spring-arch entryway beneath a large Georgian-style window, both of which are set in a projecting parapeted facade. Cost (less damages due to delays): $24,380. Downtown. *(County Profiles)*

1. For early settler Peter Looney.
2. First postmaster John T. Burks; p.o. 1892–1907.
3. H. H. Hunnewell, RR official; p.o. 1857–now.

SHERIDAN
Population: 174   Map C-1

The town was platted in 1887 just west of the Platte River along the St. Joseph, Chicago, St. Paul & Kansas City *Railroad*. Its base population came from an 1869 *gristmill* community founded at the river by mill owner Jacob Winemiller that was platted in 1872 as Defiance.[1] Sheridan, a popular place-name, honors a Civil War hero, Federal general Philip H. Sheridan (1831–1888). Post office: 1887–now.
Iowa–Missouri Marker. Iron Post, 1851. This 4.5-foot tapered post marks the original 1820 northwest Missouri *boundary*, later expanded west by the 1837 *Platte Purchase*. It was set in 1851 after the U.S. Supreme Court settled the Missouri–Iowa boundary dispute over the 1816 Sullivan survey defining the property bought in 1808 from the Osage. Missouri's original enabling act had set the northern boundary at an ill-defined rapid of the Des Moines River, before there was an Iowa. SR H, N 4.1 m.
Mural / Sculpture. Both works are by Chicago artist Clive Rickabaugh, who grew up in Sheridan. MURAL: Depicts Defiance and Sheridan. At Farmers State Bank. SCULPTURE: The Last Supper, Nativity Scene, and Apostles. At Christian Church.
Park / Petting Zoo. PARK: Millstone from Winemiller's Mill, picnic area, restrooms, playground. ZOO: Bears, buffaloes, small animals. Both in town.

Parnell, Mo. Platted in 1887 along the same railroad line as Sheridan, the town was named for Irish statesman and Home Rule advocate Charles Stewart Parnell, who was receiving international attention at the time because of London "Times" articles accusing him of Irish terrorism. Parnell's American maternal grandfather, Adm. Charles Stewart, served with distinction in the *War of 1812*. Post office: 1887–now. SR 246, E 2 m.; SR 46, S 7 m. ARCHITECTURE: The c. 1900 bandstand, a good example of its type, is located downtown across from the two-story vernacular 1889 Arlington Hotel.

1. Usually commendatory, motivation here is unknown; p.o. Winemiller 1872–1876; Defiance 1876–1887.

SHUT-INS

According to "Geologic Wonders and Curiosities of Missouri," the term "shut-in" is a southern Appalachian description of a gorge that was etymologically transmogrified in the Missouri Ozarks to describe "a gorge cut by a stream whose valley is locally constricted as it cut through or between resistant igneous knobs." There are several explanations of why shut-ins are found in the midst of otherwise placid streams. Generally, the conclusion is that erosion of sedimentary rocks left igneous knobs exposed, and further erosion sculpted the knobs into the beauty and wonder of pinnacles, potholes, and water-polished boulders that are seen today as a maze of rocks and white-water rapids constricted by a vertical-wall canyon. Whether the knobs were already exposed or were exhumed from sedimentary rocks remains debatable, as is a recent hypothesis that suggests the knobs were prominent surface features before formation of the shut-in and that headward erosion enlarged weak fracture zones in the surrounding igneous rock.

SIBLEY
Population: 367   Not on Map

The town was platted in 1836 near abandoned Fort Osage (below) by Archibald Gamble, who named it for George C. Sibley *(St. Charles: Lindenwood College)*, his brother-in-law and the fort's former government trading agent from whom he had acquired the property. Located at important cross*roads* at the only Missouri River ferry west of *Lexington*, it grew as a trading center. An 1844 flood severely damaged the town, but the 1863 destruction of it by Union forces caused its permanent decline despite the 1888 arrival of the Chicago, Santa Fe & California *Railroad,* which influenced the town's relocation to its present site. Post office: 1842–1864, 1866–now. *Santa Fe Trail* route (Fort Osage, below). Omitted from some highway maps: SR 24 at SR BB in *Buckner;* Sibley Rd. (CR 20E), N 2 m.; follow signs to Fort Osage.

Fort Osage. National Historic Landmark; picnic area, fishing access. The fort, whose future site on a high promontory above the Missouri River was noted in 1804 by William Clark during the *Lewis and Clark Expedition,* was built by Clark in 1808 and first called Fort Point and then Fort Clark until an 1808 treaty with the Osage, after which it was called Fort Osage *(Boonslick Trails).* As the first military outpost of the *Louisiana Purchase,* 230 river-miles upstream from the closest settlement, Côte sans Dessein *(Jefferson City),* its purpose was to establish an American military presence in the West and to provide protection for both westward expansion and the United States Factory System, a government trading agency for licensing private traders and for trading directly with the *Indians,* who here included both tribes of the Osage, as well as the Kansa and Pawnee. Under the direction of Maj. George C. Sibley *(St. Charles: Lindenwood College),* it was one of the government's most successful trading factories. The abandonment in 1827 of the fort was primarily due to its success (Clay County was organized in 1822, Jackson County in 1826) and to 1822 congressional lobbying by private fur traders like the American Fur Company *(Kansas City; St. Joseph)* that resented government competition. Today's replica, using original foundations when possible, was built using U.S. War Department plans; staff in 1812-period costumes demonstrate daily fort activities. Post office: 1820–1830, 1833–1853. At Old Sibley. BLOCKHOUSES: Built with gun ports and with the second story cantilevered over the first, four blockhouses were a part of, and outside, the surrounding stockade. *CEMETERY:* 3.5 acres. Some of the oldest markers are dated 1818 and 1819. FACTORY: The post (a 3.5-story building) traded items like blankets, ammunition, and kettles for hides, skins, and fur. OFFICER AND ENLISTED QUARTERS: Three officers lived in apartments; the fourth's apartment was at the mess hall/hospital; enlisted men (59 in 1812) had bunks. *SANTA FE TRAIL:* A 1919 DAR marker locates the 1821 route. VISITOR CENTER: Displays include an Osage hunter's lodge and fort artifacts.

Osage Honey Farms / Park. FARMS: Starting with one hive given to him by his grandmother, G. L. Vanarsdall created a business that now produces 230 to 330 thousand pounds of honey each year. Glass beehive, group tours. Santa Fe St. HAYES PARK: 36 acres. First county

park; picnic area, playground. Across from farm.
Sibley Generating Station. Easily located by its 700-foot stack, this coal-fired electrical generating plant owned by Missouri Public Service draws 176,000 gallons of river water per minute for cooling; maximum capacity 470 megawatts. Group tours.

SOUTH GORIN
Population: 130   Map F-1

Platted in 1887 as Gorin near the North Fabius River along the tracks of the recently arrived Atchison, Topeka & Santa Fe *Railroad,* the town was named for Henry M. Gorin, a Scotland County official and early county settler whose *gristmill* was at the townsite. By 1888 the town began having an identity crisis that continues today: it was also known as Millertown,[1] and subsequent towns were platted at the tracks in 1888 and 1889 (Octavia[2] and South Gorin, respectively), which were then incorporated with Gorin in 1889 as South Gorin. Locals still use Gorin when referring to the town, and they describe South Gorin as a relatively prosperous area on a hill at the south city limits (whose city limit sign reads Gorin), while Millertown, they say, is the area on the north side of Gorin. Contrary to federal *post office* regulations, this town has slipped between the bureaucratic cracks by maintaining its original post office name, Gorin, while legally incorporating as South Gorin, which is how the U.S. Census Bureau lists it. Regardless of its name, the town was quick to grow as a shipping point (1899 pop. 1,100) but declined after the Great Depression like many agriculturally dependent towns. (Until 1993 the official state map identified the town as Gorin; there is not, nor was there ever, a North Gorin.) Post office: 1887–now.

Ella Ewing Lake. 15 acres. Picnic, restrooms, fishing (bass, sunfish, catfish). SR U, E 1 m.; SR RA, S 1.1 m.
Mennonites. Evidence of this religious group's presence can be seen in stores like Zimmerman's at Rutledge[3] (SR A, S 6.3 m.). *(Mennonites)*
Missouri Giantess. During her lifetime, Ella K. Ewing (1872–1913) was the tallest woman in the world (8 feet, 4.5 inches, 300+ pounds), although when seated she appeared to be an average-size woman. From age 18, she toured with shows like the Barnum & Bailey Show and Buffalo Bill's Wild West Show (accompanied by her parents or friends). Beginning at $250 per week, Miss Ella earned enough to buy an 80-acre farm just south of South Gorin, where she built a house for herself and her parents, featuring 15-foot ceilings, 10-foot doors, and 7-foot windows (no longer standing). She

died of pneumonia at age 40. Her grave is outlined by a long flat cement border with a granite memorial marker, "made possible by folks that knew of Ella," which was erected in 1967 but erroneously states the year of her death as 1912. Memorabilia, including a size 24 shoe, at Boyer House *(Memphis: Scotland County Museums)*. Grave: SR A, S 3.5 m.; GR (W of bridge), S 1 m. to junction; E then S 0.2 m. to New Harmony Grove Church (Vernacular, 1870) and *cemetery*; grave NW of church.

Prairie Oil and Gas Company. The 120-foot smokestack remains as a derelict landmark of this 1906 facility that helped pump crude oil from Kansas City to Ft. Madison, Iowa. NE side.

Sand Hill, Mo. Established in 1835 at the headquarters of Cooper Settlement, Sand Hill was Scotland County's first post office and the temporary county seat (1842–1844) until after the courthouse was built in 1843 at *Memphis* (the records were removed in December 1844). Its stock place-name is descriptive. Today, Sandhill Farm, an egalitarian community, sells honey and sorghum. Post office: 1836–1903. SR A, S 6.5 m.; SR M, W 2.1 m. (to N bend of road); GR, S 0.3 m.

1. W. G. Miller, prominent landowner and first postmaster; no p.o.
2. Possibly RR official Octave Chanute, who helped plan and build the route; a town street is named Octavia; no p.o.
3. Origin unknown; p.o. 1888–now.

SPARTA
Population: 751   Map E-7

Platted in 1885 by J. J. Burton along a branch line of the St. Louis & San Francisco *Railroad* (Chadwick, below), the town was named for his mother's hometown, Sparta, Tenn., which was named for the Greek city-state whose name is usually associated with courage. Post office: 1876–now.

Chadwick, Mo. Chadwick was established in 1883 as the terminus of a branch of the St. Louis & San Francisco *Railroad*, which built a turntable here for trains hauling hardwood for railroad ties. It was named for railroad foreman John F. Chadwick, who reportedly was killed when a mule kicked him in the head. The initial population came from nearby Log Town.[1] The tracks were removed when the hardwood was depleted in 1934. Post office: 1883–now. SR 125, S 7 m. CHADWICK MOTORCYCLE TRAIL / CAMPS: 125-mile trail through steep drainages, hogback ridges, oak-hickory timber, glades, caves, springs; two annual AMA sanctioned Enduros. Two *national forest* trail camps and picnic areas: Camp Ridge (vault toilets) and Cobb Ridge (pit toilets).

Honey Branch Cave / Park. Commercial cave since 1955; half-mile guided tours, lighted. PARK: 73 acres. Fishing, camping (RV, tent), picnic area, trails, playground, 1885 log cabin. SR 14, E 10 m.; GR, county line road; S to near Ongo;[2] signs.

Recreation. *FLOAT STREAM:* Swan Creek. *TRAIL:* Hercules Glades Wilderness Trail.

1. All structures log; established 1842; no p.o.
2. Reportedly coined by a federal postal official when asked to suggest a name, based on the idea of wanting the mail to go on; 1897–1949.

SPRINGFIELD
Population: 140,494   Map E-6

The site of Missouri's third largest city was claimed in 1829 by Tennessean John Polk Campbell, who returned in 1830 with his family and relatives after the federal government began removal of Kickapoo and Delaware Indians living here. In 1833 Campbell was county clerk of newly organized Greene County, and his cabin was selected as temporary county seat. Platted in 1836 as permanent county seat on 50 acres donated by Campbell, the town was named for the post office, which was named either for its location (a spring at the base of a hill with a large field), for an early settler's former hometown, Springfield, Tenn., or for the Massachusetts hometown of James Wilson (Wilson's Creek, below). Growing at an important east–west *road* (paralleling today's I-44) that branched south into Arkansas and north to the Missouri River, Springfield dominated trade in southwest Missouri. During the *Civil War* (Wilson's Creek, below), its growth (est. 1859 pop. 2,500) was stunted despite Federals' effective control of the town in 1862–1865. Postwar westward expansion and railroad building precipitated a boom that mainly centered on shipping and commerce and was initially aided in 1870 by the arrival of the Atlantic & Pacific *Railroad* (North Springfield, below), resulting in a 1910 population of 38,000. Post office: 1834–now. Home of Southwest Missouri State University (SMSU), Drury College, Evangel College, and Willard J. Graff Area Vo-Tech. Driving and walking tour maps and information: chamber of commerce, I-44, S on Glenstone (US 65B), W on Chestnut, S on North Jefferson (320) at Park Central Square. *(Route 66)*

Architecture. Good examples of 19th- and early 20th-century styles are located in two National Historic Register districts (see map). COMMERCIAL STREET: A six-block business district, part of former North Springfield (below), extending along Commercial between Lyon and Washington. WALNUT STREET:

Residential and business structures between Glenstone and Hammons Parkway. Sites of particular interest (some of which are not in the historic district) are: CITY HALL: Richardsonian Romanesque, 1894; addition 1914; National Historic Register. Features Indiana limestone, a corner tower, a castellated central tower, gargoyles, spring arches; used for various federal government offices until acquired in 1938 by the city. I-44; US 65B, S to Chestnut, W to Boonville (830). LANDERS THEATER: Italian Renaissance, 1909; National Historic Register. Features brick, limestone, and terra-cotta with a rusticated first floor, roofline balustrade, and bracketed eaves. I-44; US 65B, S to E. Walnut (311). MUSEUM OF THE OZARKS: Below. OLD JAIL: Vernacular, 1891; remodeled 1921; National Historic Register. Two-story stone and brick with an outside chimney; used until 1955. I-44; US 65B, S to Chestnut, W to Campbell, S to W. McDaniel (409). STONE CHAPEL: Gothic Revival, 1880–1892; National Historic Register. Construction stopped in 1882 due to insufficient funds and then a fire; completed 1892. I-44; US 65B, S to Chestnut, W to Drury College. SHRINE MOSQUE: Moorish, 1923; National Historic Register. Built by Shriners in an eastern architectural style accented by colors and curves. I-44; US 65B, S to St. Louis (602).

The Arts. ART: Traditional and contemporary at city art museum; I-44; US 65B, S to Grand, W to National, S to Brookline (1111). PERFORMING ARTS CENTER: Nineties Contemporary with Art Moderne affinities, 1992. This $15-million 2,300-seat facility designed by Pellham, Phillips & Hagerman of Springfield and Jerit/Boys of Chicago combines a nostalgic 1930s sense of futuristic imagination with space-age technology: perfect acoustics without a bad seat in the house. Local, national, and international performances: theater (including Broadway shows), opera, ballet, symphony, special programs. SMSU campus.

Bass Pro Shop / Outdoor World. Outdoor World, built in 1981 by Bass Pro Shop (founded in 1971), is reportedly the world's largest sports store, with 200,000 square feet of merchandise and displays. Features include a four-story waterfall, a 64,000-gallon pool stocked with Missouri fish, a trout stream, a shark tank, four freshwater aquariums containing fish of North America, rock formations, and a two-story log cabin. WILDLIFE MUSEUM: Hundreds of taxidermy displays of birds, fish, and animals. I-44; US 65B, S to Chestnut, W to South Campbell (1935). *(Ozark: Tracker Marine)*

Caves. CRYSTAL: Open since 1893, Missouri's second oldest walk-through commercial cave features formations like the Washington Monument, as well as crinoid fossils. I-44; SR H, N 5 m. FANTASTIC CAVERNS: Billed as "The Cave You Ride Through," this is reportedly the only one of its kind in America, with jeep-drawn trams that cover a one-mile tour of natural formations. I-44; SR 13, N approx. 1.8 m.; Fantastic Caverns Rd., W 3 m.

Cave Springs, Mo. The town was established in 1839 as a brush arbor Presbyterian congregation community at a spring that appears to issue from a cave. Post offices: Willard[1] 1858–1871; Cave Spring 1871–1907. I-44 at US 160; US 160, N 8.6 m.; SR 123, N 0.6 m.; SR AC, N 1.6 m. MT. ZION PRESBYTERIAN CHURCH: Vernacular, 1869. This frame structure is the second at the site; *cemetery* adjacent. In town. THE SPRING: Beginning at a 30-foot-long, 10-foot-wide limestone crevice, it flows for about 30 feet under what appears to be a natural bridge (actually a breached cave system, not a *collapsed cave system*) and reappears in a walled basin used to pipe water. Located S of church, W of SR AC and N of road to Pearl.[2]

Cemeteries. MAPLE PARK: Established in 1876. Shaded by maples, this was a typical landscaped 19th-century cemetery, where Sunday afternoons featured buggy rides and concerts; 1890 gazebo. I-44; SR 13, S to West Grand (300). SPRINGFIELD NATIONAL: Established in 1867 for Federal soldiers killed at Wilson's Creek (below), Pea Ridge, Ark., and other regional *Civil War* battles *(Carthage; Forsyth; Newtonia)*. In 1870 a Confederate cemetery was platted adjacent; it was consolidated in 1911 with the national one through the opening of a gate in the wall between them, making this the first place where these sworn enemies were buried in the same cemetery. Of the ornate monuments, most notable are those for Confederate general Sterling Price (a larger-than-life bronze soldier), Federal general Nathaniel Lyon (10 feet tall with a knight's helmet, battle ax, and wreath), and Federal soldiers (a 20-foot granite soldier) killed at the 1863 battle of Springfield, wherein Confederate J. S. Marmaduke's vain attempt to recapture the city cost 404 combined casualties. A granite rostrum between the cemeteries features two lecterns, one facing north, the other south. Veterans of subsequent wars are also buried here. I-44; US 65B, S to East Seminole (1702). *(Cemeteries)*

Dickerson Park / Zoo. 109 acres. Established c. 1890 as a private zoological park, then acquired in 1922 by the city, it is best known for its elephant herds (rides offered), but it also has 450 other specimens, including rare and endangered species, reptiles, birds, animals, and amphibians. Picnic area, playground, concessions. I-44 at SR 13.

Exotic Animal Paradise. Billed as America's largest drive-through wild animal park, it offers a nine-mile drive leading through 400 landscaped acres containing about 3,000 exotic animals and birds (96 different

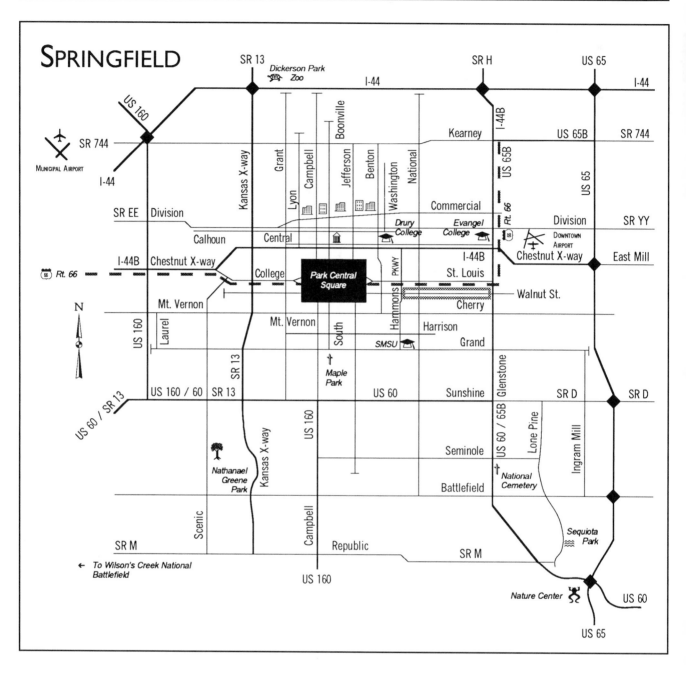

SPRINGFIELD

kinds) that roam singly and in herds, flocks, and gaggles; restrooms, concessions. I-44 at US 65; I-44, W 6.4 m. to Strafford.[3] *(Lebanon: Route 66 Sights)*

Greene County Courthouse. Italian Renaissance, 1910–1912; interior fully completed 1915. This 100-by-200-foot stone structure is the county's third courthouse at a third location: its predecessors were on the square and at College (the northwest corner of the square). Its features include belt courses, quoins, roofline balustrades, a rusticated first floor, arched entrances, pedimented windows, a different treatment of each story's windows, and four parapeted and projecting central wings with four two-story Ionic

columns. Estimated cost: $200,000. Chestnut Expressway at Park Central Square; N on Boonville to Central, then E. *(County Profiles)*

Little Sac Woods State Forest. *State Forests.*

Museum of the Ozarks. Queen Anne Free Classic, 1892; National Historic Register. This two-story 22-room house features cross gables, paired columns, wide porches, and a corner tower; inside are period furnishings and household items, stained- and leaded-glass windows, and parquet floors. Regional items include 19th-century clothing, over 3,000 photographs, china, dolls, and quilts. I-44; US 65B, S to Chestnut, W to Benton, N to East Calhoun (603).

Nathanael Greene Park. 68 acres. Features a 60-acre arboretum, an 8-acre Japanese garden with lakes, paths, and a moon bridge, and a farm replica featuring the c. 1855 Gray-Campbell house (relocated, remodeled) with plans for outbuildings; picnic area, playgrounds. I-44; SR 13, S to Sunshine, W to S. Scenic (2400).

Nature Center. The Missouri Department of Conservation offers interpretive displays, special programs, and trails (some wheelchair access). US 65 at US 60; US 60, W 0.25 m.

Needmore, Mo. While other Missouri towns *(Brumley: Ulman)* share this nickname, Greene County's post office community was the only official one. Post office: 1890–1903; ironically, defunct. SR M at S. Golden; a small shopping mall marks the site.

North Springfield, Mo. North Springfield was platted in 1870 along today's Commercial Street (Architecture, above), about one and a half miles north of Springfield's former square (Park Central Square, below), by the Ozark Land Company, which was organized by land speculators, including a congressman and railroad official, after residents refused to pay premiums to the Atlantic & Pacific *Railroad* for its right-of-way. Unlike many Missouri towns bypassed by railroads, Springfield (est. 1870 pop. 5,500) did not later move to the tracks or decline. While North Springfield grew quickly at first, the older well-established town also benefited from the increased shipping opportunities and was aided by the c. 1881 arrival of the Kansas City, Ft. Scott & Memphis *Railroad.* Both towns continued expanding, met, and consolidated in 1887. Post office: 1871–1878, 1880–1888.

Ozark Empire Fair. Late July–early August.

Park Central Square / Ozark Jubilee. The original town square was the site where, in 1867, in front of a large crowd, James Butler "Wild Bill" Hickok (1837-1876) shot and killed noted gunman Dave Tutt over a gambling argument *(County Profiles: Phelps).* Appointed U.S. Marshall a year later, a prototype of western gunslinger-sheriffs like Wyatt Earp, Hickok was shot in the back of the head at Deadwood, Dakota Territory, while holding aces and eights, thereafter known as the dead man's hand *(Princeton).* I-44; US 65B, S to St. Louis, W to square. OZARK JUBILEE: The Ozark's version of Nashville's Grand Ole Opry was hosted by Red Foley at the Jewell Theater (razed in 1961) and broadcast nationally on ABC-TV from 1954 to 1960; marker at small park. Square, 1 block S on Jefferson to McDaniel.

Route 66. The 1925–1935 city route: SR 744/US 65B (Kearney) at US 65B/I-44 Loop (Glenstone); Glenstone, S about 2 m.; St. Louis, W to the square and around it to College; College, W to Chestnut Expressway (I-44 Loop); Chestnut, W across I-44 to SR 266 to

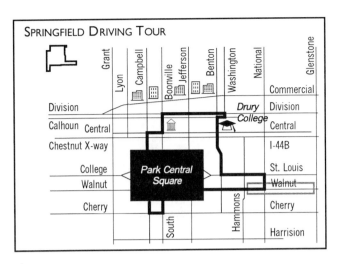

Halltown. (Route 66)

Sequoita Park. 13 acres. Formerly a private park accessible by excursion trains, it was bought by the state as a fish hatchery, then by the city as a park. Spring, cave, lake, picnic area, playgrounds. SR M at US 60; SR M, E to Lone Pine, then N; signs. (Just north of the former railroad/manufacturing town Galloway.[4])

Wilson's Creek National Battlefield. August 10, 1861; National Historic Register; *National Park.* In May 1861, three months before the battle here, at the U.S. arsenal at *St. Louis,* then-captain Nathaniel Lyon's intent to neutralize Confederate influence in Missouri *(Boonville; Carthage)* began a course of action leading him to this battlefield as a brigadier general of volunteers. On July 13, Lyon was camped at Springfield with about 6,000 soldiers when Confederate generals Ben McCulloch and N. B. Pearce joined Gen. Sterling Price in northwest Arkansas, forming a combined Arkansas-Missouri army of about 12,000 men with the purpose of destroying Lyon's army and recapturing Missouri. Neither side achieved its objective. Lyon, who had marched here the night of August 9, detached Col. Franz Sigel with 1,200 men to flank McCulloch's encamped force from the south near the Fayetteville road at Wilson's Creek.[5] Lyon struck from the north at 5:30 A.M. with 4,200 men. The fighting was intense. Sigel's troops were turned, then routed, leaving Lyon to face the brunt of the enemy force in a five-hour fight at Bloody Hill where Lyon, already wounded twice and aware that he was losing the battle, was killed at 9:30 A.M., the first Federal general to die in battle *(County Profiles: Phelps).* Federal major Samuel Sturgis assumed command at 11:00 A.M. and signaled a retreat. Confederates, erroneously believing Federal reinforcements were imminent, did not pursue. Casualties: Federal, 223 killed, 721 wounded, 291 missing; Confederates, 265 killed, 800 wounded, 30 missing. Although this was technically a Confederate victory, the Federal army remained intact.

Price occupied Springfield *(Lexington)*, then withdrew to Arkansas in February 1862 when Federal general Samuel R. Curtis approached. An 1863 Confederate counterattack failed (Cemeteries: Springfield National, above). Relative to larger Civil War battles, Wilson's Creek, Missouri's largest battle, with 17,400 combatants and 13.4 percent casualties, was one of the war's bloodiest. Visitor center: active and passive solar heating, exhibits, historic trails, self-guided tour (4.9 miles; automobile, bicycle, or hiking), featuring the Ray House *(Vernacular, c. 1852)*, which served as a post office and a Butterfield stage flag stop *(Overland Mail Company)*, as well as seven strategic battle sites, including Bloody Hill (the high ground occupied by Lyon and about 4,000 Federals). SR M at US 160; SR M, W 6.8 m.; SR FF, S 2.2 m.

1. RR Surveyor Bill Willard; p.o. 1884–now (Willard p.o. moved from Cave Spring).
2. Origin unknown; p.o. 1886–1928.
3. For 1643 Strafford, Conn., home of RR stockholders, which was named for the English Stratford-on-Avon, associated with Shakespeare; p.o. 1870–now.
4. Town founder Charles Galloway; p.o. 1883–1943.
5. Early settler James Wilson; p.o. 1856–1868, 1908–1926.

STEELVILLE
Population: 1,465   Map G-5

Settled in 1833–1837, the site was selected in 1835 as a central location for the permanent county seat of Crawford County, replacing the temporary one at James Harrison's house at Little Piney near the confluence of the Little Piney and Gasconade Rivers *(Rolla: Arlington)*. Steelville was platted in 1836 on land sold to the county court by early settler and town namesake James Steel, around whose c. 1835 store a small settlement grew at today's Main Street. Located in a valley by Yadkin Creek, it grew as a political center that was aided by an areawide 1830s–1870s iron mining boom *(St. James: Maramec Iron Works)* and the c. 1872 arrival of the St. Louis, Salem & Little Rock *Railroad*. Post offices: Davy[1] 1833–1836; Steelville 1836–now.

Crawford County Courthouse. Italianate, 1885–1886; addition 1974. The county's fourth, this 71-by-36-foot two-story brick courthouse was built with no decorative details. Its original front-gabled style with returns is reminiscent of Greek Revival, but its arched first-story windows and double doors, along with its second-story unsupported balcony and tall narrow windows, reflect an Italianate influence that today is masked by the 1974 addition of square columns and a pediment. Original cost: $7,500. Downtown. *(County Profiles)*

Crooked Creek Structure. Like the Decaturville Structure *(Camdenton)*, this complex geologic structure cannot be explained. SR 8, W 2.5 m.; SR M, S 7.8 m.; SR VV, S approx. 4.2 m.; inquire locally.

Davisville, Mo. Established c. 1880, Davisville was named for the Davis family. Post offices: Boyers Mill[2] 1878–1880; Davisville 1880–now. SR 19, S 11 m.; SR 49, S 5.2 m.; SR V, E 1.9 m. DAVISVILLE NATURAL ARCH / CAVE: Scenic; interesting formations include a natural arch (10–20 feet high, 15 feet wide) in the West bluff of Huzzah Creek; downstream 25 yards is a *cave* with an 8-by-12-foot opening and a vertical slot in the ceiling, and a few yards further is a canyon ending in a wet-weather waterfall. Warning! Climbing is difficult and dangerous; the arch can be viewed from the road. SR V, E 0.5 m. to Red Bluff Campground / Picnic Area (below) W of creek; 100 yards past first turnout. RED BLUFF CAMPGROUND / PICNIC AREA *(National Forests)*: The bluffs have been stained red and brown by iron oxides and black manganese oxide; fireplaces, tables, vault toilets, water recreation in Huzzah Creek *(Float Streams)*.

Dillard Mill. Vernacular, c. 1900; restored to working order; State Historic Site (132 acres). One of Missouri's most picturesque, this three-story red frame *gristmill* ground corn until the 1960s. Called Missouri's best preserved roller mill (it still has its original machinery), it is set at Huzzah and Indian Creeks where a rock dam creates a waterfall that cascades into the millpond. Picnic area, trail, tours. SR 19, S 11 m.; SR 49, S 11 m. to Dillard;[3] GR, S 1 m. *FLOAT STREAMS:* Courtois and Huzzah Creeks.

Peaceful Bend Winery. Locally grown French American hybrid grapes produce 12-percent-alcohol-by-volume wines named for the local creeks and river: Courtois, Huzzah, and Meramec. Vineyards, Meramec River access, tasting, picnic area. SR 8, W 2.2 m.; SR T, N 2 m.

Recreation. *FLOAT STREAMS:* Courtois and Huzzah Creeks. *NATIONAL FOREST:* Davisville, above. *STATE FOREST:* Huzzah. *WILDLIFE AREA:* Woods.

Roadside Park. Broad view of the Meramec River and valley. Picnic area. SR 19, N 1.3 m.

Steelville Museum / Park. MUSEUM: Local items, clothing, furniture, photographs. PARK: 1833 log-cabin site and *gristmill*. Spring-fed landscaped rock-enclosed pond with ducks, fish; pool, restrooms, playground, picnic area. SR 8; Spring, S 1 block to Esther. SCHWIEDER FISHING AREA: Trout fishing for children ages 12 and younger at Yadkin Creek; across from park.

USA Population Center. According to the 1990 census, the actual center of the USA is 9.7 miles southeast of Steelville, the point at which a flat U.S. map would balance perfectly, providing each person weighed a like amount and nobody moved. Since the first census in 1790, America's population center has shifted west and south from Chestertown, Md., passing through Illinois (1950–1970) to De Soto, Mo. *(Hillsboro)*, in 1980. Marker and monument, City Park (above). Incidentally, America's geographic center is just west of Castle Rock, S.D.

1. H. E. Davis, first postmaster of the former community of Davis (Davy p.o.).
2. Mill owner.
3. Mill owner Joseph Dillard Cottrell; p.o. 1886–now.

STOCKTON
Population: 1,579   Map D-6

The town was platted in 1846 as *Lancaster,* a central location for the county seat of newly organized Cedar County. That stock place-name has no recorded specific namesake, and its duplication of an existing *Lancaster* resulted in an 1847 change of names to Fremont, honoring John C. Frémont (1813–1890), who during the 1840s made newspaper headlines for his 1842–1844 exploration of the West and his 1846–1847 exploits with American Californians attempting to form a sovereign state separate from Mexico *(Mexican War).* Frémont's 1856 campaign as the Republican presidential candidate in that party's first national election so angered county residents that they petitioned to change the town name to Stockton, effective in 1859 *(Van Buren: Fremont),* honoring Commodore Robert F. Stockton, who was instrumental in capturing California during the *Mexican War* and who, ironically, had appointed Frémont commandant and civil governor of California. Landlocked and bypassed by railroads, the town grew as a county political and trading center. Incidentally, Frémont's father-in-law, influential politician Thomas Hart *Benton,* vigorously opposed Frémont's election. Post offices: Cedar[1] 1846–1847; Fremont 1847–1859; Stockton 1859–now.
Cedar County Courthouse. Moderne, 1938–1940. The county's third, this two-story monolithic courthouse of poured concrete, reportedly Missouri's first public building of this construction, creates an interesting effect with its symmetrical architectural lines emphasized by vertically aligned windows, friezes of vertical grooves, and a projecting central structure flanked by smaller complimentary wings. Cost: $122,600. Downtown. *(County Profiles)*
Jerico Springs, Mo. The town was platted in 1882 by D. G. Stratton around what were called marvelous medicinal springs. The spelling Jerico is reportedly a combination of names: the biblical town Jericho and former townsite owner Joseph B. Carico. Further playfulness with place-names here includes the stream that divides the town, Jordan Creek, and the section of town isolated by it (west of the creek), which was locally called Jerusalem. Mostly derelict. Post offices: Jericho 1882–1885; Jerico 1885–1905; Jerico Springs 1905–now. SR 39, S 6 m.; SR B, W 7.1 m. JERICO SPRINGS PARK: Located on a square bordered by a gravel street, this small plain park was once surrounded by buildings. A marker claims it was a famous health resort, drawing people from the U.S. and Europe. Today there are benches, old cedars and oaks, a historical marker, and a horseshoe-shaped cement pool containing two springs that flow from plastic pipes. Across the street are swings, a ball field, and picnic pavilions. Downtown; SR 97.
Recreation. STOCKTON LAKE: *Lakes: Corps of Engineers.* STOCKTON *STATE PARK:* SR 39, S 3.5 m.; SR 215, E 4.7 m.

1. For the county *(County Profiles).*

STREAM PIRACY

Called hydrologic short-circuiting by geologist Dr. T. R. Beveridge, stream piracy occurs when one stream, or a branch of one stream, breaches another that has a lower gradient. The more powerful, lower-gradient stream then captures the other by siphoning all or most of its upstream water to form a new, and sometimes opposite-flowing, body of water. The more obvious examples of this phenomenon create dry river valleys that are used today as highway or railroad beds *(Buckner: Lake City Stream Piracy).*

SULLIVAN
Population: 5,661   Map G-5

Established in 1856 as Mount Helicon,[1] the town was platted in 1859 as Sullivan. The Pacific *Railroad* changed the name to honor landowner Stephen Sullivan, who donated property for the depot. Post offices: Mount Helicon 1856–1860; Sullivan 1860–now. *(Route 66)*
Harney House. Vernacular, c. 1856; addition 1870. Built by the Leffingwell family as a summer home. William S. Harney (1800–1889), who served as a general in the *Mexican War* and *Civil War* and as a commander of the Department of the West at St. Louis,

A bridge across the Osage River at Warsaw.

enlarged it by 24 rooms. SW side; 332 Madison.

Japan, Mo. This 1860 community kept its name after the 1941 Japanese attack on Pearl Harbor only because locally the name is pronounced Jay'-pun and derives from the church, Holy Martyrs of Japan, which commemorates the priests and brothers crucified in 1597 during a Japanese attempt to eradicate Japanese Christianity. Post office: 1860–1868, 1887–1908. SR 185, W 3 m.; SR H, W 3.7 m. *FLOAT STREAM:* Bourbeuse River.

Meramec Upland Forest Natural Area. 461 acres. Part of Meramec *State Park* (Recreation, below). This old-growth forest with a well-developed understory and rich ground cover features dolomite glades, calcareous seeps, a sinkhole (*Collapsed Cave Systems*), and *caves*. Rt. 4, Box 4, Sullivan 63080.

Recreation. *FLOAT STREAM:* Bourbeuse River. MER-AMEC *STATE PARK:* SR 185, S 1.8 m. *STATE FORESTS:* Little Indian Creek, Meramec, Pea Ridge.

Route 66 Sights. Hand-cut-stone Shamrock Motel and a McDonald's remodeled as a memorial to Route 66. I-44 S. Outer Rd. (*Route 66*)

Stanton, Mo. The town was established c. 1859 along the Pacific *Railroad* and named for its post office, which was first established about four miles south by mine owner Peter Stanton. Post offices: Reedville[2] 1856; Stanton Copper Mines 1856–1857, 1857–1880; Stanton 1857, 1880–now. I-44, E 5 m. MERAMEC CAVERNS: Open since 1935, the cave features cave coral (grapelike clusters), a three-legged onyx table, and the stage curtain (mineral deposits 70 feet high and 60 feet wide resembling curtains), which is billed as the world's largest single cave formation. Lighted concrete walks, guided tours, camping, picnic area, Meramec River canoe rentals, concessions. I-44 exit 230. MUSEUMS: Two are easily located by I-44 bill-

boards. (1) Antique Toy: a serious toy collection, featuring modes of transportation. (2) Jesse James Wax: wax figures, a replica of the James homestead, displays including firearms. *ROUTE 66* SIGHTS: I-44 N. Outer Rd., E 8 m. (*St. Clair*).

1. Located NW of Athens, Greece, it was the legendary home of the Muses and the site of Hippocrene, a spring that inspired poetry.
2. Established by Missouri Lead Mining Co.; origin unknown.

 # SUSPENSION BRIDGES

Light and flexible suspension bridges allow engineers to cross wide distances using fewer building materials, which is not only aesthetically pleasing but also economical and presents fewer obstructions to river traffic. The best known are the 1883 Brooklyn Bridge and the 1937 Golden Gate Bridge. While Missouri has large suspension bridges, like the Paseo Bridge in Kansas City, smaller versions are more interesting because they readily reveal the basic building principles. The three essential elements are the cables, towers, and anchorages. The cables stretch rigidly from cement or masonry anchorages buried at the sides of either end of the bridge to and over the towers, between which the cables form an inverted arch. The decking and suspender cables (vertical steel cables connecting the inverted arch cables to the decking) are not as structurally important as the three essential elements, but all work together to form a flexible and integral unit. Warning! Just because a bridge is suspended does not mean that it is intended to be swung. Excessive speed, abrupt stops, and intentional tilting or swaying of a suspension bridge can be dangerous.

SWEET SPRINGS
Population: 1,595   Map E-3

Platted in 1848 by Presbyterian minister and 1826 settler John Yantis, who descriptively named it for the spring at which he settled, the site became such a popular health spa beginning in the 1870s that the politically prominent Marmaduke family built a hotel for 400 guests in 1877 and residents of the adjacent Missouri-Pacific *Railroad* town Brownsville[1] petitioned in 1887 to change their town name to Sweet Springs. Post offices: Brownsville 1840–1887; Sweet Springs 1849–1850, 1886–now.

Architecture. Despite a destructive 1882 tornado, some good examples of 19th-century styles remain, e.g. commercial buildings and churches that range from the National Historic Register 1843 Christian Church to the 1878 Lutheran Church.

Blind Pony Wildlife Area. Includes a state fish hatchery and stocked lake. (*Wildlife Areas*)

City Memorial Park. Camping, picnicking, trails, pool, fishing (small lake and Blackwater River). SR 127, S to river; signs.

Sweet Spring Site. A replica of the spring's ornate pagoda is a few feet east of the former spring. SW side; inquire locally.

---

1. Initially called Clayville for American statesman Henry Clay; reportedly changed when William Brown offered $200 for the honor.

TAOS
Population: 802   Map F-4

Platted in 1839 between the Osage and Moreau Rivers by Henry and Gertrude Haar, this predominately German and Belgian farming settlement was named Haarville (no p.o.). It was renamed for the area post office Taos c. 1866 after the office was moved here from the St. Louis *Road* (US 50) in the Schuberts, Mo., area (below). Reportedly, returning *Mexican War* veterans influenced the renaming of the post office, which was originally called Sacramento.[1] Taos, a Tewa Indian name of uncertain origin, was a 17th-century Spanish trading post north of Santa Fe, N.Mex. (*Santa Fe Trail*), and a battle site during the 1846–1848 Mexican War. Post offices: Sacramento 1848; Taos 1848–1907.

Osage City, Mo. Established as Osage in the early 1840s at an Osage River ferry and the St. Louis *Road* between and near the river's confluence with the Missouri, Osage City was named for the Osage *Indians* via the river (*County Profiles: Osage*). It grew toward the Pacific *Railroad* in the mid-1850s, culminating with an addition platted at today's site in 1867. The center span of the railroad bridge in this former steamboat-manufacturing town and port was built to lift, allowing passage underneath. Post office: 1856–1962. SR J, E 4.5 m. *LOCK AND DAM:* Concrete, 1903. The lock no longer works, but the dam still stands (some say because it was built using Osage River gravel). Inquire locally.

St. Francis Xavier Church. Gothic Revival, 1883. This red-brick church, the second (first c. 1840) to serve the area's Catholics, was established by Father Helias D'huddeghem (1796–1874), who resided here from 1842 until his death in this churchyard. Father Helias, an immigrant Belgian Jesuit of Flemish nobility (his mother was the Countess of Lens), helped organize seven churches, including those at Rich Fountain and Westphalia (*Freeburg*). He is buried in the local *cemetery;* a tall marble shaft inscribed in Latin marks his grave. Inside the church is a painting, "The Flagellation," supposedly a gift from Father Helias's mother; a small museum depicts his and the church's history. In town.

Schuberts, Mo. Established in 1844 around Point Osage Lutheran Church (St. John's, below), the community was named for landowner and general-store owner Lorenz Schubert. In 1866, Schuberts was relocated a half-mile west at today's site, probably to be closer to the St. Louis *Road* (US 50). Post office: Taos (above). SR J, E 1.4 m.; US 50, S 0.5 m. ST. JOHN'S LUTHERAN CHURCH: Gothic Revival, 1869; addition 1889. This red-brick structure replaced the original log church, Point Osage, which was moved here in 1866 and later renamed St. John's. Lancet windows, red front door, *cemetery* adjacent. In town.

Stream Piracy. One geological theory claims that the Moreau River once emptied into the Osage at Osage City until it meandered too close to the Missouri, which captured it, resulting in the abandoned valley stretching from Osage City to the Moreau, along which the railroad, taking advantage of the level terrain, was built. SR J, S 1.9 m.; GR, N and W 2.5 m. to Moreau River. (*Stream Piracy*)

---

1. The Spanish word meaning sacrament, via the California river named in 1808 and the city founded in 1839 by Capt. J. A. Sutter, which was platted in 1848, the year before gold was discovered on Sutter's property, precipitating the 1849 gold rush.

THAYER
Population: 1,996   Map G-7

George H. Nettleton, first president of the Kansas City, Springfield & Memphis Railroad Company (Ft. Scott, Memphis & Kansas City *Railroad*), had trouble with this town's location and name. The first choice in 1881 of a townsite and division point for the railroad near Mammoth Spring, Ark., proved too expensive, so in 1882 a second site was selected two miles north at the confluence of Two Mile Creek and the Warm Fork of the Spring River in Missouri, where a town was platted in February (on paper) along the east side of the Warm Fork (today's East Thayer) and reportedly named for Nettleton's wife, Augusta. However, during the spring of 1882, a small community accommodating the construction crew had begun to grow at the railroad switching yard that faced Two Mile Creek, opposite the prospective townsite. Here a post office, Division,[1] was established. Possibly because the proposed river bridge connecting the town and the railroad facilities was more expensive than first calculated or because a town was already growing, the railroad in December 1882 modified and rotated the original plat 180 degrees to fit the site at Two Mile Creek, west of the Warm Fork. Due to an existing *Augusta,* the post office was named in 1884 for recently deceased Nathaniel Thayer of Boston, Mass., a wealthy stockholder and company director. Residents petitioned in 1886 to change the town name to Thayer. Post offices: Division 1883–1884; Thayer 1884–now.

Grand Gulf State Park. National Natural Landmark. A 19th-century journalist accurately observed that, like Niagara Falls, Grand Gulf has to be seen, it cannot be described. One of the world's most spectacular examples of a *collapsed cave system,* it includes Missouri's second largest natural arch, 130-foot vertical canyon walls, a wet-weather stream, two major ruined caves, springs, a wet-weather waterfall, and a classic case of subterranean *stream piracy* that helps fuel one of America's largest single-outlet springs at Mammoth, Ark. (US 63, S 2 m.; *Van Buren: Big Spring).* Easy access, trails above and inside canyon, maps, literature. SR 19 at SR W; SR W, W 5.4 m. GRAND GULF NATURAL AREA: Part of the state park.

1. RR division point.

THONG TREE

Indians fashioned this type of tree as a trail guide to caves, springs, salt licks, medicinal herbs, etc. First, a limber sapling would be staked to grow horizontally to the ground. Then, to further identify the tree, the trunk was slit at either end of the bend and charcoal was inserted and sealed with pitch or pine rosin. As the tree grew, the slits would heal and form bumps that confirmed the bent tree was a marker and not an accident of nature.

TRENTON
Population: 6,129   Map D-2

Established in 1834 at J. S. Lomax's general store on a high bluff near the west bank of Thompson Branch of the Grand River, the community was known as Lomax's Store until platted in 1841 as Bluff Grove[1] on 80 acres donated by Lomax for county seat of newly organized Grundy County. Bluff Grove won the seat of justice in 1841 after brief competition with George Tetherow's proposed location about three miles southeast of today's Tindall[2] *(Cameron: Stewartsville).* For unknown reasons Bluff Grove's name was changed in 1842 to honor Trenton, N.J., the Revolutionary War battle site whose popular place-name represents one of the first examples of a developer naming a town for himself (William Trent, the founder in the early 1700s of Trent's Town). The arrival c. 1869 of the Chicago & Southwestern *Railroad* helped the economy (1874 est. pop. 3,000). About 1897, what is called Missouri's most ambitious cooperative community *(Utopian Societies)* was established by Walter Vrooman, a local landowner and admirer of English author and art critic John Ruskin (1819–1900), a morality-type socialist who advocated glamour, beauty, and brotherhood as the basis for economic cooperation. Vrooman's 1902 Multitude Incorporated, despite owning considerable businesses and Ruskin College, collapsed in 1905 after public disapproval of his attempt to apply Ruskin's principles to the town itself. Post offices: Bluff Grove 1840–1842; Trenton 1842–now. Home of Trenton Junior College.

Architecture. Good examples of 19th-century structures include the following, which are on the National Historic Register: the vehicle bridge at Crowder *State Park* (below); the Grundy County Library (Vernacular, c. 1890), 1331 Main; and St. Philips Episcopal Church (Gothic Revival, 1898–1899), 141 E. 9th.

Crowder State Park. SR 6, W 2.6 m.; SR 146, N 1.1 m. *(State Parks)*

Edinburg, Mo. First settled c. 1837 by Dr. W. P. Thompson,[3] Edinburg was named for the town in Scotland *(Edina).* It was the boyhood home of Enoch H. Crowder (1859–1932; Crowder *State Park),* a U.S. Army judge advocate general from 1911 to 1920 whose comprehensive military plan for WWI included the Selective Service Act (the national draft, adopted in 1917). Post office: Edinburg(h) 1857–1907. SR 6, W 2.6 m.; SR 146, N 3 m. CROWDER *STATE PARK:* SR 146, E 1.9 m.; SR 128, N 1.2 m.

Grundy County Courthouse. Richardsonian Romanesque, 1903–1905. The county's second, this imposing three-story 79-by-84-foot Bedford stone courthouse has an elaborate 106-foot central turreted tower, a hipped roof with cross gables, dormers extending through the cornice line, parapeted gables, a busy roofline, a spring-arch entrance, and walls alternating smooth and rough stone. Cost: $60,000. Downtown. *(County Profiles)*

Grundy County Museum. Vernacular, 1895. This two-story red-brick former feed and implement store exhibits the area's cultural, railroad, and agricultural influences, e.g. a Victorian parlor and a caboose. 1100 Mabel.

Parks. The town's four parks include these two. GLADYS GRIMES: Picnic shelters, ball field, basketball, playground. SR 6, E to Lake Trenton Dr., E to Hunter. MOBERLY: Pool, ball field, tennis, fitness trail, basketball, playground. SR 6, W on 9th, to S on 10th to Tindall at 22d.

1. Descriptive location.
2. J. T. Tindall, who died in Civil War battle at Shiloh; p.o. Neola, woman's name, origin unknown, 1872–1876; Tindall 1876–1967.
3. Thompson Branch namesake.

TROY

Population: 3,811   Map H-3

Platted in 1819 by Joseph Cottle and others along a north–south *road* (US 61) at the site of the derelict *War of 1812* Wood's Fort (Monroe, below), the town was named by merchant Joshua N. Robbins for 1789 Troy, N.Y., whose name probably inaugurated the use of familiar classical place-names like Troy, the site of the Trojan War first recorded in Homer's "Iliad." Selected in 1828 as county seat of Lincoln County, replacing Monroe and Alexandria (Monroe, below), it grew as a political center and as a shipping point, using the river town Cap Au Gris (Winfield, below) until the c. 1884 arrival of the St. Louis, Hannibal & Keokuk *Railroad.* Post offices: Lincoln Court House (Monroe, below) 1819; Monroe 1819–1823; Troy 1823–now.

Architecture. Good examples of 19th-century structures in the downtown area include these churches. CHRISTIAN CHURCH: Early Classical Revival, 1859; additions 1911; octagonal bell tower with spire. 2d St. PRESBYTERIAN CHURCH: Gothic Revival, 1868; remodeled 1940s; stained glass. Boone. UNIVERSALIST CHURCH / MASONIC HALL: Vernacular, 1837–1852; finished 1852 as a two-story brick building by Masons. E side of Main.

Lincoln County Courthouse. Early Classical Revival (Palladian three-part plan), 1869–1870; additions 1930s, 1974. The county's third (the second at Troy), this two-story brick courthouse, originally 70 by 80

feet, features a full-facade entry with six Corinthian columns and a triangular gable with lunette, an octagonal cupola, brackets, a semicircular fanlight over the front door, and symmetrical five-ranked arched windows. Original cost: $27,500. Downtown. *(County Profiles)*

Lincoln Hills. *Lincoln Hills Area.*

Monroe / Old Monroe, Mo. Settled c. 1800 along the Cuivre (pronounced quiver) River and known as New Spain[1] and Cuivre Settlement,[2] the town was platted in 1819 as the first county seat of Lincoln County and named for then-president James Monroe *(County Profiles: Monroe).* After county residents petitioned for a more central location, Monroe lost the seat of justice in 1823 to Alexandria[3] (formerly 5 m. N of Troy; defunct), at which time Monroe lost its post office to Troy. Alexandria was also inconvenient for county residents, and the court was moved by petition in 1828 to Troy. When Monroe reapplied for a post office c. 1863, there was an existing Monroe City in Monroe County, so the post office and, eventually, the town were renamed Old Monroe *(Old Appleton).* Post offices: Lincoln Court House 1819; Monroe 1819–1823; Old Monroe 1863–now. US 61, S 3.6 m.; SR C, E 6.5 m. CHAIN OF ROCKS, MO.: This community was named for a line of rocks in Cuivre River's streambed. The river wandered, or was forced, from its sediment-filled valley to this stretch of bedrock. The same phenomenon, evident in the Mississippi River at St. Louis (either side of the I-270 bridge), required building *Lock and Dam* #27 and dredging a canal east of the main channel for safe navigation. Post office: 1869–1907. SR C, W 3.9 m.; SR OO, S 1.9 m. CUIVRE ISLAND WILDLIFE AREA. FORT HOWARD: Site of a *War of 1812* fort. SR C at US 79 (W of town); US 79, N 2.4 m. to Bob's Creek; E of bridge, S side of creek. SQUIRE BOONE'S HOUSE SITE: The brother of Daniel Boone began a stone house here in 1800 on his Spanish land grant *(Defiance: Missouri Territory Village).* SR C at US 79; GR, N 1.2 m. to cemetery at church; site just SW of cemetery.

Moscow Mills, Mo. Platted in 1821 just east of *War of 1812* Clark's Fort[4] by Shapley (or Shipley) Ross and two other landowners who intended the site to compete for county seat, the townsite was named for Moscow, Russia, following the 19th-century fashion of using place-names of large foreign capitals or exotic names *(Callao).* After losing the competition for county seat, Moscow languished as a farming community that slowly grew into a town (1899 est. pop. 350; 1994 est. pop. 924). During the process of reapplying for a post office in 1878, Mills was added to the name because of another Moscow in Clay County. Post offices: Clark's Fort 1819–1821; Moscow 1821–1823; Moscow Mills

1878–now. US 61, S 4 m.; SR C, E 0.6 m. ARCHITEC-TURE: Good examples of 19th-century structures include the Ross House (Vernacular, 1820s; wings at side and rear added; National Historic Register), a two-story limestone structure with 18-inch-thick walls built by one of the Ross brothers, owners of the 1815 *gristmill*; 2d at Mill.

Natural Areas. All but Prairie Slough are part of Cuivre River *State Park* (below). Rt. 1, Box 25, Troy 63379. BIG SUGAR CREEK: 56 acres. An intermittent headwater stream in the *Lincoln Hills*, this picturesque creek features gravel bars, exposed limestone bedrock, small bluffs, and numerous pools. GEORGE A. HAMILTON FOREST: 40 acres. One of the finest remnant forests in the Lincoln Hills section of the glaciated plains features a mature white oak forest on a rich mesic slope with abundant spring wildflowers. PICK-ERELWEED POND: 3 acres. This quarter-acre sinkhole pond in the Lincoln Hills features aquatic plants, including American lotus and rare plants like naiad. PRAIRIE SLOUGH: 406 acres. Part of Prairie Slough *Wildlife Area*. Features include a bottomland forest, a shrub swamp, and backwater sloughs that provide winter habitat for the bald eagle. Box 324 (Tower Plaza, 655 Clinic Rd.), Hannibal 63401. US 61, N 8 m.; SR B, E 10.7 m. to Elsberry;[5] SR P, N 5 m.

Park. The marked site of Wood's Fort (Troy history, above) has a replica of the 1812 fort. Downtown; Main at Boone.

State Park / Wildlife Areas. CUIVRE RIVER *STATE PARK:* SR 47, E 3.1 m.; SR 147, N. 1.8 m. *NATIONAL WILDLIFE REFUGE:* Clarence Cannon (*Clarksville: Annada*). *WILDLIFE AREAS:* Cuivre Island, Logan, Prairie Slough, Vonaventure, White (William G. and E. P.).

US 61. *New London.*

Winfield, Mo. The town was platted in 1879 and named for Winfield Scott, a well-known soldier and politician of this era, commanding general during the *Mexican War,* 1852 Whig presidential candidate (he lost to Franklin Pierce), and architect of early Federal *Civil War* strategy. Post office: 1880–now. SR 47, E 13 m. CAP AU GRIS, MO.: This early shipping point for Troy was platted in 1845 along the Mississippi River by landowner David Bailey (p.o., below). Its descriptive French name, cap au grès (cape with the sandstone), was changed to Wiota[6] when it was incorporated in 1875, but this name was largely disregarded by residents and cartographers, who continued using Cap Au Gris. The arrival in the early 1880s of railroads at Troy and Winfield contributed to its immediate decline. Nearby (just S of town; inquire locally) is the site of *War of 1812* Fort Cap Au Gris. Post offices: Bailey's Landing 1833–1835, 1838–1845; McClain's Creek[7] 1835–1838; Cap Au Gris 1845–1883. SR N, E 2.4 m.

LOCK AND DAM #25: Built in 1935–1939. Dam: 1,140 feet long; locks: 600 feet long, 110 feet wide. Restrooms, picnic area, launch ramp, overlook. SR N, E 2.4 m. WINFIELD FERRY: SR N, E 2.4 m. at river (*Ferryboats*).

1. At the time still a Spanish possession; no p.o.
2. For the river from the French for copper; no p.o.
3. *Kahoka*, Alexandria place-name; p.o. 1823–c. 1829.
4. C. 1801 settler Maj. Christopher Clark, builder of nearby 1812 fort; inquire locally (*County Profiles: Lincoln*); p.o. Clark's Fort 1819–1821.
5. Landowner R. T. Elsberry; p.o. Nelson, origin unknown, 1877–1879; Elsberry 1879–now.
6. Algonquian, meaning uncertain; no p.o.
7. Local creek for an early settler.

TUSCUMBIA
Population: 148   Map F-5

The town was platted in 1837 along the Osage River on land donated by the Harrison brothers for the county seat of newly organized Miller County. For unknown reasons, its name honors either 1822 Tuscumbia, Ala., or its namesake, the Cherokee chief. The town, set beneath and on top of a high river bluff, initially grew as a river port but declined when bypassed by railroads (1874 est. pop. 200). It continued to prosper as a political center and milling town. Post office: 1837–now.

Anchor Mill / Museum. Vernacular, 1943. Replacing its flood-damaged predecessor, the mill now houses the county museum. Features include a one-room school, a 19th-century kitchen, tools, toys, looms, and local items. US 52, in town.

Architecture. Some interesting 19th- and early 20th-century structures are located on the hill and (as described locally) under the hill, i.e. by the river (below).

Henley Natural Arch. Easily accessible along a short trail with a broad Osage valley view, this dolomite product of subterranean *stream piracy* has a 20-foot ceiling, 20-foot span, and 50-foot passageway. SR 17, N 11 m. to Eugene;[1] SR BB, E 4.5 m. to junction of SR H; GR (opposite junction), SE 2.35 m. (bear left at Y); parking area, trail to overlook, then E on trail 50 yds.

Marshall Fields. A baseball park donated by steamboat captain Robert Melvill Marshall (1858–1954) features a community building on stilts, picnic facilities, ball field, bandstand, and covered pavilion. Under the hill (below).

Mary's Home, Mo. The proposed name for this German community established around the c. 1882 Morgan & Jenkins Store and St. Mary's Catholic Church was Morgan, honoring Robert Morgan's proposed post office. Learning of Morgan's intention,

Father Cosmos Seeberger, indignant that the site would be named for a "Protestant Yankee saloon-keeper," vigorously preached that the town belonged to the Mother of God, which eventually persuaded residents to petition for the post office name Mary's Home. Post office: 1884–1918. SR 17, N 8 m.; SR H, E 2.7 m. ARCHITECTURE: St. Mary's Church (Romanesque, 1907), stone with stained glass and a square tower. Sanning General Store (General Store, early 1900s), an excellent example with an ornamental tin front, tall storefront windows, large screen doors, a tin ceiling, and tongue-and-groove floor. TEN-MILE DRIVE: Scenic loop; gravel road. CR H-8 to CR H-14; inquire locally.

Miller County Courthouse. Vernacular, 1858–1859; enlarged, remodeled 1909–1913 with some Classical Revival elements. The county's second courthouse, originally a two-story brick 56-by-40-foot structure, was remodeled from brick to stone and enlarged to 110 by 50 feet by the addition of north and south wings, a cupola, pediments, arched doorways, and a projecting belt course a few feet beneath the roofline that hints at a balustrade. Original cost: $6,000; additions: $22,283. Off US 52, at the square. *(County Profiles)*

Old County Jail. Neoclassical, 1929. Reportedly one of the state's most modern jails when built (steam heat, running water, electric lights), the building has a hip roof, full-facade entry with Ionic columns, and cornice that identify the style. Adjacent to courthouse (above).

Saline Valley Wildlife Area. *Wildlife Areas.*

Under the Hill. Here in a romantic riverfront setting are a former bank, a frame church, old Anchor Mill, and a park (Marshall Fields, above); river access, grass banks, dramatic views of the courthouse and the 1,080-foot-long 1933 truss river bridge. US 52 at SR HH; SR HH, 0.2 m. downhill to river.

1. RR employee Eugene Simpson; p.o. 1904–now.

UNION
Population: 5,909   Map H-4

The town was platted in 1826 at the Bourbeuse River as a central location for the county seat of Franklin County, replacing Newport *(Washington: Dundee)* in 1827. Union's popular place-name reportedly commemorates reconciliation of disputes over relocating the county seat after the 1825 Missouri legislature responded to petitions by passing an act for the town's establishment. First settled by immigrants from east of the Mississippi and by Germans during the 1840s, it was slow to grow. The 1887 arrival of the St. Louis,

Kansas City & Colorado *Railroad* increased the population to 610 and helped create a building boom (40 houses in four months). Post office: 1827–now. Home of East Central Community College.

Architecture. Some good examples of 19th- and 20th-century styles are at the square. Nearby is St. John's Guildehaus Catholic Church (Romanesque, 1863), built by parishioners; *cemetery* adjacent. SR V, N 5 m.

Franklin County Courthouse. Italian Renaissance, 1922–1923. The county's fourth (the third at this site), this three-story 90-foot-square courthouse was built using reinforced concrete faced with stone. Features include roofline parapets, a different window treatment on each floor, and four full-height pedimented projecting central entries with two-story balustraded and colonnaded balconies. Cost: $200,000 (plus $42,550 for the 1975 remodeling and courtroom addition). Downtown. *(County Profiles)*

Noser Mill, Mo. US 50, W 10 m.; SR 185, S 2 m. *(Gerald)*

Parks. CLARK VITT: Five-acre fishing lake, tree house, trail, natural amphitheater, playground. State at Clark. CLEARVIEW: Bluff overlooking the river, walking trail, 20 fitness stations. SR 50 at Clearview. PARK AVENUE: Picnic facilities, ball field, basketball, pool, playground, tennis, horseshoes, dance pavilion. Park at Christina.

Robertsville State Park. US 50, E 5 m.; SR O, E 5.9 m. *(State Parks)*

UNIONVILLE
Population: 1,989   Map E-1

The town was platted in 1853 (with lots sold in 1854) as a central location for recently consolidated Dodge and Putnam Counties. Its original name, Harmony, was changed in 1855 due to an existing Harmony in Washington County. The name Unionville, like Harmony, expressed the sentiments of county residents when establishing the fifth central location for a Putnam County seat in nine years. This one was preceded by Putnamville, 1845–1847 (Livonia, below); Calhoun,[1] 1847–1848; Winchester,[2] 1849–1851; and Fair Play,[3] 1851–1853, whose name was changed in 1851 to Hartford (Livonia, below). As a county shipping point, Unionville was aided by the completion c. 1872 of the Burlington & Southwestern *Railroad*. Post office: 1854–now.

Architecture. The downtown area has good examples of 19th-century styles.

Historical Museum. Local historical items. 810 Main.

Iowa–Missouri Marker. SR 5, N 5.6 m.; SR UU, N 2.1 m.; State Line Rd., W 2.9 m.; S side. *(Sheridan)*

Lake Thunderhead. Private; members only.

Lemons, Mo. Ironically, the Missouri post office whose name changed the most times was founded by a man who wanted his name perpetuated. Abraham Lemen established the town in 1876 as Lemen along the Burlington & Southwestern *Railroad*. That same year the postmaster general, without explanation and misspelling the name, changed the post office's name to Lemon Station. In 1878 it was renamed Whiting[4] and then closed. It reopened in 1879 as Xenia,[5] which gave the site three names: the town was Lemen, the railroad station was Lemon Station, and the post office was Xenia. An attempt at consolidation (*Post Offices*) was made in 1898 with the name Lemonville, which was shortened to Lemons in 1915, leading some wag to say it was appropriate since all the name changing had left a sour taste anyway. Lemons post office was closed permanently c. 1975. Incidentally, today there are no towns on the state map or post offices in Missouri that begin with the letter X, and Xenia was one of only two post office names beginning with X; in addition to Polk County's Xerxes[6] there was another Xenia[7] in Nodaway County. Post offices: Lemen 1876; Lemon Station 1876–1878; Whiting 1878; Xenia 1879–1898; Lemonville 1898–1915; Lemons 1915–c. 1975. SR 5, S 5 m. MINERAL HILLS *STATE FOREST*.

Livonia, Mo. Livonia was platted in 1859 by Absolum Grogan. Its name, while sometimes applied to a person, is derived from a medieval Baltic country (now part of Latvia and Estonia) that during the Middle Ages formed the Livonian Knights, a branch of the Teutonic Knights. Post office: 1864–now. US 136, E 9 m. to the county's third county seat, Hartford;[8] continue US 136, E 8 m. OMAHA HOTEL: This two-story frame house, built in 1870 by G. W. Houston, was later used as a hotel by his son. Private. SR N, N 3.6 m.; SR Z, W 4 m. to Omaha.[9] REBEL'S COVE *WILDLIFE AREA*.

Putnam County Courthouse. Italian Renaissance, 1923–1924. The county's sixth, this 62-by-92-foot three-story courthouse replaced the one sold and removed in 1890, leaving the county without a courthouse for 33 years. Its style is apparent from the colonnaded entries, rusticated first floor, quoins, different treatment of each story's windows, and roofline parapet. Cost: $126,379. Downtown. (*County Profiles*)

1. Possibly just a paperwork county seat; named for statesman J. C. Calhoun; no p.o.; also known as Bryant's Station, for early settler Archibald Bryant.

2. Origin unknown, named by county court; no p.o.

3. Popular frontier place-name; named by the court, probably as a sentiment for relocating the court here; no p.o.

4. Origin unknown.

5. Greek meaning hospitality.

6. Persian king c. 485–465 B.C.; p.o. 1888–1891; defunct.

7. Both the town and post office name; p.o. 1857–1872; defunct.

8. 1637 Conn. town; p.o. Putnamville, Putnam County namesake (*County Profiles*), 1847–1851; Hartford 1851–1900.

9. Nebr. town; 1673 French for Indian tribe, extracted either directly as Omaha or as Aux Maha, i.e. to or at the place of the Maha Indians; p.o. 1860–1908.

UTOPIAN SOCIETIES

Early socialist philosophy—advocated by those believing in a planned organization that commonly owns the means of production, distribution, and exchange of goods—gained momentum as a result of the 1780–1840 Industrial Revolution. Economic writers of this era such as Swiss-Italian J. C. L. Sismondi (1773–1842), as well as activists like Robert Owen (1771–1859), were appalled at what they perceived as the Industrial Revolution's accelerating evil effect on society, including bare-minimum wages and inhumane working conditions. Many early socialists' efforts were grounded on unrealistic principles, which gave rise to communities, both secular and religious, that were based on an idyllic, usually mythical, ideal of rural society. Some sought to abolish private property, others promoted free love, and some proposed the collective rearing of children. The United Society of Believers in Christ's Second Appearance (the Shakers), America's most successful religious communitarian sect (1774–1959), stressed celibacy because of the futility of procreation when they believed the end of the world was at hand. While Karl Marx, the author with Friedrich Engels of the 1848 "Communist Manifesto," called upon the working class to overthrow the existing system, early socialists demanded the rich and educated to act more responsibly. Marx called these societies unscientific, utopian, and petit bourgeois, but their tenets of social justice are still evident in today's social-democratic parties, while communism has proved to be a social and economic failure.

VAN BUREN
Population: 893   Map H-7

First established in 1830 on the west side of the Current River along a *road* between *Potosi* and Little Rock, Ark., Van Buren was named for Martin Van Buren (1782–1862), then secretary of state in Pres. Andrew Jackson's cabinet, later vice president during Jackson's second term, and then U.S. president from 1837 to 1841 (*County Profiles: Camden*). Platted in 1834 as county seat of newly organized Ripley County, which encompassed about 20 percent of Missouri, the town languished, consisting of only a courthouse, store, *gristmill,* and a few families. When the county was reduced in size in 1847, Van Buren was replaced as county seat by the more centrally located *Doniphan,* but a further reduction in 1859 resulted in the organization of Carter County, whose commissioners selected Van Buren as county seat in 1859. A new courthouse was built in 1867 east of the river, around which the present town was platted. It grew as a political center later aided by a logging boom *(Bunker)* and automobile-era recreational attractions. Post office: 1834–now.

Big Spring / Park. National Historic Register. A state park since 1926, the site was donated in 1970 to the Ozark National Scenic Riverways *(National Parks).*

Camping in Carter County, near Van Buren.

Reportedly Big Spring is America's largest single-outlet spring (averaging 276 million gallons daily). It boils up in a mound of water from an underwater *collapsed cave* and flows to form a small river that pours into the Current River. Attempts to explore the spring have failed because of the enormous water pressure from tributaries traced as far away as *Mountain View* and the Eleven Point River watershed. River access *(Float Streams: Current River),* camping, picnic area, and lodging *(WPA* rustic cabins). US 60 at SR 103; SR 103, S 4 m.

Carter County Courthouse. Vernacular, 1871; expanded and remodeled 1935–1936. The county's second permanent courthouse, this 40-foot-square two-story frame structure was enlarged on the east side with a 30-by-70-foot addition. Native cobblestones were used as facing, making the building Missouri's only cobblestone courthouse. Original cost: $3,000; addition/remodeling: $25,000 *WPA* grant and $5,000 county funds. US 60, 1.5 m. E of river. *(County Profiles)*

Cave Spring Onyx Cavern. Shown as a religious *cave.* Guided tours by flashlight highlight formations named Angel's Wing, Jesus, and Moses; secular ones include Octopus, Monkey, and Possum. US 60, W 2 m.

Ellsinore, Mo. Established c. 1888 along the grade of the Cape Girardeau–Southwestern *Railroad,* the town immediately overshadowed nearby Crites.[1] Ellsinore was frequently spelled Elsinore, which adds to the uncertainty of its place-name. Two possibilities are that it was named (1) for the fort and Danish town in Shakespeare's "Hamlet" or (2) for local schoolteacher

Joseph Pace's two daughters, Elsie and Nora. The former is a common place-name; the latter represents a method of combining names that is also common. Both could be correct, which also is not uncommon. Post offices: Crits [*sic*] 1886–1887; Crites 1887–1888; Ellsinore 1888–now. US 60, E 21 m. OZARK *TRAIL:* Victory section. PINEWOODS LAKE CAMPGROUND / PICNIC AREA *(National Forests):* Tables, fireplaces, grills, vault toilets, 30-acre Pinewoods Lake: bass, sunfish, catfish; electric motors only.

Fremont, Mo. Established c. 1887 after completion here of the Kansas City, Fort Scott & Memphis *Railroad,* Fremont was known by its post office name, Peggy,[2] and station name, McDonald,[3] until the St. Louis & San Francisco acquired track rights and changed the name in 1907 to Fremont *(Post Offices).* Two namesakes are suggested: (1) John C. Frémont *(Stockton)* and (2) Jackie Freeman, who established a sawmill here c. 1887 and whose name was combined with a local landmark (Fre + mont for mountain). Post offices: Peggy 1888–1907; Fremont 1907–now. US 60, W 11 m. FREMONT TOWER PICNIC AREA *(National Forests):* Grills, pit toilets, water, abandoned fire tower. PECK RANCH *WILDLIFE AREA.*

Natural Areas. All except Cupola Pond and Red Maple are in Peck Ranch *Wildlife Area.* Winona 65588. CUPOLA POND: US 60, W 10 m.; SR J, S approx. 13 m.; FR 3224, E approx. 1.2 m.; FR 4823, N approx. 1.5 m. *(Doniphan).* GOLDEN SEAL: 100 acres. Along Mill Creek in a bottomland forest of well-drained soil, this wildlife refuge features witch hazel and swamp dog-wood. HEADWATERS STREAM: 486 acres; seven miles of Rogers Creek with a 200 yd. buffer zone. This is reportedly the best and least disturbed Ozark spring-fed stream, featuring shaded banks, a *shut-in*, short pools, and well-defined riffles. MULE HOLLOW GLADE: 44 acres. This wildlife refuge features about 20 acres of dolomite glade, supporting interesting plants and animals. RED MAPLE: US 60, W 5 m.; SR C, S approx. 7 m. to Eastwood;[4] continue SR C, S approx. 10.6 m. (approx. 1.7 m. S of E–W GR junction); sign *(Doniphan)*. SINKHOLE POND: 1 acre. Also known as Grassy Pond. This quarter-acre pond is a breeding place for several species of frogs and salamanders; it is thickly vegetated with only small areas of open water. **Recreation.** MILLER COMMUNITY LAKE: 27 acres. Bass, sunfish, crappie. US 60, E 7 m.; SR 21, N 1.4 m.; GR, E 0.2 m. OZARK NATIONAL SCENIC RIVER-WAYS: Includes Big Spring (above), the Current and Jacks Fork Rivers *(float streams)*, as well as campsites, picnic facilities, and river access at Cataract Landing, Chilton Creek, Hawes, Hickory Landing, and Water-cress Park *(National Parks)*. Adjacent. WATERCRESS SPRING CAMPGROUND / PICNIC AREA / TRAILS *(National Forests)*: Water, toilets, Current River fishing, swimming, boating, and Songbird Trail. Other area *trails*: the Between the Rivers section of the Ozark Trail and Skyline Trail.

Skyline Automobile Loop. 4.1 m. loop. Broad views of hardwood-pine ridges, hollows, Van Buren (1.5 m.), granite-topped Stegall Mountain (1.7 m.), a 1,020-foot ridge (2.6 m.), Spring valley (3.9 m.). Begin: SR 103, S 1.2 m. to Skyline Dr. (FR 3280). End: FR 3280 at SR 103 (1.25 m. S of beginning).

1. Early settler Solomon Crites.
2. Origin unknown.
3. Origin unknown.
4. Joint property owner H. H. Eastwood; p.o. Montay or Montag, origin unknown but possibly from Montop, an Algonquian term that via folk etymology is commonly accepted as meaning hope (e.g. Montop Hill, R.I.), 1911; Eastwood 1911–1923.

VERSAILLES

Population: 2,365   Map E-4

The town was platted in 1835 after being named and selected in 1834 as a central location for county seat of Morgan County, replacing temporary county seat Millville.[1] Versailles's namesake is disputed: it could be either (1) Versailles, France, honoring the French for aid during the Revolutionary War, and in keeping with the 19th-century style for exotic place-names *(Vienna)*, or (2) 1792 Versailles, Ky., due to the large number of

Kentucky immigrants. The Kentucky Versailles was named by town trustee Gen. Marquis Calmes, indi-rectly honoring the Marquis de La Fayette *(Fayette)*, under whom he served during the Revolutionary War, and directly honoring France for its aid during the war. Regardless, locally the name is pronounced Ver'sales, not Ver'sigh. The town grew at a major crossroads as a political and trading center aided by the c. 1872 com-pletion of a branch of the Missouri-Pacific *Railroad* con-necting it to *Boonville* at the Missouri River. Post offices: Millville 1834–1835; Versailles 1835–now.

Architecture. Two fires, in 1886 and 1887, nearly destroyed the downtown. A few good 19th-century structures remain.

Barnett, Mo. Barnett was established c. 1875 as a post office community (replacing Stone House, below) by a man named Lusk, who named it Barnettsville for his deceased son, Barnett. The name was shortened to Barnetts, then Barnett. Post offices: Barnettsville 1875–1880; Barnett 1880–now. SR 52, E 13 m. STONE HOUSE / STONE HOUSE, MO.: Vernacular, pre–1858. Built by Scottish immigrant Hiram Madole, who soon forfeited it for debts owed to Milton McDow, this two-story cut-stone house, the c. 1858 community's name-sake, also served as a post office. Post offices: Stone House 1858–1863, 1866–1875; Lodema[2] 1894–1905. SR 52, W 2.25 m., S of railroad.

Butterfield Overland Stage. Two marked sites: (1) SR 135 at Florence.[3] SR D, N 5.2 m.; SR BB, N 10 m. (2) US 50, N side of Front St. at Syracuse.[4] SR D, N 18.3 m. *(Overland Mail Company)*

Jacob's Cave. Billed as the area's largest cave with the world's largest geode; a variety of large formations, pools, a half-mile concrete walkway. SR 5, S 6.5 m.

Lake of the Ozarks. SR 5, S 8 m. to *Gravois Mills*.

Martin Hotel / Museum. Vernacular, c. 1878; National Historic Register. This 26-room two-story frame hotel and stagecoach stop replaced an 1851 log tavern that was enlarged in 1853 by Samuel Martin, who then renamed it the Martin Hotel. It remained in the family until sold in 1972 to the county as a museum. Displays include 19th-century furniture and kitchen appliances, war items (Civil War–modern), Martin family heir-looms, and local historical items. 120 N. Monroe.

Morgan County Courthouse. Second Empire, 1889; National Historic Register. The county's third, this large two-story courthouse emphasizes its style's monumental proportions with a full-height central projecting entry, four corner pavilions with mansard roofs pierced by dormers, and rows of narrow arched windows with ornate drip molding. Downtown. *(County Profiles)*

Stover, Mo. Established in 1875 on an important east–west road, the town was aided by the 1904 arrival of the St. Louis, Kansas City & Colorado *Railroad*, which also precipitated the founding of the separate railroad town Newstover.[5] Both towns were named for local congressman J. H. Stover. Post office: 1875–now. SR 52, W 8 m. BIG BUFFALO CREEK MARSH NATURAL AREA: SR FF at GR; GR, W 0.9 m. to fish hatchery (*Cole Camp*). BOYLERS MILL, MO.: The community was established c. 1852 at James Byler's first *gristmill* and named for him. The spelling of the name was corrupted by the postmaster general, who returned the approved post office application as Boylers Mill. The setting, at a bluff and Buffalo Creek, is nostalgic; derelict c. 1895. Incidentally, the mill's waterwheel still turns—at Silver Dollar City (*Branson*). Post office: 1852–1922. SR 52, W 2 m.; SR FF, S 8 m. *WILDLIFE AREAS:* Big Buffalo Creek, Carpenter.

1. J. S. Walton's mill; derelict.
2. Also spelled Loedema; origin unknown.
3. Platted in 1832 as Williamsville (town founder; no p.o.), then changed in 1840 to its post office name, Florence (origin unknown; p.o. 1839–now).
4. Named Pacific City in 1857 (for the Pacific RR); due to an existing *Pacific*, changed to Syracuse in 1858, for 1825 Syracuse, N.Y., named for the Greek city; p.o. 1858–now.
5. *Post office* 1904–1905; derelict.

VIENNA

Population: 611   Map F-5

An 1868 courthouse fire destroyed the county records. Platted in 1855 as a central location for county seat of newly organized Maries County, the town was named for the capital of Austria, following a popular 19th-century trend of choosing large foreign capitals and/or exotic place-names (*La Plata*). A local story based on a vague 19th-century historical account claims the 1855 county judge suggested the name of a deceased young woman in his family, Vie Anna, but a commissioner, "thinking the course unwise," yet wanting to avoid direct confrontation, named it for the Austrian capital. Reportedly, some old-timers still use the pronunciation Vie Anna. Vianna (but not Vie Anna) was a relatively common 19th-century feminine name, e.g. Vianna, Clark County, Ky. (named before 1860), which, while shown on postal records and maps as Vienna, was locally spelled and pronounced Vianna. Probably residents of Vienna, Mo., pronounced the town name Vie Anna for their own reasons and, later, historians tried to justify it. Poking fun at anything fancy (*Versailles*), playfulness with words (*Sparta: Honey Branch Cave: Ongo*), humor (*Springfield: Needmore*), and exasperation (*Bunker: Rat*) have inspired many Missouri place-names. Bypassed

by railroads, Vienna grew slowly as a county trading and political center. Post office: 1856–now.

Brinktown, Mo. Originally named Viessmann's Station, the settlement was established by landowner Wolfgang Viessmann, who donated land in 1874 to the Catholic church, which then established a mission here. Since no railroad is nearby, presumably "Station" was intended in its late 18th-century sense of a settlement of several families. Later shortened to Viessmann (*Post Offices*), the name was changed in 1903 to honor the local Brink family. Reportedly, Anna Marie Brink, on condition the town would be renamed Brinktown, helped finance the c. 1903 construction of the Catholic church. Post offices: Viessmann 1890–1903; Brinktown 1903–now. SR V, S 7.5 m.; SR N, W 3.1 m. TAFF SCHOOL: Log, date unknown; reroofed 1895. Built by Bill Taff, this one-room one-story one-teacher schoolhouse is a good example of its type. SR 133, N approx. 3.3 m.; W side.

City Cemetery. The older section has ornate and sentimental markers, including a nearly life-size c. 1911 statue of a grieving lady. John and Amanda Felker (Old Jail Museum, below) and their nine-month-old daughter (who died in 1858) are buried here. US 63 at SR 42; SR 42, W 0.5 m. (*Cemeteries*)

Courthouse Art Collection. About 40 original artworks by local artists focus on Maries County: its structures, environment, and people and their daily lives. In the courthouse (below).

Gasconade River. *Float Streams.*

Latham House / Park. Log, 1855; restored. Reassembled here in 1979, this two-story structure, Vienna's first, has been used as a home, polling place, icehouse, and barn. At Community Park (picnic, tennis, playground). US 63 at SR 42; US 63, N to Ballpark Rd., then E 0.25 m.

Maries County Courthouse. Moderne, 1940–1942. The county's third, this three-story 115-by-80-foot stone-and-concrete courthouse was built in two phases; the new jail is on top (Old Jail Museum, below). Cost: $76,000 ($50,000 *WPA* funding). Downtown. (*County Profiles*)

Old Jail Museum. Vernacular, 1855–1856. This two-story limestone jail served the county until c. 1941. Upstairs, the original cells still have prisoners' graffiti; the sheriff and his family lived downstairs. Displays include mastodon bones, vintage photographs, 19th-century furniture, hundreds of items such as dolls, tools, dishes, a spinning wheel, guns, and the tombstone of George Wussler, who while watching a Maries County Civil War battle was killed by a stray bullet (ironically, he was the battle's only fatality). US 63 at SR 42; E 3 blocks. FELKER HOUSE: Log, 1854–1855; restored (City Cemetery, above).

Used as a residence and a saloon; furnished. Adjacent.

Paydown, Mo. SR 42, E 5.3 m. to Bend;[1] continue SR 42, E 4.4 m. *(Belle)*

Swinging Bridge. Suspension, 1930. Built 16 feet above the Maries River, this 200-foot-long bridge is still used today. US 63 at SR 42; US 63, N to Ballpark Rd., then W 2 m. *(Suspension Bridges)*

Vichy, Mo. Platted in 1880 as a spa and named for the French resort town famous for its water, this town was destroyed by an 1886 tornado. Today, the springs barely flow. Post office: 1880–now. US 63, S 13.4 m. SPRING CREEK GAP NATURAL AREA: 40 acres. Part of Spring Creek Gap *State Forest*. Features small dolomite glades and colorful flowers, e.g. yellow coneflowers. Box 509 (Junction E and Y), Rolla 65401. US 63, N 2.5 m. to unmarked road; sign. SPRING CREEK GAP *STATE FOREST*.

1. Area known as The Bend, location at bend of Gasconade River; p.o. 1900–1917.

WAR OF 1812

This 1812–1815 war with Great Britain was primarily caused by and resolved by the 1802–1815 Napoleonic War *(Louisiana Purchase)*. Demands for war with Britain accelerated after the 1807 British Orders in Council required that anything being shipped to French territory (most of Europe at that time) first clear a British port. The 1810 U.S. congressional election sent prowar representatives to Washington, and a coalition of western and southern states helped pass a June 12, 1812, declaration of war. The senate vote was 19 to 13, with the New England states opposed because of commercial ties with England and because they thought America ill-prepared for war. Historians disagree about what motivated westerners and southerners, but the following were factors: (1) Indian attacks, intensifying after 1805 *(Black Hack War)*, blamed on British instigation *(Lancaster: Tippecanoe)*; (2) an economic depression blamed on Britain's shipping restrictions; and (3) a desire for expansion, both to Canada and to Florida (a possession of British ally Spain). Ironically, Britain repealed the Orders in Council two days before America's declaration of war, but news of it was several weeks late. Sporadic and desultory peace negotiations began in 1812, but the war continued with British sea power dominating the American coastline after 1813. Major battles were fought at Detroit (where Tecumseh was killed in 1813; *Danville: Williamsburg; Gainesville: Tecumseh)* and east along the Canadian border, at Lake Erie *(County*

Profiles: Perry), Washington, D.C. (which was partially burned), Baltimore (where Francis Scott Key wrote "The Star Spangled Banner"), and Florida (where Andrew Jackson defeated the Creek Indians who were part of Tecumseh's confederacy; *Seminole Wars)*. Peace, achieved on December 24, 1814, with the Treaty of Ghent, restored the prewar boundaries with no reparations. This treaty was signed after the May 30, 1814, Treaty of Paris, ending the Napoleonic War, which, in effect, resolved America's grievances. The Battle of New Orleans, a dramatic American victory (casualties: 2,000 British, 100 American) organized by Jackson, was fought 15 days after the Treaty of Ghent. Reportedly an incentive for Americans to forgive the British, who had dominated the war, this victory at New Orleans stimulated a surge of national pride and optimism that precipitated, among other national efforts, the movement toward western expansion, which was aided in part by government land grants called Bounty Certificates *(New Madrid: New Madrid Earthquake)*.

In Missouri, the war resulted in Indian attacks that severely restricted work, travel, and immigration to the state. The only federal help available was paperwork like that issued by Benjamin A. Howard, the 1810–1812 governor of the Territory of Upper Louisiana *(County Profiles: Howard)*, authorizing the organization of military companies but offering no supplies or equipment. Settlers built forts *(Boonville: Fort Cole)* and organized military companies like the U.S. Rangers *(Mineola: Callaway Grave Site)*. Over 30 forts were built, usually through the addition of vertical log palisades to existing log houses, but still a large number of men, women, and children were killed during the war. After Tecumseh's death in 1813, the frequency of the attacks subsided, but friction, often resulting in death, continued well after the 1814 treaty.

WARRENSBURG
Population: 15,244   Map D-4

County commissioners platted the town in 1836 (the plat was filed in 1837) as a central location for county seat of newly organized Johnson County after complaints about the inconvenient location of their first choice, Columbus.[1] According to local tradition, the future townsite was known as Warren's Corner for early settler Martin Warren, who was at the site when it was platted (Architecture, below); the commissioners changed the name to Warrensburg in 1836. Growing first as a major crossroads trading center, the town boomed after the 1864 arrival of the Pacific

Railroad despite several Civil War skirmishes and occupation of the courthouse by both sides (Old Johnson County Courthouse, below). Post office: 1837–now. Home of Central Missouri State University, founded in 1871 as State Normal School No. 2, and Warrensburg Area Vo-Tech. Historical tour maps: chamber of commerce, US 50B, S on Holden (116 N).

Architecture. Good examples of 19th- and early 20th-century styles, e.g. the courthouse (below), railroad depot (Richardsonian Romanesque, 1889), and Christ Presbyterian Church (Gothic Revival, 1910), are along a loop beginning at Holden and Gay (US 50B, S on Holden to Gay), then S on Holden, E on South, N on College, W on Gay to Holden (Warren's blacksmith's shop was at College and Gay). Examples are also on Pine (paralleling the railroad W from Holden to Water).

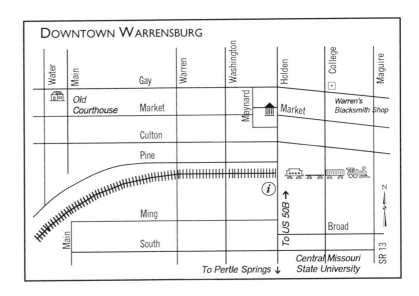

Chilhowee, Mo. Established at Simpson's Store c. 1855, Chilhowee was named for a Tennessee town whose place-name came from an important Cherokee town in Tennessee. The name's Cherokee meaning is unknown. Post offices: Simpson's Store[2] 1855–1859; Chilhowee 1859–1862, 1869–now. SR 13, S 13 m.; SR 2, W 6 m. ARCHITECTURE: Downtown proposed for National Historic Register.

Grover Memorial Park. Tennis, pool, picnic areas, volleyball, ball fields. US 50, S on Maguire, E on Gay; sign.

Heritage Museum / Library. Features statistical records, an 1866–1936 newspaper collection, and rotating exhibits of county items. US 50B, S on Holden, W on Gay to Main (300 N.).

Johnson County Courthouse. Richardsonian Romanesque, 1896–1898; National Historic Register. The county's third, this 84-by-104-foot three-story sandstone courthouse has ornate square corner towers, spring arches, arched windows, a central domed tower, and polychrome stonework. The Goddess of Liberty, a statue above the entrance, holds a silver ball that was originally gold until 1897 free-silver advocates surreptitiously replaced it. Architect G. E. McDonald designed nearly identical courthouses for Andrew, Bates, and Lawrence Counties. Cost: $50,585. Grounds: Old Drum statue (Old Johnson County Courthouse, below). US 50, S on Holden to Market. (*County Profiles*)

Knob Noster, Mo. Established c. 1846, the town was named for a nearby isolated knob (*Balds and Knobs*) on the *prairie*. While some attribute the name, originally spelled Knobnoster, to a coined English-Latin combination, meaning *our knob*, most sources believe it is a product of folk etymology based on an Indian word for the landmark. Post offices: Knobnoster 1846–1941; Knob Noster[3] 1941–now. US 50, E 9 m. KNOB NOSTER *STATE PARK*: SR 132, S 1.2 m. PIN OAK SLOUGH NATURAL AREA: 4 acres. Part of Knob Noster State Park (above). Features a mature wet-mesic forest, a buttonbush shrub swamp, silver maple, and burr, pin, and swamp white oak. Knob Noster 65336. PERRY *WILDLIFE AREA*. WHITEMAN AIR FORCE BASE: Activated in 1942 as a glider base. Today its primary mission is strategic bombing that includes use of the B-2 bomber aircraft (Stealth). Two aircraft displays: B-52 at SR J gate; B-29 at SR DD gate. Tours by arrangement. SR J, S 2 m.

Old Drum. The 1869 shooting death of a black-and-tan hound, Old Drum, and a subsequent series of trials for monetary damages culminated in the dog owner's 1870 victory and lawyer G. G. Vest's most remembered speech, wherein, after quoting the Bible and poetry (and ignoring all previous testimony), he eulogized Old Drum, raising the hound to a universal Man's Best Friend. Of the five lawyers at this trial, all were later prominent: 1881–1885 Missouri governor T. T. Crittenden, U.S. senators F. M. Cockrell and Vest, Wabash Railroad president W. H. Blodgett, and U.S. congressman and federal judge J. F. Phillips. Vest, using florid oratory, closed his summation by placing Old Drum hypothetically at his master's grave: "his head between his paws, his eyes sad but open in alert watchfulness, faithful and true even to death." Bronze statue of Old Drum and text at courthouse (above); plaque at old courthouse (below).

Old Johnson County Courthouse. Adamesque, 1838–1840; restored using original plans; National Historic Register. This simple three-ranked two-story red-brick structure (stuccoed in 1867 and 1976) has corner chimneys, a hipped roof, arched entrance, and semicircular fanlight. It served as a courthouse until 1871, when the town shifted southeast to the railroad. Owned since 1965 by the county historical society, it features 19th-century furniture (some original and pre-1870), 1840–1869 lithographs, the original north door, an 1846 public well, an 1840s brick sidewalk, locust trees planted in 1858, and pines and maples from c. 1867. US 50B; S on Holden, W on Gay to Main.

Pertle Springs. Reportedly the water from this early 1880s resort cured dyspepsia (indigestion) and kidney and liver ailments; it was bottled and shipped nationwide. The assembly hall (capacity 5,000) featured personalities like William Jennings Bryan and Carry A. Nation *(Belton)*. Decline in the belief in and popularity of mineral water ended the health resort's prosperity during the 1930s (some remnants remain along a dirt trail through woods). Today: picnic areas, small fishing and canoeing lakes, heated outdoor pool, golf, trails. SR DD at Holden; S on Pertle Springs Rd. approx. 0.4 m.

US 50 Silo. A tree inside a former grain silo has grown up and through it, bursting out like an arboreal Titan missile. US 50, E 3 m.

1. Christopher Columbus; p.o. 1837–1839, 1849–1920; Blackwater, the river, descriptive, 1839–1845; US 50, W 10.6 m.; SR M, N 3 m.

2. The store owner.

3. While this spelling flies in the face of late 19th-century *post office* directives, the name was probably made two words due to the pendulous effect on the uninitiated of trying to pronounce it all at first glance.

WARRENTON
Population: 3,596   Map G-4

The commission appointed in 1833 by the state legislature to find a site for the county seat of newly organized Warren County failed to agree unanimously on New Boston,[1] which was near today's Hopewell *(Marthasville)*. The court continued to meet at 1814 settler Mordecai Morgan's house in today's Warrenton at the *Boonslick Trail* until a second commission accepted land in 1835 donated by Morgan and Henry Walton for a county seat. Named for the county namesake *(County Profiles: Warren)*, Warrenton grew as a crossroads trading center and political center that was aided by the 1857 arrival of the North Missouri *Railroad* at Truesdale (below). Post offices: Taylor's[2] 1827–1833; Logan[3] 1833–1836; Warrenton 1836–now.

Architecture. Good examples of 19th-century structures, especially downtown, include the Schowengerdt House (Vernacular, 1867; tower added 1892; National Historic Register) on Main St.

Boonslick Trail. The route entered town from the east (SR M), then cut through town along Main. Marker across from courthouse (below). *(Boonslick Trails)*

Little Lost Creek State Forest. *State Forests.*

Truesdale, Mo. The town was platted in 1856 by railroad surveyor William Truesdale, anticipating the 1857 arrival of the North Missouri *Railroad*. Today it shares city limits with Warrenton. Post office: 1889–1979. SR M, E; adjacent. REIFSNIDER *STATE FOREST*. WHITE OAK NATURAL AREA: 22 acres. Part of Reifsnider *State Forest*. Features c. 120-year-old white oaks growing predominately in Lindley loam, a *loess* derivative. Box 147, Warrenton 63383. SR M, E 2.2 m.; Schuetzen Ground Rd., S 3.2 m.

Warren County Courthouse. Italianate, 1869–1871; National Historic Register. The county's second (a separate modern building is located behind), this two-story brick-and-stone courthouse features quoins, a cupola, brackets, first-story Corinthian columns, arched entries and windows, ornate drip molding, and a hipped roof. Downtown; SR 47, W on Main. *(County Profiles)*

Warren County Museum. Features rotating displays of local historical items and memorabil-

Pertle Springs, c. 1899. (FROM "COLUMBIA MISSOURI HERALD")

ia of Central Wesleyan College (1864–1941). S of courthouse (below); Market at Walton.

Wright City, Mo. Platted in 1857 along the North Missouri *Railroad* by Dr. H. C. Wright. Post office: 1858–now. I-70, E 7 m. HARMONY LUTHERAN CHURCH: Gothic Revival, reportedly 1843. This frame church features tall gothic windows, a gothic door, and a bell tower with an ornate cornice; the adjacent *cemetery* has old and ornate markers mostly inscribed in German. SR F, S approx. 7 m.; Strack Church Rd.; N 1.5 m. KENNEDY FORT / *CEMETERY:* Revolutionary War soldier and 1808 settler Thomas Kennedy (1739–1841) built a *War of 1812* fort about two and half miles north of the *Boonslick Trail*. He is buried, along with two War of 1812 veterans, at Kennedy Cemetery (0.3 m. N). S side; I-70 frontage road, E to city limits (approx. 1.3 m. E of downtown); GR, S 0.6 m. to just N of 1st intersection.

1. Boston, Mass.; no p.o.; defunct.
2. Early settler.
3. Early settler.

WARSAW

Population: 1,696   Map E-5

Warsaw was platted in 1837 at a bend in the Osage River as a central location for county seat of newly organized Benton County after competition with two nearby sites: Bledsoe's Ferry[1] and the original Fristoe.[2] In keeping with the early 19th century's romantic notions about revolutions, the 1838 county court named it for the capital of Poland, indirectly honoring Polish patriot Tadeusz Kosciuszko (English spelling, Thaddeus Kosciusko; e.g. Kosciusko County, Ind., whose county seat is Warsaw), who served under Greene County namesake Gen. Nathanael Greene during the American Revolution and fought unsuccessfully against the 1793 second partition of Poland by Prussia and Russia. Missouri's Warsaw, a thriving steamboat port at a major crossroads, prospered despite Union occupation during the *Civil War.* The establishment in 1879 of the short-line Sedalia, Warsaw & Southern *Railroad* to *Sedalia* helped stabilize its economic base after the decline of traffic on the unpredictable Osage River. Post offices: Benton (*Benton*) 1835–1839; Warsaw 1839–now. Butterfield (*Overland Mail Company*) stage route.

Architecture. Remodeled examples of mid-19th-century downtown structures include Christian Church (c. 1860, used as a Union hospital and stables), State St., 1 block S of courthouse; Reser Funeral Home (c. 1840, former hotel and Union commissary), 105 W.

Main; Old Dutch Fort (1845, former dry-goods store), 4 blocks N of Reser Funeral Home; and the 1856 county jail (ironically, built as the Mechanic's Bank of St. Louis; used as a Union armory), Van Buren at Washington.

Benton County Courthouse. Italianate, 1886–1887; additions 1950, 1974. The county's third (the first was log), this two-story three-ranked red-brick courthouse has typical Italianate detailing: a belt course, tall narrow arched windows with brick window crowns, and a low-pitched hip roof with brick-bracketed eaves. Cost: $9,089. Downtown; Main. (*County Profiles*)

Benton County Museum. Vernacular, 1886 (north half); additions 1907, 1915. This former two-story four-room brick schoolhouse, abandoned in 1924, has rooms and displays exhibiting 19th-century items and furnishings: a dentist's office, parlor, school, chapel, bank, bedroom, barbershop, and kitchen, as well as costumes (e.g. quilts, dresses), war memorabilia, an unusual 13-star American flag (a star in each corner and one enclosed in a circle of eight), taxidermy items, and equipment (e.g. tools, a saddle). Main at Benton; Benton N approx. 4 blocks.

Little Tebo Stream Piracy. A three-mile stretch of US 65 just north of its junction with SR 7 runs through a dry valley once occupied by Little Tebo Creek, which formerly entered the Osage River about one mile northeast of town. Captured by an Osage tributary at Kaysinger Bluff (at the dam), Little Tebo took a five-and-half-mile shortcut. Incidentally the dam at Truman Reservoir (Recreation, below), originally named Kaysinger Bluff Dam in 1964, was reportedly renamed for political reasons. (*Stream Piracy*)

Old City Cemetery. Markers date from the early 1800s; the lid of a tall zinc marker lifts, revealing an obituary and picture of the deceased. Downtown; E approx. 10 blocks on Jackson. (*Cemeteries*)

Recreation. HARRY S. TRUMAN RESERVOIR: Adjacent. Truman Visitor Center: SR 7 at US 65; US 65, N 1 m.; Dam Access Rd., W 1 m.; overlooks dam and reservoir (*Lakes: Corps of Engineers*). HARRY S. TRUMAN STATE PARK: SR 7, W 6 m.; SR UU, N 2.8 m.

Swinging Bridge / Park. BRIDGE: Repaired and replaced since 1895, it was closed in 1979 to all motorized traffic when the adjacent concrete one was completed. SR 7, W side of town (*Suspension Bridges*). PARK: Ball field, pool (and baby pool), picnic facilities, camping, boat ramp, tennis; 16-inch iron rings used for mooring steamboats (W of the bridge at river). SR 7 at Jackson.

1. Owner Lewis Bledsoe; also known as Osage, for the tribe via the river (*County Profiles: Osage*); no p.o.; defunct.
2. Located about 0.75 m. E of the Springfield *Road* and Fristoe's ferry at the Osage; owner Markham Fristoe; no p.o.; defunct.

WASHINGTON

Population: 10,704   Map H-4

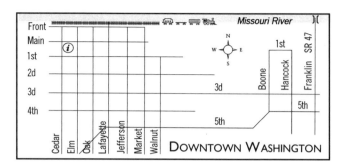

Established c. 1822 by W. G. Owens and named for George Washington, this Missouri River ferry landing was initially a business competitor of nearby Newport, the Franklin County seat (Dundee, below). Owens's plat and the 1829 sale of lots were held in abeyance by questions of clear title after his death in 1834. Mrs. Lucinda Owens successfully cleared the titles and filed the town plat in 1839. Continued immigration of Germans (Hermann), the 1849 California gold rush (St. Charles), and a successful transition in 1855 from steamboats to the Pacific Railroad helped the town prosper as a manufacturing and shipping point. Post offices: Bosscia[1] 1837–1840; Washington 1837, 1840–now. Home of Four Rivers Area Vo-Tech. Tours and maps: chamber of commerce, 323 W. Main; SR 47; W on 3d, N on Cedar to Main.

Architecture. This excellent architectural tour town has a number of structures reflecting its German heritage. The downtown area (especially between Front, Cedar, 5th, and Jefferson) has many good examples of 1830s–1880s German-style houses, buildings, and churches (older houses are set at the street with gardens and fruit trees beside and behind them).

Corncob Pipe Factory. Henry Tibbe produced the world's first lathe-turned corncob pipe in 1872 at a nearby shop and in 1878 patented a plaster of paris process for a smoother and more durable bowl. Beginning in 1883 this building, now Missouri Meerschaum, was used by Tibbe and his son Anton, whose work helped nickname the town Corncob Capital of the World. Memorabilia at office; no factory tours. Downtown; Front at Cedar.

Dundee, Mo. Originally named Newport,[2] this river port was county seat of Franklin County from 1819 to 1827 and then declined after losing the seat of justice to Union and its river trade to Washington. Platted again in 1857 along the Pacific Railroad, it was renamed for its location on Point Dundee, whose namesake is uncertain but could possibly honor Dundee, Scotland, or pre-1846 Dundee, Ky. Post offices: Newport 1820–1857; Dundee 1857–1908. SR 100, W 8 m. JOHN COLTER'S GRAVE SITE: The Pacific Railroad blasted a tunnel in 1855 under the bluff of Newport's pioneer cemetery; later, to make room for the 1926 double track of the Missouri-Pacific Railroad, most of the bluff and all of the neglected cemetery were cut away. Colter, buried here in 1818, accompanied the 1804–1806 Lewis and Clark Expedition. Leaving it on the return trip, he was the first white person to explore the Grand Tetons, the upper reaches of the Big Horn River, and Wyoming's

Yellowstone country (Defiance: Boone Home). Approx. 0.5 m. N to RR; follow the tracks W approx. 350 yds. to W side of Little Boeuf Creek.

Katy Trail State Park. SR 47 at river; SR 47, N 3 m.; SR TT, N 0.4 m. (State Parks)

Museums. CALDWELL / FRANKLIN COUNTY: Folk Victorian, 1879. This two-story side-gabled frame house contains historical items as well as memorabilia and furnishings of the Kindead Calwell family (Kindead was the county's first settler). Cemetery adjacent. SR 100 at SR 47; SR 47, S 0.9 m.; Bieker Rd., E 2.2 m. WASHINGTON HISTORICAL SOCIETY: Local historical items, tours. Downtown; Main at Cedar.

New Haven, Mo. Established in 1836 as a Missouri River port by Philip Miller and known as Millers Landing, the site was platted as such in 1856 after the 1855 arrival of the Pacific Railroad. When it was incorporated in 1858 the name was changed for unknown reasons to New Haven, honoring New Haven, Conn., which was named in 1640 for the English channel port, haven meaning port in obsolete English usage. Post offices: Blishs Mills[3] 1850–1855; Millers Landing 1855–1858; New Haven 1858–now. SR 100, W 12 m. ARCHITECTURE: Good examples of 19th-century styles, especially on the ridge overlooking town; downtown has a single line of vernacular 19th-century stores facing the railroad and bluff. EDELWEISS WINERY: Since 1979. Dry, semidry, and sweet wines; tasting. SR 100, W 0.25 m. LEVEE: Built in 1955 by the Corps of Engineers; park benches, scenic view of the river, caboose, historical marker.

Parks. KROG: Picnic facilities, playground, restrooms. SR 47 near bridge at 5th. NEW CITY PARK: 13-acre fishing lake, restrooms, ball fields, picnic shelters, playground, tennis. Adjacent to and W of Old City Park. OLD CITY PARK: Pool, ball fields, playground, restrooms, picnic area. Downtown; W on 2d to High. RENNICK RIVERFRONT: Picnic shelters, restrooms, river overlook. Downtown at river (E of Lafayette at Front).

1. P.o. for adjacent 1836 Polish town Bassora; origin unknown; also known as Goosetown for its geese; later absorbed by Washington.

2. Probably 1792 Newport, Ky., county seat of Campbell County, named for Capt. Christopher Newport, 1607 commander of ships transporting original Jamestown settlers; *Union.*

3. Mill owner.

WAYNESVILLE
Population: 3,207   Map F-5

Nearly all county records were destroyed in a 1903 courthouse fire. At nearby Roubidoux Creek a small c. 1826 settlement grew around a mill, shifting in 1831 toward squatter G. W. Gibson's site near a spring at the Kickapoo Trace (later Old Wire *Road,* then *Route 66*). As the only settlement in the county, it served as temporary county seat when Pulaski County was organized in 1833. Platted and named in 1839 for its 1834 post office, which honors Revolutionary War general Anthony Wayne *(County Profiles: Wayne),* the town was approved in 1843 as permanent county seat. Land-locked and bypassed by railroads *(Crocker),* it grew slowly (1873 est. pop. 100; 1940 pop. 468). The construction in 1940 of Fort Leonard Wood (St. Robert, below) helped create a solid economic base. Post office: Waynesville 1834–now. Home of Waynesville Area Vo-Tech. *(Route 66)*

Devils Elbow, Mo. This 1920s resort community was named for its location, a tight horseshoe bend of the Big Piney River named by frustrated loggers whose long log rafts had to be divided to negotiate the curve. Post office: 1927–now. I-44 at SR 28 (3 m. E of St. Robert, below); SR 28, S 0.1 m. to SR Z; SR Z, E 1 m. (note four-lane stretch of *Route 66* that replaced old concrete route), then SE 1 m. (note curbing that caused more accidents than it prevented). DEVILS ELBOW: Adjacent. DEVIL'S SUGAR BOWL: A massive semi-cylindrical limestone formation with a conical top was formed by weathering and jointing of the area's 200-foot dolomite bluffs. In bluffs along descent to town. *FLOAT STREAMS:* Big Piney and Gasconade Rivers. *ROUTE 66* SIGHTS: Allman's Market, Grand View Store, Munger-Moss Barbecue, Roubidoux Wood-workers, 1923 truss bridge, stone wall. In town.

Old County Courthouse / Museum. Italian Renaissance (Towered), 1903–1904; National Historic Register. The county's third courthouse, this two-story 60-by-40-foot brick structure, while departing from the pattern-book style, has all the elements: overhanging eaves, brackets, varying window treatments, arched windows with crowns (some paired), a three-story flat-roofed tower with paired arched windows, balustrades accompanied by a two-story six-sided wing with a shallow hip roof, and arched windows. Architect H. H. Hohenschild designed a similarly esoteric adaptation

for Osage County. Cost: $10,240 (insurance and general funds). MUSEUM: Displays local historical artifacts. Adjacent to new courthouse (below).

Old Stagecoach Stop. Weatherboard Log, antebellum; remodeled, additions 1894; National Historic Register. The original dogtrot log cabin had a second story and weatherboard added. This stagecoach stop and tavern served as a Union hospital in 1862–1865 after Federal colonel Franz Sigel captured the town; enlarged as a hotel in 1894. Across from old courthouse (above).

Pulaski County Courthouse. 1980s Modern; corner-stone laid 1989, dedicated 1990. The county's fourth (Old County Courthouse, above), construction for this three-story brick courthouse was barely approved by voters (1,113 to 1,000) in August 1987, after failing in February 1987 (1,249 to 1,373). State-of-the-art computers and courtroom security help place this building firmly in the 20th century. The jail, built in 1975, was incorporated into the courthouse's design. Cost: $4.4 million. Downtown; adjacent to the former courthouse. *(County Profiles)*

Route 66 Sights. ARCHITECTURE: Many bars, cafes, and other structures east and west of Roubidoux Creek. I-44 Loop and SR 17. SCENIC DRIVE: I-44 at SR 17 and Buckhorn, Mo.;[1] SR 17, S 3.5 m.; SR AB, W 7 m. to Hazelgreen.[2] In Hazelgreen are several period buildings, including Gascozark Courts; nearby (W about 1.8 m.) are remnants of Eden Resort and a Gasconade River truss bridge. *(Route 66)*

St. Robert, Mo. Originally a small community of Dunkards *(Bethel: Cherry Box),* whose reputation for piety resulted in the area being nicknamed Gospel Ridge (later Eastside, for the east side of Waynesville), the town was platted and incorporated in 1951 as St. Robert, a name inspired by Father Robert Arnold, who during the 1940s helped establish a Catholic parish for personnel at Fort Leonard Wood (below). The area's first Catholic church was dedicated in 1951 as St. Robert Bellarmine, for a Jesuit cardinal and scholar (1542–1621) who was canonized in 1930. The town name was chosen by city incorporators, some of whom were parishioners. Post office: none, mail via adjacent Waynesville. FORT LEONARD WOOD: Construction of this Army training center began in December 1940, resulting in 1,600 buildings by May 1941, with a peak labor force of 32,000. The fort eventually covered 95,000 acres, inundating, like lake projects *(Camdenton),* entire towns, farms, and cemeteries. Designed to accommodate 45,000 troops, by March 1946 it had trained over 320,000 men. In 1989 it became primarily a center for Army engineers. Incidentally, the first commandant was Gen. U. S. Grant III, grandson of the Federal general and U.S. president of the same name. I-44 spur, S 2 m. *ROUTE*

66 SIGHT: George M. Reed Wayside Park. SR Z, in town.

Stream Piracy. I-44 between Roubidoux Creek and SR H follows an abandoned stream valley that was emptied when the stream was captured east of SR H and rerouted along the south side of today's I-44 loop, where it now empties into Roubidoux Creek at the town bridge. *(Stream Piracy)*

1. Origin unknown, usually via previously named natural feature or associated with the animal; no p.o.
2. Also Hazel Green, Hazle Green, Hazlegreen; for area's hazel bushes; English spelling; p.o. Hazle Green [*sic*] 1858–1861, 1864–1895, Hazlegreen [*sic*] 1895–1958 (*Post Offices*).

WENTZVILLE
Population: 4,640   Map D-7

William M. Allen, who donated land and money for the site, platted Wentzville in 1855 as seven blocks in a row along the south side of the planned route of the North Missouri *Railroad*. Named for Allen's friend, Erasmus L. Wentz, the railroad's survey engineer, it began to grow after 1857 when the railroad arrived, bypassing the older town of Flint Hill[1] by about four miles. Post office: 1859–now.

Carr and Dula Tobacco Factory. Vernacular, 1850s; two-story brick. During the 1870s Wentzville prospered as a tobacco manufacturing center, giving rise to some of the industry's most notable capitalists, including George S. Myers (Ligget & Myers Co. began here with C. Dula as the first president) and Paul Brown (founder of Brown Tobacco Co.). Brown's estate was estimated at $16 million. First St.; S on Elm to 5th.

Foristell, Mo. The townsite was founded c. 1856 as Millville,[2] whose post office was Snow Hill.[3] The name was changed c. 1873 to honor prominent cattleman and landowner Pierre Foristell. One of the town's original mercantile stores still stands (three stories, rock, 1861). Post offices: Snow Hill 1859–1873; Foristell 1873–now. I-70, W 7 m.

New Melle, Mo. First settled c. 1840 by Ernest Bannerman and Henry Hardach, this German agricultural community, named for Melle, Germany, was platted in 1850 by F. H. Kamper around a market square and millpond. Post office: 1850–now. SR Z, S 7.3 m.

CAPPELN, MO. Founded in 1845 by Henrich Wilhelm Gerdemann, who built a general store and encouraged others from his hometown of Wester-Kappeln, Germany, to settle here. He built today's brick building (Vernacular) in 1880 to replace the original frame and log store. It was operated by the family until closed in 1926. In town. Post office: 1870–1907. SR D, W 4.1 m.

ST. JOHN'S UNITED CHURCH OF CHRIST: Gothic Revival, 1857. Built of stone quarried from bluffs near *Marthasville*, this rock structure replaced an 1840 log church near Cappeln (above). Stained-glass windows. SR D, W 2.3 m. NEARBY SIGHTS: *Defiance*.

Vietnam Memorial. First dedicated in December 1967, before the Tet Offensive, this is believed to have been America's first memorial to Vietnam veterans. The original memorial was replaced in 1985 by today's monument: a column with a red granite base and topped by an eagle. 207 W. Pearce.

1. Original settlers' former hometown, Flint Hill, Va.; p.o. 1836–now.
2. Origin unknown; often associated with a water mill, e.g. a *gristmill*, it also could be from the personal name.
3. Origin unknown, but Snow Hill, Md., is named for a place in England.

WESTON
Population: 1,528   Map C-3

Platted in 1837 along the Missouri River on property recently acquired by Joseph (or Joel) Moore, an ex-soldier from nearby 1827 Fort Leavenworth (in today's Kansas), the town was reportedly named by surveyor Tom E. Weston, who said he chose the name because, at the time, Weston was "the fartherest [*sic*] town west in trade." Like its neighbor *St. Joseph*, Weston was an outgrowth of Indian trading posts, succeeding nearby Rialto,[1] which succeeded 1819 Pensineau's Landing.[2] Settled after the *Platte Purchase* by southerners and later by German, Austrian, and Swiss immigrants, Weston boomed as a river port, relying mainly on the shipping of locally grown hemp and tobacco and the outfitting of westbound wagons (McCormick Distilling Company, below). After reaching an 1853 population of 5,000, the town suffered a series of disasters in 1853–1880, which included two business-district fires and five floods, the last of which, in 1881, rechanneled the Missouri River about two miles west, leaving the town inland. These losses were not as severe as the loss of its economic base: hemp was replaced by other products, and wagon trains and steamboats were replaced by railroads. The arrival in 1861 of the St. Joseph & Council Bluffs *Railroad* (extended in 1869 to *Kansas City*) helped supplement trade, but no new economic developments, like *St. Joseph's* stockyards, were initiated. Post office: 1838–now. Tour maps and information: Weston Historical Museum (below).

Architecture. An excellent architectural tour town, Weston has good examples of 19th-century styles, including over 100 pre–Civil War structures. Weston Historic District (National Historic Register), concentrated in a 22-block area, is roughly bounded by Summit, Rock, Market, and Ashley.

Herbert Bonnell Museum. Bonnell bequeathed this 1874 family farm to the public at his death in 1984. Features include his pencil drawings, arrowheads, a 1929 Model A Ford, tools, and late 1800s household and farm collectibles. SR 45 at SR P; SR P, N 5.5 m.; GR, E 0.5 m.

Little Bean Marsh Natural Area / Lake. 151 acres. Part of the Little Bean Marsh Natural History Area. Called the best marsh along the Missouri River, it features a slough and bottomland forest that provide breeding habitat for various marsh wildlife and a winter and migratory site for bald eagles, hawks, waterfowl, and marsh birds. 3408 Ashland, St. Joseph 64506. SR 45, N 8 m. to Bean Lake.[3] LITTLE BEAN MARSH LAKE: 400 acres. Fishing, hunting.

McCormick Distilling Company. Multiple buildings, National Historic Register. The company was established in 1856 by Benjamin J. Holliday, who later bought an interest in the Pony Express (*St. Joseph*) and whose Holliday Overland Mail and Express Company, which developed 5,000 miles of stagecoach line, was sold in 1868 for $2.3 million to Wells Fargo. The distillery, the oldest one in America still operating at its original site, offers tours that include the original spring and storage cave, Regauge House, the bottling department, and McCormick memorabilia, e.g. a decanter collection. Incidentally, the sour mash process used for making bourbon is the same as the one used for sourdough bread; the dark color of bourbon comes from aging in charred barrels, which also adds to the flavor. SR JJ, S 1.25 m.

State Parks. LEWIS AND CLARK *STATE PARK*: SR 45, N 11 m. to Lewis and Clark.[4] WESTON BEND *STATE PARK*: SR 45, S 2 m.

Weston Historical Museum. Displays housed in a remodeled 1900 Baptist church include local and county historical items, a diorama of the Hopewell *Indian* culture, furniture, Civil War and WWI items, Ben Holliday (McCormick Distilling Company, above) memorabilia, and collections such as glassware, silver, and dolls. In town, 601 Main.

Wineries. MISSION CREEK: Dry to semisweet wines; fresh fruit and fruit juices from the orchards. SR 45 at SR P. PIRTLE'S: Housed in a former 1867 Baptist church; wines from the vineyards of French-hybrid grapes and from Missouri apples, grapes, and honey (mead wine); tours and tasting. In town, 502 Spring.

1. Commendatory, made popular by Shakespeare's "Merchant of Venice" for a gathering place of businessmen; no. p.o.; defunct.

2. Also Pensen's Landing; for the creek after a Frenchman who migrated from Michigan to Indian territory with the Kickapoo; no p.o.

3. Describes its shape; p.o. 1892–1895.
4. *Lewis and Clark Expedition;* no p.o.

WEST PLAINS
Population: 8,913   Map G-7

County records were destroyed during the *Civil War*. The site was bought in 1839 from a hunter named Adams by a member of the Howell family (probably Josiah/James; *County Profiles: Howell*). Reportedly, circuit court judge John R. Woodside of Oregon County surveyed the town in 1849 or 1850, naming it, as he did the 1848 post office, for its location west of the nearest town, Thomasville (*Alton*), and for its site on rolling grassy plains (today overgrown by trees). Another history claims it was platted in 1858 after being selected county seat in 1857 of newly organized Howell County. A small town (1860 pop. 150) at a major crossroads in a sparsely populated county (1860 pop. 3,169), West Plains, like Howell County, was defenseless against Civil War regulars and irregulars from both sides. All of the town and most of the county were depopulated. West Plains was totally deserted by 1864 and burned by irregulars. The county was reorganized in 1866, and the town began to slowly grow again (1870 pop. 300). The arrival in 1883 of the Kansas City, Springfield & Memphis *Railroad* helped boost its economy (1890 pop. 2,100), establishing it as the county trading center. Post office: 1848–1864, 1866–now. Home of Southwest Missouri State University–West Plains Campus and South Central Area Vocational School.

Architecture. Some good examples of late 19th- and early 20th-century styles.

Bond Dance Hall Explosion. On a rainy Friday the 13th, in April 1928, about 50 young people were dancing to "At Sundown," an additional tune the band had decided to play, postponing its regular 11:00 P.M. intermission. Below on the first floor in a garage that stored cars, an explosion at 11:05 ripped the building apart. Three nearby brick buildings were totally destroyed, and the courthouse was damaged beyond repair. Of the estimated 50 young people and the band members, 37 were killed and at least 23 injured. No cause has ever been determined. Most of the victims were burned beyond recognition. A large memorial in the city cemetery marks the spot where all the young people were buried together. Leave a flower. *Cemetery:* SE side, US 63 at US 63B; US 63B (Bill Virdon), N then W on Lambert.

Harlin House Museum. Vernacular, 1889. Art gallery, historical items, and memorabilia of former residents, e.g. baseball players Preacher Roe and Bill Virdon and entertainers Porter Waggoner and Jan Howard. US 63 (Jan Howard), E on Broadway to Garfield, S to Lydea.

Howell County Courthouse. Moderne with Art Deco affinities, 1935–1937. The county's fourth, this building replaced its structurally damaged predecessor, which was abandoned in 1928 and razed in 1933 (Bond Dance Hall Explosion, above). The decision to finally start construction was hurried when government grants for financing new courthouses dwindled. The design for this 82-foot-square three-story *Carthage*-stone structure was probably adapted from one submitted six years previously. The stylized entrances, five-ranked two-story vertical windows, and geometric motifs along the cornice echo Art Deco. Cost: $107,000 ($45,000 grant). US 63 at SR 17; SR 17, N to square (which is actually a horseshoe shape). *(County Profiles)*

People's Park. Pool, tennis, folk-art picnic pavilion; adjacent Frisco caboose and playground. US 63 (Jan Howard), E on Broadway to US 63B (Porter Waggoner).

Recreation. CARMAN SPRINGS *WILDLIFE REFUGE:* US 63, N 11 m. to Pomona;[1] SR P, W 8 m.; SR AP, N 2.5 m. DAVIS *WILDLIFE AREA.*

1. Fruit orchards here from the Roman goddess of fruit trees; p.o. Pomo, shortened version of Pomona, 1894–1895; Pomona 1895–now.

 WPA

Originally called Works Progress Administration when created in 1935 by Pres. Franklin D. Roosevelt's New Deal, the agency was renamed the Works Projects Administration in 1939 when consolidated with the Public Works Administration, the Public Buildings Administration, and the U.S. Housing Authority as a part of Roosevelt's 1939 Reorganization Plan. The idea behind WPA programs, as well as others like the Civilian Conservation Corps (CCC), was to provide billions of dollars for employment and relief during the Depression through work-oriented agencies that sponsored building projects for dams, bridges, and parks as well as matching grants for county courthouses. The WPA was liquidated in 1942 after the United States entered WWII.

II.

Recreation

Overleaf: The Collett family gathers in Adair County *(Novinger: Cabins Historic District).*

FLOAT STREAMS

Missouri has 19,050 miles of rivers and creeks. The following float streams are some of the state's most popular. They provide varying levels of experience and easy access; nearby outfitters can supply virtually everything, including transportation, for a few hours or a few days of floating, fishing, or sight-seeing. Generally floating time is one mile per hour, three miles per hour with paddling. Necessary items include footgear, like tennis shoes, for walking through a rocky riverbed and portaging; a change of dry clothes; a spare paddle; and a waterproof container (a plastic garbage sack will do). Important safety rules include wearing a life jacket, not overloading a canoe, not paddling alone, and walking the canoe around low-water bridges. If your boat is turned broadside in the current, resist the natural impulse to lean upstream (the canoe will swamp), and lean downstream instead; if tipped over, remain upstream from the canoe to avoid being pinned by it. Detailed books about Missouri's float streams (the most notable to date is "Missouri Ozark Waterways"), are available from the Missouri Department of Conservation, Box 180, Jefferson City 65102, or from outfitters at the sites listed below.

The following streams need not be floated for their full lengths. They are graded by their degree of difficulty. Easy: occasional small rapids; the stream's course is easy to find. Medium: unobstructed rapids, easy eddies and bends; the stream's course is easy to find. Difficult: maneuvering of rapids is necessary; the stream's course is not always easy to find. Very Difficult: extended rapids, irregular waves with boulders; the stream's course is difficult to find; rough-water experience necessary.

Beaver Creek. Nearly as large as the Niangua (below), Beaver Creek is popular for fly-fishing and canoeing. GRADE: Easy to Medium. PUT IN: High water, SR 76 bridge (8 m. S of *Ava*). Low water, SR 76/125 bridge at Bradleyville (from *Forsyth:* US 160, E 4 m.; SR 76, N 13 m.). TAKEOUT: SR 160 bridge at Kissee Mills Access (picnic area, camping). LENGTH: 18.8 miles. OUTFITTERS: Brownbranch, Mo. (from put in at Bradleyville: SR 76, E 5 m.).

Big Creek. A tributary of the St. Francis River (below), but less hazardous, Big Creek also runs a tight scenic course, flowing through some swift rapids and boulder-strewn *shut-ins*. Floatable in spring and early summer. GRADE: Very Difficult. PUT IN: SR K bridge W of Annapolis (from *Arcadia:* SR 49, S 17 m.). TAKEOUT: Sam A. Baker *State Park.* LENGTH: 17.2 m. OUTFITTERS: Sam A. Baker *State Park.*

The Gasconade River at Jerome, c. 1930. (FROM "INDUSTRIAL SURVEY OF ROLLA, MISSOURI," 1931)

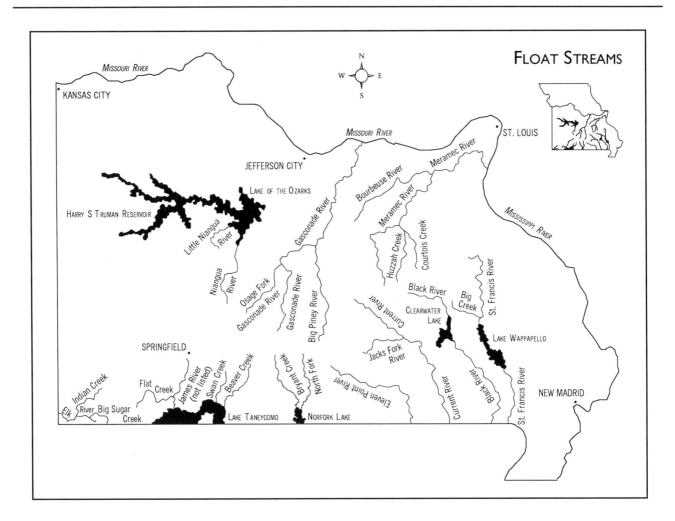

FLOAT STREAMS

Big Piney River. One of Missouri's best fishing streams and the largest tributary of the Gasconade (below), the Big Piney has many springs and spectacular bluffs. GRADE: Easy (Medium only in high water). PUT IN: Baptist Camp Access (no camping; from *Houston:* US 63, S 5.3 m.; SR RA, W 1 m.). TAKEOUT: Junction with Gasconade River at private access (lodging), just N of I-44, E side of Big Piney. LENGTH: 85.7 m. OUTFITTERS: Devils Elbow *(Waynesville),* Duke (from *Licking:* US 63, N 9 m.; SR K, W 11.8 m.), Jerome (I-44 exit 172; SR D, N 0.8 m.), and *Licking.*

Black River. The Black River is divided into two parts by Clearwater Lake *(Lakes: Corps of Engineers):* Upper, a clear fast stream with feeder springs, and Lower, a slower and less clear stream. Both offer good float fishing. GRADE: Easy (occasionally Medium). PUT IN: Upper, Mill Creek near *Lesterville* (inquire locally) is the best during normal and low-water times. Lower, Clearwater Dam (from *Piedmont:* SR HH, W 6.4 m.). TAKEOUT: Upper, SR K bridge, when the lake is high (possible campsites), and SR CC at the river when the lake is low. Lower, US 60 bridge in *Poplar Bluff.* LENGTH: Upper, 14.3 m. and 21.5 m., respectively;

lower, 46.7 m. OUTFITTERS: Annapolis *(Arcadia),* Lesterville *(Centerville), Piedmont, Mill Spring,* and Williamsville *(Mill Spring:* SR 49, S 14 m.).

Bourbeuse River. One of Missouri's crookedest streams, at one point winding 100 miles in 27 air miles, the Bourbeuse River is relatively small and slow but picturesque (until the first Union bridge), with some good bass fishing. It is a tributary of the Meramec (below). GRADE: Easy. PUT IN: The most dependable water and easiest access are at Mill Rock (from *Japan* near *Sullivan:* SR H, N 5.1 m.; GR, N 1.8 m.). TAKEOUT: US 50 bridge at *Union.* LENGTH: 66.2 m. OUTFITTERS: Leslie (from *Gerald:* US 50, E 6 m.) and *Union.*

Bryant Creek. A narrow wilderness stream with fast riffles and some obstacles, Bryant Creek offers good fishing. Inquire before floating above Aid-Hodgson Mill *(Gainesville: Mills)* during summer. GRADE: Easy to Medium. PUT IN: Vera Cruz *(Ava)* or Aid-Hodgson Mill *(Gainesville: Mills).* TAKEOUT: Corps of Engineers campground at Tecumseh *(Gainesville)* US 160 bridge. LENGTH: 43 m. and 17.1 m., respectively. OUTFITTERS: Sycamore (Aid-Hodgson Mill, above) and Tecumseh (above).

Courtois Creek. Locally pronounced Coort'a-way, the creek, like the nearby Huzzah (below), is a tributary of the Meramec River (below). These narrow clear-water streams wind through relatively unspoiled Ozark-type valleys; both can be floated only during good water. GRADE: Medium. PUT IN: Low-water bridge 0.4 m. E of Brazil (from Dillard [Steelville]: SR 49, N 5.8 m.; SR V, E 6 m.; SR Y, N 5.4 m.; GR, E 1.5 m. to Brazil). TAKEOUT: Low-water bridge at end of SR E in Huzzah *State Forest*, 0.3 m. past junction with Huzzah Creek. LENGTH: 21.5 m. OUTFITTERS: *Steelville.*

Current River. The spring-fed Current River can be floated nearly all year, especially below Welsh Spring (just above *Akers*). The best floating is above Big Spring, which is just south of *Van Buren.* Because of this stream's scenic beauty (e.g. springs, bluffs), it is part of the Ozark National Scenic Riverways *(National Parks)*, along with its tributary the Jacks Fork. GRADE: Easy (occasionally Medium). PUT IN: Montauk *State Park.* TAKEOUT: Big Spring *(Van Buren;* camping, lodging) or Currentview (from *Doniphan*: SR 142, W 8 m.; SR E, S 6.6 m.). LENGTH: 90.2 m. and 139 m., respectively. OUTFITTERS: *Akers, Doniphan, Eminence,* and *Van Buren.*

Eleven Point River. Although not a national park, a 44-mile portion of the Eleven Point River between Thomasville *(Alton)* and the SR 142 bridge was designated in 1968 as a National Scenic River *(National Parks: Ozark National Scenic Riverways)* under the jurisdiction of the Department of Agriculture. The river is fed by some of Missouri's most beautiful springs; its lower section, doubled by Greer Spring *(Alton)*, is floatable all year. Stocked with trout for the first eleven miles below the spring, this cool, fast stream flows through scenic areas like the Irish Wilderness *(Alton: Bardley)*. GRADE: Easy to Medium. PUT IN: Upper (not floatable in low water), SR 96 bridge (camping) at Thomasville *(Alton)*. Lower, SR 19 bridge (from *Alton*: SR 19, N 10 m.; camping). TAKEOUT: SR 142 bridge (limited camping; from *Doniphan*: SR 142, W 23.8 m.). LENGTH: 44.3 m. and 27.7 m., respectively. OUTFITTERS: *Alton.*

Elk River, Big Sugar and Indian Creeks. Elk River is formed by Big and Little Sugar Creeks east of Pineville and is joined north of *Noel* by Indian Creek. They can be floated individually or in combination with the Elk.

Big Sugar Creek–Elk River: Big Sugar Creek is unusually clear with good fishing. Elk River has an isolated quality below *Noel.* GRADE: Medium. PUT IN: Normal water, the low-water bridge at Cyclone (from Jane near *Pineville*: SR 90, E 4 m.; SR K, N 2 m.; GR, N 2.5 m.; camping). TAKEOUT: SR 43 bridge, Cowskin Access (from South West City near *Noel*: SR 43, N 5.2 m.) LENGTH: Big Sugar Creek: 24.3 m. Elk

River: 21 m. OUTFITTERS: Anderson (from *Pineville*: US 71, N 6 m.) for all three and *Pineville* for Elk and Big Sugar.

Indian Creek: Mainly used for spring floats, Indian Creek has the best general gradient (8.7 feet per mile) in the Missouri Ozarks and provides a steady fast run through relatively remote countryside. GRADE: Medium to Difficult. PUT IN: SR D bridge just E of Boulder City (from *Neosho*: SR H, S 7.7 m. to Boulder City). TAKEOUT: Past the confluence with the Elk at Mt. Shira Access on SR 59 south of Lanagan *(Noel: Truitt's Cave;* camping). LENGTH: 28.7 m. OUTFITTERS: Anderson (above).

Flat Creek. The creek offers good fishing from Johnboats or canoes. About the last mile is affected by Table Rock Lake *(Lakes: Corps of Engineers)*. GRADE: Easy to Medium. PUT IN: Bridge at the south edge of Jenkins (from *Cassville*: SR 248, E 14 m.; SR 39, N 1 m.; camping). TAKEOUT: SR 173 bridge (from *Reeds Spring*: SR 173, W 7 m.). LENGTH: 24 m. OUTFITTERS: Eagle Rock (from *Cassville*: SR 76, E 3 m.; SR 86, S 8 m.).

Gasconade River. The Gasconade is not only the longest river entirely within the state but also one of the most crooked (its nearly 300 river miles equal only 120 air miles). Scenic bluffs, hairpin turns, foliage, wildlife, and some fast sections help make it a family favorite. Sections south of Competition (from *Hartville*: SR Z, N 18 m.) are floatable during spring and high water. GRADE: Easy (seldom Medium). PUT IN: High water, Woods Fork of the Gasconade at SR 38 bridge east of *Hartville*. Normal water, Forest Service Access north of Competition (above; SR Z, N 2.8 m.; GR, E 0.7 m.; GR, S 1 m.; signs). TAKEOUT: Gasconade Park *(Gasconade)*. LENGTH: 252.4 m. and 219.1 m., respectively. OUTFITTERS: Devils Elbow *(Waynesville)*, Freeburg, Jerome (I-44 exit 172; SR D, N 0.8 m.), Richland *(Crocker)*, and Vienna.

Huzzah Creek. Locally pronounced Hoo'za *(County Profiles: Osage)*, the creek has the same characteristics as Courtois Creek (above). GRADE: Medium. PUT IN: SR V bridge 1.2 m. E of Davisville *(Steelville)*. TAKEOUT: SR H low-water bridge 0.3 m. past the confluence with the Meramec River (from Leasburg near *Cuba*: SR H, E 5.1 m.). LENGTH: 23.4 m. OUTFITTER: *Steelville.*

Jacks Fork River. Known as one of Missouri's most scenic Ozark streams, part of the Ozark National Scenic Riverways *(National Parks)*, the Jacks Fork flows for the first 25 miles (floatable during good water) through a deep valley that offers good fly-fishing. GRADE: Medium. PUT IN: The usual put in is at the SR 17 bridge (from *Mountain View*: SR 17, N 4.5 m.; National Park Service campground). The best low-water put in is at Alley Spring (from *Eminence*: SR 106,

W 5.3 m.; camping). TAKEOUT: Ferry landing 0.7 m. past the confluence with the Current (above), E of Jacks Fork, Mo. (from *Eminence*: SR 106, E 5.6 m.; SR V, N 3 m.). LENGTH: 38.5 and 16.3 m., respectively. OUTFITTERS: Alley Spring (above), *Eminence, Mountain View,* and *Salem.*

Little Niangua River. Fed by numerous large springs, the Little Niangua passes near several *caves.* It is notable for fishing (large-mouth bass, bluegill, black perch, crappie, walleye, channel catfish) but not always floatable; some portage may be required. GRADE: Easy (frequently Medium). PUT IN: US 54 bridge (from *Hermitage*: US 54, E 9.3 m.; approx. 0.2 m. E of county line). TAKEOUT: SR J bridge (from *Camdenton*: US 54, W 10 m.; SR J, N 8 m.). LENGTH: 31.7 m. OUTFITTERS: Roach (from *Camdenton*: US 54, W 6 m.; SR AA, N 0.7 m.).

Meramec River. Of the Meramec's 193.5 floatable miles, the first 100 offer the most wilderness scenery, including numerous *caves* and springs. Most of it is floatable all year; the most popular section is the 60 miles between Meramec Spring *(St. James)* and Meramec *State Park.* Below St. Clair, civilization is intrusive (especially real estate developments and industry), but the river can be floated to the Mississippi. The Bourbeuse River (above), its principal northern tributary, joins at Moselle *(St. Clair).* Floats above Meramec Spring are possible only during high water. GRADE: Easy (seldom Medium). PUT IN: Low-water bridge on a gravel road just east of Short Bend (from *Salem*: SR 19, N 10.3 m.). TAKEOUT: Meramec *State Park* or Chouteau Claim Access at the confluence with the Bourbeuse River (above). LENGTH: 88 m. and 132.8 m., respectively. OUTFITTERS: Meramec *State Park,* Onondaga Cave *State Park, St. Clair,* and *Steelville.*

Niangua River. The Niangua is one of Missouri's best fishing rivers. Its river fishing can be combined with trout fishing and a base camp at Bennett Spring *State Park,* but many riverside campsites are available. GRADE: Easy to Medium. PUT IN: SR 32 bridge (from *Buffalo*: SR 32, E 4 m.; Bennett Spring *State Park* is 29.5 miles north). TAKEOUT: Tunnel Dam *(Camdenton)*; approx. 2.3 m. of paddling across Niangua Lake is necessary (private takeouts at S end of lake). LENGTH: 66 m. OUTFITTERS: *Lebanon* and adjacent to Bennett Spring *State Park.*

North Fork White River. Creating some of the best white water in the Missouri Ozarks, large springs power the North Fork White River with a constant flow that is usually floatable all year from Dora (SR 181, 20 m. N of *Gainesville)* to Norfork Reservoir *(Lakes: Corps of Engineers).* The river has some wilderness character between SR 14 and SR H. GRADE: Easy to Medium (slightly Difficult in high water).

PUT IN: SR 76 bridge (from Cabool near *Mountain Grove*: SR 181, S 10 m.; SR 76, W 1.2 m.). TAKEOUT: Corps of Engineers campground at Tecumseh *(Gainesville)* US 160 bridge, 0.4 m. past junction with Bryant Creek (above). LENGTH: 49.5 m. OUTFITTERS: Caulfield (from Tecumseh, above: US 160, E 9 m.), Sycamore *(Gainesville: Mills, Aid-Hodgson),* and Tecumseh (above).

Osage Fork Gasconade River. The little-floated Osage Fork Gasconade River has excellent fishing, good floating, and pleasant scenery (flowering trees, shrubs, and *caves* along the banks). About 40 miles (from SR 5, down) of the stream's 57 miles are floatable during normal water; short sections can become log jammed. GRADE: Easy to Medium. PUT IN: High water, Rader Access (from *Marshfield*: I-44, E 13 m. to exit 113 to Conway; SR ZZ, E 8.3 m.; signs). Low water, SR 5 bridge (from *Lebanon*: SR 5, S 11 m.). TAKEOUT: Old US 66 Gasconade truss bridge 0.8 m. past the confluence with the Gasconade (from *Lebanon*: I-44, E 10 m. to exit 140; SR N, E 1.2 m.; SR AB, E 2 m.). LENGTH: 58.5 m. and 40.8 m., respectively. OUTFITTERS: *Lebanon* and Richland *(Crocker).*

St. Francis River. According to "Missouri Ozark Waterways," the upper St. Francis is not a float stream. Probably Missouri's wildest scenic run during high water, the St. Francis River's course includes boulder-strewn *shut-ins* (decked canoes advisable), gradients of 20 feet per mile, and continuous rapids with sharp drops (scouting on foot is essential). GRADE: Caution! Because some sections of the upper river can only be run in high water, it is graded exclusively for expert canoeists. The seven-mile run from the SR H put in to the SR H bridge west of Knob Lick *(Farmington)* is graded Medium. The lower section is Easy to Medium, offering a slower float through Mingo *National Wildlife Refuge* from the Sam A. Baker *State Park* put in to the takeout. PUT IN: Upper, SR H bridge at Gunner Ford Access (from *Farmington*: SR H, S 3 m.). Lower, Sam A. Baker *State Park.* TAKEOUT: Upper, Sam A. Baker *State Park,* or continue to the lower takeout, US 67 bridge at *Greenville.* LENGTH: 66.5 m. (or 78.6 m.) and 12.1 m., respectively. OUTFITTERS: Sam A. Baker *State Park.*

Swan Creek. If the gravel fields at the put in are floatable, the very clear Swan Creek provides good fly-fishing and leisurely all-day floating. During high water, it is an excellent white-water stream (decked canoe advisable). GRADE: Easy to Medium (Medium to Difficult in high water). PUT IN: SR 125 bridge at Garrison (from *Sparta*: SR 125, S 12 m.). TAKEOUT: Old *Forsyth* (camping). LENGTH: 21.2 m. OUTFITTERS: Brownbranch (from *Forsyth*: US 160, E 4 m.; SR 76, N 18 m.).

A picnic by Clearwater Lake. (MASSIE, MISSOURI RESOURCES DIVISION)

 # LAKES

Missouri has many popular public lakes, and popular does not necessarily mean crowded. Large or small, they often offer solitude: a quiet place to picnic, read, or watch the clouds change shapes. All offer fishing that includes bass, bluegill, and catfish. State and federal regulations and licensing apply.

Because of their size and complexity, Corps of Engineers lakes are listed separately on the charts in this section. Information on activities available at *wildlife area* lakes and *state park* lakes is provided on the charts included in those sections. Remember that some lakes allow hunting (Corps of Engineers Lakes Hunting chart, below) and care should be taken during those seasons (Wildlife Areas).

Other public lakes are listed in the Index under Lakes. These lakes often have stricter regulations than expected, e.g. a city lake or reservoir used by the municipal water department.

The Missouri Department of Conservation (Box 180, Jefferson City 65102) publishes an annotated Missouri map, "Outdoor Missouri," that lists by county hundreds of recreational sites, including lakes.

CORPS OF ENGINEERS LAKES HUNTING

GENERAL INFORMATION

The U.S. Army Corps of Engineers and the state of Missouri offer public hunting at the lakes listed here. All state and federal hunting regulations and licensing requirements apply, including the camping restriction that allows 14 consecutive days within a 30-day period. For information about specific regulations, contact:

Missouri Department of Conservation
Box 180
Jefferson City, Missouri 65102

LAKES See Corps *Lakes* for locations	ACRES		FACILITIES			GAME							
	CORPS HUNTING	STATE HUNTING	CAMP-GROUNDS	SEASONAL BLINDS	DAY USE BLINDS	DEER	TURKEY	DOVE	QUAIL	RABBIT	SQUIRREL	DUCK	GOOSE
LONG BRANCH	630	2,070	●	●	●	●	●	●	●	●	●	●	●
POMME DE TERRE	3,250	4,019	●		●	●	●	●	●	●	●	●	●
SMITHVILLE	8,173	0	●	●	●	●	●	●	●	●	●	●	●
STOCKTON	7,803	15,868	●		●	●	●	●	●	●	●	●	●
TRUMAN (HARRY S.)	45,534	53,875	●		●	●	●	●	●	●	●	●	●

CORPS OF ENGINEERS LAKES

FACILITIES

PICNIC - CAMPING
- D = DUMP STA.
- E = ELECTRICITY
- L = LAUNDRY
- S = SHOWERS
- W = WATER

LOCATION: General locations are given in the Lake heading. Site directions are from roads in the lake's area.

Facility columns: PICNIC | CAMPING | D/E/L/S/W | COMFORT STATION | MARINE DUMP | CAFE/SNACK NEARBY (1☆) | NATURE TRAIL | LODGING NEARBY | BEACH | BOAT RAMP | BOAT RENTAL

BULL SHOALS
Acres: 71,240 • Elev.: 695

In SW Missouri at the Missouri–Arkansas border, it was built 1947–1951 on the White River for flood control and hydroelectric power. The 2,256-foot concrete dam is America's fifth largest.
Recreation includes hunting and fishing (bass, trout, crappie, catfish, bream, and walleye).
The dam, powerhouse, and many more sites are in Arkansas.

Sites	Location	Picnic	Camping	DELSW	Comfort	Marine Dump	Cafe/Snack	Nature Trail	Lodging	Beach	Boat Ramp	Boat Rental
BEAVER CREEK	Jct. SR 76/SR O; SR O, S 2.5 m.	✓	✓	D, E, S, W	✓		☆		✓	✓	✓	
BUCK CREEK	Jct. US 60/SR 125; SR 125, S 10.1 m.	✓	✓	D, E, S, W	✓		☆		✓	✓	✓	
HIGHWAY K	Jct. SR 76/SR K; SR K, S 3.7 m.	✓	✓	D, W	✓				✓		✓	
KISSEE MILLS	SR 76/US 160 at Kissee Mills; US 160, E 1.6 m.	✓	✓	W	✓		☆		✓		✓	
PONTIAC	Jct. US 160/SR 5; SR 5, S 4.7 m.; SR W, W 7.3 m.	✓	✓	D, E, W	✓	◉	☆		✓	✓	✓	✓
RIVER RUN	Jct. SR 76/SR VV; SR VV, V 2.1 m.	✓	✓	D, E, W	✓		☆				✓	
SHADOW ROCK	SR 76 at Forsyth.	✓	✓	D, E, S, W	✓		☆				✓	
SPRING CREEK	Jct. US 160/SR HH; SR HH, S 4.2 m.	✓	✓	D	✓				✓		✓	
THEODOSIA	US 160 at Theodosia (Gainesville).	✓	✓	D, E, L, S, W	✓		★		✓	✓	✓	✓
WOODARD	Jct. SR M/SR KK; SR KK, W 1.3 m.; GR, W 6.1 m.										✓	

BLUE SPRINGS
Acres: 720 • Elev.: 820

In NW Missouri north of Lee's Summit, it was built 1982–1987 for Little Blue River area flood control and for wildlife conservation and recreation: hiking, bike trail, horse trail, and fishing (bass, bluegill, catfish, and crappie).

Sites	Location	Picnic	Camping	DELSW	Comfort	Marine Dump	Cafe/Snack	Nature Trail	Lodging	Beach	Boat Ramp	Boat Rental
NORTH SIDE	Jct. SR 5/US 40; US 40, W 2 m. to Woods Chapel Rd.; signs.	✓										
SOUTH SIDE	Same directions as North Side	✓										
EAST SIDE	Same directions as North Side	✓						✓				
WEST SIDE	Jct. US 40/I-470; I-470, S 2 m. to Bowlin Rd.; signs.	✓	✓	E, S						✓	✓	✓
PARK HQ	Same directions as North Side.											

CLEARWATER
Acres: 1,630 • Elev.: 608

In SE Missouri between Ellington and Piedmont, it was built 1940–1948 on the Black River for flood control.
Recreation includes hunting and fishing (bass, crappie, bream, catfish, and pike).
NOTE: Funk Branch and Riverside offer wilderness camping only (permit required).

Sites	Location	Picnic	Camping	DELSW	Comfort	Marine Dump	Cafe/Snack	Nature Trail	Lodging	Beach	Boat Ramp	Boat Rental
BLUFF VIEW	Jct. SR 49/SR AA; SR AA, W 6.9 m.	✓	✓	D, E, S, W	✓		☆		✓	✓	✓	✓
FUNK BRANCH	Jct. SR 49/SR BB; SR BB, W 5.3 m.; Funk Branch Rd., S 2.7 m.		✓									
HIGHWAY K	Jct. SR 49/SR K; SR K, S 5 m.	✓	✓	D, E, S	✓					✓		
PIEDMONT PARK	Jct. SR 49/SR AA; SR AA, W 5.4 m.	✓	✓	D, E, S, W	✓		☆		✓	✓	✓	
RIVER ROAD	Jct. SR 49/SR AA; SR AA, W 6 m.	✓	✓	D, E, S, W	✓		☆		✓		✓	
RIVERSIDE	Jct. SR 49/SR CC; SR CC, W 3.8 m.; Happy Hollow Rd., W 4 m.; sign.		✓									
THURMAN POINT	Jct. SR HH/SR RA; SR RA, N 1.5 m.										✓	
WEBB CREEK	Jct. SR 21/SR H; SR H, E 10.3 m.	✓	✓	D, E, S, W	✓		☆		✓	✓	✓	✓

LONG BRANCH
Acres: 2,430 • Elev.: 801

In NE Missouri near Macon. Built 1971–1980 on E. Fork Little Chariton River for flood control. Recreation: trails, hunting, and fishing (bass, catfish, and walleye). Long Branch State Park is here.

Sites	Location	Picnic	Camping	DELSW	Comfort	Marine Dump	Cafe/Snack	Nature Trail	Lodging	Beach	Boat Ramp	Boat Rental
BEE TRACE	Jct. US 36/US 63; US 63, N 5.3 m.; Axtell Rd., W 1.7 m.	✓	✓	S, W	✓			✓			✓	
BLOOMINGTON	Jct. US 36/SR O; SR O, N 2.6 m.; GR, E 1.3 m.	✓	RV Only	S, W	✓			✓		✓	✓	✓
MACON	Jct. US 36/US 63; US 63, N 3.1 m.; GR, W 1 m.				✓			✓			✓	
VISITOR CENTER	US 36 at E end of dam.											

LONGVIEW
Acres: 930 • Elev.: 909

SW of Blue Springs Lake (above), it was built 1979–1985 for flood control, wildlife conservation, and recreation: soccer, trails (horse, bike, and nature), golf, model airplane field, and fishing (bass, bluegill, catfish, and crappie).

Sites	Location	Picnic	Camping	DELSW	Comfort	Marine Dump	Cafe/Snack	Nature Trail	Lodging	Beach	Boat Ramp	Boat Rental
HIGH GROVE RD.	Jct. US 71/I-470; I-470, E 3.2 m.; Raytown Rd., S to High Grove Rd.	✓						✓				
LONGVIEW RD. EAST	Raytown Rd. (above), S to 109th; E to High View; S to Longview & Park HQ.	✓	✓	E, S								
LONGVIEW RD. WEST	Raytown Rd. (above), S to Longview Rd.	✓								✓	✓	✓
PITTENGER RD.	Raytown Rd. (above), S past Pittenger Rd.	✓										
W. 3D ST.	Raytown Rd. (above), S to 109th; E to High View; S to W 3d, then W.	✓										

NORFORK
Acres: 22,000 • Elev.: 554

In SW Missouri at the Missouri–Arkansas border. Built 1941–1944 for flood control and hydroelectric power. Recreation: hunting and fishing (bass, bream, walleye, crappie, and catfish).

Sites	Location	Picnic	Camping	DELSW	Comfort	Marine Dump	Cafe/Snack	Nature Trail	Lodging	Beach	Boat Ramp	Boat Rental
BRIDGES CREEK	Access only: Jct. SR V/SR O; SR O, W 2.4 m.; GR, N 1.7 m.											
FORD COVE	Access only: Jct. SR J/SR T; SR T, W 3.5 m.											
TECUMSEH	US 160 at Tecumseh.	✓	✓	W	✓		☆		✓			
UDALL	Jct. SR V/SR O; SR O, W 5.7 m.	✓	✓	W	✓		★		✓		✓	✓

POMME de TERRE
Acres: 7,820 • Elev.: 839

In SW Missouri south of Hermitage, it was built 1957–1961 on the

Sites	Location	Picnic	Camping	DELSW	Comfort	Marine Dump	Cafe/Snack	Nature Trail	Lodging	Beach	Boat Ramp	Boat Rental
BOLIVAR	Jct. SR PP/SR RB; SR RB, N 4.6 m.	✓	✓	D, S, W	✓						✓	
DAMSITE	From Hermitage: SR 254, S 3.8 m.	✓	✓	D, L, S, W	✓						✓	

Pomme de Terre Continued >>>

CORPS OF ENGINEERS LAKES

(CONTINUED FROM PREVIOUS CHART)

Facility legend — PICNIC-CAMPING: Picnic; Camping; D = Dump Sta., E = Electricity, L = Laundry, S = Showers, W = Water. FACILITIES: Comfort Station; Marine Dump; Cafe/Snack Nearby (★); Nature Trail; Lodging Nearby; Beach; Boat Ramp; Boat Rental.

General locations are given in the Lake heading. Site directions are from roads in the lake's area.

Lake	Sites	Location	Picnic	Camping	D/E/L/S/W	Comfort Station	Marine Dump	Cafe/Snack (★)	Nature Trail	Lodging Nearby	Beach	Boat Ramp	Boat Rental
POMME de TERRE (CONTINUED) — Pomme de Terre River for flood control along the Osage River (see Stockton, below). Recreation includes playgrounds, hunting, hiking, and fishing (bass, bluegill, crappie, catfish, and muskie). NOTE: Pomme de Terre *State Park* is located here.	LIGHTFOOT LANDING	Jct. SR 83/SR RB; SR RB, E 3.8 m.			D, E, L, S, W	✚	◉	★					
	NEMO LANDING	SR 64 at Nemo; SR 64, W 1.5 m.	P	△	D, L, S, W	✚	◉	★			☀	🚤	⛴
	OUTLET	From *Hermitage*: SR 254, S 4 m.	P	△	W	✚						🚤	
	PITTSBURG LANDING	Jct. SR 64/SR RA; SR RA, E 2.2 m.	P	△	W	✚						🚤	
	QUARRY POINT	From *Hermitage*: SR 254, S 4.8 m.	P	△	D, E, L, S, W	✚	◉	★				🚤	
	WHEATLAND	Wheatland: SR 83, S 4 m.; SR 254, E 2 m.; GR 254-25, S 1.2 m.	P	△	D, E, S, W	✚					☀	🚤	
SMITHVILLE — Acres: 7,190 • Elev.: 864. In NE Missouri N of K.C. Built in 1972–1977 on the Platte River for flood control, water supply, and recreation: golf, cross-country skiing, foot and horse trails, hunting, and fishing (bass, catfish, bluegill, crappie, muskie, and walleye).	CAMP BRANCH	Jct. US 169/SR W; SR W, E 3.6 m. to Paradise.	P	△	D, E, S, W	✚			⚑		☀	🚤	⛴
	CROWS CREEK	Jct. SR 92/SR E; SR E, N & W 3.1 m.	P	△	D, E, S, W	✚			⚑			🚤	
	LITTLE PLATTE	From *Smithville*: SR F, N 2.8 m.; GR, E 1 m.	P		W	✚			⚑		☀	🚤	⛴
	PERKINS PARK	SR 116 in *Plattsburg*.	P		W	✚							
	SMITH'S FORK	From *Smithville*: SR DD, E 2 m.	P	△	D, E, S, W	✚			⚑				
STOCKTON — Acres: 24,900 • Elev.: 867. In SW Missouri at *Stockton*, it was built 1963–1969 on the Sac River for flood control along the Osage River (see Pomme de Terre, above; Truman, below) and for hydroelectric power. Recreation includes foot and horse trails, hunting, and fishing (bass, walleye, catfish, bluegill, and crappie). NOTE: Stockton *State Park* is located here.	CEDAR RIDGE	SR 215 at Bona; SR RA, N 1.5 m.	P	△	D, E, S, W	✚					☀	🚤	
	CRABTREE COVE	From *Stockton*: SR 32, S 4.6 m.	P	△	D, S, W	✚						🚤	
	GREENFIELD	Jct. US 160/SR CC; SR CC, N 1 m.				✚						🚤	
	HAWKER POINT	Jct. SR 39/SR H; SR H, E 5.2 m.	P	△	D, S, W	✚						🚤	
	HIGH POINT	Jct. SR 123/SR VV; SR VV, W 2.5 m.; GR, S 2 m.				✚						🚤	
	MASTERS	Jct. SR 32/SR RA; SR RA, S 2.5 m.; GR, W .8 m.	P	△	D, S, W	✚					☀	🚤	
	MUTTON CREEK	Jct. SR 215/SR Y; SR Y, W 1.2 m.	P	△	D, E, L, S, W	✚		★	⚑			🚤	⛴
	OLD MILL	From *Stockton*: SR 32, E 1.6 m.	P			✚							
	ORLEANS TRAIL	From *Stockton*: city access rd., S 1 m.; inquire locally.	P	△	D, E, S, W	✚		★	⚑		☀	🚤	⛴
	RUARK BLUFF	From *Greenfield*: SR H, N 9.2 m.	P	△	D, S, W	✚					☀	🚤	
	STOCKTON	Adjacent to SE *Stockton*.	P		D, W	✚					☀	🚤	
TABLE ROCK — Area: 43,100 • Elev.: 915. In SW Missouri at the Missouri – Arkansas border, it was built 1954–1959 on the White River for flood control and hydroelectric power. Recreation includes hunting and fishing (bass, crappie, catfish, sunfish, paddlefish, and walleye). NOTE: Table Rock *State Park* is located here.	AUNTS CREEK	Jct. SR 13/SR OO; SR OO, W 2.7 m.	P	△	D, S, W	✚					☀	🚤	
	BAXTER	Jct. SR 13/SR H; SR H, W 4.8 m.	P	△	D, E, S, W	✚	◉	★			☀	🚤	⛴
	BIG BAY	Jct. SR 39/SR YY; SR YY, E 2.8 m.; GR, N 0.7 m.	P	△	W	✚						🚤	
	BIG INDIAN ACCESS	Jct. SR 39/SR H; SR H, E 4.2 m.										🚤	
	BIG M	Jct. SR E/SR M; SR M, S 1.4 m.	P	△	D, E, S, W	✚	◉	★			☀	🚤	
	CAMPBELL POINT	Jct. SR 39/SR YY; SR YY, E 5.1 m.	P	△	D, E, S, W	✚	◉	★			☀	🚤	
	CAPE FAIR	SR 76 at Cape Fair; Lake Rd. 76-82, W 1.2 m.	P	△	D, E, S, W	✚	◉	★			☀	🚤	⛴
	COOMBS FERRY	Jct. SR 86/SR JJ; SR JJ, N 6.4 m.										🚤	
	COW CREEK	Jct. SR 13/SR 86; SR 86, N 2 m.; GR, N 1.6 m.	P	△	D, S, W	✚					☀	🚤	
	EAGLE ROCK	Jct. SR F/SR 86; SR 86, S 3.6 m.	P	△	D, E, S, W	✚		★			☀	🚤	⛴
	HIGHWAY 13	SR 13 at Kimberling City, Mo.	P	△	D, E, S, W	✚		★			☀	🚤	
	INDIAN POINT	SR 76 at *Reeds Spring*; SR 76, S 6.2 m.; Lake Rd. 76-60, S 2.8 m.	P	△	D, E, S, W	✚		★			☀	🚤	
	JOE BALD	Jct. SR OO/SR 13; SR 13, S 0.3 m.; Lake Rd. 13-35, S 5.7 m.	P	△	D, S, W	✚					☀	🚤	
	KINGS RIVER ACCESS	Jct. SR J/SR RA at Golden; SR RA, N 3.4 m.										🚤	
	LONG CREEK	Jct. US 65/SR 86; SR 86, W 3.2 m.; Lake Rd. 86-26, S 1.1 m.	P	△	D, E, S, W	✚		★			☀	🚤	⛴
	MILL CREEK	Jct. SR H/SR 13 at Lampe; SR 13, N 2.4 m.; GR, W 0.5 m.	P	△	D, S, W	✚					☀	🚤	
	OLD 86	Jct. SR 86/SR UU; SR UU, E 1.8 m.	P	△	D, S, W	✚					☀	🚤	
	SHELL KNOB	Jct. SR 39/SR YY; SR YY, S 1.5 m.	P	△	W	✚							

Table Rock Continued >>>

CORPS OF ENGINEERS LAKES

(CONTINUED FROM PREVIOUS CHART)

LOCATION — General locations are given in the Lake Heading. Site directions are from roads in the lake's area.

LAKE	SITES	LOCATION	PICNIC	CAMPING	D E L S W (Dump Sta./Electricity/Laundry/Showers/Water)	COMFORT STATION	MARINE DUMP	CAFE/SNACK NEARBY (★)	NATURE TRAIL	LODGING NEARBY	BEACH	BOAT RAMP	BOAT RENTAL
TABLE ROCK (CONTINUED)	SHEPHERD OF THE HILLS	Jct. SR 76/SR 165; SR 165, S 4.3 m.		✓	W	✓						✓	
	VINEY CREEK	Jct. SR RA/SR J at Golden.; SR J, N 3.9 m.	✓	✓	D, E, S, W	✓					☼	✓	
	VIOLA	SR 39 at Viola.; SR 39, S 1.1 m.; Lake Rd. 3941, W 0.5 m.	✓	✓	D, E, S, W	✓		★			☼	✓	✓
	VISITOR CENTER	SR 265, S across dam from Shep. of the Hills Hatchery (above).	✓	✓	W	✓			✓			✓	
TRUMAN (HARRY S.)	BERRY BEND	Jct. SR 7/SR Z; SR Z, W 1 m.; GR, S 1.8 m.	✓	✓	D, E, L, S, W	✓					☼	✓	
	BLEDSOE FERRY	N of Warsaw city limits at dam's powerhouse exhibit area; signs.	✓		W	✓						✓	
	BUCKSAW	Jct. SR 7/SR U; SR U, S 3 m.		✓	D, E, L, S, W	✓		★		✓	☼	✓	✓
	BUSH CREEK	E of Osceola city limits; signs.			W							✓	
	COOPER CREEK	SR 13 at Deepwater; W of town, signs.				✓						✓	
	FAIRFIELD	Jct. SR 83/SR K; SR K, 0.9 m.	✓			✓						✓	
	KAYSINGER BLUFF	N of Warsaw city limits at Visitor Center; signs.			W				✓				
	LONG SHOAL	Jct. SR PP/SR 7 at Tightwad; SR 7, S 3.9 m.	✓	✓	D, E, L, S, W	✓		★			☼	✓	✓
	OSAGE BLUFF	Jct. SR MM/SR 83 at Whitakerville; SR 83, S 2 m.; GR, W 0.6 m.	✓	✓	D, E, L, S, W	✓		★				✓	✓
	OSCEOLA	At Osceola.	✓	✓	D, E, L, S, W	✓					☼	✓	
	ROSCOE	At Roscoe.			L							✓	
	SHAWNEE BEND	W of Warsaw city limits; adjacent to Bledsoe Ferry (above).			D, S, W								
	SPARROW FOOT	SR 13 at Clinton; SR 13, N 3.6 m.; GR, E 2.2 m.	✓	✓	D, E, L, S, W	✓					☼	✓	
	TALLEY BEND	Jct. SR HH/SR C; SR C, W 0.5 m.		✓	D, E, L, S, W	✓							
	THIBAUT POINT	Jct. US 65/SR T; SR T, W 2.5 m.; GR, S 1.2 m.	✓	✓	D, L, S, W	✓					☼	✓	
	WARSAW	At Warsaw.	✓		W	✓						✓	
	WINDSOR CROSSING	Jct. SR C/SR PP at Roseland; SR PP, S 1.8 m.	✓	✓	W	✓					☼	✓	
TWAIN (MARK)	ALLEN, ROBERT E.	Jct. SR 107/SR 154; SR 154, E 1.6 m.; GR, N 4.2 m.	✓		W	✓						✓	
	BEHRENS, RAY	Jct. SR EE/SR J; SR J, W 1.1 m.	✓	✓	D, E, S, W	✓			✓			✓	✓
	BLUFF VIEW	Jct. SR H/SR A; SR A, W 1.8 m.	✓		W	✓						✓	
	BOUDREAUX VISITOR CENTER	Jct. SR EE/SR J; SR J, N 0.4 m.	✓		W	✓							
	INDIAN CREEK	Jct. US 24/SR N; SR N, S 3.3 m.; GR, S 2.3 m.	✓	✓	D, E, S, W	✓			✓		☼	✓	✓
	RUSSELL, FRANK	Jct. SR EE/SR J; SR J, N 1.9 m.		✓	W	✓							
	SOUTH FORK	Jct. SR 107/SR 154; SR 154, W 1.4 m.	✓		W	✓						✓	
	SPALDING, JOHN F.	Jct. SR A/SR J; SR J, S 2.2 m.; GR, W & S 2.5 m.	✓		S, W	✓			✓		☼		
	STOUTSVILLE	Jct. US 24/SR 107; SR 107, S 2.2 m.; GR, W & S 2.2 m.	✓		W	✓						✓	
WAPPAPELLO	CHAONIA LANDING	Jct. SR 172/SR W; SR W, N 2 m.	✓	✓	S, W	✓						✓	✓
	EAGLE POINT	Jct. SR T/SR D at the dam; SR D, N approx. 0.2 m.	✓		W	✓							
	LOST CREEK P.A.	SR D at Shook; signs.		✓		✓						✓	
	OLD GREENVILLE	US 67 at Greenville; US 67, S 1 m.	✓	✓	D, E, W	✓						✓	
	PEOPLES CREEK	Jct. SR T/SR D at the dam; SR D, N 1 m.	✓	✓	E, S, W	✓					☼	✓	✓
	POSSUM CREEK P.A.	Jct. SR Z/SR D; SR D, N 1.2 m.; CR 523, N 1.1 m.; CR 522A, S 3.5 m.		✓		✓						✓	
	REDMAN CREEK	Jct. SR T/SR D at the dam; SR D at south end of dam.	✓	✓	D, E, S, W	✓					☼	✓	
	ROCKWOOD POINT	Jct. SR KK/SR RA; SR RA, N .8 m.	✓			✓					☼	✓	
	SPILLWAY	Jct. SR T/SR D at the dam; SR D at south end of dam.	✓		W	✓			✓			✓	
	SULPHUR SPRINGS P.A.	Jct. SR D/SR BB; SR BB, S 0.5 m.		✓		✓						✓	

TRUMAN (HARRY S.)

Acres: 55,600 • Elev.: 706

In SW Missouri in an arc from *Clinton* to *Warsaw* to *Osceola*. It was built 1964–1979 for flood control and hydroelectric power. First named Kaysinger Bluff Dam when authorized in 1954. The name was changed by Congress in 1970 to honor former U.S. president Truman. As the largest flood-control dam in Missouri, it has a storage capacity of 5 million acre-feet.

Recreation includes hunting, hiking, horseback riding, and fishing (bass, crappie, catfish, walleye, and paddlefish).

The J.M. Hooper House (Vernacular, late 19th century; National Historic Register) is on display near the Visitor Center at Kaysinger Bluff.

NOTE: Harry S Truman *State Park* is located here.

TWAIN (MARK)

Acres: 18,600 • Elev.: 606

Located in NE Missouri between *New London* and *Paris*, it was built 1970–1983 on the Salt River for flood control, water supply, hydroelectric power, and recreation that includes hiking, hunting, and fishing (bass, catfish, crappie, sunfish, and walleye).

NOTE: Mark Twain *State Park* is located here.

WAPPAPELLO

Acres: 8,400 • Elev.: 360

Located in SE Missouri at *Greenville*, it was built 1938–1941 on the St. Francis River for flood control.

Recreation includes hunting, hiking, tennis, basketball, volleyball, and fishing (bass, crappie, bluegill, and catfish).

NOTE: Remnants of historic old *Greenville* are at Old Greenville Recreation site. Wappapello *State Park* is located here. Also included here are primitive areas (P.A.) that have limited facilities.

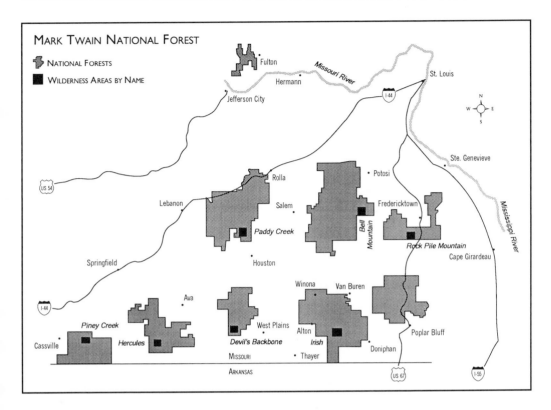

MARK TWAIN NATIONAL FOREST

NATIONAL FORESTS

WILDERNESS AREAS BY NAME

The Irish Wilderness *(Alton: Bardley).* (COURTESY "MISSOURI
CONSERVATIONIST"

NATIONAL FORESTS

The Missouri state legislature passed legislation in 1933
to restore portions of the state's wild forest land severely damaged by inappropriate timber harvesting, poor
farming practices, fires, and floods. By 1945 about 1.25
million acres were set aside, and today nearly 1.5 million acres support a wide variety of healthy flora and
fauna, including over 300 species of wildlife. Missouri's
national forests were originally divided into geographical units with various names, such as the most recent
examples, Clark *(Bowling Green: Champ Clark's Honey
Shuck)* and Mark Twain, which were consolidated as
Mark Twain National Forest in 1976.

Ninety-nine percent of Mark Twain National Forest
is spread across southern Missouri, between I-44 and
US 160, from the St. Francois Mountains in the southeast to the Ozarks in the southwest. The priorities of the
forest service, in order, are ecology, aesthetics, wildlife,
and recreation that includes camping, picnicking, hunting, fishing, and hiking. The national forest campsites
usually feature a stream, spring, lake, bluff, or other
scenic attraction. The chart lists some of the more popular and easily accessible of those sites. For other
national forest sites see *Trails.* For information and
maps for all sites and facilities, contact Mark Twain
National Forest, 401 Fairgrounds Rd., Rolla 65401.

NATIONAL FORESTS NAME	LOCATION	CAMPING•PICNIC	TRAILS	FISHING	TOILETS
BERRYMAN TRAIL CAMP	Potosi: SR 8, W 17 m.; FR 2266, N 1 m.	Camp+Picnic	Trails		T
BIG BAY CAMPGROUND/ PICNIC AREA	Shell Knob: SR 39, E 1 m.; SR YY, S 3 m. to Table Rock L.	Camp+Picnic		Fishing	T
BIG PINEY TRAIL CAMP	Paddy Creek Campground (see below): Slabtown Rd., N 1 m.	Camp+Picnic	Trails		T
BRAZIL CREEK TRAIL CAMP	Bourbon (Cuba): SR N, S 12 m.; SR W, S approx. 6.5 m.	Camp+Picnic	Trails		T
BUFFALO CREEK CAMPGROUND	Doniphan: US 160, W 16 m.; FR 3145, N 2 m.	Camp+Picnic		Fishing	T
CAMP FIVE POND TRAILHEAD / PICNIC AREA	Doniphan: US 160, W 20 m.; SR J, N 7 m.	Camp+Picnic	Trails	Fishing	T
CAMP RIDGE CAMPGROUND / PICNIC AREA	Chadwick (Sparta): SR 125, S 1.5 m.; SR H, S 1.1 m. to motorcycle trail.	Camp+Picnic	Motorcycle		T
CANEY PICNIC AREA	Ava: SR 5, S 3 m.; SR A, S 4 m.; GR, S 3 m.; FR 147, SW 6 m.	Picnic			T
CARRINGTON PITS PICNIC AREA	Fulton: SR H, W 2.25 m.; CR 159, W 0.5 m.	Picnic		Fishing	T
COBB RIDGE TRAIL CAMP	Chadwick (Sparta): SR 125, S 1.5 m.; SR H, S 2.5 m.; CR 171, W 0.5 m.	Camp	Trails		T
COUNCIL BLUFF RECREATION AREA	Caledonia: SR C, W 4.4 m.; SR DD, S 6.7 m.	Camp+Picnic		Fishing	T
CRANE LAKE PICNIC AREA	Arcadia: SR 21, S 7 m.; SR 49, S 3 m.; FR 69 at Chloride, E 4 m.; GR, S 2 m.	Picnic	Trails	Fishing	T
DEER LEAP CAMPGROUND	Doniphan: SR Y, N 5 m.; FR 4349, W 1.5 m.	Camp		Fishing	T
ELEVEN POINT NATIONAL SCENIC RIVER	Alton: (5 separate sites) Crane Bluff, Greer Crossing, Riverton, Turner N & S.	Camp+Picnic		Fishing	T
FALLING SPRING PICNIC AREA	Alton: SR 19, N 11.2 m.; FR 3170, E 0.2 m.; FR 3164, E 2.5 m.	Picnic			T
FLOAT CAMP CAMPGROUND / PICNIC AREA	Doniphan: SR Y, N 4.5 m.; FR 3210, W 0.5 m.	Camp+Picnic	Trails	Fishing	T
FREMONT TOWER PICNIC AREA	Fremont (Van Buren): US 60, W 3 m.	Picnic			T
HAZEL CREEK TRAIL CAMP	Caledonia: SR C, W 10 m.; SR Z, N 2.1 m. to Palmer; GR, N approx. 2 m.	Camp+Picnic	Trails		T
LANE SPRING CAMPGROUND / PICNIC AREA	Rolla: US 63, S 10 m.; FR 1892, W 1 m.	Camp+Picnic	Trails	Fishing	T
LITTLE SCOTIA POND CAMPGROUND / PICNIC AREA	Bunker: SR 72, N 9.2 m.; FR 2341, S 0.5 m.	Camp+Picnic			T
LOGGERS LAKE CAMPGROUND / PICNIC AREA	Bunker: SR A, W 0.2 m.; FR 2221, S 6 m.; FR 2193, S 0.5 m.	Camp+Picnic	Trails	Fishing	T
MARBLE CREEK CAMPGROUND	Arcadia: SR E, S 12 m.	Camp	Trails	Fishing	T
MARKHAM SPRING CAMPGROUND / PICNIC AREA	Mill Spring: SR 49 S & E 10.3 m.	Camp+Picnic	Trails	Fishing	T
MCCORMACK LAKE CAMPGROUND / PICNIC AREA	Alton: SR 19, N 11.2 m.; GR, S 1.8 m.	Camp+Picnic	Trails	Fishing	T
MILL CREEK CAMPGROUND / PICNIC AREA	Newburg: SR P, W & S 2.5 m.; GR, E & S 1.8 m.	Camp+Picnic	Trails	Fishing	T
NOBLETT LAKE CAMPGROUND / PICNIC AREA	Cabool (Mountain Grove): SR 181, S 16 m.; SR AP, S 4 m.	Camp+Picnic	Trails	Fishing	T
NORTH FORK CAMPGROUND / PICNIC AREA	Gainesville: SR 181, N 20 m.; SR CC, E 4 m.	Camp+Picnic	Trails	Fishing	T
PADDY CREEK CAMPGROUND / PICNIC AREA	Houston: SR 17, N 29 m.; FR 78, E approx. 4.2 m.; FR 220, S 2.2 m.	Camp+Picnic	Trails	Fishing	T
PINE RIDGE CAMPING / PICNIC AREA	Fulton: SR H, W 4.9 m.; SR J, S 3.3 m. to Guthrie; SR Y, W 2.5 m.	Camp+Picnic	Trails		T
PINEWOODS LAKE CAMPGROUND / PICNIC AREA	Ellsinore (Van Buren): SR V/US 60; US 60, W 2 m.	Camp+Picnic	Trails	Fishing	T
RED BLUFF CAMPGROUND / PICNIC AREA	Davisville (Steelville): SR V, E 1 m.	Camp+Picnic	Trails		T
RIPLEY LAKE PICNIC AREA	Doniphan: US 160, W 10 m.; SR C, N 1.5 m.; FR sign, turn E.	Picnic		Fishing	T
ROBY LAKE PICNIC AREA	Houston: SR 17, N 22 m. to Roby; SR 17, N 1 m.; FR 274, E 0.5 m.	Picnic	Trails	Fishing	T
SILVER MINES CAMPGROUND / PICNIC AREA	Fredericktown: US 72, W 5.9 m.; SR D, 3 m.	Camp+Picnic	Trails	Fishing	T
SLABTOWN PICNIC AREA	Licking: SR 32, N 4 m.; SR N, N 2 m.; SR AF, W & N 4.5 m.	Picnic	Trails	Fishing	T
SUTTON BLUFF CAMPGROUND / PICNIC AREA	Centerville: SR 21, N 3 m.; FR 2233, N 7 m.; FR 2236, S 3 m.	Camp+Picnic	Trails	Fishing	T
WATERCRESS SPRING CAMPGROUND / PICNIC AREA	Van Buren: in town; sign on US 60, approx. 0.3 m. S of jct. SR D/US 60.	Camp+Picnic	Trails	Fishing	T

NATIONAL PARKS

The National Park Service was created by a 1916 act of Congress to "conserve the scenery, the natural and historic objects and the wildlife therein." Although the name of the agency seems to imply that it administers just parks, the National Park Service has assumed responsibility for many different categories of national property, including scenic rivers, historic sites, monuments, battlefields, and even the White House. Missouri's National Parks include scenic, historic, and natural properties.

George Washington Carver National Monument. The monument preserves the birthplace of George Washington Carver, the American chemurgist (studying the utilization of raw organic materials) and educator in scientific agriculture, whose best-known work was the development of 300 by-products of the once-ignored peanut plant. Sight-seeing, museum, picnicking, hiking (*Joplin: George Washington Carver National Monument*). Superintendent: Box 38, Diamond 64840.

Jefferson National Expansion Memorial. This memorial to westward expansion, established in 1935, features the Gateway Arch, Old Courthouse, and Museum of Westward Expansion. Sight-seeing (*St. Louis: Gateway Arch Area Sights, Market Street Area Sights*). Superintendent: 11 North 4th, St. Louis 63102.

Ozark National Scenic Riverways. Protection of this scenic area began in 1920–1930 when the Missouri state parks system acquired Big Spring, Round Spring, Alley Spring, and Montauk Spring. Designation of the Mark Twain *National Forest* in 1939 introduced federal protection that was expanded in 1963–1964 by federal legislation authorizing acquisition of property along the Jacks Fork and Current Rivers under the name Ozark National Scenic Riverways. As described in the 1968 National Wild and Scenic Rivers Act, the creation of the riverways was for "preserving free-flowing

OZARK NATIONAL SCENIC RIVERWAYS

CAMPGROUNDS WITH SERVICES

All federal camping regulations apply, including a limit of 14 consecutive days within a 30-day period, quiet hours 10 p.m. — 6 a.m., no digging at the campsite, and fires only in grills. For information about specific regulations and a river map contact:

National Park Service
Ozark National Scenic Riverways
Box 490
Van Buren, Missouri 63965

NOTE: No water or electrical hookups at any campsite.

SITE	LOCATION	CANOE RENTALS	PUBLIC PHONE	STORE	LODGING	MEALS	WOODLOT	DUMP	SHOWERS
AKERS	Akers (Recreation)	✓	☎	🏕			×		
ALLEY SPRING	Eminence (Ozark)	✓	☎	🏕	🏛		×	▤	♀
BIG SPRING	Van Buren (Big)		☎		🏛	☆	×	▤	♀
POWDER MILL	From Eminence: SR 106, E 12 m.								
PULLTITE	Akers (Pulltight)	✓	☎	🏕			×		
ROUND SPRING	Eminence (Ozark)	✓	☎	🏕			×	▤	♀
TWO RIVERS	From Eminence: SR 106, E 5 m.; SR V, N 3 m.	✓	☎	🏕					♀

RIVER ACCESS, CAMPING, PICNICKING

WHEN TO COME: about 18% of visitors come in the spring, 64% in the summer, and 18% in the fall; weekdays 40%, Saturday 42%, Sunday 18%.
FLOATING: *Float Streams*
FISHING: A Missouri fishing license is required for ages 16 ≦ 64. Minimum length of fish by type: Largemouth Bass, 12 inches; Smallmouth Bass, 12 inches; Trout, ask a ranger (tag required); Goggle-eye, no minimum length.
CAMPING: Set your tent out of sight of others; use existing firepits; use the restrooms provided or dig a cathole at least 100 feet from any water; set a stick at water's edge as a gauge. The same rules apply as for Campgrounds, above.
WARNING: Locally heavy rains can cause the rivers to rise rapidly.

SITE	LOCATION	RIVER ACCESS	PICNIC AREA	CAMPSITE
BAPTIST	From Montauk *State Park*: SR 119 at SR YY; SR YY, E 1.8 m.; inquire locally.	✓		
BAY CREEK	From *Eminence*: SR 106, W 10 m.; GR/unimproved rd., S about 2.3 m.	✓		▲
BEAL LANDING	From *Ellington*: SR 106, W 10.6 m.; SR HH, S 6.3 m.; GR, E 0.5 m.	✓		
BLUE SPRING CURRENT RIVER	From *Eminence*: SR 106, E 13 m. to Current River; continue SR 106, E 2.4 m.; GR, W approx. 2.6 m.		⚶	
BLUE SPRING JACKS FORK	From *Mountian View*: US 60, E 3.1 m.; SR OO; N 2.4 m.; GR, N 2.3 m.	✓	⚶	▲
BLUFF VIEW	From *Mountain View*: SR 17, N 6 m.; SR OO, E 2.1 m.; GR, S 0.8 m.; unimproved rd., S 1.5 m.	✓		
BUCK HOLLOW	From *Mountain View*: SR 17, N 4 m. to river	✓	⚶	
CATARACT LANDING	From *Van Buren*: US 60, W 4.4 m.; SR C, S 7 m.; SR F, E 6.; GR, N 5 m.	✓		
CEDARGROVE	From *Houston*: SR B, E 23.3 m. to river.	✓	⚶	▲
CHILTON CREEK	From *Van Buren*: US 60, W 1.2 m.; SR M, N 7.8 m.; GR, N 1.2 m.	✓	⚶	▲
DEVILS WELL	From *Akers*: SR KK, E 4.9 m.; GR, S 1.5 m.		⚶	
HAWES	From *Van Buren*: US 60, W 5.4 m.; SR C, S 11 m.; GR, E 6 m.	✓	⚶	▲
HICKORY LANDING	From *Van Buren*: US 60, E 21 m.; SR 21, S 3 m; SR E, W 3.8 m.	✓		▲
HORSE CAMP	From *Eminence*: SR 106, W 3.7 m. to SR E; GR, N 1.6 m.			▲
JERKTAIL LANDING	From *Eminence*: SR 19, N 7 m.; GR, E 10 m.	✓		▲
KEATONS	From *Eminence*: SR 106, W 2.3 m.; GR, N 0.8 m.			▲
LOGYARD	From *Ellington*: SR 106, W 10.6 m.; SR HH, S 6.3 m.	✓		▲
MONTAUK STATE PARK	At Montauk *State Park*		⚶	▲
PAINT ROCK	From *Ellington*: SR 21, S 8 m.; SR D, S 1 m.; GR, W 4 m. to colorful Paint Rock.	✓		
ROBERTS FIELD	From *Eminence*: SR 106, E 7 m.; SR H, S 3.9 m.; SR NN, N 5 m.	✓		▲
ROCKY FALLS	From *Eminence*: SR 106, E 7 m.; SR H, S 3.9 m.; SR NN, N 2.2 m.; GR, S 2.8 m.			▲
RYMERS	From *Mountain View*: US 60, E 9 m.; SR M, N 3.6; GR, N 1.4 m.	✓	⚶	▲
SHAWNEE CREEK	From *Eminence*: US SR 106, E 4.7 m.; GR, N 1.6 m.	✓	⚶	▲
WATERCRESS PARK	At Van Buren.	✓	⚶	▲
WELCH LANDING	From *Akers*: SR K, N 1.4 m.; GR, W 0.6 m.	✓		

St. Louis's Gateway Arch, part of the Jefferson National Expansion Memorial.

stretches of our greatest scenic rivers." In 1969 Missouri gave ownership of Big Spring, Round Spring, and Alley Spring to the project, retaining Montauk Spring as a *state park*. Today's scenic riverways, administered by the Department of the Interior, were dedicated in 1972. They comprise 134 miles of the Jacks Fork and Current Rivers, preserving huge springs, numerous *caves*, historic structures, and interesting attractions, e.g. the Jacks Fork and Current Rivers *(Float Streams)*, Rocky Falls Shut-In *(Eminence: Ozark National Scenic Riverways)*, the Ozark *Trail*, Gravel Spring *(Ellington)*, and Devil's Well *(Akers)*, as well as natural areas like Jam Up Cave and Barn Hollow *(Mountain View: Natural Areas)*. Sight-seeing, picnicking, hiking, boating, canoeing, fishing, swimming, scuba diving, camping, horseback riding, lodging, and food service are available along the rivers. The chart provides information on specific locations; see also *Float Streams*. Superintendent: Box 490, Van Buren 63965.

Truman National Historic Sites. TRUMAN FARM HOME: *Grandview.* Superintendent: 223 N. Main, Independence 64050. TRUMAN HOME: This was the home of U.S. president Truman and his wife for over 50 years. Sight-seeing *(Independence: Truman Historic District).* 223 N. Main, Independence 64050.

Wilson's Creek National Battlefield. The 1861 site of Missouri's largest Civil War battle features seven strategic battle sites and the Ray House (Vernacular, c. 1852), used as a post office and a Butterfield stage flag stop *(Overland Mail Company).* Sight-seeing, picnicking, hiking, bicycling, fishing, horseback riding, cross-country skiing, snowshoeing *(Springfield: Wilson's Creek).* Superintendent: Postal Drawer C, Republic 65738.

 NATIONAL WILDLIFE REFUGES

Ladies' hat fashions were responsible for the creation of the first national wildlife refuge. In 1903, Pres. Theodore Roosevelt signed an executive order protecting egrets, herons, and other birds on Florida's Pelican Island whose feather plumes were being used in hat designs. The 1934 Migratory Bird Stamp Act, requiring waterfowl hunters to buy an annual duck stamp, has helped maintain an economic base for today's 430 national refuges, which comprise a nationwide network of habitats providing food, water, cover, and space totaling 90 million acres for approximately 60 endangered species and hundreds of other species of plants, animals, and birds. Administered by the U.S. Fish and Wildlife Service and set in wilderness environments, these areas offer spectacular scenery and recreational opportunities that include photography, observation, hiking, boating, and restricted hunting and fishing, as well as facilities like visitor centers, observation towers, and interpretive trails and drives (see the chart for the facilities offered at each site).

Clarence Cannon. Established in 1964 along the Mississippi River floodplain, this refuge consists of permanent and seasonally flooded impoundments, as well as forests, grasslands, and crop fields, as well as access to Long Island and Indian Grave Lakes; fish include crappie and channel catfish. Over 200 species visit annually, e.g. ducks, geese, bald eagles, herons, and egrets. Year-round residents include deer, turkey, mink, beaver, and coyote. The best times for observation are early morning and early evening in October–November and March–April. Shorebirds and warblers are best seen during the first week of May. Box 88, Annada 63330.

NATIONAL WILDLIFE REFUGES			BEST SEASON				RECREATION / FACILITIES									
		LOCATION	WINTER	SPRING	SUMMER	FALL	VISITOR CENTER	PICNIC	BICYCLING	AUTO TOUR	FOOT TRAILS	WILDERNESS USE	HUNTING	FISHING	BOAT RAMP	BOAT MOTOR (H.P.)
NAME	ACRES															
CANNON (CLARENCE)	3,747	Annada: GR, E 1 m. to HQ.		❀		❀	∱			Ⓐ				➤◀	◢	no motors
MINGO	21,676	*Bloomfield: SR J, W 15.1 m.; SR 51, N 6 m. to HQ (via Puxico).*		❀		❀	∱	⊼	⊛	Ⓐ	⋔	Å	🦌	➤◀		no motors
SQUAW CREEK	6,900	*Mound City: SR E, S 4.4 m.; SR 159, S 0.75 m. to HQ.*		❀		❀	∱	⊼	⊛	Ⓐ	⋔			➤◀		
SWAN LAKE	10,670	*Sumner: SR AA, S 1.2 m.; GR, S 1.5 m. to HQ.*		❀		❀	∱		⊛			⋔	➤	➤◀	◢	⛴ [10]

Mingo. Established in 1945, the refuge is dominated by hardwood swamplands and marshes created when the Mississippi River shifted east about 18,000 years ago. Open during daylight hours from March 15 through November 30 (check at headquarters for other times), the area offers observation towers, boardwalks, self-guided trails, horseback riding, berry and nut picking, a photography blind, fishing (bass, bluegill, catfish), and limited hunting (including bows and historic weapons), as well as canoeing on the Mingo River and Stanley Creek and along various ditches (bring your own canoe). The visitor center features wildlife exhibits and archaeological and geological displays. Rt. 1, Box 103, Puxico 63960.

Squaw Creek. Established in 1935, the area has marshes, ponds, and *loess* bluffs that provide refuge for over 200,000 geese as well as other birds, e.g. ducks, pelicans, great blue herons, sandpipers, and as many as 250 bald eagles. Other wildlife include deer, muskrat, beaver, and coyote. Viewing towers and exhibits are located at vantage points. Box 101, Mound City 64470.

Swan Lake. Established in the 1960s, this area has a migratory goose population of about 200,000 that is maintained by restricted hunting (reservations required; a ten-shell-per-day limit). These Canada geese nest along the west coast of Hudson Bay near Churchill, Manitoba, and winter near Swan Lake. Other activities include deer hunting with historic weapons (longbows, crossbows, .40 caliber black-powder single-projectile firearms; one weekend in October) and bald-eagle watch-

ing (arranged in January by reservation). Swan Lake refuge is dominated by 1,100-acre Swan Lake, 3,050-acre Silver Lake, and 800-acre South Lake (a marsh); fish include carp, buffalo, and bullhead. Goose hunting is also permitted in the Fountain Grove and Grand Pass *Wildlife Areas*. Sumner 64681.

STATE FORESTS

Managed by the Forestry Division of the Missouri Department of Conservation (Box 180, Jefferson City 65102), state forests are maintained for public uses that, along with those listed below, include hiking, orienteering, nature photography, and picnicking, all of

Camping in the early 1900s.

STATE FORESTS NAME	ACRES	LOCATION	CAMPING PICNIC	HIKING HORSE TRAILS	HUNTING WATERFOWL	C-R FISHING CREEK·RIVER
ALLEY SPRING	5,881	*Eminence:* SR 106, W 5 m.	△	HT 🚶	🦌	
BEAL	1,475	*Eminence:* SR 106, E 7 m.; SR H, S 3.9 m.; SR NN, N 4.4 m.; signs.	△	HT 🚶	🦌	R 🐟
BEAR CREEK (4 TRACTS)	720	S of *Sleeper* and I-44: just S of Old US 66 (exit 135) between SR F & SR T.	△	HT 🚶	🦌	
BIG CREEK	1,201	Jct. SR 11/SR H, S of *Kirksville;* SR H, N 1.5 m.; GR, W 1.2 m.	🏕 △	🚶	🦌	Pond 🐟
BLAIR CREEK	1,548	*Eminence:* NE side of Current R. at Jack Forks; ask locally.	△	HT 🚶	🦌	C 🐟
BLOOM CREEK	5,861	*Eminence:* SR 106, E 12.3 m. to just E of Current R.	△	HT 🚶	🦌	R 🐟
BLUFFWOODS	2,300	*St. Joseph:* US 36/US 59; US 59, S 7.8 m.	🏕 △	HT 🚶	🦌	
BOLLOW	41	*Shelbyville:* SW edge of city limits on N≡S part of Black C.; ask locally.		🐦 🚶		C 🐟
BOONE (DANIEL)	3,020	*McKittrick:* SR 95, E 2.9 m.; Daniel Boone State Forest road, N 2.2 m.	🏕 △	🚶	🦌	Pond 🐟
BUFORD	2,362	*Pilot Knob:* SR 21, N 3 m.; SR U, E 4 m.; signs.	△	🚶	🦌	
BURR OAK WOODS	1,066	*Blue Springs:* SR 7, N 1 m.	🏕	🚶		
BUSIEK	1,760	*Ozark:* US 65, S 8 m.	△	HT 🚶	🦌	C 🐟
CANAAN	1,435	*Belle:* SR 28, E 5 m.; SR A, N 1 m.; Rehmert Rd., E approx. 3.5 m.	△	HT 🚶	🦌	C 🐟
CARDAREVA	5,882	*Ellington:* SR 106, W 8.7 m.; signs.	△	HT 🚶	🦌	C 🐟
CARR CREEK	3,077	*Ellington:* SR 106, E 15 m. steep GR, W approx. 2.3 m. to Current R.	△	HT 🚶	🦌	R 🐟
CASTOR RIVER (8 TRACTS)	8,001	*Marble Hill:* SR 34, W 13 m.; tracts are N & S along SR MM & SR Y.	△	HT 🚶	🦌	R 🐟
CEDARGROVE (4 TRACTS)	1,720	See *Akers.*	△		🦌	
CLEARWATER (8 TRACTS)	6,093	SW of Clearwater *Lake* between SR H/SR RA & SR HH.	△		🐦 🦌	
CLEMENT (RICHARD F.)	520	*Anutt (Salem):* SR O, N 2.4 m.; SR OO, W 2.8 m.	△	🚶	🦌	

STATE FORESTS NAME	ACRES	LOCATION	CAMPING PICNIC	HIKING HORSE TRAILS	HUNTING WATERFOWL	C-R FISHING CREEK·RIVER
CLOW (5 TRACTS)	9,743	*Eminence:* SR 19, N 1 m. to Forest Dist. HQ.	△	HT 🚶	🦌	R
CLUBB CREEK (8 TRACTS)	622	*Zalma:* SR 51, E 4. to jct. SR W; GR, N 4 m. along Clubb C.	🏕 △	🚶	🦌	C 🐟
COLDWATER (10 TRACTS)	7,161	*Greenville:* US 67, N 13 m. to Coldwater; between US 67 & SR MM.		HT 🚶	🦌	
DAVIS (LESTER R.)	85	*Mindenmines:* US 160, E 2.6 m.; SR NN, N 1 m.; GR, W 3 m.			🦌	
DEER RUN	9,028	*Ellington:* SR 106, W 4 m.; SR 106 spur, S 1 m.; 3-acre Buford L.	🏕 △	HT 🚶	🦌	Lake 🐟
DICKENS VALLEY (3 TRACTS)	3,812	*Ellington:* SR Y, N 5.9 m.; GR, N 2.2 m.	🏕 △	HT 🚶	🦌	C 🐟
DONALDSON POINT	5,785	*New Madrid:* SR WW, E 7.8 m.; SR AB, S 3.4 m.; ponds, Mississippi R.	△	HT 🚶	🦌	R 🐟
ELMSLIE	238	*Monroe City:* SR Z, N 5.3 m.; GR, W 2 m.; GR, N 0.7 m.; lake, North River.	△	HT 🚶	🦌	R 🐟
FIERY FORK	1,286	*Climax Springs:* SR 7, E 4.8 m.; GR, S 3 m.; creek, Little Niangua R.	△	HT 🚶	🦌	R 🐟
FLAG SPRING	3,340	*Cassville:* SR 37, S 7 m.; SR 90, W 3 m.; SR UU, N 2.8 m.	△	HT 🚶	🦌	
FOURCHE CREEK (5 TRACTS)	3,767	See *Doniphan.*	△	HT 🚶	🦌	C 🐟
FOX VALLEY	1,569	*Kahoka:* SR 81, N 6 m.; SR NN, W 4.8 m.; 110-acre lake, Fox R.	△	HT 🚶	🦌	R 🐟
GOOSE CREEK (6 TRACTS)	1,040	See *Lebanon.*	△	HT	🦌	
GRAND TRACE	1,497	*Bethany:* SR W, W 3.1 m.; SR F, W 5.3 m.	△	HT 🚶	🦌	C 🐟
HARTSHORN	3,616	*Akers:* SR K, S 8.6 m.; GR, N 3 m.	△		🦌	
HEATH (CHARLIE)	1,531	*Kahoka:* SR 81, N 6 m.; SR NN, W 13.3 m.; Fox R.	△	HT 🚶	🦌	R 🐟
HENNING (RUTH & PAUL)	1,534	*Branson:* SR 76, W 5.2 m.		🚶		C 🐟
HIDDEN HOLLOW	1,228	*La Plata:* SR 156, W 7.7 m.; GR, S 1.8 m.	△	HT 🚶	🦌	C 🐟
HOLLY RIDGE	777	*Bloomfield:* SR E, E 1.2 m.; GR, S 1.4 m.	△	HT 🚶	🦌	Pond 🐟

— CONTINUED —

Predecessors of today's off-road cyclists. (FROM "ORAM CENTENNIAL, 1869–1969")

STATE FORESTS (CONTINUED FROM PREVIOUS CHART)

NAME	ACRES	LOCATION	CAMPING / PICNIC	HIKING / HORSE TRAILS	HUNTING / WATERFOWL	FISHING / CREEK·RIVER
HUCKLEBERRY RIDGE	2,066	Pineville: SR K, E 2.8 m.	△	HT ♞	🦌	C 🐟
HUZZAH	6,162	Leasburg: SR H, S 4.4 m.; Huzzah C., Meramec R., Courtois C.		HT ♞	🦌	R 🐟
INDIAN CREEK	6,092	Eminence: SR 106, E 5.2 m. to SR V; access: along SR 106 to Current R.	△		🦌	
INDIAN TRAIL	3,243	Salem: SR 19, E 14 m.; 55 ponds; State Fish Hatchery.	△	HT ♞	🦌	Pond 🐟
KETCHERSIDE MOUNTAIN	3,055	Arcadia: SR 21, S 3.6 m.	⛾△	HT ♞	🦌	C 🐟
LARSON	80	Mountain Grove: US 60, E 4 m.; SR MM, N 0.9 m.; GR, E 1.2 m.	△	HT ♞	🦌	C 🐟
LEAD MINE (3 TRACTS)	5,866	Buffalo: SR 73, N 16 m.; SR E, E 3.8 m.; Little Niangua R.	△	HT ♞	🦌	R 🐟
LITTLE BLACK	2,322	Doniphan: SR 21, N 8 m.; SR NN, N 0.3 m.; Little Black R.	△	HT ♞	🦌	R 🐟
LITTLE INDIAN CREEK (4 TRACTS)	3,362	St. Clair: SR K, S 5.8 m.; GR, S 3.2 m. to main tract (3,001 acres).	△	HT	🦌	C 🐟
LITTLE LOST CREEK	2,827	Warrenton: I-70, W 5 m.; SR BB, S 1.8 m.; SR EE, S 0.7 m.	△	HT ♞	🦌	C 🐟
LITTLE SAC WOODS	772	Springfield: SR 13, N 10 m.; SR BB, W 3 m.; FR 115, S 1.7 m.; Little Sac R.	△	♞	🦌	R 🐟
LOGAN CREEK	4,743	Ellington: SR 106, W 6 m.; SR B, N 0.3 m. (see Ellington).	△	HT ♞	🦌	C 🐟
MAGNOLIA HOLLOW	973	Ste. Genevieve: US 61, N 10 m.; SR V, E 1 m.; Establishment C.	△	HT ♞	🦌	C 🐟
MERAMEC	3,897	Sullivan: SR 185, S 4.8 m.; Meramec R.	△	♞	E side 🦌	R 🐟
MIDVALE	80	Houston: SR 17, E 18 m.; SE W, S 0.5 m.			🦌	
MILLSTREAM GARDENS	644	Fredericktown: SR 72, W 8.5 m. (W of Lance); GR, S 0.6 m.; St Francis R.		♞	Limited 🦌	
MINERAL HILLS	1,859	Unionville: SR 5, S 4 m.; SR F, E 2.9 m.; GR, N 0.8 m.; S Blackbird C.	△	HT	🦌	C 🐟
MONTGOMERY WOODS	322	Kirksville: SR 11, S 17.3 m.; GR, S 0.3 m.; Little Mussel C.	△		🦌	C 🐟
MOUNTAIN LAKE	909	Patterson: SR B, E 5 m.	△	HT ♞	🦌	
MULE MOUNTAIN (7 TRACTS)	3,050	Eminence: SR 106, E 7 m.; SR H, S 4 m.; SR NN, E (along & S of) 3.4 m.	△	HT ♞	🦌	C 🐟
NIANGUA (3 TRACTS)	837	Marshfield: (1) SR CC to Sampson; (2) I-44, S 3 m.; (3) SR CC to Niangua.	△	HT ♞	🦌	C, R 🐟
OAK RIDGE	243	Dexter: US 60, W 10 m.; SR TT, S 0.5 m.; old US 60, W 0.7 m.	⛾△	♞	🦌	Ditch
OSAGE FORK (3 TRACTS)	525	See Lebanon.	△	HT ♞	🦌	

STATE FORESTS

NAME	ACRES	LOCATION	CAMPING / PICNIC	HIKING / HORSE TRAILS	HUNTING / WATERFOWL	FISHING / CREEK·RIVER
PAINT ROCK (5 TRACTS)	6,562	Ellington: SR 21, S 8 m.; SR D, W 0.8 m.; GR, W 2.8 m. to Current R.	△	HT ♞	🦌	R 🐟
PEA RIDGE (9 TRACTS)	8,386	Sullivan: SR 185, S 16.2 m. (main tract: 5,312 acres); Indian C.	△	HT ♞	🦌	C 🐟
POOSEY	3,425	Chillicothe: SR 190, W 6 m.; SR A, N 8.9 m.; 192-acre lake.	△	HT ♞	🦌	R 🐟
POPLAR BLUFF (4 TRACTS)	952	Poplar Bluff: (1-2) at end of SR N; (3-4) SR W, N 2 m. to GR N of Hillard / RR.	△	HT ♞	🦌	C 🐟
POWDER MILL	3,355	Ellington: SR 106, W 7 m.; sign.	△	HT	🦌	
PRAIRIEWOODS	330	Nevada: US 71, N 11 m. to Horton; GR, E 0.7 m.; Hubler, Burr Lakes.	△	HT ♞	🦌	R 🐟
REIFSNIDER	1,425	Truesdale: SR M, E 2.2 m.; Schuetzen Ground Rd., S 3.2 m.	⛾△	HT ♞	🦌	C 🐟
RIVERBREAKS	2,307	Forest City: SR T, S 3.7 m.: access points along SR T from Curzon to Forbes.	△	HT ♞	🦌	C 🐟
RIVERSIDE (6 TRACTS)	2,900	Gads Hill: (3 main tracts) along SR CC & SR BB between SR 49 & Black R.	△	HT ♞	🦌	C 🐟
ROCKWOODS RESERVATION	1,898	Eureka: SR 109, N 5 m.	⛾	♞		
ROCKY CREEK (11 TRACTS)	9,296	Eminence: (2 main tracts) SR 19, S of jct. SR F to Mark Twain Nat'l Forest.	△	HT ♞	🦌	C 🐟
SHANNONDALE (5 TRACTS)	2,511	Eminence: (most accessible tract) SR 19, N 19 m.; SR A, E 0.5 m.	△	HT ♞	🦌	C 🐟
SPRING CREEK GAP	1,819	Vichy: US 63, W 2 m.; Old 63, N 1 m.	⛾△	♞	🦌	C 🐟
SUGAR CREEK	2,609	Kirksville: US 63, S 4 m.; SR 11, W 4.2 m.; SR N, S 0.5 m.	△	HT ♞	🦌	C 🐟
THREE CREEKS	1,157	Columbia: US 63, S 4 m.; SR 163, W 2 m.; GR, S 1 m.	△	HT ♞	🦌	C 🐟
UNION RIDGE	8135	Green Castle: SR D, N 2 m.	△	HT ♞	🦆🦌	C 🐟
GENERAL WATKINS	850	Benton: US 61, S 2.75 m.	⛾△	HT ♞	🦌	
WEBB CREEK (12 TRACTS)	4,621	Ellington: SR HH, S 9.5 m.; along & SW of SR HH to jct. SR 34.	△	HT	🦌	
WHITE (GEORGE O.)	754	Licking: Old US 63, N approx. 0.7 m.	⛾		🦌	Pond
WILHELMINA (2 TRACTS)	1,359	Campbell: (1) SR DD, W 4.7 m.; (2) SR 53, N 6.7 m.; CR 220, S 1.5 m.	△	HT ♞	🦆🦌	R 🐟
WYACONDA CROSSING	148	Canton: SR 81, N 4 m.; GR, W 1.1 m.	△	♞	🦌	R 🐟
YOUNG (HILDA J.)	970	Eureka: SR W, S .6 m.; SR FF, S 2.7 m.		♞	🦌	C 🐟

—— END OF LISTING ——

which are allowed in every state forest but are noted on the chart here only when facilities are provided. The following general restrictions apply in all state forests. CAMPING: Primitive only (no facilities); pack out trash, no fireworks or unattended fires, camp 100 yards from access roads and parking lots. FISHING: State laws apply. HORSEBACK RIDING: On designated two-track roads or gravel roads; groups of 10 or more need manager's permission; no commercial riding without a permit. HUNTING: Portable stands must be removed daily; shoot only when pursuing game. MOTOR VEHICLES: On main roads and two-track trails only (no use of hiking trails). VEGETATION: All cutting prohibited except for the collection of nuts, berries, and mushrooms for personal use. Note: Boundaries are marked from tree to tree with blue paint or signs; state forest signs are posted at public roads.

STATE PARKS

Beginning in 1907, nine years before the 1916 National Parks System was created to administer national sites, attempts were made to establish a Missouri state parks system. In 1917 the general assembly approved a state

parks fund that in 1924 bought the first tract of land, Big Spring State Park, which later, along with Alley Spring and Round Spring state parks, was incorporated into the Ozark National Scenic Riverways (*National Parks*). Today's 47 parks are as diverse as Missouri's geography. Together with the State Historic Sites and Natural Areas (see Index) they provide educational, scenic, and entertaining adventures. The chart provides information about picnicking, hiking, camping, water recreation, and other facilities available at each park. In the descriptions below, park locations are keyed to nearby towns, which provide directions. In all parks, pets should be kept on leashes and hunting and the discharging of firearms are prohibited. Most

campsites are on a first-come-first-served basis. Alcoholic beverages are prohibited on beaches and in parking areas. For more information, contact the Missouri Department of Natural Resources, Box 176, Jefferson City 65102.

Babler, Dr. E. A., Memorial. Established in 1937, the park was named for St. Louis surgeon Edmund A. Babler. Bounded on the west by Wild Horse Creek, it has narrow winding ridges and deep sheltered valleys that characterize this transition area between the Ozarks and the glacial plains. To the north, thick *loess* helped the growth of a diversity of wildflowers and unusually tall trees (e.g. oak, basswood, sugar maple, and walnut). To the south, erosion has exposed chert

STATE PARKS

Legend (CAMPING codes): D DUMP STATION · E ELECTRICITY · F FULL HOOKUPS · L LAUNDRY · S SHOWERS
Camping sub-columns: H HORSE · S SCOUT · G GROUP
Trails: BIKE · HIKE · HORSE · ♿ accessible
Picnic: SITES · SHELTER
Water Recreation: MOTORS H.P. / ELECTRIC ONLY · CANOEING/SAILING · TROUT FISHING · OTHER FISHING · BEACH/POOL

NAME	ACRES	BIKE	HIKE	HORSE	SITES	SHELTER	BASIC	IMPROVED	H/S/G	HOOKUP CODES	STORE	DINING	CABINS	MOTEL	BOAT RAMP	MARINA	BOAT RENTAL	MOTORS H.P.	CANOE/SAIL	TROUT FISH	OTHER FISH	BEACH/POOL
BABLER (DR. E.) MEMORIAL	2,439	●	●	H	●	●	▲	▲	S	D,E,L,S ♿												P
BAKER (SAM A.)	5,168		●	H	● ♿	●	▲	▲	H,S	D,E,L,S ♿	●	☆ ♿	●				●		●	● ♿	●	
BENNETT SPRING	3,099		●		●	●	▲	▲	S	D,E,L,S ♿	●	☆ ♿	●		●			no limit	●	● ♿		P
BIG LAKE	407				●	●	▲	▲		D,E,L,S		☆ ♿	●	●	●			no limit	●		●	P
BIG OAK TREE	1,004		● ♿		●	●			S						●				❄	●	●	
CASTLEWOOD	1,780	●	●	H	●	●									●			no limit			●	
CROWDER	1,912		●		●	●	▲	▲	S,G	D,E,L,S					●				●		●	☼
CUIVRE RIVER	6,271		●	H	●	●	▲	▲	H,S,G	D,E,F,L,S					●				❄	●	●	☼
ELEPHANT ROCKS	129		● ♿		●																●	
FINGER LAKES	1,131	motorcycle			●		▲	▲		S					●				●		●	☼
GRAHAM CAVE	357	●	● ♿		●	●	▲	▲		D,E,L,S ♿											●	
GRAND GULF	165		●		●																	
HA HA TONKA	2,817		● ♿		●	●															●	
HAWN	4,592		●		●	●	▲	▲	S	D,E,L,S											●	
JOHNSON'S SHUT-INS	2,828		● ♿		●	●	▲	▲	S	D,E,L,S ♿											●	
KATY TRAIL	262.6 miles	●	● ♿		●																	
KNOB NOSTER	3,549	●	●	H	●	●	▲	▲	H,S,G	D,E,L,S ♿									❄		●	
LAKE OF THE OZARKS	17,213	●	●	H	●	●	▲	▲	S,G	D,E,L,S ♿	●				●	●	●	no limit	●		●	☼
LAKE WAPPAPELLO	1,854	●	●		●	●	▲	▲		D,E,L,S	●		●		●	●	●	no limit	●		●	☼
LEWIS AND CLARK	121				●	●	▲	▲		D,E,L,S ♿								no limit	●			☼
LONG BRANCH	1,834	●	●		●	●		▲		D,E,S					●	●	●	no limit	●		●	☼
MASTODON	425		●		●				S												●	
MERAMEC	6,785		●		● ♿	●	▲	▲	S	D,E,F,L,S ♿	●	☆ ♿	●		●		●	no limit			●	
MONTAUK	1,353		●		●	●	▲	▲		D,E,L,S ♿	●	☆ ♿	●	●						●		
ONONDAGA CAVE	1,317		●		●		▲	▲	S	D,E,L,S	●	☆			●		●	no limit	●		●	☼
PERSHING	2,685		●		●	●	▲	▲	S	D,E,L,S									●		●	
POMME DE TERRE	734		●		●	●	▲	▲	S	D,E,L,S ♿	●				●	●	●	no limit	●		●	☼
PRAIRIE	2,982		●		●																	
ROARING RIVER	3,403		●		●	●	▲	▲		D,E,L,S	●	☆ ♿	●	●						●		P
ROBERTSVILLE	1,110		●		●		▲		S	D					●						●	
ROCK BRIDGE MEMORIAL	2,238		●		●	●			S													
ST. FRANCOIS	2,735		●	H	●	●	▲	▲	S	D,E,L,S ♿									●		●	
ST. JOE	8,238	●	●	H ♿ motorcycle	●	●	▲	▲	H	D,E,L,S					●			no limit	●		●	☼
STOCKTON	2,176	●		H	●	●	▲	▲		D,E,L,S ♿	●	☆ ♿		●	●	●	●	no limit	●			☼
TABLE ROCK	356			H	●	●	▲	▲		D,E,F,L,S	●				●	●	●	no limit	●			
TAUM SAUK MOUNTAIN	6,508		●		●		▲															
THOUSAND HILLS	3,215		●		●	●	▲	▲	S	D,E,L,S	●	☆ ♿	●		●	●		>90	●		●	☼
TRAIL OF TEARS	3,415		●	H	● ♿	●	▲	▲	S	D,E,F,L,S ♿									❄		●	☼
TRUMAN (HARRY S)	1,440			H	●	●	▲	▲		D,E,L,S ♿	●				●	●		no limit	●		●	☼
TWAIN (MARK)	2,771			H	●	●	▲	▲	G	D,E,L,S					●			no limit	●		●	☼
VAN METER	983			H	●	●	▲	▲	S	S											●	
WAKONDA	1,050				●		▲	▲		D,E,L,S			●		●		●	>10	●		●	☼
WALLACE	502		●		●		▲	▲	S	D,E,L,S									❄		●	☼
WASHINGTON	1,811		●		●	●	▲	▲	S	D,E,L,S	●	☆ ♿	●				●		●		●	☼ P
WATKINS MILL	818	●	● ♿		● ♿		▲	▲	S	D,E,L,S ♿					●			>6	●		●	☼
WESTON BEND	1,024	●	●		●		▲	▲		D,E,L,S												

and limestone soils. Park naturalist / programs. Babler Southwoods Hollow Natural Area. Near the Missouri River, approx. 20 m. W of St. Louis; near *Eureka*. Information: Chesterfield 63107.

Baker, Sam A. Established in 1926, the park was named for Sam A. Baker, Missouri governor from 1925 to 1929. Bounded on the east by the St. Francis River and by Big Creek's *shut-ins*, the park offers hiking, canoeing, and fishing (bluegill, bass, crappie). One of Missouri's oldest parks, located in the St. Francois Mountains, it is characterized by conical hills, some over 900 feet high, formed by igneous rocks that are among the continent's oldest and hardest. About 550 million years ago streams carved hills and valleys much like those seen here today, which are typified by 4,180-acre Mudlick Mountain Wild Area, where the 12-mile Mudlick National Recreation Trail offers a close look at 1,313-foot Mudlick Mountain, old-growth forests, deep canyon gorges, and open glades. Park naturalist / programs. Mudlick Mountain Natural Area. *FLOAT STREAMS*: Big Creek, St. Francis. Near Patterson *(Piedmont)*. Information: Patterson 63956.

Bennett Spring. Established in 1924, the park was named for 19th-century *gristmill* owner Peter Bennett. One of Missouri's first state parks, it is located on Ozark ridges covered by an oak-hickory forest with an understory of dogwoods and wildflowers. The spring and spring branch provide trout fishing from March to October (licenses are available at the park) and are stocked by a state hatchery there, which can be toured. The spring averages 100 million gallons daily; its output flows a mile and a half to the Niangua River. Park naturalist / programs. Bennett Spring Hanging Fern Natural Area. *FLOAT STREAM:* Niangua (park shuttle service available). East of *Lebanon*. Information: Lebanon 65536.

Big Lake. Established in 1932, the park was named for Missouri's largest natural lake (625 acres). On the eastern shoreline, it is characterized by *loess* hills that help nurture cottonwood, silver maple, and walnut trees that shade the area. The shallow oxbow lake, a former meander loop of the nearby Missouri River, is stocked with catfish, crappie, carp, bass, and bluegill and provides a migratory and winter habitat for bald eagles, white pelicans, great blue herons, ducks, geese, and cormorants. Cabins feature fireplaces and screened porches. Park naturalist / programs. Near Fortesque *(Forest City)*. Information: Bigelow 64420.

Big Oak Tree. Established in 1937, the park was named for a burr oak that stood here for 334 years. The nucleus of the park is 80 acres of virgin bottomland hardwood, one of the few remnants of the presettlement forests. With canopies averaging 120 feet, it has 12 state champion trees, 2 of which are national champions

(including a 133-foot persimmon). A half-mile boardwalk allows access to this dense swampy area, which is nationally known to bird-watchers for its 146 species, including rare ones, e.g. hooded warbler, Mississippi kite, fish crow; it is also the only known Missouri breeding site of Swanson's warbler. Big Oak Lake (22 acres) is stocked with catfish, bass, bluegill, and crappie. Big Oak Tree Natural Area. Near *East Prairie* and *Dorena*. Information: East Prairie 63845.

Big Sugar Creek. Acquired in 1992, Missouri's newest state park is named for the creek, which is lined by sugar maples. Although water-oriented, the park also has bluffs and woodlands, as well as excellent examples of oak and pine savannas. No facilities; closed to public. Near *Pineville*. Information: Box 176, Jefferson City 65102.

Castlewood. Established in 1974, the park was probably named for the wooded, white limestone bluffs along the Meramec River *(Float Streams)* that are supposedly reminiscent of medieval castle walls. A recreation and resort area from 1915 to 1940, drawing 10,000 St. Louis weekend visitors for canoeing, sunning, and dancing, Castlewood is primarily a nature park today, providing 14 miles of trails through hills, valleys, floodplains, and the Meramec River Recreation Area (108 river miles of open spaces connected by trails; located between Meramec State Park, below, and the river's confluence with the Mississippi). Near *Kirkwood*. Information: Ballwin 63021.

Crowder. Established in 1938, the park was named for Army major general Enoch H. Crowder *(Trenton: Edinburg)*. Located on gently rolling hills that become more rugged at nearby Thompson River, its nucleus is 18-acre Crowder Lake, which provides boating, canoeing, swimming, and fishing (bass, bluegill, channel catfish, crappie). It was initially developed by the CCC *(WPA)*, and some evidence of that agency's work remains. Near *Trenton*. Information: Trenton 64683.

Cuivre River. First acquired in 1936 as National Park Service property, the land was transferred to Missouri in 1946 as a state park. Although Cuivre (locally pronounced Quiver) is French, meaning copper, there is no copper here, so the derivation of the name is unknown, unless it honors, via folk etymology, French naturalist Baron Georges Cuvier (1769–1832). The site was used by prehistoric Indians (c. 10,000 B.C.), mound builders (c. A.D. 500), and more recently by the Sauk, Fox, and Illinois tribes. Its *Lincoln Hills* location offers many Ozark-like plants and animals, as well as springs, ponds, sinkholes *(Collapsed Cave Systems)*, and limestone bluffs along the river and Sugar Creek. To the north is a restored *prairie* grassland; in the middle and to the north are trails through two undeveloped areas preserved for their wilder-

Fishing at Bennett Spring. (CHARLES TREFTS PHOTOGRAPH)

ness qualities. Altogether, the park features 31 miles of connecting hiking and horse trails; 88-acre Lake Lincoln provides swimming, boating, and fishing (channel catfish, black bass, sunfish, bluegill). Park naturalist / programs. Hamilton Forest Natural Area. Near *Troy.* Information: Troy 63379.

Elephant Rocks. The area was established as a park in 1967. Most likely the size and arrangement (often end-to-end) of these rocks—and possibly their pink color—reminded the namer of elephants. Molten rock pushed to the earth surface more than a billion years ago cooled to form granite rocks that were then sculpted by surface erosion and weathering into today's extraordinary spheroidal shapes and smooth textures. Elephant Rocks Natural Area has a one-mile paved path through seven acres of the best examples of these pink geological wonders, including Dumbo, a granite "elephant" 27 feet tall, 35 feet long, 17 feet wide, and weighing 680 tons. Park naturalist / programs. Braille trail, wheelchair access, panoramic views. Near *Pilot Knob.* Information: Belleview 63623.

Finger Lakes. Established in 1973, the park was named for the shape of its lakes. Peabody Coal Company created these lakes in 1964–1967 by strip mining the acreage, which was donated by Peabody after 1972 federal reclamation laws were passed ("reclamation-for-recreation") to help reconstruct abandoned strip-mining sites for public use. About a dozen isolated lakes are connected by dams and canals. The park's barren rugged terrain, a result of the mining, provides 70 miles of ideal conditions for off-road motorcycles; four-wheel vehicles are restricted to normal park roadways (St. Joe State Park, below). Recently a motocross was developed. Near *Columbia.* Information: Columbia 65201.

Graham Cave. National Historic Landmark. Established in 1964, the park was named for the Graham family that bought the land in 1816 from Daniel Boone's son Daniel Morgan *(Defiance: Boone Fort and Cabin Site; Mineola: Architecture: Graham House).* The 60-foot flat-arched span of the entrance gives the impression, from a distance, of looking under the front end of a fossilized flying saucer. Human habitation dates from c. 7850 to c. 5950 B.C. With a southern alignment, its 16-foot-tall entrance, and a 60-foot-deep walking space, this St. Peter sandstone *cave* provides excellent solar heating. The park borders the Loutre River. Graham Cave Glades Natural Area. Near *Danville.* Information: Montgomery City 63361.

Grand Gulf. Established in 1984, the park has been nicknamed the Little Grand Canyon; its proper name is descriptive *(Thayer).* Grand Gulf Natural Area. Near *Thayer.* Information: Thayer 65791.

Ha Ha Tonka. The park was established in 1978 and named for the local post office (1895–1937) whose name was spelled Hahatonka. Reportedly the name was contrived of Indian-sounding words to mean "smiling" or "laughing waters" (unlike Minnehaha, which is a real Indian name, from the Souian word for waterfall, that was romantically misinterpreted as "laughing water"). Because of this state park's idyllic natural landscaping and the remnants of nine greenhouses, it is interesting to note that an 18th-century English garden at Stowe in Buckinghamshire is cited as one of the first to use a ha-ha, a sunk fence that leaves the landscaping visually uninterrupted while keeping livestock and other large animals away from a house. Kansas City businessman Robert M. Snyder acquired 2,500 acres at this former *gristmill* site (first used in 1830) and began to build a three-story chateauesque mansion in 1905. He died a year later. The interior was completed in 1922 by his son LeRoy. Sparks from a fireplace ignited a fire that gutted the structure, leaving only today's stark freestanding stone walls, an 80-foot-tall water tower, and trenches of the nine greenhouses. Geologically interesting, the park encompasses one of Missouri's largest springs (with a flow of 48 million gallons daily), a transition area between the Ozarks and the Salem Plateau, savannas, and a classic example of karst topography (*Camdenton: Natural Areas*). Nine connecting trails (8 m. total; none over 1.5 m.) give access to the historical and natural features. Park naturalist / programs. Near *Camdenton*. Information: Camdenton 65020.

Hawn. The park was established in 1952 by an initial donation of 1,459 acres from former *Ste. Genevieve* schoolteacher Helen Coffer Hawn. At the eastern edge of the St. Francois mountains, it is set in sandstone hills covered by oak and pine, bisected by Pickle Creek and the Aux Vases River, and dominated by outstanding sandstone formations that feature rounded knobs, canyons, and vertical cliffs. Two loop-trails (4 m., 6 m.)

in 2,080-acre Whispering Pine Wild Area, bordering the creek and river, give close-up views of fauna and flora, e.g. Missouri's only native pine, the straight shortleaf pine tree. Natural areas: *Ste. Genevieve*. Park naturalist / programs. Near *Ste. Genevieve*. Information: Ste. Genevieve 63670.

Johnson's Shut-Ins. Established in 1955, the park was named for the Johnson family (specific references are vague). Located in the St. Francois Mountains, the *shut-ins'* blue-gray rocks were formed about 1.5 billion years ago after a volcanic eruption. The rocks later cooled and were covered by an inland sea that retreated about 250 million years ago. Rain and wind then eroded a softer rock covering, exposing these volcanic rocks that have been scoured into potholes, chutes, and canyon-like gorges. Today's East Fork Black River continues to pour over them, providing visitors with white-water swimming holes and long riffles. Natural features include fens, gravel washes, igneous glades, forests, and glacier-like rocks. East Fork Wild Area (1,110 acres), ranging from bottomland woods to upland ridges, bluffs, and wet meadows, offers a pre-settlement wilderness setting that includes over 900 plant species, e.g. Missouri's largest Virginia witch hazel; access: 2.5-mile Shut-Ins Trail and the Taum Sauk section of the 500-mile Ozark *Trail*, which connects this park with the adjoining Taum Sauk Mountain State Park (below). Park naturalist / programs. Natural areas: *Centerville*. Near Lesterville (*Centerville*). Information: Middlebrook 63656.

Katy Trail. The park was established in 1987 by the Missouri Department of Natural Resources through the National Trails System Act and donations by E. D. Jones Jr. Its name comes from the nickname of the Missouri-Kansas-Texas (MKT) Railroad. At 262.6 miles long, this trail is America's largest rail-to-trail conversion. Formerly this part of the rail system ran along the north bank of the Missouri River, often paralleling the historic *Boonslick Trail*, from near Portage Des Sioux (*St.*

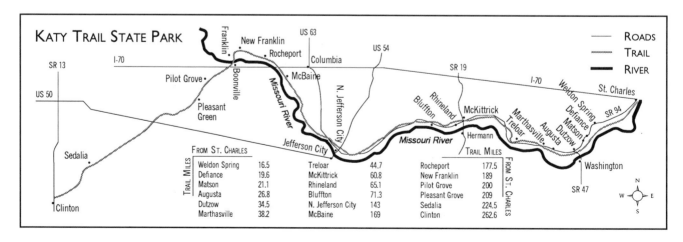

KATY TRAIL STATE PARK

ROADS
TRAIL
RIVER

FROM ST. CHARLES					
Weldon Spring	16.5	Treloar	44.7	Rocheport	177.5
Defiance	19.6	McKittrick	60.8	New Franklin	189
Matson	21.1	Rhineland	65.1	Pilot Grove	200
Augusta	26.8	Bluffton	71.3	Pleasant Grove	209
Dutzow	34.5	N. Jefferson City	143	Sedalia	224.5
Marthasville	38.2	McBaine	169	Clinton	262.6

Charles) at Machens[1] through *Boonville,* and then south through *Sedalia* to *Clinton.* Today, this 100-yard-wide 262.6-mile-long Katy railroad corridor, abandoned in 1986, provides a hiking, biking, and handicapped-use trail (no motorized vehicles allowed). Open during daylight hours; unless otherwise marked, all land beyond the 100-yard-wide corridor is private property. The trail is planned to eventually run from St. Louis to Kansas City. Information: Jefferson City 65102.

Knob Noster. Originally a 1930s federal government project called the Montserrat National Recreation Demonstration Area, the land was acquired by the state in 1946. Its namesake is disputed *(Warrensburg: Knob Noster).* Clearfork Creek flows through the park, which features prairies and savannas but is mostly covered by second-growth forests. Lake Buteo and Clearfork Lake provide fishing for channel catfish, bass, and bluegill. Seven connecting trails crisscross the park (10.5 m. total; 0.25–2 m. each); Boy Scouts maintain a compass trail. Park naturalist / programs. Pin Oak Slough Natural Area. Near Knob Noster *(Warrensburg).* Information: Knob Noster 65336.

Lake of the Ozarks. The area was established as a park by the National Park Service in the 1930s after the damming of the Osage, Niangua, and Galiza Rivers *(Camdenton: Bagnell Dam);* it was named for its location and acquired in 1946 by the state. Missouri's largest state park contains most of the area's natural features: hills and ridges covered by oak-hickory forests, *caves,* bluffs, and rocky glades. Ten trails (0.5–6 m.) explore the area. An aquatic one is marked by buoys on Grand Glaize Arm. Ozark Caverns features Angel Shower, a formation of stalactites and waterfalls. Patterson Hollow Wild Area (1,275 acres) is a wilderness setting of wooded hills, meadows, springs, and streams. The park's Lee C. Fine Airport has scheduled commercial flights. Park naturalist / programs. Coakley Hollow Fen Natural Area. Near *Linn Creek* and *Camdenton.* Information: Kaiser 65047.

Lake Wappapello. Begun when the Corps of Engineers started damming the St. Francis River in 1938 *(Greenville),* this park was acquired by the state in 1957; it was named for the nearby town (p.o. 1884–now), which, like Wapella, Ill., and Wapello, Iowa, was named for an early 19th-century Fox chief (local tradition claims the namesake was an early 19th-century Shawnee hunter in this area). Although the area is covered mostly by an oak-hickory forest, black gum and sycamore grow by the lake and have mistletoe in their branches. A cove near Asher Creek is designated a winter wildlife refuge, with eagles, osprey, and ducks. Lake fishing includes white and largemouth bass, crappie, bluegill, and catfish. Trails: Lakeview (0.5 m.), Wappapello Lake *(Lakes: Corps of Engineers)* wilderness

(15 m.), Allison *Cemetery* (3.5 m.), and Asher Creek (2 m.). Park naturalist / programs. Near *Poplar Bluff.* Information: Williamsville 63967.

Lewis and Clark. The park was established in 1933 and developed by the CCC *(WPA),* which built its picnic shelter; it was named for explorers *Lewis and Clark,* who recorded sighting today's 365-acre Sugar Lake. This oxbow lake of the Missouri River, the site of a state hatchery, provides fishing for bass, bluegill, channel catfish, and carp as well as bird-watching for geese, ducks, snowy egrets, and the great blue heron. Between *Weston* and *St. Joseph.* Information: Rushville 64484.

Long Branch. The park was established in 1982 after the Corps of Engineers dammed the East Fork of Little Chariton River to create the park's descriptive namesake Long Branch Lake *(Lakes: Corps of Engineers),* whose 24-mile shoreline (2,430 acres) provides recreation, including fishing (bass, bluegill, catfish). The topography, first shaped by glaciers *(Glacial Erratics)* and typical of the area, includes today a 40-acre remnant of *prairie* grassland. A one-mile exercise trail begins at the dam and follows the shoreline. Near *Macon* and *Callao.* Information: Macon 63552.

Mastodon. The park was established in 1976 to preserve the site of the first physical evidence found in eastern North America of the coexistence of humans and mastodons. In 1839 and the early 1900s well-preserved bones of mastodons and other extinct animals were excavated here. One large mastodon skeleton is displayed at the British Museum of Natural History. More than 60 skeletons were found in what was then called the Kimmswick Bone Bed, which was possibly a mineral spring in a formerly swampy area. A 1979 Illinois Museum dig uncovered a stone Clovis spear point dating from 10,000–14,000 B.C. that linked human habitation with the mastodon era. Museum displays include bones, tusks, teeth, human artifacts, and a full-size replica of a mastodon skeleton. Near *Kimmswick.* Information: Imperial 63052.

Meramec. Established in 1927, the park was named for the spring-fed Meramec River, whose name was derived from the Algonquian word for catfish. The river borders and bisects the park's rugged slopes, mature forests, and grassy valley. Billed as a *cave* park, Meramec has 22 caves as well as sinkholes, springs, and other karst characteristics *(Collapsed Cave Systems).* Fisher Cave (about a mile long) has guided tours. About 12 miles of hiking trails wind through the park, including one that connects with the 500-mile Ozark *Trail.* Park naturalist / programs. Meramec Upland Forest Natural Area. Meramec River Recreation Area *(Castlewood State Park, above). FLOAT STREAM:* Meramec. Near *Sullivan.* Information: Sullivan 63080.

Montauk. Established in 1926, the park was named for the site's first post office, which was established and named by New York settlers for their former hometown on Long Island *(Salem: Recreation)*. In the park, Pigeon Creek combines with Montauk's seven springs, whose flow totals 43 million gallons per day, emptying into the headwaters of the Current River at an 1896 *gristmill* (the site's fourth). Other features include a trout hatchery, a pine-oak-hickory forest, dolomite river bluffs, a bald-eagle wintering refuge, and the scenic valley setting. Park naturalist / programs. Montauk Upland Forest Natural Area. *FLOAT STREAM:* Current. Near *Licking* and *Salem*. Information: Salem 65560. OZARK NATIONAL SCENIC RIVERWAYS *(National Parks):* Baptist and Montauk river access.

Onondaga Cave. National Natural Landmark. Established in 1982, the park was named for the Indian tribe, one of the confederacy of Five Nations known as the league of the Iroquois. Not explored until 1886, the land was bought in 1900 by a mining group interested in its valuable onyx (technical and other problems stymied the group). Like visitors to the 1904 St. Louis World's Fair, today's tourists are impressed by the great abundance and quality of formations: stalactites, stalagmites, rimstone dams, cave coral, draperies, flowstone, and soda straws; guided tours are provided along lighted paved walkways. The Meramec River, bordering the park, provides recreation and broad river-bluff views of the valley. Park naturalist / programs. *FLOAT STREAM:* Meramec. Near Leasburg *(Cuba)*. Information: Leasburg 65535.

Pershing. Established in 1937 as a memorial to Gen. John J. Pershing *(Laclede)*, the park features Locust Creek (a meandering stream), oxbow sloughs, cutoffs, mature upland and bottomland forests, a 750-acre restored wet *prairie*, marshlands and swamps, as well as Woodland-era Indian burial mounds. Two small lakes provide recreation and fishing (bass, bluegill, channel catfish), as does the creek (channel catfish, bullhead, carp, drum). Cordgrass Bottoms and Locust Creek Natural Areas. Near *Laclede*. Information: Laclede 64651.

Pomme de Terre. Established in 1960, the park was named for the adjacent lake, whose name came from the river that was named "apple of the earth" (potato) by French explorers for the potato-shaped cowberry, groundnut, or wild bean eaten by local Indians. Mostly covered by a thick oak-hickory forest, the park features water-related recreation, including fishing (bass, walleye, catfish, crappie, and Missouri's only true muskie). Indian Point Trail (2 m.) leads through a cedar savanna to a scenic overlook of the lake. Cedar Bluff Trail (2 m.) follows rocky bluffs along the lake.

Park naturalist / programs. The park is divided and set on two peninsulas of the lake near *Hermitage* and Pittsburg *(Hermitage)*. Information: Pittsburg 65724.

Prairie. Established in 1980, the park was named for its setting. Encompassing an excellent example of southwest Missouri's presettlement tallgrass *prairies,* it offers three hiking trails through areas similar to those that once covered 400,000 square miles of North America: (1) Coyote (3 m.) includes portions of West and Middle Drywood Creeks, (2) Drover's (2.5 m.) has the best vistas and includes a high-quality prairie headwater stream, and (3) Gayfeather (1.5 m.) features wildflowers that bloom from late March to early November. The best hiking times are early morning and late evening; backpack camps are available. Caution! Buffalo roam the park freely. Park naturalist / programs. East Drywood Creek, Regal, and Tzi-Sho Natural Areas. Near *Liberal*. Information: Liberal 64762.

Roaring River. The park was established in 1928 when Thomas H. Sayman donated 2,400 acres of his planned resort development to the state; it was named for the river's flow, which is fed by a 20.4-million-gallon-per-day spring located in a deep canyon-like gorge. While trout fishing is the primary attraction, the park's rugged topography of steep-walled valleys supports over 600 species of plants, many of which are not found elsewhere in Missouri. About ten miles of hiking trails (0.2–3.5 m.) wind through the park and parts of the 2,075-acre Roaring River Hills Wild Area, which includes 300-foot chert-covered ridges. Trout hatchery; park naturalist / programs. Near *Cassville*. Information: Cassville 65625.

Robertsville. Established in 1979, the park was named for former 19th-century landowner Edward James Roberts, the namesake of nearby Robertsville.[2] Mostly bounded on the north and west by the Meramec River, and on the east by Calvary Creek and its oxbow sloughs, the park is water-oriented, offering fishing, swimming, canoeing, and a wetland habitat. Future plans include electrical hookups and other services. *FLOAT STREAM:* Meramec River. Near *Pacific* and *Union*. Information: Robertsville.

Rock Bridge Memorial. The park was established in 1967 through the efforts of Lewis Stoerker as a memorial to his nine-year-old daughter, Carol, who was struck and killed by a car. It was named for its featured attraction, a natural bridge (15 feet high, 150 feet long, 50–75 feet wide) that attracted various 19th-century businesses, including a *gristmill*, paper mill, and finally a distillery that burned in 1889, destroying the community of Rock Bridge.[3] The park encompasses many sinkholes, *caves*, underground streams, and springs typical of karst formations *(Collapsed Cave Systems)* that can be explored via five connected hiking trails (8.8 m.

total) that are also suitable for cross-country skiing and a map-and-compass orienteering course. Other attractions include Devil's Icebox, a double sinkhole leading to an underground cave system (experienced spelunkers only; permission required), and Gans Creek Wild Area (750 acres). Park naturalist / programs. Near *Columbia.* Information: Columbia 65201.

St. Francois. Established in 1964, the park was named for the adjacent mountains *(County Profiles: St. Francois).* It is set in the wild oak, hickory, and black gum forests and hollows of Pike Run Hills, which are bounded on the south by the Big River and its scenic dolomite bluffs. Coonville Creek Wild Area (2,101 acres) has 17 miles of hiking trails, including an 11-mile loop hiking/horse trail. Big River, a popular put-in point for the 24-mile float to Washington State Park, provides fishing (bass, catfish, sunfish). Park naturalist / programs. Coonville Creek Natural Area. *FLOAT STREAM:* Big River. Near *Bonne Terre.* Information: Bonne Terre 63628.

St. Joe. The park was established in 1976 on land donated by its namesake, the St. Joe Mineral Corporation, a lead-mining company that ceased operation in 1972 *(Flat River: Missouri Mines State Historic Site).* It is primarily dominated by oak-hickory forests, but its major attraction is an 800-acre sandflat (of tailings from the mining operation) that provides the basis for the Midwest's largest off-road-vehicle area (1,600 acres), used by motorcycles, dune buggies, four-wheel drives, snowmobiles, etc. A 23-mile series of trails forming loops through the park's wooded areas is designated for horseback riding and camping. An 11-mile paved hiking/biking/cross-county skiing trail (no motorized vehicles allowed) occupies another part of the park. Four lakes provide water recreation, including fishing (bass, bluegill, channel catfish). Park naturalist / programs. Missouri Mines State Historic Site. Near *Flat River.* Information: Elvins 63601.

Stockton. Established in 1969, the park was named for adjacent Stockton Lake, which was named for the town *Stockton.* This is primarily a water-related park set on a peninsula between the Big and Little Sac River arms of the lake, with topography ranging from Ozark hills to *prairies.* Used primarily for boating, sailing, and fishing (bass, crappie, walleye, catfish, pike, bluegill), its clear water is also popular with skin divers. Park naturalist / programs. Near *Stockton.* Information: Dadeville: 63635.

Table Rock. Established in 1957, the park was named, like adjacent Table Rock Lake *(Lakes: Corps of Engineers),* for a rock shelf above the White River about one mile downstream from the dam. Set in the White River hills of the Ozarks on the northeast side of the lake, the park focuses on water-related recreation that

includes the state's most popular scuba diving areas and fishing (bass, crappie, walleye, catfish). Park naturalist / programs. Near *Branson, Hollister,* and *Reeds Spring.* Information: Branson 65616.

Taum Sauk Mountain. The park was established in 1991 with acreage from adjoining Johnson's Shut-Ins State Park (above). Various legends try to explain the name of the park and the geological wonders of Missouri's highest mountain (1,772 feet) and highest waterfall *(Arcadia: Taum Sauk Mountain State Park).* Encompassing the rugged and scenic St. Francois Mountain landscape, it is still being developed. Today it offers picnic facilities, primitive camping, water, restrooms, and trails, e.g. a section of the Ozark *Trail* that also connects with Johnson's Shut-Ins State Park. Near *Arcadia.* Information: Middlebrook 63656.

Thousand Hills. Established in 1952, the park was named for the farm of Dr. George M. Laughlin, whose heirs' donated the first land that established it. The farm's name, Thousand Hills, describes its location here among rolling hills with steep inclines set in a patchwork of woodlands and meadows. Within the park is 573-acre Forest Lake, whose 17 miles of shoreline provide water-related attractions including fishing (crappie, large-mouth bass, bluegill, channel catfish, walleye). Indian petroglyphs here, whose rock carvings could be Woodland (A.D. 400–900) or Middle Mississippi (A.D. 1000–1600), show symbols of crosses, arrows, snakes, thunderbirds, and other animals chipped and rubbed into sandstone. A three-mile trail borders Forest Lake and also cuts through one of Missouri's last stands of bigtooth aspen. Park naturalist / programs. Near *Kirksville.* Information: Kirksville 63501.

Trail of Tears. Established in 1957, the park was named for the Trail of Tears, which was a result of the Indian Removal Act of 1830, a bitterly fought act of Congress authorizing the federal government to exchange lands with any tribe "residing within the limits of the states or otherwise." The relocation process, which mostly involved the Five Civilized Tribes of the southern states, was a vast undertaking spanning millions of square miles. Moving thousands of unwilling people required complicated logistics, wagons, boats, mules, horses, and armed military escorts. The Trail of Tears has no tidy history or specific route. For nearly 10 years it maintained what has been called a seemingly endless stream of humanity through Missouri and Arkansas to appointed lands in Indian Territory (today's Oklahoma). Thousands died of hunger, depression, and hardship. Each group followed *roads,* trails, and rivers best suited to their originating and destination locations. A group of Cherokee during the winter of 1838–1839 crossed the Mississippi, landing at

Moccasin Springs in today's park. The park is Missouri's only one located at the Mississippi River, and it is characterized by mature oak and tulip poplar forests along sharp ridges, steep ravines, and 175-foot limestone river bluffs. Peewah Trail (10 m.) leads through 1,300-acre Indian Creek Wild Area, and Sheppard Point Trail (2 m.) leads up a bluff that overlooks the river. Two other bluff overlooks (winter bald-eagle nesting sites) can be reached by car. The Mississippi offers fishing (catfish, perch, carp), as does 20-acre Lake Boutin (bass, bluegill, catfish). Park naturalist / programs. Near *Cape Girardeau*. Information: Jackson 63755.

Truman, Harry S. Established in 1976 on a peninsula of Harry S. Truman Reservoir *(Lakes: Corps of Engineers)*, the park was named for the lake, which was named for Pres. Harry S. Truman *(Independence)*. Mostly lake oriented, it is located in a transition area between prairies and ruggedly forested Ozark hills: oaks, hickories, and maples meet savannas characterized by sparsely scattered trees, no understory, and prairie ground cover (a *prairie* grassland remnant is being restored near the park entrance). Towering limestone bluffs, left above lake level after the damming of the Osage River, are visible in the park. Park naturalist / programs. Near *Warsaw*. Information: Warsaw 65355.

Twain, Mark. Established in 1924, the park was named for Mark Twain, honoring the site of his birthplace, which once overlooked the Salt River. Although this is one of the state's oldest parks, the damming of the Salt River in 1983 (construction began in 1966) to create Mark Twain Lake *(Lakes: Corps of Engineers)* resulted in a new park setting of rolling hills lined by limestone bluffs that once towered over the river. Water recreation includes fishing for bluegill, crappie, channel catfish, largemouth bass, carp, and perch. Two connected trails (0.5–6.5 miles) offer hillside hikes overlooking the lake. Park naturalist / programs. Near *Paris* and *Monroe City*. Information: Stoutsville 65283. MARK TWAIN BIRTHPLACE STATE HISTORIC SITE: Log, 1830s. Born here in 1835 (two months early and six months after his parents moved from Tennessee), Twain (born Samuel Langhorne Clemens) later described his birthplace of Florida, Mo.,[4] as a village with two streets a couple hundred yards long that consisted of tough black mud when wet and deep dust when dry. He and seven Clemenses shared this two-room 420-square-foot cabin until moving to *Hannibal* in 1839, after which he returned every summer until 12 years old. Tours; exhibits include the handwritten manuscript of "Tom Sawyer," first editions, personal household furnishings, and a full-size replica of a steamboat pilot-house. *(Hannibal: Mark Twain)*

Van Meter. National Historic Landmark. The park was established in 1932 with help from "Miss Annie" Van Meter, who donated the original 506 acres of land in memory of her husband (the Van Meter family settled here in 1834). It is characterized by tall black walnuts and steep *loess* hills that feature an extremely rugged and serrated section, the Pinnacles, accentuated by Devil's Backbone, a sharp ridge along its southern part. The park was the site of human habitation as early as 10,000 B.C.; the last *Indians* to live here were the 17th- and 18th-century Missouri Indians, who had a village of about 5,000 and built large earthworks (a fort or combination fort-ceremonial center) on the flat portion of the Pinnacles, providing a commanding view of the Missouri River three miles north. Burial mounds here probably predate the Missouri Indians. Lake Wooldridge (18 acres) offers fishing. The visitor center has exhibits and a slide show. Near *Marshall*. Information: Miami 65344.

Wakonda. The park was established in 1964; its name comes from the Souian term for spirit *(LaGrange)*. Wakonda has the park system's largest natural sand beach, which features beach sports, e.g. volleyball and badminton. Its 75-acre lake is popular for fishing (carp, buffalo, channel catfish, bullhead, crappie, yellow bass, bluegill, green sunfish, black bass). Near *LaGrange*. Information: LaGrange 63448.

Wallace. Established in 1932, the park was named for the family who formerly owned the land. Called a shady oasis in rolling farmland, it is more rugged than the surrounding land, with oak-forested hillsides, bottomland along Deer Creek, and a meadow near its center at Lake Allaman, which offers fishing for bass and channel catfish. Five miles of connected trails wind through the park, and 20 miles southwest is a 60-acre extension of it, Trice-Dedman Memorial Woods, a good example of a presettlement hardwood forest. Near *Cameron*. Information: Cameron 64429.

Washington. Established in 1932, the park was named for its county's namesake, George Washington. Set in rugged high hills forested by cedars and hardwoods, and bounded on the north by Big River and its towering bluffs, it is the site of Middle Mississippi ceremonial grounds (A.D. 1000–1600; *Kahoka*). Petroglyphs, symbols carved into dolomite rock, possibly for religious purposes, can still be seen in the park. Three trails (1.5, 3, and 10 m.) lead through limestone glades dotted with wildflowers and red cedars and along Big River's high bluffs of 100-foot hardwoods (e.g. sugar maple, slippery elm, Kentucky coffee). Big River provides water recreation. Park naturalist / programs. *FLOAT STREAM:* Big River. Near *Potosi* and De Soto *(Hillsboro)*. Information: De Soto 63020.

Watkins Mill. Established in 1964, the park was named for 19th-century plantation/mill owner

Waltus Watkins. In contrast to the adjacent farmland, it is set in wooded hills of oak, hickory, walnut, and elm. At the center, 100-acre Williams Creek Lake provides water recreation, including fishing (bass, catfish, crappie, sunfish). A 4.5-mile asphalt bike and hiking trail follows the lake's shoreline. Park naturalist / programs. Near *Kearney* and *Excelsior Springs.* Information: Lawson 64062. WATKINS WOOLEN MILL STATE HISTORIC SITE: National Landmark. Part of Waltus Watkins's 3,660-acre Bethany Plantation, a livestock farm, this site preserves his 1850 house, outbuildings, a *gristmill,* a church, an octagonal schoolhouse, and the 1860 woolen mill, the only 19th-century American one with its original machinery intact. Picnic areas.

Trailside bluffs in Pulaski County.

Weston Bend. Established in 1980, the park was named for a deep bend in the Missouri River just south of *Weston.* Set at the river's bend, the park has rich *loess* soil that formerly supported tobacco farms; a tobacco barn now contains interpretive exhibits. A shaded overlook on a bluff provides scenic views of the river, the countryside, and Fort Leavenworth, Kans.; a three-mile paved hiking/biking trail follows a creek through the woods and returns along the ridge tops. Near *Weston.* Information: Weston 64098.

1. Andrew Machens; p.o. 1895–1956.
2. P.o. 1859–1862, 1871–now; Catawissa, Algonquian probably from the words "becoming fat," and involving an incident with deer (from "American Place-Names"), 1860–now.
3. The natural bridge; p.o. Rockbridge Mills 1874–1881.
4. Territory of Florida, Spanish meaning flowered, flowery; p.o. 1832–1968.

 # TRAILS

Listed below are some of Missouri's more popular public hiking trails, which include three National Recreation Trails: Berryman, Crane Lake, and Ridge Runner. Most are located in southern Missouri, and all are excellent for short walks and picnics, as well as for backpacking. Spring and fall are popular hiking seasons, each offering its own vibrant colors.

While snakes and poison ivy are common concerns of novice hikers, chiggers and ticks are the most likely villains: use insect repellent or sulfur, wear loose clothing, inspect your entire body, and bathe daily in hot soapy water or, in warm weather, rub your body with isopropyl alcohol.

For hiking in rough terrain, it is highly recommended to have footgear that offers ankle support, a hat for shade, a walking stick for steep slopes, drinking water, and a map for unmarked trails (for topographical maps, contact the State Geological Survey, Box 25, Rolla 65401). Extended hikes should be planned, the trail supervisor notified, and proper equipment carried. A picnic lunch is not only fun, it also helps restore energy.

Other trails are listed in the charts of the appropriate agency, e.g. *state parks.* Entries here are from "Missouri Hiking Trails" by Ramond D. Gass (Missouri Department of Conservation, Box 180, Jefferson City 65102), the U.S. Forest Service (Mark Twain National Forest, 401 Fairgrounds Rd., Rolla 65401), and "The Ozark Trail" (Missouri Department of Natural Resources, Box 176, Jefferson City 65102). These agencies also have detailed maps and descriptions of the trails listed below.

Audubon, John J. 12-mile loop; map and compass recommended. Very rugged, with a 3,000-foot ascent and descent in 12 miles; perennial creeks and open glades. FR 2199 is very steep; flash floods are possible after thunderstorms. From *Fredericktown:* SR OO, N 7.9 m.; SR T, E 5.7 m.; FR 2199, N approx. 4.5 m. to Bidell Creek Ford (low-water bridge) in Mark Twain *National Forest.*

Bell Mountain Wilderness. 9,027 acres; 12 miles of trails; map and compass necessary. Rugged topography with rock outcroppings, broad views of the St. Francois Mountain countryside, *shut-ins,* steep slopes, creeks, and springs *(National Forests).* From *Caledonia:* SR 32, W 12 m.; SR A, S 0.5 m.; FR 2228, E 2 m.

Berryman. 24-mile loop; National Recreation Trail. Pine, oak, and bottomland hardwoods, switchbacks, no steep hills; also a horse trail. BEECHER CAMP: At 5.5 m. HARMON CREEK CAMP: At 9.8 m.; spring, fireplaces, tables. BRAZIL CREEK TRAIL CAMP: At 14.8 m.; a good campsite *(Cuba: Bourbon).* Berryman Trail connects with the Courtois section of the Ozark Trail (below). From *Potosi:* SR 8, W 17 m.; FR 2266, N 1 m. to Berryman Trail Camp *(Potosi: Recreation)* in Mark Twain *National Forest.*

Big Piney. 15-mile loop. A variety of Ozark terrain, e.g. bluffs, a small canyon, springs, many vistas, a waterfall, and steep climbs; also a horse trail. PICNIC SITE: At 8.3 m.; waterfall, spring. From *Houston:* SR 17, N 22 m. to Roby; continue SR 17, N approx. 2 m.; FR 78, E approx. 4.2 m.; FR 220, S approx. 2.2 m.; signs to the eastern trailhead at Paddy Creek Campground / Picnic Area (below; *Houston: Recreation)* in Mark Twain *National Forest.* Roby Lake *(Houston: Recreation)* is the western trailhead.

Blossom Rock / Twin Springs. 1-mile loop. TWIN SPRINGS: At 0.25 m. The springs flow from beneath a vertical bluff into Little Piney Creek at a rate of 1 million gallons per day. BLOSSOM ROCK: At 0.5 m. This gray sandstone rock (125 feet in diameter, 50 feet tall), the area's only outcropping, was named for the sandstone rocks that appear to blossom from the underlying dolomite. The ridges crisscrossing the rocks are mineral-filled fractures that are slightly more resistant to weathering. From *Rolla:* US 63, S 10 m.; FR 1892, W 1 m. to Lane Spring Campground / Picnic Area *(Rolla: Recreation)* in Mark Twain *National Forest.*

Blue Springs / North Fork Loop. BLUE SPRINGS: 0.5-mile loop. Named for the blue water that flows from beneath a limestone bluff (7 million gallons per day; peak flow of 19 million); small *cave.* NORTH FORK LOOP: 14-mile loop. Crosses SR CC, passes through a dense hardwood forest, parallels the North Fork River, then breaks across scenic hills and hollows. From *Gainesville:* SR 181, N 20 m.; SR CC, E 4 m. to North Fork Campground / Picnic Area *(Gainesville: Recreation)* in Mark Twain *National Forest.* See Devils Backbone Wilderness and Ridge Runner Trails (below).

Buckhorn. 8-mile loop. Passes through level to gently rolling topography. SHELTER: At 4.5 m. Caution! This is a public hunting area. Wear bright colors *(Wildlife Areas).* From *Jamestown:* SR U, W 3.3 m.; SR D, N 0.5 m.; GR, W 1 m. to campsite in Prairie Home *Wildlife Area;* signs.

Cedar Creek. 21-mile loop; map and compass recommended. Cedar Creek watershed, mature oak and hickory forests, and pastures; From *Fulton:* SR H, W 4.9 m.; SR J, S 3.3 m. to Guthrie;[1] SR Y, W 2.5 m. to Pine Ridge Camping / Picnic Area *(Fulton: Recreation)* in Mark Twain *National Forest.*

Crane Lake. National Recreation Trail. SOUTH TRAIL: 3-mile loop. Scenic overlooks, creek, glades, *shut-ins,* fields, oak-hickory forest. NORTH TRAIL: 2-mile loop. Circles the 100-acre lake *(Arcadia: Recreation),* which is impounded by an earthen dam. Warning! During high water, hiking below the dam and crossing Crane Lake Creek are not advised. The Marble Creek section of the Ozark Trail (below) connects here. From *Arcadia:* SR 21, S 7 m.; SR 49, S 3 m.; FR 69 at Chloride *(Arcadia: SR 49 Towns),* E 4 m.; GR (Crane Pond Rd.), S 2 m. to Crane Lake Picnic Area *(Arcadia: Recreation)* in Mark Twain *National Forest.*

Devils Backbone Wilderness. 6,800 acres; unmarked trails; map and compass necessary. Rugged topography with narrow ridges, hollows, and bluffs that include the North Fork River, high-quality springs, heavy forest (oak, hickory, pine), scattered limestone glades, and wild azaleas (along the river; they bloom in early May). Fishing (smallmouth bass, trout). From *Gainesville:* SR 181, N 20 m.; SR CC, E 4 m. to North Fork Campground / Picnic Area *(Gainesville: Recreation)* in Mark Twain *National Forest.* Immediately south is Ridge Runner Trail (below). Also see Blue Springs Trail (above).

Glade Top Trail / Fractures. *Ava.*

Hercules Glades Wilderness. 12,315 acres; unmarked trails; map and compass necessary. Called the most scenic and unique country in the Midwest; characterized by shallow soil and limestone outcroppings with red cedar, oak, redbud, dogwood, maple, and smoke trees, as well as open glades supporting native *prairie* grasses. From *Forsyth:* US 160, E 4 m.; SR 76, E 14 m.; SR 125, S 7 m. to Hercules Fire Tower (parking lot and trailhead) in Mark Twain *National Forest.*

Knob Lick Vista. 1,000 feet. A spectacular view of the Ozarks from the area's highest point, Knob Lick Mountain; picnic tables. From *Knob Lick:* SR 67, S 0.5 m. near the fire tower in Mark Twain *National Forest.*

Loggers Lake. 1-mile loop. Circles Loggers Lake *(Bunker)* through rolling terrain and undisturbed oak and pine forests. From *Bunker:* SR A, W 0.2 m.; FR 2221, S 6 m.; FR 2193, S 0.5 m. to Loggers Lake

Campground / Picnic Area (*Bunker: Recreation*) in Mark Twain *National Forest.*

McCormack-Greer. 7.4-mile round-trip. Generally parallels the Eleven Point River north from Greer Crossing Campground / Picnic Area to McCormack Lake Campground / Picnic Area (*Alton: Recreation*); a strenuous hike with scenic overlooks. A spur of the Ozark Trail (below) joins here. A shorter 0.75-mile loop is at the Greer end, and a 2.6-mile round-trip trail leads from Greer to the SR 19 picnic grounds. From *Alton:* SR 19, N 9.2 m. to the Eleven Point River bridge at Greer Crossing Campground / Picnic Area (*Alton: Recreation*) in Mark Twain *National Forest.*

Markham Spring. CANEBREAK INTERPRETIVE: 0.125 mile. Past Bubble Spring and a waterfall. EAGLE BLUFF: 1.5 miles. Along the banks of the Black River; bluff view of the river, bald cypress forest. RIVER: 1 mile. Along the Black River and through woods. From *Mill Spring:* SR 49 S and E 10.3 m. to Markham Spring Campground / Picnic Area (*Mill Spring: Recreation*) in Mark Twain *National Forest.*

Mill Creek Interpretive. 0.5-mile loop. Rolling to steep terrain, oak and hickory forests; a small *cave* (at 0.3 m.) and a natural bridge. From *Newburg:* SR P, W and S 2.5 m.; GR, E and S 1.8 m. to Mill Creek Campground / Picnic Area (*Newburg: Recreation*) in Mark Twain *National Forest.*

Moniteau Wilderness. 15-mile loop; map and compass recommended. Oak-hickory forests, old fields, interesting sites. MISSOURI INDIAN VILLAGE: At 3.7 m.; no remnants. INDIAN BURIAL GROUNDS: At 3.75 m.; across Moniteau Creek via a monkey bridge. HOUSE SITE: At 8 m.; the house of the aunt of Gen. Omar Bradley (*Moberly: Higbee*); he visited frequently. PIONEER *CEMETERY:* At 11.5 m.; burials include early settlers and Revolutionary War lieutenant Leonard Bradley. PERCHE CREEK: Crossed via a one-rope bridge. GULLIES / UNNAMED CREEKS: At 11.5–15 m. From *Moberly:* SR AA, S 7.6 m.; SR B, W 1.7 m.; GR, S 4.5 m. to campsite in Bennitt *Wildlife Area.*

Noblett Lake. LAKE: 0.75-mile loop. Follows the lake on the north side of the loop and crosses old-growth stands of oak and hickory on the south. LOOP TRAIL: 8.8-mile loop. Connects with Ridge Runner Trail (below). Rugged land, numerous springs, e.g. Hell-roaring Spring; crosses both Noblett and Spring Creeks. From Cabool (*Mountain Grove*): SR 181, S 16 m.; SR AP, S 4 m. to Noblett Lake Campground / Picnic Area (*Mountain Grove: Cabool*) in Mark Twain *National Forest.*

Ozark Trail. 500 miles. Not yet fully completed, this ambitious project is sponsored by private, state, and federal entities. The area covered is from St. Louis through the Ozarks to the Arkansas border, where the trail will connect with the Arkansas Highland Trail to the Oklahoma border north of the Arkansas River (*National Parks: Ozark National Scenic Riverways; National Forests*). Current information: Missouri Department of Natural Resources, Parks and Historic Preservation, Box 176, Jefferson City 65102. Completed sections include the following. BETWEEN THE RIVERS: 30 miles one way; marked. Between the Current and Eleven Point Rivers. Streams, granite barrens, panoramic views, deep forests; campsites available along the trail; also a horse trail. From *Van Buren:* US 60, W 3.5 m. BLAIR CREEK: About 26.5 miles one way; marked. Old homesites, springs, wildflower fields, panoramic views of the Current River, streams, bluffs; improved campsite at Owls Bend (SR 106 Current River bridge). From *Centerville:* SR 72, W 14 m. to SR P. COURTOIS: 22 miles one way; marked. Single-file traffic, dense hardwood forests, springs, switchbacks, ridges, rock outcroppings. Connects the Berryman Trail (above) to the Ozark Trail's Trace Creek section (below) at Hazel Creek Trail Camp. CURRENT RIVER: 30 miles one way; marked. Parallels the river for two miles, follows Indian Creek, then strikes off cross-country (traveling the hollows and ridges of Barnett, Buzzard, Mill, and Stegal Mountains, through Peck Ranch *Wildlife Area*), ending at US 60. From *Eminence:* SR 106, E 12 m. to Current River bridge at Owls Bend. ELEVEN POINT: 30 miles one way; marked; first 10 miles very rugged. Parallels the river; springs, bluffs, river overlooks; spur to McCormack Lake (above). From *Alton:* SR 19, N 9.2 m. to the Eleven Point River bridge at Greer Crossing Campground / Picnic Area (*Alton: Recreation*). From here the trail goes 10 miles east (very rugged terrain) and 20 miles west. KARKAGHNE: 12 miles one way; marked. Steep slopes, ridges, bluffs, Black River overlook, hollows, and creeks. From Sutton Bluff Campground / Picnic Area (Sutton Bluff Trail, below). MARBLE CREEK: 8 miles one way; marked. The same topography as Crane Lake Trail (above), with which it connects. TAUM SAUK: 30 miles one way; marked. Streams, granite barrens, panoramic views, deep forests; also connects two *state parks:* Johnson's Shut-Ins and Taum Sauk. From Taum Sauk *State Park.* TRACE CREEK: 24 miles one way; marked. To Bell Mountain Wilderness (above). Dense oak, hickory, and pine forests, hollows, ridge tops, creeks; also a horse trail. From *Caledonia:* SR C, W 10 m.; SR Z, N 2.1 m. to Palmer;[2] GR, N approx. 2 m. to Hazel Creek Trail Camp (*Caledonia: Recreation*). VICTORY: 30 miles one way; marked. Generally the same topography as Victory Horse Trail (below), with which it connects. From *Ellsinore (Van Buren):* SR V, N 2.7 m. to Brushy Creek trailhead.

Paddy Creek. 1.25-mile loop; described clockwise.

Reportedly one of Mark Twain National Forest's most scenic areas. The trail follows Paddy Creek, crossing it twice; scenic overlooks, steep but easy slopes. Big Piney Trail (above) leaves from Paddy Creek Trail's north leg at the junction of gravel roads (hike N road approx. 0.3 m.). At Paddy Creek Campground / Picnic Area *(Houston: Recreation)*.

Piney Creek Wilderness. 8,400 acres; unmarked network of well-used trails; map and compass necessary. Narrow ridge tops and hollows, long steep slopes, a few cedar glades, forests (oak, cedar, hickory, pine), and old fields; blue heron habitat, bald eagle winter nesting. No formal trails; hikers may devise their own routes. From *Shell Knob (Cassville):* SR 39, N 3 m.; SR 76, E 5 m.; GR, S approx. 1 m. to Pine View Lookout Tower (main trailhead) in Mark Twain *National Forest.*

Ridge Runner. 46-mile round-trip; National Recreation Trail. Runs between Noblett Lake Recreational Area (Noblett, above) near Sugar Hill Campground (swimming beach, picnic area, fishing, water) and North Fork Campground / Picnic Area *(Gainesville: Recreation;* Blue Springs, above). Mileage is from the Noblett Lake and North Fork Trails, respectively. Sites and checkpoints include: HORTON (PARRISH) *CEMETERY:* At 3 and 20 m. The only remnant of the timber boomtowns Horton[3] and Cordz,[4] whose peak population was 1,500 *(Bunker).* A 1902 plague is recorded by the cemetery markers. The trail crosses new pine and hardwood forest (burned in 1965). TRAIL CAMP: At 6 and 17 m. Open land, dry creek. TRAIL CAMP: At 14 and 9 m. A narrow razorback ridge overlooking Tabor Creek. STREAM MILL HOLLOW: At 20 and 3 m. Deep hollow, small spring branches; overlooking North Fork River. Trailhead locations: see Noblett Lake and Blue Springs, both of which have loop trails connecting to Ridge Runner Trail; in Mark Twain *National Forest.*

Rock Pile Mountain Wilderness. 4,159 acres; unmarked trails; map and compass necessary. Scenic views, steep limestone bluffs, black granite streambed, St. Francis River, *shut-ins,* scattered granite glades, *caves,* 1,305-foot Rock Pile Mountain and its namesake, a presettlement circle of granite rocks *(Fredericktown: Chimney Rock Bluff).* Hikers may design their own routes. From *Fredericktown:* US 67, S 3 m.; SR C, S 8.7 m.; SR CC, W 0.7 m.; GR (Trace Creek Rd.), N approx. 0.5 m. to small parking lot. Rock Pile Mountain is due west; in Mark Twain *National Forest.*

Rockwoods Reservation. Established in 1938 by St. Louis businessmen, the reservation offers a variety of trails through Ozark-like terrain that includes creeks, ravines, rocky ridge tops, and remnants of limestone, clay, and gravel quarries. LIME KILN: 3.25-mile loop. Late 1800s–early 1900s limestone mining. ROCK QUARRY: 2.25-mile loop. Late 1800s–early 1900s lime-

stone mining. TRAIL AMONG THE TREES: 1.5-mile loop. Designed for easy access: wooden steps in steep areas, bridges across creeks, asphalt or wood-bark surfaces; interpretive brochures. From *Eureka:* SR 109, N 5 m.

Silver Mines. 1-mile loop with a 2-mile round-trip spur. The spur leads upstream from the dam. Scenic overlooks, Silver Mine and St. Francis River *shut-ins,* abandoned silver mines, townsite. At Silver Mines Shut-Ins *(Fredericktown).* Between SR D parking lot and nearby picnic area; sign.

Skyline / Songbird. SKYLINE: 2.6-mile round-trip. Typical Ozark scenery. From *Van Buren:* SR 103, S 1.2 m. to Skyline Dr. (FR 3280), W 2.9 m.; in Mark Twain *National Forest.* SONGBIRD: 1.2-mile loop. Spring, *cave,* Civil War gun emplacements, views of the Current River when trees lose their leaves. In *Van Buren:* sign on US 60, approx. 0.3 m. S of junction of SR D and US 60; near ranger station at Watercress Spring Campground / Picnic Area *(Van Buren: Recreation)* in Mark Twain *National Forest.*

Slabtown Bluff. 3-mile loop. Follows the Big Piney River about a mile, then begins a wide turn that climbs a ridge, giving scenic views of the river bottoms. From *Licking:* SR 32, N 4 m.; SR N, N 2 m.; SR AF, W and N 4.5 m. to Slabtown Picnic Area *(Licking: Recreation)* in Mark Twain *National Forest.*

Sutton Bluff. 1.5-mile loop. Travels a ridge top and a bluff along the West Fork of the Black River; interesting rocks and plants, scenic overlooks. Connects with the Karkaghne section of the Ozark Trail (above). From *Centerville:* SR 21, N 3 m.; FR 2233, N 7 m.; FR 2236, S 3 m. to Sutton Bluff Campground / Picnic Area *(Centerville: Recreation)* in Mark Twain *National Forest.*

Victory Horse. VICTORY HORSE TRAIL LOOP: 8-mile loop; part of the main trail. Begins and ends at Victory School site (below). VICTORY HORSE TRAIL: Excluding the 8-mile loop, approx. 60 mile round-trip. Because of the many roads crossing this trail, the distances vary. Popular for horseback riding and hiking; a variety of terrains, long views, thick oak-hickory forests. Connects with the Victory section of the Ozark Trail (above). There are two trailheads. (1) From *Poplar Bluff* to Victory School site trailhead: US 67, N 7 m.; US 60, W 4.2 m.; GR (0.8 m. E of junction with SR PP), N 1.5 m. to hitching rack. (2) From *Leeper (Mill Spring)* to SR KK trailhead: SR 34, W 2.7 m.; SR KK, S 3.5 m. to hitching rack; in Mark Twain *National Forest.* Checkpoints (where the trail crosses roads) traveling from Victory School site to SR KK: FR 3526 (at 4 m.), FR 3111 (at 8 m.), SR A (at 12 m.), FR 3129 (at 17 m.), and SR KK (at end).

White Oak Forest / WoodChuck. WHITE OAK FOREST: 1.5-mile loop. Demonstration project in watershed management, showing how planting trees can prevent soil erosion; benches, restrooms. Joins Woodchuck. WOODCHUCK: 0.5-mile open loop. Current River, giant sycamores, oaks, pines, 8,000-gallon-per-day Malden Spring, woodchuck dens; self-guided, scenic overlooks, restrooms. Joins White Oak. From *Doniphan:* SR Y, N 4.5 m.; FR 3210, W 0.5 m. to Float Camp Campground / Picnic Area *(Doniphan: Recreation)* in Mark Twain *National Forest.*

Whites Creek. 18-mile loop; map and compass recommended. In the heart of the Irish Wilderness *(Alton: Bardley).* Representative Ozark plant communities and contrasts, e.g. cedar glades, oak-hickory forests, pine forests, river bottoms. START OF LOOP: At 4 m. is a fork. To avoid more hills take the right-hand fork and hike the trail counterclockwise. BLISS SPRING CAMPGROUND: At 9 m.; Eleven Point River, latrine, picnic tables, fireplace pits, no drinking water. WHITES CREEK CAVE: At 12.2 m.; from here the creek is W 0.5 m. (1 m. round-trip, or continue 2.2 m. to rejoin main trail, then turn NE). FIDDLER SPRING: At 13.2 m.; a 40-foot-wide bluff hole. END OF LOOP: At 14.2 m.; turn east to trailhead. From Bardley *(Alton):* SR J, N 5.5 m. to Camp Five Pond Picnic Area *(Alton: Recreation)* in Mark Twain *National Forest.*

1. Town founders S. N. and John Guthrie; p.o. Bigbee, origin unknown, formerly spelled Big Bee, 1872–1874; Guthrie 1875–1954.
2. Palmer Lead Co.; p.o. Harmony, the ideal, 1827–1874; Palmer 1874–1955.

3. RR surveyor who platted it in 1883; p.o. 1885–1886; later Drew for mill manager W. H. Drew; no p.o.
4. Mill manager Henry Cordz, whose wife was postmaster; p.o. 1886–1914.

WILDLIFE AREAS

The Missouri Department of Conservation (MDC) manages more than 800 areas. These include wildlife areas as well as *state forests*, river access points, and natural areas, some of which are combined. If a wildlife area is combined with another MDC area and is subordinate to it, the wildlife area will not be listed on the chart here, e.g. Huzzah State Forest, which is also a wildlife area. Rules, posted at access points, specify use limitations. Missouri hunting and fishing laws apply to all areas, and some areas may have stricter regulations. While the wildlife areas are mainly used for hunting, fishing, and boating, other outdoor activities are also available. Generally, these areas are set in wilderness environments that provide excellent conditions for observation, photography, picnicking, and hiking. Most have designated areas for primitive campsites that usually require campers to supply everything, including firewood. Some of the areas are mixed with parcels of private property. Be certain the land is public before entering. During hunting seasons, nonhunters should (1) dress in bright colors, (2) avoid traveling through dense underbrush, and (3) be aware that the sound of close gunfire is serious; stay alert and in the open. The chart lists the more popular recreational activities of the most accessible wildlife areas. For specific information and a detailed highway map to all MDC areas, contact the department at Box 180, Jefferson City 65102. Note: (1) Sites named after individuals are alphabetized by that person's last name. (2) Directions are keyed to towns listed in the Index; when the town's name appears in italics, it can be found as a main entry. (3) The heading Lakes/Rivers/Acres indicates the number of lakes and the acreage of the largest lake (for example, 12 lakes, the largest of which is 280 acres, would be shown as a fraction, 12 L / 280).

Waterfowl hunters.

Wildlife Areas

Name	Acres	Location	Boat Rental Ramp	Lake•River Acres (L/R)	Hunting/Waterfowl	Fishing
ALLEN (WILBUR) MEMORIAL	380	Hartville: SR Z, N 11.7 m.; SR H, E 2.6 m.; SR T, N 4 m.		R	deer	fish
AMARUGIA HIGHLANDS	881	Archie: SR A, W 5 m.; SR A, N 3.5 m.; sign.	ramp	L 55	deer, duck	fish
ANDERSON (EDWARDS)	1,046	New London: SR V, E 4.5 m.; SR T, E 7.9 to jct. SR 79.			duck	
ASHE JUNIPER NATURAL AREA	31	Hollister: US 65, S 7 m.; SR 86, W 11 m.; SR JJ, N 3.9 m.			duck	
ATLANTA	2,017	Macon: US 63, N 8 m.		2L 2/2	duck	fish
BAGLEY NATURAL AREA	20	13 m. NW of Princeton off SR P (private property access).			duck	
BANGERT (LOUIS H.)	160	St. Charles: I-70, E at Missouri R.		R		fish
BARNES (P.F.)	120	Houston: SR 17, W 7 m.; SR 38, W 8 m. to Fairview; ask locally.			duck	
BENNITT (RUDOLF)	3,444	Moberly: SR AA, S 7.6 m.; SR T, S 1.6 m.			duck	
BIG BUFFALO CREEK	1,556	Stover: SR 52, W 2 m.; SR FF, S 8 m. to GR near Boylers Mill.			duck	
BILBY RANCH	4,548	Maryville: SR 46, W 13 m. at SR HH.			deer, duck	
BIRDSONG	430	Osceola: SR 13, S 11 m.; US 54, W 5 m.; SR J, S 2.2 m. to Brush C.			duck	fish
BISMARCK LAKE	1,188	Bismarck: SR N, S of town; ask locally.	ramp	L 210	duck	fish
BLIND PONY	1,683	Marshall: SR 20, W 6.7 m.; SR EE, S 3.5 m., GR, W 1.5 m.	rental, ramp	L 195	duck	fish
BOIS D'ARC	2,892	Bois D'Arc: 2 m. NW of town; ask locally.		3L 1/40	deer, duck	fish
BONANZA	1,496	Kingston: SR F, E 3 m.			duck	fish
BRICKYARD HILL	2,102	Rock Port: I-29, N 5 m. to jct. SR A/SR RA, E to Charity Lake.		L 28	duck	fish
BROWN (BOB)	3,302	Forest City: marked GR, W 2.5 m. to Missouri R.		R	deer	
BUCK & DOE RUN	192	St. Patrick: SR Z, E 3.9 m.; US 61, S 2.4 m.; GR, E 1.2 m.; Miss. R.		R	deer	
BUNCH HOLLOW	3,189	Coloma: SR Z, N 3.8 m.; GR, W 1.8 m..			deer, duck	fish
BUSCH (AUGUST A.)	6,987	Weldon Spring: adjacent; along SR 94 & US 61.		32L 500	duck	fish
BUSHWHACKER	3,223	Liberal: SR 43, N 5 m.; GR, E 1 m.	ramp	9L 175	deer, duck	fish
BUSIEK	2,505	Ozark: US 65, S 8 m.; Woods Fork C.			duck	fish
CARPENTER (FRANK E.)	366	Stover: SR 135, S 6.8 m.; SR T, S 5.6 m.			duck	
CASH (BEN)	1,258	Kennett: SR 25, S 2.9 m.; SR A, W 2.1 m.; GR, W 1.5 m.		R	deer	fish
CATAWISSA	199	Pacific: SR N, S 2.5 m.	ramp	R	duck	
CHRISTIE (JAMES D.)	182	Savannah: SR C, N 8 m.; SR 48, E 2 m.		2L .5	duck	fish
CLEMENT (RICHARD F.)	520	Anutt: SR O, N 2.4 m.; SR OO, W 4.8 m.			duck	
COOLEY LAKE	917	Missouri City: SR 210, E 2.5 m.		L 300	duck	fish
COON ISLAND	3,138	Poplar Bluff: SR 142, S 14 m.; SR HH, E 2.6 m.; GR, E 1.2 m.	ramp	R	deer	fish
CROOKED RIVER	1,400	Richmond: SR 13, N 6.1 m.; SR FF, W 3.1 m.; GR, N 0.5 m.		R	duck	fish
CROWLEY'S RIDGE	1,878	Bloomfield: SR AC, W 5 m.; GR, N 1.1 m.		4L 10	duck	fish
CUIVRE ISLAND	1,341	Old Monroe: E of town at the Mississippi R.; Cuivre R.		R	deer	fish
DANVILLE	2,654	Danville: SR RB, S 2 m.			duck	
DARK CYPRESS SWAMP	460	Zalma: US 51, S 3 m., SR C, E 2.8 m.; near Greenbrier Rd.	ramp		deer	fish
DAVIS (DEAN)	177	West Plains: US 63, N 13.6 m.		L 3	duck	fish
DAVISDALE	2,398	New Franklin: SR P, E 7.8 m. to jct. SR P/SR 240; GR, S 1 m.		L 3	duck	
DEER RIDGE	4,524	Monticello: SR Y, N 10 m.; N. Fabius R.	ramp	L 48	duck	
DIGGS (MARSHALL I.)	1,017	Wellsville: SR ZZ, W 2.6 m.; SR RA, W 2.7 m.	ramp	2L 15	duck	fish
DRURY - MINCEY	4,088	Branson: SR 76, S 4.6 m.; SR J, S 5.5 m. Bull Shoals Lake		16400	deer, duck	
DUCK CREEK	6,072	Zalma: US 51, S 5.5 m.		L 1713	duck	fish
DUPONT RESERVATION	1,320	Louisana: SR 79, N 14 m. to Ashburn; adjacent.	ramp	R	deer	fish
ELAM BEND	1,402	Gentryville: SR T, E 3.7 m.; SR A, S 1.5 m.; Grand R.		R	duck	fish
FEWEL (CONNOR O.)	320	Clinton: SR 52, E 6 m.; SR AC, N 3.6 m.		3L 8	duck	fish
FLOYD (NANNIE B.)	20	Mendon: SR 11, N 7 m.; SR E, E 1.2 m. to Rothville; GR, N 0.25 m.			duck	
FORT CROWDER	2,363	Neosho: SR HH, E 4 m.			duck	
FOUNTAIN GROVE	6,714	Laclede: SR 36, W 6.8; SR W, S 4.6 m. Grand R.; Parson C.		L 30	deer, duck	fish
FOUR RIVERS	6,218	Rich Hill: US 71, S 3.7 m.; SR TT, E 2.7 m.; Osage & Little Osage R.		R	deer, duck	fish
FRANKLIN ISLAND	1,528	New Franklin: US 40/SR 5; US 40 E 1.3 m.; GR, S 0.7 m.; Mo. R.	ramp	R	duck	fish
FUNK	180	Piedmont: SR 49, N 14 m.; SR BB, W approx. 2.5 m.; ask locally.		L 1	duck	fish
GALLATIN	650	Gallatin: SR 13, S 6.3 m.; SR M, E 0.7 m.			duck	
GRAND PASS	4,711	Malta Bend: US 65, E 3 m.; SR N, N 5.5 m.		2L 2	deer, duck	fish
GRIFFITH	128	New Cambria: SR 149, N 3 m.			duck	
HAPPY HOLLER	1,820	Savannah: SR C, N 1.1 m.; GR, E 1.2 m.		R	deer	fish
HARMONY MISSION	1,080	Rich Hill: SR PP, S 4 m.	ramp	L 96	deer, duck	fish
HEATH (CHARLIE) MEMORIAL	1,531	Kahoka: SR 81, N 6 m.; SR NN, W 12.3 m.			duck	
HELTON (WAYNE)	2,560	Bethany: US 136, E 9 m.; SR CC, S 2.8 m.; GR, W 2 m.		7L 3	duck	fish
HONEY CREEK	1,448	Savannah: US 71, N 3 m.; US 59, W 5.9 m.; SR RA, S 0.5 m.		R	duck	fish
HORNERSVILLE SWAMP	3,166	Cardwell: SR 164, E 11 m. to Hornersville.	ramp		deer	
HOWELL ISLAND	2,548	Chesterfield: Airport Rd. W to Olive Rd. to Eatherton Rd.; signs.		R	deer, duck	fish
HUNGRY MOTHER	274	Fayette: SR H, N 2.6 m.; SR O, N 4.1 m.; SR BB, N 3.6 m.			duck	
HUNNEWELL	1,390	Shelbina: US 36, E 10 m.; SR Z, N 2.5 m.	rental, ramp	L 228	duck	fish
HUZZAH	6,162	Leasburg: SR H, S 4.4 m.		R	duck	fish
HYER WOODS	30	Salem: SR 72, N 11 m.			duck	
INDIAN HILLS	3,304	1 m. E of Bible Grove at Middle Fork of Fabius R.; ask locally.		L 5	deer	fish
KING LAKE	1,273	King City: SR Z, E 2.5 m.; GR, S 0.5 m.	ramp	L 200	duck	fish
LAKE GIRARDEAU	351	Jackson: SR 34, W 9 m.; SR U, S 5.9 m.	rental, ramp	L 162	duck	fish
LAKE PAHO	1,606	Princeton: SR 136, W 4 m.	rental, ramp	L 273	duck	fish
LAMINE RIVER	5,692	Otterville: SR A, E 1 m.; ask locally.	ramp	R	duck	fish
—— CONTINUED ——						

Wildlife Areas

(CONTINUED FROM PREVIOUS CHART)

Name	Acres	Location	Boat Rental/Ramp	Lake•River Acres	Hunting/Waterfowl	Fishing
LEACH (B.K.)	690	Troy: US 61, N 8 m.; SR B, E 10.7 m.; SR 79, S 3 m.; SR M, E 3 m.			waterfowl	fish
LITTLE COMPTON	345	Carrollton: SR 24, E 9 m.; SR 139, N 10; SR NN, N 3.6 m.; Grand R.	boat	L 40	deer	fish
LITTLE DIXIE ♿	467	Fulton: SR F, W 10.9 m.; SR J, N 0.2 m.	ramp	L 205		fish
LOCUST CREEK	3,164	Milan: SR 5, S 0.5 m.			waterfowl	fish
LOGAN (WILLIAM) R.	1,798	Troy: SR 47/US 61; US 61, N 10 m.; SR E, W 1 m.; SR RA, N 3 m.		7 L 7	deer	fish
LONE JACK ♿	295	Lone Jack: 1 m. NW of town; ask locally.		L 35		fish
LOWER TAUM SAUK	1,340	Lesterville: SR 49, E 1 m.; SR U, N 1 m.	boat	L 200		fish
MANITO LAKE ♿	851	Tipton: US 50 at SR 5; SR 5, S 4.5 m.	boat	L 77		fish
MARAIS TEMPS CLAIR	918	Portage Des Sioux: SR J, S 1 m.; SR H, S 5.7 m.; GR, N 1.3 m.		L Marsh	waterfowl	fish
MARSHALL JUNCTION ♿	774	Marshall: US 65, S 11 m.; SR CW, W 1.9 m.; SR RB, N 0.6 m.		R	deer	fish
MONKEY MOUNTAIN	788	Forest City: SR T, S 10.5 m.; GR, E 1.7 m.; Nodaway R.		R	deer	
MONTROSE LAKE ♿	3,600	Clinton: SR 18, W 15.2 m.; SR RA, S 3.3 m.	boat, ramp	L 1600	deer	fish
MORA	320	Cole Camp: SR U, N 4.6 m.			deer	
MUSSEL FORK	1,951	Marceline: SR WW, E 4.5 m.			waterfowl	fish
NEEPER	227	Kahoka: SR 81, S 6.5 m.; GR, W 1.5 m.			waterfowl	
NORTHCUFF (D.L.)	80	Mexico: SR 22, W 7 m.; SR E, N appx. 1.5 m.			deer	
OTTER SLOUGH	4,821	Dexter: SR 25, S 5 m.; SR H, W 6.7; SR ZZ, N 1.3 m.; GR, W 1 m.		L 250	waterfowl	fish
PACIFIC PALISADES	695	Pacific: SR F, S approx. 1.5 m.	boat	2 L 60		fish
PEABODY	299	Rich Hill: SR A, W 4 m.		3 L 35	deer	fish
PECK RANCH	22,969	Fremont: US 60, W 2.1 m.; SR P, N 2.7 m.			deer	
PERRY (RALPH & MARTHA)	3,852	Knob Noster: SR 23, N 9 m.; Blackwater R.		4 L 7		fish
PIGEON HILL	366	Agency: SR FF, N 3 m.; SR O, W 1.2 m.; GR, S 0.5 m.			deer	
PLATTE FALLS	2,308	Platte City: SR HH, E 5 m.; Interurban Rd., N to river.		L 1.5	deer	
PLEASANT HOPE	1,106	Brighton: SR 215, E 2.8 m.			deer	
POAGUE (HAYSLER A.)	879	Clinton: SR 7, W 6 m.; SR O, N 0.8 m.; GR, E 1.4 m.	ramp	20 L 77	deer	fish
PONY EXPRESS ♿	3,030	Maysville: SR 33, S 7.1 m.; SR RA, W 1 m.	boat, ramp	L 240	deer	fish
PRAIRIE HOME	1,461	Prairie Home: SR W, S 2 m.			deer	
PRAIRIE SLOUGH	584	Troy: US 61, N 8 m.; SR B, E 10.7 m.; SR P, N 5 m.		7 L 10	waterfowl	fish
RANACKER	1,618	Bowling Green: US 61, N 11 m.; SR RA, S 0.25 m.			deer	
REBEL'S COVE	3,919	Livonia: SR N, N 4.4 m.; Chariton R.		R	waterfowl	fish
REED (JAMES A.)	2,456	Lee's Summit: US 50/SR 291; US 50, E 2.1 m.; SR RA, S 1.5 m.	ramp	9 L 42	deer	fish
REFORM	6,800	Fulton: US 54B; SR O, E 11.1 m.		35 L 7	deer	fish
RIPPEE	408	Ava: SR 14, E approx. 11.1 m., GR, S 0.8 m.			deer	
RIVER 'ROUND	302	St. Clair: SR TT, E 5.3 m.; GR, S appx. 1 m.; Meramec R.	boat	R	deer	fish

Wildlife Areas

Name	Acres	Location	Boat Rental/Ramp	Lake•River Acres	Hunting/Waterfowl	Fishing
ROARING RIVER	439	Cassville: SR 112, S 6 m.; next to Roaring River State Park.		R	deer	fish
ROCKY FORKS LAKE	2,024	Columbia: US 63, N 6.1 m.	boat	25 L 50	deer	fish
SALINE VALLEY	4,250	Eldon: SR M, E 7 m.; Saline C., Osage R.		8 L 5	deer	fish
SCHELL-OSAGE ♿	8,633	El Dorado: SR 82, N 3 m.; SR H, N 6.2 m.; SR Y, W approx. 1.3 m.	boat, ramp	2 L 816	deer	fish
SCHIFFERDECKER (W.L.)	241	Carrollton: SR E, W 11.3 m. to jct. SR D.		L 15		fish
SCRIVNER ROAD	919	Jefferson City: SR C, W 14.3 m.; SR AA, S 2.2 m.; GR, E 1.7 m.		L 12	deer	fish
SEAT (EMMETT & LEAH)	3,084	Denver: SR M, E 4.8 m.	ramp	10 L 1	deer	fish
SETTLE'S FORD	6,056	Adrian: SR N, N 6 m.; SR B, E 8.3 m.; S. Grand R.		R	deer	fish
SEVEN ISLAND	1,376	Dorena: SR PP, W 2.1 m.; SR A, W 0.5 m.; Mississippi R.	boat	R	deer	fish
SEVER (HENRY)	1,115	Newark: SR KK, N 1 m.	boat, ramp	L 158	deer	fish
SHANKS (TED)	6,636	Ashburn: SR 79, N 14 m.; Mississippi R.	boat	14 L 60	deer	fish
SHEPHERD OF THE HILLS	211	Branson: US 65, S 2.6 m.; SR 165, W 5.7 m.; White R.	boat	L 1700		fish
SWIFTWATER BEND	69	Pacific: SR F, E 2 m.	boat	R		
TALBOT (ROBERT E.)	4,239	Vernon: I-44, W 6 m.; SR 97, N 4 m.; Spring R.		5 L 4	deer	
TEN MILE POND	2,227	East Prairie: SR 102, S 4 m.; drainage ditch.			waterfowl	fish
THOMAS HILL	11,000	Macon: US 63, S 5 m.; SR T, W 9.1 m.; Thomas Hill Res.	boat, ramp	L 4400	deer	fish
THURNAU (H. F.)	366	Craig: SR 111, W 3.8 m.; GR, S 0.5 m.; Missouri R.	boat	R	deer	fish
TORONTO SPRINGS	532	Brumley: SR C, S 5.5 m.			deer	fish
UPPER MISSISSIPPI	12,420	Mississippi R. islands from near Portage Des Sioux to LaGrange.		R	deer	fish
URICH	480	Urich: SR 7, E 1.6 m.; GR, E 1.6 m.; GR, N 1.3 m.; Big Creek.			deer	fish
VONAVENTURE	203	Troy: US 63, N 10.2 m.; SR E, W 5.3 m.; SR UU, N 2 m.			deer	fish
WAPPAPELLO	44,396	Greenville: W of US 67, N & S of city; Current R.; Wappapello Res.	boat, ramp	L 8400	deer	fish
WELDON SPRING	7,356	Weldon Spring: adjacent; along SR 94 and US 61.		2 L 30	deer	fish
WELLSVILLE LAKE ♿	120	Wellsville: GR, 2 m. S of town; ask locally.	boat	L 14		fish
WHETSTONE CREEK	5,147	Fulton: SR Z, E 9.7 m.; I-70, E 6 m.; GR, N 1.3 m.	boat	30 L 15	deer	fish
WHITE (ROBERT M. II)	1,038	Mexico: SR 15, N 9 m.; SR Z, E 1.7 m.; SR ZZ, E & N 2 m.			deer	fish
WHITE (WM. G. & E. P.)	810	Troy: US 61, N 14 m.; SR Z, W 1.5 m.	boat		deer	fish
WHITE RIVER TRACE ♿	257	Salem: SR 32, E 2 m.; GR, N approx. 0.7 m.		2 L 30	deer	fish
WILLINGHAM (RUBY CLARK)	70	Paris: SR 32, W approx. 1.7 m.			deer	fish
WIRE ROAD	730	Galena: SR 13, N 10 m. to Crane; ask locally; Crane C.			deer	fish
WOLF BAYOU	268	Hayti: I-55 exit 19, N 7.5 m.; SR BB, E 3.2 m.; sign.; Wolf Bayou.		3 L 35	deer	fish
WOODS (WOODSON K.)	5,680	St. James: Maramec Iron Works, adjacent; Meramec R., Dry Fork C.		R	deer	fish
WORTHWINE ISLAND	430	St. Joseph: I-29/SR K; SR K, N 2 m.; GR, W 2.5 m.; Missouri R.		R	deer	fish

—— END OF LISTING ——

Acknowledgments

SPECIAL ATTENTION should be drawn to Jane Lago, managing editor of the University of Missouri Press, who spent many months on the manuscript for this book—unraveling ravels, chasing countless anomalies through more than 300,000 words, and streamlining my work to bring clarity and consistency to the text, footnotes, maps, and charts. Thanks, Jane.

The following list is based on the best records I could keep. If someone has been inadvertently omitted, I am truly sorry because without their help this book would not have been written. Although this list is alphabetical by last name, I need to begin with my wife, Mary Sims, my daughter, Emma Earngey, and my friends Pat Sims and Gary Green, who helped me explore the roads. Jim Abernathy, O. E. Adams, Roy E. Adams, Velma E. Adams, W. E. Alexander, Terry Allan, Gerrie Anderson, Fern Angus, Leo Archer, Clyde Ardrey, Robert F. Arndt, Marty Asel, James S. Ashbury, Dale Atha, David Attlesey, Artie Ayers, Michaelle L. Baird, Reva Baker, Judi Baldwin, Ruth Bales, R. T. Bamber, Leota Barron, Sharon Bart, Vicki Barton, John Bashan, Sam W. Baugh, Patricia Bausch, Marjorie Beenders, Ellen Bern, Nellie C. Best, Angeline Bigbee, Clifford Bins, Jeanie Bissell, Viola M. Blechle, Regenia Blum, Lynn Bock, Marian Bock, Deas Bohn, Rev. W. Bok, Father John Bolderson, Sharon K. Boles, Jean Bolte, Kathy Borgman, R. Boudreau, Paul Bowden, Lucile Boyer, David R. Bradley, Barbara Bregant, Chet F. Breitwieser, Alice Bremer, Chris Brewer, R. W. Bricken, Francis L. Brillhart, Al Britton, Harry Broermann, Rob Brooks, Joy Broombaugh, Jim Bross, Dona Brown, Jerry Brown, Carol Bruce, Inez Bryant, Gordon B. Buckner, Ann Bullock, Jackie Bullock, E. R. Bunn, Clyde Burch, Marion J. Burns, Frank Burrell, Genevieve Butler, J. D. Byrne, William Caine, Becky Campbell, Neil Campbell, Bob Caps, Thomas Carneal, Pauline Carnell, Rowe Carney Jr., Robin Carolus, Ruth Carr, Lynn Cassidy, Brooks Chambers, Lorene Chambers, Wayne R. Chandler, Dorothy Childress, Harold Childress, Eric Chism, Mildred Church, Nan Cocke, Eleanor Coeffield, Jerry Coleman, Bob Collins, L. L. Combs, Michael A. Comer, Bernice Conley, Will Connaghan, John Conner, Willis Conner, Jim Conti, Daniel E. Coomer, Herbert B. Cooper, Anne B. Cope, Joe A. Corbin, Robert J. Corcoran, William J. Cotton, Mark Cox, Joe D. Coy, Bill T. Crawford, James T. Crenshaw, John Crouch, Bill Crow, Joe Clay Crum, Sam L. Currier, Charles R. Curry, Rev. Charles D'Arcy, Leroy Danz, Janie Daughtery, Gene Davis, Rosemary Davison, Betty J. Dawson, Mark Dawson, Avanell Dedman, Carol Demaree, Ray A. Denney, W. R. Denslow, Wilmer Diedrich, Gary D. Diehl, Leonard Doerhoff, Kay Doran, Ruth Drosselmeyer, Ed Dust, Wencil Eads, Harold Eckerson, Alice Eddleman, Goldie M. Edelblute, Charles N. Edwards, Tressie Eichenberger, James Ellis, Alfred M. Ems, Thomas Enderle, Roland Epperson, Bob Esworthy, Chester Ewart, Clara Faatz, Virgil Farthing, Elizabeth Faulkenberry, Maria Faulkner, Michael Feeback, Grace Ferrier, Al Fisch, Joyce Fisher, Robert Flanders, Beverly Fleming, Jack A. Fly, Billie K. Forbes, Buford Foster, Shirley Foster, Bill Free, Ron Fuenfhausen, Julie Moberly Fuller, Eldred E. Gallagher, Bruce Gamet, Lloyd J. Gantt, Nadine Gardner, Marian Gaskill, Barbara J. Gates, Steve Gaynor, Mary Ann Geile, Nelle V. George, Anton Gerbe, David W. Gessert, Ronald Gillman, Robert Gilmore, Warren Ray Giver, Fred Gladbach, Sally Ann Gladden, Helen Glasson, Victor Gloe, James W. Goodrich, Bruce E. Graham, Floyd Graham, Kevn Greene, Steve Grider, Tommy L. Griffith, Sharon Grimes, Paul Grimwood, Dorthy Groeteke, Cathy S. Grove, Richard B. Groves, Barbara J. Hall, Nancy Halliday, Ernest J. Hamilton, Rosella Hamilton, T. M. Hamilton, Robert G. Harmon, Leola Harris, Gale Harrison, Gary Harrison, Tom Hartman, Keith Hassler, Douglas Hauth, Arch Hayes, Carolee Hazlet, Mary Heeren, Olene Heflin, Marie Heinemann, Mark A. Heins, Mary Heinsz, Mildred Helms, Wilma Henbest, Vyra Hendrickson, Randy Hendrix, Genevieve Hickey, Barbara Hill, Leron L. Hill, Lee

Hines, Erma Hinkle, John W. Hodde, James Hofherr, James Holland, James W. Holloway, Lawrence Holt, Wayne Hoover, Janet Hopkins, Mildred Horton, William A. Hoskins, Mary Hotterster, Ann Huck, Delores Hudson, Larry E. Hughes, Carl James Hullinger, David R. Humes, Cecil L. Humphrey, Cindy Hutchcraft, Winston Hutsell, Larry and Marie Hyde, Lee Imler, Michael Jefferies, Clyde Lee Jenkins, Dale Jennings, Ben Johnson, Evelyn Johnson, Philip R. Johnson, Linda Jones, Reita Juliette, Steve Kappler, Warren Karstern Jr., Tom and Mims Keedy, V. Kelly, Carl Kemna, Wayne Killebrew, Rebecca Kistler, Marjorie Klick, Lavern Kling, F. D. Kneibert, Charles Knorp, Martha Knox, Barbara and Frank Koeing, Bill Kolas, Lorraine Krewson, Sylvia Krueger, Larry Kruger, Gloria Krumsiek, James C. Laflin, Betty J. LaJaunie, B. G. Landolt, Becky Lang, Ed Langenberg, Josephine Lawrence, Joan (Smith) Lawson, Bill Lay, Richard L. Lay, Nancy K. Lewis, Bud Lillard, Ralph M. Lindsey Jr., Sheridan A. Logan, Carol Long, Ben B. Loudermilk, Jack Lovelace, Crystal Lyda, James Lynch, Doris McBride, Margaret McBride, Sandra McCarty, Shari K. McClanahan, Ronald D. McCullough, Richard McGonegal, David R. Mack, Laura E. McKeever, Earnie W. McMullen Jr., Donald T. McNeely, Charles McQuiggan, Hames H. Maenner, Sherry Mahnken, Willard Main, Bonnie Mallory, Pat Marble, Guss W. Marcum, Larry M. Marcum, Patricia Marsh, John Martin, Jack B. Mathis, Madeline Matson, David May, J. Hoyle Mayfield, Minta Maze, Rolland Meador, John Meffert, Tracy Mehan III, Mildred Melton, Stephanie Menke, Jay Mermoud, Josephine Merrill, Robert J. Miget, Norma Lea Mihalevich, Kathleen W. Miles, James Millan, Betty Miller, Galen L. Miller, Harold W. Miller, William L. Miller, John Mills, Melvin A. Moldenhauer, Nancy Monachino, Thomas Monks, Jean Montgomery, Judy A. Moon, Ada Moore, Nancy Moore, Tom Moore, Ann Morris, Meredith Moser, Bette Mueller, Stephen E. Muich, Bill Murrell, Murl Nash, Shirley Needy, Michael Nelson, Jennie Newby, Ken Newton, Michile Newton, Bill Nichols, Al Nilges, Tom Norris, Ruth Ann Northcutt, J. T. Offineer, Kelli Offutt, William Olenyik, John C. O'Renick, Rick Orton, Tracey Osborne, Vicki Ott, Pat Parr, Ron and Margaret Parsons, Ursa Parsons, Robert I. Patterson, Clayton Paul, David Pearce, Clare Pelzel, Milton F. Perry, Thomas D. Perry Jr., Virginia Peterson, Scott and Carol Phillips, Barbara Pickering, A. D. Pierce, Tommy Pike, Shirley Piland, Marshall Pile, Vickie Pingel, Aileen Pippins, Elbert Pirtle, Leo Pitts, Randy Poe, Vaughn Poertner, Larry Ponder, Daniel S. Potter, Francis O. Potts, Dorothy Presson, David S. Price, William Price, Gordon W. Proctor, Marvin E. Proffer, Carroll E. Rainwater, Joyce Rayfield, Ionamae Rebenstorf, Howard Reddick, Roger Redmon, Mabel Reed, Connie Reichhart, Joe A. Reilly, Patty Reisenbichler, A. O. Rekate, Thomas P. Risher, Everett J. Ritchie, Janet Robert, Tommy Roberts, Ed Robertson, Jim Robertson, John Robinson, W. Curtis Rogers, Don Roney, Rocky Roost, Clyde A. Rowan, Melanie A. Rowe, Ruth L. Rubenstein, James G. Russell, William M. Ryan, Kelly Salsbury, Milo R. Salyer, Paul Sampson, Denise Sanders, Laura L. Sandy, Ethel Sanning, James R. Santmyer, Cindy Sarber, Rev. Gerald Scheperle, Robert W. Schlingmann, Joan Schmelig, Jim Schmitz, Linda Schneider, Ruben Schnurbusch, Vincent C. Schoemehl, Blake Schreck, Gail Schrivener, Donald R. Schroeger, Robert G. Schultz, Richard Schwartz, Elenore Schwene, Vancell Scifres, Gordon Scruggs, Dan Searcy, Henry H. Seibel, Sara Seidel, Hope Regina Seider, Harold G. Sellers, Jerome J. Selsor, Mildred Shell, Charles Shepherd, Barbara Sherman, Chet Shoemaker, Firmin Showalter, Jill Shriver, Laura L. Simmons, John Paul Skaggs, Wicky Sleight, Art Smith, Clifford B. Smith, Doris Smith, Dorothy Smith, Harold Smith, Howard M. Smith, Larry Smith, Loretta B. Smith, P. Glenn Smith, Vi Smith, Mark Snow, Kathryn C. Snyder, Vic Snyder, Irene Solter, Glenns Southard, Bill Southerland, Stephen E. Sowers, Lance Spears, Dean Sprague, David Spurlock, John R. Stanard, Nicole Standish, Edna Staples, Earle Staponski, Mark C. Stauter, Maple Z. Stearns, Beverly Steffens, Walter Stemmes, Linda Stephenson, Carol Stevens, Richards Stevens, Al Stewart, Floyd V. Stewart, Audrey Stigall, Doris Stockman, Jim Stokes, Huber L. Stover, Tom B. Stow, Kathtrn Strong, Patricia Strouse, Gil Stuenkel, Sylvia Sturgeon, R. Joe Sullivan, Dorothy Summers, Jo Ann Sumner, Howard (Jack) Sutor, Ed E. Swain, Robert L. Swank, Arleene Sweet, Carolyn Taffner, Jim Tally, David L. Tennison, Kenneth Terry, Pat Teter, Gilbert Theiss, Sheila Tracy, Harry Travis, Charles Tripp, Ruth Tucker, Fred Vahle, Leon Vanderfeltz, Mary Lou Veirs, Joyce Vinson, Harvey E. Wadleigh, Ross Wagner, Diana Walker, Lester Walker, Bob Wall, Thomas W. Wallace, David R. Waller, Lee Ward, Donald Washam, Colleen M. Washburn, Neva Wasson, Everett Watson, Jackie Wayman, Curtis G. Weeks, Diana Weidinger, Ron Weir, Chris Wessel, B. J. Wessing, Virginia West, Joyce Whelchel, Jerry White, Robert M. White, Robert Whitehead, James R. Whitley, Lou Ann Wibe, Marilyn Wilde, Kathleen Wilham, Rita Williams, Nellie Stites Wills, Dave Wilson, Diane Winegar, Edwin E. Winfrey, Burnis Winger, Anna Marie Wingron, Kay E. Winn, Bub and Nina Winters, Blanch Wisehart, Anne Wolfe, Joyce Wood, Marilyn Woods, Betty Wortham, Homer Clay Wright, I. L. Young III, Juanita J. Young, Louise Yusko.

Special recognition is owed to the following people, whose independent research helped answer questions not found in standard source material: Jeanne M. Adams, Thomas J. Aiken, Muriel E. Akers, Gerald E. Angel, Claudia Baker, Thelma Ball, Wilma Barber, Hayward Barnett, Guy D. Barrett, Mary Alice Beemer, John Bowers, Mrs. Wallace Boyer, Patrick Brophy, Carol Brunner, Patricia A. Brush, L. L. Buchheit, Patricia Bufka, Sally Burg, Arthur Cahill, Virginia Carlson, Dorothy Childress, Gerald Cohen, Ramona Coleman, Harold Corse, Willanna Crank, J. Daugherty, H. Denny Davis, Gavin L. Doughty, Dorothy Downing, Virginia Duffield, Gayla Dunn, Dan Dywer, Raymond Edwards, Betty Eldridge, Gary and Carol Ellis, Mary Ann Frazee, Marguerette Gallager, Nelle V. George, Ruth Gladstone, Emil Green, Ralph Gregory, Jan Gross, Jim Hagler, Peggy Smith Hake, Harold Hamilton, Terry Hampton, Viola Hartman, Nora K. Hartwig, Lawrence A. Haslag, Art Hebrank, J. G. Heinlein, Kara Helmandollar, Leta Hodge, Mary Hogan, Lois Holman, George F. Hooper, Tim Houtchens, Goldena Howard, Mrs. Leni Howe, Mary Jo Hulsey, Freeda Huskey, Mozelle Hutchison, Larry A. James, Ralph Jobe III, Carolyn Johnson, Iscle Johnson, Judy Kallenbach, Ken Kamper, Brenton Karhoff, Patty Kinder, James B. King Jr., Leonard A. Kuehnert, Russell D. Leek, Sheridan A. Logan, Kathy Love, Virginia McBee, James L. Martin, Dodie Mauer, Homer May, James Mayo, Edward P. Milbank, Marjorie M. Miller, Dorothy Minear, Chris Montgomery, Benjamin Bird Moore, Francis Moore, Naomi Morgan, Dorothy Mount, Patty Mulkey, Steve Oldfield, Rita Patterson, Roy C. Payton, Le Roy Pickett, Peggy Platner, Virginia Poehlman, James R. Powell, Jean Purvines, Bonnie Rapp, Doris Reed, Cecy Rice, B. J. Ripley, Ruby M. Robbins, Mrs. Laurence Sanders, Mrs. Orrie Schaeffer, Karen Schwadron, Judy Shields, Kathie Simpkins, Rhonda Sisemore, Jean Snider, Betty Soper, Fae Sotham, Earl Strebeck, Art Taylor, Shari Thomas, Earline Vaughn, Helen Vogt, Ina C. Wachtel, Carol Watkins, Bill and Sandra Wayne, Lydia White, Robin Wilcox, Bette Wiley, Darryl K. Wilkinson, Marilyn Williams, Rosena Willis, Ruth Womack, Dale Wooton.

Selected Bibliography

Note: Book titles mentioned in the entries are given in quotation marks, in order to avoid confusion with the cross references.

Arthurs, Royce. "Family Tree of Missouri Pacific Railroad." 1938 Thesis. University of Arkansas Special Collections.

Battles and Leaders of the Civil War, Vol. 1. New York: Thomas Yoseloff, Inc., 1956.

Beveridge, Thomas R. *Geologic Wonders and Curiosities of Missouri*. Rolla: Missouri Division of Geology and Land Survey, 1978.

Caldwell, Dorothy J. *Missouri Historic Sites Catalogue*. Columbia: State Historical Society of Missouri, 1963.

Chapman, Carl H. and Eleanor F. *Indians and Archaeology of Missouri*. Columbia: University of Missouri Press, 1983.

Church, William. "Little River Valley & Arkansas Railroad: Cotton Belt's Bird Point Branch." Arkansas Railway Historical Association Newsletter, 1990.

Cohen, Gerald Leonard. *Interesting Missouri Place Names*. Vols. 1 and 2. Rolla: Published by the editor, 1982 and 1987.

Earngey, Bill. *Arkansas Roadsides*. Eureka Springs: East Mountain Press / August House Publishers, 1987.

Farmer, David Hugh. *The Oxford Dictionary of Saints*. Oxford and New York: Oxford University Press, 1987.

Flader, Susan, ed. *Exploring Missouri's Legacy: State Parks and Historic Sites*. With essays by R. Roger Pryor, John A. Karal, Charles Callison, and Susan Flader. Columbia: University of Missouri Press, 1992.

Franzwa, Gregory M. *The Oregon Trail Revisited*. St. Louis: Patrice Press, 1972.

———. *The Story of Old Genevieve*. St. Louis: Patrice Press, 1967.

Gass, Ramond D. *Missouri Hiking Trails*. Jefferson City: Missouri Department of Conservation, 1984.

History of the Frisco. N.p.: The Frisco Railroad Museum, 1958.

Holtz, William. *The Ghost in the Little House: A Life of Rose Wilder Lane*. Columbia: University of Missouri Press, 1993.

Jones, Alexander. *The Jerusalem Bible*. Garden City: Doubleday and Co., 1970.

Kamper, Ken. "Booneslick Settlement and Trails." Hazelwood: from his notes, 1990–1993.

Lass, Abraham H., David Kiremidjian, and Ruth M. Goldstein. *The Dictionary of Classical, Biblical, and Literary Allusions*. New York: Ballantine Books, 1988.

Logan, Sheridan A. *The Story of Old Saint Jo: Gateway to the West, 1799–1932*. Lunenburg, Vt.: Stinehour Press, 1979.

McAlester, Virginia and Lee. *A Field Guide to American Houses*. New York: Alfred A. Knopf, 1989.

Masterson, V. V. *The KATY Railroad and the Last Frontier*. Columbia: University of Missouri Press, 1978.

Missouri: A Guide to the "Show Me" State. Duell, Sloan and Pearce, 1941. Reprinted as *The WPA Guide to 1930s Missouri*. Lawrence: University Press of Kansas, 1986.

Morris, William and Mary. *Dictionary of Word and Phrase Origins*. New York: Harper and Row, 1962.

Moser, Arthur Paul. "A Directory of Towns, Villages and Hamlets, Past and Present." 1981. Manuscript on file at the Springfield–Greene County Library, Springfield, Mo.

National Trust for Historic Preservation in the United States. *What Style Is It?* Washington: Preservation Press, 1983.

Ohman, Marian M. *Encyclopedia of Missouri Courthouses*. Columbia: University of Missouri–Columbia Extension Division, 1981.

———. *A History of Missouri's Counties, County Seats, and Courthouse Squares*. Columbia: University of

Missouri–Columbia Extension Division, 1983.

Ostertag, John and Enid. *Tracing Your Roots in the Missouri River Valley from Sioux City, Iowa, to Independence, Missouri*. St. Joseph: Ostertag, 1987.

Overton, Richard C. *Burlington Route*. New York: Alfred A. Knopf, 1965.

Panati, Charles. *Panati's Browser's Book of Beginnings*. Boston: Houghton Mifflin Co., 1984.

———. *Panati's Extraordinary Endings of Practically Everything and Everybody*. New York: Harper and Row, 1989.

Partridge, Eric. *Origins: A Short Etymological Dictionary of Modern English*. New York: Greenwich House, 1983.

Pierce, Don. *Exploring Missouri River Country*. Jefferson City: Missouri Department of Natural Resources, Division of Parks and Historic Preservation, n.d.

Rafferty, Milton D. *Historical Atlas of Missouri*. Norman: University of Oklahoma Press, 1981.

Ramsay, Robert L. *Our Storehouse of Missouri Place Names*. Columbia: University of Missouri Press, 1973.

Rennick, Robert M. *Kentucky Place Names*. Lexington: University Press of Kentucky, 1984.

Ruth, Kent. *Oklahoma Travel Handbook*. Norman: University of Oklahoma Press, 1977.

Schlissel, Lillian. *Women's Diaries of the Westward Journey*. New York: Schocken Books, 1982.

Schultz, Robert G. *Missouri Post Offices, 1804–1981*. St. Louis: American Philatelic Society, St. Louis Branch, 1982.

Sharpe, Patricia, and Robert S. Weddle. *Texas*. Austin: Texas Monthly Press, 1982.

Stewart, George R. *American Place-Names*. Oxford and New York: Oxford University Press, 1970.

Steyermark, Julian A. *Flora of Missouri*. Ames: Iowa State University Press, 1963.

Thom, Richard H., and Greg Iffrig. *Directory of Missouri Natural Areas*. Jefferson City: Missouri Department of Conservation and Department of Natural Resources, 1985.

Wentworth, Harold, and Stuart Berg Flexner. *Thomas Dictionary of American Slang*. New York: Y. Crowell, 1975.

Williams, Edwin B. *The New College Spanish and English Dictionary*. New York: Amsco School Publications, 1968.

Williams, Walter. *The State of Missouri*. The Missouri Commission to the Louisiana Purchase Exposition, Columbia: Press of E. W. Stevens, 1904.

Wilson, D. Ray. *Missouri Historical Tour Guide*. Carpentersville: Crossroads Communications. 1988.

Zim, Herbert S., and Paul R. Shaffer. *Rocks and Minerals*. Racine: Western Publishing Co., 1957.

Index

— M —

(CHARLES TREFTS COLLECTION)

Mini-Finder